FORD WINDSTAR
1995-98 REPAIR MANUAL

D0825178

CHILTON'S

President	Dean F. Morgantini, S.A.E.
Vice President–Finance	Barry L. Beck
Vice President–Sales	Glenn D. Potere
Executive Editor	Kevin M. G. Maher
Production Manager	Ben Greisler, S.A.E.
Project Managers	Michael Abraham, George B. Heinrich III, S.A.E., Will Kessler, A.S.E., S.A.E., Richard Schwartz
Schematics Editor	Christopher G. Ritchie
Editor	James R. Marotta

PUBLISHED BY **W. G. NICHOLS, INC.**

Manufactured in USA
© 1998 W. G. Nichols
1020 Andrew Drive
West Chester, PA 19380
ISBN 0-8019-8969-8
Library of Congress Catalog Card No. 97-77882
1234567890 7654321098

Contents

Contents

DRIVE TRAIN **7**

SUSPENSION AND STEERING **8**

BRAKES **9**

BODY & TRIM **10**

GLOSSARY

MASTER INDEX

SAFETY NOTICE

Proper service and repair procedures are vital to the safe, reliable operation of all motor vehicles, as well as the personal safety of those performing repairs. This manual outlines procedures for servicing and repairing vehicles using safe, effective methods. The procedures contain many NOTES, CAUTIONS and WARNINGS which should be followed, along with standard procedures, to eliminate the possibility of personal injury or improper service which could damage the vehicle or compromise its safety.

It is important to note that repair procedures and techniques, tools and parts for servicing motor vehicles, as well as the skill and experience of the individual performing the work, vary widely. It is not possible to anticipate all of the conceivable ways or conditions under which vehicles may be serviced, or to provide cautions as to all possible hazards that may result. Standard and accepted safety precautions and equipment should be used during cutting, grinding, chiseling, prying, or any other process that can cause material removal or projectiles.

Some procedures require the use of tools specially designed for a specific purpose. Before substituting another tool or procedure, you must be completely satisfied that neither your personal safety, nor the performance of the vehicle, will be endangered.

Although information in this manual is based on industry sources and is complete as possible at the time of publication, the possibility exists that some vehicle manufacturers made later changes which could not be included here. While striving for total accuracy, NP/Chilton cannot assume responsibility for any errors, changes or omissions that may occur in the compilation of this data.

PART NUMBERS

Part numbers listed in this reference are not recommendations by Chilton for any product brand name. They are references that can be used with interchange manuals and aftermarket supplier catalogs to locate each brand supplier's discrete part number.

SPECIAL TOOLS

Special tools are recommended by the vehicle manufacturer to perform their specific job. Use has been kept to a minimum, but, where absolutely necessary, they are referred to in the text by the part number of the tool manufacturer. These tools can be purchased, under the appropriate part number, from your local dealer or regional distributor, or an equivalent tool can be purchased locally from a tool supplier or parts outlet. Before substituting any tool for the one recommended, read the SAFETY NOTICE at the top of this page.

ACKNOWLEDGMENTS

NP/Chilton expresses appreciation to Ford Motor Company for their generous assistance.

A special thanks to the fine companies who supported the production of this book. Hand tools, supplied by Craftsman, were used during all phases of vehicle teardown and photography. A Rotary lift, the largest automobile lift manufacturer in the world offering the biggest variety of surface and inground lifts available, was also used.

1

GENERAL INFORMATION AND MAINTENANCE

HOW TO USE THIS BOOK

Chilton's Total Car Care manual for the 1995–98 Ford Windstar is intended to help you learn more about the inner workings of your vehicle while saving you money on its upkeep and operation.

The beginning of the book will likely be referred to the most, since that is where you will find information for maintenance and tune-up. The other sections deal with the more complex systems of your vehicle. Operating systems from engine through brakes are covered to the extent that the average do-it-yourselfer becomes mechanically involved. This book will not explain such things as rebuilding a differential for the simple reason that the expertise required and the investment in special tools make this task uneconomical. It will, however, give you detailed instructions to help you change your own brake pads and shoes, replace spark plugs, and perform many more jobs that can save you money, give you personal satisfaction and help you avoid expensive problems.

A secondary purpose of this book is a reference for owners who want to understand their vehicle and/or their mechanics better. In this case, no tools at all are required.

Where to Begin

Before removing any bolts, read through the entire procedure. This will give you the overall view of what tools and supplies will be required. There is nothing more frustrating than having to walk to the bus stop on Monday morning because you were short one bolt on Sunday afternoon. So read ahead and plan ahead. Each operation should be approached logically and all procedures thoroughly understood before attempting any work.

All sections contain adjustments, maintenance, removal and installation procedures, and in some cases, repair or overhaul procedures. When repair is not considered practical, we tell you how to remove the part and then how to install the new or rebuilt replacement. In this way, you at least save the labor costs. Backyard repair of some components is just not practical.

Avoiding Trouble

Many procedures in this book require you to "label and disconnect . . ." a group of lines, hoses or wires. Don't be lulled into thinking you can remember where everything goes—you won't. If you hook up vacuum or fuel lines incorrectly, the vehicle will run poorly, if at all. If you hook up electrical wiring incorrectly, you may instantly learn a very expensive lesson.

You don't need to know the official or engineering name for each hose or line. A piece of masking tape on the hose and a piece on its fitting will allow you to assign your own label such as the letter A or a short name. As long as you remember your own code, the lines can be reconnected by matching similar letters or names. Do remember that tape will dissolve in gasoline or other fluids; if a component is to be washed or cleaned, use another method of identification. A permanent felt-tipped marker can be very handy for marking metal parts. Remove any tape or paper labels after assembly.

Maintenance or Repair?

It's necessary to mention the difference between maintenance and repair. Maintenance includes routine inspections, adjustments, and replacement of parts which show signs of normal wear. Maintenance compensates for wear or deterioration. Repair implies that something has broken or is not working. A need for repair is often caused by lack of maintenance. Example: draining and refilling the automatic transmission fluid is maintenance recommended by the manufacturer at specific mileage intervals. Failure to do this can ruin the transmission/transaxle, requiring very expensive repairs. While no maintenance program can prevent items from breaking or wearing out, a general rule can be stated: MAINTENANCE IS CHEAPER THAN REPAIR.

Two basic mechanic's rules should be mentioned here. First, whenever the left side of the vehicle or engine is referred to, it is meant to specify the driver's side. Conversely, the right side of the vehicle means the passenger's side. Second, most screws and bolts are removed by turning counterclockwise, and tightened by turning clockwise.

Safety is always the most important rule. Constantly be aware of the dangers involved in working on an automobile and take the proper precautions. See the information in this section regarding SERVICING YOUR VEHICLE SAFELY and the SAFETY NOTICE on the acknowledgment page.

Avoiding the Most Common Mistakes

Pay attention to the instructions provided. There are 3 common mistakes in mechanical work:

1. Incorrect order of assembly, disassembly or adjustment. When taking something apart or putting it together, performing steps in the wrong order usually just costs you extra time; however, it CAN break something. Read the entire procedure before beginning disassembly. Perform everything in the order in which the instructions say you should, even if you can't immediately see a reason for it. When you're taking apart something that is very intricate, you might want to draw a picture of how it looks when assembled at one point in order to make sure you get everything back in its proper position. We will supply exploded views whenever possible. When making adjustments, perform them in the proper order; often, one adjustment affects another, and you cannot expect even satisfactory results unless each adjustment is made only when it cannot be changed by any other.

2. Overtorquing (or undertorquing). While it is more common for overtorquing to cause damage, undertorquing may allow a fastener to vibrate loose causing serious damage. Especially when dealing with aluminum parts, pay attention to torque specifications and utilize a torque wrench in assembly. If a torque figure is not available, remember that if you are using the right tool to perform the job, you will probably not have to strain yourself to get a fastener tight enough. The pitch of most threads is so slight that the tension you put on the wrench will be multiplied many times in actual force on what you are tightening. A good example of how critical torque is can be seen in the case of spark plug installation, especially where you are putting the plug into an aluminum cylinder head. Too little torque can fail to crush the gasket, causing leakage of combustion gases and consequent overheating of the plug and engine parts. Too much torque can damage the threads or distort the plug, changing the spark gap.

There are many commercial products available for ensuring that fasteners won't come loose, even if they are not torqued just right (a very common brand is Loctite®). If you're worried about getting something together tight enough to hold, but loose enough to avoid mechanical damage during assembly, one of these products might offer substantial insurance. Before choosing a threadlocking compound, read the label on the package and make sure the product is compatible with the materials, fluids, etc. involved.

3. Crossthreading. This occurs when a part such as a bolt is screwed into a nut or casting at the wrong angle and forced. Crossthreading is more likely to occur if access is difficult. It helps to clean and lubricate fasteners, then to start threading with the part to be installed positioned straight in. Then, start the bolt, spark plug, etc. with your fingers. If you encounter resistance, unscrew the part and start over again at a different angle until it can be inserted and turned several times without much effort. Keep in mind that many parts, especially spark plugs, have tapered threads, so that gentle turning will automatically bring the part you're threading to the proper angle, but only if you don't force it or resist a change in angle. Don't put a wrench on the part until it's been tightened a couple of turns by hand. If you suddenly encounter resistance, and the part has not seated fully, don't force it. Pull it back out to make sure it's clean and threading properly.

Always take your time and be patient; once you have some experience, working on your vehicle may well become an enjoyable hobby.

TOOLS AND EQUIPMENT

♦ **See Figures 1 thru 17**

Naturally, without the proper tools and equipment it is impossible to properly service your vehicle. It would also be virtually impossible to catalog every tool that you would need to perform all of the operations in this book. Of course, It would be unwise for the amateur to rush out and buy an expensive set of tools on the theory that he/she may need one or more of them at some time.

The best approach is to proceed slowly, gathering a good quality set of those tools that are used most frequently. Don't be misled by the low cost of bargain tools. It is far better to spend a little more for better quality. Forged wrenches, 6 or 12-point sockets and fine tooth ratchets are by far preferable to their less expensive counterparts. As any good mechanic can tell you, there are few worse experiences than trying to work on a vehicle with bad tools. Your monetary savings will be far outweighed by frustration and mangled knuckles.

Begin accumulating those tools that are used most frequently: those associated with routine maintenance and tune-up. In addition to the normal assortment of screwdrivers and pliers, you should have the following tools:

• Wrenches/sockets and combination open end/box end wrenches in sizes from 1/8–3/4 in. or 3mm–19mm (depending on whether your vehicle uses standard or metric fasteners) and a 13/16 in. or 5/8 in. spark plug socket (depending on plug type).

TCCS1202

Fig. 3 A hydraulic floor jack and a set of jackstands are essential for lifting and supporting the vehicle

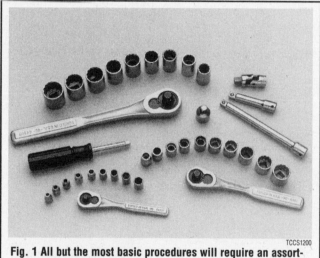

TCCS1200

Fig. 1 All but the most basic procedures will require an assortment of ratchets and sockets

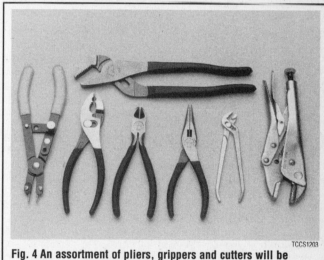

TCCS1203

Fig. 4 An assortment of pliers, grippers and cutters will be handy for old rusted parts and stripped bolt heads

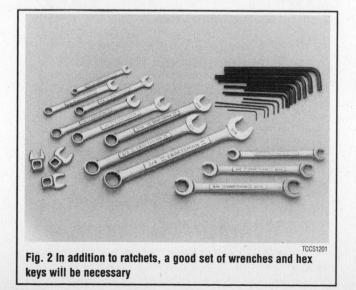

TCCS1201

Fig. 2 In addition to ratchets, a good set of wrenches and hex keys will be necessary

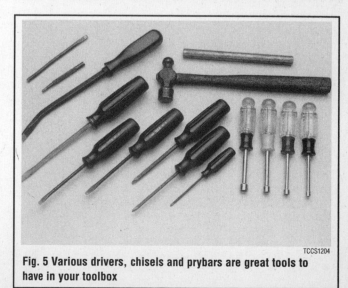

TCCS1204

Fig. 5 Various drivers, chisels and prybars are great tools to have in your toolbox

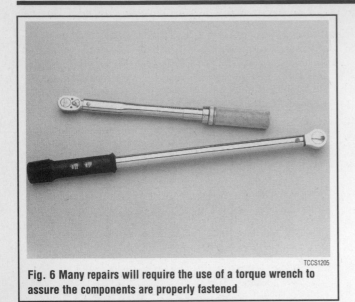

Fig. 6 Many repairs will require the use of a torque wrench to assure the components are properly fastened

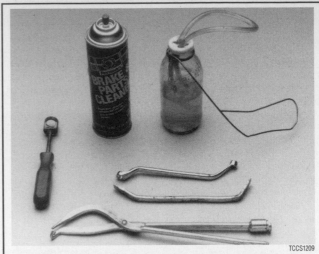

Fig. 9 Although not always necessary, using specialized brake tools will save time

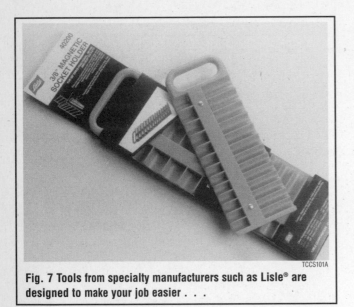

Fig. 7 Tools from specialty manufacturers such as Lisle® are designed to make your job easier . . .

Fig. 10 A few inexpensive lubrication tools will make maintenance easier

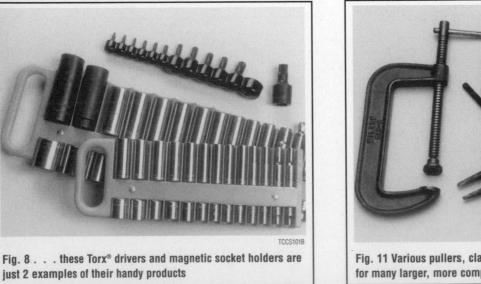

Fig. 8 . . . these Torx® drivers and magnetic socket holders are just 2 examples of their handy products

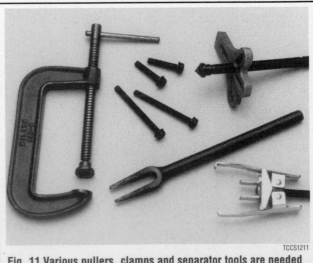

Fig. 11 Various pullers, clamps and separator tools are needed for many larger, more complicated repairs

Fig. 12 A variety of tools and gauges should be used for spark plug gapping and installation

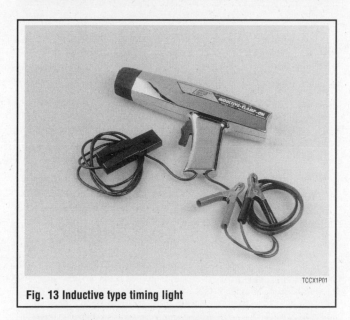

Fig. 13 Inductive type timing light

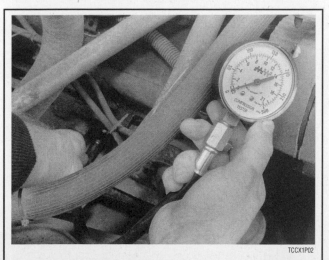

Fig. 14 A screw-in type compression gauge is recommended for compression testing

➥If possible, buy various length socket drive extensions. Universal-joint and wobble extensions can be extremely useful, but be careful when using them, as they can change the amount of torque applied to the socket.

- Jackstands for support.
- Oil filter wrench.
- Spout or funnel for pouring fluids.
- Grease gun for chassis lubrication (unless your vehicle is not equipped with any grease fittings—for details, please refer to information on Fluids and Lubricants found later in this section).

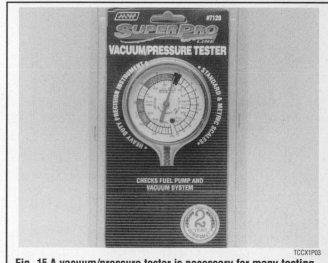

Fig. 15 A vacuum/pressure tester is necessary for many testing procedures

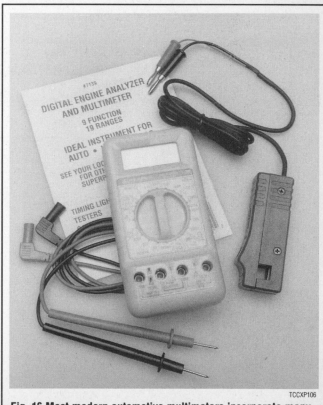

Fig. 16 Most modern automotive multimeters incorporate many helpful features

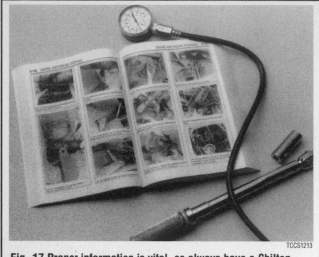

Fig. 17 Proper information is vital, so always have a Chilton Total Car Care manual handy

TCCS1213

• Hydrometer for checking the battery (unless equipped with a sealed, maintenance-free battery).
• A container for draining oil and other fluids.
• Rags for wiping up the inevitable mess.

In addition to the above items there are several others that are not absolutely necessary, but handy to have around. These include Oil Dry® (or an equivalent oil absorbent gravel—such as cat litter) and the usual supply of lubricants, antifreeze and fluids, although these can be purchased as needed. This is a basic list for routine maintenance, but only your personal needs and desire can accurately determine your list of tools.

After performing a few projects on the vehicle, you'll be amazed at the other tools and non-tools on your workbench. Some useful household items are: a large turkey baster or siphon, empty coffee cans and ice trays (to store parts), ball of twine, electrical tape for wiring, small rolls of colored tape for tagging lines or hoses, markers and pens, a note pad, golf tees (for plugging vacuum lines), metal coat hangers or a roll of mechanic's wire (to hold things out of the way), dental pick or similar long, pointed probe, a strong magnet, and a small mirror (to see into recesses and under manifolds).

A more advanced set of tools, suitable for tune-up work, can be drawn up easily. While the tools are slightly more sophisticated, they need not be outrageously expensive. There are several inexpensive tach/dwell meters on the market that are every bit as good for the average mechanic as a professional model. Just be sure that it goes to a least 1200–1500 rpm on the

tach scale and that it works on 4, 6 and 8-cylinder engines. (If you have one or more vehicles with a diesel engine, a special tachometer is required since diesels don't use spark plug ignition systems). The key to these purchases is to make them with an eye towards adaptability and wide range. A basic list of tune-up tools could include:
• Tach/dwell meter.
• Spark plug wrench and gapping tool.
• Feeler gauges for valve or point adjustment. (Even if your vehicle does not use points or require valve adjustments, a feeler gauge is helpful for many repair/overhaul procedures).

A tachometer/dwell meter will ensure accurate tune-up work on vehicles without electronic ignition. The choice of a timing light should be made carefully. A light which works on the DC current supplied by the vehicle's battery is the best choice; it should have a xenon tube for brightness. On any vehicle with an electronic ignition system, a timing light with an inductive pickup that clamps around the No. 1 spark plug cable is preferred.

In addition to these basic tools, there are several other tools and gauges you may find useful. These include:
• Compression gauge. The screw-in type is slower to use, but eliminates the possibility of a faulty reading due to escaping pressure.
• Manifold vacuum gauge.
• 12V test light.
• A combination volt/ohmmeter
• Induction Ammeter. This is used for determining whether or not there is current in a wire. These are handy for use if a wire is broken somewhere in a wiring harness.

As a final note, you will probably find a torque wrench necessary for all but the most basic work. The beam type models are perfectly adequate, although the newer click types (breakaway) are easier to use. The click type torque wrenches tend to be more expensive. Also keep in mind that all types of torque wrenches should be periodically checked and/or recalibrated. You will have to decide for yourself which better fits your purpose.

Special Tools

Normally, the use of special factory tools is avoided for repair procedures, since these are not readily available for the do-it-yourself mechanic. When it is possible to perform the job with more commonly available tools, it will be pointed out, but occasionally, a special tool was designed to perform a specific function and should be used. Before substituting another tool, you should be convinced that neither your safety nor the performance of the vehicle will be compromised.

Special tools can usually be purchased from an automotive parts store or from your dealer. In some cases special tools may be available directly from the tool manufacturer.

SERVICING YOUR VEHICLE SAFELY

▶ **See Figures 18, 19, 20 and 21**

It is virtually impossible to anticipate all of the hazards involved with automotive maintenance and service, but care and common sense will prevent most accidents.

The rules of safety for mechanics range from "don't smoke around gasoline," to "use the proper tool(s) for the job." The trick to avoiding injuries is to develop safe work habits and to take every possible precaution.

Do's

- Do keep a fire extinguisher and first aid kit handy.
- Do wear safety glasses or goggles when cutting, drilling, grinding or prying, even if you have 20–20 vision. If you wear glasses for the sake of vision, wear safety goggles over your regular glasses.
- Do shield your eyes whenever you work around the battery. Batteries contain sulfuric acid. In case of contact with the eyes or skin, flush the area with water or a mixture of water and baking soda, then seek immediate medical attention.

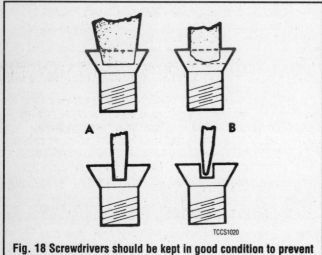

Fig. 18 Screwdrivers should be kept in good condition to prevent injury or damage which could result if the blade slips from the screw

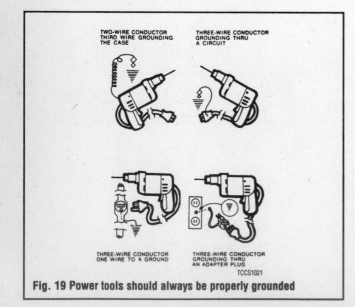

Fig. 19 Power tools should always be properly grounded

Fig. 20 Using the correct size wrench will help prevent the possibility of rounding off a nut

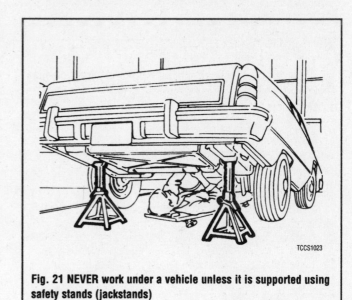

Fig. 21 NEVER work under a vehicle unless it is supported using safety stands (jackstands)

- Do use safety stands (jackstands) for any undervehicle service. Jacks are for raising vehicles; jackstands are for making sure the vehicle stays raised until you want it to come down. Whenever the vehicle is raised, block the wheels remaining on the ground and set the parking brake.
- Do use adequate ventilation when working with any chemicals or hazardous materials. Like carbon monoxide, the asbestos dust resulting from some brake lining wear can be hazardous in sufficient quantities.
- Do disconnect the negative battery cable when working on the electrical system. The secondary ignition system contains EXTREMELY HIGH VOLTAGE. In some cases it can even exceed 50,000 volts.
- Do follow manufacturer's directions whenever working with potentially hazardous materials. Most chemicals and fluids are poisonous if taken internally.
- Do properly maintain your tools. Loose hammerheads, mushroomed punches and chisels, frayed or poorly grounded electrical cords, excessively worn screwdrivers, spread wrenches (open end), cracked sockets, slipping ratchets, or faulty droplight sockets can cause accidents.
- Likewise, keep your tools clean; a greasy wrench can slip off a bolt head, ruining the bolt and often harming your knuckles in the process.

• Do use the proper size and type of tool for the job at hand. Do select a wrench or socket that fits the nut or bolt. The wrench or socket should sit straight, not cocked.

• Do, when possible, pull on a wrench handle rather than push on it, and adjust your stance to prevent a fall.

• Do be sure that adjustable wrenches are tightly closed on the nut or bolt and pulled so that the force is on the side of the fixed jaw.

• Do strike squarely with a hammer; avoid glancing blows.

• Do set the parking brake and block the drive wheels if the work requires a running engine.

Don'ts

• Don't run the engine in a garage or anywhere else without proper ventilation—EVER! Carbon monoxide is poisonous; it takes a long time to leave the human body and you can build up a deadly supply of it in your system by simply breathing in a little every day. You may not realize you are slowly poisoning yourself. Always use power vents, windows, fans and/or open the garage door.

• Don't work around moving parts while wearing loose clothing. Short sleeves are much safer than long, loose sleeves. Hard-toed shoes with neoprene soles protect your toes and give a better grip on slippery surfaces. Jewelry such as watches, fancy belt buckles, beads or body adornment of any kind is not safe working around a vehicle. Long hair should be tied back under a hat or cap.

• Don't use pockets for toolboxes. A fall or bump can drive a screwdriver deep into your body. Even a rag hanging from your back pocket can wrap around a spinning shaft or fan.

• Don't smoke when working around gasoline, cleaning solvent or other flammable material.

• Don't smoke when working around the battery. When the battery is being charged, it gives off explosive hydrogen gas.

• Don't use gasoline to wash your hands; there are excellent soaps available. Gasoline contains dangerous additives which can enter the body through a cut or through your pores. Gasoline also removes all the natural oils from the skin so that bone dry hands will suck up oil and grease.

• Don't service the air conditioning system unless you are equipped with the necessary tools and training. When liquid or compressed gas refrigerant is released to atmospheric pressure it will absorb heat from whatever it contacts. This will chill or freeze anything it touches. Although refrigerant is normally non-toxic, R-12 becomes a deadly poisonous gas in the presence of an open flame. One good whiff of the vapors from burning refrigerant can be fatal.

• Don't use screwdrivers for anything other than driving screws! A screwdriver used as an prying tool can snap when you least expect it, causing injuries. At the very least, you'll ruin a good screwdriver.

• Don't use a bumper or emergency jack (that little ratchet, scissors, or pantograph jack supplied with the vehicle) for anything other than changing a flat! These jacks are only intended for emergency use out on the road; they are NOT designed as a maintenance tool. If you are serious about maintaining your vehicle yourself, invest in a hydraulic floor jack of at least a 1½ ton capacity, and at least two sturdy jackstands.

FASTENERS, MEASUREMENTS AND CONVERSIONS

Bolts, Nuts and Other Threaded Retainers

▶ See Figures 22, 23, 24 and 25

Although there are a great variety of fasteners found in the modern car or truck, the most commonly used retainer is the threaded fastener (nuts, bolts, screws, studs, etc). Most threaded retainers may be reused, provided that they are not damaged in use or during the repair. Some retainers (such as stretch bolts or torque prevailing nuts) are designed to deform when tightened or in use and should not be reinstalled.

Whenever possible, we will note any special retainers which should be replaced during a procedure. But you should always inspect the condition of a retainer when it is removed and replace any that show signs of damage. Check all threads for rust or corrosion which can increase the torque necessary to achieve the desired clamp load for which that

fastener was originally selected. Additionally, be sure that the driver surface of the fastener has not been compromised by rounding or other damage. In some cases a driver surface may become only partially rounded, allowing the driver to catch in only one direction. In many of these occurrences, a fastener may be installed and tightened, but the driver would not be able to grip and loosen the fastener again. (This could lead to frustration down the line should that component ever need to be disassembled again).

If you must replace a fastener, whether due to design or damage, you must ALWAYS be sure to use the proper replacement. In all cases, a retainer of the same design, material and strength should be used. Markings on the heads of most bolts will help determine the proper strength of the fastener. The same material, thread and pitch must be selected to assure proper installation and safe operation of the vehicle afterwards.

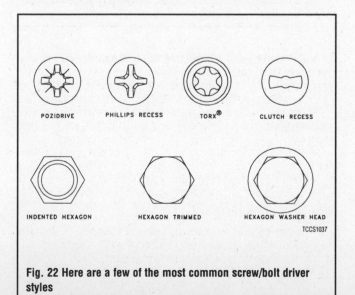

Fig. 22 Here are a few of the most common screw/bolt driver styles

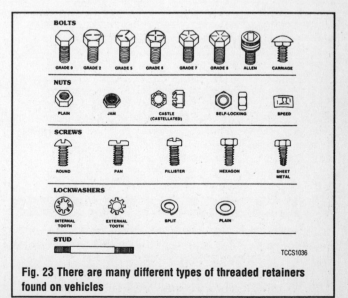

Fig. 23 There are many different types of threaded retainers found on vehicles

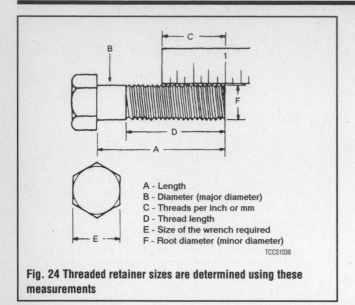

A - Length
B - Diameter (major diameter)
C - Threads per inch or mm
D - Thread length
E - Size of the wrench required
F - Root diameter (minor diameter)

TCCS1038

Fig. 24 Threaded retainer sizes are determined using these measurements

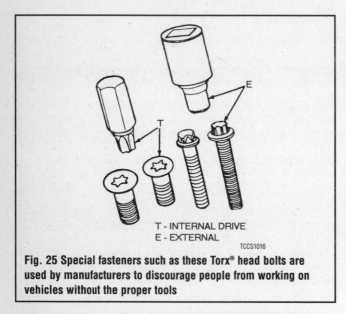

T - INTERNAL DRIVE
E - EXTERNAL

TCCS1016

Fig. 25 Special fasteners such as these Torx® head bolts are used by manufacturers to discourage people from working on vehicles without the proper tools

Thread gauges are available to help measure a bolt or stud's thread. Most automotive and hardware stores keep gauges available to help you select the proper size. In a pinch, you can use another nut or bolt for a thread gauge. If the bolt you are replacing is not too badly damaged, you can select a match by finding another bolt which will thread in its place. If you find a nut which threads properly onto the damaged bolt, then use that nut to help select the replacement bolt. If however, the bolt you are replacing is so badly damaged (broken or drilled out) that its threads cannot be used as a gauge, you might start by looking for another bolt (from the same assembly or a similar location on your vehicle) which will thread into the damaged bolt's mounting. If so, the other bolt can be used to select a nut; the nut can then be used to select the replacement bolt.

In all cases, be absolutely sure you have selected the proper replacement. Don't be shy, you can always ask the store clerk for help.

❋❋ WARNING

Be aware that when you find a bolt with damaged threads, you may also find the nut or drilled hole it was threaded into has also been damaged. If this is the case, you may have to drill and tap the hole, replace the nut or otherwise repair the threads. NEVER try to force a replacement bolt to fit into the damaged threads.

Torque

Torque is defined as the measurement of resistance to turning or rotating. It tends to twist a body about an axis of rotation. A common example of this would be tightening a threaded retainer such as a nut, bolt or screw. Measuring torque is one of the most common ways to help assure that a threaded retainer has been properly fastened.

When tightening a threaded fastener, torque is applied in three distinct areas, the head, the bearing surface and the clamp load. About 50 percent of the measured torque is used in overcoming bearing friction. This is the friction between the bearing surface of the bolt head, screw head or nut face and the base material or washer (the surface on which the fastener is rotating). Approximately 40 percent of the applied torque is used in overcoming thread friction. This leaves only about 10 percent of the applied torque to develop a useful clamp load (the force which holds a joint together). This means that friction can account for as much as 90 percent of the applied torque on a fastener.

TORQUE WRENCHES

◆ See Figures 26 and 27

In most applications, a torque wrench can be used to assure proper installation of a fastener. Torque wrenches come in various designs and most automotive supply stores will carry a variety to suit your needs. A torque wrench should be used any time we supply a specific torque value for a fastener. A torque wrench can also be used if you are following the general guidelines in the accompanying charts. Keep in mind that because there is no worldwide standardization of fasteners, the charts are a general guideline and should be used with caution. Again, the general rule of "if you are using the right tool for the job, you should not have to strain to tighten a fastener" applies here.

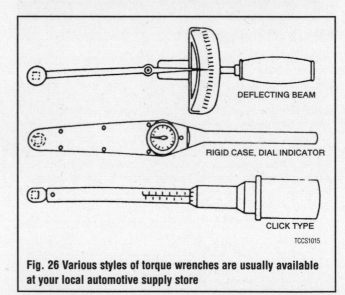

DEFLECTING BEAM

RIGID CASE, DIAL INDICATOR

CLICK TYPE

TCCS1015

Fig. 26 Various styles of torque wrenches are usually available at your local automotive supply store

Beam Type

◆ See Figure 28

The beam type torque wrench is one of the most popular types. It consists of a pointer attached to the head that runs the length of the flexible beam (shaft) to a scale located near the handle. As the wrench is pulled, the beam bends and the pointer indicates the torque using the scale.

Click (Breakaway) Type

◆ See Figure 29

Another popular design of torque wrench is the click type. To use the click type wrench you pre-adjust it to a torque setting. Once the torque is reached, the wrench has a reflex signaling feature that causes a momentary breakaway of the torque wrench body, sending an impulse to the operator's hand.

Standard Torque Specifications and Fastener Markings

In the absence of specific torques, the following chart can be used as a guide to the maximum safe torque of a particular size/grade of fastener.
- There is no torque difference for fine or coarse threads.
- Torque values are based on clean, dry threads. Reduce the value by 10% if threads are oiled prior to assembly.
- The torque required for aluminum components or fasteners is considerably less.

U.S. Bolts

SAE Grade Number	1 or 2			5			6 or 7		
Number of lines always 2 less than the grade number.									
Bolt Size (Inches)—(Thread)	Maximum Torque			Maximum Torque			Maximum Torque		
	Ft./Lbs.	Kgm	Nm	Ft./Lbs.	Kgm	Nm	Ft./Lbs.	Kgm	Nm
¼ — 20	5	0.7	6.8	8	1.1	10.8	10	1.4	13.5
— 28	6	0.8	8.1	10	1.4	13.6			
⁵⁄₁₆ — 18	11	1.5	14.9	17	2.3	23.0	19	2.6	25.8
— 24	13	1.8	17.6	19	2.6	25.7			
⅜ — 16	18	2.5	24.4	31	4.3	42.0	34	4.7	46.0
— 24	20	2.75	27.1	35	4.8	47.5			
⁷⁄₁₆ — 14	28	3.8	37.0	49	6.8	66.4	55	7.6	74.5
— 20	30	4.2	40.7	55	7.6	74.5			
½ — 13	39	5.4	52.8	75	10.4	101.7	85	11.75	115.2
— 20	41	5.7	55.6	85	11.7	115.2			
⁹⁄₁₆ — 12	51	7.0	69.2	110	15.2	149.1	120	16.6	162.7
— 18	55	7.6	74.5	120	16.6	162.7			
⅝ — 11	83	11.5	112.5	150	20.7	203.3	167	23.0	226.5
— 18	95	13.1	128.8	170	23.5	230.5			
¾ — 10	105	14.5	142.3	270	37.3	366.0	280	38.7	379.6
— 16	115	15.9	155.9	295	40.8	400.0			
⅞ — 9	160	22.1	216.9	395	54.6	535.5	440	60.9	596.5
— 14	175	24.2	237.2	435	60.1	589.7			
1 — 8	236	32.5	318.6	590	81.6	799.9	660	91.3	894.8
— 14	250	34.6	338.9	660	91.3	849.8			

Metric Bolts

Relative Strength Marking	4.6, 4.8			8.8		
Bolt Markings						
Bolt Size Thread Size x Pitch (mm)	Maximum Torque			Maximum Torque		
	Ft./Lbs.	Kgm	Nm	Ft./Lbs.	Kgm	Nm
6 x 1.0	2–3	.2–.4	3–4	3–6	4–.8	5–8
8 x 1.25	6–8	.8–1	8–12	9–14	1.2–1.9	13–19
10 x 1.25	12–17	1.5–2.3	16–23	20–29	2.7–4.0	27–39
12 x 1.25	21–32	2.9–4.4	29–43	35–53	4.8–7.3	47–72
14 x 1.5	35–52	4.8–7.1	48–70	57–85	7.8–11.7	77–110
16 x 1.5	51–77	7.0–10.6	67–100	90–120	12.4–16.5	130–160
18 x 1.5	74–110	10.2–15.1	100–150	130–170	17.9–23.4	180–230
20 x 1.5	110–140	15.1–19.3	150–190	190–240	26.2–46.9	160–320
22 x 1.5	150–190	22.0–26.2	200–260	250–320	34.5–44.1	340–430
24 x 1.5	190–240	26.2–46.9	260–320	310–410	42.7–56.5	420–550

TCCS1098

Fig. 27 Standard and metric bolt torque specifications based on bolt strengths

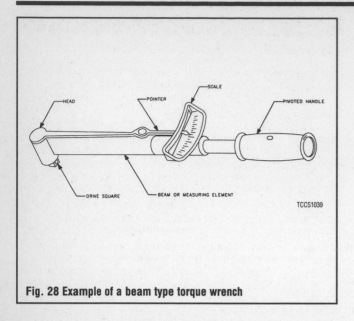

Fig. 28 Example of a beam type torque wrench

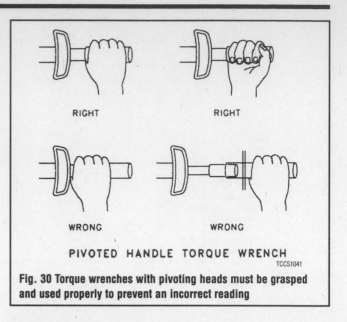

Fig. 30 Torque wrenches with pivoting heads must be grasped and used properly to prevent an incorrect reading

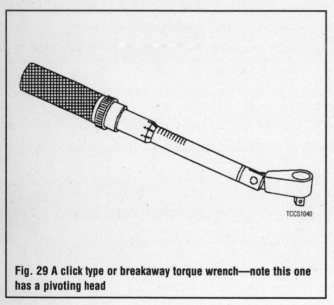

Fig. 29 A click type or breakaway torque wrench—note this one has a pivoting head

Pivot Head Type

▶ See Figure 30

Some torque wrenches (usually of the click type) may be equipped with a pivot head which can allow it to be used in areas of limited access. BUT, it must be used properly. To hold a pivot head wrench, grasp the handle lightly, and as you pull on the handle, it should be floated on the pivot point. If the handle comes in contact with the yoke extension during the process of pulling, there is a very good chance the torque readings will be inaccurate because this could alter the wrench loading point. The design of the handle is usually such as to make it inconvenient to deliberately misuse the wrench.

➡ It should be mentioned that the use of any U-joint, wobble or extension will have an effect on the torque readings, no matter what type of wrench you are using. For the most accurate readings, install the socket directly on the wrench driver. If necessary, straight extensions (which hold a socket directly under the wrench driver) will have the least effect on the torque reading. Avoid any extension that alters the length of the wrench from the handle to the head/driving point (such as a crow's foot). U-joint or Wobble extensions can greatly affect the readings; avoid their use at all times.

Rigid Case (Direct Reading)

▶ See Figure 31

A rigid case or direct reading torque wrench is equipped with a dial indicator to show torque values. One advantage of these wrenches is that they can be held at any position on the wrench without affecting accuracy. These wrenches are often preferred because they tend to be compact, easy to read and have a great degree of accuracy.

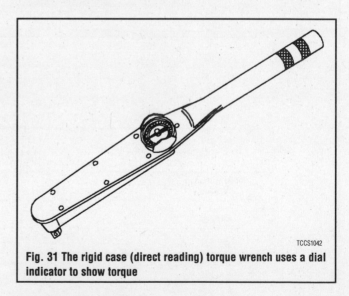

Fig. 31 The rigid case (direct reading) torque wrench uses a dial indicator to show torque

TORQUE ANGLE METERS

▶ See Figure 32

Because the frictional characteristics of each fastener or threaded hole will vary, clamp loads which are based strictly on torque will vary as well. In most applications, this variance is not significant enough to cause worry. But, in certain applications, a manufacturer's engineers may determine that more precise clamp loads are necessary (such is the case with many aluminum cylinder heads). In these cases, a torque angle method of installation would be specified. When installing fasteners which are torque angle tightened, a predetermined seating torque and standard torque wrench are usually used first to remove any compliance from the joint. The fastener is

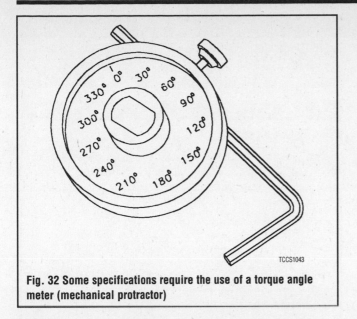

Fig. 32 Some specifications require the use of a torque angle meter (mechanical protractor)

Standard and Metric Measurements

♦ See Figure 33

Throughout this manual, specifications are given to help you determine the condition of various components on your vehicle, or to assist you in their installation. Some of the most common measurements include length (in. or cm/mm), torque (ft. lbs., inch lbs. or Nm) and pressure (psi, in. Hg, kPa or mm Hg). In most cases, we strive to provide the proper measurement as determined by the manufacturer's engineers.

Though, in some cases, that value may not be conveniently measured with what is available in your toolbox. Luckily, many of the measuring devices which are available today will have two scales so the Standard or Metric measurements may easily be taken. If any of the various measuring tools which are available to you do not contain the same scale as listed in the specifications, use the accompanying conversion factors to determine the proper value.

The conversion factor chart is used by taking the given specification and multiplying it by the necessary conversion factor. For instance, looking at the first line, if you have a measurement in inches such as "free-play should be 2 in." but your ruler reads only in millimeters, multiply 2 in. by the conversion factor of 25.4 to get the metric equivalent of 50.8mm. Likewise, if the specification was given only in a Metric measurement, for example in Newton Meters (Nm), then look at the center column first. If the measurement is 100 Nm, multiply it by the conversion factor of 0.738 to get 73.8 ft. lbs.

then tightened the specified additional portion of a turn measured in degrees. A torque angle gauge (mechanical protractor) is used for these applications.

CONVERSION FACTORS

LENGTH–DISTANCE

Inches (in.)	x 25.4	= Millimeters (mm)	x .0394	= Inches
Feet (ft.)	x .305	= Meters (m)	x 3.281	= Feet
Miles	x 1.609	= Kilometers (km)	x .0621	= Miles

VOLUME

Cubic Inches (in3)	x 16.387	= Cubic Centimeters	x .061	= in3
IMP Pints (IMP pt.)	x .568	= Liters (L)	x 1.76	= IMP pt.
IMP Quarts (IMP qt.)	x 1.137	= Liters (L)	x .88	= IMP qt.
IMP Gallons (IMP gal.)	x 4.546	= Liters (L)	x .22	= IMP gal.
IMP Quarts (IMP qt.)	x 1.201	= US Quarts (US qt.)	x .833	= IMP qt.
IMP Gallons (IMP gal.)	x 1.201	= US Gallons (US gal.)	x .833	= IMP gal.
Fl. Ounces	x 29.573	= Milliliters	x .034	= Ounces
US Pints (US pt.)	x .473	= Liters (L)	x 2.113	= Pints
US Quarts (US qt.)	x .946	= Liters (L)	x 1.057	= Quarts
US Gallons (US gal.)	x 3.785	= Liters (L)	x .264	= Gallons

MASS–WEIGHT

Ounces (oz.)	x 28.35	= Grams (g)	x .035	= Ounces
Pounds (lb.)	x .454	= Kilograms (kg)	x 2.205	= Pounds

PRESSURE

Pounds Per Sq. In. (psi)	x 6.895	= Kilopascals (kPa)	x .145	= psi
Inches of Mercury (Hg)	x .4912	= psi	x 2.036	= Hg
Inches of Mercury (Hg)	x 3.377	= Kilopascals (kPa)	x .2961	= Hg
Inches of Water (H_2O)	x .07355	= Inches of Mercury	x 13.783	= H_2O
Inches of Water (H_2O)	x .03613	= psi	x 27.684	= H_2O
Inches of Water (H_2O)	x .248	= Kilopascals (kPa)	x 4.026	= H_2O

TORQUE

Pounds–Force Inches (in–lb)	x .113	= Newton Meters (N·m)	x 8.85	= in–lb
Pounds–Force Feet (ft–lb)	x 1.356	= Newton Meters (N·m)	x .738	= ft–lb

VELOCITY

Miles Per Hour (MPH)	x 1.609	= Kilometers Per Hour (KPH)	x .621	= MPH

POWER

Horsepower (Hp)	x .745	= Kilowatts	x 1.34	= Horsepower

FUEL CONSUMPTION*

Miles Per Gallon IMP (MPG)	x .354	= Kilometers Per Liter (Km/L)
Kilometers Per Liter (Km/L)	x 2.352	= IMP MPG
Miles Per Gallon US (MPG)	x .425	= Kilometers Per Liter (Km/L)
Kilometers Per Liter (Km/L)	x 2.352	= US MPG

*It is common to covert from miles per gallon (mpg) to liters/100 kilometers (1/100 km), where mpg (IMP) x 1/100 km = 282 and mpg (US) x 1/100 km = 235.

TEMPERATURE

Degree Fahrenheit (°F)	= (°C x 1.8) + 32
Degree Celsius (°C)	= (°F – 32) x .56

TCCS1044

Fig. 33 Standard and metric conversion factors chart

SERIAL NUMBER IDENTIFICATION

Vehicle

◆ See Figure 34

The Vehicle Identification Number (VIN) is located at two positions on the vehicle. The first is at the top left of the dash, viewable through the windshield. The second location is at the driver side door jamb, on the certification label.

The seventeen-digit vehicle number is composed of an identification number and a six-digit serial number.

The two most important digits are the eighth and tenth. The eighth digit identifies the engine type. This will be used later in the book to identify the engines in the specification charts. The tenth digit identifies the model year.

Engine

◆ See Figures 35 and 36

The engine code information label is located on the valve cover. The label contains information on engine calibration, build date, plant code and engine code.

The certification label, located on the driver's door jamb, contains a wealth of vehicle information

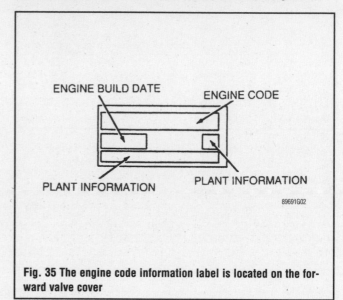

Fig. 35 The engine code information label is located on the forward valve cover

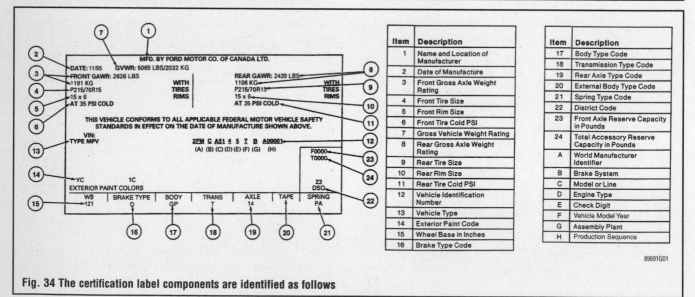

Fig. 34 The certification label components are identified as follows

Item	Description
1	Name and Location of Manufacturer
2	Date of Manufacture
3	Front Gross Axle Weight Rating
4	Front Tire Size
5	Front Rim Size
6	Front Tire Cold PSI
7	Gross Vehicle Weight Rating
8	Rear Gross Axle Weight Rating
9	Rear Tire Size
10	Rear Rim Size
11	Rear Tire Cold PSI
12	Vehicle Identification Number
13	Vehicle Type
14	Exterior Paint Code
15	Wheel Base in Inches
16	Brake Type Code

Item	Description
17	Body Type Code
18	Transmission Type Code
19	Rear Axle Type Code
20	External Body Type Code
21	Spring Type Code
22	District Code
23	Front Axle Reserve Capacity in Pounds
24	Total Accessory Reserve Capacity in Pounds
A	World Manufacturer Identifier
B	Brake System
C	Model or Line
D	Engine Type
E	Check Digit
F	Vehicle Model Year
G	Assembly Plant
H	Production Sequence

VEHICLE IDENTIFICATION CHART

	Engine Code					Model Year	
Code	Liters	Cu. In. (cc)	Cyl.	Fuel Sys.	Eng. Mfg.	Code	Year
U	3.0	182 (2966)	6	SEFI	Ford	S	1995
4	3.8	232 (3802)	6	SEFI	Ford	T	1996
						V	1997
						W	1998

SEFI - Sequential Electronic Fuel Injection

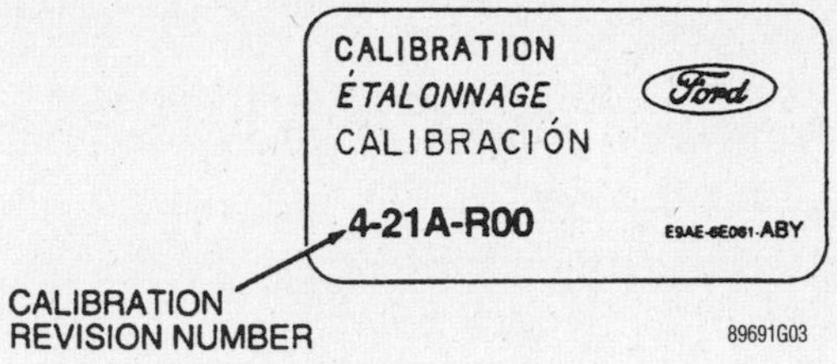

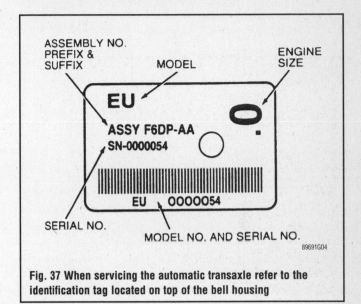

Fig. 36 The emission calibration label is located on the driver door or driver door post pillar and should be used when purchasing any emission control or fuel system component

Another important label is the emission calibration label, located on the on either the driver's or passenger's door or door jamb. This label identifies the engine calibration, engine code and revision numbers. These numbers are used to determine if parts are unique to specific engines.

➡It is imperative that the engine codes and calibration number be used when ordering parts or making inquiries about the engine.

Transaxle

▶ **See Figure 37**

The transaxle identification number is located on the top of the bell housing. The label contains information about assembly number, model, engine size and serial number.

➡It is imperative that the transaxle code number be used when ordering parts or making inquiries about the transaxle.

Fig. 37 When servicing the automatic transaxle refer to the identification tag located on top of the bell housing

ENGINE IDENTIFICATION

Year	Model	Engine Displacement Liters (cc)	Engine Series (ID/VIN)	Fuel System	No. of Cylinders	Engine Type
1995	Windstar	3.0 (2966)	U	SEFI	6	OHV
		3.8 (3802)	4	SEFI	6	OHV
1996	Windstar	3.0 (2966)	U	SEFI	6	OHV
		3.8 (3802)	4	SEFI	6	OHV
1997	Windstar	3.0 (2966)	U	SEFI	6	OHV
		3.8 (3802)	4	SEFI	6	OHV
1998	Windstar	3.0 (2966)	U	SEFI	6	OHV
		3.8 (3802)	4	SEFI	6	OHV

SEFI - Sequential Electronic Fuel Injection

89691C02

GENERAL ENGINE SPECIFICATIONS

Year	Engine ID/VIN	Engine Displacement Liters (cc)	Fuel System Type	Net Horsepower @ rpm	Net Torque @ rpm (ft. lbs.)	Bore x Stroke (in.)	Compression Ratio	Oil Pressure @ rpm
1995	U	3.0(2966)	SEFI	147@5000	170@3250	3.50x3.14	9.2:1	40-60@2500
	4	3.8(3802)	SEFI	155@4000	220@3000	3.81x3.39	9.0:1	40-60@2500
1996	U	3.0(2966)	SEFI	150@5000	170@3250	3.50x3.14	9.3:1	40-60@2500
	4	3.8(3802)	SEFI	200@5000	230@3000	3.81x3.39	9.3:1	40-60@2500
1997	U	3.0(2966)	SEFI	150@5000	170@3250	3.50x3.14	9.3:1	40-60@2500
	4	3.8(3802)	SEFI	200@5000	230@3000	3.81x3.39	9.3:1	40-60@2500
1998	U	3.0(2966)	SEFI	150@5000	172@3300	3.50x3.14	9.3:1	40-60@2500
	4	3.8(3802)	SEFI	200@5000	225@3000	3.81x3.39	9.3:1	40-60@2500

SEFI - Sequential Electronic Fuel Injection

89691C03

ROUTINE MAINTENANCE AND TUNE-UP

Proper maintenance and tune-ups are the keys to long and trouble-free vehicle life, and the work can yield its own rewards. Studies have shown that a properly tuned and maintained vehicle can achieve better gas mileage than an out-of-tune vehicle. As a conscientious owner and driver, set aside a Saturday morning, say once a month, to check or replace items which could cause major problems later. Keep your own personal log to jot down which services you performed, how much the parts cost you, the date, and the exact odometer reading at the time. Keep all receipts for such items as engine oil and filters, so that they may be referred to in case of related problems or to determine operating expenses. As a do-it-yourselfer, these receipts are the only proof you have that the required maintenance was performed. In the event of a warranty problem, these receipts will be invaluable.

The literature provided with your vehicle when it was originally delivered includes the factory recommended maintenance schedule. If you no longer have this literature, replacement copies are usually available from the dealer. A maintenance schedule is provided later in this section, in case you do not have the factory literature.

Air Cleaner

The air cleaner contains a dry paper element that keeps most dirt and dust from entering the engine. The paper element should be replaced every 60,000 miles (96,000 km) under normal conditions or 30,000 miles (48,000 km) under severe conditions.

REMOVAL & INSTALLATION

3.0L Engine

▶ See Figure 38

1. Loosen and remove the air cleaner tube clamp at the mass air flow sensor.
2. Release the retaining clips and remove the air cleaner cover.
3. Position the cover aside.
4. Remove the air cleaner element.
5. Clean the air filter box of debris.
6. Install the air cleaner element and tighten the tube clamp to 27–44 inch lbs. (3–5 Nm).

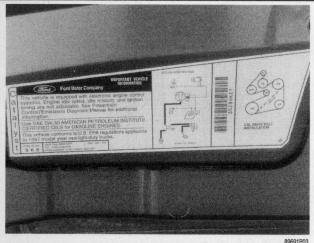

89691P03

Emissions control systems information is found on the Vehicle Emissions Control Information (VECI) label in the engine compartment

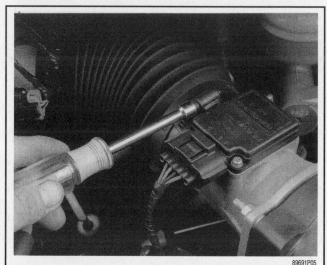

89691P05

A nut driver comes in handy to loosen the air cleaner tube clamp—3.0L engine

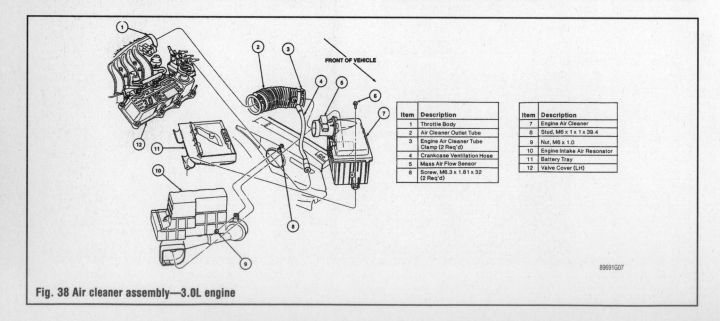

Item	Description
1	Throttle Body
2	Air Cleaner Outlet Tube
3	Engine Air Cleaner Tube Clamp (2 Req'd)
4	Crankcase Ventilation Hose
5	Mass Air Flow Sensor
6	Screw, M6.3 x 1.81 x 32 (2 Req'd)

Item	Description
7	Engine Air Cleaner
8	Stud, M6 x 1 x 1 x 39.4
9	Nut, M6 x 1.0
10	Engine Intake Air Resonator
11	Battery Tray
12	Valve Cover (LH)

89691G07

Fig. 38 Air cleaner assembly—3.0L engine

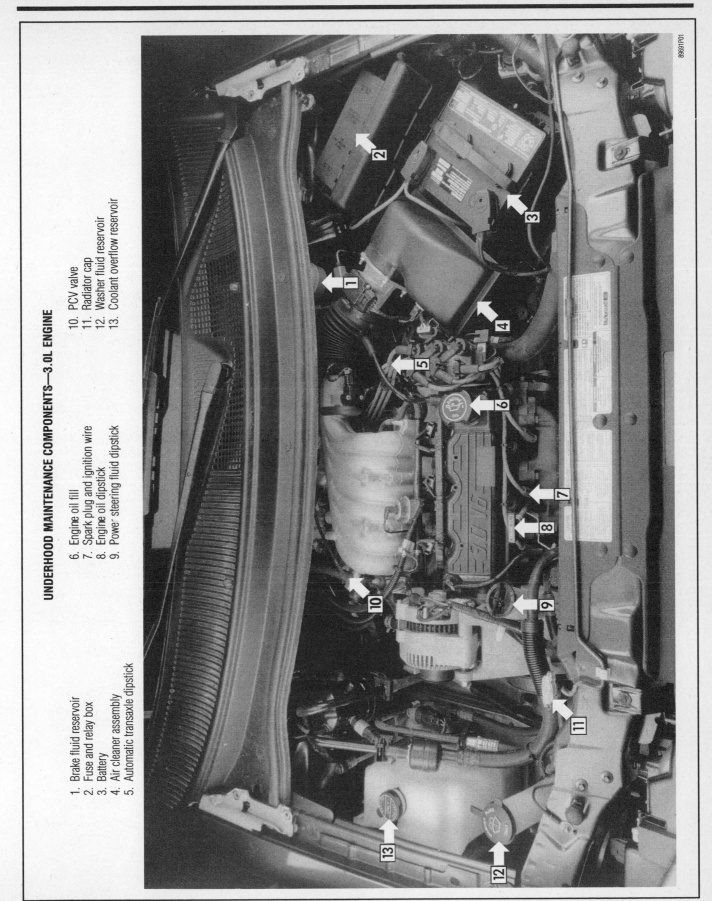

UNDERHOOD MAINTENANCE COMPONENTS—3.0L ENGINE

1. Brake fluid reservoir
2. Fuse and relay box
3. Battery
4. Air cleaner assembly
5. Automatic transaxle dipstick
6. Engine oil fill
7. Spark plug and ignition wire
8. Engine oil dipstick
9. Power steering fluid dipstick
10. PCV valve
11. Radiator cap
12. Washer fluid reservoir
13. Coolant overflow reservoir

89691P01

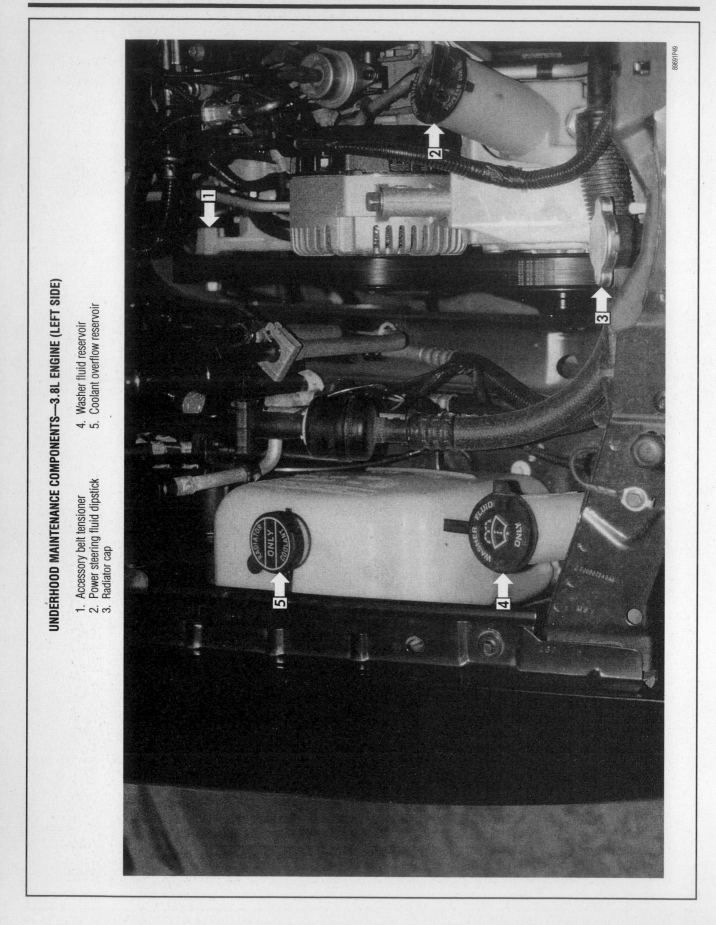

UNDERHOOD MAINTENANCE COMPONENTS—3.8L ENGINE (LEFT SIDE)

1. Accessory belt tensioner
2. Power steering fluid dipstick
3. Radiator cap
4. Washer fluid reservoir
5. Coolant overflow reservoir

89691P49

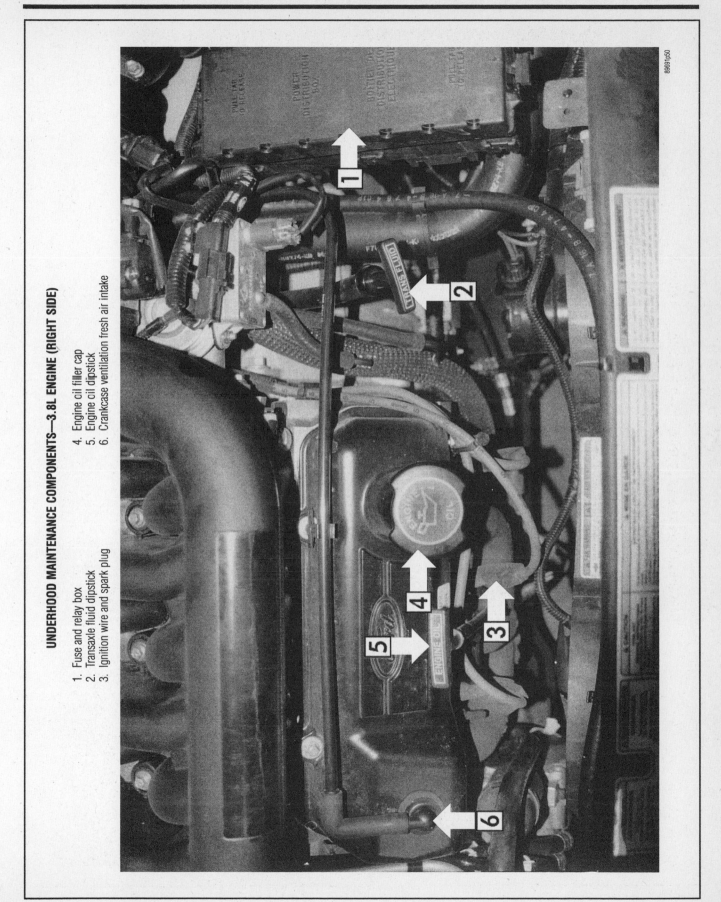

UNDERHOOD MAINTENANCE COMPONENTS—3.8L ENGINE (RIGHT SIDE)

1. Fuse and relay box
2. Transaxle fluid dipstick
3. Ignition wire and spark plug
4. Engine oil filler cap
5. Engine oil dipstick
6. Crankcase ventilation fresh air intake

89691p50

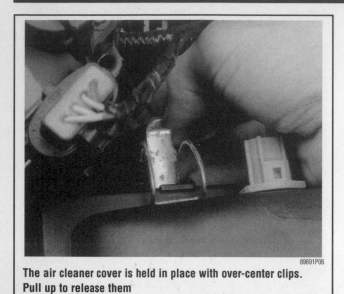

The air cleaner cover is held in place with over-center clips. Pull up to release them

89691P06

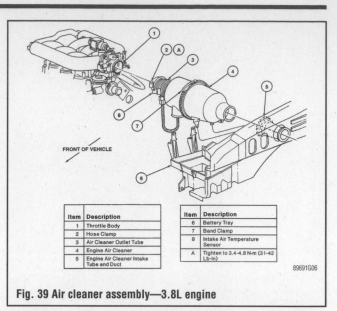

Item	Description
1	Throttle Body
2	Hose Clamp
3	Air Cleaner Outlet Tube
4	Engine Air Cleaner
5	Engine Air Cleaner Intake Tube and Duct

Item	Description
6	Battery Tray
7	Band Clamp
8	Intake Air Temperature Sensor
A	Tighten to 3.4-4.8 N·m (31-42 Lb-in)

89691G06

Fig. 39 Air cleaner assembly—3.8L engine

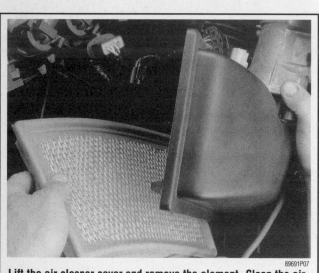

Lift the air cleaner cover and remove the element. Clean the air filter box of debris as necessary

89691P07

The air cleaner cover is held in place with an over-center clamp. Pull up on the lever to release the clamp

89691P08

3.8L Engine

▶ See Figure 39

1. Release the lever on the over-center band clamp.
2. Pull the engine side half of the air cleaner housing forward, while leaving the air cleaner element in the end half of the housing.

➡️**It may be necessary to remove the air cleaner tube clamp at the mass air flow sensor.**

3. Position the engine side half of the air cleaner housing aside.
4. Remove the air cleaner element.
5. Install the air cleaner element and align the air cleaner housing halves.
6. Install the over-center band clamp and fasten securely.

Removing the air cleaner tube from the throttle body makes the job easier. Just loosen the clamp . . .

89691P09

. . . and slide the air cleaner tube off the throttle body

Separate the cover halves and move the engine side half out of the way

The air cleaner element is contained inside the outer half of the air cleaner cover

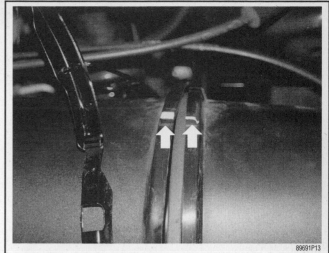

When assembling the cover halves, note the alignment notch at the top of the housing

Fuel Filter

▶ See Figure 40

Although the manufacturer does not specify a replacement interval for fuel filters, we at Chilton feel the fuel filter should be replaced every 60,000 miles (96,000 km) under normal conditions or 30,000 miles (48,000 km) under severe conditions.

➡**For fuel pressure relief and push connector fitting removal, please refer to Section 5.**

1. Relieve the fuel system pressure.
2. Raise and support the vehicle safely.
3. Place a rag under the fuel filter to catch any residual fuel that may leak out when the filter is removed.
4. Remove the push connect fittings at both ends of the fuel filter.
5. Install retainer clips in each connect fitting.
6. Note the flow arrow direction for installation reference.
7. Remove the fuel filter by pulling from the bracket.

To install:

8. Install the fuel filter in its bracket, ensuring proper direction of flow as noted earlier.

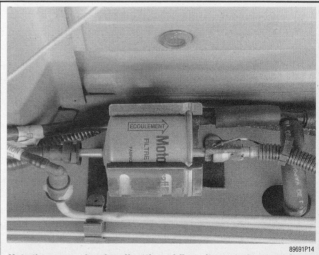

Note the arrow showing direction of flow. It must always point toward the front of the vehicle

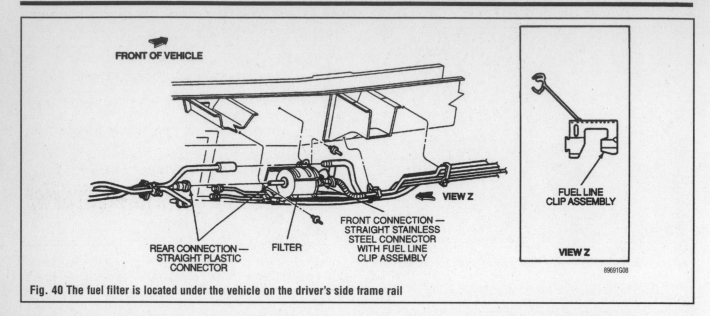

Fig. 40 The fuel filter is located under the vehicle on the driver's side frame rail

9. Install push connect fittings at both ends of the fuel filter.
10. Lower the vehicle.
11. Start the engine and check the filter connections for leaks by running the tip of your finger around each connection.

PCV Valve

▶ **See Figures 41, 42 and 43**

The PCV system should be inspected and the PCV valve replaced at 60,000 miles (96,000 km) and then every 40,000 miles (64,000 km) afterwards.

A Positive Crankcase Ventilation (PCV) system is used to prevent pollutants (blow-by gases) from being released into the atmosphere. The PCV system supplies fresh air to the crankcase through the air cleaner. The fresh air mixes with the gases and is passed through the PCV valve to the intake manifold; the gases are then reburned in the combustion process.

➡ **For more information on the Positive Crankcase Ventilation (PCV) system, please refer to Section 4 of this manual.**

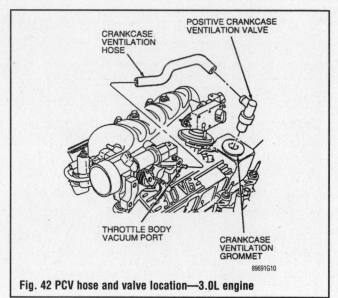

Fig. 42 PCV hose and valve location—3.0L engine

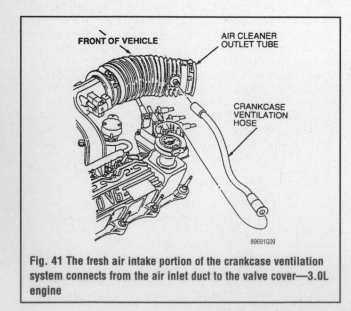

Fig. 41 The fresh air intake portion of the crankcase ventilation system connects from the air inlet duct to the valve cover—3.0L engine

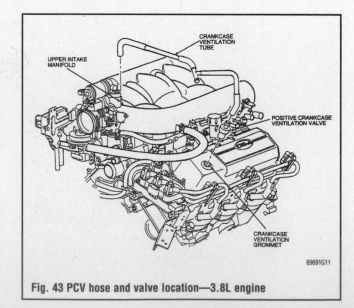

Fig. 43 PCV hose and valve location—3.8L engine

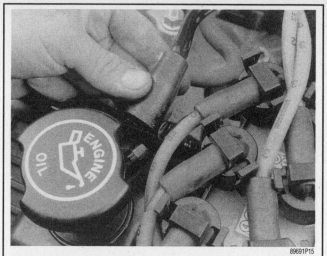

Carefully inspect the fresh air intake for blockage each time the PCV valve is serviced—3.0L engine

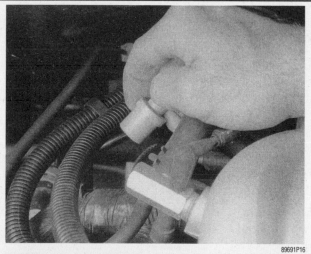

The PCV valve is located on the valve cover at the rear of the engine compartment

The fitting and hose on the front valve cover of the 3.8L engine is the fresh air intake, not the PCV valve

REMOVAL & INSTALLATION

1. Disconnect the hose from the PCV valve.
2. Remove the valve from the grommet on the valve cover.
To install:
3. Inspect the PCV valve and grommet. Inspect the hose for obstructions. Replace as necessary.
4. The PCV valve may be tested by shaking. If a rattle is heard, the valve is operating properly.
5. Connect the hose to the PCV valve.
6. Insert the PCV valve into the grommet on the valve cover.

Evaporative Canister

SERVICING

The evaporative canister requires no periodic servicing. However, a careful inspection of the canister and hoses should be made frequently. Replace damaged components as required.

The canister is located on the driver's side frame rail in the engine compartment.

REMOVAL & INSTALLATION

1. Disconnect the vapor hose from the canister.
2. Remove the bolts retaining the canister.
3. Lift the canister to disengage the tab on the back.
4. Remove the canister from the engine compartment.
To install:
5. Installation is the reverse of removal.
6. Tighten the canister retaining bolts to 17–20 ft. lbs. (22–28 Nm).

Battery

The battery should be serviced at least once a year. The battery case, tray and terminals should be cleaned and inspected for damage. The electrolyte level should be checked and specific gravity tested.

PRECAUTIONS

Always use caution when working on or near the battery. Never allow a tool to bridge the gap between the negative and positive battery terminals. Also, be careful not to allow a tool to provide a ground between the positive cable/terminal and any metal component on the vehicle. Either of these conditions will cause a short circuit, leading to sparks and possible personal injury.

Do not smoke, have an open flame or create sparks near a battery; the gases contained in the battery are very explosive and, if ignited, could cause severe injury or death.

All batteries, regardless of type, should be carefully secured by a battery hold-down device. If this is not done, the battery terminals or casing may crack from stress applied to the battery during vehicle operation. A battery which is not secured may allow acid to leak out, making it discharge faster; such leaking corrosive acid can also eat away at components under the hood.

Always visually inspect the battery case for cracks, leakage and corrosion. A white corrosive substance on the battery case or on nearby components would indicate a leaking or cracked battery. If the battery is cracked, it should be replaced immediately.

GENERAL MAINTENANCE

▶ **See Figure 44**

A battery that is not sealed must be checked periodically for electrolyte level. You cannot add water to a sealed maintenance-free battery (though not all maintenance-free batteries are sealed); however, a sealed battery must also be checked for proper electrolyte level, as indicated by the color of the built-in hydrometer "eye."

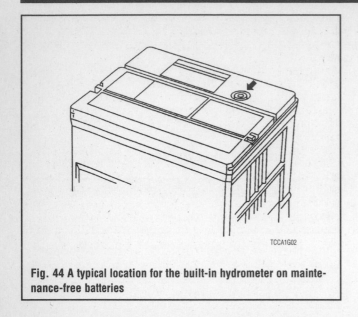

Fig. 44 A typical location for the built-in hydrometer on maintenance-free batteries

Always keep the battery cables and terminals free of corrosion. Check these components about once a year. Refer to the removal, installation and cleaning procedures outlined in this section.

Keep the top of the battery clean, as a film of dirt can help completely discharge a battery that is not used for long periods. A solution of baking soda and water may be used for cleaning, but be careful to flush this off with clear water. DO NOT let any of the solution into the filler holes. Baking soda neutralizes battery acid and will de-activate a battery cell.

Batteries in vehicles which are not operated on a regular basis can fall victim to parasitic loads (small current drains which are constantly drawing current from the battery). Normal parasitic loads may drain a battery on a vehicle that is in storage and not used for 6–8 weeks. Vehicles that have additional accessories such as a cellular phone, an alarm system or other devices that increase parasitic load may discharge a battery sooner. If the vehicle is to be stored for 6–8 weeks in a secure area and the alarm system, if present, is not necessary, the negative battery cable should be disconnected at the onset of storage to protect the battery charge.

Remember that constantly discharging and recharging will shorten battery life. Take care not to allow a battery to be needlessly discharged.

BATTERY FLUID

Check the battery electrolyte level at least once a month, or more often in hot weather or during periods of extended vehicle operation. On non-sealed batteries, the level can be checked either through the case on translucent batteries or by removing the cell caps on opaque-cased types. The electrolyte level in each cell should be kept filled to the split ring inside each cell, or the line marked on the outside of the case.

If the level is low, add only distilled water through the opening until the level is correct. Each cell is separate from the others, so each must be checked and filled individually. Distilled water should be used, because the chemicals and minerals found in most drinking water are harmful to the battery and could significantly shorten its life.

If water is added in freezing weather, the vehicle should be driven several miles to allow the water to mix with the electrolyte. Otherwise, the battery could freeze.

Although some maintenance-free batteries have removable cell caps for access to the electrolyte, the electrolyte condition and level on all sealed maintenance-free batteries must be checked using the built-in hydrometer "eye." The exact type of eye varies between battery manufacturers, but most apply a sticker to the battery itself explaining the possible readings. When in doubt, refer to the battery manufacturer's instructions to interpret battery condition using the built-in hydrometer.

➡Although the readings from built-in hydrometers found in sealed batteries may vary, a green eye usually indicates a properly charged battery with sufficient fluid level. A dark eye is normally an indicator of a battery with sufficient fluid, but one which may be low in charge. And a light or yellow eye is usually an indication that electrolyte supply has dropped below the necessary level for battery (and hydrometer) operation. In this last case, sealed batteries with an insufficient electrolyte level must usually be discarded.

Checking the Specific Gravity

▶ See Figure 45

A hydrometer is required to check the specific gravity on all batteries that are not maintenance-free. On batteries that are maintenance-free, the specific gravity is checked by observing the built-in hydrometer "eye" on the top of the battery case. Check with your battery's manufacturer for proper interpretation of its built-in hydrometer readings.

On non-maintenance-free batteries, the fluid level can be checked through the case on translucent models; the cell caps must be removed on other models

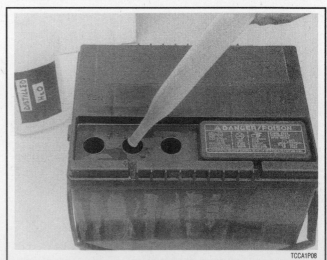

If the fluid level is low, add only distilled water through the opening until the level is correct

Battery electrolyte contains sulfuric acid. If you should splash any on your skin or in your eyes, flush the affected area with plenty of clear water. If it lands in your eyes, get medical help immediately.

The fluid (sulfuric acid solution) contained in the battery cells will tell you many things about the condition of the battery. Because the cell plates must be kept submerged below the fluid level in order to operate, maintaining the fluid level is extremely important. And, because the specific gravity of the acid is an indication of electrical charge, testing the fluid can be an aid in determining if the battery must be replaced. A battery in a vehicle with a properly operating charging system should require little maintenance, but careful, periodic inspection should reveal problems before they leave you stranded.

As stated earlier, the specific gravity of a battery's electrolyte level can be used as an indication of battery charge. At least once a year, check the specific gravity of the battery. It should be between 1.20 and 1.26 on the gravity scale. Most auto supply stores carry a variety of inexpensive battery testing hydrometers. These can be used on any non-sealed battery to test the specific gravity in each cell.

The battery testing hydrometer has a squeeze bulb at one end and a nozzle at the other. Battery electrolyte is sucked into the hydrometer until the float is lifted from its seat. The specific gravity is then read by noting the position of the float. If gravity is low in one or more cells, the battery should be slowly charged and checked again to see if the gravity has come up. Generally, if after charging, the specific gravity between any two cells varies more than 50 points (0.50), the battery should be replaced, as it can no longer produce sufficient voltage to guarantee proper operation.

CABLES

▶ **See Figures 46, 47, 48, 49 and 50**

Once a year (or as necessary), the battery terminals and the cable clamps should be cleaned. Loosen the clamps and remove the cables, negative cable first. On batteries with posts on top, the use of a puller specially made for this purpose is recommended. These are inexpensive and available in most auto parts stores. Side terminal battery cables are secured with a small bolt.

Clean the cable clamps and the battery terminal with a wire brush, until all corrosion, grease, etc., is removed and the metal is shiny. It is especially important to clean the inside of the clamp thoroughly (an old knife is useful here), since a small deposit of foreign material or oxidation there will prevent a sound electrical connection and inhibit either starting or charging. Special tools are available for cleaning these parts, one type for conventional top post batteries and another type for side terminal batteries. It is also a good idea to apply some dielectric grease to the terminal, as this will aid in the prevention of corrosion.

After the clamps and terminals are clean, reinstall the cables, negative cable last; DO NOT hammer the clamps onto battery posts. Tighten the clamps securely, but do not distort them. Give the clamps and terminals a thin external coating of grease after installation, to retard corrosion.

Check the cables at the same time that the terminals are cleaned. If the cable insulation is cracked or broken, or if the ends are frayed, the cable should be replaced with a new cable of the same length and gauge.

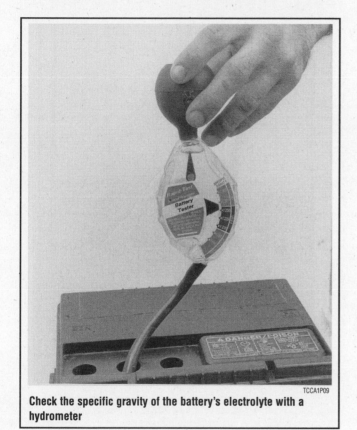

Check the specific gravity of the battery's electrolyte with a hydrometer

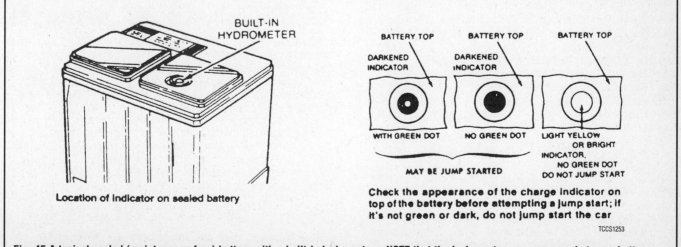

Location of indicator on sealed battery

BATTERY TOP — DARKENED INDICATOR — WITH GREEN DOT

BATTERY TOP — DARKENED INDICATOR — NO GREEN DOT

MAY BE JUMP STARTED

BATTERY TOP — LIGHT YELLOW OR BRIGHT INDICATOR, NO GREEN DOT — DO NOT JUMP START

Check the appearance of the charge indicator on top of the battery before attempting a jump start; if it's not green or dark, do not jump start the car

TCCS1253

Fig. 45 A typical sealed (maintenance-free) battery with a built-in hydrometer—NOTE that the hydrometer eye may vary between battery manufacturers; always refer to the battery's label

Fig. 46 Maintenance is performed with household items and with special tools like this post cleaner

Fig. 47 The underside of this special battery tool has a wire brush to clean post terminals

Fig. 48 Place the tool over the battery posts and twist to clean until the metal is shiny

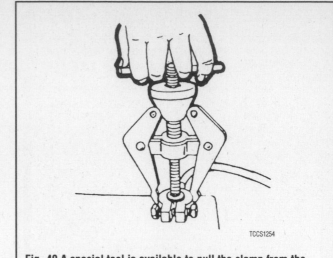

Fig. 49 A special tool is available to pull the clamp from the post

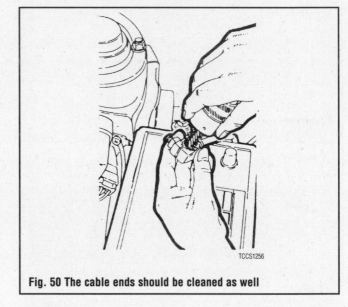

Fig. 50 The cable ends should be cleaned as well

CHARGING

❊❊ CAUTION

The chemical reaction which takes place in all batteries generates explosive hydrogen gas. A spark can cause the battery to explode and splash acid. To avoid serious personal injury, be sure there is proper ventilation and take appropriate fire safety precautions when connecting, disconnecting, or charging a battery and when using jumper cables.

A battery should be charged at a slow rate to keep the plates inside from getting too hot. However, if some maintenance-free batteries are allowed to discharge until they are almost "dead," they may have to be charged at a high rate to bring them back to "life." Always follow the charger manufacturer's instructions on charging the battery.

REMOVAL & INSTALLATION

◆ See Figures 51 thru 56

1. Disconnect the negative and then the positive battery cables.
2. Loosen the hold-down clamp or strap retainers.

Fig. 51 Loosen the battery hold-down device retainer . . .

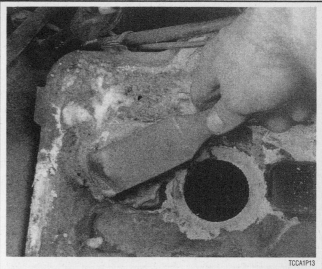

Fig. 54 Use a wire brush to clean any rust from the battery tray

Fig. 52 . . . then remove the battery hold-down device

Fig. 55 Brush on a solution of baking soda and water to clean the tray

Fig. 53 Remove the battery from the vehicle

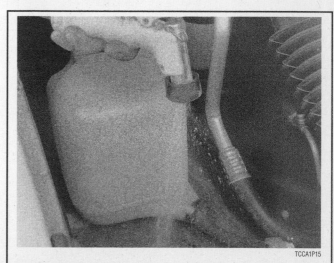

Fig. 56 After cleaning the tray thoroughly, wash it off with some water

3. Remove the battery hold-down device.
4. Remove the battery from the vehicle.

While the battery is removed, it is a good idea and opportunity to check the condition of the battery tray. Clear it of any debris, and check it for soundness (the battery tray can be cleaned with a baking soda and water solution). Rust should be wire brushed away, and the metal given a couple coats of anti-rust paint.

To install:

5. Install the battery and tighten the hold-down clamp or strap securely. Do not overtighten, as this can crack the battery case.
6. Connect the positive and then the negative battery cables.

REPLACEMENT

When it becomes necessary to replace the battery, select one with an amperage rating equal to or greater than the battery originally installed. Deterioration and just plain aging of the battery cables, starter motor, and associated wires makes the battery's job harder in successive years. The slow increase in electrical resistance over time makes it prudent to install a new battery with a greater capacity than the old.

Belts

INSPECTION

▶ **See Figures 57, 58, 59, 60 and 61**

Inspect the belts for signs of glazing or cracking at least once a year. A glazed belt will be perfectly smooth from slippage, while a good belt will have a slight texture of fabric visible. Cracks will usually start at the inner edge of the belt and run outward. All worn or damaged drive belts should be replaced immediately. It is best to replace all drive belts at one time, as a preventive maintenance measure, during this service operation.

ADJUSTMENT

All engines use an automatic drive belt tensioner. No adjustment is necessary. It is recommended that the belt tension indicator mark be inspected with the engine **OFF** at 60,000 mile (96,000 km) intervals. If the indicator mark is not between the MIN and MAX marks, the drive belt is worn or an incorrect drive belt has been installed.

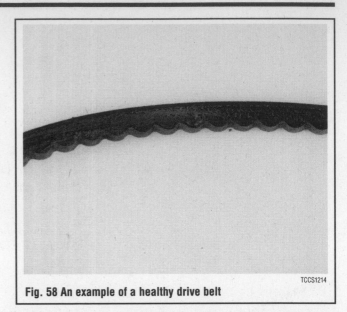

TCCS1214

Fig. 58 An example of a healthy drive belt

TCCS1215

Fig. 59 Deep cracks in this belt will cause flex, building up heat that will eventually lead to belt failure

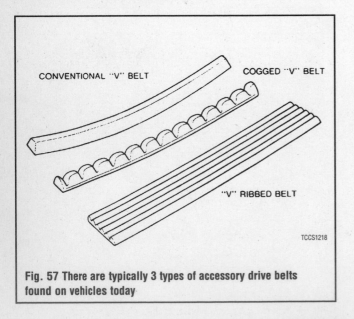

CONVENTIONAL "V" BELT   COGGED "V" BELT

"V" RIBBED BELT

TCCS1218

Fig. 57 There are typically 3 types of accessory drive belts found on vehicles today

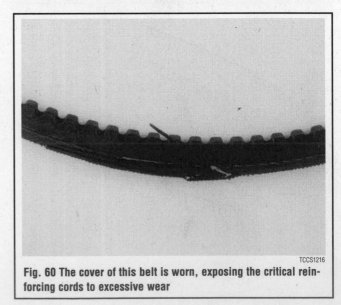

TCCS1216

Fig. 60 The cover of this belt is worn, exposing the critical reinforcing cords to excessive wear

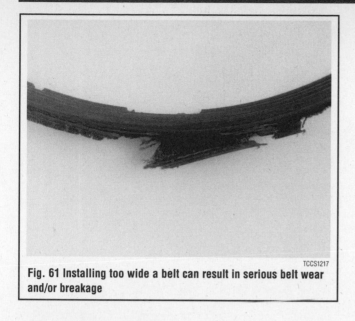

TCCS1217

Fig. 61 Installing too wide a belt can result in serious belt wear and/or breakage

REMOVAL & INSTALLATION

▶ See Figures 62, 63 and 64

Using a 15mm wrench attached to the drive belt tensioner pulley, rotate the tensioner clockwise to release the tension. Remove the drive belt from the pulley. When installing the new drive belt, ensure that the drive belt is routed correctly and note the position of the indicator mark on the tensioner.

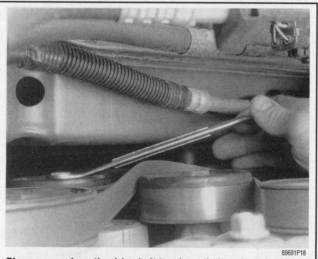

89691P18

Place a wrench on the drive belt tensioner bolt and rotate the assembly clockwise to relieve belt tension

Hoses

INSPECTION

▶ See Figures 65, 66, 67 and 68

Upper and lower radiator hoses, along with the heater hoses, should be checked for deterioration, leaks and loose hose clamps at least every 15,000 miles (24,000 km). It is also wise to check the hoses periodically in early spring and at the beginning of the fall or winter when you are performing other maintenance. A quick visual inspection could discover a weakened hose which might have left you stranded if it had remained unrepaired.

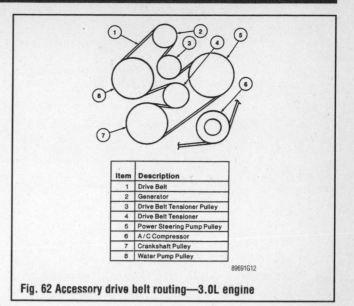

Item	Description
1	Drive Belt
2	Generator
3	Drive Belt Tensioner Pulley
4	Drive Belt Tensioner
5	Power Steering Pump Pulley
6	A / C Compressor
7	Crankshaft Pulley
8	Water Pump Pulley

89691G12

Fig. 62 Accessory drive belt routing—3.0L engine

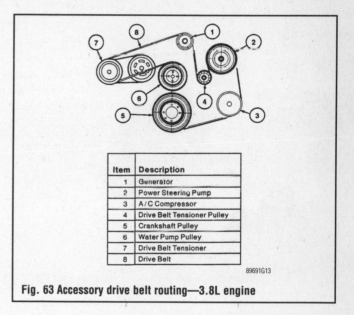

Item	Description
1	Generator
2	Power Steering Pump
3	A / C Compressor
4	Drive Belt Tensioner Pulley
5	Crankshaft Pulley
6	Water Pump Pulley
7	Drive Belt Tensioner
8	Drive Belt

89691G13

Fig. 63 Accessory drive belt routing—3.8L engine

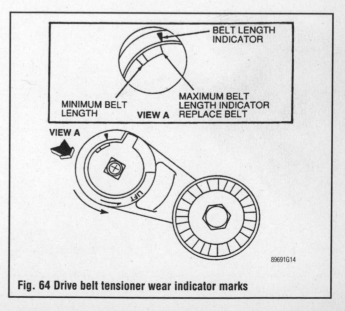

89691G14

Fig. 64 Drive belt tensioner wear indicator marks

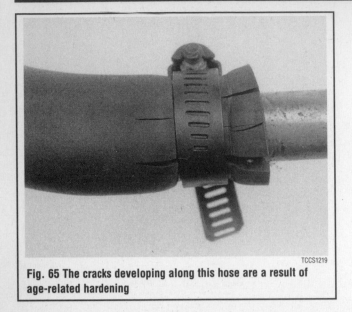

Fig. 65 The cracks developing along this hose are a result of age-related hardening

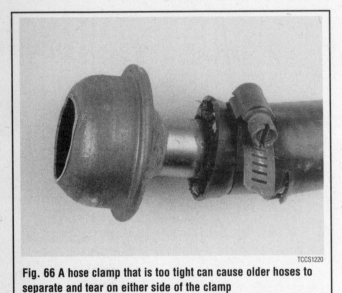

Fig. 66 A hose clamp that is too tight can cause older hoses to separate and tear on either side of the clamp

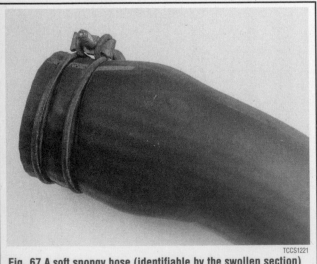

Fig. 67 A soft spongy hose (identifiable by the swollen section) will eventually burst and should be replaced

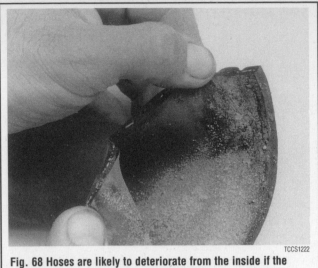

Fig. 68 Hoses are likely to deteriorate from the inside if the cooling system is not periodically flushed

Whenever you are checking the hoses, make sure the engine and cooling system are cold. Visually inspect for cracking, rotting or collapsed hoses, and replace as necessary. Run your hand along the length of the hose. If a weak or swollen spot is noted when squeezing the hose wall, the hose should be replaced.

REMOVAL & INSTALLATION

1. Remove the radiator pressure cap.

✳✳ CAUTION

Never remove the pressure cap while the engine is running, or personal injury from scalding hot coolant or steam may result. If possible, wait until the engine has cooled to remove the pressure cap. If this is not possible, wrap a thick cloth around the pressure cap and turn it slowly to the stop. Step back while the pressure is released from the cooling system. When you are sure all the pressure has been released, use the cloth to turn and remove the cap.

2. Position a clean container under the radiator and/or engine draincock or plug, then open the drain and allow the cooling system to drain to an appropriate level. For some upper hoses, only a little coolant must be drained. To remove hoses positioned lower on the engine, such as a lower radiator hose, the entire cooling system must be emptied.

✳✳ CAUTION

When draining coolant, keep in mind that cats and dogs are attracted by ethylene glycol antifreeze, and are quite likely to drink any that is left in an uncovered container or in puddles on the ground. This will prove fatal in sufficient quantity. Always drain coolant into a sealable container. Coolant may be reused unless it is contaminated or several years old.

3. Loosen the hose clamps at each end of the hose requiring replacement. Clamps are usually either of the spring tension type (which require pliers to squeeze the tabs and loosen) or of the screw tension type (which require screw or hex drivers to loosen). Pull the clamps back on the hose away from the connection.

4. Twist, pull and slide the hose off the fitting, taking care not to damage the neck of the component from which the hose is being removed.

➡If the hose is stuck at the connection, do not try to insert a screwdriver or other sharp tool under the hose end in an effort to free it, as the connection and/or hose may become damaged. Heater connections especially may be easily damaged by such a procedure. If the hose is to be replaced, use a single-edged razor blade to make a slice along the portion of the hose which is stuck on the connection, perpendicular to the end of the hose. Do not cut deep so as to prevent damaging the connection. The hose can then be peeled from the connection and discarded.

5. Clean both hose mounting connections. Inspect the condition of the hose clamps and replace them, if necessary.

To install:

6. Dip the ends of the new hose into clean engine coolant to ease installation.

7. Slide the clamps over the replacement hose, then slide the hose ends over the connections into position.

8. Position and secure the clamps at least ¼ in. (6.35mm) from the ends of the hose. Make sure they are located beyond the raised bead of the connector.

9. Close the radiator or engine drains and properly refill the cooling system with the clean drained engine coolant or a suitable mixture of ethylene glycol coolant and water.

10. If available, install a pressure tester and check for leaks. If a pressure tester is not available, run the engine until normal operating temperature is reached (allowing the system to naturally pressurize), then check for leaks.

✳✴ CAUTION

If you are checking for leaks with the system at normal operating temperature, BE EXTREMELY CAREFUL not to touch any moving or hot engine parts. Once temperature has been reached, shut the engine OFF, and check for leaks around the hose fittings and connections which were removed earlier.

CV-Boots

INSPECTION

♦ See Figures 69 and 70

The CV (Constant Velocity) boots should be checked for damage each time the oil is changed and any other time the vehicle is raised for service. These boots keep water, grime, dirt and other damaging matter from entering the CV-joints. Any of these could cause early CV-joint failure which can be expensive to repair. Heavy grease thrown around the inside of the front wheel(s) and on the brake caliper/drum can be an indication of a torn boot.

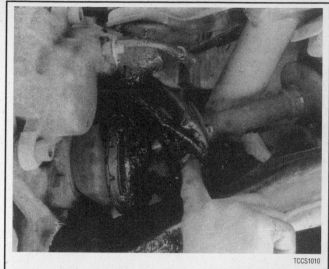

TCCS1010

Fig. 70 A torn boot should be replaced immediately

Thoroughly check the boots for missing clamps and tears. If the boot is damaged, it should be replaced immediately. Please refer to Section 7 for procedures.

Spark Plugs

♦ See Figure 71

The spark plugs should be replaced every 100,000 miles (160,000 km).

A typical spark plug consists of a metal shell surrounding a ceramic insulator. A metal electrode extends downward through the center of the insulator and protrudes a small distance. Located at the end of the plug and attached to the side of the outer metal shell is the side electrode. The side electrode bends in at a 90° angle so that its tip is just past and parallel to the tip of the center electrode. The distance between these two electrodes (measured in thousandths of an inch or hundredths of a millimeter) is called the spark plug gap.

The spark plug does not produce a spark but instead provides a gap across which the current can arc. The coil produces anywhere from 20,000 to 50,000 volts (depending on the type and application) which travels through the wires to the spark plugs. The current passes along the center electrode and jumps the gap to the side electrode, and in doing so, ignites the air/fuel mixture in the combustion chamber.

TCCS1011

Fig. 69 CV-boots must be inspected periodically for damage

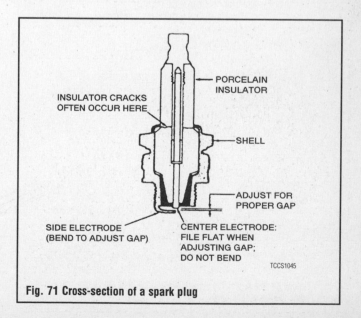

PORCELAIN INSULATOR

INSULATOR CRACKS OFTEN OCCUR HERE

SHELL

ADJUST FOR PROPER GAP

SIDE ELECTRODE (BEND TO ADJUST GAP)

CENTER ELECTRODE: FILE FLAT WHEN ADJUSTING GAP; DO NOT BEND

TCCS1045

Fig. 71 Cross-section of a spark plug

SPARK PLUG HEAT RANGE

▶ **See Figure 72**

Spark plug heat range is the ability of the plug to dissipate heat. The longer the insulator (or the farther it extends into the engine), the hotter the plug will operate; the shorter the insulator (the closer the electrode is to the block's cooling passages) the cooler it will operate. A plug that absorbs little heat and remains too cool will quickly accumulate deposits of oil and carbon since it is not hot enough to burn them off. This leads to plug fouling and consequently to misfiring. A plug that absorbs too much heat will have no deposits but, due to the excessive heat, the electrodes will burn away quickly and might possibly lead to preignition or other ignition problems. Preignition takes place when plug tips get so hot that they glow sufficiently to ignite the air/fuel mixture before the actual spark occurs. This early ignition will usually cause a pinging during low speeds and heavy loads.

The general rule of thumb for choosing the correct heat range when picking a spark plug is: if most of your driving is long distance, high speed travel, use a colder plug; if most of your driving is stop and go, use a hotter plug. Original equipment plugs are generally a good compromise between the 2 styles and most people never have the need to change their plugs from the factory-recommended heat range.

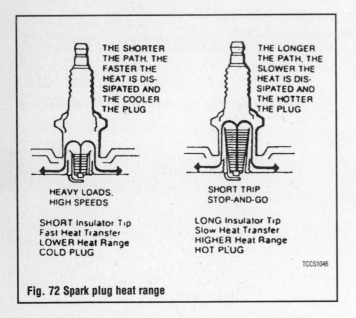

THE SHORTER THE PATH, THE FASTER THE HEAT IS DISSIPATED AND THE COOLER THE PLUG

THE LONGER THE PATH, THE SLOWER THE HEAT IS DISSIPATED AND THE HOTTER THE PLUG

HEAVY LOADS.
HIGH SPEEDS

SHORT Insulator Tip
Fast Heat Transfer
LOWER Heat Range
COLD PLUG

SHORT TRIP
STOP-AND-GO

LONG Insulator Tip
Slow Heat Transfer
HIGHER Heat Range
HOT PLUG

TCCS1046

Fig. 72 Spark plug heat range

REMOVAL & INSTALLATION

When you're removing spark plugs, work on one at a time. Don't start by removing the plug wires all at once, because, unless you number them, they may become mixed up. Take a minute before you begin and number the wires with tape.

1. Disconnect the negative battery cable, and if the vehicle has been run recently, allow the engine to thoroughly cool.

2. Carefully twist the spark plug wire boot to loosen it, then pull upward and remove the boot from the plug. Be sure to pull on the boot and not on the wire, otherwise the connector located inside the boot may become separated.

3. Using compressed air, blow any water or debris from the spark plug well to assure that no harmful contaminants are allowed to enter the combustion chamber when the spark plug is removed. If compressed air is not available, use a rag or a brush to clean the area.

➡**Remove the spark plugs when the engine is cold, if possible, to prevent damage to the threads. If removal of the plugs is difficult, apply a few drops of penetrating oil or silicone spray to the area around the base of the plug, and allow it a few minutes to work.**

89691P19

Twist and remove the spark plug boots one at a time

89691P20

Using a special spark plug socket, carefully remove the spark plug from the engine

89691P21

Inspect each spark plug as you remove it. Such analysis gives a good indication of engine condition

4. Using a spark plug socket that is equipped with a rubber insert to properly hold the plug, turn the spark plug counterclockwise to loosen and remove the spark plug from the bore.

✳✳ WARNING

Be sure not to use a flexible extension on the socket. Use of a flexible extension may allow a shear force to be applied to the plug. A shear force could break the plug off in the cylinder head, leading to costly and frustrating repairs.

To install:

5. Inspect the spark plug boot for tears or damage. If a damaged boot is found, the spark plug wire must be replaced.

6. Using a wire feeler gauge, check and adjust the spark plug gap. When using a gauge, the proper size should pass between the electrodes with a slight drag. The next larger size should not be able to pass while the next smaller size should pass freely.

7. Carefully thread the plug into the bore by hand. If resistance is felt before the plug is almost completely threaded, back the plug out and begin threading again. In small, hard to reach areas, an old spark plug wire and boot could be used as a threading tool. The boot will hold the plug while you twist the end of the wire and the wire is supple enough to twist before it would allow the plug to crossthread.

✳✳ WARNING

Do not use the spark plug socket to thread the plugs. Always carefully thread the plug by hand or using an old plug wire to prevent the possibility of crossthreading and damaging the cylinder head bore.

8. Carefully tighten the spark plug. If the plug you are installing is equipped with a crush washer, seat the plug, then tighten about ¼ turn to crush the washer. If you are installing a tapered seat plug, tighten the plug to specifications provided by the vehicle or plug manufacturer.

9. Apply a small amount of silicone dielectric compound to the end of the spark plug lead or inside the spark plug boot to prevent sticking, then install the boot to the spark plug and push until it clicks into place. The click may be felt or heard, then gently pull back on the boot to assure proper contact.

INSPECTION & GAPPING

▶ **See Figures 73 thru 84**

Check the plugs for deposits and wear. If they are not going to be replaced, clean the plugs thoroughly. Remember that any kind of deposit will decrease the efficiency of the plug. Plugs can be cleaned on a spark plug cleaning machine, which can sometimes be found in service stations, or you can do an acceptable job of cleaning with a stiff brush. If the plugs are cleaned, the electrodes must be filed flat. Use an ignition points file, not an emery board or the like, which will leave deposits. The electrodes must be filed perfectly flat with sharp edges; rounded edges reduce the spark plug voltage by as much as 50%.

Check spark plug gap before installation. The ground electrode (the L-shaped one connected to the body of the plug) must be parallel to the center electrode and the specified size wire gauge (please refer to the Tune-Up Specifications chart for details) must pass between the electrodes with a slight drag.

➡ **NEVER adjust the gap on a used platinum type spark plug.**

Always check the gap on new plugs as they are not always set correctly at the factory. Do not use a flat feeler gauge when measuring the gap on a used plug, because the reading may be inaccurate. A round-wire type gapping tool is the best way to check the gap. The correct gauge should pass through the electrode gap with a slight drag. If you're in doubt, try one size smaller and one larger. The smaller gauge should go through easily, while the larger one shouldn't go through at all. Wire gapping tools usually have a bending tool attached. Use that to adjust the side electrode until the proper distance is obtained. Absolutely never attempt to bend the center electrode. Also, be careful not to bend the side electrode too far or too often as it may weaken and break off within the engine, requiring removal of the cylinder head to retrieve it.

TCCS2135

Fig. 73 A normally worn spark plug should have light tan or gray deposits on the firing tip

TCCS2136

Fig. 74 A carbon fouled plug, identified by soft, sooty, black deposits, may indicate an improperly tuned vehicle. Check the air cleaner, ignition components and engine control system

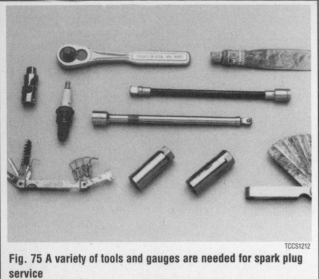

Fig. 75 A variety of tools and gauges are needed for spark plug service

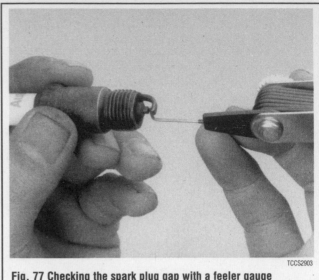

Fig. 77 Checking the spark plug gap with a feeler gauge

Fig. 76 A physically damaged spark plug may be evidence of severe detonation in that cylinder. Watch that cylinder carefully between services, as a continued detonation will not only damage the plug, but could also damage the engine

Fig. 78 An oil fouled spark plug indicates an engine with worn piston rings and/or bad valve seals, allowing excessive oil to enter the chamber

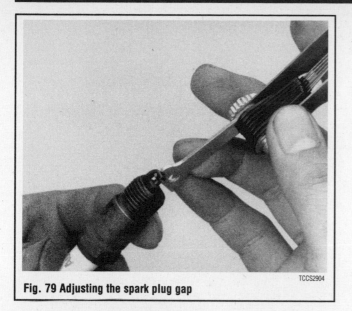

Fig. 79 Adjusting the spark plug gap

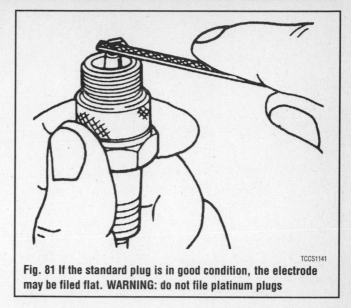

Fig. 81 If the standard plug is in good condition, the electrode may be filed flat. WARNING: do not file platinum plugs

Fig. 80 This spark plug has been left in the engine too long, as evidenced by the extreme gap. Plugs with such an extreme gap can cause misfiring and stumbling, accompanied by a noticeable lack of power

Fig. 82 A bridged or almost bridged spark plug, identified by a build-up between the electrodes caused by excessive carbon or oil build-up on the plug

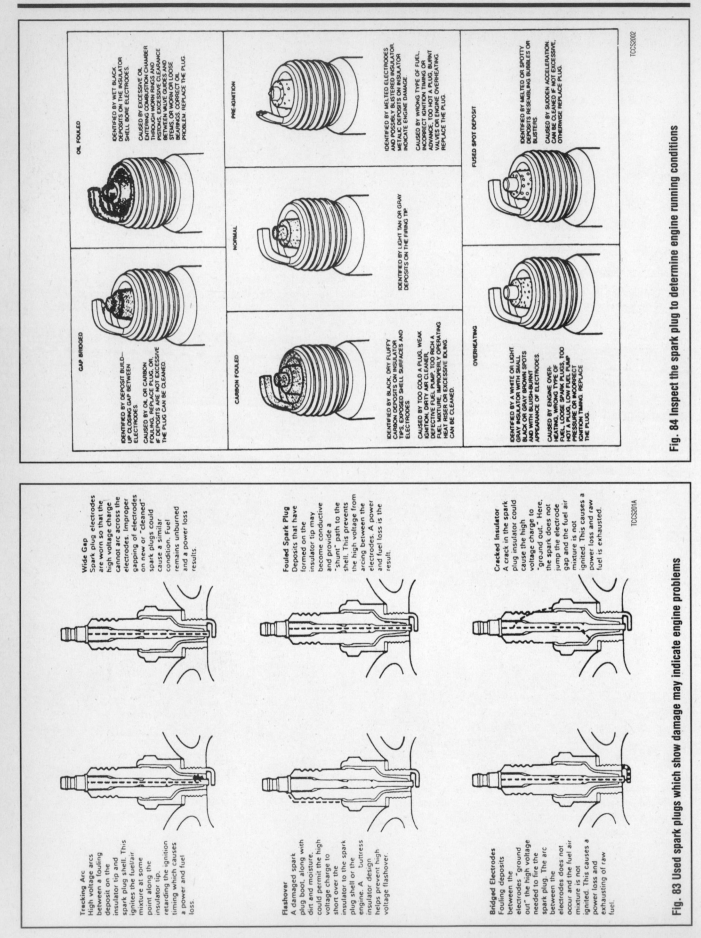

OIL FOULED

IDENTIFIED BY WET BLACK DEPOSITS ON THE INSULATOR SHELL BORE ELECTRODES.

CAUSED BY EXCESSIVE OIL ENTERING COMBUSTION CHAMBER THROUGH WORN RINGS AND PISTONS, EXCESSIVE CLEARANCE BETWEEN VALVE GUIDES AND STEMS, OR WORN OR LOOSE BEARINGS. CORRECT OIL PROBLEM. REPLACE THE PLUG.

GAP BRIDGED

IDENTIFIED BY DEPOSIT BUILD-UP CLOSING GAP BETWEEN ELECTRODES.

CAUSED BY OIL OR CARBON FOULING. REPLACE PLUG, OR, IF DEPOSITS ARE NOT EXCESSIVE THE PLUG CAN BE CLEANED.

PRE-IGNITION

IDENTIFIED BY MELTED ELECTRODES AND POSSIBLY BLISTERED INSULATOR. METALLIC DEPOSITS ON INSULATOR INDICATE ENGINE DAMAGE.

CAUSED BY WRONG TYPE OF FUEL, INCORRECT IGNITION TIMING OR ADVANCE, TOO HOT A PLUG, BURNT VALVES OR ENGINE OVERHEATING. REPLACE THE PLUG.

NORMAL

IDENTIFIED BY LIGHT TAN OR GRAY DEPOSITS ON THE FIRING TIP.

CARBON FOULED

IDENTIFIED BY BLACK, DRY FLUFFY CARBON DEPOSITS ON INSULATOR TIPS, EXPOSED SHELL SURFACES AND ELECTRODES

CAUSED BY TOO COLD A PLUG, WEAK IGNITION, DIRTY AIR CLEANER, DEFECTIVE FUEL PUMP, TOO RICH A FUEL MIXTURE, IMPROPERLY OPERATING HEAT RISER OR EXCESSIVE IDLING CAN BE CLEANED.

FUSED SPOT DEPOSIT

IDENTIFIED BY MELTED OR SPOTTY DEPOSITS RESEMBLING BUBBLES OR BLISTERS

CAUSED BY SUDDEN ACCELERATION. CAN BE CLEANED IF NOT EXCESSIVE, OTHERWISE REPLACE PLUG.

OVERHEATING

IDENTIFIED BY A WHITE OR LIGHT GRAY INSULATOR WITH SMALL BLACK OR GRAY BROWN SPOTS AND WITH BLUISH-BURNT APPEARANCE OF ELECTRODES.

CAUSED BY ENGINE OVER-HEATING, WRONG TYPE OF FUEL, LOOSE SPARK PLUGS, TOO HOT A PLUG, LOW FUEL PUMP PRESSURE OR INCORRECT IGNITION TIMING. REPLACE THE PLUG.

TCCS2002

Fig. 84 Inspect the spark plug to determine engine running conditions

Tracking Arc
High voltage arcs between a fouling deposit on the insulator tip and spark plug shell. This ignites the fuel/air mixture at some point along the insulator tip, retarding the ignition timing which causes a power and fuel loss.

Wide Gap
Spark plug electrodes are worn so that the high voltage charge cannot arc across the electrodes. Improper gapping of electrodes on new or "cleaned" spark plugs could cause a similar condition. Fuel remains unburned and a power loss results.

Flashover
A damaged spark plug boot, along with dirt and moisture, could permit the high voltage charge to short over the insulator to the spark plug shell or the engine. A buttress insulator design helps prevent high voltage flashover.

Fouled Spark Plug
Deposits that have formed on the insulator tip may become conductive and provide a "shunt" path to the shell. This prevents the high voltage from arcing between the electrodes. A power and fuel loss is the result.

Bridged Electrodes
Fouling deposits between the electrodes "ground out" the high voltage needed to fire the spark plug. The arc between the electrodes does not occur and the fuel air mixture is not ignited. This causes a power loss and exhausting of raw fuel.

Cracked Insulator
A crack in the spark plug insulator could cause the high voltage charge to "ground out". Here, the spark does not jump the electrode gap and the fuel air mixture is not ignited. This causes a power loss and raw fuel is exhausted.

TCCS201A

Fig. 83 Used spark plugs which show damage may indicate engine problems

Spark Plug Wires

TESTING

▶ **See Figure 85**

At every tune-up/inspection, visually check the spark plug cables for burns, cuts, or breaks in the insulation. Check the boots and the nipples on the distributor cap and/or coil. Replace any damaged wiring.

Every 100,000 miles (160,000 km), the resistance of the wires should be checked with an ohmmeter. Wires with excessive resistance will cause misfiring, and may make the engine difficult to start in damp weather.

1. Disconnect the spark plug wire at the spark plug and the coil pack.
2. Measure and note the length of the spark plug wire.
3. Using a ohmmeter, measure the resistance between the spark plug wire terminals.
4. Resistance should be less than 7000 ohms per foot of spark plug wire.

➡**If one spark plug wire is found to be out of specification, it is a good idea to replace the entire set.**

5. If resistance is excessive, the spark plug wire is faulty.

REMOVAL & INSTALLATION

▶ **See Figures 86 and 87**

1. Label each spark plug wire and make a note of its routing.

➡**Don't rely on wiring diagrams or sketches for spark plug wire routing. Improper arrangement of spark plug wires will induce volt-**

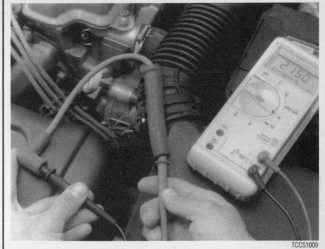

Fig. 85 Checking individual plug wire resistance with a digital ohmmeter

TCCS1009

age between wires, causing misfiring and surging. Be careful to arrange spark plug wires properly.

2. Starting with the longest wire, disconnect the spark plug wire from the spark plug and then from the coil pack.
3. Disconnect the ignition wire from the coil pack by squeezing the locking tabs and twisting while pulling upward.

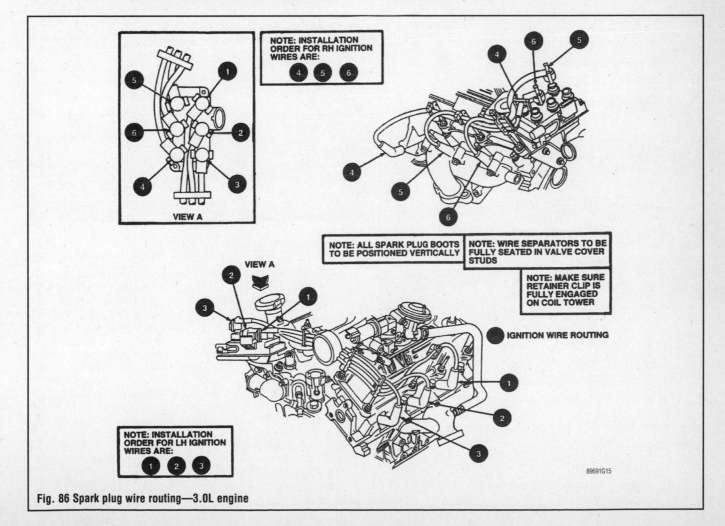

NOTE: INSTALLATION ORDER FOR RH IGNITION WIRES ARE: ④ ⑤ ⑥

VIEW A

NOTE: ALL SPARK PLUG BOOTS TO BE POSITIONED VERTICALLY

NOTE: WIRE SEPARATORS TO BE FULLY SEATED IN VALVE COVER STUDS

NOTE: MAKE SURE RETAINER CLIP IS FULLY ENGAGED ON COIL TOWER

IGNITION WIRE ROUTING

VIEW A

NOTE: INSTALLATION ORDER FOR LH IGNITION WIRES ARE: ① ② ③

89691G15

Fig. 86 Spark plug wire routing—3.0L engine

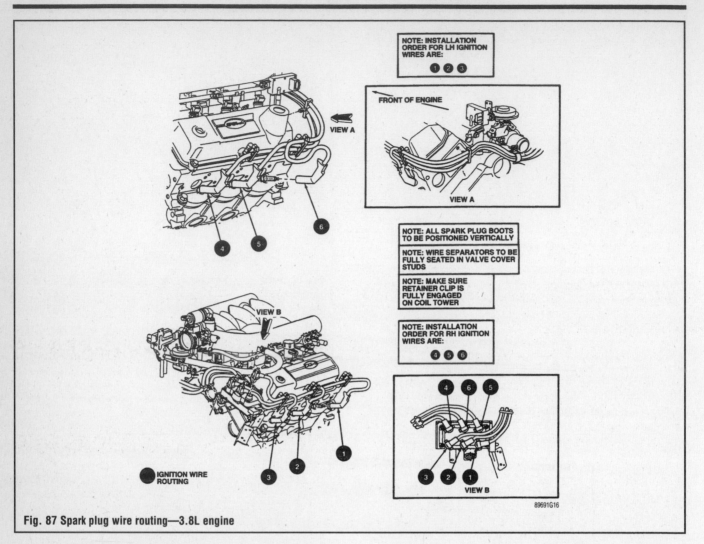

NOTE: INSTALLATION ORDER FOR LH IGNITION WIRES ARE:
① ② ③

FRONT OF ENGINE

VIEW A

VIEW A

NOTE: ALL SPARK PLUG BOOTS TO BE POSITIONED VERTICALLY

NOTE: WIRE SEPARATORS TO BE FULLY SEATED IN VALVE COVER STUDS

NOTE: MAKE SURE RETAINER CLIP IS FULLY ENGAGED ON COIL TOWER

NOTE: INSTALLATION ORDER FOR RH IGNITION WIRES ARE:
④ ⑤ ⑥

VIEW B

IGNITION WIRE ROUTING

VIEW B

Fig. 87 Spark plug wire routing—3.8L engine

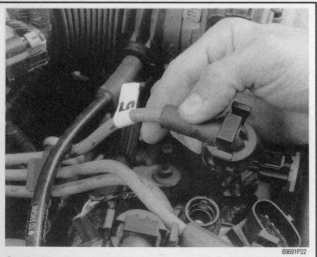

Spark plug wires are attached to the coil pack with special clips. Squeeze the clips to disconnect the wire

To install:

4. If replacing the spark plug wires, match the old wire with an appropriately sized wire in the new set.

5. Lubricate the boots and terminals with dielectric grease and install the wire on the coil pack. Make sure the wire snaps into place.

6. Route the wire in the exact path as the original and connect the wire to the spark plug.

7. Repeat the process for each remaining wire, working from the longest wire to the shortest.

Ignition Timing

GENERAL INFORMATION

Periodic adjustment of the ignition timing is not necessary for any engine covered by this manual. If ignition timing is not within specification, there is a fault in the engine control system. Diagnose and repair the problem as necessary.

Ignition timing is the measurement, in degrees of crankshaft rotation, of the point at which the spark plugs fire in each of the cylinders. It is measured in degrees before or after Top Dead Center (TDC) of the compression stroke.

Ideally, the air/fuel mixture in the cylinder will be ignited by the spark plug just as the piston passes TDC of the compression stroke. If this happens, the piston will be at the beginning of the power stroke just as the compressed and ignited air/fuel mixture forces the piston down and turns the crankshaft. Because it takes a fraction of a second for the spark plug to ignite the mixture in the cylinder, the spark plug must fire a little before the piston reaches TDC. Otherwise, the mixture will not be completely ignited as the piston passes TDC and the full power of the explosion will not be used by the engine.

The timing measurement is given in degrees of crankshaft rotation before the piston reaches TDC (BTDC). If the setting for the ignition timing is 10 BTDC, each spark plug must fire 10 degrees before each piston reaches TDC. This only holds true, however, when the engine is at idle speed.

As the engine speed increases, the pistons go faster. The spark plugs have to ignite the fuel even sooner if it is to be completely ignited when the piston reaches TDC. On all engines covered in this manual, spark timing changes are accomplished electronically by the Powertrain Control Module (PCM), based on input from engine sensors.

If the ignition is set too far advanced (BTDC), the ignition and expansion of the fuel in the cylinder will occur too soon and tend to force the piston down while it is still traveling up. This causes engine ping. If the ignition spark is set too far retarded, or after TDC (ATDC), the piston will have already started on its way down when the fuel is ignited. The piston will be forced down for only a portion of its travel, resulting in poor engine performance and lack of power.

Timing marks or scales can be found on the rim of the crankshaft pulley and the timing cover. The marks on the pulley correspond to the position of the piston in the No. 1 cylinder. A stroboscopic (dynamic) timing light is hooked onto the No. 1 cylinder spark plug wire. Every time the spark plug fires, the timing light flashes. By aiming the light at the timing marks while the engine is running, the exact position of the piston within the cylinder can be easily read (the flash of light makes the mark on the pulley appear to be standing still). Proper timing is indicated when the mark and scale are in specified alignment.

✳✳ WARNING

When checking timing with the engine running, take care not to get the timing light wires tangled in the fan blades and/or drive belts.

INSPECTION

▶ **See Figure 88**

1. Place the vehicle in **P** or **N** with the parking brake applied and the drive wheels blocked.
2. Start the engine and allow it reach normal operating temperature. Make sure all accessories are off.
3. Connect a suitable tachometer and timing light to the engine, as per the manufacturer's instructions.
4. Check that the idle speed is within the specified rpm range.
5. Following the manufacturer's instructions, aim the timing light and check the ignition timing. As the light flashes, note the position of the mark on the crankshaft pulley against the scale on the timing cover. Timing should be 8–12 degrees BTDC.
6. If ignition timing is not within specification, there is a fault in the engine control system. Diagnose and repair the problem as necessary.
7. Stop the engine and remove the tachometer and timing light.

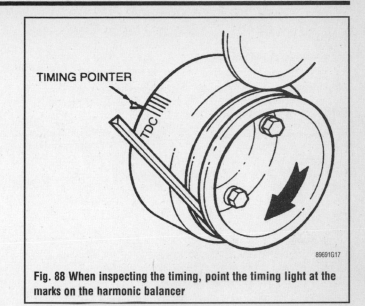

Fig. 88 When inspecting the timing, point the timing light at the marks on the harmonic balancer

Valve Lash

All engines covered in this manual use hydraulic valve tappets. Periodic valve lash adjustments are not necessary. If it is determined that the engine has a valve tap, a complete inspection of the valve train must be made to determine the faulty components.

Idle Speed and Mixture Adjustments

All engines covered in this manual utilize sophisticated multi-port fuel injection systems. Based on information from various sensors, the powertrain control module constantly adjusts and maintains proper idle speed and mixture to meet driving conditions.

Periodic adjustment of the idle speed and fuel mixture is not necessary for any engine covered by this manual. If ignition timing is not within specification, there is a fault in the engine control system. Diagnose and repair the problem as necessary.

GASOLINE ENGINE TUNE-UP SPECIFICATIONS

Year	Engine ID/VIN	Engine Displacement Liters (cc)	Spark Plugs Gap (in.)	Ignition Timing (deg.) MT	AT	Fuel Pump (psi)	Idle Speed (rpm) MT	AT	Valve Clearance In.	Ex.
1995	U	3.0(2966)	0.052–0.046	—	8–12 ①	35–40	—	675–725	HYD	HYD
	4	3.8(3802)	0.052–0.056	—	8–12 ①	35–40	—	675–725	HYD	HYD
1996	U	3.0(2966)	0.052–0.046	—	8–12 ①	35–40	—	675–725	HYD	HYD
	4	3.8(3802)	0.052–0.056	—	8–12 ①	35–40	—	675–725	HYD	HYD
1997	U	3.0(2966)	0.052–0.046	—	8–12 ①	35–40	—	675–725	HYD	HYD
	4	3.8(3802)	0.052–0.056	—	8–12 ①	35–40	—	675–725	HYD	HYD
1998	U	3.0(2966)	0.052–0.046	—	8–12 ①	35–40	—	675–725	HYD	HYD
	4	3.8(3802)	0.052–0.056	—	8–12 ①	35–40	—	675–725	HYD	HYD

NOTE: The Vehicle Emission Control Information label often reflects specification changes made during production. Label figures must be used if they differ from those in this chart.

① Ignition timing is controlled by the powertrain control module and is not adjustable.

89691C04

Air Conditioning System

SYSTEM SERVICE & REPAIR

➡ **It is recommended that the A/C system be serviced by an EPA Section 609 certified automotive technician utilizing a refrigerant recovery/recycling machine.**

The do-it-yourselfer should not service his/her own vehicle's A/C system for many reasons, including legal concerns, personal injury, environmental damage and cost. The following are some of the reasons why you may decide not to service your own vehicle's A/C system.

According to the U.S. Clean Air Act, it is a federal crime to service or repair (involving the refrigerant) a Motor Vehicle Air Conditioning (MVAC) system for money without being EPA certified. It is also illegal to vent R-134a refrigerant into the atmosphere.

State and/or local laws may be more strict than the federal regulations, so be sure to check with your state and/or local authorities for further information. For further federal information on the legality of servicing your A/C system, call the EPA Stratospheric Ozone Hotline.

➡ **Federal law dictates that a fine of up to $25,000 may be leveled on people convicted of venting refrigerant into the atmosphere. Additionally, the EPA may pay up to $10,000 for information or services leading to a criminal conviction of the violation of these laws.**

When servicing an A/C system, you run the risk of handling or coming in contact with refrigerant, which may result in skin or eye irritation or frostbite. Although low in toxicity (due to chemical stability), inhalation of concentrated refrigerant fumes is dangerous and can result in death; cases of fatal cardiac arrhythmia have been reported in people accidentally subjected to high levels of refrigerant. Some early symptoms include loss of concentration and drowsiness.

Also, refrigerants can decompose at high temperatures (near gas heaters or open flame), which may result in hydrofluoric acid, hydrochloric acid and phosgene (a fatal nerve gas).

R-134a refrigerant is a greenhouse gas which, if allowed to vent into the atmosphere, will contribute to global warming (the Greenhouse Effect).

It is usually more economically feasible to have a certified MVAC automotive technician perform A/C system service on your vehicle. While it is illegal to service an A/C system without the proper equipment, the home mechanic would have to purchase an expensive refrigerant recovery/recycling machine to service his/her own vehicle.

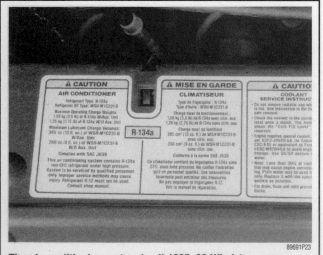

The air conditioning system in all 1995–98 Windstars uses R-134a refrigerant

PREVENTIVE MAINTENANCE

Although the A/C system should not be serviced by the do-it-yourselfer, preventive maintenance can be practiced and A/C system inspections can be performed to help maintain the efficiency of the vehicle's A/C system. For preventive maintenance, perform the following:

• The easiest and most important preventive maintenance for your A/C system is to be sure that it is used on a regular basis. Running the system for five minutes each month (no matter what the season) will help ensure that the seals and all internal components remain lubricated.

➡ **Some newer vehicles automatically operate the A/C system compressor whenever the windshield defroster is activated. When running, the compressor lubricates the A/C system components; therefore, the A/C system would not need to be operated each month.**

• In order to prevent heater core freeze-up during A/C operation, it is necessary to maintain a proper antifreeze protection. Use a hand-held coolant tester (hydrometer) to periodically check the condition of the antifreeze in your engine's cooling system.

➡ **Antifreeze should not be used longer than the manufacturer specifies.**

• For efficient operation of an air conditioned vehicle's cooling system, the radiator cap should have a holding pressure which meets manufacturer's specifications. A cap which fails to hold these pressures should be replaced.

• Any obstruction of or damage to the condenser configuration will restrict air flow which is essential to its efficient operation. It is, therefore, a good rule to keep this unit clean and in proper physical shape.

➡ **Bug screens which are mounted in front of the condenser (unless they are original equipment) are regarded as obstructions.**

• The condensation drain tube expels any water, which accumulates on the bottom of the evaporator housing, into the engine compartment. If this tube is obstructed, the air conditioning performance can be restricted and condensation buildup can spill over onto the vehicle's floor.

SYSTEM INSPECTION

Although the A/C system should not be serviced by the do-it-yourselfer, preventive maintenance can be practiced and A/C system inspections can be performed to help maintain the efficiency of the vehicle's A/C system. For A/C system inspection, perform the following:

The easiest and often most important check for the air conditioning system consists of a visual inspection of the system components. Visually inspect the air conditioning system for refrigerant leaks, damaged compressor clutch, abnormal compressor drive belt tension and/or condition, plugged evaporator drain tube, blocked condenser fins, disconnected or broken wires, blown fuses, corroded connections and poor insulation.

A refrigerant leak will usually appear as an oily residue at the leakage point in the system. The oily residue soon picks up dust or dirt particles from the surrounding air and appears greasy. Through time, this will build up and appear to be a heavy, dirt impregnated grease.

For a thorough visual and operational inspection, check the following:

• Check the surface of the radiator and condenser for dirt, leaves or other material which might block air flow.

• Check for kinks in hoses and lines. Check the system for leaks.

• Make sure the drive belt is properly tensioned. When the air conditioning is operating, make sure the drive belt is free of noise or slippage.

• Make sure the blower motor operates at all appropriate positions, then check for distribution of the air from all outlets with the blower on **HIGH** or **MAX**.

➡ **Keep in mind that under conditions of high humidity, air discharged from the A/C vents may not feel as cold as expected, even if the system is working properly. This is because vaporized moisture in humid air retains heat more effectively than dry air, thereby making humid air more difficult to cool.**

• Make sure the air passage selection lever is operating correctly. Start the engine and warm it to normal operating temperature, then make sure the temperature selection lever is operating correctly.

Windshield Wipers

Although the manufacturer does not specify a replacement interval for windshield wipers, we at Chilton feel the wipers should be replaced at least once a year, or whenever the wipers do not effectively clear the windshield.

ELEMENT (REFILL) CARE & REPLACEMENT

▶ **See Figures 89 thru 98**

For maximum effectiveness and longest element life, the windshield and wiper blades should be kept clean. Dirt, tree sap, road tar and so on will cause streaking, smearing and blade deterioration if left on the glass. It is advisable to wash the windshield carefully with a commercial glass cleaner at least once a month. Wipe off the rubber blades with the wet rag afterwards. Do not attempt to move wipers across the windshield by hand; damage to the motor and drive mechanism will result.

To inspect and/or replace the wiper blade elements, place the wiper switch in the **LOW** speed position and the ignition switch in the **ACC** position. When the wiper blades are approximately vertical on the windshield, turn the ignition switch to **OFF**.

Examine the wiper blade elements. If they are found to be cracked, broken or torn, they should be replaced immediately. Replacement intervals will vary with usage, although ozone deterioration usually limits element life to about one year. If the wiper pattern is smeared or streaked, or if the blade chatters across the glass, the elements should be replaced. It is easiest and most sensible to replace the elements in pairs.

If your vehicle is equipped with aftermarket blades, there are several different types of refills and your vehicle might have any kind. Aftermarket blades and arms rarely use the exact same type blade or refill as the original equipment. Here are some typical aftermarket blades; not all may be available for your vehicle:

The Anco® type uses a release button that is pushed down to allow the refill to slide out of the yoke jaws. The new refill slides back into the frame and locks in place.

Some Trico® refills are removed by locating where the metal backing strip or the refill is wider. Insert a small screwdriver blade between the frame and metal backing strip. Press down to release the refill from the retaining tab.

Other types of Trico® refills have two metal tabs which are unlocked by squeezing them together. The rubber filler can then be withdrawn from the

Fig. 90 Lexor® wiper blade and fit kit

TCCS1224

Fig. 91 Pylon® wiper blade and adapter

TCCS1225

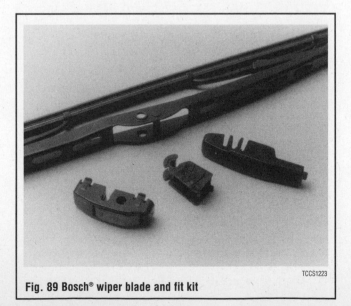

Fig. 89 Bosch® wiper blade and fit kit

TCCS1223

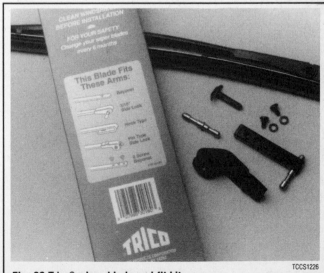

Fig. 92 Trico® wiper blade and fit kit

TCCS1226

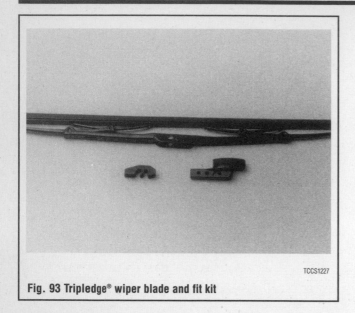

Fig. 93 Tripledge® wiper blade and fit kit

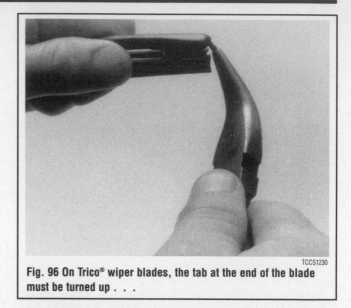

Fig. 96 On Trico® wiper blades, the tab at the end of the blade must be turned up . . .

Fig. 94 To remove and install a Lexor® wiper blade refill, slip out the old insert and slide in a new one

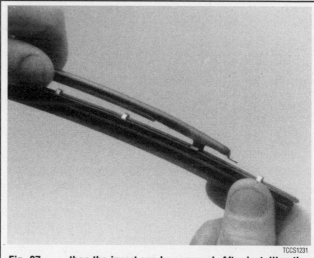

Fig. 97 . . . then the insert can be removed. After installing the replacement insert, bend the tab back

Fig. 95 On Pylon® inserts, the clip at the end has to be removed prior to sliding the insert off

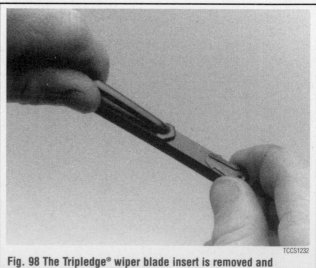

Fig. 98 The Tripledge® wiper blade insert is removed and installed using a securing clip

frame jaws. A new refill is installed by inserting the refill into the front frame jaws and sliding it rearward to engage the remaining frame jaws. There are usually four jaws; be certain when installing that the refill is engaged in all of them. At the end of its travel, the tabs will lock into place on the front jaws of the wiper blade frame.

Another type of refill is made from polycarbonate. The refill has a simple locking device at one end which flexes downward out of the groove into which the jaws of the holder fit, allowing easy release. By sliding the new refill through all the jaws and pushing through the slight resistance when it reaches the end of its travel, the refill will lock into position.

To replace the Tridon® refill, it is necessary to remove the wiper blade. This refill has a plastic backing strip with a notch about 1 in. (25mm) from the end. Hold the blade (frame) on a hard surface so that the frame is tightly bowed. Grip the tip of the backing strip and pull up while twisting counter-clockwise. The backing strip will snap out of the retaining tab. Do this for the remaining tabs until the refill is free of the blade. The length of these refills is molded into the end and they should be replaced with identical types.

Regardless of the type of refill used, be sure to follow the part manufacturer's instructions closely. Make sure that all of the frame jaws are engaged as the refill is pushed into place and locked. If the metal blade holder and frame are allowed to touch the glass during wiper operation, the glass will be scratched.

Tires and Wheels

Tires should be inspected frequently and rotated every 5,000 miles (8,000 km).

Common sense and good driving habits will afford maximum tire life. Fast starts, sudden stops and hard cornering are hard on tires and will shorten their useful life span. Make sure that you don't overload the vehicle or run with incorrect pressure in the tires. Both of these practices will increase tread wear.

➡**For optimum tire life, keep the tires properly inflated, rotate them often and have the wheel alignment checked periodically.**

Be especially careful to watch for bubbles in the tread or sidewall, deep cuts or underinflation. Replace any tires with bubbles in the sidewall. If cuts are so deep that they penetrate to the cords, discard the tire. Any cut in the sidewall of a radial tire renders it unsafe. Also look for uneven tread wear patterns that may indicate the front end is out of alignment or that the tires are out of balance.

TIRE ROTATION

▶ **See Figures 99, 100 and 101**

Tires must be rotated periodically to equalize wear patterns that vary with a tire's position on the vehicle. Tires will also wear in an uneven way as the front steering/suspension system wears to the point where the alignment should be reset.

Rotating the tires will ensure maximum life for the tires as a set, so you will not have to discard a tire early due to wear on only part of the tread. Regular rotation is required to equalize wear.

When rotating "unidirectional tires," make sure that they always roll in the same direction. This means that a tire used on the left side of the vehicle must not be switched to the right side and vice-versa. Such tires should only be rotated front-to-rear or rear-to-front, while always remaining on the same side of the vehicle. These tires are marked on the sidewall as to the direction of rotation; observe the marks when reinstalling the tire(s).

Some styled or "mag" wheels may have different offsets front to rear. In these cases, the rear wheels must not be used up front and vice-versa. Furthermore, if these wheels are equipped with unidirectional tires, they cannot be rotated unless the tire is remounted for the proper direction of rotation.

➡**The compact or space-saver spare is strictly for emergency use. It must never be included in the tire rotation or placed on the vehicle for everyday use.**

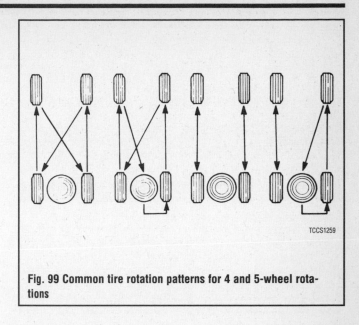

Fig. 99 Common tire rotation patterns for 4 and 5-wheel rotations

TCCS1259

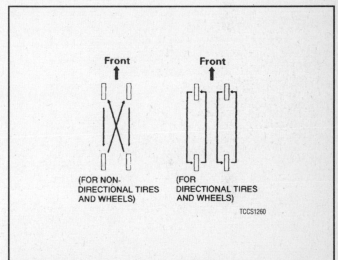

Fig. 100 Compact spare tires must NEVER be used in the rotation pattern

TCCS1260

Fig. 101 Unidirectional tires are identifiable by sidewall arrows and/or the word "rotation"

TCCS1234

TIRE DESIGN

▶ **See Figure 102**

For maximum satisfaction, tires should be used in sets of four. Mixing of different types (radial, bias-belted, fiberglass belted) must be avoided. In most cases, the vehicle manufacturer has designated a type of tire on which the vehicle will perform best. Your first choice when replacing tires should be to use the same type of tire that the manufacturer recommends.

When radial tires are used, tire sizes and wheel diameters should be selected to maintain ground clearance and tire load capacity equivalent to the original specified tire. Radial tires should always be used in sets of four.

✷✷ CAUTION

Radial tires should never be used on only the front axle.

When selecting tires, pay attention to the original size as marked on the tire. Most tires are described using an industry size code sometimes referred to as P-Metric. This allows the exact identification of the tire specifications, regardless of the manufacturer. If selecting a different tire size or brand, remember to check the installed tire for any sign of interference with the body or suspension while the vehicle is stopping, turning sharply or heavily loaded.

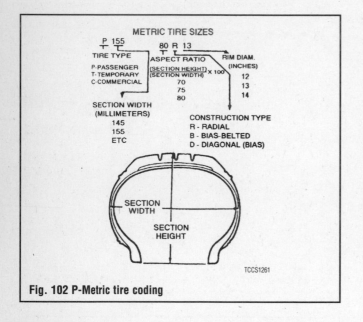

Fig. 102 P-Metric tire coding

Snow Tires

Good radial tires can produce a big advantage in slippery weather, but in snow, a street radial tire does not have sufficient tread to provide traction and control. The small grooves of a street tire quickly pack with snow and the tire behaves like a billiard ball on a marble floor. The more open, chunky tread of a snow tire will self-clean as the tire turns, providing much better grip on snowy surfaces.

To satisfy municipalities requiring snow tires during weather emergencies, most snow tires carry either an M + S designation after the tire size stamped on the sidewall, or the designation "all-season." In general, no change in tire size is necessary when buying snow tires.

Most manufacturers strongly recommend the use of 4 snow tires on their vehicles for reasons of stability. If snow tires are fitted only to the drive wheels, the opposite end of the vehicle may become very unstable when braking or turning on slippery surfaces. This instability can lead to unpleasant endings if the driver can't counteract the slide in time.

Note that snow tires, whether 2 or 4, will affect vehicle handling in all non-snow situations. The stiffer, heavier snow tires will noticeably change the turning and braking characteristics of the vehicle. Once the snow tires are installed, you must re-learn the behavior of the vehicle and drive accordingly.

➥Consider buying extra wheels on which to mount the snow tires. Once done, the "snow wheels" can be installed and removed as needed. This eliminates the potential damage to tires or wheels from seasonal removal and installation. Even if your vehicle has styled wheels, see if inexpensive steel wheels are available. Although the look of the vehicle will change, the expensive wheels will be protected from salt, curb hits and pothole damage.

TIRE STORAGE

If they are mounted on wheels, store the tires at proper inflation pressure. All tires should be kept in a cool, dry place. If they are stored in the garage or basement, do not let them stand on a concrete floor; set them on strips of wood, a mat or a large stack of newspaper. Keeping them away from direct moisture is of paramount importance. Tires should not be stored upright, but in a flat position.

INFLATION & INSPECTION

▶ **See Figures 103 thru 110**

The importance of proper tire inflation cannot be overemphasized. A tire employs air as part of its structure. It is designed around the sup-

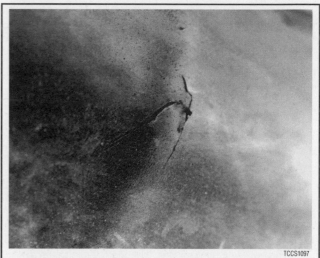

Fig. 103 Tires should be checked frequently for any sign of puncture or damage

Fig. 104 Tires with deep cuts, or cuts which show bulging should be replaced immediately

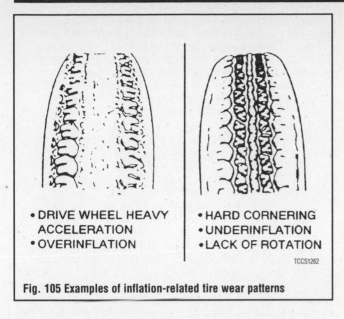

- DRIVE WHEEL HEAVY ACCELERATION
- OVERINFLATION

- HARD CORNERING
- UNDERINFLATION
- LACK OF ROTATION

TCCS1262

Fig. 105 Examples of inflation-related tire wear patterns

porting strength of the air at a specified pressure. For this reason, improper inflation drastically reduces the tire's ability to perform as intended. A tire will lose some air in day-to-day use; having to add a few pounds of air periodically is not necessarily a sign of a leaking tire.

Two items should be a permanent fixture in every glove compartment: an accurate tire pressure gauge and a tread depth gauge. Check the tire pressure (including the spare) regularly with a pocket type gauge. Too often, the gauge on the end of the air hose at your corner garage is not accurate because it suffers too much abuse. Always check tire pressure when the tires are cold, as pressure increases with temperature. If you must move the vehicle to check the tire inflation, do not drive more than a mile before checking. A cold tire is generally one that has not been driven for more than three hours.

A plate or sticker is normally provided somewhere in the vehicle (door post, hood, tailgate or trunk lid) which shows the proper pressure for the tires. Never counteract excessive pressure build-up by bleeding off air pressure (letting some air out). This will cause the tire to run hotter and wear quicker.

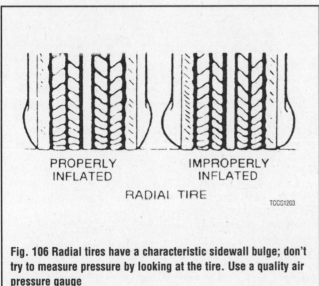

PROPERLY INFLATED   IMPROPERLY INFLATED

RADIAL TIRE

TCCS1203

Fig. 106 Radial tires have a characteristic sidewall bulge; don't try to measure pressure by looking at the tire. Use a quality air pressure gauge

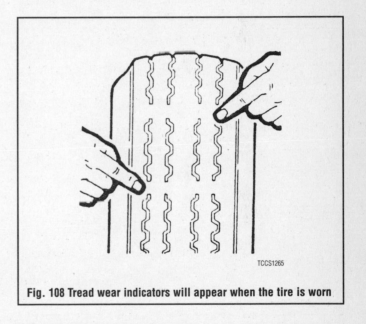

TCCS1265

Fig. 108 Tread wear indicators will appear when the tire is worn

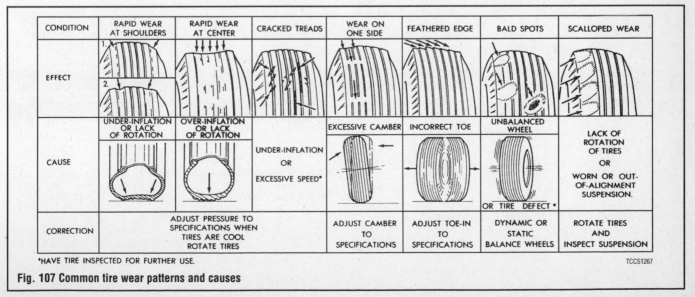

CONDITION	RAPID WEAR AT SHOULDERS	RAPID WEAR AT CENTER	CRACKED TREADS	WEAR ON ONE SIDE	FEATHERED EDGE	BALD SPOTS	SCALLOPED WEAR
EFFECT							
CAUSE	UNDER-INFLATION OR LACK OF ROTATION	OVER-INFLATION OR LACK OF ROTATION	UNDER-INFLATION OR EXCESSIVE SPEED*	EXCESSIVE CAMBER	INCORRECT TOE	UNBALANCED WHEEL OR TIRE DEFECT *	LACK OF ROTATION OF TIRES OR WORN OR OUT-OF-ALIGNMENT SUSPENSION.
CORRECTION	ADJUST PRESSURE TO SPECIFICATIONS WHEN TIRES ARE COOL ROTATE TIRES			ADJUST CAMBER TO SPECIFICATIONS	ADJUST TOE-IN TO SPECIFICATIONS	DYNAMIC OR STATIC BALANCE WHEELS	ROTATE TIRES AND INSPECT SUSPENSION

*HAVE TIRE INSPECTED FOR FURTHER USE.

TCCS1267

Fig. 107 Common tire wear patterns and causes

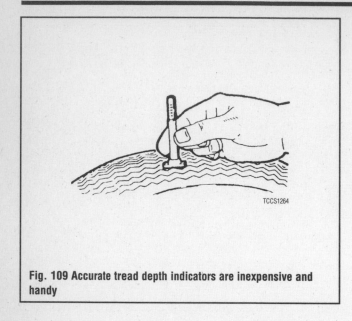

Fig. 109 Accurate tread depth indicators are inexpensive and handy

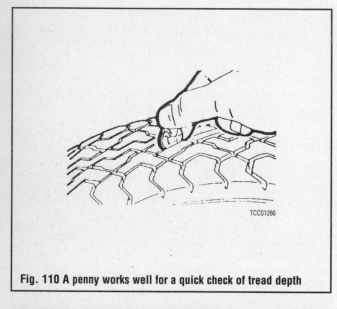

Fig. 110 A penny works well for a quick check of tread depth

❊❊ CAUTION

Never exceed the maximum tire pressure embossed on the tire! This is the pressure to be used when the tire is at maximum

loading, but it is rarely the correct pressure for everyday driving. Consult the owner's manual or the tire pressure sticker for the correct tire pressure.

Once you've maintained the correct tire pressures for several weeks, you'll be familiar with the vehicle's braking and handling personality. Slight adjustments in tire pressures can fine-tune these characteristics, but never change the cold pressure specification by more than 2 psi. A slightly softer tire pressure will give a softer ride but also yield lower fuel mileage. A slightly harder tire will give crisper dry road handling but can cause skidding on wet surfaces. Unless you're fully attuned to the vehicle, stick to the recommended inflation pressures.

All tires made since 1968 have built-in tread wear indicator bars that show up as ½ in. (13mm) wide smooth bands across the tire when $\frac{1}{16}$ in. (1.5mm) of tread remains. The appearance of tread wear indicators means that the tires should be replaced. In fact, many states have laws prohibiting the use of tires with less than this amount of tread.

You can check your own tread depth with an inexpensive gauge or by using a Lincoln head penny. Slip the Lincoln penny (with Lincoln's head upside-down) into several tread grooves. If you can see the top of Lincoln's head in 2 adjacent grooves, the tire has less than $\frac{1}{16}$ in. (1.5mm) tread left and should be replaced. You can measure snow tires in the same manner by using the "tails" side of the Lincoln penny. If you can see the top of the Lincoln memorial, it's time to replace the snow tire(s).

CARE OF SPECIAL WHEELS

If you have invested money in magnesium, aluminum alloy or sport wheels, special precautions should be taken to make sure your investment is not wasted and that your special wheels look good for the life of the vehicle.

Special wheels are easily damaged and/or scratched. Occasionally check the rims for cracking, impact damage or air leaks. If any of these are found, replace the wheel. But in order to prevent this type of damage and the costly replacement of a special wheel, observe the following precautions:

• Use extra care not to damage the wheels during removal, installation, balancing, etc. After removal of the wheels from the vehicle, place them on a mat or other protective surface. If they are to be stored for any length of time, support them on strips of wood. Never store tires and wheels upright; the tread may develop flat spots.

• When driving, watch for hazards; it doesn't take much to crack a wheel.

• When washing, use a mild soap or non-abrasive dish detergent (keeping in mind that detergent tends to remove wax). Avoid cleansers with abrasives or the use of hard brushes. There are many cleaners and polishes for special wheels.

• If possible, remove the wheels during the winter. Salt and sand used for snow removal can severely damage the finish of a wheel.

• Make certain the recommended lug nut torque is never exceeded or the wheel may crack. Never use snow chains on special wheels; severe scratching will occur.

FLUIDS AND LUBRICANTS

Fluid Disposal

Used fluids such as engine oil, transmission fluid, antifreeze and brake fluid are hazardous wastes and must be disposed of properly. Before draining any fluids, consult with your local authorities; in many areas, waste oil, antifreeze, etc. are being accepted as a part of recycling programs. A number of service stations and auto parts stores are also accepting waste fluids for recycling.

Be sure of the recycling center's policies before draining any fluids, as many will not accept different fluids that have been mixed together.

Fuel and Engine Oil Recommendations

FUEL

➡Some fuel additives contain chemicals that can damage the catalytic converter and/or oxygen sensor. Read all of the labels carefully before using any additive in the engine or fuel system.

All vehicles covered by this manual are designed to run on unleaded fuel. The use of a leaded fuel in a vehicle requiring unleaded fuel will plug the catalytic converter and render it inoperative. It will also increase exhaust backpressure to the point where engine output will be severely reduced. Obviously, use of leaded fuel should not be a problem, since most companies have stopped selling it for quite some time.

The minimum octane rating of the unleaded fuel being used must be at least 87 (as listed on the pumps), which usually means regular unleaded. Some areas may have even lower octanes available, which would make 87 a midgrade fuel. In these cases a minimum fuel octane of 87 should STILL be used.

Fuel should be selected for the brand and octane which performs best with your engine. Judge a gasoline by its ability to prevent pinging, its engine starting capabilities (cold and hot) and general all weather performance. The use of a fuel too low in octane (a measurement of anti-knock quality) will result in spark knock. Since many factors such as altitude, terrain, air temperature and humidity affect operating efficiency, knocking may result even though the recommended fuel is being used. If persistent knocking occurs, it may be necessary to switch to a different brand or grade of fuel. Continuous or heavy knocking may result in engine damage.

➡ **Your engine's fuel requirement can change with time, mainly due to carbon buildup, which will in turn change the compression ratio. If your engine pings or knocks switch to a higher grade of fuel. Sometimes just changing brands will cure the problem.**

The other most important quality you should look for in a fuel is that it contains detergents designed to keep fuel injection systems clean. Many of the major fuel companies will display information right at the pumps telling you that their fuels contain these detergents. The use of a high-quality fuel which contains detergents will help assure trouble-free operation of your vehicle's fuel system.

OIL

♦ **See Figures 111 and 112**

The recommended oil viscosities for sustained temperatures ranging from below -20°F (-30°C) to above 100°F (40°C) are listed in the section. The only oil type shown is multi-viscosity. Multi-viscosity oils are recommended because of their wider range of acceptable temperatures and driving conditions.

When adding oil to the crankcase or changing the oil and filter, it is important that oil of an equal quality to original equipment be used in your vehicle. The use of inferior oils may void the warranty, damage your engine, or both.

The Society of Automotive Engineers (SAE) grade number of the oil indicates the viscosity of the oil—its ability to lubricate at a given temperature. The lower the SAE number, the lighter the oil; the lower the viscosity, the

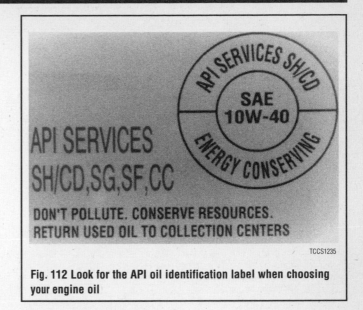

Fig. 112 Look for the API oil identification label when choosing your engine oil

easier it is to crank the engine in cold weather, but the less the oil will lubricate and protect the engine at high temperatures. This number is marked on every oil container.

When using engine oil, there are two types of ratings with which you should be familiar: viscosity and service (quality). There are several service ratings, resulting from tests established by the American Petroleum Institute. The most current rating, SH, is recommended for use in all engines. The SH rating superceeds all other ratings.

Oil viscosities should be chosen from those oils recommended for the lowest anticipated temperatures during the oil change interval. Due to the need for an oil that embodies both good lubrication at high temperature and easy cranking in cold weather, multi-grade oils have been developed. Basically, a multi-grade oil is thinner at low temperatures and thicker at high temperatures. For example, a 10W-40 oil (the W stands for winter) exhibits the characteristics of a 10-weight (SAE 10) oil when the vehicle is first started and the oil is cold. Its lighter weight allows it to travel to the lubricating surfaces quicker and offer less resistance to starter motor cranking than a heavier oil. But after the engine reaches operating temperature, the 10W-40 oil begins acting like straight 40-weight (SAE 40) oil. It behaves as a heavier oil, providing greater lubrication and protection against foaming than lighter oils.

The American Petroleum Institute (API) designations, also found on oil containers, indicates the classification of engine oil used for given operating conditions. Only oils designated Service SH (or the latest superseding designation) heavy-duty detergent should be used in your vehicle. Oils of the SH-type perform many functions inside the engine besides their basic lubrication. Through a balanced system of metallic detergents and polymeric dispersants, the oil prevents high and low temperature deposits and also keeps sludge and dirt particles in suspension. Acids, particularly sulfuric, as well as other by-products of engine combustion are neutralized by the oil. If these acids are allowed to concentrate, they can cause corrosion and rapid wear of the internal engine parts.

Engine

OIL LEVEL CHECK

Engine oil level should be checked every time you put fuel in the vehicle or are under the hood performing other maintenance.

1. Park the vehicle on a level surface.
2. The engine may be either hot or cold when checking oil level. However, if it is hot, wait a few minutes after the engine has been turned **OFF** to allow the oil to drain back into the crankcase. If the engine is cold, do not start it before checking the oil level.

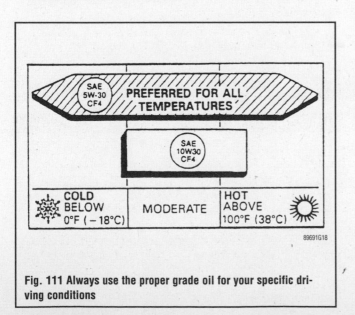

Fig. 111 Always use the proper grade oil for your specific driving conditions

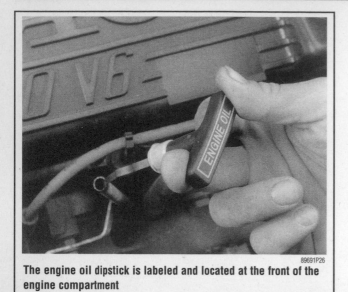

The engine oil dipstick is labeled and located at the front of the engine compartment

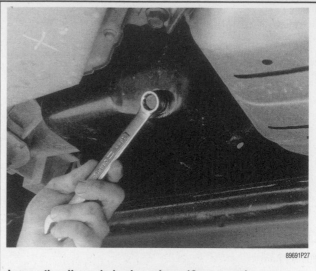

Loosen the oil pan drain plug using a 16mm wrench

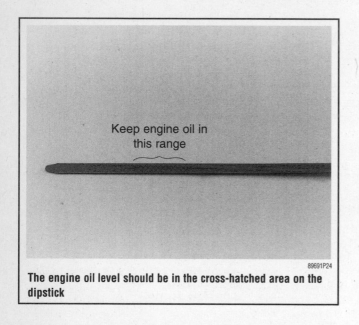

Keep engine oil in this range

The engine oil level should be in the cross-hatched area on the dipstick

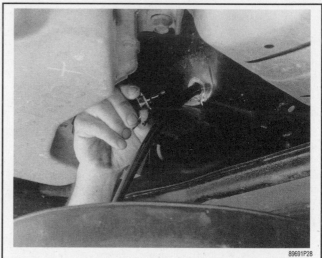

Remove the drain plug carefully and allow the engine to drain fully

3. Open the hood and locate the engine oil dipstick. Pull the dipstick from its tube, wipe it clean, and reinsert it. Make sure the dipstick is fully inserted.

4. Pull the dipstick from its tube again. Holding it horizontally, read the oil level. The oil should be between the MIN and MAX mark. If the oil is below the MIN mark, add oil of the proper viscosity through the capped opening of the valve cover.

5. Replace the dipstick, and check the level again after adding any oil. Be careful not to overfill the crankcase. Approximately one quart of oil will raise the level from the low mark to the high mark. Excess oil will generally be consumed at an accelerated rate even if no damage to the engine seals occurs.

OIL & FILTER CHANGE

The oil and filter should be changed every 5,000 miles (8,000 km) under normal service and every 3,000 miles (6,000 km) under severe service.

✳✳ CAUTION

Prolonged and repeated skin contact with used engine oil, may be harmful.

The oil filter on the 3.0L engine is located above the starter, at the front of the engine compartment

The oil filter on the 3.8L engine is located on the passenger's side of the vehicle, near the catalytic converter

Remove the engine oil cap, located on the valve cover at the front of the engine compartment . . .

. . . and, using a funnel, fill the engine with the proper amount and grade of clean engine oil

➡The engine oil and oil filter should be changed at the recommended intervals on the Maintenance Chart. Though some manufacturer's have at times recommended changing the filter only at every other oil change, Chilton recommends that you always change the filter with the oil. The benefit of fresh oil is quickly lost if the old filter is clogged and unable to do its job. Also, leaving the old filter in place leaves a significant amount of dirty oil in the system.

The oil should be changed more frequently if the vehicle is being operated in a very dusty area. Before draining the oil, make sure that the engine is at operating temperature. Hot oil will hold more impurities in suspension and will flow better, allowing the removal of more oil and dirt.

It is a good idea to warm the engine oil first so it will flow better. This can be accomplished by 15–20 miles of highway driving. Fluid which is warmed to normal operating temperature will flow faster, drain more completely and remove more contaminants from the engine.

1. Raise and support the vehicle safely on jackstands. Make sure the oil drain plug is at the lowest point on the oil pan. If not, you may have to raise the vehicle slightly higher on one jackstand (side) than the other.

2. Before you crawl under the vehicle, take a look at where you will be working and gather all the necessary tools, such as a few wrenches or a ratchet and strip of sockets, the drain pan, some clean rags and, if the oil filter is more accessible from underneath the vehicle, you will also want to grab a bottle of oil, the new filter and a filter wrench at this time.

3. Position the drain pan beneath the oil pan drain plug. Keep in mind that the fast flowing oil, which will spill out as you pull the plug from the pan, will flow with enough force that it could miss the pan. Position the drain pan accordingly and be ready to move the pan more directly beneath the plug as the oil flow lessens to a trickle.

4. Loosen the drain plug with a wrench (or socket and driver), then carefully unscrew the plug with your fingers. Use a rag to shield your fingers from the heat. Push in on the plug as you unscrew it so you can feel when all of the screw threads are out of the hole (and so you will keep the oil from seeping past the threads until you are ready to remove the plug). You can then remove the plug quickly to avoid having hot oil run down your arm. This will also help assure that have the plug in your hand, not in the bottom of a pan of hot oil.

✳✳ CAUTION

Be careful of the oil; when at operating temperature, it is hot enough to cause a severe burn.

5. Allow the oil to drain until nothing but a few drops come out of the drain hole. Check the drain plug to make sure the threads and sealing surface are not damaged. Carefully thread the plug into position and tighten it

Before installing a new oil filter, lightly coat the rubber gasket with clean oil

with a torque wrench to 9–11 ft. lbs. (11–16 Nm). If a torque wrench is not available, snug the drain plug and give a slight additional turn. You don't want the plug to fall out (as you would quickly become stranded), but the pan threads are EASILY stripped from overtightening (and this can be time consuming and/or costly to fix).

6. To remove the filter, you may need an oil filter wrench since the filter may have been fitted too tightly and/or the heat from the engine may have made it even tighter. A filter wrench can be obtained at any auto parts store and is well-worth the investment. Loosen the filter with the filter wrench. With a rag wrapped around the filter, unscrew the filter from the boss on the side of the engine. Be careful of hot oil that will run down the side of the filter. Make sure that your drain pan is under the filter before you start to remove it from the engine; should some of the hot oil happen to get on you, there will be a place to dump the filter in a hurry and the filter will usually spill a good bit of dirty oil as it is removed.

7. Wipe the base of the mounting boss with a clean, dry cloth. When you install the new filter, smear a small amount of fresh oil on the gasket with your finger, just enough to coat the entire contact surface. When you tighten the filter, rotate it about a quarter-turn after it contacts the mounting boss (or follow any instructions which are provided on the filter or parts box).

❋❋ WARNING

Never operate the engine without engine oil, otherwise SEVERE engine damage will be the result.

8. Remove the jackstands and carefully lower the vehicle, then IMMEDIATELY refill the engine crankcase with the proper amount of oil. DO NOT WAIT TO DO THIS because if you forget and someone tries to start the vehicle, severe engine damage will occur.

9. Refill the engine crankcase slowly, checking the level often. You may notice that it usually takes less than the amount of oil listed in the capacity chart to refill the crankcase. But, that is only until the engine is run and the oil filter is filled with oil. To make sure the proper level is obtained, run the engine to normal operating temperature, shut the engine **OFF**, allow the oil to drain back into the oil pan, and recheck the level. Top off the oil at this time to the fill mark.

➡If the vehicle is not resting on level ground, the oil level reading on the dipstick may be slightly off. Be sure to check the level only when the vehicle is sitting level.

10. Drain your used oil in a suitable container for recycling.

Automatic Transaxle

The automatic transaxle fluid should be replaced every 30,000 miles (48,000 km) under normal conditions or 21,000 miles (34,000 km) under severe conditions.

FLUID RECOMMENDATIONS

Ford recommends the use of Mercon® automatic transmission fluid.

LEVEL CHECK

1. Park the vehicle on a level surface.
2. The transaxle should be at normal operating temperature when checking fluid level. To ensure the fluid is at normal operating temperature, drive the vehicle at least 20 miles.
3. With the selector lever in **P** and the parking brake applied, start the engine.
4. Open the hood and locate the transaxle fluid dipstick. Pull the dipstick from its tube, wipe it clean, and reinsert it. Make sure the dipstick is fully inserted.
5. Pull the dipstick from its tube again. Holding it horizontally, read the fluid level. The fluid should be between the MIN and MAX mark. If the fluid is below the MIN mark, add fluid through the dipstick tube.
6. Replace the dipstick, and check the level again after adding any fluid. Be careful not to overfill the transaxle.

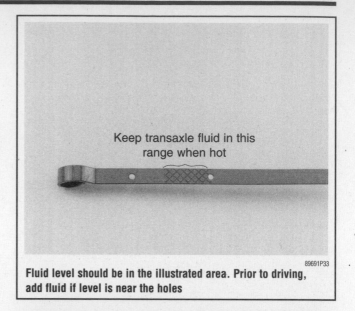

Fluid level should be in the illustrated area. Prior to driving, add fluid if level is near the holes

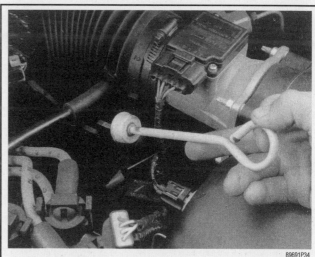

The transaxle dipstick on 3.0L engines is under the air cleaner tube at the rear of the engine compartment

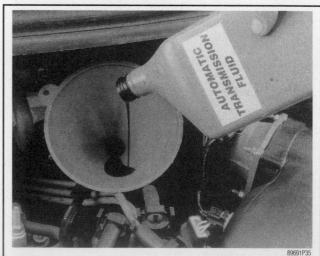

Using a flexible neck funnel, fill the transaxle through the dipstick tube

DRAIN & REFILL

1. Place the transaxle range selector lever in **P** and set the parking brake.
2. Start the engine and check transaxle fluid level.

➡The amount of fluid in the transaxle will affect the time it takes to drain the transaxle. Make sure to check the fluid level before proceeding.

3. Turn the engine **OFF**.
4. Raise and support the vehicle safely.
5. Remove the retainer clip from the lower transaxle fluid cooler line and fitting.
6. Pinch the plastic retaining tabs of the push connect fitting and pull the cooler line to separate it from the cooler line fitting.
7. Disconnect the lower transaxle cooler line from the transaxle cooler line fitting at the transaxle.
8. Attach a 3 foot long flexible hose to the end of the transaxle cooler line and gently fasten the hose with a clamp.
9. Place the opposite end of the hose in a 15 quart container.

➡When plugging the transaxle cooler line fitting, make sure the plug is mad of soft material to prevent damage to the internal seal of the cooler line fitting.

10. Insert a plug into the transaxle cooler line fitting at the transaxle to prevent any residual fluid leakage.
11. Lower the vehicle.

➡When the steady stream of transaxle fluid stops flowing the engine should be turned OFF immediately to prevent damage to the transaxle. Engine rpm should not exceed curb idle speed while draining fluid.

12. Place selector lever in **P** and start the engine. Run the engine at idle while observing the flexible hose attached to the cooler line.
13. Run the engine at idle for approximately 40–60 seconds until the steady stream of transaxle fluid stops flowing. This step will drain approximately 2–3 quarts (1.9–2.8 liters).
14. Fill the transaxle with 10 quarts (9.5 liters) of Mercon® transmission fluid.
15. Run the engine at idle for approximately 2–3 minutes until the steady stream of transaxle fluid stops flowing. This step will drain approximately 10 quarts (9.5 liters) of transmission fluid.
16. Remove the plug from the transaxle cooler line fitting at the transaxle.
17. Remove the flexible hose from the cooler line.

➡Carefully clean the cooler line prior to installing it. This will ensure a good connection and prevent leaks.

18. Install the cooler line into the transaxle cooler fitting by pushing straight into the cooler line fitting until a click is heard. then, gently pull on the cooler line to make sure the line is locked in place in the cooler line fitting.
19. Install the retaining clip over the cooler line and fitting.
20. Add 2 quarts (1.9 liters) of Mercon® transmission fluid.
21. Move the range selector lever through all ranges allowing the transaxle to engage in each position and return the selector lever to **P**.
22. Check the transaxle fluid level. The fluid level at normal operating temperature should read within the cross hatched area of the fluid level dipstick.
23. If the fluid level read below the cross hatched area, adjust the level by adding fluid in small increments until the correct fluid level is obtained.

PAN & FILTER SERVICE

▸ **See Figures 113 and 114**

1. Drain and flush the transaxle fluid.
2. Raise and support the vehicle safely.
3. Place a drain pan under the transaxle.

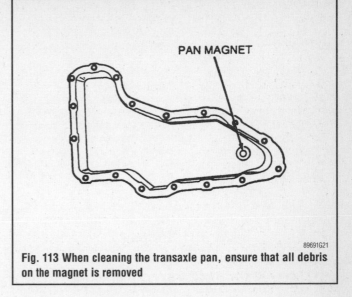

Fig. 113 When cleaning the transaxle pan, ensure that all debris on the magnet is removed

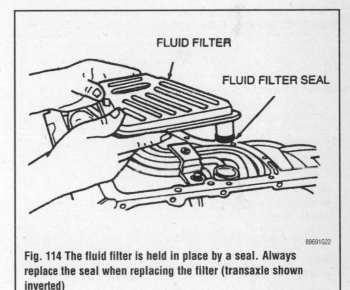

Fig. 114 The fluid filter is held in place by a seal. Always replace the seal when replacing the filter (transaxle shown inverted)

When lowering the pan, it must be level to prevent fluid spillage

To remove the transaxle fluid filter, grasp it from both sides and pull straight down

The pan magnet catches and holds metallic debris so it cannot be circulated back into the transaxle

4. Remove the transaxle pan cover bolts.
5. Carefully lower the pan, keeping it level.
6. Remove the filter by pulling it away from the transaxle.

To install:

7. Throughly clean the pan and pan magnet of debris.
8. Install the new filter using a new O-ring.
9. Replace the pan using a new gasket.
10. Tighten the pan bolts to 9–11 ft. lbs. (6–8 Nm).
11. Lower the vehicle.
12. Refill the transaxle with fluid.

Cooling System

Any time you have the hood open, glance at the coolant reserve tank to make sure it is properly filled. Coolant should be replaced at 50,000 miles (80,000 km) and then every 30,000 miles (48,000 km) thereafter.

FLUID RECOMMENDATIONS

Ford recommends the use of a good quality ethylene glycol based or other aluminum compatible antifreeze. It is best to add a 50/50 mix of antifreeze and water to avoid diluting the coolant in the system.

LEVEL CHECK

The proper coolant level is slightly above the FULL COLD marking when the engine is cold. Top off the cooling system using the recovery tank and its marking as a guideline.

➡**Never overfill the reserve tank.**

A coolant level that consistently drops is usually a sign of a small, hard to detect leak, although in the worst case it could be a sign of an internal engine leak. In most cases, you will be able to trace the leak to a loose fitting or damaged hose.

Evaporating ethylene glycol antifreeze will have a sweet smell and leave small, white (salt-like) deposits, which can be helpful in tracing a leak.

❄❄ CAUTION

When draining coolant, keep in mind that cats and dogs are attracted to ethylene glycol antifreeze, and are likely to drink any that is left in an uncovered container or in puddles on the ground. This will prove fatal in sufficient quantity. Always drain coolant into a sealable container. Coolant may be reused unless it is contaminated or several years old.

DRAIN & REFILL

Ensure that the engine is completely cool prior to starting this service.

1. Remove the radiator and reserve tank caps.
2. Place a drain pan of sufficient capacity under the radiator and open the petcock (drain).

➡**Plastic petcocks easily bind. Before opening a plastic radiator petcock, spray it with some penetrating lubricant.**

3. Drain the cooling system completely.
4. Close the petcock.
5. Determine the capacity of the coolant system, then properly refill the cooling system with a 50/50 mixture of fresh coolant and water.
6. Fill the radiator with coolant until it reaches the radiator filler neck seat.
7. Start the engine and allow it to idle until the thermostat opens (the upper radiator hose will become hot).
8. Turn the engine **OFF** and refill the radiator until the coolant level is at the filler neck seat.
9. Once the engine has cooled completely, fill the engine coolant overflow tank with coolant to the FULL COLD mark, then install the radiator cap.

Never remove the radiator cap when the engine is hot

To adjust the level of coolant in the system, add coolant into the overflow tank

10. Check the level of protection with an antifreeze/coolant hydrometer and adjust as necessary.

11. Start the engine and allow it to reach operating temperature. Check for leaks.

FLUSHING & CLEANING THE SYSTEM

1. Drain the cooling system completely.

2. Close the petcock and fill the system with a cooling system flush (clean water may also be used, but is not as efficient).

When refilling the system, add coolant directly into the radiator

3. Idle the engine until the upper radiator hose gets hot.
4. Allow the engine to cool completely and drain the system again.
5. Repeat this process until the drained water is clear and free of scale.
6. Flush the reserve tank with water and leave empty.
7. Fill the cooling system.

Brake Master Cylinder

Ford recommends that the fluid level in the brake master cylinder reservoir be checked at least once a year.

➡**Brake fluid is hydroscopic, that is to say it readily absorbs water. As water is absorbed into the fluid, it becomes contaminated. Contaminated brake fluid has a lower boiling point and will corrode vital brake system components. This may result in reduced braking performance and/or the need to replace expensive brake system components. It is highly recommended that the entire brake system be drained, flushed and refilled with fresh brake fluid when recommended by the manufacturer, or at least every 2 years.**

FLUID RECOMMENDATIONS

Ford recommends the use of only fresh, uncontaminated brake fluid meeting or exceeding DOT 3 standards.

LEVEL CHECK

1. Check the level of brake fluid in the brake fluid reservoir. The fluid should be maintained at the MAX line on the reservoir. Brake fluid should be added if fluid level is more than 0.30 in. (7mm) below the MAX line.

➡**Any sudden decrease in fluid level indicates a probable leak in the system and should be inspected immediately.**

2. Clean around the reservoir cap with a shop rag to prevent contaminating the fluid with dirt.
3. Remove the cap and add the required amount of fluid to the system.

➡**When making additions of fluid, use only fresh, uncontaminated brake fluid meeting or exceeding DOT 3 standards. Be careful not to spill any brake fluid on painted surfaces, because it will damage the paint. Do not allow the fluid container or brake fluid reservoir to remain open any longer than necessary; brake fluid absorbs moisture from the air, reducing its effectiveness and causing brake line corrosion.**

4. Install the reservoir cap.

The master cylinder reservoir is located under the cowl on the driver's side. Note the MAX fill line (arrow)

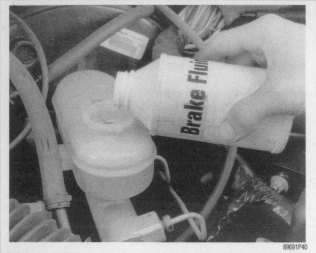

Wipe around the reservoir cap to prevent the entry of dirt, then open and fill the reservoir with fresh fluid

Power steering reservoir location—3.8L engine

Power Steering Pump

Ford recommends that the fluid level in the power steering pump reservoir be checked at least twice a year.

FLUID RECOMMENDATIONS

Ford recommends the use of Motorcraft Type "F", or equivalent power steering fluid.

LEVEL CHECK

1. Park the vehicle on a level surface.
2. Start the engine and allow it to run for at least 5 minutes to heat the power steering fluid to operating temperature.
3. Turn the steering wheel back and forth several times.
4. Turn the engine **OFF**.
5. Clean around the reservoir cap with a shop rag to prevent contaminating the fluid with dirt.
6. Remove the dipstick from the reservoir. The level should be between the illustrated marks on the FULL HOT side of the dipstick.
7. As required, add the required amount of fluid to the system.

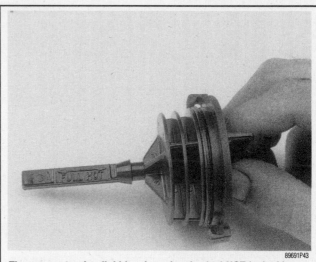

The power steering fluid level can be checked HOT by looking on one side of the dipstick . . .

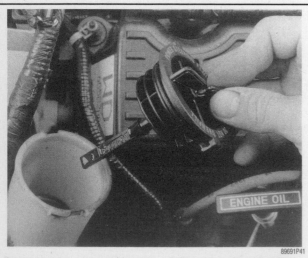

Power steering reservoir location—3.0L engine. Note that the cap has a built-in dipstick

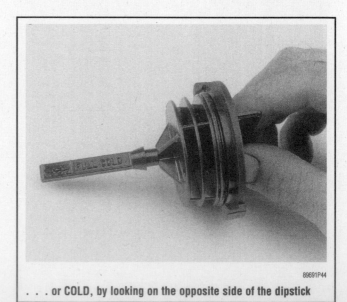

. . . or COLD, by looking on the opposite side of the dipstick

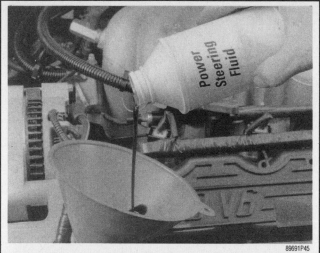

89691P45

When adjusting fluid level, only pour in a little fluid at a time. Overfilling the system can damage the pump

➡**The power steering fluid should only be checked cold if absolutely necessary. When checking the level cold, ensure it is at least up to the bottom of the FULL COLD marks on the dipstick.**

Chassis Greasing

Ball joints, suspension bushings and driveline joints are permanently lubricated at the factory and require no periodic lubrication. However, many aftermarket parts used to replace these components will contain a provision for lubrication. The easiest way to determine if a component can be lubricated is to look for a grease (Zerk®) fitting.

Although the manufacturer does not recommend an interval, we at Chilton feel the chassis should be lubricated every 10,000 miles (16,000 km)

PROCEDURE

1. Raise and support the vehicle safely.
2. Locate all grease fittings on the vehicle. They are usually located on the at ball joints, suspension bushings and universal joints.

➡**Some grease fittings may be obscured by road dirt or grease from an over zealous chassis lubrication.**

3. Inspect the boot or seal for damage and replace as necessary. It is useless to attempt filling a damaged boot with grease as it will probably leak out.
4. Remove the grease fitting cap.
5. Clean the area around the grease fitting with a rag.
6. Connect a grease gun to the fitting and pump grease into the joint until the boot or seal swells slightly. On a well maintained vehicle, this should be no more than 3–4 pumps.

➡**Do not overfill the component with grease. If grease exits the boot or seal, it is overfill.**

7. Remove the grease gun and install the grease fitting cap.
8. Lower the vehicle.

Body Lubrication and Maintenance

Treat the specified components as follows:
• Lock cylinders—apply graphite lubricant sparingly through the key slot. Insert the key and operate the lock several times to be sure that the lubricant is worked into the lock cylinder.

• Hinges—spray a silicone lubricant or white lithium grease on the hinge pivot points to eliminate any binding conditions. Open and close the door several times to be sure that the lubricant is evenly and thoroughly distributed.
• Latches—spray a silicone lubricant or white lithium grease on the latch mechanism and friction surfaces to eliminate squeaks and binding. Operate the latch to distribute the lubricant.
• Door seals—spray a silicone lubricant or a rubber protectant on the door seals and wipe the excess with a rag. This will eliminate squeaks and prevent the rubber from sticking to the metal.

Rear Wheel Bearings

REPACKING

➡**Sodium based grease is not compatible with lithium based grease. Read the package labels and be careful not to mix the two types. If there is any doubt as to the type of grease used, completely clean the old grease from the bearing and hub before replacing.**

Before handling the bearings, there are several things that you should remember to do and not to do:
DO THE FOLLOWING:
• Remove all outside dirt from the housing before exposing the bearing.
• Treat a used bearing as gently as you would a new one.
• Work with clean tools in clean surroundings.
• Use clean, dry canvas gloves, or at least clean, dry hands.
• Clean solvents and flushing fluids are a must.
• Use clean paper when laying out the bearings to dry.
• Protect disassembled bearings from rust and dirt. Cover them up.
• Use clean rags to wipe bearings.
• Keep the bearings in oil-proof paper when they are to be stored or are not in use.
• Clean the inside of the housing before replacing the bearing.
DO NOT DO THE FOLLOWING:
• Work In dirty surroundings.
• Use dirty, chipped or damaged tools.
• Work on wooden work benches or use wooden mallets.
• Handle bearings with dirty or moist hands.
• Use gasoline for cleaning. Use a safe solvent.
• Spin dry bearings with compressed air. They will be damaged.
• Use cotton waste or dirty cloths to wipe bearings.
• Scratch or nick bearing surfaces.
• Allow the bearing to come in contact with dirt or rust at any time.

➡**Only the rear wheel bearings require periodic maintenance. A premium high melting point grease is recommended. This service should be performed every time the rear hub is removed.**

1. Raise and support the vehicle safely.
2. Remove the wheel bearings.
3. Clean all parts in a non-flammable solvent and let them air dry.

➡**Only use lint free rags to dry the bearings. Never spin-dry a bearing with compressed air, as this will damage the rollers!**

4. Check for excessive wear and damage. Replace the bearing as necessary.
5. Packing wheel bearings with grease is best accomplished by using a wheel bearing packer (available at most automotive stores). If one is not available they may be packed by hand.
6. Place a healthy glob of grease in the palm of one hand and force the edge of the bearing into it so that the grease fills the space between the rollers and the bearing cage. Do this until the whole bearing is packed.
7. Place the packed bearing on a clean sheet of paper until time for installation.
8. Install the wheel bearing.
Refer to Section 8 of this manual for information on servicing wheel bearings.

TRAILER TOWING

▶ **See Figure 115**

General Recommendations

Your vehicle was primarily designed to carry passengers and cargo. It is important to remember that towing a trailer will place additional loads on your vehicles engine, drivetrain, steering, braking and other systems. However, if you decide to tow a trailer, using the proper equipment is a must.

Local laws may require specific equipment such as trailer brakes or fender mounted mirrors. Check your local laws prior to purchasing trailer equipment.

Trailer Weight

The weight of the trailer is the most important factor. A good weight-to-horsepower ratio is about 35:1, 35 lbs. of Gross Combined Weight (GCW) for every horsepower your engine develops. Multiply the engine's rated horsepower by 35 and subtract the weight of the vehicle passengers and luggage. The number remaining is the approximate maximum weight you should tow, although a numerically higher axle ratio can help compensate for heavier weight.

Hitch (Tongue) Weight

Calculate the hitch weight in order to select a proper hitch. The weight of the hitch is usually 10% of the trailer gross weight and should be measured with the trailer loaded. Hitches fall into various categories: those that mount on the frame and rear bumper, the bolt-on type, or the weld-on distribution type used for larger trailers. Axle mounted or clamp-on bumper hitches should never be used.

Check the gross weight rating of your trailer. Tongue weight is usually figured as 10% of gross trailer weight. Therefore, a trailer with a maximum gross weight of 2000 lbs. will have a maximum tongue weight of 200 lbs. Class I trailers fall into this category. Class II trailers are those with a gross weight rating of 2000–3000 lbs., while Class III trailers fall into the 3500–6000 lbs. category. Class IV trailers are those over 6000 lbs.

When you've determined the hitch that you'll need, follow the manufacturer's installation instructions, exactly, especially when it comes to fas-

tener torques. The hitch will subjected to a lot of stress and good hitches come with hardened bolts. Never substitute an inferior bolt for a hardened bolt.

Drive Train Recommendation

ENGINE

Cooling System

One of the most common, if not THE most common, problems associated with trailer towing is engine overheating. Cleaning and flushing the cooling system is good preventative maintenance. Ensure all cooling system components are functioning properly. If your vehicle is not equipped with a factory towing package, installation of aftermarket high capacity radiators, high flow water pumps and auxiliary electric cooling fans will all help keeping your vehicle running cool.

Oil Cooler

Aftermarket engine oil coolers are helpful for prolonging engine oil life and reducing overall engine temperatures. Both of these factors increase engine life. While not absolutely necessary in towing a Class I trailer, all vehicles towing Class II trailers and above should be equipped with an engine oil cooler. Engine oil cooler systems usually consist of an adapter, screwed on in place of the oil filter, a remote filter mounting and a multi-tube, finned heat exchanger, which is mounted in front of the radiator or air conditioning condenser.

TRANSAXLE

Transaxle Cooler

An automatic transaxle is recommended for trailer towing. Modern automatics have proven reliable and, of course, easy to operate, in trailer towing. The increased load of a trailer, however, causes an increase in the temperature of the automatic transmission fluid. Heat is the worst enemy of an automatic transaxle. As the temperature of the fluid increases, the life of the fluid decreases.

It is essential, therefore, that you install an automatic transaxle cooler. The cooler, which consists of a multi-tube, finned heat exchanger, is usually installed in front of the radiator or air conditioning condenser, and hooked in-line with the transaxle cooler tank inlet line. Follow the cooler manufacturer's installation instructions.

Select a cooler of at least adequate capacity, based upon the combined gross weights of the vehicle and trailer.

➡**A transaxle cooler can, sometimes, cause slow or harsh shifting in the cold weather, until the fluid has a chance to come up to normal operating temperature. Some coolers can be purchased with or retrofitted with a temperature bypass valve which will allow fluid flow through the cooler only when the fluid has reached above a certain operating temperature.**

Handling A Trailer

Towing a trailer with ease and safety requires a certain amount of experience. The handling and brakinbg characteristics of any tow vehicle may be radically changed by the added weight of a trailer. It a good idea to learn the feel of a trailer by practicing turning, stopping and backing in an open area such as an empty parking lot. Make mental notes of space requirements and trailer response while praticing turning and braking. Follow these notes while on the road to help avoid accidents.

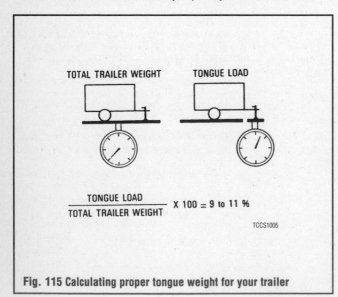

TOTAL TRAILER WEIGHT   TONGUE LOAD

$$\frac{\text{TONGUE LOAD}}{\text{TOTAL TRAILER WEIGHT}} \times 100 = 9 \text{ to } 11 \text{ \%}$$

TCCS1005

Fig. 115 Calculating proper tongue weight for your trailer

TOWING THE VEHICLE

Preferred Towing Method—Flatbed

For maximum safety to the components of your drive train and chassis, it is most desirable to have your vehicle towed by on a flatbed or whole vehicle trailer. The only way to properly place the vehicle on a flatbed is to have it pulled on from the front.

Alternate Towing Method—T-Hook

If a flatbed is unavailable, your vehicle can be towed using a T-hook wrecker. In this case, it is best to tow from the front, with the front wheels off the ground, as this will prevent wear and tear on the drive train. Tow vehicle speed should not exceed 35 mph (56 km/h) when using this method.

When necessary, you can tow using the T-hook in the rear, with the front wheels on the ground. All of the previous conditions for front towing are applicable AND the total distance towed should NOT EXCEED 50 miles (80 km), otherwise transaxle damage may occur.

Last Chance Towing Method—Dolly

If absolutely necessary, you can tow your vehicle with either the front or rear wheels on a dolly. Again, the preferred method would be to leave the rear wheels on the ground and the front on the dolly, so the drive train is not turning. All conditions which apply to the T-hook method also apply for the dolly method.

JUMP STARTING A DEAD BATTERY

▶ **See Figure 116**

Whenever a vehicle is jump started, precautions must be followed in order to prevent the possibility of personal injury. Remember that batteries contain a small amount of explosive hydrogen gas which is a by-product of battery charging. Sparks should always be avoided when working around batteries, especially when attaching jumper cables. To minimize the possibility of accidental sparks, follow the procedure carefully.

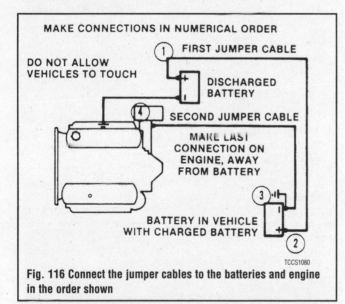

Fig. 116 Connect the jumper cables to the batteries and engine in the order shown

✳✳ CAUTION

NEVER hook the batteries up in a series circuit or the entire electrical system will go up in smoke, including the starter!

Vehicles equipped with a diesel engine may utilize two 12 volt batteries. If so, the batteries are connected in a parallel circuit (positive terminal to positive terminal, negative terminal to negative terminal). Hooking the batteries up in parallel circuit increases battery cranking power without increasing total battery voltage output. Output remains at 12 volts. On the other hand, hooking two 12 volt batteries up in a series circuit (positive terminal to negative terminal, positive terminal to negative terminal) increases total battery output to 24 volts (12 volts plus 12 volts).

Jump Starting Precautions

- Be sure that both batteries are of the same voltage. Vehicles covered by this manual and most vehicles on the road today utilize a 12 volt charging system.
- Be sure that both batteries are of the same polarity (have the same terminal, in most cases NEGATIVE grounded).
- Be sure that the vehicles are not touching or a short could occur.
- On serviceable batteries, be sure the vent cap holes are not obstructed.
- Do not smoke or allow sparks anywhere near the batteries.
- In cold weather, make sure the battery electrolyte is not frozen. This can occur more readily in a battery that has been in a state of discharge.
- Do not allow electrolyte to contact your skin or clothing.

Jump Starting Procedure

1. Make sure that the voltages of the 2 batteries are the same. Most batteries and charging systems are of the 12 volt variety.
2. Pull the jumping vehicle (with the good battery) into a position so the jumper cables can reach the dead battery and that vehicle's engine. Make sure that the vehicles do NOT touch.
3. Place the transmission/transaxle of both vehicles in **N** (MT) or **P** (AT), as applicable, then firmly set their parking brakes.

➡**If necessary for safety reasons, the hazard lights on both vehicles may be operated throughout the entire procedure without significantly increasing the difficulty of jumping the dead battery.**

4. Turn all lights and accessories OFF on both vehicles. Make sure the ignition switches on both vehicles are turned to the **OFF** position.
5. Cover the battery cell caps with a rag, but do not cover the terminals.
6. Make sure the terminals on both batteries are clean and free of corrosion or proper electrical connection will be impeded. If necessary, clean the battery terminals before proceeding.
7. Identify the positive (+) and negative (-) terminals on both batteries.
8. Connect the first jumper cable to the positive (+) terminal of the dead battery, then connect the other end of that cable to the positive (+) terminal of the booster (good) battery.
9. Connect one end of the other jumper cable to the negative (-) terminal on the booster battery and the final cable clamp to an engine bolt head, alternator bracket or other solid, metallic point on the engine with the dead battery. Try to pick a ground on the engine that is positioned away from the battery in order to minimize the possibility of the 2 clamps touching should one loosen during the procedure. DO NOT connect this clamp to the negative (-) terminal of the bad battery.

✲✲✲ CAUTION

Be very careful to keep the jumper cables away from moving parts (cooling fan, belts, etc.) on both engines.

10. Check to make sure that the cables are routed away from any moving parts, then start the donor vehicle's engine. Run the engine at moderate speed for several minutes to allow the dead battery a chance to receive some initial charge.

11. With the donor vehicle's engine still running slightly above idle, try to start the vehicle with the dead battery. Crank the engine for no more than 10 seconds at a time and let the starter cool for at least 20 seconds between tries. If the vehicle does not start in 3 tries, it is likely that something else is also wrong or that the battery needs additional time to charge.

12. Once the vehicle is started, allow it to run at idle for a few seconds to make sure that it is operating properly.

13. Turn ON the headlights, heater blower and, if equipped, the rear defroster of both vehicles in order to reduce the severity of voltage spikes and subsequent risk of damage to the vehicles' electrical systems when the cables are disconnected. This step is especially important to any vehicle equipped with computer control modules.

14. Carefully disconnect the cables in the reverse order of connection. Start with the negative cable that is attached to the engine ground, then the negative cable on the donor battery. Disconnect the positive cable from the donor battery and finally, disconnect the positive cable from the formerly dead battery. Be careful when disconnecting the cables from the positive terminals not to allow the alligator clips to touch any metal on either vehicle or a short and sparks will occur.

JACKING

Your vehicle was supplied with a jack for emergency road repairs. This jack is fine for changing a flat tire or other short term procedures not requiring you to go beneath the vehicle. If it is used in an emergency situation, carefully follow the instructions provided either with the jack or in your owner's manual. Do not attempt to use the jack on any portions of the vehicle other than specified by the vehicle manufacturer. Always block the diagonally opposite wheel when using a jack.

A more convenient way of jacking is the use of a garage or floor jack. You may use the floor jack at the illustrated jacking locations.

Never place the jack under the radiator, engine or transmission components. Severe and expensive damage will result when the jack is raised. Additionally, never jack under the floorpan or bodywork; the metal will deform.

Whenever you plan to work under the vehicle, you must support it on jackstands or ramps. Never use cinder blocks or stacks of wood to support the vehicle, even if you're only going to be under it for a few minutes. Never crawl under the vehicle when it is supported only by the tire-changing jack or other floor jack.

➡ Always position a block of wood or small rubber pad on top of the jack or jackstand to protect the lifting point's finish when lifting or supporting the vehicle.

Small hydraulic, screw, or scissors jacks are satisfactory for raising the vehicle. Drive-on trestles or ramps are also a handy and safe way to both raise and support the vehicle. Be careful though, some ramps may be too steep to drive your vehicle onto without scraping the front bottom

panels. Never support the vehicle on any suspension member (unless specifically instructed to do so by a repair manual) or by an underbody panel.

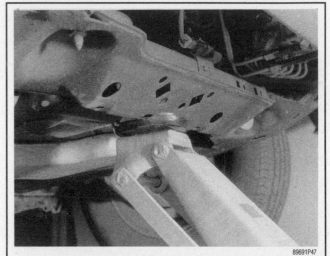

89691P47

To raise the front of the vehicle, place the jack beneath the front subframe

89691P46

This vehicle has been raised and properly supported

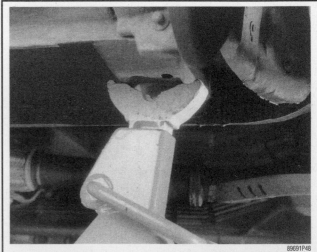

89691P48

Support the vehicle with jackstands placed beneath the frame, just behind the front wheels

Jacking Precautions

The following safety points cannot be overemphasized:
- Always block the opposite wheel or wheels to keep the vehicle from rolling off the jack.
- When raising the front of the vehicle, firmly apply the parking brake.

- When the drive wheels are to remain on the ground, leave the vehicle in gear to help prevent it from rolling.
- Always use jackstands to support the vehicle when you are working underneath. Place the stands beneath the vehicle's jacking brackets. Before climbing underneath, rock the vehicle a bit to make sure it is firmly supported.

CAPACITIES

Year	Model	Engine ID/VIN	Engine Displacement Liters (cc)	Engine Oil with Filter	Transmission (pts.)			Transfer Case (pts.)	Drive Axle		Fuel Tank (gal.)	Cooling System (qts.)
					4-Spd	5-Spd	Auto.		Front (pts.)	Rear (pts.)		
1995	Windstar	U	3.0(2966)	4.5	—	—	24.5	—	—	—	20.0 ①	12.1
	Windstar	4	3.8(3802)	4.5	—	—	24.5	—	—	—	20.0 ①	12.1
1996	Windstar	U	3.0(2966)	4.5	—	—	24.5	—	—	—	20.0 ①	12.1
	Windstar	4	3.8(3802)	4.5	—	—	24.5	—	—	—	20.0 ①	12.1
1997	Windstar	U	3.0(2966)	4.5	—	—	24.5	—	—	—	20.0 ①	12.1
	Windstar	4	3.8(3802)	4.5	—	—	24.5	—	—	—	20.0 ①	12.1
1998	Windstar	U	3.0(2966)	4.5	—	—	24.5	—	—	—	20.0 ①	12.1
	Windstar	4	3.8(3802)	4.5	—	—	24.5	—	—	—	20.0 ①	12.1

① Optional 26.0 gal

89691C05

MANUFACTURER RECOMMENDED NORMAL MAINTENANCE INTERVALS

Vehicle Maintenance Interval

Component	Type of Service	Miles (x1000) 5 / km 8	10 / 16	15 / 24	20 / 32	25 / 40	30 / 48	35 / 56	40 / 64	45 / 72	50 / 80	55 / 88	60 / 96	65 / 104	70 / 112	75 / 120	80 / 128
Accessory Drive Belts	I												✓				
Air Cleaner	R						✓						✓				
Automatic Transaxle Fluid	R						✓						✓				
Brakes	I						✓						✓				
Coolant ①	R										✓						✓
Cooling System Components	I			✓			✓			✓			✓			✓	
Engine Oil and Filter	R	✓	✓	✓	✓	✓	✓	✓	✓	✓	✓	✓	✓	✓	✓	✓	✓
Exhaust System	I						✓						✓				
PCV valve	R										✓		✓				
Rotate Tires	I	✓		✓		✓		✓		✓		✓		✓		✓	
Spark Plugs ②	R																

I – Inspect and correct or replace, if necessary.

R – Replace or change.

① Change coolant at 50,000 miles (80,000 km) and then every 30,000 miles (48,000 km) afterwards

② Replace spark plugs at 100,000 miles (160,000 km)

89691C06

MANUFACTURER RECOMMENDED SEVERE MAINTENANCE INTERVALS

Component	Type of Service	Vehicle Maintenance Interval ①
Accessory Drive Belts	I	Inspect every 60,000 miles (96,000 km)
Air Cleaner	R	Replace every 30,000 miles (48,000 km)
Automatic Transaxle Fluid	R	Replace every 21,000 miles (34,000 km)
Brakes	I	Inspect every 30,000 miles (48,000 km)
Coolant	R	Change at 50,000 miles (80,000 km) and then every 30,000 miles (48,000 km) afterwards
Cooling System Components	I	Inspect every 15,000 miles (24,000 km)
Engine Oil and Filter	R	Replace every 3,000 miles (5,000 km)
Exhaust System	I	Inspect every 30,000 miles (48,000 km)
PCV valve	R	Replace at 60,000 miles (96,000 km)
Rotate Tires	I	Inspect every 6,000 miles (9,500 km)
Spark Plugs	R	Replace at 100,000 miles (160,000 km)

I – Inspect and correct or replace, if necessary.

R – Replace or change.

① If a vehicle is operated under any of the following conditions it is considered severe service:

- Towing a trailer.
- Repeated short trips.
- Driving on rough, dusty and/or muddy roads.
- Driving in extremely cold weather and/or on salted roads.

All other maintenance service procedures should be performed according to the normal maintenance interval chart.

89691C07

ENGLISH TO METRIC CONVERSION: MASS (WEIGHT)

Current **mass** measurement is expressed in pounds and ounces (lbs. & ozs.). The metric unit of mass (or weight) is the kilogram (kg). Even although this table does not show conversion of masses (weights) larger than 15 lbs, it is easy to calculate larger units by following the data immediately below.

To convert ounces (oz.) to grams (g): multiply th number of ozs. by 28
To convert grams (g) to ounces (oz.): multiply the number of grams by .035

To convert pounds (lbs.) to kilograms (kg): multiply the number of lbs. by .45
To convert kilograms (kg) to pounds (lbs.): multiply the number of kilograms by 2.2

lbs	kg	lbs	kg	oz	kg	oz	kg
0.1	0.04	0.9	0.41	0.1	0.003	0.9	0.024
0.2	0.09	1	0.4	0.2	0.005	1	0.03
0.3	0.14	2	0.9	0.3	0.008	2	0.06
0.4	0.18	3	1.4	0.4	0.011	3	0.08
0.5	0.23	4	1.8	0.5	0.014	4	0.11
0.6	0.27	5	2.3	0.6	0.017	5	0.14
0.7	0.32	10	4.5	0.7	0.020	10	0.28
0.8	0.36	15	6.8	0.8	0.023	15	0.42

ENGLISH TO METRIC CONVERSION: TEMPERATURE

To convert Fahrenheit ("F) to Celsius (°C): take number of °F and subtract 32; multiply result by 5; divide result by 9

To convert Celsius (°C) to Fahrenheit (°F): take number of °C and multiply by 9; divide result by 5; add 32 to total

Fahrenheit (F)		Celsius (C)		Fahrenheit (F)		Celsius (C)		Fahrenheit (F)		Celsius (C)	
°F	°C	°C	°F	°F	°C	°C	°F	°F	°C	°C	°F
−40	−40	−38	−36.4	80	26.7	18	64.4	215	101.7	80	176
−35	−37.2	−36	−32.8	85	29.4	20	68	220	104.4	85	185
−30	−34.4	−34	−29.2	90	32.2	22	71.6	225	107.2	90	194
−25	−31.7	−32	−25.6	95	35.0	24	75.2	230	110.0	95	202
−20	−28.9	−30	−22	100	37.8	26	78.8	235	112.8	100	212
−15	−26.1	−28	−18.4	105	40.6	28	82.4	240	115.6	105	221
−10	−23.3	−26	−14.8	110	43.3	30	86	245	118.3	110	230
−5	−20.6	−24	−11.2	115	46.1	32	89.6	250	121.1	115	239
0	−17.8	−22	−7.6	120	48.9	34	93.2	255	123.9	120	248
1	−17.2	−20	−4	125	51.7	36	96.8	260	126.6	125	257
2	−16.7	−18	−0.4	130	54.4	38	100.4	265	129.4	130	266
3	−16.1	−16	3.2	135	57.2	40	104	270	132.2	135	275
4	−15.6	−14	6.8	140	60.0	42	107.6	275	135.0	140	284
5	−15.0	−12	10.4	145	62.8	44	112.2	280	137.8	145	293
10	−12.2	−10	14	150	65.6	46	114.8	285	140.6	150	302
15	−9.4	−8	17.6	155	68.3	48	118.4	290	143.3	155	311
20	−6.7	−6	21.2	160	71.1	50	122	295	146.1	160	320
25	−3.9	−4	24.8	165	73.9	52	125.6	300	148.9	165	329
30	−1.1	−2	28.4	170	76.7	54	129.2	305	151.7	170	338
35	1.7	0	32	175	79.4	56	132.8	310	154.4	175	347
40	4.4	2	35.6	180	82.2	58	136.4	315	157.2	180	356
45	7.2	4	39.2	185	85.0	60	140	320	160.0	185	365
50	10.0	6	42.8	190	87.8	62	143.6	325	162.8	190	374
55	12.8	8	46.4	195	90.6	64	147.2	330	165.6	195	383
60	15.6	10	50	200	93.3	66	150.8	335	168.3	200	392
65	18.3	12	53.6	205	96.1	68	154.4	340	171.1	205	401
70	21.1	14	57.2	210	98.9	70	158	345	173.9	210	410
75	23.9	16	60.8	212	100.0	75	167	350	176.7	215	414

TCCS1C01

ENGLISH TO METRIC CONVERSION: LENGTH

To convert inches (ins.) to millimeters (mm): multiply number of inches by 25.4

To convert millimeters (mm) to inches (ins.): multiply number of millimeters by .04

Inches		Decimals	Milli-meters	Inches to millimeters inches	mm		Inches		Decimals	Milli-meters	Inches to millimeters inches	mm
	1/64	0.051625	0.3969	0.0001	0.00254			33/64	0.515625	13.0969	0.6	15.24
1/32		0.03125	0.7937	0.0002	0.00508		17/32		0.53125	13.4937	0.7	17.78
	3/64	0.046875	1.1906	0.0003	0.00762			35/64	0.546875	13.8906	0.8	20.32
1/16		0.0625	1.5875	0.0004	0.01016	9/16			0.5625	14.2875	0.9	22.86
	5/64	0.078125	1.9844	0.0005	0.01270			37/64	0.578125	14.6844	1	25.4
3/32		0.09375	2.3812	0.0006	0.01524		19/32		0.59375	15.0812	2	50.8
	7/64	0.109375	2.7781	0.0007	0.01778			39/64	0.609375	15.4781	3	76.2
1/8		0.125	3.1750	0.0008	0.02032	5/8			0.625	15.8750	4	101.6
	9/64	0.140625	3.5719	0.0009	0.02286			41/64	0.640625	16.2719	5	127.0
5/32		0.15625	3.9687	0.001	0.0254		21/32		0.65625	16.6687	6	152.4
	11/64	0.171875	4.3656	0.002	0.0508			43/64	0.671875	17.0656	7	177.8
3/16		0.1875	4.7625	0.003	0.0762	11/16			0.6875	17.4625	8	203.2
	13/64	0.203125	5.1594	0.004	0.1016			45/64	0.703125	17.8594	9	228.6
7/32		0.21875	5.5562	0.005	0.1270		23/32		0.71875	18.2562	10	254.0
	15/64	0.234375	5.9531	0.006	0.1524			47/64	0.734375	18.6531	11	279.4
1/4		0.25	6.3500	0.007	0.1778	3/4			0.75	19.0500	12	304.8
	17/64	0.265625	6.7469	0.008	0.2032			49/64	0.765625	19.4469	13	330.2
9/32		0.28125	7.1437	0.009	0.2286		25/32		0.78125	19.8437	14	355.6
	19/64	0.296875	7.5406	0.01	0.254			51/64	0.796875	20.2406	15	381.0
5/16		0.3125	7.9375	0.02	0.508	13/16			0.8125	20.6375	16	406.4
	21/64	0.328125	8.3344	0.03	0.762			53/64	0.828125	21.0344	17	431.8
11/32		0.34375	8.7312	0.04	1.016		27/32		0.84375	21.4312	18	457.2
	23/64	0.359375	9.1281	0.05	1.270			55/64	0.859375	21.8281	19	482.6
3/8		0.375	9.5250	0.06	1.524	7/8			0.875	22.2250	20	508.0
	25/64	0.390625	9.9219	0.07	1.778			57/64	0.890625	22.6219	21	533.4
13/32		0.40625	10.3187	0.08	2.032		29/32		0.90625	23.0187	22	558.8
	27/64	0.421875	10.7156	0.09	2.286			59/64	0.921875	23.4156	23	584.2
7/16		0.4375	11.1125	0.1	2.54	15/16			0.9375	23.8125	24	609.6
	29/64	0.453125	11.5094	0.2	5.08			61/64	0.953125	24.2094	25	635.0
15/32		0.46875	11.9062	0.3	7.62		31/32		0.96875	24.6062	26	660.4
	31/64	0.484375	12.3031	0.4	10.16			63/64	0.984375	25.0031	27	690.6
1/2		0.5	12.7000	0.5	12.70							

ENGLISH TO METRIC CONVERSION: TORQUE

To convert foot-pounds (ft. lbs.) to Newton-meters: multiply the number of ft. lbs. by 1.3

To convert inch-pounds (in. lbs.) to Newton-meters: multiply the number of in. lbs. by .11

in lbs	N-m	in lbs	N-m	in lbs	N-m	in lbs	N-m	in lbs	N-m
0.1	0.01	1	0.11	10	1.13	19	2.15	28	3.16
0.2	0.02	2	0.23	11	1.24	20	2.26	29	3.28
0.3	0.03	3	0.34	12	1.36	21	2.37	30	3.39
0.4	0.04	4	0.45	13	1.47	22	2.49	31	3.50
0.5	0.06	5	0.56	14	1.58	23	2.60	32	3.62
0.6	0.07	6	0.68	15	1.70	24	2.71	33	3.73
0.7	0.08	7	0.78	16	1.81	25	2.82	34	3.84
0.8	0.09	8	0.90	17	1.92	26	2.94	35	3.95
0.9	0.10	9	1.02	18	2.03	27	3.05	36	4.0

TCCS1C02

ENGLISH TO METRIC CONVERSION: TORQUE

Torque is now expressed as either foot-pounds (ft./lbs.) or inch-pounds (in./lbs.). The metric measurement unit for torque is the Newton-meter (Nm). This unit—the Nm—will be used for all SI metric torque references, both the present ft./lbs. and in./lbs.

ft lbs	N-m	ft lbs	N-m	ft lbs	N-m	ft lbs	N-m
0.1	0.1	33	44.7	74	100.3	115	155.9
0.2	0.3	34	46.1	75	101.7	116	157.3
0.3	0.4	35	47.4	76	103.0	117	158.6
0.4	0.5	36	48.8	77	104.4	118	160.0
0.5	0.7	37	50.7	78	105.8	119	161.3
0.6	0.8	38	51.5	79	107.1	120	162.7
0.7	1.0	39	52.9	80	108.5	121	164.0
0.8	1.1	40	54.2	81	109.8	122	165.4
0.9	1.2	41	55.6	82	111.2	123	166.8
1	1.3	42	56.9	83	112.5	124	168.1
2	2.7	43	58.3	84	113.9	125	169.5
3	4.1	44	59.7	85	115.2	126	170.8
4	5.4	45	61.0	86	116.6	127	172.2
5	6.8	46	62.4	87	118.0	128	173.5
6	8.1	47	63.7	88	119.3	129	174.9
7	9.5	48	65.1	89	120.7	130	176.2
8	10.8	49	66.4	90	122.0	131	177.6
9	12.2	50	67.8	91	123.4	132	179.0
10	13.6	51	69.2	92	124.7	133	180.3
11	14.9	52	70.5	93	126.1	134	181.7
12	16.3	53	71.9	94	127.4	135	183.0
13	17.6	54	73.2	95	128.8	136	184.4
14	18.9	55	74.6	96	130.2	137	185.7
15	20.3	56	75.9	97	131.5	138	187.1
16	21.7	57	77.3	98	132.9	139	188.5
17	23.0	58	78.6	99	134.2	140	189.8
18	24.4	59	80.0	100	135.6	141	191.2
19	25.8	60	81.4	101	136.9	142	192.5
20	27.1	61	82.7	102	138.3	143	193.9
21	28.5	62	84.1	103	139.6	144	195.2
22	29.8	63	85.4	104	141.0	145	196.6
23	31.2	64	86.8	105	142.4	146	198.0
24	32.5	65	88.1	106	143.7	147	199.3
25	33.9	66	89.5	107	145.1	148	200.7
26	35.2	67	90.8	108	146.4	149	202.0
27	36.6	68	92.2	109	147.8	150	203.4
28	38.0	69	93.6	110	149.1	151	204.7
29	39.3	70	94.9	111	150.5	152	206.1
30	40.7	71	96.3	112	151.8	153	207.4
31	42.0	72	97.6	113	153.2	154	208.8
32	43.4	73	99.0	114	154.6	155	210.2

TCCS1C03

ENGLISH TO METRIC CONVERSION: FORCE

Force is presently measured in pounds (lbs.). This type of measurement is used to measure spring pressure, specifically how many pounds it takes to compress a spring. Our present force unit (the pound) will be replaced in SI metric measurements by the Newton (N). This term will eventually see use in specifications for electric motor brush spring pressures, valve spring pressures, etc.

To convert pounds (lbs.) to Newton (N): multiply the number of lbs. by 4.45

lbs	N	lbs	N	lbs	N	oz	N
0.01	0.04	21	93.4	59	262.4	1	0.3
0.02	0.09	22	97.9	60	266.9	2	0.6
0.03	0.13	23	102.3	61	271.3	3	0.8
0.04	0.18	24	106.8	62	275.8	4	1.1
0.05	0.22	25	111.2	63	280.2	5	1.4
0.06	0.27	26	115.6	64	284.6	6	1.7
0.07	0.31	27	120.1	65	289.1	7	2.0
0.08	0.36	28	124.6	66	293.6	8	2.2
0.09	0.40	29	129.0	67	298.0	9	2.5
0.1	0.4	30	133.4	68	302.5	10	2.8
0.2	0.9	31	137.9	69	306.9	11	3.1
0.3	1.3	32	142.3	70	311.4	12	3.3
0.4	1.8	33	146.8	71	315.8	13	3.6
0.5	2.2	34	151.2	72	320.3	14	3.9
0.6	2.7	35	155.7	73	324.7	15	4.2
0.7	3.1	36	160.1	74	329.2	16	4.4
0.8	3.6	37	164.6	75	333.6	17	4.7
0.9	4.0	38	169.0	76	338.1	18	5.0
1	4.4	39	173.5	77	342.5	19	5.3
2	8.9	40	177.9	78	347.0	20	5.6
3	13.4	41	182.4	79	351.4	21	5.8
4	17.8	42	186.8	80	355.9	22	6.1
5	22.2	43	191.3	81	360.3	23	6.4
6	26.7	44	195.7	82	364.8	24	6.7
7	31.1	45	200.2	83	369.2	25	7.0
8	35.6	46	204.6	84	373.6	26	7.2
9	40.0	47	209.1	85	378.1	27	7.5
10	44.5	48	213.5	86	382.6	28	7.8
11	48.9	49	218.0	87	387.0	29	8.1
12	53.4	50	224.4	88	391.4	30	8.3
13	57.8	51	226.9	89	395.9	31	8.6
14	62.3	52	231.3	90	400.3	32	8.9
15	66.7	53	235.8	91	404.8	33	9.2
16	71.2	54	240.2	92	409.2	34	9.4
17	75.6	55	244.6	93	413.7	35	9.7
18	80.1	56	249.1	94	418.1	36	10.0
19	84.5	57	253.6	95	422.6	37	10.3
20	89.0	58	258.0	96	427.0	38	10.6

TCCS1C04

ENGLISH TO METRIC CONVERSION: LIQUID CAPACITY

Liquid or fluid capacity is presently expressed as pints, quarts or gallons, or a combination of all of these. In the metric system the liter (l) will become the basic unit. Fractions of a liter would be expressed as deciliters, centiliters, or most frequently (and commonly) as milliliters.

To convert pints (pts.) to liters (l): multiply the number of pints by .47
To convert liters (l) to pints (pts.): multiply the number of liters by 2.1
To convert quarts (qts.) to liters (l): multiply the number of quarts by .95

To convert liters (l) to quarts (qts.): multiply the number of liters by 1.06
To convert gallons (gals.) to liters (l): multiply the number of gallons by 3.8
To convert liters (l) to gallons (gals.): multiply the number of liters by .26

gals	liters	qts	liters	pts	liters
0.1	0.38	0.1	0.10	0.1	0.05
0.2	0.76	0.2	0.19	0.2	0.10
0.3	1.1	0.3	0.28	0.3	0.14
0.4	1.5	0.4	0.38	0.4	0.19
0.5	1.9	0.5	0.47	0.5	0.24
0.6	2.3	0.6	0.57	0.6	0.28
0.7	2.6	0.7	0.66	0.7	0.33
0.8	3.0	0.8	0.76	0.8	0.38
0.9	3.4	0.9	0.85	0.9	0.43
1	3.8	1	1.0	1	0.5
2	7.6	2	1.9	2	1.0
3	11.4	3	2.8	3	1.4
4	15.1	4	3.8	4	1.9
5	18.9	5	4.7	5	2.4
6	22.7	6	5.7	6	2.8
7	26.5	7	6.6	7	3.3
8	30.3	8	7.6	8	3.8
9	34.1	9	8.5	9	4.3
10	37.8	10	9.5	10	4.7
11	41.6	11	10.4	11	5.2
12	45.4	12	11.4	12	5.7
13	49.2	13	12.3	13	6.2
14	53.0	14	13.2	14	6.6
15	56.8	15	14.2	15	7.1
16	60.6	16	15.1	16	7.6
17	64.3	17	16.1	17	8.0
18	68.1	18	17.0	18	8.5
19	71.9	19	18.0	19	9.0
20	75.7	20	18.9	20	9.5
21	79.5	21	19.9	21	9.9
22	83.2	22	20.8	22	10.4
23	87.0	23	21.8	23	10.9
24	90.8	24	22.7	24	11.4
25	94.6	25	23.6	25	11.8
26	98.4	26	24.6	26	12.3
27	102.2	27	25.5	27	12.8
28	106.0	28	26.5	28	13.2
29	110.0	29	27.4	29	13.7
30	113.5	30	28.4	30	14.2

TCCS1C05

2

ENGINE ELECTRICAL

DISTRIBUTORLESS IGNITION SYSTEM

▶ See Figures 1 and 2

The distributorless ignition is referred to as the Electronic Ignition (EI) system, and eliminates the conventional distributor by utilizing a multiple ignition coil pack. The EI system consists of the following components:

- Crankshaft Position (CKP) sensor
- Ignition Control Module (ICM)
- Ignition coil pack
- Powertrain Control Module (PCM)
- Related wiring

➡**Only 1995–96 3.0L engines use an external ICM. 1997–98 3.0L and all 3.8L engines have the ICM incorporated into the Power Control Module (PCM).**

The CKP sensor is a variable reluctance sensor, mounted near the crankshaft damper and pulley.

The crankshaft damper has a "36 minus 1 tooth" wheel (data wheel)

mounted on it. When this wheel rotates, the magnetic field (reluctance) of the CKP sensor changes in relationship with the passing of the teeth on the data wheel. This change in the magnetic field is called the CKP signal.

➡**The base ignition timing is set at 10 (plus or minus 2 degrees) degrees Before Top Dead Center (BTDC) and is not adjustable.**

The CKP signal is sent to the PCM, which uses the signal to determine base ignition timing and rpm calculations.

The one missing tooth on the data wheel creates one large space between two of the teeth. The PCM utilizes this large space as a reference to help determine base ignition timing and engine speed (rpm), and to synchronize the ignition coils for the proper spark timing sequence.

A coil pack, which contains three separate ignition coils is used on both engines. Each ignition coil fires two spark plugs simultaneously. One of the two plugs being fired is on the compression stroke (this plug uses most of

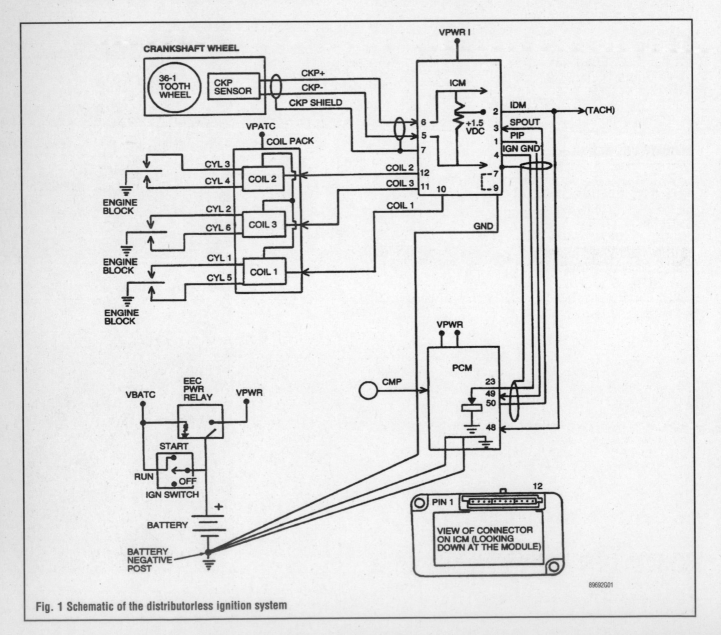

Fig. 1 Schematic of the distributorless ignition system

89692G01

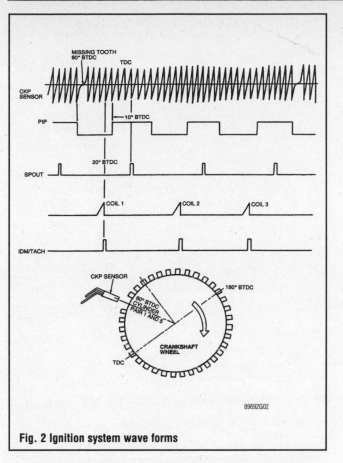

Fig. 2 Ignition system wave forms

the voltage) and the other plug is on the exhaust stroke (this plug uses very little of the voltage). Since these two plugs are connected in series, the firing voltage of one plug is negative (with respect to ground) and the other plug is positive.

Diagnosis and Testing

SECONDARY SPARK TEST

The best way to perform this procedure is to use a spark tester (available at most automotive parts stores). Two types of spark testers are commonly available. The Neon Bulb type is connected to the spark plug wire and flashes with each ignition pulse. The Air Gap type must be adjusted to the individual spark plug gap specified for the engine. This type of tester allows the user to not only detect the presence of spark, but also the intensity (orange/yellow is weak, blue is strong).

1. Disconnect a spark plug wire at the spark plug end.
2. Connect the plug wire to the spark tester and ground the tester to an appropriate location on the engine.
3. Crank the engine and check for spark at the tester.
4. If spark exists at the tester, the ignition system is functioning properly.
5. If spark does not exist at the spark tester, there is a fault in the ignition system.
6. Test the spark plug wires, ignition coil, crankshaft position sensor and related wiring. Repair or replace components as necessary.

Adjustments

All adjustments in the ignition system are controlled by the Powertrain Control Module (PCM) for optimum performance. No adjustments are possible.

Ignition Coil Pack(s)

TESTING

◆ **See Figure 3**

1. Turn the ignition OFF.
2. Disconnect the negative battery cable.
3. Disconnect the wiring harness from the ignition coil.
4. Check for dirt, corrosion or damage on the terminals and repair as necessary.
5. Measure coil primary resistance between ignition coil pin 4 (B+) and pins 1 (coil 2), 2 (coil 3) and 3 (coil 1).
6. Resistance should be 0.3–1.0 ohms.
7. Measure coil secondary resistance between ignition coil terminals and their corresponding spark plug wire towers on the coil.
- Pin 3 (coil 1)—spark plugs 1 and 5
- Pin 2 (coil 3)—spark plugs 2 and 6
- Pin 1 (coil 2)—spark plugs 3 and 4

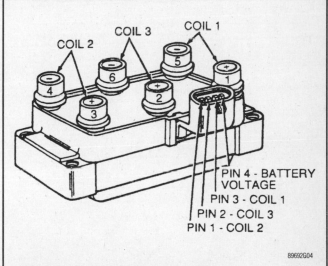

Fig. 3 Ignition coil pack terminal designations

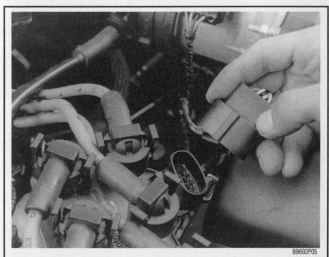

The ignition coil is connected to the vehicle wiring harness with a four terminal plug

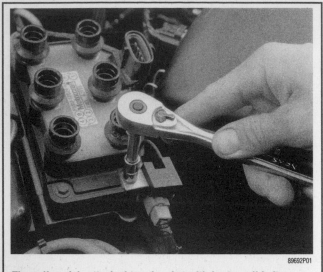

The coil pack is attached to a bracket with four small bolts

89692P01

The coil pack contains the coils and the ignition control module. It is removed as an assembly

89692P02

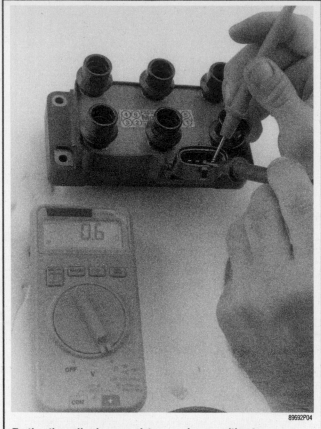

Testing the coil primary resistance using a multimeter

89692P04

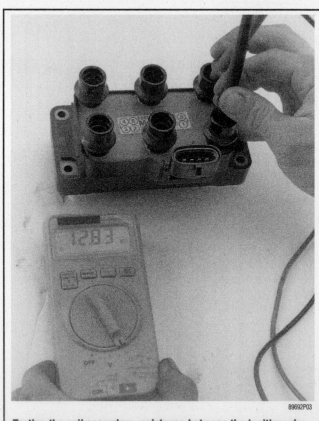

Testing the coil secondary resistance between the ignition wire terminals

89692P03

8. Resistance should be 12.8–13.1 kilohms.
9. If either primary or secondary resistance is not within specification, the coil may be faulty.

REMOVAL & INSTALLATION

▶ See Figures 4 and 5

1. Disconnect the negative battery cable.
2. Disconnect the electrical harness from the coil pack.
3. Label and remove the spark plug wires from the ignition coil terminal towers. To remove the wires, squeeze the locking tabs to release the coil boot retainers.
4. Remove the coil pack mounting screws and remove the coil pack.
To install:
5. Install the coil pack and the retaining screws. Tighten the retaining screws to 44–61 inch lbs. (5–7 Nm).

➡**Lubricate the terminals with dielectric compound prior to installing the spark plug wires.**

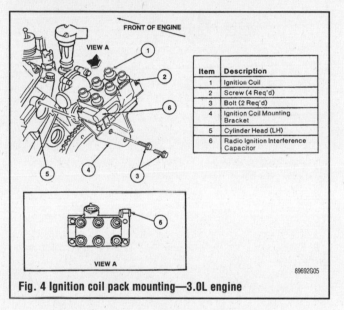

Item	Description
1	Ignition Coil
2	Screw (4 Req'd)
3	Bolt (2 Req'd)
4	Ignition Coil Mounting Bracket
5	Cylinder Head (LH)
6	Radio Ignition Interference Capacitor

89692G05

Fig. 4 Ignition coil pack mounting—3.0L engine

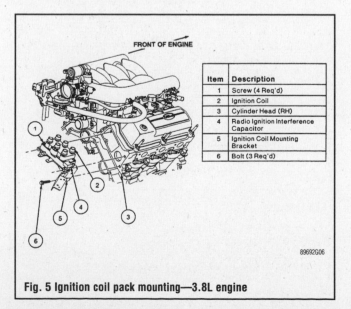

Item	Description
1	Screw (4 Req'd)
2	Ignition Coil
3	Cylinder Head (RH)
4	Radio Ignition Interference Capacitor
5	Ignition Coil Mounting Bracket
6	Bolt (3 Req'd)

89692G06

Fig. 5 Ignition coil pack mounting—3.8L engine

6. Connect the spark plug wires and electrical harness to the coil pack.
7. Connect the negative battery cable.

Ignition Control Module (ICM)

REMOVAL & INSTALLATION

▶ See Figure 6

➡**Only 1995–96 3.0L engines use an external ICM. 1997–98 3.0L and all 3.8L engines have the ICM incorporated into the Power Control Module (PCM).**

1. Disconnect the negative battery cable.
2. Disconnect the wiring harness from the ICM.
3. Remove the ICM.
To install:
4. Position the ICM onto the inner fender apron and install the mounting bolts. Tighten the bolts to 27–35 inch lbs. (3–4 Nm).

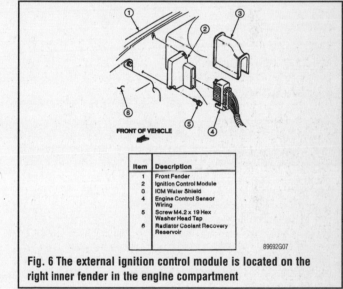

Item	Description
1	Front Fender
2	Ignition Control Module
3	ICM Water Shield
4	Engine Control Sensor Wiring
5	Screw M4.2 x 19 Hex Washer Head Tap
6	Radiator Coolant Recovery Reservoir

89692G07

Fig. 6 The external ignition control module is located on the right inner fender in the engine compartment

5. Connect the wiring harness to the ICM.
6. Connect the negative battery cable.

Camshaft Position (CMP) Sensor

For Camshaft Position (CMP) sensor procedures, please refer to Section 4 in this manual.

Crankshaft Position (CKP) Sensor

For Crankshaft Position (CKP) sensor procedures, please refer to Section 4 in this manual.

See Figures 7 and 8

➡To avoid confusion, remove and tag the spark plug wires one at a time, for replacement.

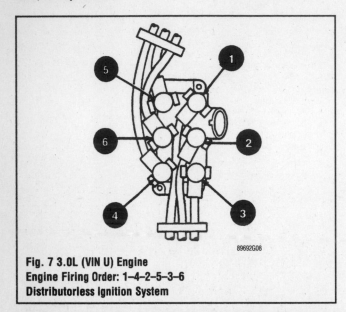

Fig. 7 3.0L (VIN U) Engine
Engine Firing Order: 1–4–2–5–3–6
Distributorless Ignition System

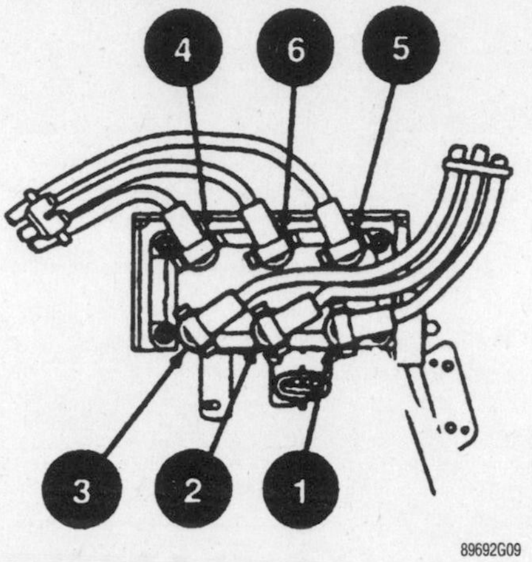

Fig. 8 3.8L (VIN 4) Engine
Engine Firing Order: 1–4–2–5–3–6
Distributorless Ignition System

CHARGING SYSTEM

General Information

The charging system is a negative (-) ground system which consists of an alternator, a regulator, a charge indicator lamp, a storage battery, circuit protection and wiring connecting the components.

The alternator is belt-driven from the engine. Energy is supplied from the alternator (with integral regulator) to the rotating field through brushes to slip-rings. The slip-rings are mounted on the rotor shaft and are connected to the field coil. This energy supplied to the rotating field from the battery is called excitation current and is used to initially energize the field to begin the generation of electricity. Once the alternator starts to generate electricity, the excitation current comes from its own output rather than the battery.

The alternator produces power in the form of alternating current. The alternating current is rectified by diodes into direct current. The direct current is used to charge the battery and power the rest of the electrical system. When the ignition key is turned on, current flows from the battery, through the charging system indicator light on the instrument panel, to the voltage regulator, and to the alternator. Since the alternator is not producing any current, the alternator warning light comes on. When the engine is started, the alternator begins to produce current and turns the alternator light off.

As the alternator turns and produces current, the current is divided in two ways: charging the battery and powering the electrical components of the vehicle. Part of the current is returned to the alternator to enable it to increase its output. In this situation, the alternator is receiving current from the battery and from itself. A voltage regulator is wired into the current supply to the alternator to prevent it from receiving too much current, which would cause it to overproduce current. Conversely, if the voltage regulator does not allow the alternator to receive enough current, the battery will not be fully charged and will eventually go dead.

The battery is connected to the alternator at all times, whether the ignition key is turned on or off. If the battery were shorted to ground, the alternator would also be shorted. This would damage the alternator. To prevent this, circuit protection (usually in the form of a fuse link) is installed in the wiring between the battery and the alternator. If the battery is shorted, the circuit protection will protect the alternator.

PRECAUTIONS

- NEVER ground or short out the alternator or regulator terminals.
- NEVER operate the alternator with any of its or the battery's lead wires disconnected.
- NEVER use a fast battery charger to jump start a dead battery.
- NEVER attempt to polarize an alternator.
- NEVER subject the alternator to excessive heat or dampness (for instance, steam cleaning the engine).
- NEVER use arc welding equipment on the car with the alternator connected.
- ALWAYS observe proper polarity of the battery connections; be especially careful when jump starting the car.
- ALWAYS remove the battery or at least disconnect the ground cable while charging.
- ALWAYS disconnect the battery ground cable while repairing or replacing an electrical components.

Alternator

TESTING

▶ **See Figures 9 and 10**

The easiest way to test the performance of the alternator is to perform a regulated voltage test.

1. Start the engine and allow it to reach operating temperature.
2. Connect a voltmeter between the positive and negative terminals of the battery.
3. Voltage should be 14.1–14.7 volts.
4. If voltage is higher or lower than specification, connect a voltmeter

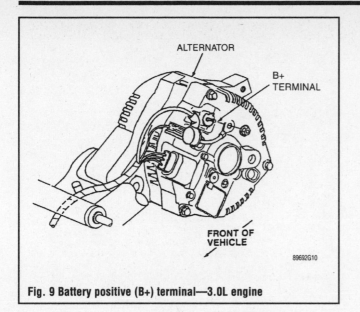

Fig. 9 Battery positive (B+) terminal—3.0L engine

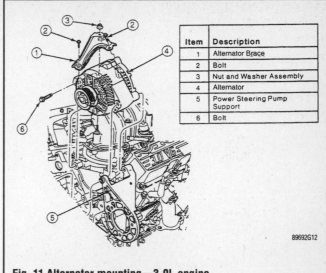

Item	Description
1	Alternator Brace
2	Bolt
3	Nut and Washer Assembly
4	Alternator
5	Power Steering Pump Support
6	Bolt

Fig. 11 Alternator mounting—3.0L engine

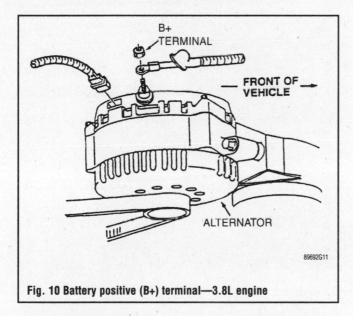

Fig. 10 Battery positive (B+) terminal—3.8L engine

After disconnecting the negative battery cable, remove the alternator B+ wire

between the battery positive (B+) voltage output terminal of the alternator and a good engine ground.

5. Voltage should be 14.1–14.7 volts.

6. If voltage is still out of specification, a problem exists in the alternator or voltage regulator.

7. If voltage is now within specification, a problem exists in the wiring to the battery or in the battery itself.

➡Many automotive parts stores have alternator bench testers available for use by customers. An alternator bench test is the most definitive way to determine the condition of your alternator.

REMOVAL & INSTALLATION

3.0L Engine

♦ See Figure 11

1. Disconnect the negative battery cable.
2. Disconnect the alternator wiring harness.
3. Detach the alternator drive belt.
4. Loosen the alternator pivot bolt.
5. Remove the alternator brace.

Unplug the remaining connectors from the back of the alternator

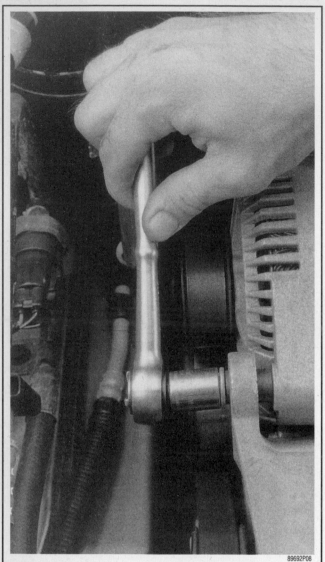

A large bolt is used as a pivot for the alternator. Loosen it first, but do not remove it

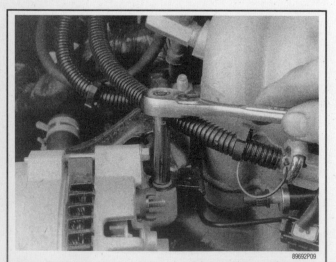

Remove the bolt attaching the rear of the alternator to the bracket—3.0L engine

Remove the bolt attaching the bracket to the intake manifold—3.0L engine

Remove the bracket from the engine—3.0L engine

6. Remove the alternator pivot bolt.
7. Remove the alternator.
To install:
8. Position the alternator on the engine.
9. Install the alternator pivot bolt and brace.
10. Tighten the alternator brace to 15–22 ft. lbs. (20–30 Nm) and the pivot bolt to 30–41 ft. lbs. (40–55 Nm).
11. Install and tension the alternator drive belt.
12. Connect the alternator wiring harness. Tighten the output terminal nut to 80–97 inch lbs. (9–11 Nm).
13. Connect the negative battery cable.

Once the alternator is loose, remove the accessory drive belt

Now remove the alternator pivot bolt . . .

. . . and carefully lift the alternator from the engine

3.8L Engine

▶ See Figure 12

1. Disconnect the negative battery cable.
2. Disconnect the alternator wiring harness.
3. Detach the alternator drive belt.
4. Remove the three alternator attaching bolts.
5. Remove the alternator.

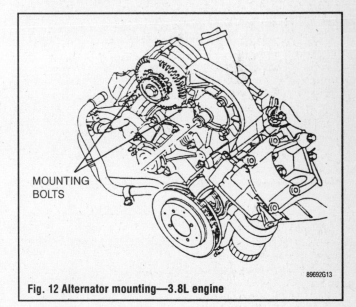

MOUNTING BOLTS

Fig. 12 Alternator mounting—3.8L engine

To install:

6. Position the alternator on the engine.
7. Install the three alternator attaching bolts. Tighten the bolts 30–41 ft. lbs. (40–55 Nm).
8. Install and tension the alternator drive belt.
9. Connect the alternator wiring harness. Tighten the output terminal nut to 80–97 inch lbs. (9–11 Nm).
10. Connect the negative battery cable.

Voltage Regulator

REMOVAL & INSTALLATION

▶ **See Figure 13**

1. Remove the alternator from the vehicle, as previously described.
2. Remove the four regulator attaching bolts.
3. Remove the regulator with the brush and terminal holder attached.

To install:

4. Transfer the brush and terminal holder to the new regulator, as necessary.
5. Push the brushes back into the holder and insert a thin wire or toothpick through the access hole in the regulator. This will keep the brushes retracted during installation.
6. Install the regulator assembly. Tighten the attaching bolts to 20–30 inch lbs. (2–3 Nm).
7. Remove the thin wire or toothpick from the access hole.
8. Install the alternator on the vehicle.

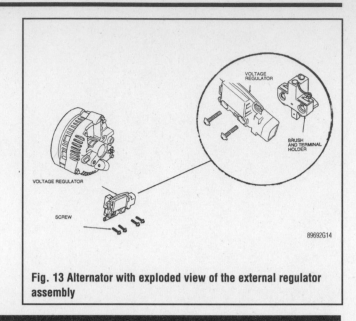

Fig. 13 Alternator with exploded view of the external regulator assembly

STARTING SYSTEM

General Information

The starting system includes the battery, starter motor, solenoid, ignition switch, circuit protection and wiring connecting the components. An inhibitor switch is included in the starting system to prevent the vehicle from being started with the vehicle in gear.

When the ignition key is turned to the **START** position, current flows and energizes the starter's solenoid coil. The solenoid plunger and clutch shift lever are activated and the clutch pinion engages the ring gear on the flywheel. The switch contacts close and the starter cranks the engine until it starts.

To prevent damage caused by excessive starter armature rotation when the engine starts, the starter incorporates an over-running clutch in the pinion gear.

TESTING

The easiest way to test the performance of the starter is to perform a voltage drop test.

➡**The battery must be in good condition and fully charged prior to performing this test.**

1. Connect a voltmeter between the positive and negative terminals of the battery.
2. Turn the ignition key to the **START** position and note the voltage drop on the meter.
3. If voltage drops below 11.5 volts, there is high resistance in the starting system.
4. Check for proper connections at the battery and starter.
5. Check the resistance of the battery cables and replace as necessary.
6. If all other components in the system are functional, the starter may be faulty.

➡**Many automotive parts stores have starter bench testers available for use by customers. A starter bench test is the most definitive way to determine the condition of your starter.**

REMOVAL & INSTALLATION

1. Disconnect the negative battery cable.
2. Raise and support the vehicle safely.

➡**When removing the hard shell connector at terminal "S", grasp the plastic shell. Do not pull on the wire.**

3. . Disconnect the starter electrical harness.
4. Remove the upper starter bolt.
5. Support the starter and remove the lower bolt.
6. Remove the starter from the vehicle.

To install:

7. Position the starter in the vehicle.
8. Install the upper and lower bolts. Tighten to 15–20 ft. lbs. (20–27 Nm).
9. Connect the starter electrical harness. Tighten the starter cable nut to 80–124 inch lbs. (9–14 Nm).

➡**When installing the hard shell connector, be careful to push it straight on and make sure it locks in position with a notable click or detent.**

10. Lower the vehicle.
11. Connect the negative battery cable.

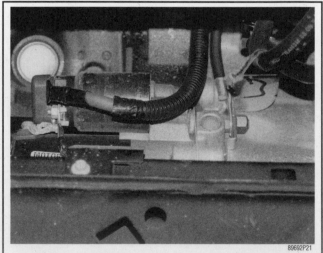

The starter is located at the lower front of the engine, and is visible through the air duct

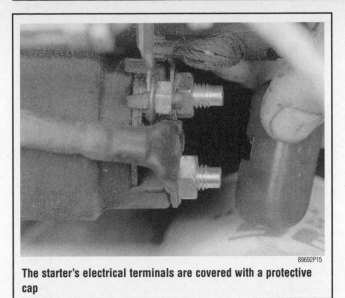

The starter's electrical terminals are covered with a protective cap

Remove the starter's lower mounting bolt . . .

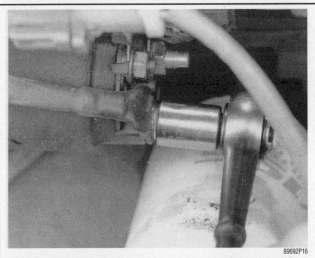

After disconnecting the negative battery cable, detach the wire from the starter's B+ terminal

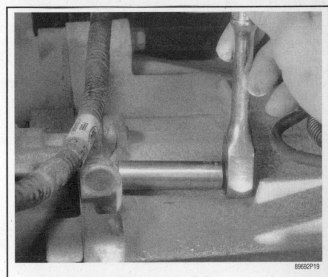

. . . followed by the upper mounting bolt

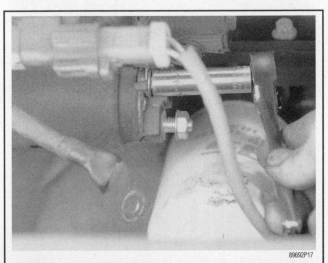

The ignition wire is the smaller of the two wires leading to the starter

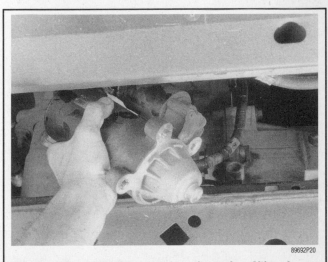

Take care when lifting the starter from the engine. Although small, it is very heavy

SENDING UNITS

➡ This section describes the operating principles of sending units, warning lights and gauges. Sensors which provide information to the Electronic Control Module (ECM) are covered in Section 4 of this manual.

Instrument panels contain a number of indicating devices (gauges and warning lights). These devices are composed of two separate components. One is the sending unit, mounted on the engine or other remote part of the vehicle, and the other is the actual gauge or light in the instrument panel.

Several types of sending units exist, however most can be characterized as being either a pressure type or a resistance type. Pressure type sending units convert liquid pressure into an electrical signal which is sent to the gauge. Resistance type sending units are most often used to measure temperature and use variable resistance to control the current flow back to the indicating device. Both types of sending units are connected in series by a wire to the battery (through the ignition switch). When the ignition is turned **ON**, current flows from the battery through the indicating device and on to the sending unit.

Coolant Temperature Sender

TESTING

1. Disconnect the sending unit electrical harness.
2. Remove the radiator cap and place a mechanic's thermometer in the coolant.
3. Using an ohmmeter, check the resistance between the sending unit terminals.
4. Resistance should be high (375 ohms) with engine coolant cold and low (180 ohms) with engine coolant hot.

➡ It is best to check resistance with the engine cool, then start the engine and watch the resistance change as the engine warms.

5. If resistance does not drop as engine temperature rises, the sending unit is faulty.

REMOVAL & INSTALLATION

1. Locate the coolant temperature sending unit on the engine.
2. Disconnect the sending unit electrical harness.

3. Drain the engine coolant below the level of the switch.
4. Unfasten and remove the sending unit from the engine.
5. Coat the new sending unit with Teflon® tape or electrically conductive sealer.
6. Install the sending unit and tighten to 11–15 ft. lbs. (15–20 Nm).
7. Attach the sending unit's electrical connector.
8. Fill the engine with coolant.
9. Start the engine, allow it to reach operating temperature and check for leaks.
10. Check for proper sending unit operation.

Oil Pressure Sender

TESTING

1. Disconnect the sending unit electrical harness.
2. Using an ohmmeter, check continuity between the sending unit terminals.
3. With the engine stopped, continuity should exist.

➡ The switch inside the oil pressure sending unit closes at 6 psi or less of pressure.

4. With the engine running, continuity should not exist.
5. If continuity does not exist as stated, the sending unit is faulty.

REMOVAL & INSTALLATION

1. Locate the oil pressure sending unit on the engine.
2. Disconnect the sending unit electrical harness.
3. Unfasten and remove the sending unit from the engine.
To install:
4. Coat the new sending unit with Teflon® tape or electrically conductive sealer.
5. Install the sending unit and tighten to 11–15 ft. lbs. (15–20 Nm).
6. Attach the sending unit's electrical connector.
7. Start the engine, allow it to reach operating temperature and check for leaks.
8. Check for proper sending unit operation.

Troubleshooting Basic Starting System Problems

Problem	Cause	Solution
Starter motor rotates engine slowly	• Battery charge low or battery defective	• Charge or replace battery
	• Defective circuit between battery and starter motor	• Clean and tighten, or replace cables
	• Low load current	• Bench-test starter motor. Inspect for worn brushes and weak brush springs.
	• High load current	• Bench-test starter motor. Check engine for friction, drag or coolant in cylinders. Check ring gear-to-pinion gear clearance.
Starter motor will not rotate engine	• Battery charge low or battery defective	• Charge or replace battery
	• Faulty solenoid	• Check solenoid ground. Repair or replace as necessary.
	• Damaged drive pinion gear or ring gear	• Replace damaged gear(s)
	• Starter motor engagement weak	• Bench-test starter motor
	• Starter motor rotates slowly with high load current	• Inspect drive yoke pull-down and point gap, check for worn end bushings, check ring gear clearance
	• Engine seized	• Repair engine
Starter motor drive will not engage (solenoid known to be good)	• Defective contact point assembly	• Repair or replace contact point assembly
	• Inadequate contact point assembly ground	• Repair connection at ground screw
	• Defective hold-in coil	• Replace field winding assembly
Starter motor drive will not disengage	• Starter motor loose on flywheel housing	• Tighten mounting bolts
	• Worn drive end busing	• Replace bushing
	• Damaged ring gear teeth	• Replace ring gear or driveplate
	• Drive yoke return spring broken or missing	• Replace spring
Starter motor drive disengages prematurely	• Weak drive assembly thrust spring	• Replace drive mechanism
	• Hold-in coil defective	• Replace field winding assembly
Low load current	• Worn brushes	• Replace brushes
	• Weak brush springs	• Replace springs

TCCS2C01

Troubleshooting Basic Charging System Problems

Problem	Cause	Solution
Noisy alternator	• Loose mountings • Loose drive pulley • Worn bearings • Brush noise • Internal circuits shorted (High pitched whine)	• Tighten mounting bolts • Tighten pulley • Replace alternator • Replace alternator • Replace alternator
Squeal when starting engine or accelerating	• Glazed or loose belt	• Replace or adjust belt
Indicator light remains on or ammeter indicates discharge (engine running)	• Broken belt • Broken or disconnected wires • Internal alternator problems • Defective voltage regulator	• Install belt • Repair or connect wiring • Replace alternator • Replace voltage regulator/alternator
Car light bulbs continually burn out—battery needs water continually	• Alternator/regulator overcharging	• Replace voltage regulator/alternator
Car lights flare on acceleration	• Battery low • Internal alternator/regulator problems	• Charge or replace battery • Replace alternator/regulator
Low voltage output (alternator light flickers continually or ammeter needle wanders)	• Loose or worn belt • Dirty or corroded connections • Internal alternator/regulator problems	• Replace or adjust belt • Clean or replace connections • Replace alternator/regulator

TCCS2C02

3

ENGINE AND ENGINE OVERHAUL

ENGINE MECHANICAL

Engine

REMOVAL & INSTALLATION

▶ **See Figures 1 thru 6**

In the process of removing the engine, you will come across a number of steps which call for the removal of a separate component or system, such as "disconnect the exhaust system" or "remove the radiator." In most instances, a detailed removal procedure can be found elsewhere in this manual.

It is virtually impossible to list each individual wire and hose which must be disconnected, simply because so many different model and engine combinations have been manufactured. Careful observation and common sense are the best possible approaches to any repair procedure.

Removal and installation of the engine can be made easier if you follow these basic points:

- If you have to drain any of the fluids, use a suitable container.
- Always any wires or hoses and, if possible, the components they came from before disconnecting them.

- Because there are so many bolts and fasteners involved, store and label the retainers from components separately in muffin pans, jars or coffee cans. This will prevent confusion during installation.
- After unbolting the transmission or transaxle, always make sure it is properly supported.
- If it is necessary to disconnect the air conditioning system, have this service performed by a qualified technician using a recovery/recycling station. If the system does not have to be disconnected, unbolt the compressor and set it aside.
- When unbolting the engine mounts, always make sure the engine is properly supported. When removing the engine, make sure that any lifting devices are properly attached to the engine. It is recommended that if your engine is supplied with lifting hooks, your lifting apparatus be attached to them.
- Lift the engine from its compartment slowly, checking that no hoses, wires or other components are still connected.
- After the engine is clear of the compartment, place it on an engine stand or workbench.
- After the engine has been removed, you can perform a partial or full teardown of the engine using the procedures outlined in this manual.

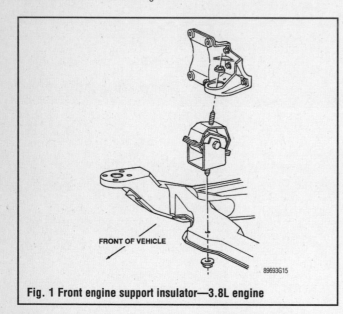

Fig. 1 Front engine support insulator—3.8L engine

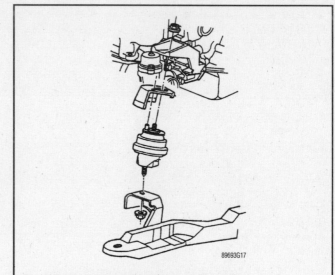

Fig. 3 Transaxle support insulator—3.8L engine

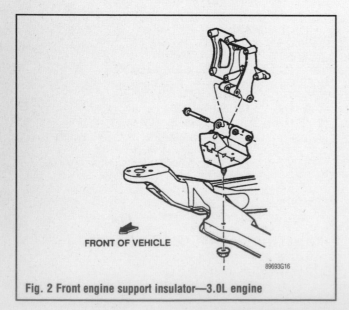

Fig. 2 Front engine support insulator—3.0L engine

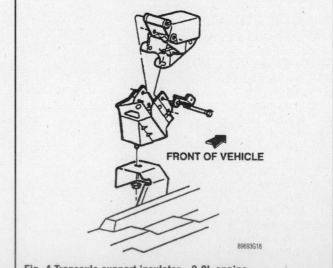

Fig. 4 Transaxle support insulator—3.0L engine

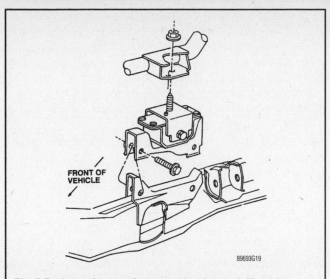

Fig. 5 Engine and transaxle support insulator—3.8L engine

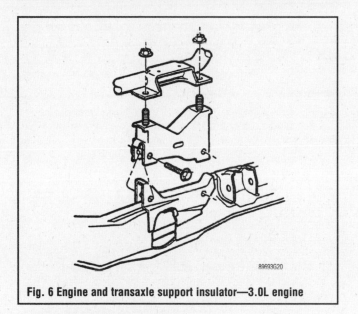

Fig. 6 Engine and transaxle support insulator—3.0L engine

1. Disconnect the negative battery cable.
2. Drain and recycle the engine coolant.
3. Recover and recycle the refrigerant from the A/C system.
4. Remove the cowl top vent panel.
5. Diconnect the wiring from the alternator.
6. Loosen the air cleaner outlet tube clamp at the throttle body and remove the engine air cleaner assembly.
7. Disconnect the upper and lower radiator hoses and secure to engine.
8. Disconnect the heater water hoses and secure to body.
9. Disconnect and plug the A/C discharge and suction hoses and secure to engine.
10. Disconnect accelerator cable and speed control cable from the throttle body lever.
11. Remove the accelerator cable bracket from the throttle body.
12. Disconnect fuel supply and return lines from the fuel injection supply manifold.
13. Label and disconnect all engine wiring harnesses from the engine and secure to the body.
14. Label and disconnect all vacuum hoses from the engine.
15. Remove the gear shift cable from the transaxle.

➡**Damage to the steering column air bag wiring cab result if the steering wheel is allowed to rotate freely. The wire is wound like a watch spring and can be overtightened and break of the steering wheel is rotated too far in either direction.**

16. Lock the steering wheel with wheels in the straight ahead position by turning the ignition to the **OFF** position.
17. Raise and support the vehicle safely.
18. Remove the front wheels.
19. Drain and recycle the engine oil.
20. Disconnect and plug the transaxle cooler lines at the transaxle. Secure the lines to the radiator.
21. Disconnect the heated oxygen sensor wiring harness.

➡**Do not allow the flex connector of the duel converter Y-pipe to hang unsupported or damage to the flex joint will result.**

22. Disconnect the dual converter Y-pipe and support to the body.

➡**The routing of the battery ground cable to the cylinder block is critical. It should go between the transaxle and the bracket. Take note during disassembly.**

23. Disconnect the starter motor wires and secure out of the way.
24. Remove the starter motor.
25. Remove the engine rear plate and torque converter-to-flywheel nuts.
26. Disconnect and plug the power steering cooler lines.
27. Remove the upper bolt from the sway bar links.
28. Remove the dust boot from the steering rack pinion support by gently spreading the integral tension ring and pushing upward.
29. Remove the steering coupling pinch bolt form the steering column intermediate shaft at the steering gear.
30. Remove the intermediate shaft from the steering gear.
31. Remove the front stabilizer bar links.
32. Separate the front suspension lower arms from the knuckles at the ball joint.
33. Separate the tie rod ends from the knuckle.
34. Remove the front axle wheel hub retainers from the halfshaft ends.
35. Remove the halfshafts from the front wheel knuckle.
36. Support the front subframe, engine and transaxle assembly.
37. Remove the four retaining bolts and lower the engine transaxle and front subframe from vehicle.
38. Disconnect the power steering pressure hose from the power steering pump.
39. Attach and engine hoist and lift the engine slightly.
40. Remove the engine support insulators.
41. Lift the engine and transaxle assembly from the front subframe.
42. Lower engine and transaxle.
43. Supprot transaxle on a level stationary surface and separate the engine from the transaxle.
To install:
44. Installation is the reverse of removal.
45. Please note the following torque specifications:
- Engine-to-transaxle—30–44 ft. lbs. (40–60 Nm)
- Torque converter nuts—20–34 ft. lbs. (27–46 Nm)
- Subframe-to-body bolts—57–76 ft. lbs. (77–103 Nm)
- Steering coupling pinch bolt—25–34 ft. lbs. (34–46 Nm)
- Dual converter Y-pipe-to-exhaust manifold—25–34 ft. lbs. (34–46 Nm)
- Flex pipe retaining bolts—25–34 ft. lbs. (34–46 Nm)
- Accelerator cable bracket retaining bolts—71–106 inch lbs. (8–12 Nm)
- Front engine support insulator-to-subframe (3.8L engine)—50–68 ft. lbs. (68–92 Nm)
- Front engine support insulator-to-subframe (3.0L engine)—65–87 ft. lbs. (88–119 Nm)
- Transmission insulator-to-subframe—65–87 ft. lbs. (88–119 Nm)
- Rear engine and transaxle support insulator-to-subframe—56–75 ft. lbs. (76–103 Nm)

Valve Cover

REMOVAL & INSTALLATION

3.0L Engine

▶ See Figures 7 and 8

1. Disconnect the negative battery cable.
2. Label and disconnect the ignition wires from the spark plugs.
3. Remove the ignition wire brackets from the valve cover retaining studs.
4. To remove the forward valve cover:
   a. Disconnect the crankcase ventilation tube.
   b. Remove the oil filler cap (if replacing the valve cover).
   c. Remove the fuel charging wiring harness from the valve cover studs. Move the fuel charging wiring out of the way.
5. To remove the rear valve cover:
   a. Remove the cowl vent panel.
   b. Remove the throttle body.
   c. Loosen the lower EGR valve to exhaust manifold tube retaining nut and rotate the tube out of the way.

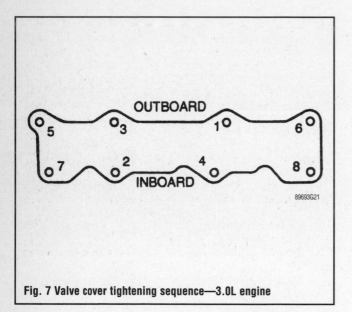

Fig. 7 Valve cover tightening sequence—3.0L engine

d. Remove the PCV valve (if replacing the valve cover).
e. Remove the fuel charging wiring harness from the valve cover studs. Move the fuel charging wiring out of the way.

➡Note the bolt and stud locations prior to removing the valve cover.

6. Loosen the valve cover retaining bolts and studs.
7. Carefully slide a sharp, thin bladed knife between the cylinder head and valve cover gasket at the step where the intake manifold mates to the cylinder head.

➡Cut only the silicone sealer and not the integral valve cover gasket.

8. Remove the valve cover making sure the silicone sealer does not pull the valve cover gasket from the valve cover.
9. Remove the valve cover gasket by pulling it from its channel.

To install:

10. Clean all gasket mating surfaces thoroughly.
11. Lubricate all bolt and stud threads prior to installation.
12. Install new valve cover gasket and align fastener holes.

➡Check valve cover gasket for correct installation. New valve cover gasket will lay flat to the valve cover in both the channel and fastener areas. If the valve cover gasket is installed incorrectly, oil leakage will occur.

13. Install valve cover gasket to each fastener by securing fastener head with a nut driver or socket. Seat fastener against valve cover and at the same time, roll gasket around fastener collar. If installed correctly, all fasteners will be secured by the gasket and will not fall out.
14. Apply a bead of silicone rubber sealer at the cylinder head to intake manifold step.

➡Use a straight down approach when installing valve cover. Any adjustment after sealer contact can roll gasket from the channel in the valve cover.

15. Position valve cover on cylinder head and tighten bolts in sequence to 96–120 inch lbs. (10–14 Nm).
16. To install the forward valve cover:
   a. Install the fuel charging wiring harness on the valve cover studs.
   b. Install the oil filler cap.
   c. Connect the crankcase ventilation tube.
17. To install the rear valve cover:
   a. Install the throttle body.
   b. Rotate the EGR tube into position and tighten the lower EGR valve to exhaust manifold tube retaining nut to 26–48 ft. lbs. (35–65 Nm).

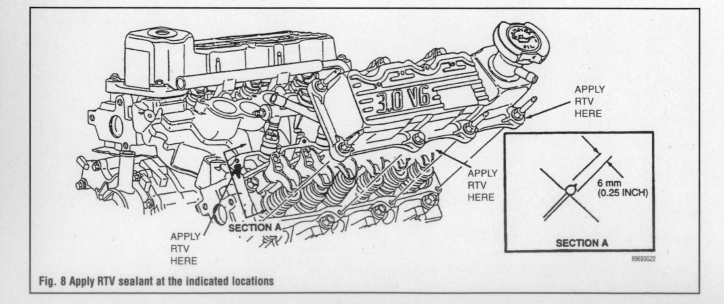

Fig. 8 Apply RTV sealant at the indicated locations

The ignition wire holders slip over the stud portion of the valve cover attaching bolt

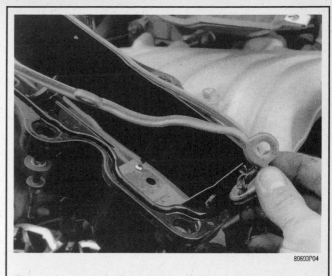

The valve cover gasket may be reused if it is not damaged

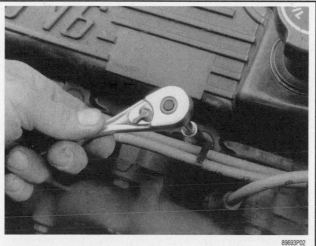

The valve covers are plastic; take care when removing or installing the attaching hardware

With the valve cover off, take time to inspect the valve train and oil drainback holes

c. Install the PCV valve.
d. Install the fuel charging wiring harness on the valve cover studs.
e. Install the cowl vent panel.
18. Connect the negative battery cable.
19. Start the engine and check for leaks.

3.8L Engine

♦ **See Figure 9**

1. Disconnect the negative battery cable.
2. Label and disconnect the ignition wires from the spark plugs.
3. Remove the ignition wire brackets from the valve cover retaining studs.
4. Remove the upper intake manifold.
5. To remove the forward valve cover:
   a. Disconnect the crankcase ventilation tube.
   b. Remove the oil filler cap.
   c. Remove the alternator wiring harness from the valve cover studs.
6. To remove the rear valve cover:
   a. Remove the cowl vent panel.
   b. Position the air cleaner assembly aside.
   c. Remove the PCV valve.

Remove the valve cover carefully. Do not pry on the cover to loosen it from the engine

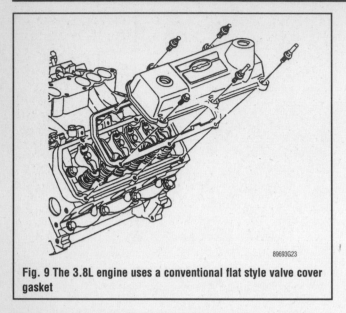

Fig. 9 The 3.8L engine uses a conventional flat style valve cover gasket

➡ **Note bolt and stud locations prior to removing the valve cover.**

7. Loosen the valve cover retaining bolts and studs
8. Remove the valve cover.

To install:

9. Clean all gasket mating surfaces thoroughly.
10. Lubricate all bolt and stud threads prior to installation.
11. Install new valve cover gasket and align fastener holes.
12. Position valve cover on cylinder head and tighten bolts in sequence to 71–97 inch lbs. (8–11 Nm).
13. To install the forward valve cover:
   a. Install the alternator wiring harness on the valve cover studs.
   b. Install the oil filler cap.
   c. Connect the crankcase ventilation tube.
14. To install the rear valve cover:
   a. Install the air cleaner assembly.
   b. Install the PCV valve.
   c. Install the cowl vent panel.
15. Install the upper intake manifold.
16. Install the ignition wires.
17. Connect the negative battery cable.
18. Start the engine and check for leaks.

Rocker Arms

REMOVAL & INSTALLATION

1. Remove the valve cover.
2. Remove the rocker arm retaining bolt.

➡ **Rocker arms should be installed in their original location and position during assembly.**

3. Remove rocker arms. If more than one rocker arm is to be removed, identify rocker arm location.

To install:

4. Lubricate pushrods and rocker arms with Engine Assembly Lubricant (D9AZ-19579-D), or equivalent. Lubricate the retaining bolts with engine oil.

➡ **Prior to final tightening, the rocker arm seats must be fully seated into the cylinder head. The pushrods must be fully seated in the rocker arm and valve tappet sockets.**

5. Install the rocker arms into position with the pushrods and snug the retaining bolt.
6. Rotate the crankshaft until the lifter is on base circle (heel) of the cam lobe.

7. Tighten the rocker arm retaining bolt to 60–132 inch lbs. (7–15 Nm) on 3.0L engine or 44 inch lbs. (5 Nm) maximum on 3.8L engine.
8. Final tighten bolt with camshaft in any position to 20–28 ft. lbs. (26–38 Nm).
9. Install valve cover.

VALVE CLEARANCE

▶ **See Figure 10**

If a pushrod, rocker arm or valve tappet must be replaced, the engine should not be cranked or rotated until the valve tappets have an opportunity to leak down to their normal operating position. The leakdown rate can be accelerated by using a Valve Tappet Bleed Down Wrench, or equivalent, on the rocker arm and applying pressure in a direction to collapse the valve tappet.

With the tappet fully collapsed and the camshaft on the base circle of the valve being checked, clearance between the rocker arm and valve head should be 0.09–0.19 in. (2.25–4.79mm).

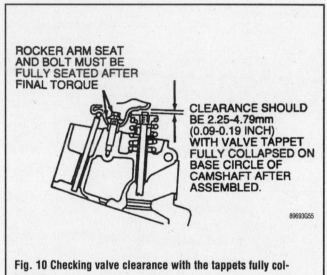

ROCKER ARM SEAT AND BOLT MUST BE FULLY SEATED AFTER FINAL TORQUE

CLEARANCE SHOULD BE 2.25-4.79mm (0.09-0.19 INCH) WITH VALVE TAPPET FULLY COLLAPSED ON BASE CIRCLE OF CAMSHAFT AFTER ASSEMBLED.

Fig. 10 Checking valve clearance with the tappets fully collapsed

Thermostat

REMOVAL & INSTALLATION

▶ **See Figures 11 and 12**

1. Disconnect the negative battery cable.

✳✳ CAUTION

Never remove the radiator cap when the engine is HOT. Serious personal injury can result.

2. Drain and recycle the engine coolant.
3. Remove the upper radiator hose at the thermostat housing.
4. Remove the thermostat housing from the engine.
5. Remove the thermostat from the housing with a counterclockwise twist.

To install:

6. Clean all gasket mating surfaces thoroughly.
7. Install the thermostat in the housing and rotate clockwise to lock into place.
8. Using a new gasket, install the housing and tighten the bolts to 96–120 inch lbs. (10–14 Nm) on the 3.0L engine, or 72–96 inch lbs. (8–10 Nm) on the 3.8L engine.

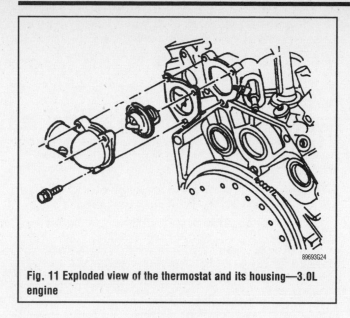

Fig. 11 Exploded view of the thermostat and its housing—3.0L engine

Take care to not strip the thermostat housing bolts. The cylinder head and housing are aluminum

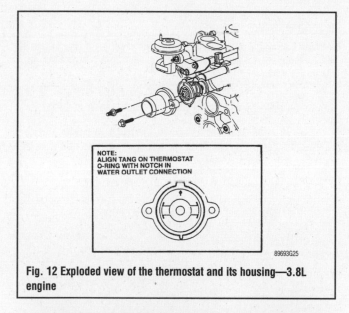

Fig. 12 Exploded view of the thermostat and its housing—3.8L engine

Note the position of the thermostat. Some sit above the gasket, and some sit below it

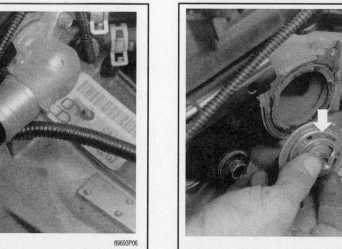

The thermostat housing is located on the cylinder head, near the coil pack

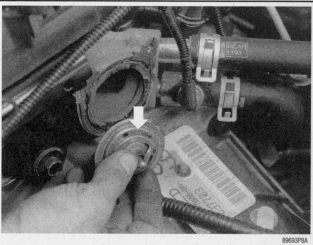

The thermostat temperature rating is usually stamped into the top of the thermostat

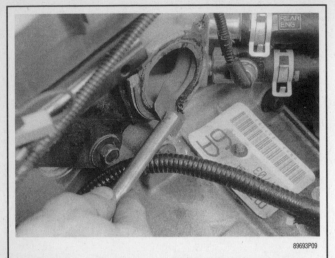

Scrape the old gasket material carefully. Do not damage the aluminum intake manifold

9. Install the upper radiator hose.
10. Fill and bleed the cooling system.
11. Connect the negative battery cable.
12. Start the engine and check for leaks.
13. Check and adjust the coolant level once the engine has cooled.

Intake Manifold

REMOVAL & INSTALLATION

3.0L Engine

♦ See Figures 13 and 14

1. Disconnect the negative battery cable.
2. Drain and recycle the engine coolant.
3. Remove the crankcase ventilation tube from the valve cover.
4. Remove the air cleaner inlet and outlet tube.
5. Properly relieve the fuel system pressure.
6. Remove the fuel line safety clips and disconnect the fuel lines.
7. Label and disconnect the vacuum lines.
8. Label and disconnect electrical wiring.

9. Label and disconnect control cables.
10. Disconnect the radiator and heater hoses.
11. Remove the alternator brace.
12. Remove the EGR tube and EGR valve.
13. Remove the fuel charging assembly.
14. Label and remove the ignition wires. Remove the ignition coil pack.
15. Remove the camshaft position sensor.
16. Remove the valve covers.
17. Loosen cylinder No. 3 intake valve rocker arm seating retaining bolt. Rotate the rocker arm off its pushrod and away from the top of the valve stem. Remove the pushrod.

➡The lower intake manifold may be removed with the fuel injection supply manifold and fuel injectors in place as an assembly.

18. Remove the lower intake manifold retaining bolts using a Torx® head socket.
19. Break the seal between the intake manifold and cylinder block. Wedge a prybar between the intake manifold and cylinder block. Pry upward on tool using area between water hose connection and transaxle as a leverage point.
20. Remove the intake manifold.
To install:
21. Throughly clean all gasket mating surfaces on the intake manifold and cylinder head.

➡When cleaning cylinder head gasket surfaces, lay a clean cloth in the valve tappet area to prevent any particles from entering the oil drainback area.

22. Apply a 0.25 in. (5–6mm) bead of silicone rubber sealant to the intersection of the cylinder block and cylinder head at the four corners of the intake manifold.
23. Install the intake manifold gaskets, aligning the intake gasket locking tabs to provisions on the head. Install the front and rear intake manifold end seals and secure with retainers.
24. Install the intake manifold.
25. Install intake bolts No. 1, 2, 3, and 4. Tighten by hand.
26. Install the remaining intake bolts and tighten all bolts in sequence to 15–22 ft. lbs. (20–30 Nm). Tighten again in sequence to 20–23 ft. lbs. (26–32 Nm).
27. Install No. 3 intake valve rocker arm.
28. Install the valve covers.
29. Lubricate camshaft position sensor and install.
30. Install the ignition coil pack and tighten retaining bolts to 30–41 ft. lbs. (40–55 Nm). Install the ignition wires.

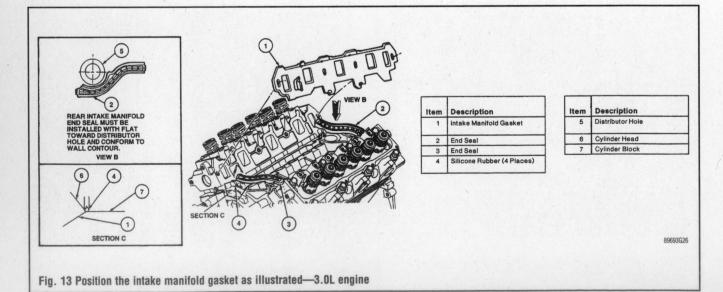

REAR INTAKE MANIFOLD END SEAL MUST BE INSTALLED WITH FLAT TOWARD DISTRIBUTOR HOLE AND CONFORM TO WALL CONTOUR.

VIEW B

VIEW B

SECTION C

SECTION C

Item	Description
1	Intake Manifold Gasket
2	End Seal
3	End Seal
4	Silicone Rubber (4 Places)

Item	Description
5	Distributor Hole
6	Cylinder Head
7	Cylinder Block

Fig. 13 Position the intake manifold gasket as illustrated—3.0L engine

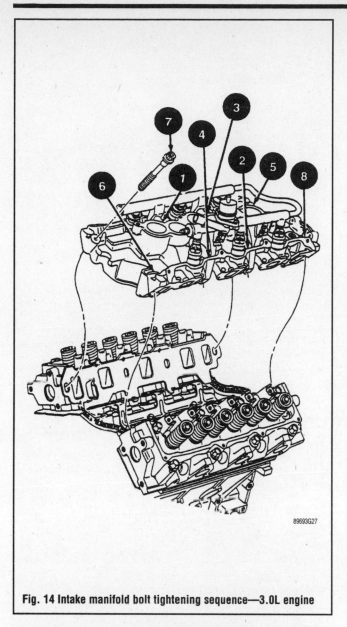

Fig. 14 Intake manifold bolt tightening sequence—3.0L engine

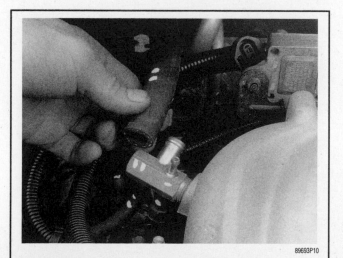

When performing a large job, it is imperative that all connections be matchmarked

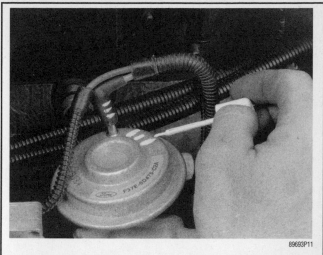

A handy tool for matchmarking components is brush-on correction fluid

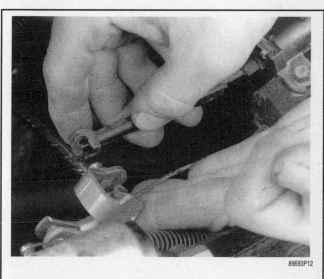

Disconnect the transaxle control cable . . .

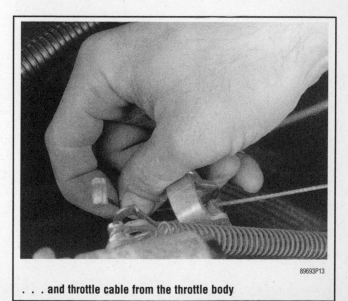

. . . and throttle cable from the throttle body

Remove the bolts attaching the upper intake manifold to the lower intake manifold

The fuel charging assembly can be removed as an assembly

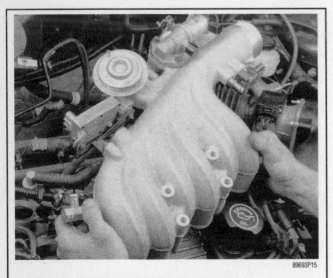

Lift the upper intake manifold from the engine . . .

The valve covers are attached to the intake manifold, as well as to the cylinder head

. . . and remove the gasket

The valve covers must be removed to gain clearance for intake manifold removal

Two pushrods, one in each cylinder head, pass through the intake manifold and must be removed

Carefully lift the intake manifold from the engine

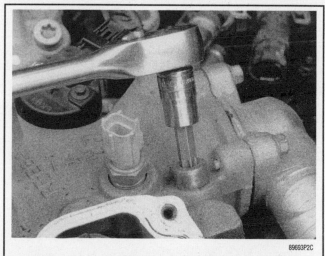

The intake bolts have a Torx® head and require a special driver for removal

Inspect the gaskets for defects and carefully remove them from the engine

It is a good practice to remove intake bolts in the reverse order of the tightening sequence

Rubber end seals are used in conjunction with the intake manifold gaskets to seal the top of the engine

31. Install the fuel charging assembly and tighten bolts to 71–106 inch lbs. (8–12 Nm).
32. Install the EGR tube and EGR valve.
33. Install the alternator brace.
34. Connect the radiator and heater hoses.
35. Connect and adjust the control cables.
36. Connect electrical wiring
37. Connect the vacuum lines.
38. Conenct the fuel lines and install the fuel line safety clips.
39. Install the air cleaner inlet and outlet tube.
40. Install the crankcase ventilation tube.
41. Fill and bleed engine cooling system.
42. Connect the negative battery cable.
43. Start engine and check for leaks.

3.8L Engine

UPPER MANIFOLD

▶ **See Figure 15**

1. Remove the air cleaner outlet tube.
2. Disconnect the accelerator cable and speed control actuator cable at the throttle body.
3. Remove the accelerator cable bracket and position it aside.
4. Label and disconnect the vacuum lines.
5. Label and disconnect the necessary electrical harnesses.
6. Disconnect the crankcase ventilation tube from the PCV valve.
7. Remove the throttle body.
8. Remove the idle air control valve.
9. Remove the intake manifold retaining bolts, noting their positions.

➡**Keep the intake manifold bolts in order, so they can be installed in their original positions.**

10. Remove the upper intake manifold.
To install:
11. Inspect the intake gasket to ensure seals are completely installed in manifold groove and seals show no signs of damage.
12. Install intake manifold and tighten bolts to 71–106 inch lbs. (8–12 Nm) in the sequence shown.
13. Install the idle air control valve.
14. Install the throttle body.
15. Connect the crankcase ventilation tube to the PCV valve.
16. Connect the electrical harnesses.
17. Connect the vacuum lines.

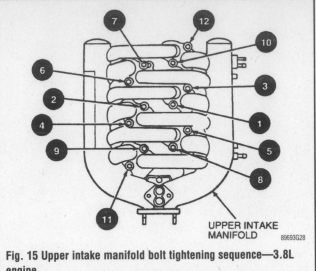

Fig. 15 Upper intake manifold bolt tightening sequence—3.8L engine

18. Install the accelerator cable bracket and tighten bolts to 71–106 inch lbs. (8–12 Nm).
19. Connect the accelerator cable and speed control actuator cable at the throttle body.
20. Install the air cleaner outlet tube.

LOWER MANIFOLD

▶ **See Figures 16 and 17**

1. Drain and recycle the engine coolant.
2. Remove the upper intake manifold.
3. Disconnect the water bypass hose from the heater water outlet tube.
4. Remove the bypass hose from the lower intake manifold.
5. Properly relieve the fuel system pressure.
6. Label and disconnect the electrical wiring harnesses.
7. Remove the fuel injectors and fuel charging assembly.
8. Disconnect the vacuum motor and bracket assemblies.
9. Disconnect the valve assembly and linkage from the Intake Manifold Runner Control (IMRC) lever and bushing by using a pry tool.
10. Remove the tube retaining bolts.
11. Remove the old bushing from the lever.
12. Remove the EGR valve and adapter.
13. Remove the lower intake manifold retaining bolts.

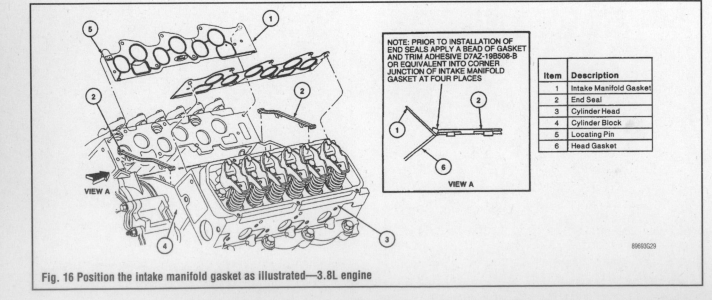

Fig. 16 Position the intake manifold gasket as illustrated—3.8L engine

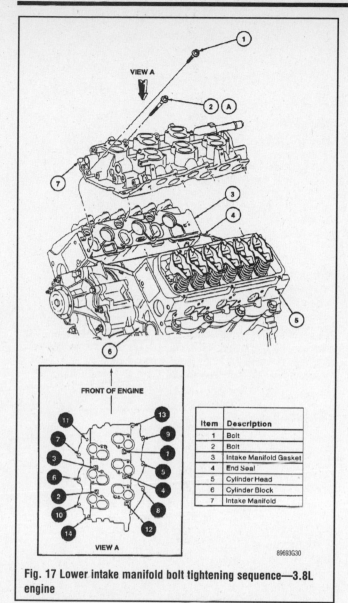

Fig. 17 Lower intake manifold bolt tightening sequence—3.8L engine

Item	Description
1	Bolt
2	Bolt
3	Intake Manifold Gasket
4	End Seal
5	Cylinder Head
6	Cylinder Block
7	Intake Manifold

➡The lower intake manifold is sealed at each corner with sealer. To break the seal it may be necessary to pry on the front of the intake manifold with a prybar. If it is necessary, use care to prevent damage to the machined surfaces.

14. Remove the lower intake manifold.
To install:
15. Throughly clean all gasket mating surfaces.

➡When using silicone rubber sealer, assembly must occur within 15 minutes after sealer application. After this time, the sealer may start to set up and its sealing effectiveness may be reduced.

16. Install new bushings into the IMRC levers.
17. Apply a 0.125 in. (3mm) bead of silicone rubber sealer at each corner where the cylinder head joins the engine block.
18. Install the front and rear intake manifold seals.
19. Using new gaskets, carefully install the lower intake manifold into position on the cylinder block.
20. Apply pipe sealant to the intake bolts and install in their original locations. Tighten in sequence to 71–106 inch lbs. (8–12 Nm).
21. Install the EGR valve and adapter.
22. Install the IMRC vacuum motors and tighten retaining bolts to 71–106 inch lbs. (8–12 Nm).

23. Install fuel injectors and charging assembly. Tighten retaining bolts to 71–97 inch lbs. (8–11 Nm).
24. Install the water bypass tube to the lower intake manifold. Tighten the retaining bolts to 71–97 inch lbs. (8–11 Nm).
25. Connect the water bypass tube hose to the outlet tube and tighten the hose clamp securely.
26. Connect the electrical wiring harnesses.
27. Connect the vacuum lines to the IMRC motors.
28. Connect the upper radiator hose to water hose connection and tighten the hose clamp securely.
29. Install the upper intake manifold.
30. Fill and bleed the cooling system.
31. Start the engine and check for leaks.

Exhaust Manifold

REMOVAL & INSTALLATION

3.0L Engine

◆ See Figure 18

REAR MANIFOLD

1. Disconnect the negative battery cable.
2. Remove the cowl vent panel.
3. Label and disconnect the EGR backpressure transducer hoses.
4. Remove the EGR valve tube from the exhaust manifold.

➡Use a backup wrench to prevent damaging the tube.

5. Raise and support the vehicle safely.
6. Disconnect the dual converter Y-pipe from the exhaust manifold.
7. Lower the vehicle.
8. Remove the exhaust manifold.
To install:
9. Clean all mating surfaces thoroughly.
10. Position the exhaust manifold and tighten the bolts to 15–22 ft. lbs. (20–30 Nm).
11. Raise and support the vehicle safely.
12. Connect the dual converter Y-pipe and tighten bolts to 25–34 ft. lbs. (34–47 Nm).
13. Lower the vehicle.
14. Install the EGR valve tube and tighten the fitting to 26–48 ft. lbs. (35–65 Nm).

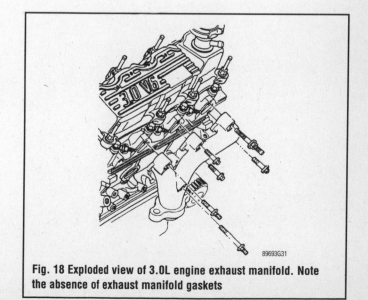

Fig. 18 Exploded view of 3.0L engine exhaust manifold. Note the absence of exhaust manifold gaskets

15. Connect the EGR backpressure transducer hoses.
16. Install the cowl vent panel.
17. Connect the negative battery cable.
18. Start the engine and check for exhaust leaks.

FRONT MANIFOLD

1. Disconnect the negative battery cable.
2. Remove the oil level indicator tube support bracket and retaining nut.
3. Remove the oil level dipstick and oil level indicator tube.
4. Raise and support the vehicle safely.
5. Disconnect the dual converter Y-pipe from the exhaust manifold.
6. Lower the vehicle.
7. Remove the exhaust manifold.

To install:

8. Clean all mating surfaces thoroughly.
9. Position exhaust manifold and tighten bolts to 15–22 ft. lbs. (20–30 Nm).
10. Raise and support the vehicle safely.
11. Connect the dual converter Y-pipe and tighten bolts to 25–34 ft. lbs. (34–47 Nm).

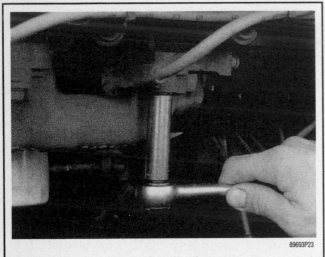

Spraying the exhaust manifold bolts with liquid penetrant makes removal of rusted bolts much easier

The front exhaust manifold is easily removed from above, while the rear must be removed from below

12. Lower the vehicle.
13. Install the oil level dipstick and oil level indicator tube. Tighten nut to 11–14 ft. lbs. (15–20 Nm).
14. Connect the negative battery cable.
15. Start the engine and check for exhaust leaks.

3.8L Engine

REAR MANIFOLD

▶ **See Figure 19**

1. Disconnect the negative battery cable.
2. Remove the cowl vent panel.
3. Remove the engine air cleaner and air cleaner outlet tube.
4. Disconnect the ignition wires from the rear cylinder head and ignition coil.
5. Remove the spark plugs from the rear cylinder head.
6. Raise and support the vehicle safely.
7. Disconnect the dual converter Y-pipe from the exhaust manifold.
8. Lower the vehicle.
9. Remove the exhaust manifold.

To install:

10. Clean all gasket mating surfaces thoroughly.

➡**A slight warpage in the exhaust manifold may cause a misalignment between the bolt holes in the cylinder head and exhaust manifold. Elongate the holes in the exhaust manifold as necessary to correct the misalignment. Do not elongate the pilot hole.**

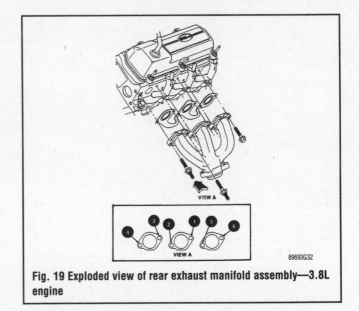

Fig. 19 Exploded view of rear exhaust manifold assembly—3.8L engine

11. Position exhaust manifold gasket and exhaust manifold. Start two bolts to hold manifold in position.
12. Install the remaining bolts and tighten bolts in sequence to 15–22 ft. lbs. (20–30 Nm).
13. Raise and support the vehicle safely.
14. Connect the dual converter Y-pipe and tighten bolts to 25–34 ft. lbs. (34–47 Nm).
15. Lower the vehicle.
16. Install the spark plugs in the rear cylinder head.
17. Connect the ignition wires.
18. Install the engine air cleaner and air cleaner outlet tube.
19. Install the cowl vent panel.
20. Connect the negative battery cable.
21. Start the engine and check for exhaust leaks.

FRONT MANIFOLD

▶ See Figure 20

1. Disconnect the negative battery cable.
2. Remove the oil level indicator tube.
3. Label and disconnect the ignition wires from the front cylinder head.
4. Disconnect the EGR to exhaust manifold tube.
5. Raise and support the vehicle safely.
6. Disconnect the dual converter Y-pipe from the exhaust manifold.
7. Lower the vehicle.
8. Remove the exhaust manifold.

To install:

9. Clean all gasket mating surfaces thoroughly.

➡**A slight warpage in the exhaust manifold may cause a misalignment between the bolt holes in the cylinder head and exhaust manifold. Elongate the holes in the exhaust manifold as necessary to correct the misalignment. Do not elongate the pilot hole.**

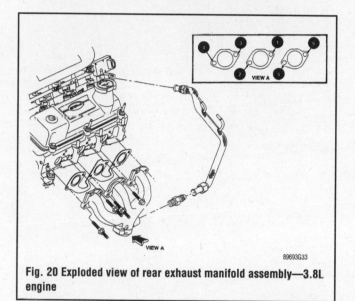

Fig. 20 Exploded view of rear exhaust manifold assembly—3.8L engine

10. Position exhaust manifold gasket and exhaust manifold. Start two bolts to hold the manifold in position.
11. Install the remaining bolts and tighten bolts in sequence to 15–22 ft. lbs. (20–30 Nm).
12. Raise and support the vehicle safely.
13. Connect the dual converter Y-pipe and tighten bolts to 25–34 ft. lbs. (34–47 Nm).
14. Lower the vehicle.
15. Connect the EGR to the exhaust manifold tube.
16. Connect the ignition wires.
17. Install the oil level indicator tube.
18. Connect the negative battery cable.
19. Start the engine and check for exhaust leaks.

Radiator

REMOVAL & INSTALLATION

1. Disconnect the negative battery cable.
2. Drain and recycle the engine coolant.
3. Disengage the grille opening panel pushpins.
4. Label and disconnect cooling fan motor wiring harness.
5. Position wiring harness out of the way and remove the cooling fan motor assembly.

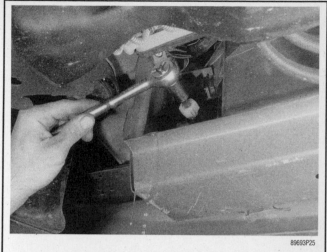

The radiator drain petcock is located at the bottom of the radiator on the driver's side

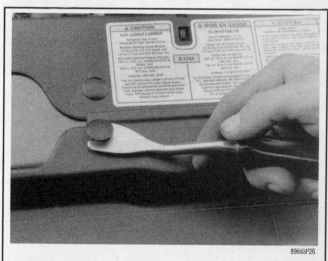

The grille opening panel pushpins can be removed with a clip removal tool

Don't forget to disconnect the radiator overflow tube

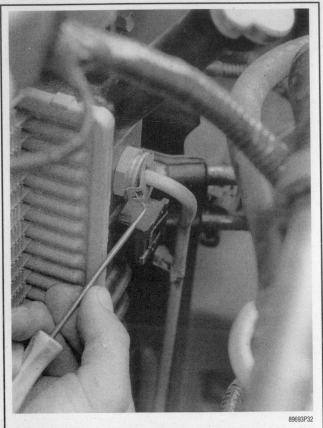

The transaxle cooler lines are held in place by special clips

Insert the tool into the fitting and pull the tube from the radiator

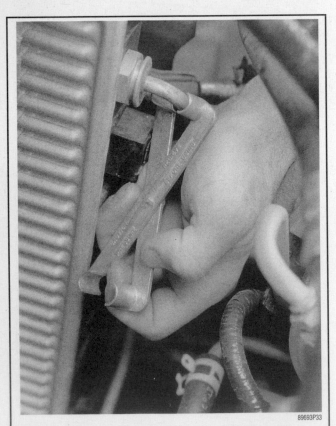

Once the clips are removed, a special tool must be used to release the tube from the radiator

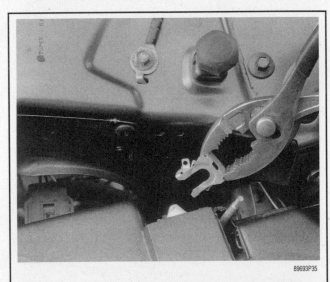

The headlight assemblies are attached to the vehicle with clips

6. Disconnect the overflow hose and the upper and lower radiator hoses.

7. Disconnect and plug the transaxle cooler lines at the radiator.

8. Remove the headlamp mounting clips.

9. Remove the turn signal lamp retaining nuts and position the turn signal and headlamp out of the way.

10. Remove the grille opening panel bracket bolts (4 per side).

➡Grille reinforcements are easily bent. Take extra care when removing the grille.

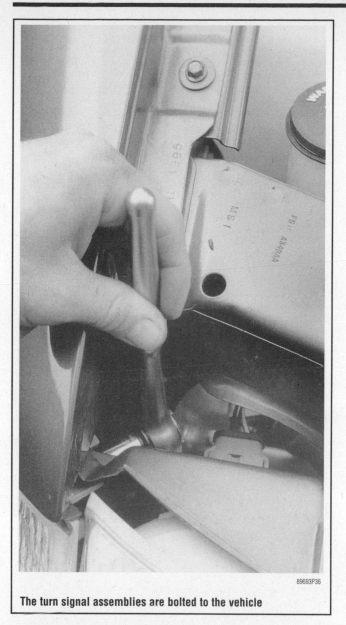

The turn signal assemblies are bolted to the vehicle

89693P36

The turn signal . . .

89693P37

89693P38

. . . and headlight assemblies must be removed to gain access to mounting bolts

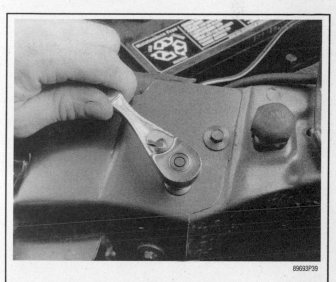

89693P39

Remove the grille opening panel bracket bolts

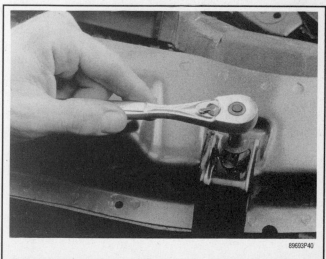

89693P40

Take care when removing these brackets, as they are easily bent

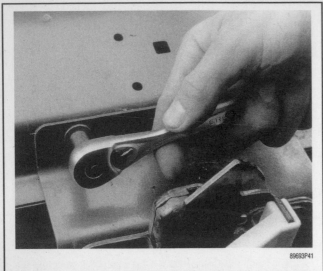

89693P41

The hood latch must be disconnected from the radiator support

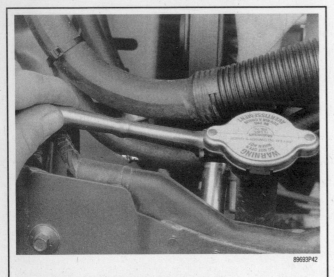

89693P42

The radiator is bolted in from the engine side

89693P43

The radiator must first be pushed down to disengage it from the mounting clips, then lifted up and out

11. Remove the radiator grille opening panel brackets.

12. Remove the hood latch support mounting bolts and pull the support forward.

13. Remove the radiator mounting bolts.

14. Remove the grill opening reinforcement retaining screws (3 per side). Remove the radiator grille opening panel reinforcement from the vehicle.

15. Remove the top condenser mounting screws. Lift up the A/C condenser core while pushing down on the radiator to disengage the clips on the bottom.

16. Remove the radiator from the vehicle.

To install:

17. Position the radiator in the vehicle.

18. Position the A/C condenser.

19. Install the top condenser mounting screws and tighten to 89–106 inch lbs. (10–12 Nm).

20. Install the grill opening panel reinforcement screws and tighten securely.

21. Install the radiator mounting bolts and tighten to 45–61 inch lbs. (5–7 Nm).

22. Install the hood latch support. Tighten mounting bolts to 19–25 ft. lbs. (25–35 Nm).

23. Install the radiator grille opening panel brackets and tighten screws securely.

24. Install the turn signal and headlamp assembly. Tighten turn signal retaining screw to 45–61 inch lbs. (5–7 Nm). Install the headlamp mounting clips.

25. Connect the transaxle cooler lines at the radiator.

26. Connect the overflow hose and the upper and lower radiator hoses.

27. Install the cooling fan motor assembly. Tighten bolts to 89–106 inch lbs. (10–12 Nm).

28. Connect cooling fan motor wiring harness.

29. Install the grille opening panel pushpins.

30. Fill and bleed the cooling system.

31. Connect the negative battery cable.

32. Start the engine and check for leaks.

Engine Cooling Fan

REMOVAL & INSTALLATION

▶ **See Figures 21 and 22**

1. Disconnect the negative battery cable.

2. Remove the constant control relay module, located on the driver's side of the engine compartment.

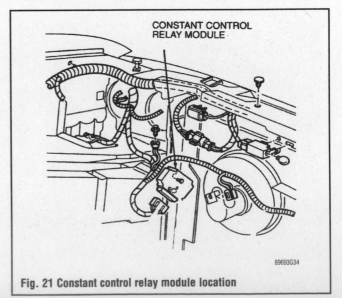

89693G34

Fig. 21 Constant control relay module location

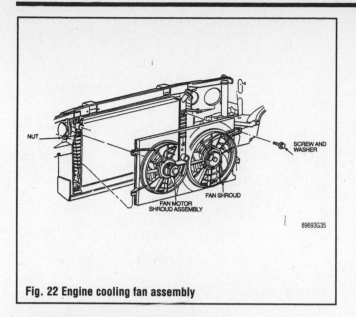

Fig. 22 Engine cooling fan assembly

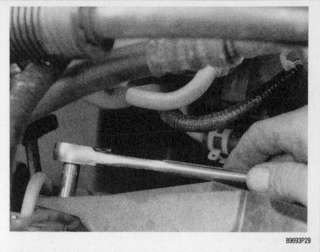

The cooling fan is bolted directly to the radiator. Take care when removing and installing the bolts

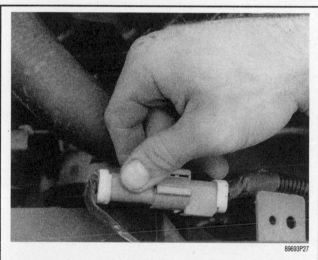

One cooling fan electrical connector is located at the top of the fan shroud . . .

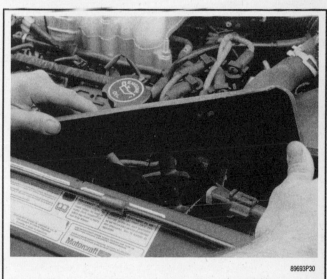

The cooling fan and shroud are removed as an assembly

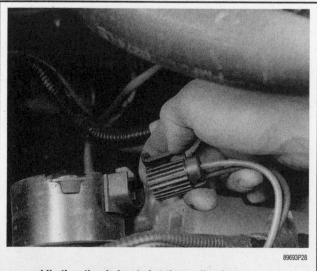

. . . while the other is located at the cooling fan

3. Disconnect the cooling fan electrical harness.
4. Remove the fan shroud mounting bolts.
5. Slide the engine cooling fan assembly clear of the radiator tank hose connector and lift up past the radiator.

To install:

6. Position the engine cooling fan on the radiator.
7. Install the fan shroud mounting bolts and tighten to 89–106 inch lbs. (8–12 Nm).
8. Connect the cooling fan electrical harness.
9. Install the constant control relay module.
10. Connect the negative battery cable.

TESTING

The PCM determines when fan operation is required by monitoring coolant temperature, vehicle speed and air conditioning status. When operation is required, the PCM signals the Constant Control Relay Module (CCRM) to turn on fans to desired speed.

Water Pump

REMOVAL & INSTALLATION

3.0L Engine

▶ **See Figure 23**

1. Disconnect the negative battery cable.
2. Drain and recycle the engine coolant.
3. Loosen the four water pump pulley retaining bolts while the accessory drive belts are still tight.
4. Rotate the automatic tensioner down and to the left.
5. Remove the accessory drive belt.
6. Remove the two nuts and bolt retaining the drive belt automatic tensioner to the engine, then remove the tensioner.
7. Disconnect and remove the lower radiator and heater hose from the water pump.
8. Remove the eleven water pump-to-engine retaining bolts, then lift the water pump and pulley up and out of the vehicle.
9. Remove the water pump pulley retaining bolts, then remove the pulley from the water pump.

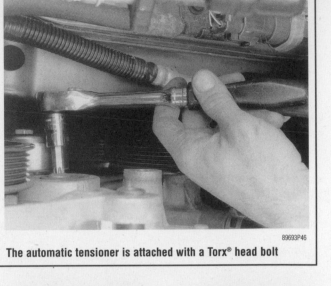

The automatic tensioner is attached with a Torx® head bolt

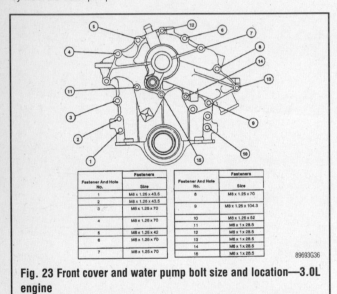

Fastener And Hole No.	Size	Fastener And Hole No.	Size
1	M8 x 1.25 x 43.5	8	M8 x 1.25 x 70
2	M8 x 1.25 x 43.5	9	M8 x 1.25 x 104.3
3	M8 x 1.25 x 70	10	M8 x 1.25 x 52
4	M8 x 1.25 x 70	11	M6 x 1 x 28.5
5	M8 x 1.25 x 42	12	M6 x 1 x 28.5
6	M8 x 1.25 x 70	13	M6 x 1 x 28.5
7	M8 x 1.25 x 70	14	M6 x 1 x 28.5
		15	M6 x 1 x 28.5

Fig. 23 Front cover and water pump bolt size and location—3.0L engine

Note the tensioner position for installation reference and remove it from the vehicle

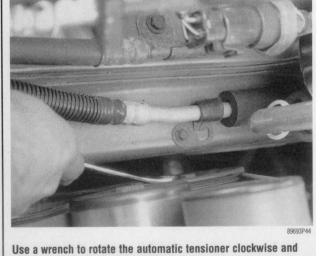

Use a wrench to rotate the automatic tensioner clockwise and remove the accessory drive belt

Label and disconnect the radiator and heater hoses from the water pump

After removing the water pump attaching bolts, remove the water pump and pulley

Clean the gasket mating surfaces thoroughly, but take care not to gouge the aluminum

The water pump works in conjunction with passages in the timing cover to circulate coolant

To install:

➡ Be careful not to gouge the aluminum surfaces when scraping the old gasket material from the mating surfaces of the water pump and front cover.

10. Clean the gasket surfaces on the water pump and front cover. Lightly oil all bolt and stud threads except those requiring special sealant.

11. Position a new water pump housing gasket on the water pump sealing surface using gasket sealant to hold the gasket in place.

12. With the water pump pulley and retaining bolts loosely installed on the water pump, align the water pump-to-engine front cover, then install the retaining bolts.

13. Tighten the bolts to the following specifications:
   a. Bolt numbers 1–10: 15–22 ft. lbs. (20–30 Nm).
   b. Bolt numbers 11–15: 71–106 inch lbs (8–12 Nm).

14. Hand-tighten the water pump pulley retaining bolts.

15. Install the automatic belt tensioner assembly. Tighten the two retaining nuts and bolt to 35 ft. lbs. (47 Nm).

16. Install the alternator and power steering belts. Final tighten the water pump pulley retaining bolts to 15–22 ft. lbs. (22–30 Nm).

17. Position the hose clamps between the alignment marks on both ends of the hose, then slide the hose on the connection. Tighten the hose clamps to 20–30 inch lbs. (2.2–3.4 Nm).

18. Fill and bleed the cooling system.

19. Connect the negative battery cable.

20. Start the engine and check for leaks.

3.8L Engine

◆ See Figure 24

1. Disconnect the negative battery cable.
2. Drain and recycle the engine coolant.
3. Loosen the drive belt tensioner, then remove the drive belts.
4. Remove the lower radiator hose.
5. Remove the lower nut on both front engine supports.
6. Remove the alternator.
7. Position a drain pan under the power steering pump.
8. Disconnect power steering pressure line from pump using a fuel line disconnect tool (T90T-9550-S), or equivalent.
9. Remove the power steering reservoir filler cap.
10. Disconnect the water bypass hose and oil cooler hose from the heater water outlet tube.
11. Remove the retaining bolt and disconnect the heater water outlet tube from the water pump.
12. Remove the A/C bracket brace.

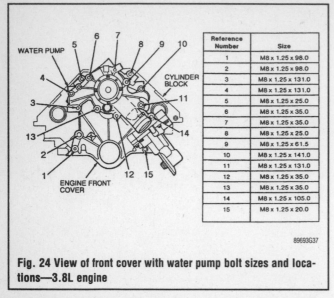

Reference Number	Size
1	M8 x 1.25 x 98.0
2	M8 x 1.25 x 98.0
3	M8 x 1.25 x 131.0
4	M8 x 1.25 x 131.0
5	M8 x 1.25 x 25.0
6	M8 x 1.25 x 35.0
7	M8 x 1.25 x 35.0
8	M8 x 1.25 x 25.0
9	M8 x 1.25 x 61.5
10	M8 x 1.25 x 141.0
11	M8 x 1.25 x 131.0
12	M8 x 1.25 x 35.0
13	M8 x 1.25 x 35.0
14	M8 x 1.25 x 105.0
15	M8 x 1.25 x 20.0

89693G37

Fig. 24 View of front cover with water pump bolt sizes and locations—3.8L engine

13. Raise the engine approximately 2 inches (51mm) to provide necessary clearance for water pump removal.

14. Remove the water pump pulley.

15. Remove the drive belt tensioner form the power steering pump support.

16. Remove the power steering pump support and place the pump and support aside in the engine compartment.

17. Remove the water pump.

To install:

18. Clean all gasket mating surfaces thoroughly.

➡**Be careful not to gouge the aluminum surfaces when scraping the old gasket material from the mating surfaces of the water pump and front cover.**

19. Coat the threads of the No. 1 engine front cover stud with Teflon® pipe sealant, or equivalent.

20. Position a new water pump housing gasket on the water pump sealing surface using gasket sealant to hold the gasket in place.

21. Install the water pump and tighten bolts to 15–22 ft. lbs. (20–30 Nm) and nuts to 71–106 inch lbs. (8–12 Nm).

22. Install the power steering pump support.

23. Install the drive belt tensioner.

24. Install the water pump pulley.

25. Lower the engine.

26. Install the A/C bracket brace.

27. Connect the heater water outlet tube.

28. Connect the water bypass hose and oil cooler hose.

29. Install the power steering reservoir filler cap.

30. Connect power steering pressure line using fuel line connect tool (T90T-9550-S), or equivalent.

31. Install the alternator.

32. Install the lower nut on both front engine supports.

33. Install the lower radiator hose.

34. Install the drive belts.

35. Fill and bleed the cooling system.

36. Connect the negative battery cable.

Cylinder Head

REMOVAL & INSTALLATION

3.0L Engine

♦ **See Figures 25, 26 and 27**

1. Rotate the crankshaft to 0° TDC on the compression stroke.

2. Disconnect the negative battery cable.

3. Drain and recycle the engine coolant.

4. Remove the cowl top vent panel.

5. Remove the air cleaner outlet tube to the throttle body.

6. Label and disconnect all necessary vacuum lines.

7. Disconnect the EGR backpressure transducer from the EGR valve.

8. Loosen the lower EGR valve to exhaust manifold tube nut and rotate the EGR valve tube away from the valve.

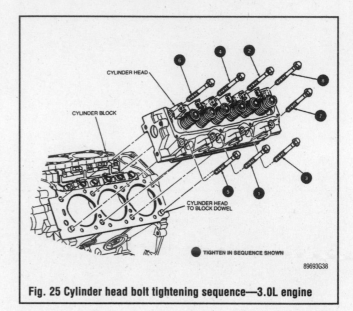

89693G38

Fig. 25 Cylinder head bolt tightening sequence—3.0L engine

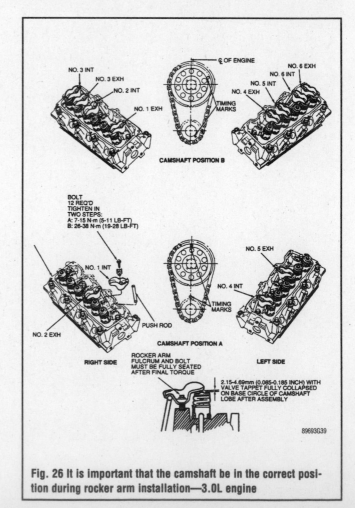

89693G39

Fig. 26 It is important that the camshaft be in the correct position during rocker arm installation—3.0L engine

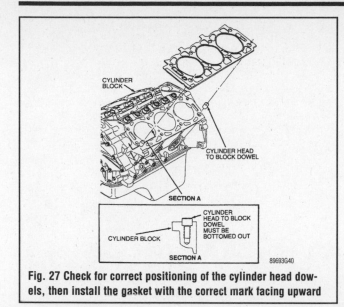

Fig. 27 Check for correct positioning of the cylinder head dowels, then install the gasket with the correct mark facing upward

Matchmark the rocker arms for installation reference

1. Pushrod
2. Hydraulic roller valve tappet
3. Rocker arm
4. Valve spring
5. Rocker arm retaining bolt
6. Valve tappet guide plate
7. Valve tappet retainer

Valve Train Components

A piece of cardboard with holes punched in it makes a handy tool for keeping pushrods in order

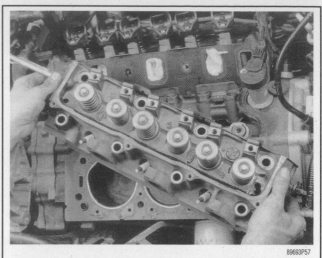

Carefully remove the cylinder head from the vehicle. Take care to not allow dirt to enter the engine

If removing the front cylinder head, remove the alternator and bracket assembly to gain clearance

Inspect the cylinder head and intake gaskets for damage or leakage as indicated by the arrows

Removing the cylinder head bolts in reverse order of the torque sequence is a good idea

Place paper towels or rags in the intake valley and cylinders to prevent the entry of dirt

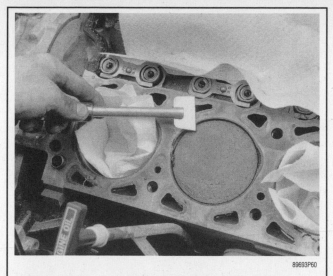

Clean the gasket mating surfaces thoroughly with a scraper

9. Label and disconnect the all necessary engine wiring.
10. Properly relieve the fuel system pressure.
11. Remove the fuel line safety clips and disconnect the fuel lines.

→The fuel injectors and fuel injection supply manifold may be removed with the lower intake manifold as an assembly.

12. Remove the ignition wires and ignition coil pack.
13. Disconnect the upper radiator and heater hoses.
14. Remove the camshaft position sensor.
15. If the front cylinder head is being removed, perform the following:
  a. Disconnect the alternator electrical harness.
  b. Rotate the tensioner clockwise and remove the accessory drive belt.
  c. Remove the automatic belt tensioner assembly.
  d. Remove the alternator.
  e. Remove the power steering mounting bracket retaining bolts. Leave the hoses connected and place the pump aside in a position to prevent fluid from leaking out.
  f. Remove the engine oil dipstick tube from the exhaust manifold.
16. If the rear cylinder head is being removed, perform the following:
  a. Remove the alternator belt tensioner bracket.
  b. Remove the heater supply tube retaining brackets from the exhaust manifold.
  c. Remove the vehicle speed sensor cable retaining bolt.
  d. Remove the EGR vacuum regulator sensor and bracket.
17. Remove the valve covers.

→Pushrods must be installed in their original position. Note pushrod location during removal.

18. Loosen rocker arm seat retaining bolts and remove the pushrods.
19. Remove the lower intake manifold.
20. Remove the spark plugs.
21. Remove the exhaust manifolds.
22. Remove cylinder head bolts.
23. Lift cylinder head from engine block and discard gaskets.
To install:
24. The cylinder head should be cleaned and inspected by a competent machinist prior to installation. For general cylinder head inspection and overhaul procedures, refer to Engine Reconditioning in this section.
25. Lightly oil all bolt and stud bolt threads before installation.
26. Clean all gasket mating surfaces thoroughly.
27. Position new head gaskets on the cylinder block, noting the UP position on the gasket face, using the dowels in the engine block for alignment. If the dowels are damaged, they must be replaced.

✳✳ WARNING

Always use new cylinder head bolts when installing cylinder head or damage to engine may occur.

28. Position the cylinder head on the cylinder block. Tighten the cylinder head bolts in 2 steps following the proper torque sequence. The first step is 37 ft. lbs. (50 Nm) and the second step is 68 ft. lbs. (92 Nm).

→When cylinder head attaching bolts have been tightened using the above procedure, it is not necessary to retighten the bolts after extended engine operation. The bolts can be rechecked for tightness if desired.

29. Install the intake manifold.
30. Connect all engine wiring harnesses previously disconnected.
31. Install the lower intake manifold.
32. Dip each pushrod end in engine assembly lubricant. Install the pushrods in their original position.
33. Rotate the crankshaft clockwise one full turn (360 degrees) to camshaft position "A", as illustrated.
34. Lubricate all rocker arm components with engine assembly lubricant.
35. Install the illustrated rocker arms, seats and retaining bolts. Tighten bolts to 62–132 inch lbs. (7–15 Nm).
36. Rotate crankshaft clockwise 120 degrees to camshaft position "B", as illustrated.
37. Install the illustrated rocker arms, seats and retaining bolts. Tighten bolts to 62–132 inch lbs. (7–15 Nm).

→The rocker arm seats must be fully seated in the cylinder head and the pushrods must be seated in the rocker arm sockets prior to the final tightening.

38. Final tighten all rocker arm retaining bolts to 20–28 ft. lbs. (26–38 Nm).
39. Install spark plugs.
40. Install the exhaust manifolds.
41. Install the spark plugs.
42. Install the valve covers.
43. If the rear cylinder head is being installed, perform the following:
  a. Install the EGR vacuum regulator sensor and bracket.
  b. Install the vehicle speed sensor cable retaining bolt.
  c. Install the heater supply tube retaining brackets from the exhaust manifold.
  d. Install the alternator belt tensioner bracket.
  e. Install the engine oil dipstick tube from the exhaust manifold.
44. If the front cylinder head is being installed, perform the following:
  a. Install the power steering mounting bracket retaining bolts. Leave the hoses connected and place the pump aside in a position to prevent fluid from leaking out.
  b. Install the alternator.
  c. Install the automatic belt tensioner assembly.
  d. Rotate the tensioner clockwise and install the accessory drive belt.
  e. Connect the alternator electrical harness.
45. Install the camshaft position sensor.
46. Connect the upper radiator and heater hoses.
47. Install the ignition wires and ignition coil pack. Tighten coil pack mounting bolts to 30–40 ft. lbs. (40–55 Nm).
48. Connect the fuel lines and install the fuel line safety clips.
49. Loosen the lower EGR valve to exhaust manifold tube nut and rotate the EGR valve tube away from the valve.
50. Connect the EGR backpressure transducer from the EGR valve.
51. Connect all necessary vacuum lines.
52. Install the air cleaner outlet tube to the throttle body.
53. Install the cowl top vent panel.
54. Fill and bleed the cooling system.

➥Engine coolant is corrosive to engine bearing material. Replace the engine oil after removal of any coolant carrying component to help prevent potential bearing damage.

55. Change engine oil and filter
56. Connect the negative battery cable.
57. Start the engine and check for leaks.

3.8L Engine

◆ See Figure 28

1. Disconnect the negative battery cable.
2. Drain and recycle the engine coolant.
3. Remove the air cleaner assembly.
4. Remove the cowl top vent panel.
    a. Rotate the tensioner clockwise and remove the accessory drive belt.
5. If the front cylinder head is being removed, perform the following:
    a. Remove the oil filler cap.
    b. Remove the A/C compressor mounting bracket and set A/C compressor aside with refrigerant lines still connected.
    c. Remove the power steering pump and bracket. Leave power steering hoses connected and place the pump aside in the engine compartment.
    d. Remove the alternator and alternator mounting bracket.
6. If the rear cylinder head is being removed, perform the following:
    a. Remove the accessory drive belt tensioner.
    b. Remove the PCV valve.
    c. Remove the power steering line bracket.
    d. Remove the tensioner bracket.
    e. Remove the coil pack assembly.
7. Remove the upper intake manifold.
8. Remove the valve cover.
9. Properly relieve the fuel system pressure.
10. Remove the fuel charging assembly.
11. Remove the lower intake manifold.
12. Remove the exhaust manifolds.

➥Pushrods must be installed in their original position. Note pushrod location during removal.

13. Loosen rocker arm seat retaining bolts and remove the pushrods.

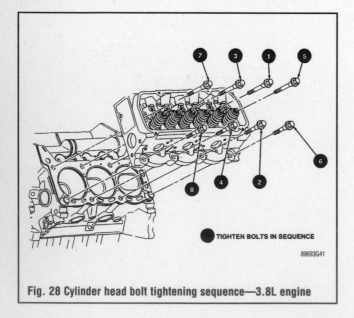

TIGHTEN BOLTS IN SEQUENCE

89693G41

Fig. 28 Cylinder head bolt tightening sequence—3.8L engine

14. Remove cylinder head bolts.
15. Lift cylinder head from engine block and discard gaskets.

To install:

16. The cylinder head should be cleaned and inspected by a competent machinist prior to installation. For general cylinder head inspection and overhaul procedures, refer to Engine Reconditioning in this section.
17. Lightly oil all bolt and stud bolt threads before installation.
18. Clean all gasket mating surfaces thoroughly.
19. Position new head gaskets on the cylinder block, noting the UP position on the gasket face, using the dowels in the engine block for alignment. If the dowels are damaged, they must be replaced.

✳✳ WARNING

Always use new cylinder head bolts when installing cylinder head or damage to engine may occur.

20. Position the cylinder head on the cylinder block.
21. Lubricate cylinder head bolts with 50 weight oil and install. Tighten the cylinder head bolts in 3 steps following the proper torque sequence. The first step is 15 ft. lbs. (20 Nm), the second step is 29 ft. lbs. (40 Nm) and the third step is 37 ft. lbs. (50 Nm).

➥Do not loosen all of the cylinder head bolts at once. Only work on one bolt at a time or damage to the engine may occur.

22. In sequence, loosen the cylinder head bolt 2–3 turns and retighten in 2 steps.
    a. On long bolts, the first step is 29–37 ft. lbs. (40–50 Nm). The second step is tighten additional 175–185 degrees.
    b. On short bolts, the first step is 15–22 ft. lbs. (20–30 Nm). The second step is tighten additional 175–185 degrees.
23. Dip each pushrod end in engine assembly lubricant. Install the pushrods in their original position.
24. Lubricate all rocker arm components with engine assembly lubricant.
25. Rotate the engine clockwise until the valve tappet rests on the heel (base circle) of the camshaft lobe.
26. Install rocker arms, seats and bolts and tighten to 44 inch lbs. (5 Nm). After all rocker arms have been installed, final tighten all bolts to 22–29 ft. lbs. (30–40 Nm).
27. Install exhaust manifolds.
28. Install lower intake manifold.
29. Install fuel injection charging assembly.
30. Install valve covers with new gaskets. Tighten bolts to 71–97 inch lbs. (8–11 Nm).
31. Install upper intake manifold.
32. Install spark plugs and ignition wires.
33. If the front cylinder head is being removed, perform the following:
    a. Install the alternator and alternator mounting bracket.
    b. Install the power steering pump and bracket
    c. Install the A/C compressor mounting bracket
    d. Install the oil filler cap.
34. If the rear cylinder head is being removed, perform the following:
    a. Install the coil pack assembly.
    b. Install the tensioner bracket.
    c. Install the power steering line bracket.
    d. Install the PCV valve
    e. Install the accessory drive belt tensioner.
    f. Rotate the tensioner clockwise and remove the accessory drive belt.
35. Install the cowl top vent panel.
36. Install the air cleaner assembly.
37. Fill and bleed the cooling system.
38. Connect the negative battery cable.

Oil Pan

✳ CAUTION

The EPA warns that prolonged contact with used engine oil may cause a number of skin disorders, including cancer! You should make every effort to minimize your exposure to used engine oil. Protective gloves should be worn when changing the oil. Wash your hands and any other exposed skin areas as soon as possible after exposure to used engine oil. Soap and water, or waterless hand cleaner, should be used.

REMOVAL & INSTALLATION

3.0L Engine

▶ **See Figure 29**

1. Disconnect the negative battery cable.
2. Remove the oil level dipstick.
3. Raise and safely support the vehicle.
4. Remove the retainer clip at the sensor. Disconnect the wiring harness from the sensor.
5. Drain the crankcase.
6. Disconnect the wiring harness from the oxygen sensors.
7. Remove the dual converter Y-pipe.
8. Remove the starter motor.
9. Remove the lower engine/flywheel dust cover from the torque converter housing.
10. Remove the oil pan bolts, then slowly remove the oil pan, making sure the internal pan baffle does not snag the oil pump screen cover and tube.
11. Remove the oil pan gasket.

To install:

12. Clean the gasket mating surfaces thoroughly.

➡When using a silicone sealer, the assembly process should occur within 15 minutes after the sealer has been applied. After this time, the sealer may start to set-up and its sealing effectiveness may be affected.

13. Apply a 0.25 in. (6mm) bead of silicone sealer to the junction of the rear main bearing cap and cylinder block junction of the front cover assembly and cylinder block.
14. Position the oil pan gasket to the oil pan with sealing bends against the oil pan surface and secure with gasket adhesive.
15. Position the oil pan on the engine block and install the oil pan attaching bolts. Tighten the bolts to 8–10 ft. lbs. (10–14 Nm).
16. Back off all of the bolts and retighten them.
17. Install the lower engine/flywheel dust cover to the torque converter housing.
18. Install the starter motor.
19. Install the dual converter Y-pipe.
20. Connect the wiring harness to the oxygen sensors.
21. Connect the low oil level sensor wiring harness and install the retainer clip.
22. Lower the vehicle.
23. Install the oil level dipstick.
24. Connect the negative battery cable.

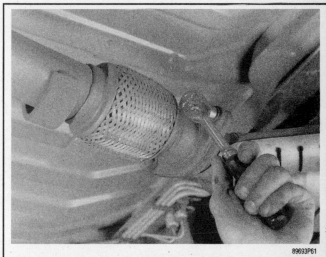

89693P61

Unfasten the exhaust system bolts after spraying them with an anti-seize penetrant

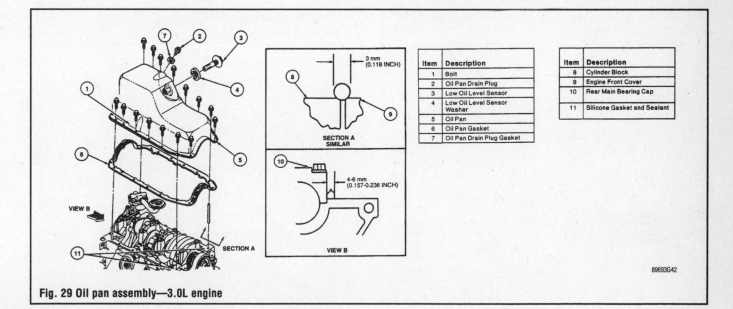

Item	Description
1	Bolt
2	Oil Pan Drain Plug
3	Low Oil Level Sensor
4	Low Oil Level Sensor Washer
5	Oil Pan
6	Oil Pan Gasket
7	Oil Pan Drain Plug Gasket

Item	Description
8	Cylinder Block
9	Engine Front Cover
10	Rear Main Bearing Cap
11	Silicone Gasket and Sealant

89693G42

Fig. 29 Oil pan assembly—3.0L engine

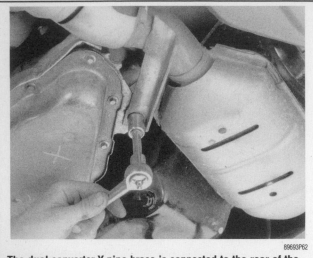

The dual converter Y-pipe brace is connected to the rear of the transaxle assembly

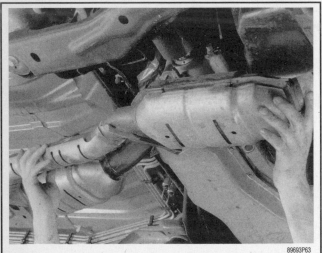

Carefully lower the dual converter Y-pipe after disconnecting it from the engine and exhaust system

Pay special attention to the oxygen sensors (arrows) during removal of the exhaust pipe

Loosen the oil pan bolts a few turns at a time to prevent bending the oil pan rail

The oil pan may need to be maneuvered to clear the oil pump pickup

Note the dab of silicone gasket sealant at the junction of the front cover and the engine block (arrow)

89693P67

This shield protects the torque converter and is located at the rear of the oil pan

89693P68

25. Fill the engine with oil.
26. Start the engine and check leaks.

3.8L Engine

▶ See Figure 30

1. Disconnect the negative battery cable.
2. Raise and support the vehicle safely.
3. Drain and recycle the engine oil.
4. Remove the oil filter.
5. Remove the dual converter Y-pipe assembly.
6. Remove the starter motor.
7. Remove the engine rear plate/converter housing cover.
8. Remove the retaining bolts and remove the oil pan.

To install:

9. Clean the gasket mating surfaces thoroughly.
10. Trial fit oil pan to cylinder block. Ensure that enough clearance has been provided to allow the oil pan to be installed without sealant being scraped off when pan is positioned under the engine.
11. Apply a bead of silicone sealer to the oil pan flange. Also apply a bead of sealer to the front cover/cylinder block joint and fill the grooves on both sides of the rear main seal cap.

➡When using silicone rubber sealer, assembly must occur within 15 minutes after sealer application. After this time, the sealer may start to harden and its sealing effectiveness may be reduced.

12. Install the oil pan and secure to the block with the attaching screws. Tighten the screws to 80–106 inch lbs. (9–12 Nm).
13. Install a new oil filter.
14. Install the engine rear plate/converter housing cover.
15. Install the starter motor.
16. Install the Y-pipe converter assembly.
17. Lower the vehicle.
18. Fill the engine with oil.
19. Connect the negative battery cable.
20. Start the engine and check for leaks.

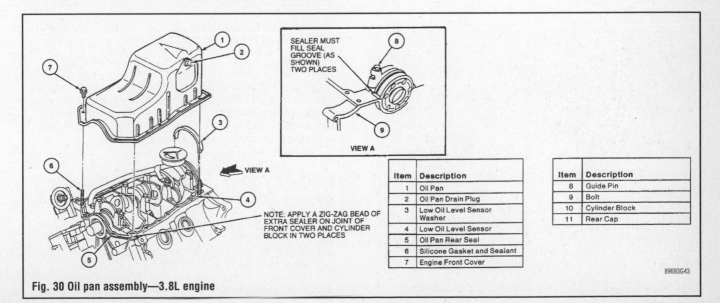

SEALER MUST FILL SEAL GROOVE (AS SHOWN) TWO PLACES

VIEW A

VIEW A

NOTE: APPLY A ZIG-ZAG BEAD OF EXTRA SEALER ON JOINT OF FRONT COVER AND CYLINDER BLOCK IN TWO PLACES

Item	Description
1	Oil Pan
2	Oil Pan Drain Plug
3	Low Oil Level Sensor Washer
4	Low Oil Level Sensor
5	Oil Pan Rear Seal
6	Silicone Gasket and Sealant
7	Engine Front Cover

Item	Description
8	Guide Pin
9	Bolt
10	Cylinder Block
11	Rear Cap

Fig. 30 Oil pan assembly—3.8L engine

89693G43

Oil Pump

REMOVAL & INSTALLATION

3.0L Engine

▶ See Figure 31

1. Disconnect the negative battery cable.
2. Remove the oil pan.
3. Remove the oil pump attaching bolts. Lift the oil pump from the engine.
4. If replacing the oil pump, remove the oil pump intermediate shaft.

To install:

5. Prime the oil pump by filling either the inlet or the outlet port with engine oil. Rotate the pump shaft to distribute the oil within the oil pump body cavity.
6. Insert the oil pump intermediate shaft assembly into the hex drive hole in the oil pump assembly until the retainer "clicks" into place.
7. Place the oil pump in the proper position with a new gasket and install the retaining bolt.

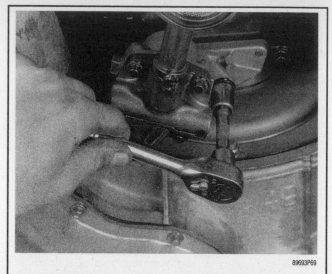

89693P69

The oil pump is secured to the engine with a single bolt

89693P70

The oil pump shaft (arrow) drives the camshaft position sensor

8. Tighten the oil pump retaining bolt to 30–40 ft. lbs. (40–55 Nm).
9. Install the oil pan.
10. Fill the engine with oil.
11. Connect the negative battery cable.

➡️**Check for proper engine oil pressure immediately after starting engine. If engine oil pressure is not within specification a few seconds after starting the engine, stop the engine and determine the reason for the low oil pressure condition. Running an engine with low oil pressure may result in serious engine damage.**

12. Start the engine and check for leaks.

3.8L Engine

▶ See Figure 32

The oil pump, oil pressure relief valve and drive intermediate shaft are contained in the front cover assembly.

1. Disconnect the negative battery cable.
2. If necessary for access, remove the oil filter.
3. Remove the oil pump and filter body-to-engine front cover retaining bolts, them remove the oil pump and filter body from the engine front cover.

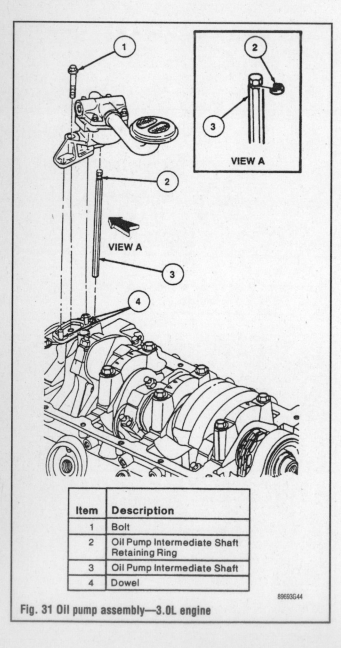

Item	Description
1	Bolt
2	Oil Pump Intermediate Shaft Retaining Ring
3	Oil Pump Intermediate Shaft
4	Dowel

89693G44

Fig. 31 Oil pump assembly—3.0L engine

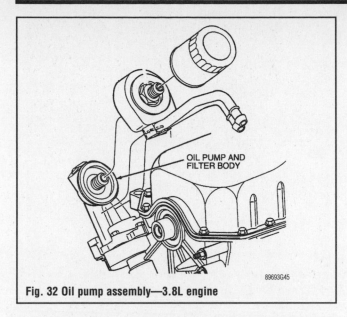

Fig. 32 Oil pump assembly—3.8L engine

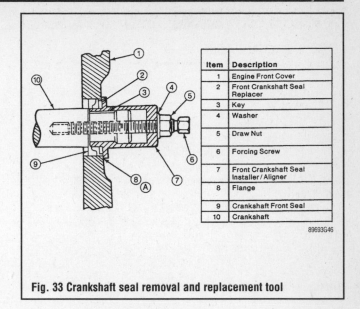

Item	Description
1	Engine Front Cover
2	Front Crankshaft Seal Replacer
3	Key
4	Washer
5	Draw Nut
6	Forcing Screw
7	Front Crankshaft Seal Installer / Aligner
8	Flange
9	Crankshaft Front Seal
10	Crankshaft

Fig. 33 Crankshaft seal removal and replacement tool

4. Inspect the oil pump body seal, oil pump and filter body, and engine front cover for distortion. Replace damaged components as necessary.

To install:

5. Position the oil pump and filter body on the engine front cover, then install the retaining bolts.

6. Tighten the four large engine front cover retaining bolts to 17–23 ft. lbs. (23–32 Nm), then tighten the remaining retaining bolts to 71–97 ft. lbs. (8–11 Nm).

7. If removed, install the oil filter.

8. Connect the negative battery cable.

➡**Check for proper engine oil pressure immediately after starting engine. If engine oil pressure is not within specification a few seconds after starting the engine, stop the engine and determine the reason for the low oil pressure condition. Running an engine with low oil pressure may result in serious engine damage.**

9. Start engine and check for leaks.

Crankshaft Damper

REMOVAL & INSTALLATION

▶ **See Figures 33 and 34**

1. Disconnect the negative battery cable.
2. Remove the accessory drive belt.
3. Raise and support the vehicle safely.
4. Remove the passengers side front wheel.

➡**The vibration damper and crankshaft pulley are a balanced at the factory as a unit and must be installed in the same relative position as before removal.**

5. Matchmark the crankshaft pulley and damper for installation reference.

6. Remove the crankshaft pulley.

7. Remove the crankshaft damper retaining bolt and washer.

➡**It is important to use the proper tools to remove and install the crankshaft damper. Improper removal or installation could damage the damper and cause serious engine damage.**

8. Remove the damper from the crankshaft by using a Crankshaft Damper Remover (T58P-63-16-D) or equivalent.

➡**Take care when removing the damper to not damage the crankshaft snout, engine front cover or crankshaft position sensor.**

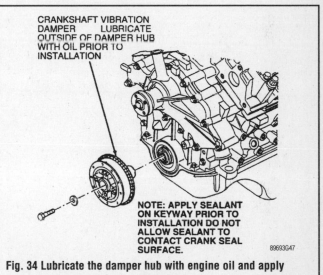

Fig. 34 Lubricate the damper hub with engine oil and apply sealer to the keyway prior to installation

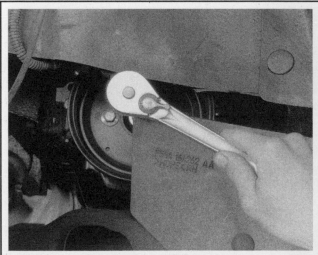

Remove the crankshaft damper center bolt

Remove the crankshaft pulley retaining bolts

89693P72

Note the position of the pulley to the balancer, as they must be reinstalled in the same relative position

889693P73

A crankshaft damper removal tool must be used to prevent damage to the damper

89693P74

Remove the damper carefully as to not damage the crankshaft position sensor tone wheel (arrow)

89693P75

9. Remove the damper from the engine.
10. Remove the crankshaft front seal.
To install:
11. Inspect the engine front cover for damage which may cause the new crankshaft front seal to fail. Service or replace components as necessary.
12. Lubricate the crankshaft oil seal lip with engine oil and install using a seal driver.
13. Lubricate the damper sealing surface with engine oil.
14. Apply silicone sealer to the keyway of the damper.
15. Install the damper using a Crankshaft Damper Replacer (T82L-6316-A) or equivalent.
16. Install the damper retaining bolt and washer. Tighten the bolt to 93–121 ft. lbs (125–165 Nm) on 3.0L engine and 103–132 ft. lbs. (140–180 Nm) on 3.8L engine.
17. Align and install the crankshaft pulley. Tighten bolts to 30–44 ft. lbs. (40–60 Nm) on 3.0L engine and 19–28 ft. lbs. (26–38 Nm).
18. Install the front wheel.
19. Lower the vehicle.
20. Install accessory drive belt.
21. Connect the negative battery cable.
22. Start the engine and check for oil leaks.
23. Road test the vehicle and check for abnormal vibration.

Engine Front Cover and Seal

REMOVAL & INSTALLATION

3.0L Engine

▶ See Figure 23

1. Disconnect the negative battery cable.
2. Drain and recycle the engine coolant.
3. Loosen the four water pump pulley retaining bolts while the accessory drive belts are still tight.
4. Rotate the automatic tensioner down and to the left.
5. Remove the accessory drive belt.
6. Remove the two nuts and bolt retaining the drive belt automatic tensioner to the engine, then remove the tensioner.
7. Disconnect and remove the lower radiator and heater hose from the water pump.
8. Remove the crankshaft pulley and damper.

➡ Do not cut and seal the oil pan gasket. Always replace it with a new oil pan gasket.

The crankshaft position sensor is bolted to the engine front cover

Remove the engine front cover bolts

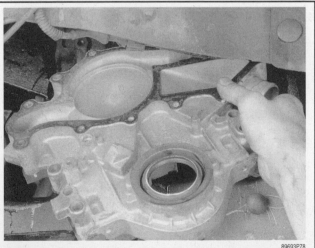

By first removing the water pump, front cover removal will be easier

9. Drain and recycle the engine oil.
10. Remove the oil pan.
11. Remove the screw securing the power steering line bracket to the front subframe at the right front of the engine.
12. Remove the water pump pulley.
13. Disconnect the crankshaft position sensor electrical harness.

➡The engine front cover and water pump may be removed as an assembly by not removing bolt numbers 11–15 as illustrated.

14. Remove front cover bolts and lift the front cover from the engine.
15. Using a seal puller, remove the front cover seal.
   To install:

➡Be careful not to gouge the aluminum surfaces when scraping the old gasket material from the mating surfaces of the water pump and front cover.

16. Clean all gasket mating surfaces thoroughly.
17. Lightly oil all bolt and stud threads except those requiring thread sealant.
18. Using a seal driver, install a new front cover seal.
19. Align and install a new front cover gasket.
20. Install the engine front cover and water pump as an assembly with the water pump pulley loosely attached.
21. Hand start the engine front cover bolts after applying Teflon® pipe sealant to bolts No. 1, 2 and 3 as illustrated. Tighten bolts 1–10 to 15–22 ft. lbs. (20–30 Nm).
22. If the water pump was removed separately, tighten bolts 11 through 15 to 71–106 inch lbs. (8–12 Nm).
23. Install oil pan using a new gasket.
24. Install crankshaft damper and pulley.
25. Hand tighten the water pump pulley retaining bolts.
26. Install the automatic belt tensioner assembly. Tighten the two retaining nuts and bolt to 35 ft. lbs. (47 Nm).
27. Install the accessory drive belt.
28. Final tighten the water pump pulley retaining bolts to 15–22 ft. lbs. (22–30 Nm).
29. Connect the lower radiator and heater hoses.
30. Fill and bleed the cooling system.
31. Connect the negative battery cable.
32. Start the engine and check for leaks.

3.8L Engine

▶ **See Figure 24**

1. Disconnect the negative battery cable.
2. Drain and recycle the engine coolant.
3. Loosen the drive belt tensioner, then remove the drive belts.
4. Remove the lower radiator hose.
5. Remove the lower nut on both front engine supports.
6. Remove the alternator.
7. Position a drain pan under the power steering pump.
8. Disconnect power steering pressure line from pump using a fuel line disconnect tool (T90T-9550-S), or equivalent.
9. Remove the power steering reservoir filler cap.
10. Disconnect the water bypass hose and oil cooler hose from the heater water outlet tube.
11. Remove the retaining bolt and disconnect the heater water outlet tube from the water pump.
12. Remove the A/C bracket brace.
13. Raise the engine approximately 2 inches (51mm) to provide necessary clearance for water pump removal.
14. Remove the water pump pulley.
15. Remove the drive belt tensioner form the power steering pump support.
16. Remove the power steering pump support and place the pump and support aside in the engine compartment.
17. Remove the crankshaft pulley and vibration damper.
18. Remove the oil bypass filter and oil cooler assembly.
19. Remove the oil pan.

➡ Do not overlook the engine front cover retaining bolt located behind the oil pump and filter body. The engine front cover will break if pried upon and all retaining bolts are not removed.

20. Remove the engine front cover.

➡ It is not necessary to remove the water pump. The water pump and front cover may be removed as an assembly.

To install:

➡ Be careful not to gouge the aluminum surfaces when scraping the old gasket material from the mating surfaces of the water pump and front cover.

21. Clean all gasket mating surfaces thoroughly.

➡ Install the bolt nearest the oil bypass filter flange last and tighten last. Apply Loctite® or equivalent thread locker to bolt prior to installation.

22. Install the engine front cover and tighten bolts to 15–22 ft. lbs. (20–30 Nm) and nuts to 71–106 inch lbs. (8–12 Nm).
23. Install the oil pan.
24. Install the oil bypass filter and oil cooler assembly.
25. Install the crankshaft pulley and vibration damper.
26. Install the power steering pump support.
27. Install the drive belt tensioner.
28. Install the water pump pulley.
29. Lower the engine.
30. Install the A/C bracket brace.
31. Connect the heater water outlet tube.
32. Connect the water bypass hose and oil cooler hose.
33. Install the power steering reservoir filler cap.
34. Connect power steering pressure line using fuel line connect tool (T90T-9550-S), or equivalent.
35. Install the alternator.
36. Install the lower nut on both front engine supports.
37. Install the lower radiator hose.
38. Install the drive belts.
39. Fill and bleed the cooling system.
40. Connect the negative battery cable.

Timing Chain and Gears

REMOVAL & INSTALLATION

3.0L Engine

▶ **See Figures 35 and 36**

1. Remove the engine front cover.
2. Rotate the crankshaft until the No. 1 piston is at the TDC on its compression stroke and the timing marks are aligned.
3. Remove the camshaft sprocket attaching bolt and washer.
4. Slide both sprockets and timing chain forward and remove as an assembly.

To install:

➡ Be careful not to gouge the aluminum surfaces when scraping the old gasket material from the gasket mating surfaces.

5. Clean all gasket mating surfaces thoroughly.
6. Slide both sprockets and timing chain onto the camshaft and crankshaft with the timing marks aligned as illustrated.
7. Install the camshaft bolt and washer and tighten to 37–51 ft. lbs. (50–70 Nm).

➡ The camshaft bolt has a drilled oil passage in it for timing chain lubrication. If the bolt is damaged, do not replace it with a standard bolt.

8. Lubricate the timing chain and sprockets with clean engine oil.

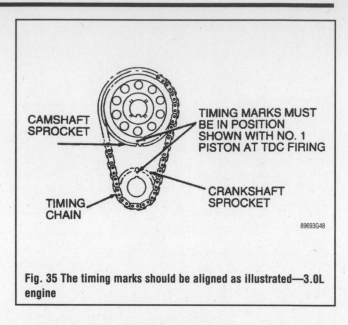

Fig. 35 The timing marks should be aligned as illustrated—3.0L engine

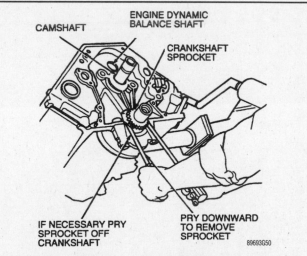

Fig. 36 If the crankshaft sprocket is difficult to remove, it can be loosened with two large prybars as illustrated

Align the camshaft and crankshaft timing marks as illustrated

➡Check the timing mark alignment again prior to installing the engine front cover. Misaligned timing marks will result in decreased engine performance, difficulty starting and may cause serious engine damage.

9. Install the engine front cover.

3.8L Engine

▶ See Figures 37

1. Remove the engine front cover.
2. Rotate the crankshaft until the No. 1 piston is at the TDC on its compression stroke and the timing marks are aligned.
3. Compress the timing chain vibration damper and insert a pin through the hole in the brace to relieve tension on the timing chain.
4. Remove the camshaft sprocket attaching bolt and washer.

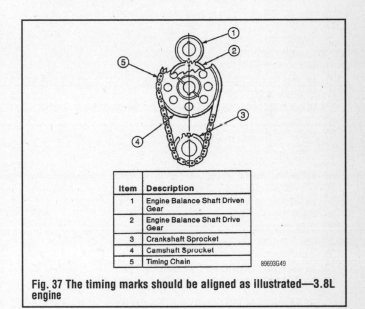

Item	Description
1	Engine Balance Shaft Driven Gear
2	Engine Balance Shaft Drive Gear
3	Crankshaft Sprocket
4	Camshaft Sprocket
5	Timing Chain

Fig. 37 The timing marks should be aligned as illustrated—3.8L engine

➡If the crankshaft sprocket is difficult to remove, carefully pry to sprocket off of the shaft using a pair of large prybars positioned on both sides of the crankshaft sprocket.

5. Slide the sprockets and timing chain forward and remove as an assembly.

To install:

➡Be careful not to gouge the aluminum surfaces when scraping the old gasket material from the gasket mating surfaces.

6. Clean all gasket mating surfaces thoroughly.
7. Slide the sprockets and timing chain onto the engine with the timing marks aligned as illustrated.
8. Check for proper alignment of the balance shaft gear prior to tightening the camshaft bolt.
9. Install the camshaft bolt and washer and tighten to 29–37 ft. lbs. (40–50 Nm).
10. Lubricate the timing chain and sprockets with clean engine oil.
11. Remove the timing chain vibration damper pin.

➡Check the timing mark alignment again prior to installing the engine front cover. Misaligned timing marks will result in decreased engine performance, difficulty starting and may cause serious engine damage.

12. Install the engine front cover.

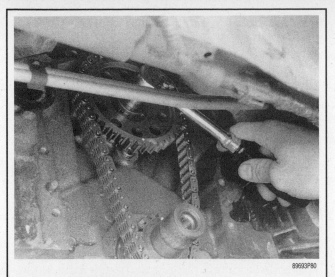

Remove the camshaft sprocket and washer . . .

. . . then remove the camshaft sprocket and timing chain

The crankshaft sprocket can then be removed

Camshaft and Lifters

REMOVAL & INSTALLATION

▶ **See Figures 38, 39 and 40**

3.0L Engine

1. Remove the engine from the vehicle.
2. Rotate the crankshaft until the No. 1 piston is at the TDC on its compression stroke and the timing marks are aligned.
3. Remove the throttle body.
4. Label and remove the ignition wires.
5. Remove the camshaft position sensor.
6. Remove the ignition coil.
7. Remove the valve covers.
8. Loosen the cylinder No. 3 intake valve rocker arm seat retaining bolt and rotate the rocker arm off of the pushrod and away from the top of the valve stem, then remove the pushrod.
9. Remove the alternator and mounting brackets.
10. Remove the drive belt tensioner and drive belt.
11. Remove the intake manifold.
12. Loosen the rocker arm fulcrum nuts and position the rocker arms to the side for easy access to the pushrods.
13. Remove the pushrods and label so they may be installed in their original positions.
14. Remove the tappet guide plate from the valve tappets by lifting straight up.
15. Using a suitable magnet or tappet removal tool, remove the hydraulic tappets and keep them in order so they can be installed in their original positions.
16. Remove the crankshaft pulley and damper.
17. Remove the oil pan assembly.
18. Remove the engine front cover assembly.
19. Align the timing marks on the camshaft and crankshaft sprockets as illustrated.
20. Check the camshaft end-play as follows:

    a. Push the camshaft toward the rear of the engine and install a dial indicator, so the indicator point is on the camshaft sprocket attaching screw.

    b. Zero the dial indicator. Position a small prybar or equivalent, between the camshaft sprocket or gear and block.

    c. Pull the camshaft forward and release it. Camshaft end-play should be 0.007 in. (0.17mm).

    d. If the camshaft end-play is not within specification, replace the thrust plate.

21. Remove the timing chain and sprockets.
22. Remove the camshaft thrust plate.
23. Carefully remove the camshaft by pulling it toward the front of the engine. Remove it slowly to avoid damaging the bearings, journals and lobes.

To install:

24. Clean and inspect all parts before installation.
25. Lubricate camshaft lobes and journals with Molylube or heavy engine oil.
26. Carefully install camshaft.

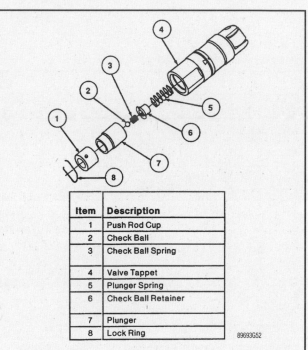

Item	Description
1	Push Rod Cup
2	Check Ball
3	Check Ball Spring
4	Valve Tappet
5	Plunger Spring
6	Check Ball Retainer
7	Plunger
8	Lock Ring

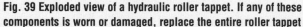

Fig. 39 Exploded view of a hydraulic roller tappet. If any of these components is worn or damaged, replace the entire roller tappet

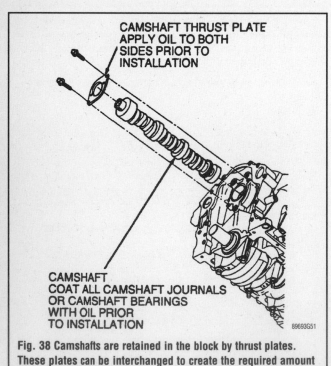

Fig. 38 Camshafts are retained in the block by thrust plates. These plates can be interchanged to create the required amount of camshaft end-play

CAMSHAFT THRUST PLATE APPLY OIL TO BOTH SIDES PRIOR TO INSTALLATION

CAMSHAFT COAT ALL CAMSHAFT JOURNALS OR CAMSHAFT BEARINGS WITH OIL PRIOR TO INSTALLATION

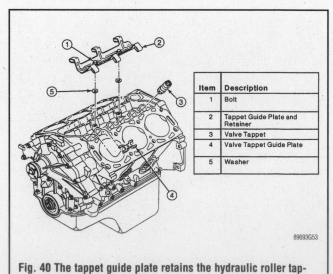

Item	Description
1	Bolt
2	Tappet Guide Plate and Retainer
3	Valve Tappet
4	Valve Tappet Guide Plate
5	Washer

Fig. 40 The tappet guide plate retains the hydraulic roller tappets in their proper orientation

The tappet retainer is attached to the cylinder block with two bolts

Once the tappet retainer is removed, individual lifters can be removed

The tappet guides are marked for position. Always install them with the appropriate mark facing up

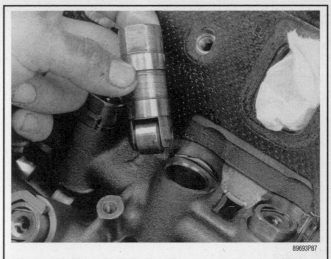

If any part of the roller tappet is damaged, replace the tappet with a new one

➡ **If a new camshaft is being installed, recheck camshaft endplay.**

27. Lubricate the engine thrust plate with Engine Assembly Lubricant D9AZ-19579-D, then install the thrust plate. Tighten the retaining bolts to 7 ft. lbs. (10 Nm).

28. Install the timing chain and sprockets.

➡ **Check the camshaft sprocket bolt for blockage of drilled oil passages prior to installation and clean, if necessary.**

29. Install the engine front cover.
30. Install the crankshaft damper and pulley.
31. Lubricate and install the hydraulic tappets into their original bores.
32. Align valve tappet flats and install the tappet guide plate with the word "UP" facing you.
33. Install the intake manifold assembly.
34. Lubricate and install the pushrods and rocker arms.
35. Install the oil pan.
36. Install the valve covers.
37. Install the alternator and brackets.
38. Install the drive belt tensioner and the drive belt.
39. Install the throttle body.
40. Connect the ignition wires.
41. Install the engine assembly into the vehicle.

3.8L Engine

1. Remove the engine from the vehicle.
2. Rotate the crankshaft until the No. 1 piston is at the TDC on its compression stroke and the timing marks are aligned.
3. Remove the valve covers.
4. Remove the intake manifolds.
5. Loosen the rocker arm bolts and position the rocker arms to the side for easy access to the pushrods.
6. Label and remove the pushrods so they may be installed in their original positions.
7. Remove the tappet guide plate from the valve tappets by lifting straight up.
8. Using a suitable magnet or tappet removal tool, remove the hydraulic tappets and keep them in order so they can be installed in their original positions.
9. Remove the crankshaft pulley and damper.
10. Remove the oil pan assembly.
11. Remove the engine front cover assembly.
12. Align the timing marks on the camshaft and crankshaft sprockets as illustrated.

13. Check the camshaft end-play as follows:

    a. Push the camshaft toward the rear of the engine and install a dial indicator, so the indicator point is on the camshaft sprocket attaching screw.

    b. Zero the dial indicator. Position a small prybar or equivalent, between the camshaft sprocket or gear and block.

    c. Pull the camshaft forward and release it. Camshaft end-play should be 0.001–0.006 in. (0.025–0.15mm).

    d. If the camshaft end-play is not within specification, replace the thrust plate.

14. Remove the timing chain and sprockets.

15. Remove the camshaft thrust plate.

16. Carefully remove the camshaft by pulling it toward the front of the engine. Remove it slowly to avoid damaging the bearings, journals and lobes.

To install:

17. Clean and inspect all parts before installation.

18. Lubricate camshaft lobes and journals with Molylube or heavy engine oil.

19. Carefully install camshaft.

➡**If a new camshaft is being installed, recheck camshaft endplay.**

20. Lubricate the engine thrust plate with Engine Assembly Lubricant D9AZ-19579-D, then install the thrust plate. Tighten the retaining bolts to 71–124 inch lbs. (8–14 Nm).

21. Install the timing chain and sprockets.

➡**Check the camshaft sprocket bolt for blockage of drilled oil passages prior to installation and clean, if necessary.**

22. Install the engine front cover.

23. Install the crankshaft damper and pulley.

24. Lubricate and install the hydraulic tappets into their original bores.

25. Align valve tappet flats and install the tappet guide plate with the word "UP" facing you.

26. Install the intake manifold assembly.

27. Lubricate and install the pushrods and rocker arms.

28. Install the oil pan.

29. Install the valve covers.

30. Install the engine assembly into the vehicle.

INSPECTION

Clean the camshaft with solvent and wipe it dry. Remove light scuffs, scores or nicks from the camshaft machined surfaces with a smooth oil stone.

The camshaft must be replaced if the journals are excessively worn or scored. Camshaft journals can be refinished to accommodate 0.015 in. (0.38mm) undersize bearings. If the journals do not clean up the camshaft must be replaced.

Check camshaft bores for size, taper, roundness, alignment and finish. If any of these exceed specification, install new camshaft bearings.

Inspect the camshaft runout by setting the No. 1 and No. 4 journals on V-blocks and using a dial indicator. If maximum runout of camshaft is not within specification, replace the camshaft.

Inspect the camshaft lobes for scoring and signs of abnormal wear. Lobe pitting in the general area of the lobe toe does not harm camshaft operation. The camshaft should not be replaced unless the lobe lift loss has exceeded specification or pitting has occurred in the lobe lift area.

➡**If any part of the valve tappet needs replacement, the entire valve tappet should be replaced.**

Inspect the valve tappet and discard the entire tappet if it shows signs of pitting, scoring or excessive wear.

Inspect the valve tappet plunger and make sure it is free in the body. The plunger should drop to the bottom of the body by its own weight when assembled dry.

Inspect the roller on the valve tappet for flat spots or scoring. If a flat spot is found, check the camshaft lobes for proper height or wear.

Balance Shaft

REMOVAL & INSTALLATION

▶ **See Figure 41**

3.8L Engine

1. Remove the engine from the vehicle.
2. Remove the intake manifold.
3. Remove the oil pan.
4. Remove the engine front cover.
5. Remove timing chain and sprockets.
6. Remove the balance shaft drive gear and spacer.
7. Remove the balance shaft gear, thrust plate and shaft assembly.

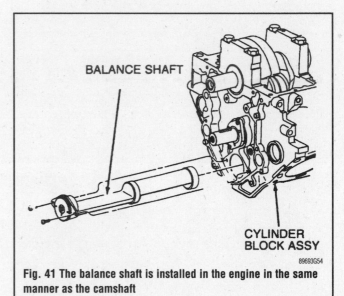

Fig. 41 The balance shaft is installed in the engine in the same manner as the camshaft

To install:

8. Thoroughly coat the balance shaft bearings with engine oil.
9. Install the balance shaft gear.
10. Install the balance shaft, thrust plate and gear, then tighten the retaining bolts to 6–10 ft. lbs. (8–14 Nm).
11. Install the timing chain and sprockets.
12. Install the oil pan.
13. Install the engine front cover.
14. Install the intake manifold.
15. Install the engine in the vehicle.

Rear Main Seal

REMOVAL & INSTALLATION

▶ **See Figure 42**

1. Disconnect the negative battery cable.
2. Raise and support the vehicle safely.
3. Remove the transaxle.
4. Remove the flywheel and the rear cover plate, if necessary.
5. Using a sharp awl, punch one hole into the crankshaft rear oil seal metal surface between the seal lip and the cylinder block.

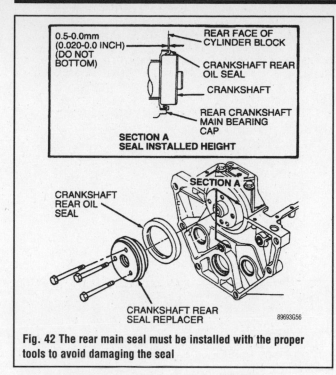

Fig. 42 The rear main seal must be installed with the proper tools to avoid damaging the seal

➡Use caution to avoid damaging the oil seal surface.

6. Screw in the threaded end of crankshaft rear seal replacer (T88L-6701-A) or equivalent, then use the tool to remove the seal.

To install:

7. Inspect the crankshaft seal area for any damage which may cause the seal to leak. If damage is evident, service or replace the crankshaft as necessary.

8. Coat the crankshaft seal area and the lip with engine oil.

9. Using a Rear Crankshaft Seal Replacer T88P-6701-A, or equivalent, install the seal. Tighten the bolts of the seal installer tool evenly so the seal is straight and seats without misalignment.

10. Install the flywheel.

11. Install the rear cover plate, if necessary.

12. Install the transaxle.

EXHAUST SYSTEM

Inspection

➡Safety glasses should be worn at all times when working on or near the exhaust system. Older exhaust systems will almost always be covered with loose rust particles which will shower you when disturbed. These particles are more than a nuisance and could injure your eye.

✶✶ CAUTION

Do NOT perform exhaust repairs or inspection with the engine or exhaust hot. Allow the system to cool completely before attempting any work. Exhaust systems are noted for sharp edges, flaking metal and rusted bolts. Gloves and eye protection are required. A healthy supply of penetrating oil and rags is highly recommended.

Your vehicle must be raised and supported safely to inspect the exhaust system properly. By placing 4 safety stands under the vehicle for support should provide enough room for you to slide under the vehicle and inspect the system completely. Start the inspection at the exhaust manifold or turbocharger pipe where the header pipe is attached and work your way to the

Flywheel/Flexplate

REMOVAL & INSTALLATION

◆ **See Figure 43**

➡The flywheel is individually balanced. Balance weights should not be added to new flywheels.

1. Remove the transaxle from the vehicle.
2. Matchmark the flywheel to the crankshaft for installation reference.
3. Remove the flywheel retaining bolts.
4. Remove the flywheel.

To install:

5. Inspect the rear main seal thoroughly. This is the time to replace a leaky seal.

6. Position the flywheel on the crankshaft and install the retaining bolts.

7. Tighten bolts to 54–64 ft. lbs. (73–87 Nm) in a star pattern.

8. Install the transaxle.

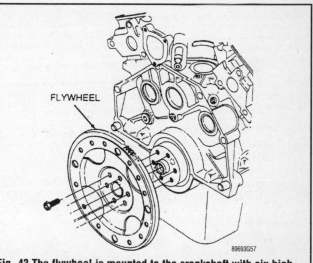

Fig. 43 The flywheel is mounted to the crankshaft with six high strength bolts. Always tighten the flywheel bolts to specification

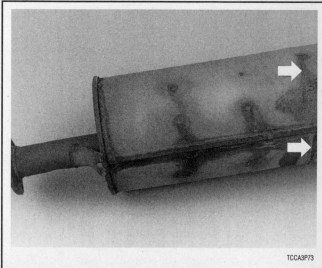

Cracks in the muffler are a guaranteed leak

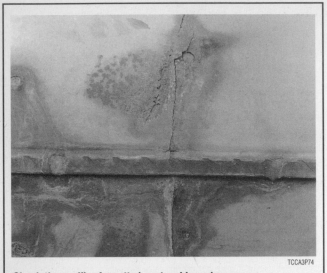

Check the muffler for rotted spot welds and seams

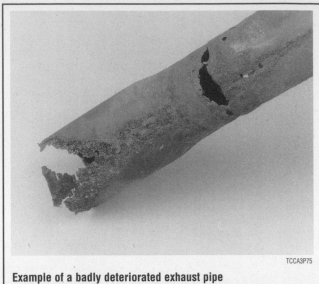

Example of a badly deteriorated exhaust pipe

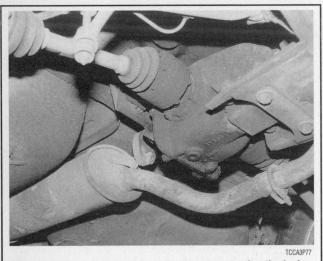

Make sure the exhaust components are not contacting the body or suspension

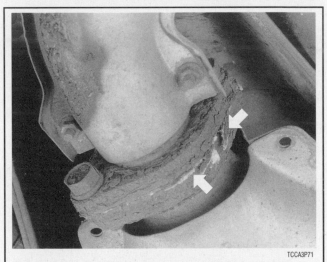

Inspect flanges for gaskets that have deteriorated and need replacement

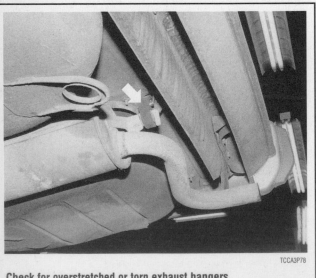

Check for overstretched or torn exhaust hangers

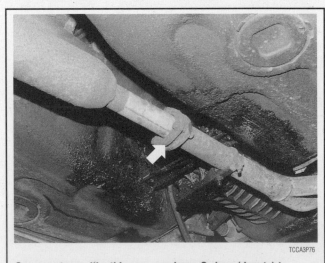

Some systems, like this one, use large O-rings (donuts) in between the flanges

back of the vehicle. On dual exhaust systems, remember to inspect both sides of the vehicle. Check the complete exhaust system for open seams, holes loose connections, or other deterioration which could permit exhaust fumes to seep into the passenger compartment. Inspect all mounting brackets and hangers for deterioration, some models may have rubber O-rings that can be overstretched and non-supportive. These components will need to be replaced if found. It has always been a practice to use a pointed tool to poke up into the exhaust system where the deterioration spots are to see whether or not they crumble. Some models may have heat shield covering certain parts of the exhaust system , it will be necessary to remove these shields to have the exhaust visible for inspection also.

REPLACEMENT

There are basically two types of exhaust systems. One is the flange type where the component ends are attached with bolts and a gasket in-between. The other exhaust system is the slip joint type. These components slip into one another using clamps to retain them together.

✳✳ CAUTION

Allow the exhaust system to cool sufficiently before spraying a solvent exhaust fasteners. Some solvents are highly flammable and could ignite when sprayed on hot exhaust components.

Before removing any component of the exhaust system, ALWAYS squirt a liquid rust dissolving agent onto the fasteners for ease of removal. A lot of knuckle skin will be saved by following this rule. It may even be wise to spray the fasteners and allow them to sit overnight.

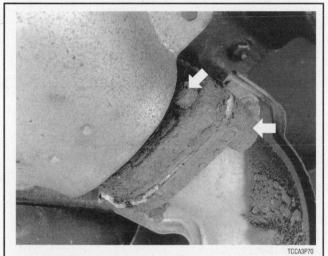

TCCA3P70

Nuts and bolts will be extremely difficult to remove when deteriorated with rust

Flange Type

✳✳ CAUTION

Do NOT perform exhaust repairs or inspection with the engine or exhaust hot. Allow the system to cool completely before attempting any work. Exhaust systems are noted for sharp edges, flaking metal and rusted bolts. Gloves and eye protection are required. A healthy supply of penetrating oil and rags is highly recommended. Never spray liquid rust dissolving agent onto a hot exhaust component.

Before removing any component on a flange type system, ALWAYS squirt a liquid rust dissolving agent onto the fasteners for ease of removal. Start by unbolting the exhaust piece at both ends (if required). When unbolting the headpipe from the manifold, make sure that the bolts are free before trying to remove them. if you snap a stud in the exhaust manifold, the

TCCA3P72

Example of a flange type exhaust system joint

stud will have to be removed with a bolt extractor, which often means removal of the manifold itself. Next, disconnect the component from the mounting; slight twisting and turning may be required to remove the component completely from the vehicle. You may need to tap on the component with a rubber mallet to loosen the component. If all else fails, use a hacksaw to separate the parts. An oxy-acetylene cutting torch may be faster but the sparks are DANGEROUS near the fuel tank, and at the very least, accidents could happen, resulting in damage to the under-car parts, not to mention yourself.

Slip Joint Type

Before removing any component on the slip joint type exhaust system, ALWAYS squirt a liquid rust dissolving agent onto the fasteners for ease of removal. Start by unbolting the exhaust piece at both ends (if required). When unbolting the headpipe from the manifold, make sure that the bolts are free before trying to remove them. if you snap a stud in the exhaust manifold, the stud will have to be removed with a bolt extractor, which often means removal of the manifold itself. Next, remove the mounting U-bolts from around the exhaust pipe you are extracting from the vehicle. Don't be surprised if the U-bolts break while removing the nuts. Loosen the exhaust pipe from any mounting brackets retaining it to the floor pan and separate the components.

TCCA3P79

Example of a common slip joint type system

Determining Engine Condition

Anything that generates heat and/or friction will eventually burn or wear out (i.e. a light bulb generates heat, therefore its life span is limited). With this in mind, a running engine generates tremendous amounts of both; friction is encountered by the moving and rotating parts inside the engine and heat is created by friction and combustion of the fuel. However, the engine has systems designed to help reduce the effects of heat and friction and provide added longevity. The oiling system reduces the amount of friction encountered by the moving parts inside the engine, while the cooling system reduces heat created by friction and combustion. If either system is not maintained, a break-down will be inevitable. Therefore, you can see how regular maintenance can affect the service life of your vehicle. If you do not drain, flush and refill your cooling system at the proper intervals, deposits will begin to accumulate in the radiator, thereby reducing the amount of heat it can extract from the coolant. The same applies to your oil and filter; if it is not changed often enough it becomes laden with contaminates and is unable to properly lubricate the engine. This increases friction and wear.

There are a number of methods for evaluating the condition of your engine. A compression test can reveal the condition of your pistons, piston rings, cylinder bores, head gasket(s), valves and valve seats. An oil pressure test can warn you of possible engine bearing, or oil pump failures. Excessive oil consumption, evidence of oil in the engine air intake area and/or bluish smoke from the tail pipe may indicate worn piston rings, worn valve guides and/or valve seals. As a general rule, an engine that uses no more than one quart of oil every 1000 miles is in good condition. Engines that use one quart of oil or more in less than 1000 miles should first be checked for oil leaks. If any oil leaks are present, have them fixed before determining how much oil is consumed by the engine, especially if blue smoke is not visible at the tail pipe.

COMPRESSION TEST

A noticeable lack of engine power, excessive oil consumption and/or poor fuel mileage measured over an extended period are all indicators of internal engine wear. Worn piston rings, scored or worn cylinder bores, blown head gaskets, sticking or burnt valves, and worn valve seats are all possible culprits. A check of each cylinder's compression will help locate the problem.

➡A screw-in type compression gauge is more accurate than the type you simply hold against the spark plug hole. Although it takes slightly longer to use, it's worth the effort to obtain a more accurate reading.

TCCS3801

A screw-in type compression gauge is more accurate and easier to use without an assistant

1. Make sure that the proper amount and viscosity of engine oil is in the crankcase, then ensure the battery is fully charged.
2. Warm-up the engine to normal operating temperature, then shut the engine **OFF**.
3. Disable the ignition system.
4. Label and disconnect all of the spark plug wires from the plugs.
5. Thoroughly clean the cylinder head area around the spark plug ports, then remove the spark plugs.
6. Set the throttle plate to the fully open (wide-open throttle) position. You can block the accelerator linkage open for this, or you can have an assistant fully depress the accelerator pedal.
7. Install a screw-in type compression gauge into the No. 1 spark plug hole until the fitting is snug.

❊❊ WARNING

Be careful not to crossthread the spark plug hole.

8. According to the tool manufacturer's instructions, connect a remote starting switch to the starting circuit.
9. With the ignition switch in the **OFF** position, use the remote starting switch to crank the engine through at least five compression strokes (approximately 5 seconds of cranking) and record the highest reading on the gauge.
10. Repeat the test on each cylinder, cranking the engine approximately the same number of compression strokes and/or time as the first.
11. Compare the highest readings from each cylinder to that of the others. The indicated compression pressures are considered within specifications if the lowest reading cylinder is within 75 percent of the pressure recorded for the highest reading cylinder. For example, if your highest reading cylinder pressure was 150 psi (1034 kPa), then 75 percent of that would be 113 psi (779 kPa). So the lowest reading cylinder should be no less than 113 psi (779 kPa).
12. If a cylinder exhibits an unusually low compression reading, pour a tablespoon of clean engine oil into the cylinder through the spark plug hole and repeat the compression test. If the compression rises after adding oil, it means that the cylinder's piston rings and/or cylinder bore are damaged or worn. If the pressure remains low, the valves may not be seating properly (a valve job is needed), or the head gasket may be blown near that cylinder. If compression in any two adjacent cylinders is low, and if the addition of oil doesn't help raise compression, there is leakage past the head gasket. Oil and coolant in the combustion chamber, combined with blue or constant white smoke from the tail pipe, are symptoms of this problem. However, don't be alarmed by the normal white smoke emitted from the tail pipe during engine warm-up or from cold weather driving. There may be evidence of water droplets on the engine dipstick and/or oil droplets in the cooling system if a head gasket is blown.

OIL PRESSURE TEST

Check for proper oil pressure at the sending unit passage with an externally mounted mechanical oil pressure gauge (as opposed to relying on a factory installed dash-mounted gauge). A tachometer may also be needed, as some specifications may require running the engine at a specific rpm.

1. With the engine cold, locate and remove the oil pressure sending unit.
2. Following the manufacturer's instructions, connect a mechanical oil pressure gauge and, if necessary, a tachometer to the engine.
3. Start the engine and allow it to idle.
4. Check the oil pressure reading when cold and record the number. You may need to run the engine at a specified rpm, so check the specifications chart located earlier in this section.
5. Run the engine until normal operating temperature is reached (upper radiator hose will feel warm).
6. Check the oil pressure reading again with the engine hot and record the number. Turn the engine **OFF**.

7. Compare your hot oil pressure reading to that given in the chart. If the reading is low, check the cold pressure reading against the chart. If the cold pressure is well above the specification, and the hot reading was lower than the specification, you may have the wrong viscosity oil in the engine. Change the oil, making sure to use the proper grade and quantity, then repeat the test.

Low oil pressure readings could be attributed to internal component wear, pump related problems, a low oil level, or oil viscosity that is too low. High oil pressure readings could be caused by an overfilled crankcase, too high of an oil viscosity or a faulty pressure relief valve.

Buy or Rebuild?

Now that you have determined that your engine is worn out, you must make some decisions. The question of whether or not an engine is worth rebuilding is largely a subjective matter and one of personal worth. Is the engine a popular one, or is it an obsolete model? Are parts available? Will it get acceptable gas mileage once it is rebuilt? Is the car it's being put into worth keeping? Would it be less expensive to buy a new engine, have your engine rebuilt by a pro, rebuild it yourself or buy a used engine from a salvage yard? Or would it be simpler and less expensive to buy another car? If you have considered all these matters and more, and have still decided to rebuild the engine, then it is time to decide how you will rebuild it.

➡The editors at Chilton feel that most engine machining should be performed by a professional machine shop. Don't think of it as wasting money, rather, as an assurance that the job has been done right the first time. There are many expensive and specialized tools required to perform such tasks as boring and honing an engine block or having a valve job done on a cylinder head. Even inspecting the parts requires expensive micrometers and gauges to properly measure wear and clearances. Also, a machine shop can deliver to you clean, and ready to assemble parts, saving you time and aggravation. Your maximum savings will come from performing the removal, disassembly, assembly and installation of the engine and purchasing or renting only the tools required to perform the above tasks. Depending on the particular circumstances, you may save 40 to 60 percent of the cost doing these yourself.

A complete rebuild or overhaul of an engine involves replacing all of the moving parts (pistons, rods, crankshaft, camshaft, etc.) with new ones and machining the non-moving wearing surfaces of the block and heads. Unfortunately, this may not be cost effective. For instance, your crankshaft may have been damaged or worn, but it can be machined undersize for a minimal fee.

So, as you can see, you can replace everything inside the engine, but, it is wiser to replace only those parts which are really needed, and, if possible, repair the more expensive ones. Later in this section, we will break the engine down into its two main components: the cylinder head and the engine block. We will discuss each component, and the recommended parts to replace during a rebuild on each.

Engine Overhaul Tips

Most engine overhaul procedures are fairly standard. In addition to specific parts replacement procedures and specifications for your individual engine, this section is also a guide to acceptable rebuilding procedures. Examples of standard rebuilding practice are given and should be used along with specific details concerning your particular engine.

Competent and accurate machine shop services will ensure maximum performance, reliability and engine life. In most instances it is more profitable for the do-it-yourself mechanic to remove, clean and inspect the component, buy the necessary parts and deliver these to a shop for actual machine work.

Much of the assembly work (crankshaft, bearings, piston rods, and other components) is well within the scope of the do-it-yourself mechanic's tools and abilities. You will have to decide for yourself the depth of involvement you desire in an engine repair or rebuild.

TOOLS

The tools required for an engine overhaul or parts replacement will depend on the depth of your involvement. With a few exceptions, they will be the tools found in a mechanic's tool kit (see Section 1 of this manual). More in-depth work will require some or all of the following:
- A dial indicator (reading in thousandths) mounted on a universal base
- Micrometers and telescope gauges
- Jaw and screw-type pullers
- Scraper
- Valve spring compressor
- Ring groove cleaner
- Piston ring expander and compressor
- Ridge reamer
- Cylinder hone or glaze breaker
- Plastigage®
- Engine stand

The use of most of these tools is illustrated in this section. Many can be rented for a one-time use from a local parts jobber or tool supply house specializing in automotive work.

Occasionally, the use of special tools is called for. See the information on Special Tools and the Safety Notice in the front of this book before substituting another tool.

OVERHAUL TIPS

Aluminum has become extremely popular for use in engines, due to its low weight. Observe the following precautions when handling aluminum parts:
- Never hot tank aluminum parts (the caustic hot tank solution will eat the aluminum.
- Remove all aluminum parts (identification tag, etc.) from engine parts prior to the tanking.
- Always coat threads lightly with engine oil or anti-seize compounds before installation, to prevent seizure.
- Never overtighten bolts or spark plugs especially in aluminum threads.

When assembling the engine, any parts that will be exposed to frictional contact must be prelubed to provide lubrication at initial start-up. Any product specifically formulated for this purpose can be used, but engine oil is not recommended as a prelube in most cases.

When semi-permanent (locked, but removable) installation of bolts or nuts is desired, threads should be cleaned and coated with Loctite® or another similar, commercial non-hardening sealant.

CLEANING

Before the engine and its components are inspected, they must be thoroughly cleaned. You will need to remove any engine varnish, oil sludge and/or carbon deposits from all of the components to insure an accurate inspection. A crack in the engine block or cylinder head can easily become overlooked if hidden by a layer of sludge or carbon.

Most of the cleaning process can be carried out with common hand tools and readily available solvents or solutions. Carbon deposits can be chipped away using a hammer and a hard wooden chisel. Old gasket material and varnish or sludge can usually be removed using a scraper and/or cleaning solvent. Extremely stubborn deposits may require the use of a power drill with a wire brush. If using a wire brush, use extreme care around any critical machined surfaces (such as the gasket surfaces, bearing saddles, cylinder bores, etc.). USE OF A WIRE BRUSH IS NOT RECOMMENDED ON ANY ALUMINUM COMPONENTS. Always follow any safety recommendations given by the manufacturer of the tool and/or solvent. You should always wear eye protection during any cleaning process involving scraping, chipping or spraying of solvents.

An alternative to the mess and hassle of cleaning the parts yourself is to drop them off at a local garage or machine shop. They will, more than likely, have the necessary equipment to properly clean all of the parts for a nominal fee.

TCCS3132

Use a gasket scraper to remove the old gasket material from the mating surfaces

TCCS3208

Clean the piston ring grooves using a ring groove cleaner tool, or . . .

✲✲ CAUTION

Always wear eye protection during any cleaning process involving scraping, chipping or spraying of solvents.

Remove any oil galley plugs, freeze plugs and/or pressed-in bearings and carefully wash and degrease all of the engine components including the fasteners and bolts. Small parts such as the valves, springs, etc., should be placed in a metal basket and allowed to soak. Use pipe cleaner type brushes, and clean all passageways in the components. Use a ring expander and remove the rings from the pistons. Clean the piston ring grooves with a special tool or a piece of broken ring. Scrape the carbon off of the top of the piston. You should never use a wire brush on the pistons. After preparing all of the piston assemblies in this manner, wash and degrease them again.

✲✲ WARNING

Use extreme care when cleaning around the cylinder head valve seats. A mistake or slip may cost you a new seat.

When cleaning the cylinder head, remove carbon from the combustion chamber with the valves installed. This will avoid damaging the valve seats.

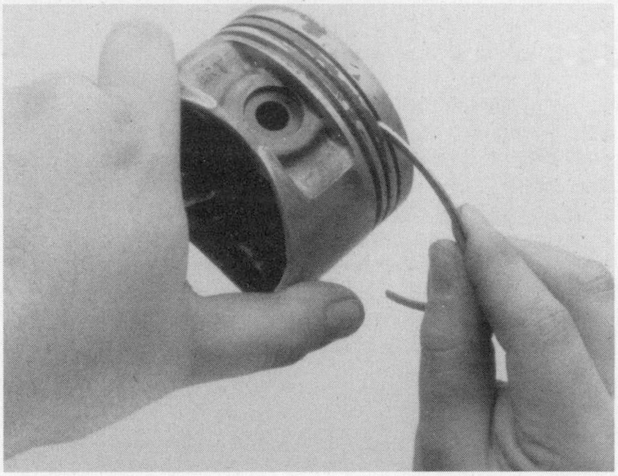
TCCS3911

. . . use a piece of an old ring to clean the grooves. Be careful, the ring can be quite sharp

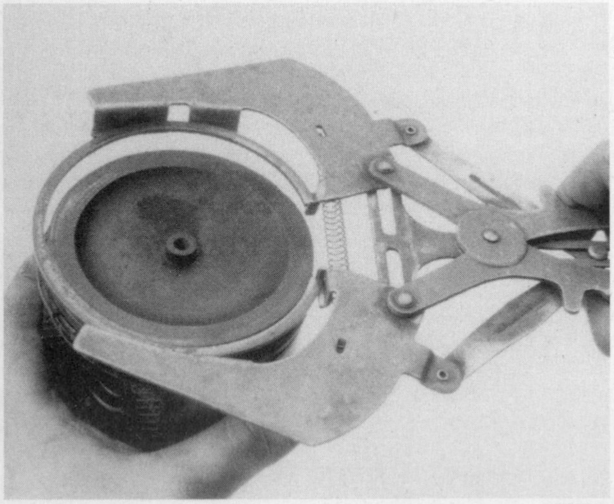
TCCS3211

Use a ring expander tool to remove the piston rings

REPAIRING DAMAGED THREADS

See Figures 44, 45, 46, 47 and 48

Several methods of repairing damaged threads are available. Heli-Coil® (shown here), Keenserts® and Microdot® are among the most widely used. All involve basically the same principle—drilling out stripped threads, tapping the hole and installing a prewound insert—making welding, plugging and oversize fasteners unnecessary.

Two types of thread repair inserts are usually supplied: a standard type for most inch coarse, inch fine, metric course and metric fine thread sizes and a spark lug type to fit most spark plug port sizes. Consult the individual tool manufacturer's catalog to determine exact applications. Typical thread repair kits will contain a selection of prewound threaded inserts, a tap (corresponding to the outside diameter threads of the insert) and an installation tool. Spark plug inserts usually differ because they require a tap equipped with pilot threads and a combined reamer/tap section. Most manufacturers also supply blister-packed thread repair inserts separately in addition to a master kit containing a variety of taps and inserts plus installation tools.

Before attempting to repair a threaded hole, remove any snapped, broken or damaged bolts or studs. Penetrating oil can be used to free frozen threads. The offending item can usually be removed with locking pliers or

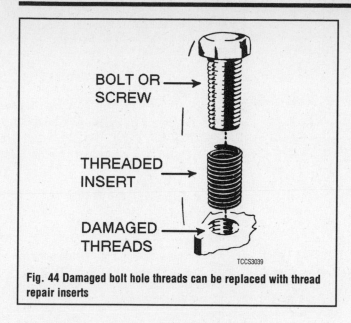

Fig. 44 Damaged bolt hole threads can be replaced with thread repair inserts

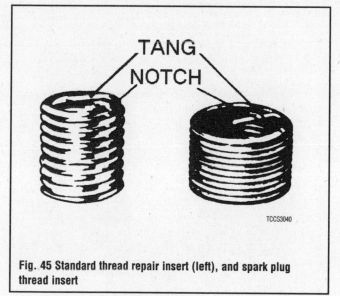

Fig. 45 Standard thread repair insert (left), and spark plug thread insert

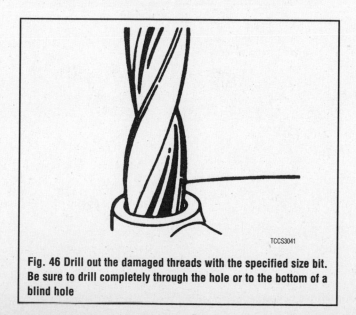

Fig. 46 Drill out the damaged threads with the specified size bit. Be sure to drill completely through the hole or to the bottom of a blind hole

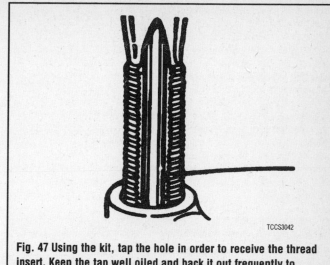

Fig. 47 Using the kit, tap the hole in order to receive the thread insert. Keep the tap well oiled and back it out frequently to avoid clogging the threads

Fig. 48 Screw the insert onto the installer tool until the tang engages the slot. Thread the insert into the hole until it is ¼–½ turn below the top surface, then remove the tool and break off the tang using a punch

using a screw/stud extractor. After the hole is clear, the thread can be repaired, as shown in the series of accompanying illustrations and in the kit manufacturer's instructions.

Engine Preparation

To properly rebuild an engine, you must first remove it from the vehicle, then disassemble and diagnose it. Ideally you should place your engine on an engine stand. This affords you the best access to the engine components. Follow the manufacturer's directions for using the stand with your particular engine. Remove the flywheel or flexplate before installing the engine to the stand.

Now that you have the engine on a stand, and assuming that you have drained the oil and coolant from the engine, it's time to strip it of all but the necessary components. Before you start disassembling the engine, you may want to take a moment to draw some pictures, or fabricate some labels or containers to mark the locations of various components and the bolts and/or studs which fasten them. Modern day engines use a lot of little brackets and clips which hold wiring harnesses and such, and these holders are often mounted on studs and/or bolts that can be easily mixed up. The manufacturer spent a lot of time and money designing your vehicle, and they wouldn't have wasted any of it by haphazardly placing brackets, clips or fasteners on the vehicle. If it's present when you disassemble it, put it back when you assemble, you will regret not remembering that little bracket which holds a wire harness out of the path of a rotating part.

You should begin by unbolting any accessories still attached to the engine, such as the water pump, power steering pump, alternator, etc. Then, unfasten any manifolds (intake or exhaust) which were not removed during the engine removal procedure. Finally, remove any covers remaining on the engine such as the rocker arm, front or timing cover and oil pan. Some front covers may require the vibration damper and/or crank pulley to be removed beforehand. The idea is to reduce the engine to the bare necessities (cylinder head(s), valve train, engine block, crankshaft, pistons and connecting rods), plus any other `in block' components such as oil pumps, balance shafts and auxiliary shafts.

Finally, remove the cylinder head(s) from the engine block and carefully place on a bench. Disassembly instructions for each component follow later in this section.

Cylinder Head

There are two basic types of cylinder heads used on today's automobiles: the Overhead Valve (OHV) and the Overhead Camshaft (OHC). The latter can also be broken down into two subgroups: the Single Overhead Camshaft (SOHC) and the Dual Overhead Camshaft (DOHC). Generally, if there is only a single camshaft on a head, it is just referred to as an OHC head. Also, an engine with a OHV cylinder head is also known as a pushrod engine.

Most cylinder heads these days are made of an aluminum alloy due to its light weight, durability and heat transfer qualities. However, cast iron was the material of choice in the past, and is still used on many vehicles today. Whether made from aluminum or iron, all cylinder heads have valves and seats. Some use two valves per cylinder, while the more hi-tech engines will utilize a multi-valve configuration using 3, 4 and even 5 valves per cylinder. When the valve contacts the seat, it does so on precision machined surfaces, which seals the combustion chamber. All cylinder heads have a valve guide for each valve. The guide centers the valve to the seat and allows it to move up and down within it. The clearance between the valve and guide can be critical. Too much clearance and the engine may consume oil, lose vacuum and/or damage the seat. Too little, and the valve can stick in the guide causing the engine to run poorly if at all, and possibly causing severe damage. The last component all cylinder heads have are valve springs. The spring holds the valve against its seat. It also returns the valve to this position when the valve has been opened by the valve train or camshaft. The spring is fastened to the valve by a retainer and valve locks (sometimes called keepers). Aluminum heads will also have a valve spring shim to keep the spring from wearing away the aluminum.

An ideal method of rebuilding the cylinder head would involve replacing all of the valves, guides, seats, springs, etc. with new ones. However, depending on how the engine was maintained, often this is not necessary. A major cause of valve, guide and seat wear is an improperly tuned engine. An engine that is running too rich, will often wash the lubricating oil out of the guide with gasoline, causing it to wear rapidly. Conversely, an engine which is running too lean will place higher combustion temperatures on the valves and seats allowing them to wear or even burn. Springs fall victim to the driving habits of the individual. A driver who often runs the engine rpm to the redline will wear out or break the springs faster then one that stays well below it. Unfortunately, mileage takes it toll on all of the parts. Generally, the valves, guides, springs and seats in a cylinder head can be machined and re-used, saving you money. However, if a valve is burnt, it may be wise to replace all of the valves, since they were all operating in the same environment. The same goes for any other component on the cylinder head. Think of it as an insurance policy against future problems related to that component.

Unfortunately, the only way to find out which components need replacing, is to disassemble and carefully check each piece. After the cylinder head(s) are disassembled, thoroughly clean all of the components.

DISASSEMBLY

Before disassembling the cylinder head, you may want to fabricate some containers to hold the various parts, as some of them can be quite small (such as keepers) and easily lost. Also keeping yourself and the components

organized will aid in assembly and reduce confusion. Where possible, try to maintain a components original location; this is especially important if there is not going to be any machine work performed on the components.

1. If you haven't already removed the rocker arms and/or shafts, do so now.
2. Position the head so that the springs are easily accessed.
3. Use a valve spring compressor tool, and relieve spring tension from the retainer.

➡️**Due to engine varnish, the retainer may stick to the valve locks. A gentle tap with a hammer may help to break it loose.**

4. Remove the valve locks from the valve tip and/or retainer. A small magnet may help in removing the locks.
5. Lift the valve spring, tool and all, off of the valve stem.
6. If equipped, remove the valve seal. If the seal is difficult to remove with the valve in place, try removing the valve first, then the seal. Follow the steps below for valve removal.
7. Position the head to allow access for withdrawing the valve.

➡️**Cylinder heads that have seen a lot of miles and/or abuse may have mushroomed the valve lock grove and/or tip, causing difficulty in removal of the valve. If this has happened, use a metal file to carefully remove the high spots around the lock grooves and/or tip. Only file it enough to allow removal.**

TCCS3137

When removing an OHV valve spring, use a compressor tool to relieve the tension from the retainer

TCCS3138

A small magnet will help in removal of the valve locks

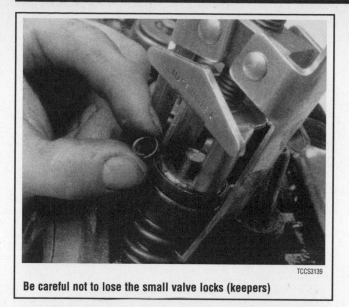

Be careful not to lose the small valve locks (keepers)

Remove the valve seal from the valve stem—O-ring type seal shown

Removing an umbrella/positive type seal

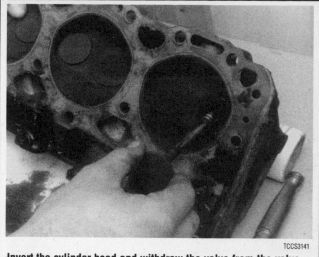

Invert the cylinder head and withdraw the valve from the valve guide bore

8. Remove the valve from the cylinder head.

9. If equipped, remove the valve spring shim. A small magnetic tool or screwdriver will aid in removal.

10. Repeat Steps 3 though 9 until all of the valves have been removed.

INSPECTION

Now that all of the cylinder head components are clean, it's time to inspect them for wear and/or damage. To accurately inspect them, you will need some specialized tools:

- A 0–1 inch micrometer for the valves
- A dial indicator or inside diameter gauge for the valve guides
- A spring pressure test gauge

If you do not have access to the proper tools, you may want to bring the components to a shop that does.

Valves

The first thing to inspect are the valve heads. Look closely at the head, margin and face for any cracks, excessive wear or burning. The margin is the best place to look for burning. It should have a squared edge with an even width all around the diameter. When a valve burns, the margin will look melted and the edges rounded. Also inspect the valve head for any signs of tulipping. This will show as a lifting of the edges or dishing in the center of the head and will usually not occur to all of the valves. All of the heads should look the same, any that seem dished more than others are probably bad. Next, inspect the valve lock grooves and valve tips. Check for any burrs around the lock grooves, especially if you had to file them to remove the valve. Valve tips should appear flat, although slight rounding with high mileage engines is normal. Slightly worn valve tips will need to be machined flat. Last, measure the valve stem diameter with the micrometer. Measure the area that rides within the guide, especially towards the tip where most of the wear occurs. Take several measurements along its length and compare them to each other. Wear should be even along the length with little to no taper. If no minimum diameter is given in the specifications, then the stem should not read more than 0.001 in. (0.025mm) below the specification. Any valves that fail these inspections should be replaced.

Springs, Retainers and Valve Locks

The first thing to check is the most obvious, broken springs. Next check the free length and squareness of each spring. If applicable, insure to distinguish between intake and exhaust springs. Use a ruler and/or carpenters square to measure the length. A carpenters square should be used to check the springs for squareness. If a spring pressure test gauge is available, check each springs rating and compare to the specifications chart. Check

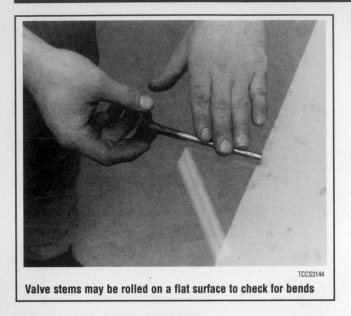

Valve stems may be rolled on a flat surface to check for bends

TCCS3144

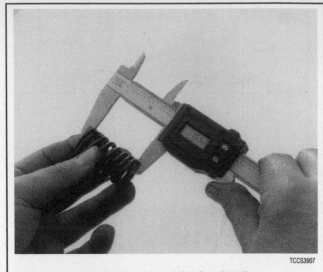

Use a caliper to check the valve spring free-length

TCCS3907

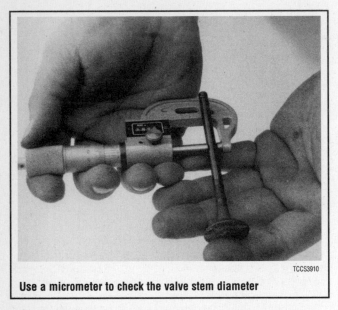

Use a micrometer to check the valve stem diameter

TCCS3910

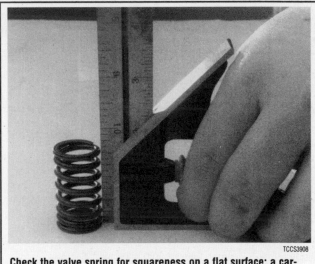

Check the valve spring for squareness on a flat surface; a carpenter's square can be used

TCCS3908

the readings against the specifications given. Any springs that fail these inspections should be replaced.

The spring retainers rarely need replacing, however they should still be checked as a precaution. Inspect the spring mating surface and the valve lock retention area for any signs of excessive wear. Also check for any signs of cracking. Replace any retainers that are questionable.

Valve locks should be inspected for excessive wear on the outside contact area as well as on the inner notched surface. Any locks which appear worn or broken and its respective valve should be replaced.

Cylinder Head

There are several things to check on the cylinder head: valve guides, seats, cylinder head surface flatness, cracks and physical damage.

VALVE GUIDES

Now that you know the valves are good, you can use them to check the guides, although a new valve, if available, is preferred. Before you measure anything, look at the guides carefully and inspect them for any cracks, chips or breakage. Also if the guide is a removable style (as in most aluminum heads), check them for any looseness or evidence of movement. All of the guides should appear to be at the same height from the spring seat. If

any seem lower (or higher) from another, the guide has moved. Mount a dial indicator onto the spring side of the cylinder head. Lightly oil the valve stem and insert it into the cylinder head. Position the dial indicator against the valve stem near the tip and zero the gauge. Grasp the valve stem and wiggle towards and away from the dial indicator and observe the readings. Mount the dial indicator 90 degrees from the initial point and zero the gauge and again take a reading. Compare the two readings for a out of round condition. Check the readings against the specifications given. An Inside Diameter (I.D.) gauge designed for valve guides will give you an accurate valve guide bore measurement. If the I.D. gauge is used, compare the readings with the specifications given. Any guides that fail these inspections should be replaced or machined.

VALVE SEATS

A visual inspection of the valve seats should show a slightly worn and pitted surface where the valve face contacts the seat. Inspect the seat carefully for severe pitting or cracks. Also, a seat that is badly worn will be recessed into the cylinder head. A severely worn or recessed seat may need to be replaced. All cracked seats must be replaced. A seat concentricity gauge, if available, should be used to check the seat run-out. If run-out exceeds specifications the seat must be machined (if no specification is given use 0.002 in. or 0.051mm).

A dial gauge may be used to check valve stem-to-guide clearance; read the gauge while moving the valve stem

TCCS3142

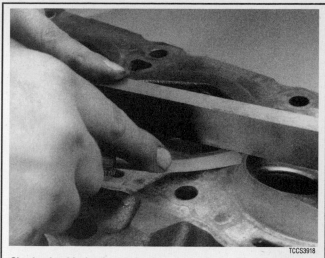

Checks should also be made along both diagonals of the head surface

TCCS3918

CYLINDER HEAD SURFACE FLATNESS

After you have cleaned the gasket surface of the cylinder head of any old gasket material, check the head for flatness.

Place a straightedge across the gasket surface. Using feeler gauges, determine the clearance at the center of the straightedge and across the cylinder head at several points. Check along the centerline and diagonally on the head surface. If the warpage exceeds 0.003 in. (0.076mm) within a 6.0 in. (15.2cm) span, or 0.006 in. (0.152mm) over the total length of the head, the cylinder head must be resurfaced. After resurfacing the heads of a V-type engine, the intake manifold flange surface should be checked, and if necessary, milled proportionally to allow for the change in its mounting position.

CRACKS AND PHYSICAL DAMAGE

Generally, cracks are limited to the combustion chamber, however, it is not uncommon for the head to crack in a spark plug hole, port, outside of the head or in the valve spring/rocker arm area. The first area to inspect is always the hottest: the exhaust seat/port area.

A visual inspection should be performed, but just because you don't see a crack does not mean it is not there. Some more reliable methods for inspecting for cracks include Magnaflux®, a magnetic process or Zyglo®, a dye penetrant. Magnaflux® is used only on ferrous metal (cast iron) heads. Zyglo® uses a spray on fluorescent mixture along with a black light to

reveal the cracks. It is strongly recommended to have your cylinder head checked professionally for cracks, especially if the engine was known to have overheated and/or leaked or consumed coolant. Contact a local shop for availability and pricing of these services.

Physical damage is usually very evident. For example, a broken mounting ear from dropping the head or a bent or broken stud and/or bolt. All of these defects should be fixed or, if unrepairable, the head should be replaced.

REFINISHING & REPAIRING

Many of the procedures given for refinishing and repairing the cylinder head components must be performed by a machine shop. Certain steps, if the inspected part is not worn, can be performed yourself inexpensively. However, you spent a lot of time and effort so far, why risk trying to save a couple bucks if you might have to do it all over again?

Valves

Any valves that were not replaced should be refaced and the tips ground flat. Unless you have access to a valve grinding machine, this should be done by a machine shop. If the valves are in extremely good condition, as well as the valve seats and guides, they may be lapped in without performing machine work.

It is a recommended practice to lap the valves even after machine work has been performed and/or new valves have been purchased. This insures a positive seal between the valve and seat.

LAPPING THE VALVES

➡Before lapping the valves to the seats, read the rest of the cylinder head section to insure that any related parts are in acceptable enough condition to continue.

➡Before any valve seat machining and/or lapping can be performed, the guides must be within factory recommended specifications.

1. Invert the cylinder head.
2. Lightly lubricate the valve stems and insert them into the cylinder head in their numbered order.
3. Raise the valve from the seat and apply a small amount of fine lapping compound to the seat.
4. Moisten the suction head of a hand-lapping tool and attach it to the head of the valve.
5. Rotate the tool between the palms of both hands, changing the position of the valve on the valve seat and lifting the tool often to prevent grooving.
6. Lap the valve until a smooth, polished circle is evident on the valve and seat.
7. Remove the tool and the valve. Wipe away all traces of the grinding compound and store the valve to maintain its lapped location.

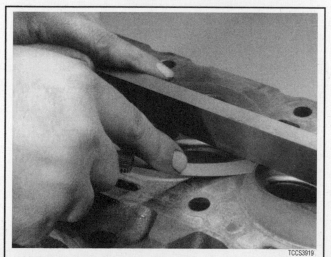

Check the head for flatness across the center of the head surface using a straightedge and feeler gauge

TCCS3919

Do not get the valves out of order after they have been lapped. They must be put back with the same valve seat they were lapped with.

Springs, Retainers and Valve Locks

There is no repair or refinishing possible with the springs, retainers and valve locks. If they are found to be worn or defective, they must be replaced with new (or known good) parts.

Cylinder Head

Most refinishing procedures dealing with the cylinder head must be performed by a machine shop. Read the sections below and review your inspection data to determine whether or not machining is necessary.

VALVE GUIDE

➤**If any machining or replacements are made to the valve guides, the seats must be machined.**

Unless the valve guides need machining or replacing, the only service to perform is to thoroughly clean them of any dirt or oil residue.

There are only two types of valve guides used on automobile engines: the replaceable-type (all aluminum heads) and the cast-in integral-type (most cast iron heads). There are four recommended methods for repairing worn guides.

* Knurling
* Inserts
* Reaming oversize
* Replacing

Knurling is a process in which metal is displaced and raised, thereby reducing clearance, giving a true center, and providing oil control. It is the least expensive way of repairing the valve guides. However, it is not necessarily the best, and in some cases, a knurled valve guide will not stand up for more than a short time. It requires a special knurlizer and precision reaming tools to obtain proper clearances. It would not be cost effective to purchase these tools, unless you plan on rebuilding several of the same cylinder head.

Installing a guide insert involves machining the guide to accept a bronze insert. One style is the coil-type which is installed into a threaded guide. Another is the thin-walled insert where the guide is reamed oversize to accept a split-sleeve insert. After the insert is installed, a special tool is then run through the guide to expand the insert, locking it to the guide. The insert is then reamed to the standard size for proper valve clearance.

Reaming for oversize valves restores normal clearances and provides a true valve seat. Most cast-in type guides can be reamed to accept an valve with an oversize stem. The cost factor for this can become quite high as you will need to purchase the reamer and new, oversize stem valves for all guides which were reamed. Oversizes are generally 0.003 to 0.030 in. (0.076 to 0.762mm), with 0.015 in. (0.381mm) being the most common.

To replace cast-in type valve guides, they must be drilled out, then reamed to accept replacement guides. This must be done on a fixture which will allow centering and leveling off of the original valve seat or guide, otherwise a serious guide-to-seat misalignment may occur making it impossible to properly machine the seat.

Replaceable-type guides are pressed into the cylinder head. A hammer and a stepped drift or punch may be used to install and remove the guides. Before removing the guides, measure the protrusion on the spring side of the head and record it for installation. Use the stepped drift to hammer out the old guide from the combustion chamber side of the head. When installing, determine whether or not the guide also seals a water jacket in the head, and if it does, use the recommended sealing agent. If there is no water jacket, grease the valve guide and its bore. Use the stepped drift, and hammer the new guide into the cylinder head from the spring side of the cylinder head. A stack of washers the same thickness as the measured protrusion may help the installation process.

VALVE SEATS

➤**Before any valve seat machining can be performed, the guides must be within factory recommended specifications.**

➤**If any machining or replacements were made to the valve guides, the seats must be machined.**

If the seats are in good condition, the valves can be lapped to the seats, and the cylinder head assembled. See the valves section for instructions on lapping.

If the valve seats are worn, cracked or damaged, they must be serviced by a machine shop. The valve seat must be perfectly centered to the valve guide, which requires very accurate machining.

CYLINDER HEAD SURFACE

If the cylinder head is warped, it must be machined flat. If the warpage is extremely severe, the head may need to be replaced. In some instances, it may be possible to straighten a warped head enough to allow machining. In either case, contact a professional machine shop for service.

CRACKS AND PHYSICAL DAMAGE

Certain cracks can be repaired in both cast iron and aluminum heads. For cast iron, a tapered threaded insert is installed along the length of the crack. Aluminum can also use the tapered inserts, however welding is the preferred method. Some physical damage can be repaired through brazing or welding. Contact a machine shop to get expert advice for your particular dilemma.

ASSEMBLY

The first step for any assembly job is to have a clean area in which to work. Next, thoroughly clean all of the parts and components that are to be assembled. Finally, place all of the components onto a suitable work space and, if necessary, arrange the parts to their respective positions.

1. Lightly lubricate the valve stems and insert all of the valves into the cylinder head. If possible, maintain their original locations.
2. If equipped, install any valve spring shims which were removed.
3. If equipped, install the new valve seals, keeping the following in mind:
* If the valve seal presses over the guide, lightly lubricate the outer guide surfaces.
* If the seal is an O-ring type, it is installed just after compressing the spring but before the valve locks.
4. Place the valve spring and retainer over the stem.
5. Position the spring compressor tool and compress the spring.
6. Assemble the valve locks to the stem.
7. Relieve the spring pressure slowly and insure that neither valve lock becomes dislodged by the retainer.
8. Remove the spring compressor tool.
9. Repeat Steps 2 through 8 until all of the springs have been installed.

Engine Block

GENERAL INFORMATION

A thorough overhaul or rebuild of an engine block would include replacing the pistons, rings, bearings, timing belt/chain assembly and oil pump. For OHV engines also include a new camshaft and lifters. The block would then have the cylinders bored and honed oversize (or if using removable cylinder sleeves, new sleeves installed) and the crankshaft would be cut undersize to provide new wearing surfaces and perfect clearances. However, your particular engine may not have everything worn out. What if only the piston rings have worn out and the clearances on everything else are still within factory specifications? Well, you could just replace the rings and put it back together, but this would be a very rare example. Chances are, if one component in your engine is worn, other components are sure to follow, and soon. At the very least, you should always replace the rings, bearings and oil pump. This is what is commonly called a "freshen up".

Cylinder Ridge Removal

Because the top piston ring does not travel to the very top of the cylinder, a ridge is built up between the end of the travel and the top of the cylinder bore.

Pushing the piston and connecting rod assembly past the ridge can be difficult, and damage to the piston ring lands could occur. If the ridge is not removed before installing a new piston or not removed at all, piston ring breakage and piston damage may occur.

➡**It is always recommended that you remove any cylinder ridges before removing the piston and connecting rod assemblies. If you know that new pistons are going to be installed and the engine block will be bored oversize, you may be able to forego this step. However, some ridges may actually prevent the assemblies from being removed, necessitating its removal.**

There are several different types of ridge reamers on the market, none of which are inexpensive. Unless a great deal of engine rebuilding is anticipated, borrow or rent a reamer.

1. Turn the crankshaft until the piston is at the bottom of its travel.
2. Cover the head of the piston with a rag.
3. Follow the tool manufacturers instructions and cut away the ridge, exercising extreme care to avoid cutting too deeply.
4. Remove the ridge reamer, the rag and as many of the cuttings as possible. Continue until all of the cylinder ridges have been removed.

DISASSEMBLY

The engine disassembly instructions following assume that you have the engine mounted on an engine stand. If not, it is easiest to disassemble the engine on a bench or the floor with it resting on the bellhousing or transmission mounting surface. You must be able to access the connecting rod fasteners and turn the crankshaft during disassembly. Also, all engine covers (timing, front, side, oil pan, whatever) should have already been removed. Engines which are seized or locked up may not be able to be completely disassembled, and a core (salvage yard) engine should be purchased.

Pushrod Engines

If not done during the cylinder head removal, remove the pushrods and lifters, keeping them in order for assembly. Remove the timing gears and/or timing chain assembly, then remove the oil pump drive assembly and withdraw the camshaft from the engine block. Remove the oil pick-up and pump assembly. If equipped, remove any balance or auxiliary shafts. If necessary, remove the cylinder ridge from the top of the bore. See the cylinder ridge removal procedure earlier in this section.

Rotate the engine over so that the crankshaft is exposed. Use a number punch or scribe and mark each connecting rod with its respective cylinder number. The cylinder closest to the front of the engine is always number 1. However, depending on the engine placement, the front of the engine could either be the flywheel or damper/pulley end. Generally the front of the engine faces the front of the vehicle. Use a number punch or scribe and also mark the main bearing caps from front to rear with the front most cap being number 1 (if there are five caps, mark them 1 through 5, front to rear).

✳✳ WARNING

Take special care when pushing the connecting rod up from the crankshaft because the sharp threads of the rod bolts/studs will score the crankshaft journal. Insure that special plastic caps are installed over them, or cut two pieces of rubber hose to do the same.

Again, rotate the engine, this time to position the number one cylinder bore (head surface) up. Turn the crankshaft until the number one piston is at the bottom of its travel, this should allow the maximum access to its connecting rod. Remove the number one connecting rods fasteners and cap and place two lengths of rubber hose over the rod bolts/studs to protect the crankshaft from damage. Using a sturdy wooden dowel and a ham-

TCCS3803

Place rubber hose over the connecting rod studs to protect the crankshaft and cylinder bores from damage

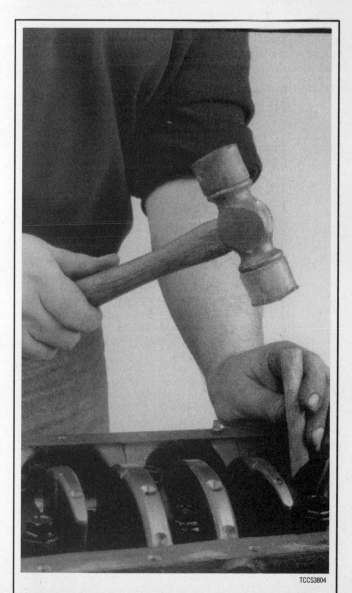

TCCS3804

Carefully tap the piston out of the bore using a wooden dowel

mer, push the connecting rod up about 1 in. (25mm) from the crankshaft and remove the upper bearing insert. Continue pushing or tapping the connecting rod up until the piston rings are out of the cylinder bore. Remove the piston and rod by hand, put the upper half of the bearing insert back into the rod, install the cap with its bearing insert installed, and hand-tighten the cap fasteners. If the parts are kept in order in this manner, they will not get lost and you will be able to tell which bearings came form what cylinder if any problems are discovered and diagnosis is necessary. Remove all the other piston assemblies in the same manner. On V-style engines, remove all of the pistons from one bank, then reposition the engine with the other cylinder bank head surface up, and remove that banks piston assemblies.

The only remaining component in the engine block should now be the crankshaft. Loosen the main bearing caps evenly until the fasteners can be turned by hand, then remove them and the caps. Remove the crankshaft from the engine block. Thoroughly clean all of the components.

INSPECTION

Now that the engine block and all of its components are clean, it's time to inspect them for wear and/or damage. To accurately inspect them, you will need some specialized tools:

- Two or three separate micrometers to measure the pistons and crankshaft journals
- A dial indicator
- Telescoping gauges for the cylinder bores
- A rod alignment fixture to check for bent connecting rods

If you do not have access to the proper tools, you may want to bring the components to a shop that does.

Generally, you shouldn't expect cracks in the engine block or its components unless it was known to leak, consume or mix engine fluids, it was severely overheated, or there was evidence of bad bearings and/or crankshaft damage. A visual inspection should be performed on all of the components, but just because you don't see a crack does not mean it is not there. Some more reliable methods for inspecting for cracks include Magnaflux®, a magnetic process or Zyglo®, a dye penetrant. Magnaflux® is used only on ferrous metal (cast iron). Zyglo® uses a spray on fluorescent mixture along with a black light to reveal the cracks. It is strongly recommended to have your engine block checked professionally for cracks, especially if the engine was known to have overheated and/or leaked or consumed coolant. Contact a local shop for availability and pricing of these services.

Engine Block

ENGINE BLOCK BEARING ALIGNMENT

Remove the main bearing caps and, if still installed, the main bearing inserts. Inspect all of the main bearing saddles and caps for damage, burrs or high spots. If damage is found, and it is caused from a spun main bearing, the block will need to be align-bored or, if severe enough, replacement. Any burrs or high spots should be carefully removed with a metal file.

Place a straightedge on the bearing saddles, in the engine block, along the centerline of the crankshaft. If any clearance exists between the straightedge and the saddles, the block must be align-bored.

Align-boring consists of machining the main bearing saddles and caps by means of a flycutter that runs through the bearing saddles.

DECK FLATNESS

The top of the engine block where the cylinder head mounts is called the deck. Insure that the deck surface is clean of dirt, carbon deposits and old gasket material. Place a straightedge across the surface of the deck along its centerline and, using feeler gauges, check the clearance along several points. Repeat the checking procedure with the straightedge placed along both diagonals of the deck surface. If the reading exceeds 0.003 in. (0.076mm) within a 6.0 in. (15.2cm) span, or 0.006 in. (0.152mm) over the total length of the deck, it must be machined.

CYLINDER BORES

The cylinder bores house the pistons and are slightly larger than the pistons themselves. A common piston-to-bore clearance is 0.0015–0.0025 in. (0.0381mm–0.0635mm). Inspect and measure the cylinder bores. The bore should be checked for out-of-roundness, taper and size. The results of this inspection will determine whether the cylinder can be used in its existing size and condition, or a rebore to the next oversize is required (or in the case of removable sleeves, have replacements installed).

The amount of cylinder wall wear is always greater at the top of the cylinder than at the bottom. This wear is known as taper. Any cylinder that has a taper of 0.0012 in. (0.305mm) or more, must be rebored. Measurements are taken at a number of positions in each cylinder: at the top, middle and bottom and at two points at each position; that is, at a point 90 degrees from the crankshaft centerline, as well as a point parallel to the crankshaft centerline. The measurements are made with either a special dial indicator or a telescopic gauge and micrometer. If the necessary precision tools to check the bore are not available, take the block to a machine shop and have them mike it. Also if you don't have the tools to check the cylinder bores, chances are you will not have the necessary devices to check the pistons, connecting rods and crankshaft. Take these components with you and save yourself an extra trip.

For our procedures, we will use a telescopic gauge and a micrometer. You will need one of each, with a measuring range which covers your cylinder bore size.

1. Position the telescopic gauge in the cylinder bore, loosen the gauges lock and allow it to expand.

➡**Your first two readings will be at the top of the cylinder bore, then proceed to the middle and finally the bottom, making a total of six measurements.**

2. Hold the gauge square in the bore, 90 degrees from the crankshaft centerline, and gently tighten the lock. Tilt the gauge back to remove it from the bore.
3. Measure the gauge with the micrometer and record the reading.
4. Again, hold the gauge square in the bore, this time parallel to the crankshaft centerline, and gently tighten the lock. Again, you will tilt the gauge back to remove it from the bore.
5. Measure the gauge with the micrometer and record this reading. The difference between these two readings is the out-of-round measurement of the cylinder.
6. Repeat steps 1 through 5, each time going to the next lower position, until you reach the bottom of the cylinder. Then go to the next cylinder, and continue until all of the cylinders have been measured.

TCCS3209

Use a telescoping gauge to measure the cylinder bore diameter—take several readings within the same bore

The difference between these measurements will tell you all about the wear in your cylinders. The measurements which were taken 90 degrees from the crankshaft centerline will always reflect the most wear. That is because at this position is where the engine power presses the piston against the cylinder bore the hardest. This is known as thrust wear. Take your top, 90 degree measurement and compare it to your bottom, 90 degree measurement. The difference between them is the taper. When you measure your pistons, you will compare these readings to your piston sizes and determine piston-to-wall clearance.

Crankshaft

Inspect the crankshaft for visible signs of wear or damage. All of the journals should be perfectly round and smooth. Slight scores are normal for a used crankshaft, but you should hardly feel them with your fingernail. When measuring the crankshaft with a micrometer, you will take readings at the front and rear of each journal, then turn the micrometer 90 degrees and take two more readings, front and rear. The difference between the front-to-rear readings is the journal taper and the first-to-90 degree reading is the out-of-round measurement. Generally, there should be no taper or out-of-roundness found, however, up to 0.0005 in. (0.0127mm) for either can be overlooked. Also, the readings should fall within the factory specifications for journal diameters.

If the crankshaft journals fall within specifications, it is recommended that it be polished before being returned to service. Polishing the crankshaft insures that any minor burrs or high spots are smoothed, thereby reducing the chance of scoring the new bearings.

Pistons and Connecting Rods

PISTONS

The piston should be visually inspected for any signs of cracking or burning (caused by hot spots or detonation), and scuffing or excessive wear on the skirts. The wristpin attaches the piston to the connecting rod. The piston should move freely on the wrist pin, both sliding and pivoting. Grasp the connecting rod securely, or mount it in a vise, and try to rock the piston back and forth along the centerline of the wristpin. There should not be any excessive play evident between the piston and the pin. If there are C-clips retaining the pin in the piston then you have wrist pin bushings in the rods. There should not be any excessive play between the wrist pin and the rod bushing. Normal clearance for the wrist pin is approx. 0.001–0.002 in. (0.025mm–0.051mm).

Use a micrometer and measure the diameter of the piston, perpendicu-

Measure the piston's outer diameter, perpendicular to the wrist pin, with a micrometer

TCCS3210

lar to the wrist pin, on the skirt. Compare the reading to its original cylinder measurement obtained earlier. The difference between the two readings is the piston-to-wall clearance. If the clearance is within specifications, the piston may be used as is. If the piston is out of specification, but the bore is not, you will need a new piston. If both are out of specification, you will need the cylinder rebored and oversize pistons installed. Generally if two or more pistons/bores are out of specification, it is best to rebore the entire block and purchase a complete set of oversize pistons.

CONNECTING ROD

You should have the connecting rod checked for straightness at a machine shop. If the connecting rod is bent, it will unevenly wear the bearing and piston, as well as place greater stress on these components. Any bent or twisted connecting rods must be replaced. If the rods are straight and the wrist pin clearance is within specifications, then only the bearing end of the rod need be checked. Place the connecting rod into a vice, with the bearing inserts in place, install the cap to the rod and torque the fasteners to specifications. Use a telescoping gauge and carefully measure the inside diameter of the bearings. Compare this reading to the rods original crankshaft journal diameter measurement. The difference is the oil clearance. If the oil clearance is not within specifications, install new bearings in the rod and take another measurement. If the clearance is still out of specifications, and the crankshaft is not, the rod will need to be reconditioned by a machine shop.

➡**You can also use Plastigage® to check the bearing clearances. The assembling section has complete instructions on its use.**

Camshaft

Inspect the camshaft and lifters/followers as described earlier in this section.

Bearings

All of the engine bearings should be visually inspected for wear and/or damage. The bearing should look evenly worn all around with no deep scores or pits. If the bearing is severely worn, scored, pitted or heat blued, then the bearing, and the components that use it, should be brought to a machine shop for inspection. Full-circle bearings (used on most camshafts, auxiliary shafts, balance shafts, etc.) require specialized tools for removal and installation, and should be brought to a machine shop for service.

Oil Pump

➡**The oil pump is responsible for providing constant lubrication to the whole engine and so it is recommended that a new oil pump be installed when rebuilding the engine.**

Completely disassemble the oil pump and thoroughly clean all of the components. Inspect the oil pump gears and housing for wear and/or damage. Insure that the pressure relief valve operates properly and there is no binding or sticking due to varnish or debris. If all of the parts are in proper working condition, lubricate the gears and relief valve, and assemble the pump.

REFINISHING

Almost all engine block refinishing must be performed by a machine shop. If the cylinders are not to be rebored, then the cylinder glaze can be removed with a ball hone. When removing cylinder glaze with a ball hone, use a light or penetrating type oil to lubricate the hone. Do not allow the hone to run dry as this may cause excessive scoring of the cylinder bores and wear on the hone. If new pistons are required, they will need to be installed to the connecting rods. This should be performed by a machine shop as the pistons must be installed in the correct relationship to the rod or engine damage can occur.

Use a ball type cylinder hone to remove any glaze and provide a new surface for seating the piston rings

Pistons and Connecting Rods

Only pistons with the wrist pin retained by C-clips are serviceable by the home-mechanic. Press fit pistons require special presses and/or heaters to remove/install the connecting rod and should only be performed by a machine shop.

All pistons will have a mark indicating the direction to the front of the engine and the must be installed into the engine in that manner. Usually it is a notch or arrow on the top of the piston, or it may be the letter F cast or stamped into the piston.

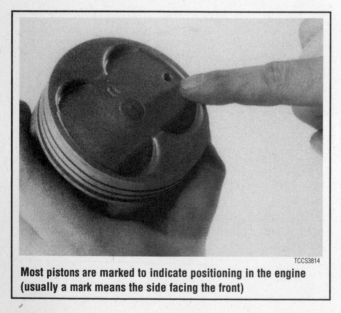

Most pistons are marked to indicate positioning in the engine (usually a mark means the side facing the front)

ASSEMBLY

Before you begin assembling the engine, first give yourself a clean, dirt free work area. Next, clean every engine component again. The key to a good assembly is cleanliness.

Mount the engine block into the engine stand and wash it one last time using water and detergent (dishwashing detergent works well). While washing it, scrub the cylinder bores with a soft bristle brush and thoroughly clean all of the oil passages. Completely dry the engine and spray the entire assembly down with an anti-rust solution such as WD-40® or similar product. Take a clean lint-free rag and wipe up any excess anti-rust solution from the bores,

bearing saddles, etc. Repeat the final cleaning process on the crankshaft. Replace any freeze or oil galley plugs which were removed during disassembly.

Crankshaft

1. Remove the main bearing inserts from the block and bearing caps.
2. If the crankshaft main bearing journals have been refinished to a definite undersize, install the correct undersize bearing. Be sure that the bearing inserts and bearing bores are clean. Foreign material under inserts will distort bearing and cause failure.
3. Place the upper main bearing inserts in bores with tang in slot.

➡**The oil holes in the bearing inserts must be aligned with the oil holes in the cylinder block.**

4. Install the lower main bearing inserts in bearing caps.
5. Clean the mating surfaces of block and rear main bearing cap.
6. Carefully lower the crankshaft into place. Be careful not to damage bearing surfaces.
7. Check the clearance of each main bearing by using the following procedure:

    a. Place a piece of Plastigage® or its equivalent, on bearing surface across full width of bearing cap and about ¼ in. off center.

    b. Install cap and tighten bolts to specifications. Do not turn crankshaft while Plastigage® is in place.

    c. Remove the cap. Using the supplied Plastigage® scale, check width of Plastigage® at widest point to get maximum clearance. Difference between readings is taper of journal.

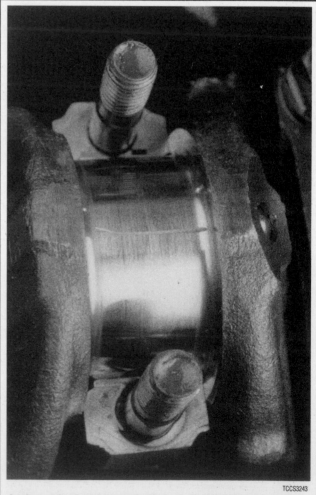

Apply a strip of gauging material to the bearing journal, then install and torque the cap

After the cap is removed again, use the scale supplied with the gauging material to check the clearance

TCCS3912

A dial gauge may be used to check crankshaft end-play

TCCS3805

Carefully pry the crankshaft back and forth while reading the dial gauge for end-play

TCCS3806

d. If clearance exceeds specified limits, try a 0.001 in. or 0.002 in. undersize bearing in combination with the standard bearing. Bearing clearance must be within specified limits. If standard and 0.002 in. undersize bearing does not bring clearance within desired limits, refinish crankshaft journal, then install undersize bearings.

8. After the bearings have been fitted, apply a light coat of engine oil to the journals and bearings. Install the rear main bearing cap. Install all bearing caps except the thrust bearing cap. Be sure that main bearing caps are installed in original locations. Tighten the bearing cap bolts to specifications.

9. Install the thrust bearing cap with bolts finger-tight.

10. Pry the crankshaft forward against the thrust surface of upper half of bearing.

11. Hold the crankshaft forward and pry the thrust bearing cap to the rear. This aligns the thrust surfaces of both halves of the bearing.

12. Retain the forward pressure on the crankshaft. Tighten the cap bolts to specifications.

13. Measure the crankshaft end-play as follows:

a. Mount a dial gauge to the engine block and position the tip of the gauge to read from the crankshaft end.

b. Carefully pry the crankshaft toward the rear of the engine and hold it there while you zero the gauge.

c. Carefully pry the crankshaft toward the front of the engine and read the gauge.

d. Confirm that the reading is within specifications. If not, install a new thrust bearing and repeat the procedure. If the reading is still out of specifications with a new bearing, have a machine shop inspect the thrust surfaces of the crankshaft, and if possible, repair it.

14. Rotate the crankshaft so as to position the first rod journal to the bottom of its stroke.

15. Install the rear main seal.

Pistons and Connecting Rods

1. Before installing the piston/connecting rod assembly, oil the pistons, piston rings and the cylinder walls with light engine oil. Install connecting rod bolt protectors or rubber hose onto the connecting rod bolts/studs. Also perform the following:

a. Select the proper ring set for the size cylinder bore.

b. Position the ring in the bore in which it is going to be used.

c. Push the ring down into the bore area where normal ring wear is not encountered.

d. Use the head of the piston to position the ring in the bore so that the ring is square with the cylinder wall. Use caution to avoid damage to the ring or cylinder bore.

e. Measure the gap between the ends of the ring with a feeler gauge. Ring gap in a worn cylinder is normally greater than specification. If the ring gap is greater than the specified limits, try an oversize ring set.

f. Check the ring side clearance of the compression rings with a feeler gauge inserted between the ring and its lower land according to specification. The gauge should slide freely around the entire ring circumference without binding. Any wear that occurs will form a step at the inner portion of the lower land. If the lower lands have high steps, the piston should be replaced.

2. Unless new pistons are installed, be sure to install the pistons in the cylinders from which they were removed. The numbers on the connecting rod and bearing cap must be on the same side when installed in the cylinder bore. If a connecting rod is ever transposed from one engine or cylinder to another, new bearings should be fitted and the connecting rod should be numbered to correspond with the new cylinder number. The notch on the piston head goes toward the front of the engine.

3. Install all of the rod bearing inserts into the rods and caps.

4. Install the rings to the pistons. Install the oil control ring first, then the second compression ring and finally the top compression ring. Use a piston ring expander tool to aid in installation and to help reduce the chance of breakage.

5. Make sure the ring gaps are properly spaced around the circumference of the piston. Fit a piston ring compressor around the piston and slide the piston and connecting rod assembly down into the cylinder bore, pushing

Checking the piston ring-to-ring groove side clearance using the ring and a feeler gauge

TCCS3923

The notch on the side of the bearing cap matches the tang on the bearing insert

TCCS3917

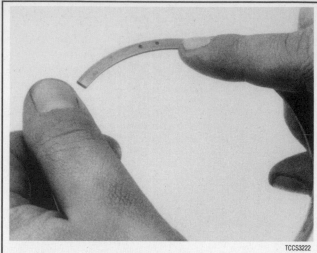

Most rings are marked to show which side of the ring should face up when installed to the piston

TCCS3222

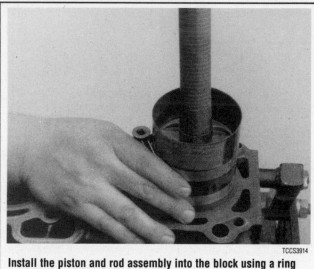

Install the piston and rod assembly into the block using a ring compressor and the handle of a hammer

TCCS3914

it in with the wooden hammer handle. Push the piston down until it is only slightly below the top of the cylinder bore. Guide the connecting rod onto the crankshaft bearing journal carefully, to avoid damaging the crankshaft.

6. Check the bearing clearance of all the rod bearings, fitting them to the crankshaft bearing journals. Follow the procedure in the crankshaft installation above.

7. After the bearings have been fitted, apply a light coating of assembly oil to the journals and bearings.

8. Turn the crankshaft until the appropriate bearing journal is at the bottom of its stroke, then push the piston assembly all the way down until the connecting rod bearing seats on the crankshaft journal. Be careful not to allow the bearing cap screws to strike the crankshaft bearing journals and damage them.

9. After the piston and connecting rod assemblies have been installed, check the connecting rod side clearance on each crankshaft journal.

10. Prime and install the oil pump and the oil pump intake tube.

11. Install the auxiliary/balance shaft(s)/assembly(ies).

12. Install the camshaft.

13. Install the lifters/followers into their bores.

14. Install the timing gears/chain assembly.

15. Install the cylinder head(s) using new gaskets.

16. Assemble the rest of the valve train (pushrods and rocker arms and/or shafts).

Engine Start-up and Break-in

STARTING THE ENGINE

Now that the engine is installed and every wire and hose is properly connected, go back and double check that all coolant and vacuum hoses are connected. Check that you oil drain plug is installed and properly tightened. If not already done, install a new oil filter onto the engine. Fill the crankcase with the proper amount and grade of engine oil. Fill the cooling system with a 50/50 mixture of coolant/water.

1. Connect the vehicle battery.
2. Start the engine. Keep your eye on your oil pressure indicator; if it does not indicate oil pressure within 10 seconds of starting, turn the vehicle off.

✳✳ WARNING

Damage to the engine can result if it is allowed to run with no oil pressure. Check the engine oil level to make sure that it is full. Check for any leaks and if found, repair the leaks before continuing. If there is still no indication of oil pressure, you may need to prime the system.

3. Confirm that there are no fluid leaks (oil or other).
4. Allow the engine to reach normal operating temperature (the upper radiator hose will be hot to the touch).
5. If necessary, set the ignition timing.
6. Install any remaining components such as the air cleaner (if removed for ignition timing) or body panels which were removed.

BREAKING IT IN

Make the first miles on the new engine, easy ones. Vary the speed but do not accelerate hard. Most importantly, do not lug the engine, and avoid sustained high speeds until at least 100 miles. Check the engine oil and coolant levels frequently. Expect the engine to use a little oil until the rings seat. Change the oil and filter at 500 miles, 1500 miles, then every 3000 miles past that.

KEEP IT MAINTAINED

Now that you have just gone through all of that hard work, keep yourself from doing it all over again by thoroughly maintaining it. Not that you may not have maintained it before, heck you could have had one to two hundred thousand miles on it before doing this. However, you may have bought the vehicle used, and the previous owner did not keep up on maintenance. Which is why you just went through all of that hard work. See?

TORQUE SPECIFICATIONS

Components	Ft. Lbs.	Nm
Engine Assembly		
Engine-to-transaxle	30–44 ft. lbs.	40–60 Nm
Torque converter nuts	20–34 ft. lbs.	27–46 Nm
Subframe-to-body bolts	57–76 ft. lbs.	77–103 Nm
Steering coupling pinch bolt	25–34 ft. lbs.	34–46 Nm
Dual converter Y-pipe-to-exhaust manifold	25–34 ft. lbs.	34–46 Nm
Flex pipe retaining bolts	25–34 ft. lbs.	34–46 Nm
Accelerator cable bracket retaining bolts	71–106 inch lbs.	8–12 Nm
Front engine support insulator-to-subframe		
3.8L Engine	50–68 ft. lbs.	68–92 Nm
3.0L Engine	65–87 ft. lbs.	88–119 Nm
Transmission insulator-to-subframe	65–87 ft. lbs.	00–110 Nm
Rear engine and transaxle support insulator-to-subframe	56–75 ft. lbs.	76–103 Nm
Valve Cover		
3.0L Engine	96–120 inch lbs.	10–14 Nm
3.8L Engine	71–97 inch lbs.	8–11 Nm
Rocker Arm		
3.0L Engine		
First step	60–132 inch lbs.	7–15Nm
Second step	20–28 ft. lbs.	26–38 Nm
3.8L engine		
First step	44 inch lbs.	5 Nm
Second step	20–28 ft. lbs.	26–38 Nm
Thermostat		
3.0L Engine	96–120 inch lbs.	10–14 Nm
3.8L engine	72–96 inch lbs.	8–10 Nm
Intake Manifold		
3.0L Engine		
First step	15–22 ft. lbs.	20–30 Nm
Second step	20–23 ft. lbs.	26–32 Nm
3.8L Engine		
Upper	71–106 inch lbs.	8–12 Nm
Lower	71–106 inch lbs.	8–12 Nm
Exhaust Manifold		
3.0L Engine	15–22 ft. lbs.	20–30 Nm
3.8L Engine	15–22 ft. lbs.	20–30 Nm
Radiator	45–61 inch lbs.	5–7 Nm
Cooling Fan		
Cooling fan motor	89–106 inch lbs.	10–12 Nm
Fan shroud	71–106 inch lbs.	8–12 Nm
Water Pump		
3.0L Engine		
Numbers 1–10	15–22 ft. lbs.	20–30 Nm
Numbers 11–15	71–106 in. lbs	8–12 Nm
3.8L Engine		
Bolts	15–22 ft. lbs.	20–30 Nm
Nuts	71–106 inch lbs.	8–12 Nm
Cylinder Head		
3.0L Engine		
First step	37 ft. lbs.	50 Nm
Second step	68 ft. lbs.	92 Nm

89693C58

TORQUE SPECIFICATIONS

Components	Ft. Lbs.	Nm
Cylinder Head		
3.8L Engine		
First step	15 ft. lbs.	20 Nm
Second step	29 ft. lbs.	40 Nm
Third step	37 ft. lbs.	50 Nm
Fourth step	Loosen the cylinder head bolt 2–3 turns	
Fifth step (Long Bolts)	29–37 ft. lbs. plus 175–185 °	40–50 Nm plus 175–185 °
Sixth (Short Bolts)	15–22 ft. lbs. plus 175–185 °	20–30 Nm plus 175–185 °
Rocker arms		
3.0L Engine		
First step	62–132 inch lbs.	7–15 Nm
Second step	20–28 ft. lbs.	26–38 Nm
3.8L Engine		
First step	44 inch lbs.	5 Nm
Second step	22–29 ft. lbs.	30–40 Nm
Oil Pan bolts	80–106 inch lbs.	9–12 Nm
Oil Pump		
3.0L Engine	30–40 ft. lbs.	40–55 Nm
3.8L Engine		
Four large engine front cover retaining bolts	17–23 ft. lbs.	23–32 Nm
Remaining retaining bolts	71–97 ft. lbs.	8–11 Nm
Damper		
3.0L Engine	93–121 ft. lbs	126–164 Nm
3.8L Engine	103–132 ft. lbs.	140–180 Nm
Crankshaft pulley		
3.0L Engine	30–44 ft. lbs.	40–60 Nm
3.8L Engine	19–28 ft. lbs.	26–38 Nm
Front Cover		
3.0L Engine		
Bolts 1-10	15–22 ft. lbs.	20–30 Nm
Bolts 11–15	71–106 inch lbs.	8–12 Nm
3.8L Engine		
Bolts	15–22 ft. lbs.	20–30 Nm
Nuts	71–106 inch lbs.	8–12 Nm
Camshaft Sprocket		
3.0L Engine	37–51 ft. lbs.	50–70 Nm
3.8L Engine	29–37 ft. lbs.	40–50 Nm
Thrust plate	71–124 inch lbs.	8–14 Nm
Balance Shaft	6–10 ft. lbs.	8–14 Nm
Flywheel bolts	54–64 ft. lbs.	73–87 Nm

89693C59

3.0L (2966cc) ENGINE SPECIFICATIONS

Description	English Specifications	Metric Specifications
SPECIFICATIONS		
Displacement	3.0L	
Number of Cylinders	6	
Bore and Stroke		
Bore	3.50 in.	89.00mm
Stroke	3.14 in.	80.00mm
Firing Order	1-4-2-5-3-6	
Oil Pressure (Hot 2500 rpm)	40-60 psi	276-414 kPa
CYLINDER HEAD AND VALVE TRAIN		
Combustion Chamber Volume	2.874 cu. in.	47.1-50.1 cm3
Valve Guide Bore Diameter		
Intake and Exhaust	9.3433-0.3443 in.	8.720-8.745mm
Valve Seats		
Width-Intake and Exhaust	0.06-0.08 in.	1.5-2.0mm
Angle	45 degrees	
Run-out (T.I.R.)	0.003 in.	0.976mm
Bore Diameter (Insert Counterbore Diameter)	1.8542 in. max.	47.097mm
Intake	1.8532 in. min.	47.072mm
Exhaust	1.5645 in. max.	39.730mm
Gasket Surface Flatness	0.003 in. per 6.00 in.	0.08mm per 152.0mm
Valve Stem to Guide Clearance		
Intake	0.001-0.0027 in.	0.026-0.068mm
Exhaust	0.0015-0.0032 in.	0.038-0.081mm
Valve Head Diameter		
Intake	1.57 in.	40.0mm
Exhaust	1.30 in.	33.0mm
Valve Face Run-out Limit	0.002 in.	0.05mm
Valve Face Angle	44 degrees	
Valve Stem Diameter		
Standard		
Intake	0.3126-0.3134 in.	7.940-7.960mm
Exhaust	0.3121-0.3129 in.	7.928-7.948mm
Oversize		
Intake	0.3276-0.3283 in.	8.320-8.340mm
Exahust	0.3271-0.3279 in.	8.308-8.328mm
Oversize		
Intake	0.3425-0.3433 in.	8.700-8.720mm
Exhaust	0.3420-0.3428 in.	90.688-8.708mm
Valve Springs		
Compression Pressure (pressure @ spec.length)		
Valve Open to maximum Lift	180 Lbs@1.16 in.	800.6 N@29.5mm
Valve Closed	65 Lb@1.58 in.	288.1 N@40.1mm
Free Length (Approximate)	1.84 in.	46.7mm
Installed Spring Height	1650-1.736 in.	41.98-44.17mm
Service Limit	10% Force Loss @ Specified Height	
Rocker Arm Ratio	1.61	
Valve Tappet, Hydraulic		
Diameter (Std.)	0.874 in.	22.206mm
Clearance to Bore	0.0007-0.0027 in.	0.018-0.069mm
Service Limit	0.005 in.	0.127mm
Hydraulic Leakdown Rate	①	
Collapsed Tappet Gap		
Intake	0.088-0.189 in.	2.23-4.77mm
Exhaust	0.088-0.189 in.	2.23-4.77mm

3.0L (2966cc) ENGINE SPECIFICATIONS

Camshaft Bore inside Diameter		
No. 1	2.1531-2.1541 in.	54.688-54.713mm
No. 2	2.1334-2.1344 in.	54.188-54.213mm
No. 3	2.1334-2.1344 in	54.188-54.213mm
No. 4	2.1531-2.1541 in.	54.688-54.713mm
① 20-200 seconds to leakdown 3.18mm (0.125 in. with 225 Newtons (50 pounds) load and tappet filled with leak-down fluid.		
CAMSHAFT		
Theoretical Valve Life @ Zero Lash		
Intake	0.419 in.	10.65mm
Exhaust	0.419 in.	10.65mm
End-Play	0.007 in.	0.003mm
Journal to Bearing Clearance	0.001-0.003 in.	0.025-0.076mm
Journal Diameter	2.0074-2.0084 in.	50.987-51.013mm
Cam Bearing I.D.	2.0094-2.0104 in.	51.038-51.063mm
Run-out Limit	0.002 in.	0.05mm
Out-of-Round-Limit	0.001 in.	0.025mm
CYLINDER BLOCK		
Head Gasket Surface Flatness	0.003 in. per 6.00 in.	0.08mm per 152.0mm
Head Gasket Surface Finish (RMS)	1.0-3.3 Micrometers	
Cylinder Bore		
Diameter	3.504 in.	89.00mm
Surface Finish (RMS)	0.45-0.96 Micrometers	
Out-of-Round Limit	0.001 in.	0.025mm
Out-of-Round Service Limit	0.002 in.	0.050mm
Taper Service Limit	0.002 in.	0.050mm
Main. Bearing Bore Diameter	2.713 in.	68.905mm
CRANKSHAFT AND FLYWHEEL		
Main. Bearing Journal Diameter	2.5190-2.5198 in.	63.983-64.003mm
Out-of-Round Limit	0.0003 in.	0.008mm
Taper Limit	0.0005 in. Total	0.06mm
	0.0003 in. per inch	0.013mm per 25mm
Journal Run-out Limit	0.002 in.	0.05mm
Surface Finish (RMS)	0.25 Micrometers	
Thrust Bearing Journal Length	1.0148-1.067 in.	25.775-25.825mm
Connecting Rod Journal		
Diameter	2.1253-2.1261 in.	53.983-54.003mm
Out-of-Round Limit (max)	0.0003 in.	0.006mm
Out-of-Round Limit (Total)	0.0006 in.	0.015mm
Taper Limit	0.0003 in. per inch	0.008mm per 25mm
Surface Limit (RMS)	0.25 Micrometers	
Main. Bearing Thrust Face		
Surface Finish (RMS)	0.4 Micrometers	
Run-out Limit	0.001 in.	0.025mm
Flywheel Ring Gear Lateral Run-out (T.I.R.) Automatic Transmission	0.07 in.	1.778mm
Crankshaft End-Play	0.004-0.008 in.	0.10-0.20mm
Connecting Rod Bearings		
Clearance to Crankshaft		
Desired	0.001-0.0015 in.	0.025-0.035mm
Allowable	0.00086-0.0027in.	0.020-0.066mm
Bearing Wall Thickness Std	0.0612-0.0618 in.	1.557-1.570mm
Main. Bearings		
Clearance to Crankshaft		
Desired	0.001-0.0014 in.	0.25-0.035mm
Allowable	0.0005-0.0023 in.	0.020-0.066mm
Bearing Wall Thickness	0.0962-0.0976 in.	2.444-2.481mm

89693C61

3.0L (2966cc) ENGINE SPECIFICATIONS

CONNECTING ROD		
Piston Pin. Bore Diameter	0.9096-0.9112 in.	23.105-23.145mm
Crankshaft Bearing Bore Diameter	2.250-2.251 in.	57.15-57.17mm
Length (Center-to-Center)	5.530-5.533 in.	140.46-140.54mm
Alignment (Bore-to-Bore max. Diff.)		
Twist	0.003 per in.	0.075 per 25mm
Bend	0.0016 per in.	0.04 per 25mm
Side Clearance (Assembled to Crank)		
Standard	0.006-0.014 in.	0.15-0.35mm
Service Limit	0.014 in. max.	0.36mm max.
PISTON		
Diameter		
Coded Red	3.5024-3.5031 in.	88.962-88.978mm
Coded Blue	3.5035-3.5041 in.	88.988-89.004mm
Coded Yellow	3.5045-3.5051 in.	89.014-89.030mm
Piston-to-Bore Clearance	0.0012-0.0022 in.	0 030-0.056mm
Service Limit	0.0031 in. max.	0.081mm
Ring Groove Width		
Compression (Top)	0.0602-0.0612 in.	1.530-1.555mm
Compression (Bottom)	0.0602-0.0612 in.	1.530-1.555mm
Oil	4.030-4.055mm	
Piston Pin		
Length	3.012-3.039 in.	76.5-77.2mm
Diameter	0.9119-0.9124 in.	23.162-23.175mm
Pin. to Piston Clearance	0.002-0.0005 in.	0.005-0.012mm
Pin. to Rod Clearance	Press Fit	
Piston Rings		
Ring Width		
Compression (Top)	0.0575-1.0587 in.	1.460-1.490mm
Compression (Bottom)	0.0575-0.0587 in.	1.460-1.490mm
Oil Ring	Snug Fit	
Ring Gap		
Compression (Top)	0.01-0.02 in.	0.25-0.50mm
Compression (Bottom)	0.01-0.02 in.	0.25-0.50mm
Oil Ring (Steel Rail)	0.010-0.049 in.	0.25-1.25mm
Side Clearance		
1st Ring	0.0016-0.0037 in.	0.040-0.095mm
2nd Ring	0.0016-0.0037 in.	0.040-0.095mm
LUBRICATION SYSTEM		
Oil Pump		
Relief Valve Spring Tension (Force @ Length)	10.1-9.1 lb.@1.11 in.	44.9-40.5 N@28.2mm
Relief Valve to Bore Clearance	0.0029-0.0017 in.	0.073-0.043mm
Oil Pump Gear Backlash	0.008-0.012 in.	0.02-0.03mm
Oil Pump Gear Radial Clearance (Idler and Driver)	0.0055-0.002 in.	0.125-0.050mm
Oil Pump Gear Height Clearance	0.0032-0.0003 in.	0.0825-0.010mm
Idler Shaft to Idler Gear Clearance	0.0027-0.0015 in.	0.069-0.039mm
Driver Shaft to Housing Clearance	0.0019-0.0005 in.	0.073-0.038mm
Oil Capacity	4.5 Quarts with Filter Change	4.25 Liters

89693C62

3.8L (3802cc) ENGINE SPECIFICATIONS

Description	English Specifications	Metric Specifications
SPECIFICATIONS		
Displacement	3.8L	
Number of Cylinders	6	
Bore	3.81 in.	96.8325mm
Stroke	3.39 in.	86.0mm
Firing Order	1-4-2-5-3-6	
Oil Pressure (Hot 2500 RPM)	40-60 psi	
CYLINDER HEAD AND VALVE TRAIN		
Combustion Chamber Volume (cc)	59.7-67.7	
Valve Guide Bore Diameter	0.3443-0.3433 in.	8.745-8.720mm
Valve Seats		
Width - Intake and Exhaust	0.06-0.08 in.	1.5-2.0mm
Angle	44.75 degrees	
Run-out (T.I.R.)	0.003 in.	0.076mm
Bore Diameter (Insert Counterbore Diameter)		
Intake	1.8532–1.8542 in.	47.072–47.097mm
Exhaust	1.5635–1.5645 in. Max.	39.714 –39.739mm
Gasket Surface Flatness	0.007 in.	0.018mm
Valve Stem To Guide Clearance		
Intake	0.001-0.0028 in.	0.026-0.071mm
Exhaust	0.0015-0.0033 in.	0.038-0.083mm
Valve Head Diameter		
Intake	1.78 in.	45.3mm
Exhaust	1.45 in.	37.1mm
Valve Face Run-out Limit	0.002 in.	0.05mm
Valve Face Angle	45.8 degrees	
Valve Stem Diameter (Std.)		
Intake	0.3423-0.3415 in.	8.694.8.674mm
Exhaust	0.3418-0.3410 in.	8.682-8.662mm
Valve Springs		
Compression Pressure (pressure@spec. length)		
Valve Open (Without Damper)	220 Lbs.@1.18 in.	979N@30.0mm
Valve Closed (Without Damper)	85 Lbs.@1.65 in.	378N@41.9mm
Free Length (Approximate)		
Assembled Height	1.97 in.	50.1mm
Service Limit	10% Force Loss @Specified Length	
Rocker Arm		
Ratio	1.73	
Valve Tappet, Hydraulic		
Diameter (Std.)	0.8740-8745 in.	22.212-22.195mm
Clearance to Bore	0.0007-0.0027 in.	0.018-0.068mm
Service Limit	0.005 in.	0.127mm
Hydraulic Leakdown Rate	①	
Collapsed Tappet Gap	0.09-0.19 in.	2.25-4.79mm
Camshaft Postion	0.8767-0.8752 in.	22.268-22.230mm

① 20-200 seconds to leakdown 3.18mm (0.125 in. with 225 Newtons (50 pounds) load and tappet filled with leak-down fluid.

3.8L (3802cc) ENGINE SPECIFICATIONS

Camshaft Bore Inside Diameter		
No. 1	2.192-2.191 in.	55.689-55.664mm
No. 2	2.177-2.176 in.	55.308-55.283mm
No. 3	2.177-2.176 in.	55.308-55.283mm
No. 4	2.192-2.191 in.	55.684-55.664mm
Balance Shaft Bore		
Inside Diameter	2.192-2.191 in.	55.689-55.664mm
End Plug	0.003-0.006 in.	0.16-0.075mm
Balance Shaft		
End Play	2.192-2.191 in.	0.075-0.21mm
Journal Diameter	2.0515-2.0505 in.	52.108-52.082mm
Run-out	0.001 in.	0.025mm
CAMSHAFT		
Lobe Lift		
Intake	0.245 in.	6.22mm
Exhaust	0.259 in.	6.57mm
Allowable Lobe Lift Loss Theoretical Valve Lift @ Zero Lash	0.005 in.	0.127mm
Intake	0.426 in.	10.83mm
Exhaust	0.451 in.	11.47mm
End Play		
Service Limit	0.001-0.006 in.	0.025-0.150mm
Journal to Bearing Clearance	2.0515-2.0505 in.	0.025-0.076mm
Journal Diameter		
All	2.0515-2.0505 in.	52.108-52.082mm
Cam Bearing I.D.	2.0535-2.0525 in.	52.158-52.133mm
Run-out Limit	0.002 in.	0.05mm
Out-of-Round Limit	0.001 in.	0.025mm
CAMSHAFT DRIVE		
Assembled Gear Face Run-out		
Crankshaft	0.004 in.	0.10mm
Camshaft	0.010 in.	0.25mm
Timing Chain Deflection	0.5 in.	12.7mm
CYLINDER BLOCK		
Head Gasket Surface Flatness	0.003 in.. per 6.00 in..	0.08mm per 52.0mm
Head Gasket Surface Finish (RMS)	1.0-3.3 Micrometers	
Cylinder Bore		
Diameter	3.81 in.	96.80mm
Surface Finish (RMS)	0.45-0.96 Micrometers	
Out-of-Round Limit	0.001 in.	0.025mm
Out-of-Round Service Limit	0.002 in.	0.050mm
Taper Service Unit	0.002 in.	0.050mm
Main Bearing Bore	2.713 in.	68.905mm
Diameter	2.712 in.	68.885mm
CRANKSHAFT AND FLYWHEEL		
Main Bearing Journal		
Diameter	2.5190-2.5198 in.	68.983-64.003mm
Out-of-Round Limit	0.003 in..Max. in..45 degrees,	0.008mm Max. in 45 degrees,
Surface Finish (RMS)	11.8 Micro in..	0.3 Micrometers
Thrust Bearing Journal Length	1.703-1.722 in.	29.725-29.775mm
Connecting Rod Journal Diameter	2.3103-2.3111 In.	58.682-58.702mm

89693C64

USING A VACUUM GAUGE

White needle = steady needle   *Dark needle = drifting needle*

The vacuum gauge is one of the most useful and easy-to-use diagnostic tools. It is inexpensive, easy to hook up, and provides valuable information about the condition of your engine.

Indication: Normal engine in good condition

Gauge reading: Steady, from 17–22 in./Hg.

Indication: Sticking valve or ignition miss

Gauge reading: Needle fluctuates from 15–20 in./Hg. at idle

Indication: Late ignition or valve timing, low compression, stuck throttle valve, leaking carburetor or manifold gasket.

Gauge reading: Low (15–20 in./Hg.) but steady

Indication: Improper carburetor adjustment, or minor intake leak at carburetor or manifold

NOTE: Bad fuel injector O-rings may also cause this reading.

Gauge reading: Drifting needle

Indication: Weak valve springs, worn valve stem guides, or leaky cylinder head gasket (vibrating excessively at all speeds).

NOTE: A plugged catalytic converter may also cause this reading.

Gauge reading: Needle fluctuates as engine speed increases

Indication: Burnt valve or improper valve clearance. The needle will drop when the defective valve operates.

Gauge reading: Steady needle, but drops regularly

Indication: Choked muffler or obstruction in system. Speed up the engine. Choked muffler will exhibit a slow drop of vacuum to zero.

Gauge reading: Gradual drop in reading at idle

Indication: Worn valve guides

Gauge reading: Needle vibrates excessively at idle, but steadies as engine speed increases

TCCS3C01

Troubleshooting Engine Mechanical Problems

Problem	Cause	Solution
External oil leaks	• Cylinder head cover RTV sealant broken or improperly seated	• Replace sealant; inspect cylinder head cover sealant flange and cylinder head sealant surface for distortion and cracks
	• Oil filler cap leaking or missing	• Replace cap
	• Oil filter gasket broken or improperly seated	• Replace oil filter
	• Oil pan side gasket broken, improperly seated or opening in RTV sealant	• Replace gasket or repair opening in sealant; inspect oil pan gasket flange for distortion
	• Oil pan front oil seal broken or improperly seated	• Replace seal; inspect timing case cover and oil pan seal flange for distortion
	• Oil pan rear oil seal broken or improperly seated	• Replace seal; inspect oil pan rear oil seal flange; inspect rear main bearing cap for cracks, plugged oil return channels, or distortion in seal groove
	• Timing case cover oil seal broken or improperly seated	• Replace seal
	• Excess oil pressure because of restricted PCV valve	• Replace PCV valve
	• Oil pan drain plug loose or has stripped threads	• Repair as necessary and tighten
	• Rear oil gallery plug loose	• Use appropriate sealant on gallery plug and tighten
	• Rear camshaft plug loose or improperly seated	• Seat camshaft plug or replace and seal, as necessary
Excessive oil consumption	• Oil level too high	• Drain oil to specified level
	• Oil with wrong viscosity being used	• Replace with specified oil
	• PCV valve stuck closed	• Replace PCV valve
	• Valve stem oil deflectors (or seals) are damaged, missing, or incorrect type	• Replace valve stem oil deflectors
	• Valve stems or valve guides worn	• Measure stem-to-guide clearance and repair as necessary
	• Poorly fitted or missing valve cover baffles	• Replace valve cover
	• Piston rings broken or missing	• Replace broken or missing rings
	• Scuffed piston	• Replace piston
	• Incorrect piston ring gap	• Measure ring gap, repair as necessary
	• Piston rings sticking or excessively loose in grooves	• Measure ring side clearance, repair as necessary
	• Compression rings installed upside down	• Repair as necessary
	• Cylinder walls worn, scored, or glazed	• Repair as necessary

TCCS3C02

Troubleshooting Engine Mechanical Problems

Problem	Cause	Solution
Excessive oil consumption (cont.)	• Piston ring gaps not properly staggered	• Repair as necessary
	• Excessive main or connecting rod bearing clearance	• Measure bearing clearance, repair as necessary
No oil pressure	• Low oil level	• Add oil to correct level
	• Oil pressure gauge, warning lamp or sending unit inaccurate	• Replace oil pressure gauge or warning lamp
	• Oil pump malfunction	• Replace oil pump
	• Oil pressure relief valve sticking	• Remove and inspect oil pressure relief valve assembly
	• Oil passages on pressure side of pump obstructed	• Inspect oil passages for obstruction
	• Oil pickup screen or tube obstructed	• Inspect oil pickup for obstruction
	• Loose oil inlet tube	• Tighten or seal inlet tube
Low oil pressure	• Low oil level	• Add oil to correct level
	• Inaccurate gauge, warning lamp or sending unit	• Replace oil pressure gauge or warning lamp
	• Oil excessively thin because of dilution, poor quality, or improper grade	• Drain and refill crankcase with recommended oil
	• Excessive oil temperature	• Correct cause of overheating engine
	• Oil pressure relief spring weak or sticking	• Remove and inspect oil pressure relief valve assembly
	• Oil inlet tube and screen assembly has restriction or air leak	• Remove and inspect oil inlet tube and screen assembly. (Fill inlet tube with lacquer thinner to locate leaks.)
	• Excessive oil pump clearance	• Measure clearances
	• Excessive main, rod, or camshaft bearing clearance	• Measure bearing clearances, repair as necessary
High oil pressure	• Improper oil viscosity	• Drain and refill crankcase with correct viscosity oil
	• Oil pressure gauge or sending unit inaccurate	• Replace oil pressure gauge
	• Oil pressure relief valve sticking closed	• Remove and inspect oil pressure relief valve assembly
Main bearing noise	• Insufficient oil supply	• Inspect for low oil level and low oil pressure
	• Main bearing clearance excessive	• Measure main bearing clearance, repair as necessary
	• Bearing insert missing	• Replace missing insert
	• Crankshaft end-play excessive	• Measure end-play, repair as necessary
	• Improperly tightened main bearing cap bolts	• Tighten bolts with specified torque
	• Loose flywheel or drive plate	• Tighten flywheel or drive plate attaching bolts
	• Loose or damaged vibration damper	• Repair as necessary

Troubleshooting Engine Mechanical Problems

Problem	Cause	Solution
Connecting rod bearing noise	• Insufficient oil supply	• Inspect for low oil level and low oil pressure
	• Carbon build-up on piston	• Remove carbon from piston crown
	• Bearing clearance excessive or bearing missing	• Measure clearance, repair as necessary
	• Crankshaft connecting rod journal out-of-round	• Measure journal dimensions, repair or replace as necessary
	• Misaligned connecting rod or cap	• Repair as necessary
	• Connecting rod bolts tightened improperly	• Tighten bolts with specified torque
Piston noise	• Piston-to-cylinder wall clearance excessive (scuffed piston)	• Measure clearance and examine piston
	• Cylinder walls excessively tapered or out-of-round	• Measure cylinder wall dimensions, rebore cylinder
	• Piston ring broken	• Replace all rings on piston
	• Loose or seized piston pin	• Measure piston-to-pin clearance, repair as necessary
	• Connecting rods misaligned	• Measure rod alignment, straighten or replace
	• Piston ring side clearance excessively loose or tight	• Measure ring side clearance, repair as necessary
	• Carbon build-up on piston is excessive	• Remove carbon from piston
Valve actuating component noise	• Insufficient oil supply	• Check for: (a) Low oil level (b) Low oil pressure (c) Wrong hydraulic tappets (d) Restricted oil gallery (e) Excessive tappet to bore clearance
	• Rocker arms or pivots worn	• Replace worn rocker arms or pivots
	• Foreign objects or chips in hydraulic tappets	• Clean tappets
	• Excessive tappet leak-down	• Replace valve tappet
	• Tappet face worn	• Replace tappet; inspect corresponding cam lobe for wear
	• Broken or cocked valve springs	• Properly seat cocked springs; replace broken springs
	• Stem-to-guide clearance excessive	• Measure stem-to-guide clearance, repair as required
	• Valve bent	• Replace valve
	• Loose rocker arms	• Check and repair as necessary
	• Valve seat runout excessive	• Regrind valve seat/valves
	• Missing valve lock	• Install valve lock
	• Excessive engine oil	• Correct oil level

TCCS3C04

Troubleshooting Engine Performance

Problem	Cause	Solution
Hard starting (engine cranks normally)	• Faulty engine control system component • Faulty fuel pump • Faulty fuel system component • Faulty ignition coil • Improper spark plug gap • Incorrect ignition timing • Incorrect valve timing	• Repair or replace as necessary • Replace fuel pump • Repair or replace as necessary • Test and replace as necessary • Adjust gap • Adjust timing • Check valve timing; repair as necessary
Rough idle or stalling	• Incorrect curb or fast idle speed • Incorrect ignition timing • Improper feedback system operation • Faulty EGR valve operation • Faulty PCV valve air flow • Faulty TAC vacuum motor or valve • Air leak into manifold vacuum • Faulty distributor rotor or cap • Improperly seated valves • Incorrect ignition wiring • Faulty ignition coil • Restricted air vent or idle passages • Restricted air cleaner	• Adjust curb or fast idle speed (If possible) • Adjust timing to specification • Refer to Chapter 4 • Test EGR system and replace as necessary • Test PCV valve and replace as necessary • Repair as necessary • Inspect manifold vacuum connections and repair as necessary • Replace rotor or cap (Distributor systems only) • Test cylinder compression, repair as necessary • Inspect wiring and correct as necessary • Test coil and replace as necessary • Clean passages • Clean or replace air cleaner filter element
Faulty low-speed operation	• Restricted idle air vents and passages • Restricted air cleaner • Faulty spark plugs • Dirty, corroded, or loose ignition secondary circuit wire connections • Improper feedback system operation • Faulty ignition coil high voltage wire • Faulty distributor cap	• Clean air vents and passages • Clean or replace air cleaner filter element • Clean or replace spark plugs • Clean or tighten secondary circuit wire connections • Refer to Chapter 4 • Replace ignition coil high voltage wire (Distributor systems only) • Replace cap (Distributor systems only)
Faulty acceleration	• Incorrect ignition timing • Faulty fuel system component • Faulty spark plug(s) • Improperly seated valves • Faulty ignition coil	• Adjust timing • Repair or replace as necessary • Clean or replace spark plug(s) • Test cylinder compression, repair as necessary • Test coil and replace as necessary

Troubleshooting Engine Performance

Problem	Cause	Solution
Faulty acceleration (cont.)	• Improper feedback system operation	• Refer to Chapter 4
Faulty high speed operation	• Incorrect ignition timing • Faulty advance mechanism	• Adjust timing (if possible) • Check advance mechanism and repair as necessary (Distributor systems only)
	• Low fuel pump volume • Wrong spark plug air gap or wrong plug • Partially restricted exhaust manifold, exhaust pipe, catalytic converter, muffler, or tailpipe • Restricted vacuum passages • Restricted air cleaner	• Replace fuel pump • Adjust air gap or install correct plug • Eliminate restriction • Clean passages • Cleaner or replace filter element as necessary
	• Faulty distributor rotor or cap • Faulty ignition coil • Improperly seated valve(s) • Faulty valve spring(s) • Incorrect valve timing • Intake manifold restricted • Worn distributor shaft • Improper feedback system operation	• Replace rotor or cap (Distributor systems only) • Test coil and replace as necessary • Test cylinder compression, repair as necessary • Inspect and test valve spring tension, replace as necessary • Check valve timing and repair as necessary • Remove restriction or replace manifold • Replace shaft (Distributor systems only) • Refer to Chapter 4
Misfire at all speeds	• Faulty spark plug(s) • Faulty spark plug wire(s) • Faulty distributor cap or rotor • Faulty ignition coil • Primary ignition circuit shorted or open intermittently • Improperly seated valve(s) • Faulty hydraulic tappet(s) • Improper feedback system operation • Faulty valve spring(s) • Worn camshaft lobes • Air leak into manifold • Fuel pump volume or pressure low • Blown cylinder head gasket • Intake or exhaust manifold passage(s) restricted	• Clean or relace spark plug(s) • Replace as necessary • Replace cap or rotor (Distributor systems only) • Test coil and replace as necessary • Troubleshoot primary circuit and repair as necessary • Test cylinder compression, repair as necessary • Clean or replace tappet(s) • Refer to Chapter 4 • Inspect and test valve spring tension, repair as necessary • Replace camshaft • Check manifold vacuum and repair as necessary • Replace fuel pump • Replace gasket • Pass chain through passage(s) and repair as necessary
Power not up to normal	• Incorrect ignition timing • Faulty distributor rotor	• Adjust timing • Replace rotor (Distributor systems only)

TCCS3C06

Troubleshooting Engine Performance

Problem	Cause	Solution
Power not up to normal (cont.)	• Incorrect spark plug gap	• Adjust gap
	• Faulty fuel pump	• Replace fuel pump
	• Faulty fuel pump	• Replace fuel pump
	• Incorrect valve timing	• Check valve timing and repair as necessary
	• Faulty ignition coil	• Test coil and replace as necessary
	• Faulty ignition wires	• Test wires and replace as necessary
	• Improperly seated valves	• Test cylinder compression and repair as necessary
	• Blown cylinder head gasket	• Replace gasket
	• Leaking piston rings	• Test compression and repair as necessary
	• Improper feedback system operation	• Refer to Chapter 4
Intake backfire	• Improper ignition timing	• Adjust timing
	• Defective EGR component	• Repair as necessary
	• Defective TAC vacuum motor or valve	• Repair as necessary
Exhaust backfire	• Air leak into manifold vacuum	• Check manifold vacuum and repair as necessary
	• Faulty air injection diverter valve	• Test diverter valve and replace as necessary
	• Exhaust leak	• Locate and eliminate leak
Ping or spark knock	• Incorrect ignition timing	• Adjust timing
	• Distributor advance malfunction	• Inspect advance mechanism and repair as necessary (Distributor systems only)
	• Excessive combustion chamber deposits	• Remove with combustion chamber cleaner
	• Air leak into manifold vacuum	• Check manifold vacuum and repair as necessary
	• Excessively high compression	• Test compression and repair as necessary
	• Fuel octane rating excessively low	• Try alternate fuel source
	• Sharp edges in combustion chamber	• Grind smooth
	• EGR valve not functioning properly	• Test EGR system and replace as necessary
Surging (at cruising to top speeds)	• Low fuel pump pressure or volume	• Replace fuel pump
	• Improper PCV valve air flow	• Test PCV valve and replace as necessary
	• Air leak into manifold vacuum	• Check manifold vacuum and repair as necessary
	• Incorrect spark advance	• Test and replace as necessary
	• Restricted fuel filter	• Replace fuel filter
	• Restricted air cleaner	• Clean or replace air cleaner filter element
	• EGR valve not functioning properly	• Test EGR system and replace as necessary
	• Improper feedback system operation	• Refer to Chapter 4

Troubleshooting the Serpentine Drive Belt

Problem	Cause	Solution
Tension sheeting fabric failure (woven fabric on outside circumference of belt has cracked or separated from body of belt)	• Grooved or backside idler pulley diameters are less than minimum recommended • Tension sheeting contacting (rubbing) stationary object • Excessive heat causing woven fabric to age • Tension sheeting splice has fractured	• Replace pulley(s) not conforming to specification • Correct rubbing condition • Replace belt • Replace belt
Noise (objectional squeal, squeak, or rumble is heard or felt while drive belt is in operation)	• Belt slippage • Bearing noise • Belt misalignment • Belt-to-pulley mismatch • Driven component inducing vibration • System resonant frequency inducing vibration	• Adjust belt • Locate and repair • Align belt/pulley(s) • Install correct belt • Locate defective driven component and repair • Vary belt tension within specifications. Replace belt.
Rib chunking (one or more ribs has separated from belt body)	• Foreign objects imbedded in pulley grooves • Installation damage • Drive loads in excess of design specifications • Insufficient internal belt adhesion	• Remove foreign objects from pulley grooves • Replace belt • Adjust belt tension • Replace belt
Rib or belt wear (belt ribs contact bottom of pulley grooves)	• Pulley(s) misaligned • Mismatch of belt and pulley groove widths • Abrasive environment • Rusted pulley(s) • Sharp or jagged pulley groove tips • Rubber deteriorated	• Align pulley(s) • Replace belt • Replace belt • Clean rust from pulley(s) • Replace pulley • Replace belt
Longitudinal belt cracking (cracks between two ribs)	• Belt has mistracked from pulley groove • Pulley groove tip has worn away rubber-to-tensile member	• Replace belt • Replace belt
Belt slips	• Belt slipping because of insufficient tension • Belt or pulley subjected to substance (belt dressing, oil, ethylene glycol) that has reduced friction • Driven component bearing failure • Belt glazed and hardened from heat and excessive slippage	• Adjust tension • Replace belt and clean pulleys • Replace faulty component bearing • Replace belt
"Groove jumping" (belt does not maintain correct position on pulley, or turns over and/or runs off pulleys)	• Insufficient belt tension • Pulley(s) not within design tolerance • Foreign object(s) in grooves	• Adjust belt tension • Replace pulley(s) • Remove foreign objects from grooves

TCCS3C09

Troubleshooting the Serpentine Drive Belt

Problem	Cause	Solution
"Groove jumping" (belt does not maintain correct position on pulley, or turns over and/or runs off pulleys)	• Excessive belt speed • Pulley misalignment • Belt-to-pulley profile mismatched • Belt cordline is distorted	• Avoid excessive engine acceleration • Align pulley(s) • Install correct belt • Replace belt
Belt broken (Note: identify and correct problem before replacement belt is installed)	• Excessive tension • Tensile members damaged during belt installation • Belt turnover • Severe pulley misalignment • Bracket, pulley, or bearing failure	• Replace belt and adjust tension to specification • Replace belt • Replace belt • Align pulley(s) • Replace defective component and belt
Cord edge failure (tensile member exposed at edges of belt or separated from belt body)	• Excessive tension • Drive pulley misalignment • Belt contacting stationary object • Pulley irregularities • Improper pulley construction • Insufficient adhesion between tensile member and rubber matrix	• Adjust belt tension • Align pulley • Correct as necessary • Replace pulley • Replace pulley • Replace belt and adjust tension to specifications
Sporadic rib cracking (multiple cracks in belt ribs at random intervals)	• Ribbed pulley(s) diameter less than minimum specification • Backside bend flat pulley(s) diameter less than minimum • Excessive heat condition causing rubber to harden • Excessive belt thickness • Belt overcured • Excessive tension	• Replace pulley(s) • Replace pulley(s) • Correct heat condition as necessary • Replace belt • Replace belt • Adjust belt tension

TCCS3C10

Troubleshooting the Cooling System

Problem	Cause	Solution
High temperature gauge indication—overheating	• Coolant level low • Improper fan operation • Radiator hose(s) collapsed • Radiator airflow blocked • Faulty pressure cap • Ignition timing incorrect • Air trapped in cooling system • Heavy traffic driving • Incorrect cooling system component(s) installed • Faulty thermostat • Water pump shaft broken or impeller loose • Radiator tubes clogged • Cooling system clogged • Casting flash in cooling passages • Brakes dragging • Excessive engine friction • Antifreeze concentration over 68% • Missing air seals • Faulty gauge or sending unit • Loss of coolant flow caused by leakage or foaming • Viscous fan drive failed	• Replenish coolant • Repair or replace as necessary • Replace hose(s) • Remove restriction (bug screen, fog lamps, etc.) • Replace pressure cap • Adjust ignition timing • Purge air • Operate at fast idle in neutral intermittently to cool engine • Install proper component(s) • Replace thermostat • Replace water pump • Flush radiator • Flush system • Repair or replace as necessary. Flash may be visible by removing cooling system components or removing core plugs. • Repair brakes • Repair engine • Lower antifreeze concentration percentage • Replace air seals • Repair or replace faulty component • Repair or replace leaking component, replace coolant • Replace unit
Low temperature indication—undercooling	• Thermostat stuck open • Faulty gauge or sending unit	• Replace thermostat • Repair or replace faulty component
Coolant loss—boilover	• Overfilled cooling system • Quick shutdown after hard (hot) run • Air in system resulting in occasional "burping" of coolant • Insufficient antifreeze allowing coolant boiling point to be too low • Antifreeze deteriorated because of age or contamination • Leaks due to loose hose clamps, loose nuts, bolts, drain plugs, faulty hoses, or defective radiator	• Reduce coolant level to proper specification • Allow engine to run at fast idle prior to shutdown • Purge system • Add antifreeze to raise boiling point • Replace coolant • Pressure test system to locate source of leak(s) then repair as necessary

TCCS3C11

Troubleshooting the Cooling System (cont.)

Problem	Cause	Solution
Coolant loss—boilover	• Faulty head gasket • Cracked head, manifold, or block • Faulty radiator cap	• Replace head gasket • Replace as necessary • Replace cap
Coolant entry into crankcase or cylinder(s)	• Faulty head gasket • Crack in head, manifold or block	• Replace head gasket • Replace as necessary
Coolant recovery system inoperative	• Coolant level low • Leak in system • Pressure cap not tight or seal missing, or leaking • Pressure cap defective • Overflow tube clogged or leaking • Recovery bottle vent restricted	• Replenish coolant to FULL mark • Pressure test to isolate leak and repair as necessary • Repair as necessary • Replace cap • Repair as necessary • Remove restriction
Noise	• Fan contacting shroud • Loose water pump impeller • Glazed fan belt • Loose fan belt • Rough surface on drive pulley • Water pump bearing worn • Belt alignment	• Reposition shroud and inspect engine mounts (on electric fans inspect assembly) • Replace pump • Apply silicone or replace belt • Adjust fan belt tension • Replace pulley • Remove belt to isolate. Replace pump. • Check pulley alignment. Repair as necessary.
No coolant flow through heater core	• Restricted return inlet in water pump • Heater hose collapsed or restricted • Restricted heater core • Restricted outlet in thermostat housing • Intake manifold bypass hole in cylinder head restricted • Faulty heater control valve • Intake manifold coolant passage restricted	• Remove restriction • Remove restriction or replace hose • Remove restriction or replace core • Remove flash or restriction • Remove restriction • Replace valve • Remove restriction or replace intake manifold

NOTE: *Immediately after shutdown, the engine enters a condition known as heat soak. This is caused by the cooling system being inoperative while engine temperature is still high. If coolant temperature rises above boiling point, expansion and pressure may push some coolant out of the radiator overflow tube. If this does not occur frequently it is considered normal.*

TCCS3C12

4

DRIVEABILITY AND EMISSIONS CONTROLS

AIR POLLUTION

The earth's atmosphere, at or near sea level, consists approximately of 78 percent nitrogen, 21 percent oxygen and 1 percent other gases. If it were possible to remain in this state, 100 percent clean air would result. However, many varied sources allow other gases and particulates to mix with the clean air, causing our atmosphere to become unclean or polluted.

Some of these pollutants are visible while others are invisible, with each having the capability of causing distress to the eyes, ears, throat, skin and respiratory system. Should these pollutants become concentrated in a specific area and under certain conditions, death could result due to the displacement or chemical change of the oxygen content in the air. These pollutants can also cause great damage to the environment and to the many man made objects that are exposed to the elements.

To better understand the causes of air pollution, the pollutants can be categorized into 3 separate types, natural, industrial and automotive.

Natural Pollutants

Natural pollution has been present on earth since before man appeared and continues to be a factor when discussing air pollution, although it causes only a small percentage of the overall pollution problem. It is the direct result of decaying organic matter, wind born smoke and particulates from such natural events as plain and forest fires (ignited by heat or lightning), volcanic ash, sand and dust which can spread over a large area of the countryside.

Such a phenomenon of natural pollution has been seen in the form of volcanic eruptions, with the resulting plume of smoke, steam and volcanic ash blotting out the sun's rays as it spreads and rises higher into the atmosphere. As it travels into the atmosphere the upper air currents catch and carry the smoke and ash, while condensing the steam back into water vapor. As the water vapor, smoke and ash travel on their journey, the smoke dissipates into the atmosphere while the ash and moisture settle back to earth in a trail hundreds of miles long. In some cases, lives are lost and millions of dollars of property damage result.

Industrial Pollutants

Industrial pollution is caused primarily by industrial processes, the burning of coal, oil and natural gas, which in turn produce smoke and fumes. Because the burning fuels contain large amounts of sulfur, the principal ingredients of smoke and fumes are sulfur dioxide and particulate matter. This type of pollutant occurs most severely during still, damp and cool weather, such as at night. Even in its less severe form, this pollutant is not confined to just cities. Because of air movements, the pollutants move for miles over the surrounding countryside, leaving in its path a barren and unhealthy environment for all living things.

Working with Federal, State and Local mandated regulations and by carefully monitoring emissions, big business has greatly reduced the amount of pollutant introduced from its industrial sources, striving to obtain an acceptable level. Because of the mandated industrial emission clean up, many land areas and streams in and around the cities that were formerly barren of vegetation and life, have now begun to move back in the direction of nature's intended balance.

Automotive Pollutants

The third major source of air pollution is automotive emissions. The emissions from the internal combustion engines were not an appreciable problem years ago because of the small number of registered vehicles and the nation's small highway system. However, during the early 1950's, the trend of the American people was to move from the cities to the surrounding suburbs. This caused an immediate problem in transportation because the majority of suburbs were not afforded mass transit conveniences. This lack of transportation created an attractive market for the automobile manufacturers, which resulted in a dramatic increase in the number of vehicles produced and sold, along with a marked increase in highway construction between cities and the suburbs. Multi-vehicle families emerged with a growing emphasis placed on an individual vehicle per family member. As the increase in vehicle ownership and usage occurred, so did pollutant levels in and around the cities, as suburbanites drove daily to their businesses and employment, returning at the end of the day to their homes in the suburbs.

It was noted that a smoke and fog type haze was being formed and at times, remained in suspension over the cities, taking time to dissipate. At first this "smog," derived from the words "smoke" and "fog," was thought to result from industrial pollution but it was determined that automobile emissions shared the blame. It was discovered that when normal automobile emissions were exposed to sunlight for a period of time, complex chemical reactions would take place.

It is now known that smog is a photo chemical layer which develops when certain oxides of nitrogen (NOx) and unburned hydrocarbons (HC) from automobile emissions are exposed to sunlight. Pollution was more severe when smog would become stagnant over an area in which a warm layer of air settled over the top of the cooler air mass, trapping and holding the cooler mass at ground level. The trapped cooler air would keep the emissions from being dispersed and diluted through normal air flows. This type of air stagnation was given the name "Temperature Inversion."

TEMPERATURE INVERSION

In normal weather situations, surface air is warmed by heat radiating from the earth's surface and the sun's rays. This causes it to rise upward, into the atmosphere. Upon rising it will cool through a convection type heat exchange with the cooler upper air. As warm air rises, the surface pollutants are carried upward and dissipated into the atmosphere.

When a temperature inversion occurs, we find the higher air is no longer cooler, but is warmer than the surface air, causing the cooler surface air to become trapped. This warm air blanket can extend from above ground level to a few hundred or even a few thousand feet into the air. As the surface air is trapped, so are the pollutants, causing a severe smog condition. Should this stagnant air mass extend to a few thousand feet high, enough air movement with the inversion takes place to allow the smog layer to rise above ground level but the pollutants still cannot dissipate. This inversion can remain for days over an area, with the smog level only rising or lowering from ground level to a few hundred feet high. Meanwhile, the pollutant levels increase, causing eye irritation, respiratory problems, reduced visibility, plant damage and in some cases, even disease.

This inversion phenomenon was first noted in the Los Angeles, California area. The city lies in terrain resembling a basin and with certain weather conditions, a cold air mass is held in the basin while a warmer air mass covers it like a lid.

Because this type of condition was first documented as prevalent in the Los Angeles area, this type of trapped pollution was named Los Angeles Smog, although it occurs in other areas where a large concentration of automobiles are used and the air remains stagnant for any length of time.

HEAT TRANSFER

Consider the internal combustion engine as a machine in which raw materials must be placed so a finished product comes out. As in any machine operation, a certain amount of wasted material is formed. When we relate this to the internal combustion engine, we find that through the input of air and fuel, we obtain power during the combustion process to drive the vehicle. The by-product or waste of this power is, in part, heat and exhaust gases with which we must dispose.

The heat from the combustion process can rise to over 4000°F (2204°C). The dissipation of this heat is controlled by a ram air effect, the use of cooling fans to cause air flow and a liquid coolant solution surrounding the combustion area to transfer the heat of combustion through the cylinder walls and into the coolant. The coolant is then directed to a thin-finned, multi-tubed radiator, from which the excess heat is transferred to the atmosphere by 1 of the 3 heat transfer methods, conduction, convection or radiation.

The cooling of the combustion area is an important part in the control of exhaust emissions. To understand the behavior of the combustion and transfer of its heat, consider the air/fuel charge. It is ignited and the flame front burns progressively across the combustion chamber until the burning charge reaches the cylinder walls. Some of the fuel in contact with the walls is not hot enough to burn, thereby snuffing out or quenching the combustion process. This leaves unburned fuel in the combustion chamber. This unburned fuel is then forced out of the cylinder and into the exhaust system, along with the exhaust gases.

Many attempts have been made to minimize the amount of unburned fuel in the combustion chambers due to quenching, by increasing the coolant temperature and lessening the contact area of the coolant around the combustion area.

However, design limitations within the combustion chambers prevent the complete burning of the air/fuel charge, so a certain amount of the unburned fuel is still expelled into the exhaust system, regardless of modifications to the engine.

AUTOMOTIVE EMISSIONS

Before emission controls were mandated on internal combustion engines, other sources of engine pollutants were discovered along with the exhaust emissions. It was determined that engine combustion exhaust produced approximately 60 percent of the total emission pollutants, fuel evaporation from the fuel tank and carburetor vents produced 20 percent, with the final 20 percent being produced through the crankcase as a by-product of the combustion process.

Exhaust Gases

The exhaust gases emitted into the atmosphere are a combination of burned and unburned fuel. To understand the exhaust emission and its composition, we must review some basic chemistry.

When the air/fuel mixture is introduced into the engine, we are mixing air, composed of nitrogen (78 percent), oxygen (21 percent) and other gases (1 percent) with the fuel, which is 100 percent hydrocarbons (HC), in a semi-controlled ratio. As the combustion process is accomplished, power is produced to move the vehicle while the heat of combustion is transferred to the cooling system. The exhaust gases are then composed of nitrogen, a diatomic gas (N_2), the same as was introduced in the engine, carbon dioxide (CO_2), the same gas that is used in beverage carbonation, and water vapor (H_2O). The nitrogen (N_2), for the most part, passes through the engine unchanged, while the oxygen (O_2) reacts (burns) with the hydrocarbons (HC) and produces the carbon dioxide (CO_2) and the water vapors (H_2O). If this chemical process would be the only process to take place, the exhaust emissions would be harmless. However, during the combustion process, other compounds are formed which are considered dangerous. These pollutants are hydrocarbons (HC), carbon monoxide (CO), oxides of nitrogen (NOx) oxides of sulfur (SOx) and engine particulates.

HYDROCARBONS

Hydrocarbons (HC) are essentially fuel which was not burned during the combustion process or which has escaped into the atmosphere through fuel evaporation. The main sources of incomplete combustion are rich air/fuel mixtures, low engine temperatures and improper spark timing. The main sources of hydrocarbon emission through fuel evaporation on most vehicles used to be the vehicle's fuel tank and carburetor float bowl.

To reduce combustion hydrocarbon emission, engine modifications were made to minimize dead space and surface area in the combustion chamber. In addition, the air/fuel mixture was made more lean through the improved control which feedback carburetion and fuel injection offers and by the addition of external controls to aid in further combustion of the hydrocarbons outside the engine. Two such methods were the addition of air injection systems, to inject fresh air into the exhaust manifolds and the installation of catalytic converters, units that are able to burn traces of hydrocarbons without affecting the internal combustion process or fuel economy.

To control hydrocarbon emissions through fuel evaporation, modifications were made to the fuel tank to allow storage of the fuel vapors during periods of engine shut-down. Modifications were also made to the air intake system so that at specific times during engine operation, these vapors may be purged and burned by blending them with the air/fuel mixture.

CARBON MONOXIDE

Carbon monoxide is formed when not enough oxygen is present during the combustion process to convert carbon (C) to carbon dioxide (CO_2). An increase in the carbon monoxide (CO) emission is normally accompanied by an increase in the hydrocarbon (HC) emission because of the lack of oxygen to completely burn all of the fuel mixture.

Carbon monoxide (CO) also increases the rate at which the photo chemical smog is formed by speeding up the conversion of nitric oxide (NO) to nitrogen dioxide (NO_2). To accomplish this, carbon monoxide (CO) combines with oxygen (O_2) and nitric oxide (NO) to produce carbon dioxide (CO_2) and nitrogen dioxide (NO_2). ($CO + O_2 + NO = CO_2 + NO_2$).

The dangers of carbon monoxide, which is an odorless and colorless toxic gas are many. When carbon monoxide is inhaled into the lungs and passed into the blood stream, oxygen is replaced by the carbon monoxide in the red blood cells, causing a reduction in the amount of oxygen supplied to the many parts of the body. This lack of oxygen causes headaches, lack of coordination, reduced mental alertness and, should the carbon monoxide concentration be high enough, death could result.

NITROGEN

Normally, nitrogen is an inert gas. When heated to approximately 2500°F (137°C) through the combustion process, this gas becomes active and causes an increase in the nitric oxide (NO) emission.

Oxides of nitrogen (NOx) are composed of approximately 97–98 percent nitric oxide (NO). Nitric oxide is a colorless gas but when it is passed into the atmosphere, it combines with oxygen and forms nitrogen dioxide (NO_2). The nitrogen dioxide then combines with chemically active hydrocarbons (HC) and when in the presence of sunlight, causes the formation of photo-chemical smog.

Ozone

To further complicate matters, some of the nitrogen dioxide (NO_2) is broken apart by the sunlight to form nitric oxide and oxygen. ($NO_2 +$ sunlight $= NO + O$). This single atom of oxygen then combines with diatomic (meaning 2 atoms) oxygen (O_2) to form ozone (O_3). Ozone is one of the smells associated with smog. It has a pungent and offensive odor, irritates the eyes and lung tissues, affects the growth of plant life and causes rapid deterioration of rubber products. Ozone can be formed by sunlight as well as electrical discharge into the air.

The most common discharge area on the automobile engine is the secondary ignition electrical system, especially when inferior quality spark plug cables are used. As the surge of high voltage is routed through the secondary cable, the circuit builds up an electrical field around the wire, which acts upon the oxygen in the surrounding air to form the ozone. The faint glow along the cable with the engine running that may be visible on a dark night, is called the "corona discharge." It is the result of the electrical field passing from a high along the cable, to a low in the surrounding air, which forms the ozone gas. The combination of corona and ozone has been a major cause of cable deterioration. Recently, different and better quality insulating materials have lengthened the life of the electrical cables.

Although ozone at ground level can be harmful, ozone is beneficial to the earth's inhabitants. By having a concentrated ozone layer called the "ozonosphere," between 10 and 20 miles (16–32 km) up in the atmosphere, much of the ultra violet radiation from the sun's rays are absorbed and screened. If this ozone layer were not present, much of the earth's surface would be burned, dried and unfit for human life.

OXIDES OF SULFUR

Oxides of sulfur (SOx) were initially ignored in the exhaust system emissions, since the sulfur content of gasoline as a fuel is less than $\frac{1}{10}$ of 1 percent. Because of this small amount, it was felt that it contributed very little to the overall pollution problem. However, because of the difficulty in solving the sulfur emissions in industrial pollutions and the introduction of catalytic converter to the automobile exhaust systems, a change was mandated. The automobile exhaust system, when equipped with a catalytic converter, changes the sulfur dioxide (SO_2) into sulfur trioxide (SO_3).

When this combines with water vapors (H_2O), a sulfuric acid mist

(H_2SO_4) is formed and is a very difficult pollutant to handle since it is extremely corrosive. This sulfuric acid mist that is formed, is the same mist that rises from the vents of an automobile battery when an active chemical reaction takes place within the battery cells.

When a large concentration of vehicles equipped with catalytic converters are operating in an area, this acid mist may rise and be distributed over a large ground area causing land, plant, crop, paint and building damage.

PARTICULATE MATTER

A certain amount of particulate matter is present in the burning of any fuel, with carbon constituting the largest percentage of the particulates. In gasoline, the remaining particulates are the burned remains of the various other compounds used in its manufacture. When a gasoline engine is in good internal condition, the particulate emissions are low but as the engine wears internally, the particulate emissions increase. By visually inspecting the tail pipe emissions, a determination can be made as to where an engine defect may exist. An engine with light gray or blue smoke emitting from the tail pipe normally indicates an increase in the oil consumption through burning due to internal engine wear. Black smoke would indicate a defective fuel delivery system, causing the engine to operate in a rich mode. Regardless of the color of the smoke, the internal part of the engine or the fuel delivery system should be repaired to prevent excess particulate emissions.

Diesel and turbine engines emit a darkened plume of smoke from the exhaust system because of the type of fuel used. Emission control regulations are mandated for this type of emission and more stringent measures are being used to prevent excess emission of the particulate matter. Electronic components are being introduced to control the injection of the fuel at precisely the proper time of piston travel, to achieve the optimum in fuel ignition and fuel usage. Other particulate after-burning components are being tested to achieve a cleaner emission.

Good grades of engine lubricating oils should be used, which meet the manufacturers specification. Cut-rate oils can contribute to the particulate emission problem because of their low flash or ignition temperature point. Such oils burn prematurely during the combustion process causing emission of particulate matter.

The cooling system is an important factor in the reduction of particulate matter. The optimum combustion will occur, with the cooling system operating at a temperature specified by the manufacturer. The cooling system must be maintained in the same manner as the engine oiling system, as each system is required to perform properly in order for the engine to operate efficiently for a long time.

Crankcase Emissions

Crankcase emissions are made up of water, acids, unburned fuel, oil fumes and particulates. These emissions are classified as hydrocarbons (HC) and are formed by the small amount of unburned, compressed air/fuel mixture entering the crankcase from the combustion area (between the cylinder walls and piston rings) during the compression and power strokes. The head of the compression and combustion help to form the remaining crankcase emissions.

Since the first engines, crankcase emissions were allowed into the atmosphere through a road draft tube, mounted on the lower side of the engine block. Fresh air came in through an open oil filler cap or breather. The air passed through the crankcase mixing with blow-by gases. The motion of the vehicle and the air blowing past the open end of the road draft tube caused a low pressure area (vacuum) at the end of the tube. Crankcase emissions were simply drawn out of the road draft tube into the air.

To control the crankcase emission, the road draft tube was deleted. A hose and/or tubing was routed from the crankcase to the intake manifold so the blow-by emission could be burned with the air/fuel mixture. However, it was found that intake manifold vacuum, used to draw the crankcase emissions into the manifold, would vary in strength at the wrong time and not allow the proper emission flow. A regulating valve was needed to control the flow of air through the crankcase.

Testing, showed the removal of the blow-by gases from the crankcase as quickly as possible, was most important to the longevity of the engine. Should large accumulations of blow-by gases remain and condense, dilution of the engine oil would occur to form water, soots, resins, acids and lead salts, resulting in the formation of sludge and varnishes. This condensation of the blow-by gases occurs more frequently on vehicles used in numerous starting and stopping conditions, excessive idling and when the engine is not allowed to attain normal operating temperature through short runs.

Evaporative Emissions

Gasoline fuel is a major source of pollution, before and after it is burned in the automobile engine. From the time the fuel is refined, stored, pumped and transported, again stored until it is pumped into the fuel tank of the vehicle, the gasoline gives off unburned hydrocarbons (HC) into the atmosphere. Through the redesign of storage areas and venting systems, the pollution factor was diminished, but not eliminated, from the refinery standpoint. However, the automobile still remained the primary source of vaporized, unburned hydrocarbon (HC) emissions.

Fuel pumped from an underground storage tank is cool but when exposed to a warmer ambient temperature, will expand. Before controls were mandated, an owner might fill the fuel tank with fuel from an underground storage tank and park the vehicle for some time in warm area, such as a parking lot. As the fuel would warm, it would expand and should no provisions or area be provided for the expansion, the fuel would spill out of the filler neck and onto the ground, causing hydrocarbon (HC) pollution and creating a severe fire hazard. To correct this condition, the vehicle manufacturers added overflow plumbing and/or gasoline tanks with built in expansion areas or domes.

However, this did not control the fuel vapor emission from the fuel tank. It was determined that most of the fuel evaporation occurred when the vehicle was stationary and the engine not operating. Most vehicles carry 5–25 gallons (19–95 liters) of gasoline. Should a large concentration of vehicles be parked in one area, such as a large parking lot, excessive fuel vapor emissions would take place, increasing as the temperature increases.

To prevent the vapor emission from escaping into the atmosphere, the fuel systems were designed to trap the vapors while the vehicle is stationary, by sealing the system from the atmosphere. A storage system is used to collect and hold the fuel vapors from the carburetor (if equipped) and the fuel tank when the engine is not operating. When the engine is started, the storage system is then purged of the fuel vapors, which are drawn into the engine and burned with the air/fuel mixture.

EMISSION CONTROLS

Positive Crankcase Ventilation (PCV) System

OPERATION

▶ **See Figures 1, 2, 3 and 4**

The PCV valve system vents crankcase gases into the engine air intake where they are burned with the fuel and air mixture. The PCV valve system keeps pollutants from being released into the atmosphere, and also helps to keep the engine oil clean, by ridding the crankcase of moisture and corrosive fumes. The PCV valve system consists of the PCV valve, its mounting grommet, the nipple in the air intake and the connecting hoses. On some engine applications, the PCV valve system is connected with the evaporative emission system.

The PCV valve controls the amount of vapors pulled into the intake manifold from the crankcase and acts as a check valve by preventing air flow from entering the crankcase in the opposite direction. The PCV valve also prevents combustion backfiring from entering the crankcase in order to prevent detonation of the accumulated crankcase gases.

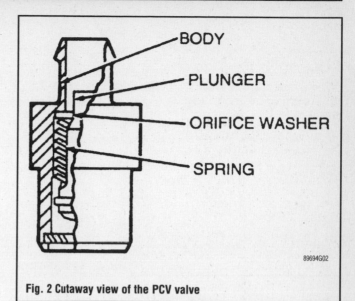

Fig. 2 Cutaway view of the PCV valve

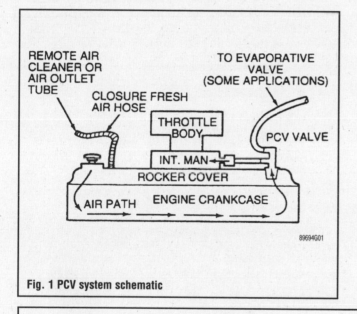

Fig. 1 PCV system schematic

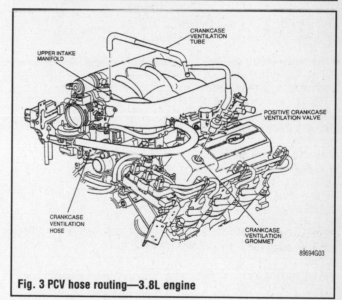

Fig. 3 PCV hose routing—3.8L engine

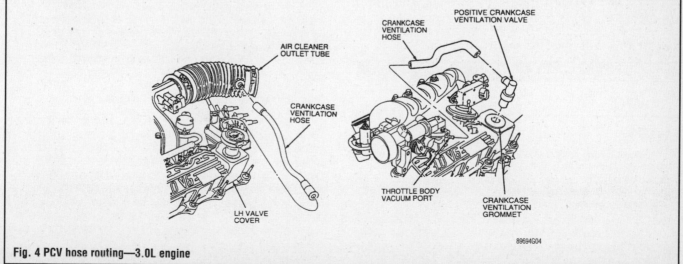

Fig. 4 PCV hose routing—3.0L engine

TESTING

▶ See Figure 5

1. Remove the PCV valve from the valve cover grommet.
2. Shake the PCV valve.
   a. If the valve rattles when shaken, reinstall it and proceed to Step 3.
   b. If the valve does not rattle, it is sticking and must be replaced.
3. Start the engine and allow it to reach normal operating temperature.
4. Check the PCV valve for vacuum by placing your finger over the end of the valve.
   a. If vacuum exists, proceed to Step 5.
   b. If vacuum does not exist, check for loose hose connections, vacuum leaks or blockage. Correct as necessary.
5. Disconnect the fresh air intake hose from the air inlet tube (connects the air cleaner housing to the throttle body).
6. Place a stiff piece of paper over the hose end and wait 1 minute.
   a. If vacuum holds the paper in place, the system is OK; reconnect the hose.
   b. If the paper is not held in place, check for loose hose connections, vacuum leaks or blockage. Correct as necessary.

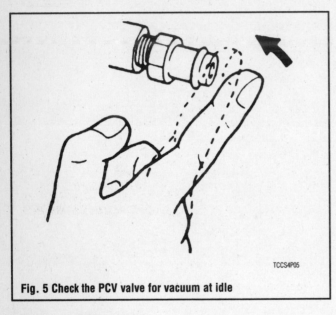

Fig. 5 Check the PCV valve for vacuum at idle

REMOVAL & INSTALLATION

1. Disconnect the vacuum hose from the PCV valve.
2. Remove the PCV valve from its mounting grommet.
3. To install, attach the PCV vacuum hose to the PCV valve, then insert the valve into its mounting grommet.

Evaporative Emission Controls

OPERATION

▶ See Figure 6

Fuel vapors trapped in the sealed fuel tank are vented through the Evaporative Emission Valve orifice in the top of the tank. The vapors leave the valve assembly through a single vapor line and continue through the Vapor Control Valve to the Evaporative Emission Canister for storage until they are purged to the engine for burning.

Purging removes the fuel vapor stored in the canister. The fuel vapor is purged via a Vapor Management Valve (VMV) or vacuum controlled purge valve. Purging occurs when the engine is at normal operating temperature and off idle.

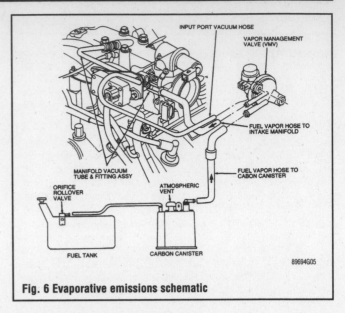

Fig. 6 Evaporative emissions schematic

Evaporative Emissions Canister

The fuel vapors from the fuel tank are stored in the fuel vapor canister until the vehicle is operated, at which time, the vapors will purge from the canister into the engine for consumption. The fuel vapor canister contains activated carbon, which absorbs the fuel vapor. The canister is located in the engine compartment or along the frame rail.

Evaporative Emission Valve

Fuel vapors in the tank are vented through the Evaporative Emission Valves in the top of the fuel tank. The vapors are transmitted through a single vapor tube to the canister at the front of the vehicle. A spring loaded poppet valve provides relief ahead of the orifice to the canister. This valve gradually opens above 20–25 in. Hg (5–6 kPa) to vent fuel vapors to the canister.

Vapor Control Valve

The vapor system also includes an inline vapor control valve mounted centrally on the top of the fuel tank. During refueling, the valve inhibits flow of vapor through the vapor valves to keep the tank from overfilling.

Vapor Management Valve (VMV)

The VMV is inline with the carbon canister and controls the flow of fuel vapors out of the canister. It is normally closed. When the engine is **OFF**, the vapors from the fuel tank flow into the canister. After the engine is started, the solenoid is engaged and opens, purging the vapors into the engine. With the solenoid open, vapors from the fuel tank are routed directly into the engine.

Pressure/Vacuum Relief Fuel Tank Filler Cap

The fuel cap contains an integral pressure and vacuum relief valve. The vacuum valve acts to allow air into the fuel tank to replace the fuel as it is used, while preventing vapors from escaping the tank through the atmosphere. The vacuum relief valve opens after a vacuum of 0.25 psi (1.7 kPa). The pressure valve acts as a backup pressure relief valve in the event the normal venting system is overcome by excessive generation of internal pressure or restriction of the normal venting system. The pressure relief is 2 psi (14 kPa). Fill cap damage or contamination that stops the pressure vacuum valve from working may result in deformation of the fuel tank.

COMPONENT TESTING

Evaporative Emissions Canister

Generally, the only testing done to the canister is a visual inspection. Look the canister over and replace it with a new one if there is any evidence of cracks or other damage.

Evaporative Emissions Valve

Inspect the valve for open air passage through the orifice. The valve is molded directly to the fuel tank and is not serviceable separately. If the orifice is blocked, replace the fuel tank.

Vapor Management Valve (VMV)

▶ See Figure 7

1. Remove the VMV.
2. Measure the resistance between the two VMV terminals.
   a. If the resistance is between 30–36 ohms, proceed to the Step 3.
   b. If the resistance is not between 30–36 ohms, replace the VMV.
3. Attach a hand-held vacuum pump to the intake manifold vacuum side of the VMV, then apply 16 in. Hg (53 kPa) of vacuum to the solenoid.

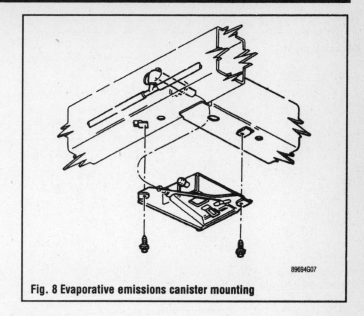

Fig. 8 Evaporative emissions canister mounting

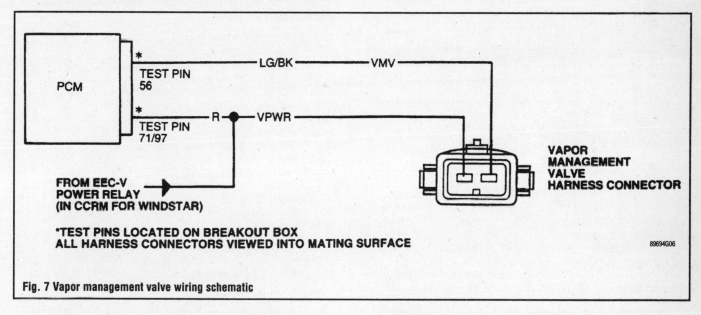

Fig. 7 Vapor management valve wiring schematic

a. If the solenoid will not hold vacuum for at least 20 seconds replace it with a new one.
b. If the solenoid holds vacuum, proceed to Step 4. Keep the vacuum applied to the solenoid.
4. Using an external voltage source, apply 9–14 DC volts to the VMV electrical terminals.
   a. If the solenoid opens and the vacuum drops, the solenoid is working properly. Check power and ground circuits.
   b. If the solenoid does not open and the vacuum remains, replace the solenoid is faulty.

REMOVAL & INSTALLATION

Evaporative Emissions Canister

▶ See Figure 8

1. Disconnect the vapor hose from the canister.
2. Remove the bolt retaining the canister and bracket assembly to the frame rail.
3. Lift the canister to disengage the tab on the back side of the canister and remove from the vehicle.

4. Installation is the reverse of removal. Tighten bolt to 17–20 ft. lbs. (22–28 Nm)

Evaporative Emissions Valve

The valve is an integral part of the fuel tank and is not serviceable separately. If replacement is required, the valve must be replaced as part of the fuel tank assembly.

Vapor Control Valve

1. Remove the fuel tank.
2. Disconnect the vapor hose from the valve.
3. Remove the valve.
4. Installation is the reverse of removal.

Vapor Management Valve (VMV)

▶ See Figure 9

1. Remove the cowl top vent panel.
2. Disconnect the electrical harness from the VMV.
3. Disconnect the fuel vapor hoses.

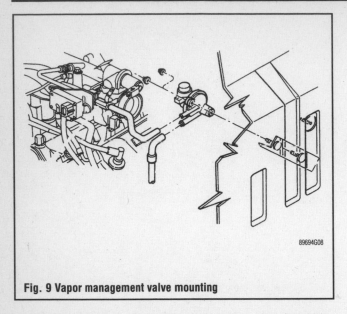

Fig. 9 Vapor management valve mounting

4. Loosen the two nuts securing the valve and remove from the vehicle.
5. Installation is the reverse of removal. Tighten the nuts to 98–115 inch lbs. (11–13 Nm).

Exhaust Gas Recirculation (EGR) System

OPERATION

▶ See Figure 10

The Exhaust Gas Recirculation (EGR) system is designed to reintroduce exhaust gas into the combustion chambers, thereby lowering combustion temperatures and reducing the formation of Oxides of Nitrogen (NO_x).

The amount of exhaust gas that is reintroduced into the combustion cycle is determined by several factors, such as: engine speed, engine vacuum, exhaust system backpressure, coolant temperature, throttle position. All EGR valves are vacuum operated. The EGR vacuum diagram for your particular vehicle is displayed on the Vehicle Emission Control Information (VECI) label.

The EGR system is Differential Pressure Feedback EGR (DPFE) system, controlled by the Powertrain Control Module (PCM) and composed of the following components: DPFE sensor (also referred to as the backpressure transducer), EGR Vacuum Regulator (EVR) solenoid, EGR valve, and assorted hoses.

COMPONENT TESTING

DPFE Sensor

▶ See Figure 11

1. Disconnect the pressure hoses at the DPFE sensor.
2. Connect a hand vacuum pump to the downstream pickup marked **REF** on the sensor.
3. Using a multimeter, backprobe the SIG RTN circuit at the DPFE connector.
4. With the ignition **ON**, signal voltage should be 0.20–0.70 volts.
5. Apply 8–9 in. Hg of vacuum to the sensor. Voltage should be greater than 4 volts.
6. Quickly release the vacuum from the sensor. Voltage should drop to less than 1 volt in 3 seconds.
7. If the sensor does not respond as specified, check the power and ground circuits.
8. If power and ground circuits are functional, the sensor is faulty.

EVR Solenoid

▶ See Figure 12

1. Remove the EVR solenoid.
2. Attempt to lightly blow air into the EVR solenoid.
   a. If air blows through the solenoid, replace the solenoid with a new one.
   b. If air does not pass freely through the solenoid, continue with the test.
3. Apply battery voltage (approximately 12 volts) and a ground to the EVR solenoid electrical terminals. Attempt to lightly blow air, once again, through the solenoid.
   a. If air does not pass through the solenoid, replace the solenoid with a new one.
   b. If air does not flow through the solenoid, the solenoid is OK.
4. If the solenoid is functional but the problem still exists, check the power and ground circuits.

EGR Valve

1. Install a tachometer on the engine, following the manufacturer's instructions.
2. Detach the engine wiring harness connector from the Idle Air Control (IAC) solenoid.

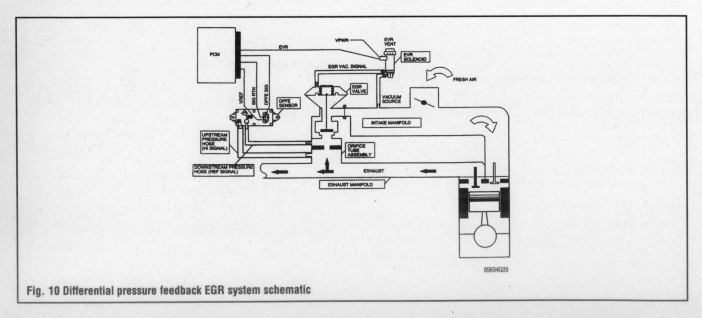

Fig. 10 Differential pressure feedback EGR system schematic

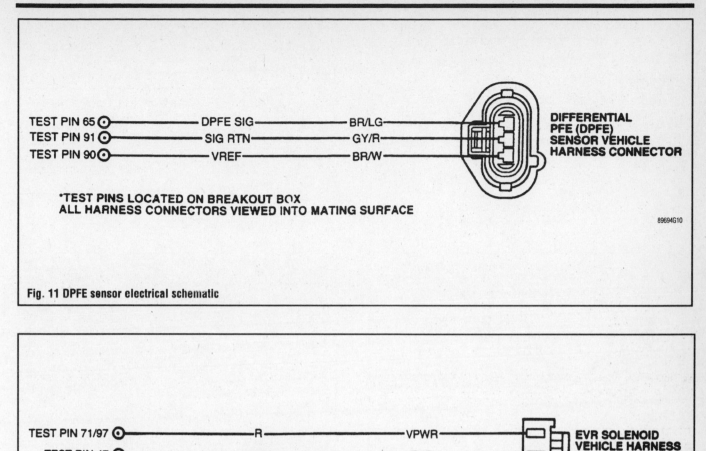

TEST PIN 65 ⊙────────DPFE SIG────────BR/LG────────
TEST PIN 91 ⊙────────SIG RTN────────GY/R────────
TEST PIN 90 ⊙────────VREF────────BR/W────────

DIFFERENTIAL PFE (DPFE) SENSOR VEHICLE HARNESS CONNECTOR

***TEST PINS LOCATED ON BREAKOUT BOX
ALL HARNESS CONNECTORS VIEWED INTO MATING SURFACE**

89694G10

Fig. 11 DPFE sensor electrical schematic

TEST PIN 71/97 ⊙────────R────────VPWR────────
TEST PIN 47 ⊙────────BR/PK────────EVR────────

EVR SOLENOID VEHICLE HARNESS CONNECTOR

***TEST PINS LOCATED ON BREAKOUT BOX
ALL HARNESS CONNECTORS VIEWED INTO MATING SURFACE**

89694G11

Fig. 12 EVR solenoid electrical schematic

3. Disconnect and plug the vacuum supply hose from the EGR valve.

4. Start the engine, then apply the parking brake, block the rear wheels and position the transmission in Neutral.

5. Observe and note the idle speed.

➡**If the engine will not idle with the IAC solenoid disconnected, provide an air bypass to the engine by slightly opening the throttle plate or by creating an intake vacuum leak. Do not allow the idle speed to exceed typical idle rpm.**

6. Using a hand-held vacuum pump, slowly apply 5–10 in. Hg (17–34 kPa) of vacuum to the EGR valve nipple.

a. If the idle speed drops more than 100 rpm with the vacuum applied and returns to normal after the vacuum is removed, the EGR valve is OK.

b. If the idle speed does not drop more than 100 rpm with the vacuum applied and return to normal after the vacuum is removed, inspect the EGR valve for a blockage; clean it if a blockage is found. Replace the EGR valve if no blockage is found, or if cleaning the valve does not remedy the malfunction.

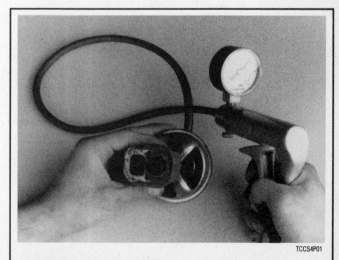

TCCS4P01

Some EGR valves may be tested using a vacuum pump by watching for diaphragm movement

REMOVAL & INSTALLATION

DPFE Sensor

▶ **See Figures 13 and 14**

1. Disconnect the negative battery cable.
2. Label and disconnect the wiring harness from the DPFE sensor.
3. Label and disconnect the vacuum hoses.
4. Remove the mounting nuts, then separate the sensor from the mounting bracket.

To install:

5. Position the DPFE sensor on the mounting bracket, then install and tighten the mounting nuts until snug.
6. Attach all necessary hoses and wiring to the sensor.
7. Connect the negative battery cable.

EVR Solenoid

➡ The EVR solenoid is mounted either on the same bracket as the PFE/DPFE sensor, attached to the upper intake manifold, or near the EGR valve on its own bracket.

1. Disconnect the negative battery cable.
2. Label and detach the wiring harness connector from the EVR solenoid.
3. Detach the main emission vacuum control connector from the solenoid.
4. Remove the retaining nuts, then separate the solenoid from the mounting bracket.

To install:

5. Position the solenoid on its mounting bracket and install the retaining nuts.
6. Attach the main emission vacuum control connector and the wiring harness connector to the EVR solenoid.
7. Connect the negative battery cable.

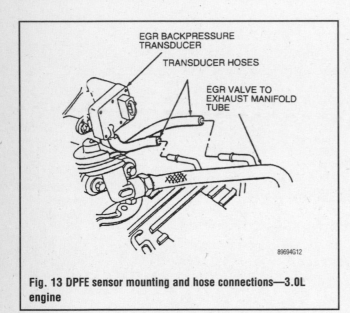

EGR BACKPRESSURE
TRANSDUCER

TRANSDUCER HOSES

EGR VALVE TO
EXHAUST MANIFOLD
TUBE

89694G12

Fig. 13 DPFE sensor mounting and hose connections—3.0L engine

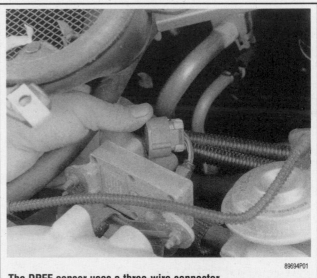

89694P01

The DPFE sensor uses a three-wire connector

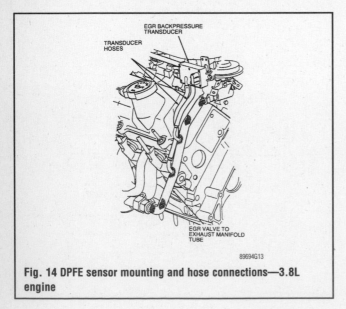

EGR BACKPRESSURE
TRANSDUCER

TRANSDUCER
HOSES

EGR VALVE TO
EXHAUST MANIFOLD
TUBE

89694G13

Fig. 14 DPFE sensor mounting and hose connections—3.8L engine

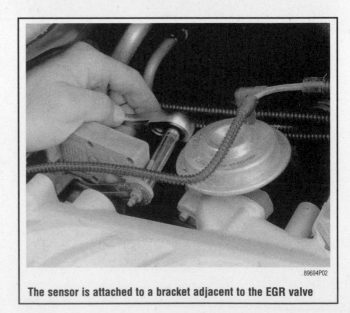

89694P02

The sensor is attached to a bracket adjacent to the EGR valve

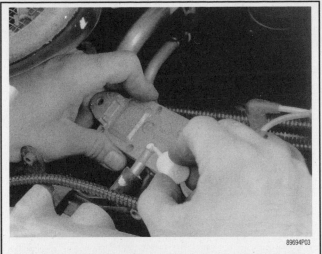

It is always a good idea to matchmark hoses for installation reference

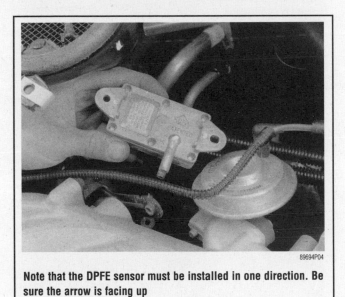

Note that the DPFE sensor must be installed in one direction. Be sure the arrow is facing up

EGR Valve

▶ See Figures 15 and 16

1. Disconnect the negative battery cable.
2. If necessary, remove the air inlet tube from the throttle body and air cleaner housing.
3. Label and detach all vacuum hoses from the EGR valve.
4. Label and detach any electrical wiring harness connectors from the EGR valve.
5. Disconnect the EGR valve-to-exhaust manifold tube from the EGR valve.
6. Remove the EGR valve mounting fasteners, then separate the valve from the upper intake manifold.
7. Remove and discard the old EGR valve gasket, and clean the gasket mating surfaces on the valve and the intake manifold.

To install:

8. Install the EGR valve, along with a new gasket, on the upper intake manifold, then install and tighten the mounting bolts to 15–22 ft. lbs. (20–30 Nm) on 3.8L engines, or to 106–159 inch lbs. (12–18 Nm) on 5.0L engines.
9. Connect the EGR valve-to-exhaust manifold tube to the valve, then tighten the tube nut to 30 ft. lbs. (41 Nm).
10. Connect all wiring or hoses to the EGR valve.
11. Install the air inlet tube.
12. Connect the negative battery cable.

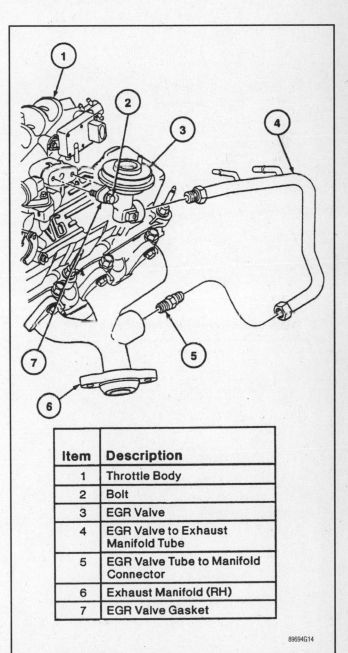

Item	Description
1	Throttle Body
2	Bolt
3	EGR Valve
4	EGR Valve to Exhaust Manifold Tube
5	EGR Valve Tube to Manifold Connector
6	Exhaust Manifold (RH)
7	EGR Valve Gasket

Fig. 15 EGR valve and component mounting—3.0L engine

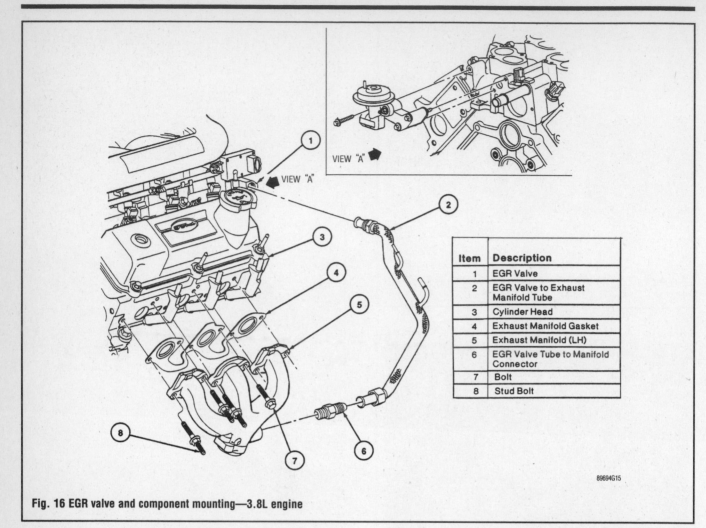

Item	Description
1	EGR Valve
2	EGR Valve to Exhaust Manifold Tube
3	Cylinder Head
4	Exhaust Manifold Gasket
5	Exhaust Manifold (LH)
6	EGR Valve Tube to Manifold Connector
7	Bolt
8	Stud Bolt

Fig. 16 EGR valve and component mounting—3.8L engine

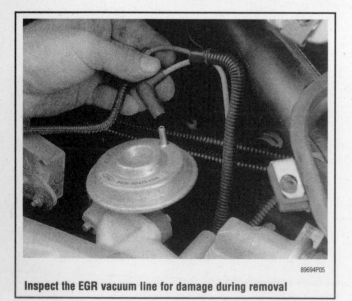

Inspect the EGR vacuum line for damage during removal

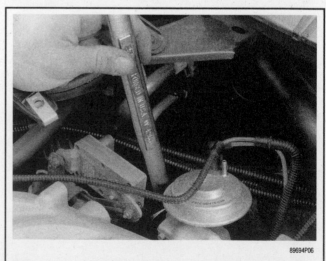

The exhaust manifold tube must be disconnected to remove the EGR valve

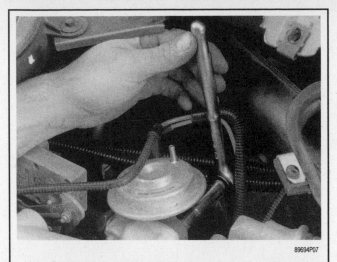

89694P07

It may be necessary to spray the EGR attaching bolts with penetrant prior to removal

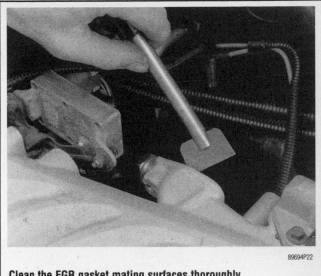

89694P22

Clean the EGR gasket mating surfaces thoroughly

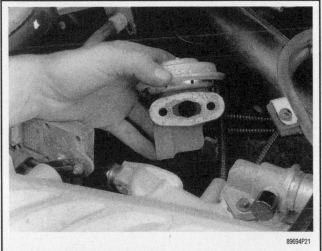

89694P21

Inspect the EGR passages for blockage. If deposits cannot be removed, replace the EGR valve

ELECTRONIC ENGINE CONTROLS

Electronic Engine Control 5 (EEC-V) System

▶ **See Figures 17 and 18**

The EEC-5 system is the latest generation of Ford's engine control technology. EEC-5 is compliant with the latest OBD-II regulations set forth by the government. When a system or component exceeds emission thresholds or a component operates outside of tolerance, a Diagnostic Trouble Code (DTC) will be stored in the Powertrain Control Module (PCM) and the Malfunction Indicator Lamp (MIL) will be illuminated.

The PCM is the heart of the EEC-5 system. It receives data from a number of sensors and other electronic components (switches, relay, etc.). Based on information received and programs mapped into the PCM's memory, it generates output signals to control various relay, solenoids and other actuators. The PCM in the EEC-5 system has calibration modules, located inside the assembly, that contain calibration specifications for optimizing emissions, fuel economy and driveability. The calibration module is called a PROM.

The EEC-5 system consists of the following components:
- Powertrain Control Module (PCM)
- Throttle Position (TP) sensor
- Mass Air Flow (MAF) sensor
- Intake Air Temperature (IAT) sensor
- Idle Air Control (IAC) valve
- Engine Coolant Temperature (ECT) sensor
- Heated Oxygen Sensor (HO2S)
- Camshaft Position (CMP) sensor
- Knock Sensor (KS)
- Vehicle Speed Sensor (VSS)
- Crankshaft Position (CKP) sensor

The MAF sensor (a potentiometer) senses the position of the airflow in the engine's air induction system and generates a voltage signal that varies with the amount of air drawn into the engine. The IAT sensor (a sensor in the area of the MAF sensor) measures the temperature of the incoming air and transmits a corresponding electrical signal. Another temperature sensor (the ECT sensor) inserted in the engine coolant tells if the engine is cold or warmed up. The TP sensor, a switch that senses throttle plate position, pro-

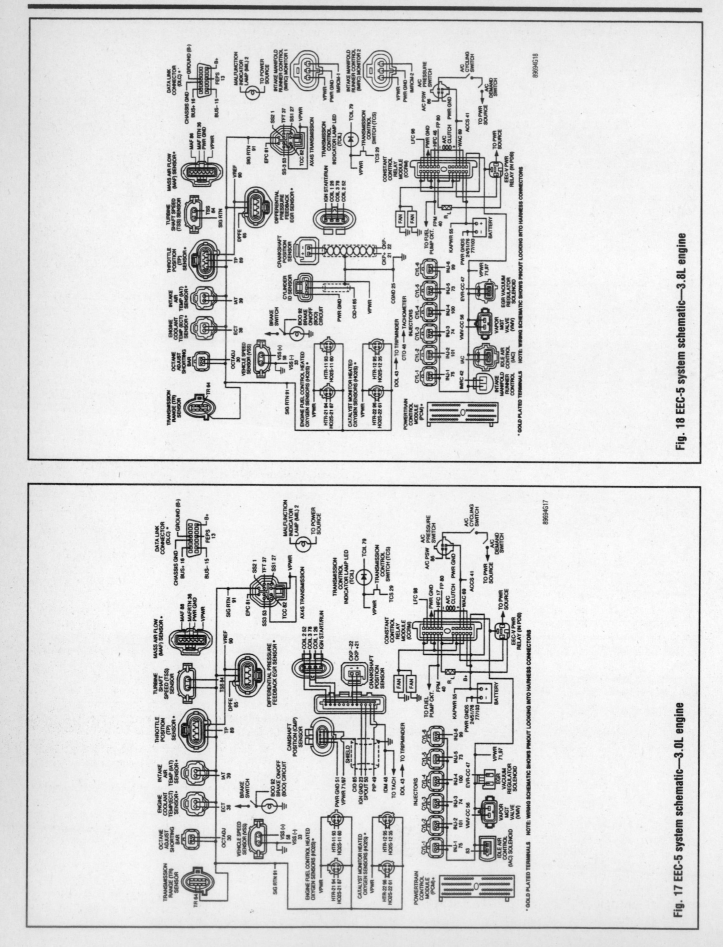

Fig. 18 EEC-5 system schematic—3.8L engine

Fig. 17 EEC-5 system schematic—3.0L engine

duces electrical signals that tell the PCM when the throttle is closed or wide open. A special probe (the HO2S) in the exhaust manifold measures the amount of oxygen in the exhaust gas, which is in indication of combustion efficiency, and sends a signal to the PCM. The sixth signal, camshaft position information, is transmitted by the CMP sensor, installed in place of the distributor.

The EEC-5 microcomputer circuit processes the input signals and produces output control signals to the fuel injectors to regulate fuel discharged to the injectors. It also adjusts ignition spark timing to provide the best balance between driveability and economy, and controls the IAC valve to maintain the proper idle speed.

→**Because of the complicated nature of the EEC-5 OBD II system, special tools such as a Break Out Box (BOB) and a Generic Scan Tool (GST) are necessary for testing and troubleshooting.**

Powertrain Control Module (PCM)

OPERATION

The Powertrain Control Module (PCM) performs many functions on your vehicle. The module accepts information from various engine sensors and computes the required fuel flow rate necessary to maintain the correct amount of air/fuel ratio throughout the entire engine operational range.

Based on the information that is received and programmed into the PCM's memory, the PCM generates output signals to control relays, actuators and solenoids. The PCM also sends out a command to the fuel injectors that meters the appropriate quantity of fuel. The module automatically senses and compensates for any changes in altitude when driving your vehicle.

The PCM is located behind the passenger's side of the firewall.

REMOVAL & INSTALLATION

▸ **See Figure 19**

→**When the battery has been disconnected, some abnormal driving symptoms may occur while the PCM relearns its fuel trim. The vehicle may need to be driven 10 miles (16 km) or more to relearn the fuel trim.**

1. Disconnect the negative battery cable.
2. Remove the cowl top vent panel.
3. Loosen the engine control sensor wiring to PCM connector retaining bolt.
4. Remove the engine control sensor wiring connector form the PCM.
5. Remove the PCM cover nuts.

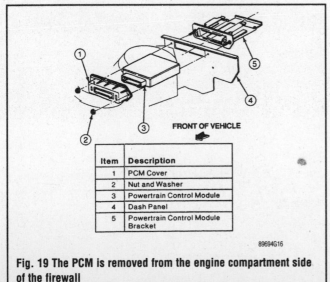

Item	Description
1	PCM Cover
2	Nut and Washer
3	Powertrain Control Module
4	Dash Panel
5	Powertrain Control Module Bracket

89694G16

Fig. 19 The PCM is removed from the engine compartment side of the firewall

89694P08

The PCM is located behind the passenger's side of the firewall

6. Remove PCM cover.
7. Pull the PCM out of the bracket.

To install:

8. Position the PCM in the bracket.
9. Install PCM cover and tighten nuts to 35–49 inch lbs. (4–7 Nm).
10. Install the engine control sensor wiring connector and tighten the bolt to 32 inch lbs. (4 Nm).
11. Install the cowl top vent panel.
12. Connect the negative battery cable.

Heated Oxygen Sensors (HO2S)

OPERATION

The heated oxygen sensor supplies the PCM with a signal which indicates a rich or lean condition during engine operation. The input information assists the computer in determining the proper air/fuel ratio. A low voltage signal from the sensor indicates too much oxygen in the exhaust (lean condition) and a high voltage signal indicates too little oxygen in the exhaust (rich condition).

The sensors are threaded into the dual converter Y-pipe. Heated oxygen sensors are used on all models to allow the engine to reach the closed loop state faster.

Heated oxygen sensors are located in the dual converter Y-pipe both before and after the catalyst.

TESTING

✳ WARNING

Do not pierce the wires when testing this sensor; this can lead to wiring harness damage. Backprobe the connector to properly read the voltage of the HO2S.

1. Disconnect the HO2S.
2. Measure the resistance between PWR and GND terminals of the sensor. Resistance should be approximately 6 ohms at 68°F (20°C). If resistance is not within specification, the sensor's heater element is faulty.
3. With the HO2S connected and engine running, measure the voltage with a Digital Volt-Ohmmeter (DVOM) between terminals **HO2S** and **SIG RTN** (GND) of the oxygen sensor connector. Voltage should fluctuate between 0.01–1.1 volts. If voltage fluctuation is slow or voltage is not within specification, the sensor may be faulty.

REMOVAL & INSTALLATION

1. Disconnect the negative battery cable.
2. Raise and support the vehicle safely.
3. Label and disconnect the HO2S from the engine control wiring harness.

→**Lubricate the sensor with penetrating oil prior to removal.**

4. Remove the sensor using an Oxygen Sensor Wrench (T94P-9472-A), or equivalent.
To install:
5. Install the sensor in the mounting boss and tighten to 27–33 ft. lbs. (37–45 Nm).
6. Connect the engine control wiring harness to the sensor.
7. Lower the vehicle.
8. Connect the negative battery cable.

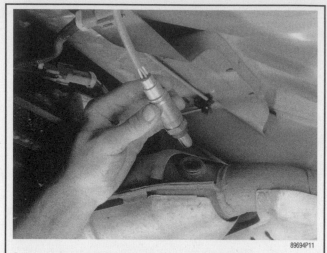

If reinstalling an old oxygen sensor, coat the threads with anti-seize compound. New sensors are already coated

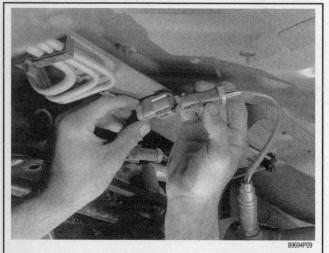

Never detach the oxygen sensor connector while the engine is running

Oxygen sensors are located in the dual converter Y-pipe

Idle Air Control (IAC) Valve

OPERATION

The IAC valve adjusts the engine idle speed. The valve is located on the side of the throttle body. The valve is controlled by a duty cycle signal from the PCM and allows air to bypass the throttle plate in order to maintain the proper idle speed.

The IAC is located at the top of the upper intake manifold adjacent to the throttle body.

→**Do not attempt to clean the IAC valve. Carburetor tune-up cleaners or any type of solvent cleaners will damage the internal components of the valve.**

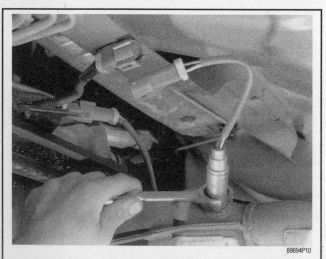

An oxygen sensor wrench is available from Ford or aftermarket manufacturers to ease sensor removal

TESTING

▶ **See Figures 20 and 21**

1. Turn the ignition switch to the **OFF** position.
2. Disconnect the wiring harness from the IAC valve .
3. Measure the resistance between the terminals of the valve.

➡**Due to the diode in the solenoid, place the ohmmeter positive lead on the VPWR terminal and the negative lead on the ISC terminal.**

4. Resistance should be 6–13 ohms.
5. If resistance is not within specification, the valve may be faulty.

REMOVAL & INSTALLATION

1. Disconnect the negative battery cable.
2. Disconnnect the wiring harness from the IAC valve.
3. Remove the two retaining bolts.
4. Remove the IAC valve and discard the old gasket.

To install:

5. Clean the gasket mating surfaces thoroughly.
6. Using a new gasket, position the IAC valve on the throttle body.
7. Install and tighten the retaining bolts to 71–106 inch lbs. (8–12 Nm).
8. Connect the wiring harness to the IAC valve.
9. Connect the negative battery cable.

The IAC connector is held in place by a clip which must be carefully lifted to disengage the connector

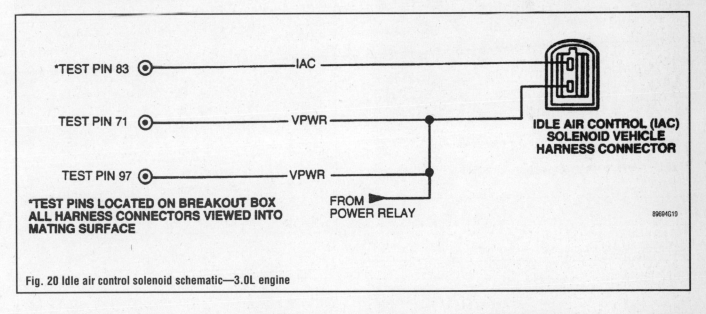

Fig. 20 Idle air control solenoid schematic—3.0L engine

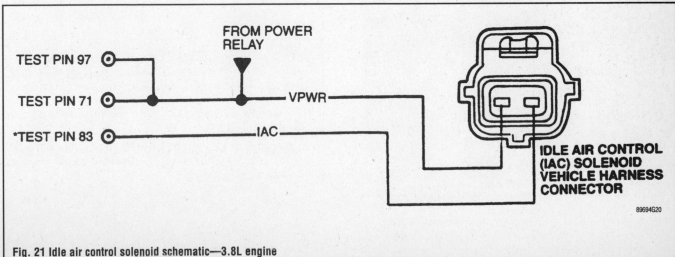

Fig. 21 Idle air control solenoid schematic—3.8L engine

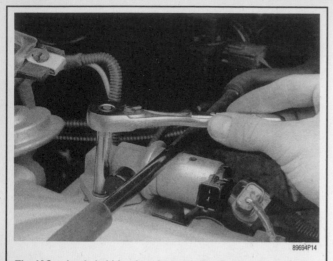

The IAC valve is held in place by two bolts. Remove them carefully, as to not strip the aluminum intake manifold

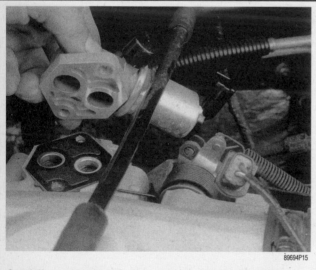

Carefully remove the IAC valve as to not damage the gasket

Inspect the IAC gasket carefully for leaks or damage. A leaky gasket can result in idle speed problems

Engine Coolant Temperature (ECT) Sensor

OPERATION

▶ **See Figures 22 and 23**

The engine coolant temperature sensor resistance changes in response to engine coolant temperature. The sensor resistance decreases as the coolant temperature increases. This provides a reference signal to the PCM, which indicates engine coolant temperature.

On 3.0L engines, the ECT is mounted at the top of the water outlet housing on the lower intake manifold. The second sensor (green) mounted to the lower intake manifold is the coolant temperature sender for the coolant gauge on the instrument panel.

On 3.8L engines, the ECT is mounted to the side of the water outlet housing on the lower intake manifold.

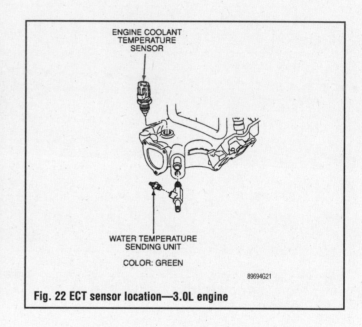

Fig. 22 ECT sensor location—3.0L engine

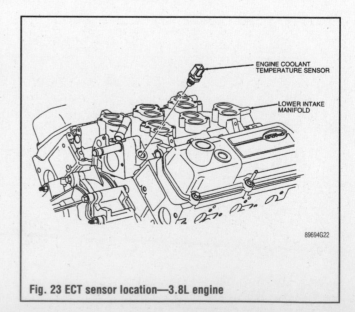

Fig. 23 ECT sensor location—3.8L engine

TESTING

▶ **See Figure 24**

1. Disconnect the engine wiring harness from the ECT sensor.
2. Connect an ohmmeter between the ECT sensor terminals.
3. With the engine cold and the ignition switch in the **OFF** position, measure and note the ECT sensor resistance.
4. Connect the engine wiring harness to the sensor.
5. Start the engine and allow the engine to reach normal operating temperature.
6. Once the engine has reached normal operating temperature, turn the engine **OFF**.
7. Once again, disconnect the engine wiring harness from the ECT sensor.
8. Measure and note the ECT sensor resistance with the engine hot.
9. Compare the cold and hot ECT sensor resistance measurements with the accompanying chart.
10. If readings do not approximate those in the chart, the sensor may be faulty.

REMOVAL & INSTALLATION

1. Partially drain the engine cooling system until the coolant level is below the ECT sensor mounting hole.
2. Disconnect the negative battery cable.
3. Disconnect the wiring harness from the ECT sensor.
4. Remove the coolant temperature sensor from the intake manifold.

To install:

5. Coat the sensor threads with Teflon® sealant.
6. Thread the sensor into the intake manifold and tighten to 71–115 inch lbs. (8–13 Nm).
7. Connect the negative battery cable.
8. Refill the engine cooling system.
9. Start the engine and check for coolant leaks. Top off the cooling system.

Temperature		Engine Coolant/Intake Air Temperature Sensor Values
		Resistance (K ohms)
°F	°C	
248	120	1.18
230	110	1.55
212	100	2.07
194	90	2.80
176	80	3.84
158	70	5.37
140	60	7.70
122	50	10.97
104	40	16.15
86	30	24.27
68	20	37.30
50	10	58.75

89694G23

Fig. 24 ECT and IAT sensor resistance-to-temperature specifications

TCCS4P02

Another method of testing the ECT sensor is to submerge it in cold or hot water and check resistance

Intake Air Temperature (IAT) Sensor

OPERATION

▶ **See Figures 25 and 26**

The Intake Air Temperature (IAT) sensor resistance changes in response to the ambient air temperature. The sensor resistance decreases as the air temperature increases. This provides a signal to the PCM indicating the temperature of the incoming air charge.

The 3.0L engine sensor is mounted in the air cleaner-to-throttle body supply tube, while the 3.8L engine sensor is mounted in the air cleaner box.

TESTING

1. Turn the ignition switch **OFF**.
2. Disconnect the wiring harness from the IAT sensor.
3. Measure the resistance between the sensor terminals.
4. Compare the resistance reading with the accompanying chart.
5. If the resistance is not within specification, the IAT may be faulty.
6. Connect the wiring harness to the sensor.

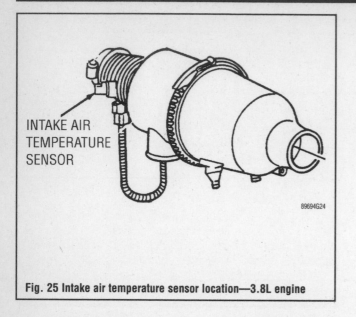

Fig. 25 Intake air temperature sensor location—3.8L engine

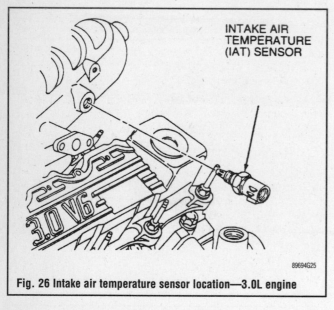

Fig. 26 Intake air temperature sensor location—3.0L engine

REMOVAL & INSTALLATION

1. Disconnect the negative battery cable.
2. Disconnect the wiring harness from the IAT sensor.
3. Remove the sensor.

To install:

4. Clean the air cleaner outlet tube or air cleaner box of all dirt and grime.
5. Install the sensor and tighten securely on the 3.8L engine. Tighten the sensor to 12–17 ft. lbs. (16–24 Nm) on the 3.0L engine.
6. Connect the wiring harness to the sensor.
7. Connect the negative battery cable.

Mass Air Flow (MAF) Sensor

OPERATION

▶ **See Figure 27**

The MAF sensor directly measures the amount of the air flowing into the engine. The sensor is mounted between the air cleaner assembly and the air cleaner outlet tube.

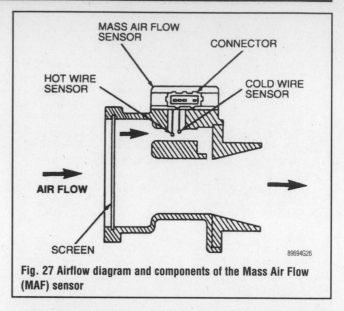

Fig. 27 Airflow diagram and components of the Mass Air Flow (MAF) sensor

The sensor utilizes a hot wire sensing element to measure the amount of air entering the engine. The sensor does this by sending a signal, generated by the sensor when the incoming air cools the hot wire down, to the PCM. The signal is used by the PCM to calculate the injector pulse width, which controls the air/fuel ratio in the engine. The sensor and plastic housing are integral and must be replaced if found to be defective.

The sensing element (hot wire) is one thin platinum wire wound on a ceramic bobbin and coated with glass. This hot wire is maintained at 392°F (200°C) above the ambient temperature as measured by a constant "cold wire".

TESTING

▶ **See Figure 28**

1. Using a multimeter, check for voltage by backprobing the MAF sensor connector.
2. With the engine running at idle, verify that there is at least 10.5 volts between the VPWR and PWR GND terminals of the MAF sensor connector. If voltage is not within specification, check power and ground circuits and repair as necessary.
3. Check voltage between the MAF and MAF RTN terminals. Voltage should be approximately 0.34–1.96 volts. If voltage is not within specification, the sensor may be faulty.

REMOVAL & INSTALLATION

✳✳ CAUTION

Do not tamper with the sensing element located in the MAF sensor.

3.0L Engine

1. Disconnect the negative battery cable.
2. Disconnect the wiring harness from the MAF sensor.
3. Loosen the engine air cleaner outlet tube clamps, then remove the tube from the engine.
4. Remove the MAF retaining nuts.
5. Remove the MAF sensor and discard the gasket.

To install:

6. Install the MAF sensor using a new gasket and tighten nuts to 71–106 inch lbs. (8–12 Nm).
7. Install the air cleaner outlet tube, then tighten the outlet tube clamps to 18–27 inch lbs. (2–3 Nm).
8. Connect the wiring harness to the MAF sensors.
9. Connect the negative battery cable.

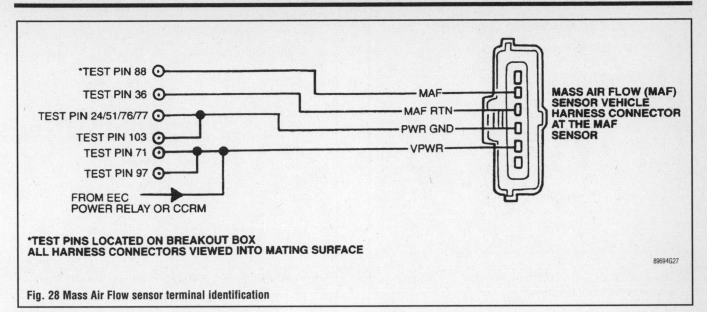

Fig. 28 Mass Air Flow sensor terminal identification

3.8L Engine

1. Disconnect the negative battery cable.
2. Release the band clamp to separate the outer cover from the engine air cleaner.
3. Pull back the wire convolute near the grommet of the intake air system.
4. Pull the grommet out of the cover and slide down the wire.
5. Remove the inner flange cover containing the MAF within the intake air system outer cover.
6. Disconnect the wiring harness from the MAF sensor.
7. Remove the MAF retaining nuts.
8. Remove the MAF sensor and discard the gasket.

To install:
9. Inspect the MAF screen and replace as necessary.
10. Install the MAF and tighten retaining nuts to 71–106 inch lbs. (8–12 Nm).
11. Connect the wiring harness to the MAF sensors.
12. Align the notch of the inner flange cover with the actual notch in the outer cover and install. The mass air flow sensor connector will align with the opening in the outer cover.

➡**The grommet used to seal the opening in the outer cover for the electrical wire must be fully installed and the air outlet tube must be securely fastened. Otherwise, unmetered air will enter the engine.**

13. Slide the grommet up the wire and insert into the cover.
14. Cover the wire with the convolute.
15. Align the engine air cleaner with the outer cover and secure with band clamp.
16. Connect the negative battery cable.

Throttle Position (TP) Sensor

OPERATION

The TP sensor is a potentiometer that provides a signal to the PCM that is directly proportional to the throttle plate position. The TP sensor is mounted on the side of the throttle body and is connected to the throttle plate shaft. The TP sensor monitors throttle plate movement and position, and transmits an appropriate electrical signal to the PCM. These signals are used by the PCM to adjust the air/fuel mixture, spark timing and EGR operation according to engine load at idle, part throttle, or full throttle. The TP sensor is not adjustable.

TESTING

1. Disconnect the negative battery cable.
2. Disconnect the wiring harness from the sensor.
3. Check resistance between terminals TP (br/w wire) and the VREF (gy/w wire), on the TP sensor.

➡**Do not measure the wiring harness connector terminals, rather the terminals on the sensor itself.**

4. Slowly rotate the throttle shaft and monitor the ohmmeter for a continuous, steady change in resistance. Any sudden jumps, or irregularities (such as jumping back and forth) in resistance indicates a malfunctioning sensor.
5. Reconnect the negative battery cable.
6. Turn the ignition switch **ON** and using the DVOM on voltmeter function, measure the voltage between terminals 89 and 90 of the breakout box. The specification is 0.9 volts.
7. If the voltage is outside the standard value or if it does not change smoothly, inspect the circuit wiring and/or replace the TP sensor.

REMOVAL & INSTALLATION

1. Disconnect the negative battery cable.
2. Disconnect the wiring harness from the TP sensor.

The throttle position sensor uses a three-terminal connector

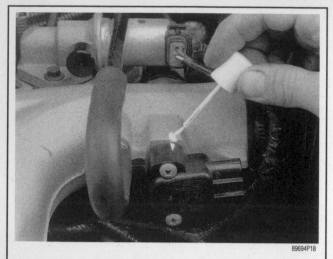

If the sensor has adjustment slots, it is a good idea to match-mark the sensor to the throttle body

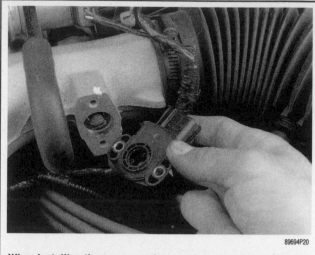

When installing the sensor, make sure the tang properly aligns with the slot in the sensor

The throttle position sensor is secured by two screws

3. Remove the two sensor mounting screws, then pull the TP sensor out of the throttle body housing.

To install:

4. Position the sensor against the throttle body housing, ensuring that the mounting screw holes are aligned.

5. When positioning the TP sensor against the throttle body, slide the sensor straight onto the housing.

6. Install and tighten the sensor mounting screws to 25–34 inch lbs. (3–4 Nm).

7. Connect the wiring harness to the sensor.

8. Connect the negative battery cable.

Camshaft Position (CMP) Sensor

OPERATION

The CMP sensor, also known as the Cylinder Identification (CID) sensor, provides camshaft position information, called the CMP or CID signal, which is used by the Powertrain Control Module (PCM) for fuel and ignition system synchronization.

The sensor is located at the front of the engine in the bore formerly occupied by the distributor.

TESTING

▶ **See Figure 29**

1. Check voltage between the camshaft position sensor terminals PWR GND and CID.

2. With engine running, voltage should be greater than 0.1 volt AC and vary with engine speed.

3. If voltage is not within specification, check for proper voltage at the VPWR terminal.

4. If VPWR voltage is greater than 10.5 volts, sensor may be faulty.

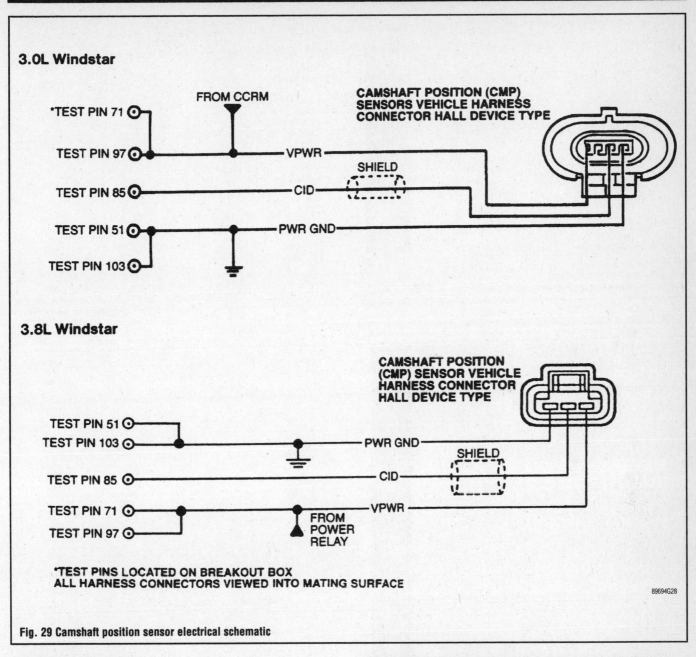

Fig. 29 Camshaft position sensor electrical schematic

REMOVAL & INSTALLATION

♦ See Figures 30 and 31

1. Rotate the engine so that the No. 1 piston is at TDC of the compression stroke and the timing pointer is at 0 degrees on the scale.
2. Matchmark the position of the camshaft position sensor electrical connector.
3. Disconnect the negative battery cable.
4. Disconnect the fuel charging electrical harness from the CMP sensor.
5. Remove the CMP sensor retaining screws and lift the sensor from the housing.
6. If the CMP housing is to be removed, proceed as follows:
   a. Remove the housing hold down clamp.
   b. Lift the sensor housing and oil pump intermediate shaft from the engine as an assembly.

To install:

➡ When replacing the CMP housing with a new housing, the replacement should contain a plastic locator cover tool. If the plastic cover tool is missing, a special service tool must be obtained prior to installation of the replacement sensor. Failure to follow this procedure will result in improper camshaft position sensor alignment. This will result in the ignition system and fuel system being out of time with the engine and possibly cause severe engine damage.

7. If the plastic locator cover tool is not attached to the replacement camshaft position sensor, attach Syncro Positioning Tool (T95T-12200-A) for a 3.0L engine or (T89T-12200-A) for a 3.8L engine as follows:
   a. Engage CMP sensor housing vane into the radial slot of the tool.
   b. Rotate tool on CMP sensor housing until tool boss engages notch in CMP sensor housing.
8. Transfer oil pump intermediate shaft from old CMP sensor housing to replacement housing.
9. Install CMP sensor housing so drive gear engagement occurs when arrow on locator tool is pointed approximately as shown in the illustrations. This step should align the CMP sensor electrical connector with the matchmark made during removal.
10. Install the hold down clamp and tighten bolt to 15–22 ft. lbs. (20–30 Nm).
11. Remove the syncro positioning tool.

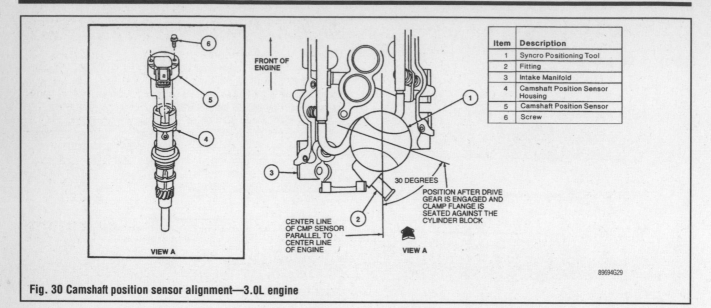

Item	Description
1	Syncro Positioning Tool
2	Fitting
3	Intake Manifold
4	Camshaft Position Sensor Housing
5	Camshaft Position Sensor
6	Screw

89694G29

Fig. 30 Camshaft position sensor alignment—3.0L engine

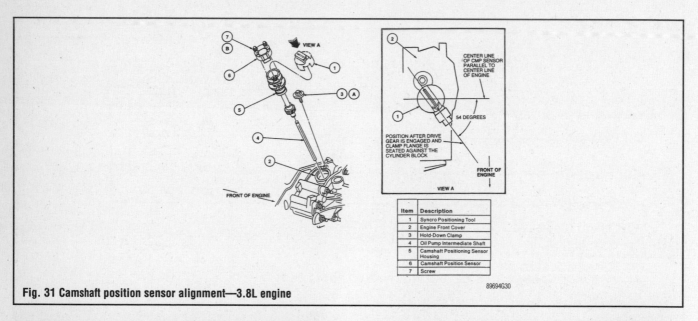

Item	Description
1	Syncro Positioning Tool
2	Engine Front Cover
3	Hold-Down Clamp
4	Oil Pump Intermediate Shaft
5	Camshaft Positioning Sensor Housing
6	Camshaft Position Sensor
7	Screw

89694G30

Fig. 31 Camshaft position sensor alignment—3.8L engine

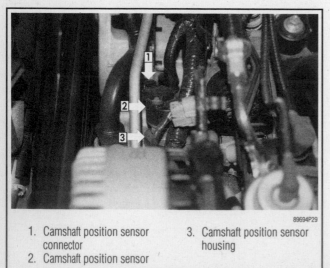

89694P29

1. Camshaft position sensor connector
2. Camshaft position sensor
3. Camshaft position sensor housing

Camshaft position sensor components

89694P23

The CMP sensor is attached to the fuel charging wiring harness with a three-terminal connector

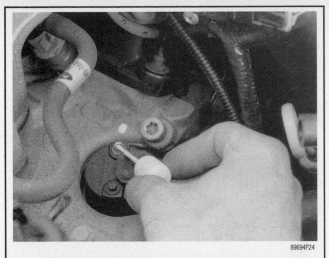

It is extremely important to matchmark the position of the CMP sensor to the engine

If the sensor and housing are to be removed as an assembly, loosen the housing retaining bolt . . .

. . . then remove the housing with the sensor and oil pump intermediate shaft

✳✳ CAUTION

If the CMP sensor electrical connector is not positioned properly, do not reposition the connector by rotating the CMP sensor housing. This will result in improper camshaft position sensor alignment. This will result in the ignition system and fuel system being out of time with the engine and possibly cause severe engine damage. Remove the CMP housing and repeat installation.

12. Install the CMP sensor and retaining screws. Tighten the sensor screws to 22–31 inch lbs. (3–4 Nm) for a 3.0L engine or 40–62 inch lbs. (5–7 Nm) for a 3.8L engine.
13. Conenct CMP sensor wiring harness.
14. Connect the negative battery cable.

Crankshaft Position (CKP) Sensor

OPERATION

▶ See Figures 32 and 33

The CKP sensor, located on the engine front cover near the crankshaft pulley, is used to determine crankshaft position and crankshaft rpm. The

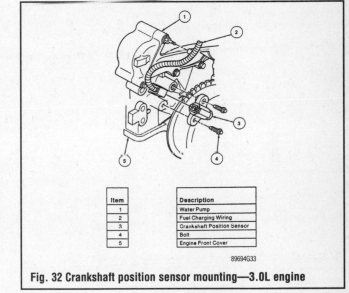

Item	Description
1	Water Pump
2	Fuel Charging Wiring
3	Crankshaft Position Sensor
4	Bolt
5	Engine Front Cover

Fig. 32 Crankshaft position sensor mounting—3.0L engine

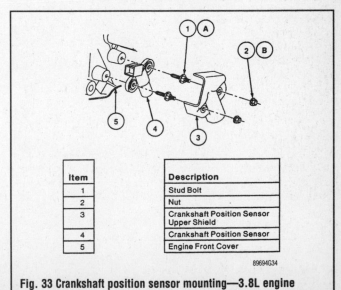

Item	Description
1	Stud Bolt
2	Nut
3	Crankshaft Position Sensor Upper Shield
4	Crankshaft Position Sensor
5	Engine Front Cover

Fig. 33 Crankshaft position sensor mounting—3.8L engine

sensor is a magnetic reluctance type which senses the passing of teeth on a tone wheel because the teeth disrupt the magnetic field of the sensor. This disruption creates a voltage fluctuation, which is monitored by the PCM.

TESTING

▶ **See Figures 34 and 35**

1. Measure the voltage between the sensor CKP sensor terminals by backprobing the sensor connector.

➡**If the connector cannot be backprobed, fabricate or purchase a test harness.**

2. Sensor voltage should be more than 0.1 volt DC with the engine running and should vary with engine RPM.

3. If voltage is not within specification, the sensor may be faulty.

REMOVAL & INSTALLATION

1. Disconnect the negative battery cable.
2. Disconnect the wiring harness from the CKP sensor.
3. Loosen the CKP sensor mounting stud/bolts, then separate the sensor form the engine front cover.
To install:
4. Position the sensor against the engine front cover.
5. Install ad tighten the mounting stud/bolts.
6. Connect the wiring harness to the CKP sensor.
7. Connect the negative battery cable.

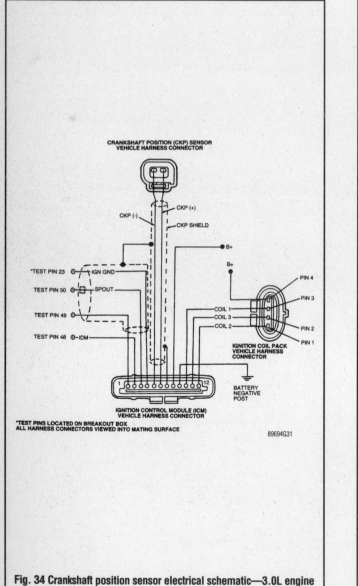

Fig. 34 Crankshaft position sensor electrical schematic—3.0L engine

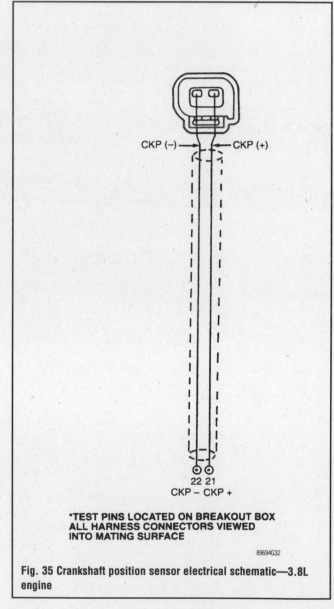

Fig. 35 Crankshaft position sensor electrical schematic—3.8L engine

COMPONENT LOCATIONS

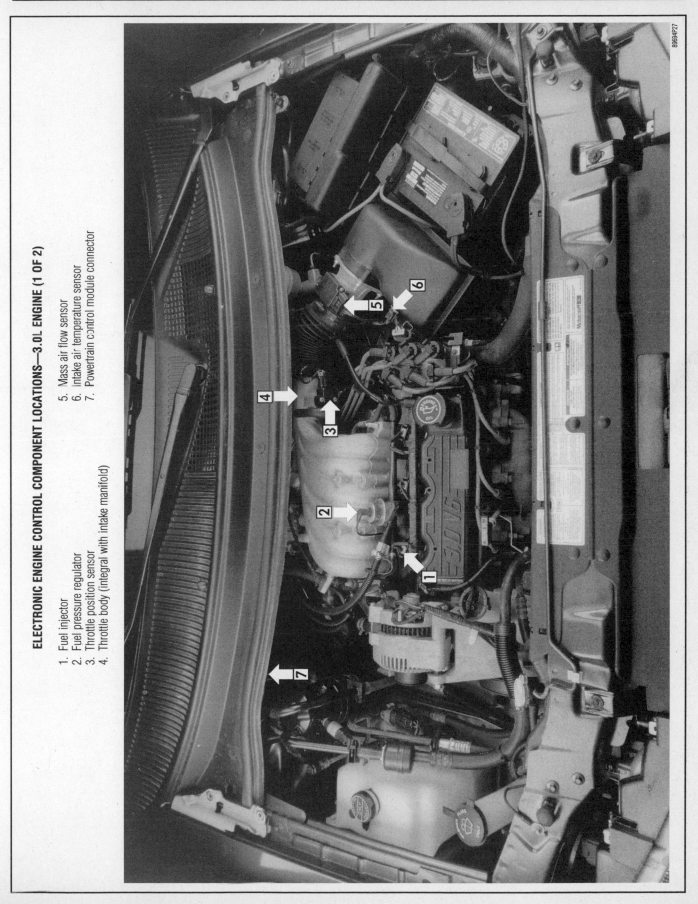

ELECTRONIC ENGINE CONTROL COMPONENT LOCATIONS—3.0L ENGINE (1 OF 2)

1. Fuel injector
2. Fuel pressure regulator
3. Throttle position sensor
4. Throttle body (integral with intake manifold)
5. Mass air flow sensor
6. Intake air temperature sensor
7. Powertrain control module connector

ELECTRONIC ENGINE CONTROL COMPONENT LOCATIONS—3.0L ENGINE (2 of 2)

1. Pre-catalytic converter heated oxygen sensor
2. Crankshaft position sensor tone wheel
3. Post-catalytic converter heated oxygen sensor
4. Dual catalytic converter Y-pipe

ELECTRONIC ENGINE CONTROL COMPONENT LOCATIONS—3.8L ENGINE

1. Idle air control valve
2. Throttle body
3. Throttle position sensor
4. EGR valve
5. Differential pressure feedback sensor
6. Fuel injector
7. Idle air temperature sensor

Diagnostic Trouble Code (DTC) Definitions

DTC	Definitions
P0102	Mass Air Flow (MAF) sensor circuit low input
P0103	Mass Air Flow (MAF) sensor circuit high input
P0106	Barometric Pressure (BP) sensor circuit performance
P0107	Barometric Pressure (BP) sensor circuit low input
P0108	Barometric Pressure (BP) sensor circuit high input
P0112	Intake Air Temperature (IAT) sensor circuit low input
P0113	Intake Air Temperature (IAT) sensor circuit high input
P0117	Engine Coolant Temperature (ECT) sensor circuit low input
P0118	Engine Coolant Temperature (ECT) sensor circuit high input
P0121	In-range operating Throttle Position (TP) sensor circuit failure
P0122	Throttle Position (TP) sensor circuit low input
P0123	Throttle Position (TP) sensor circuit high input
P0125	Insufficient coolant temperature to enter closed loop fuel control
P0131	Upstream Heated Oxygen Sensor (HO2S 11) circuit out of range low voltage (Bank #1)
P0133	Upstream Heated Oxygen Sensor (HO2S 11) circuit slow response (Bank #1)
P0135	Upstream Heated Oxygen Sensor Heater (HTR 11) circuit malfunction (Bank #1)
P0136	Downstream Heated Oxygen Sensor (HO2S 12) circuit malfunction (Bank #1)
P0141	Downstream Heated Oxygen Sensor Heater (HTR 12) circuit malfunction (Bank #1)
P0151	Upstream Heated Oxygen Sensor (HO2S 21) circuit out of range low voltage (Bank #2)
P0153	Upstream Heated Oxygen Sensor (HO2S 21) circuit slow response (Bank #2)
P0155	Upstream Heated Oxygen Sensor Heater (HTR 21) circuit malfunction (Bank #2)
P0156	Downstream Heated Oxygen Sensor (HO2S 22) circuit malfunction (Bank #2)
P0161	Downstream Heated Oxygen Sensor Heater (HTR 22) circuit malfunction (Bank #2)
P0171	System (adaptive fuel) too lean (Bank #1)
P0172	System (adaptive fuel) too rich (Bank #1)
P0174	System (adaptive fuel) too lean (Bank #2)
P0175	System (adaptive fuel) too rich (Bank #2)
P0176	Fuel Composition sensor (FCS) circuit malfunction
P0182	Fuel Temperature sensor A circuit low input
P0183	Fuel Temperature sensor A circuit high input
P0187	Fuel Temperature sensor B circuit low input
P0188	Fuel Temperature sensor B circuit high input
P0191	Injector Pressure sensor circuit performance
P0192	Injector Pressure sensor circuit low input
P0193	Injector Pressure sensor circuit high input
P0222	Throttle Position Sensor B (TP-B) circuit low input
P0223	Throttle Position Sensor B (TP-B) circuit high input
P0230	Fuel Pump primary circuit malfunction
P0231	Fuel Pump secondary circuit low
P0232	Fuel Pump secondary circuit high
P0300	Random Misfire detected
P0301	Cylinder #1 Misfire detected
P0302	Cylinder #2 Misfire detected
P0303	Cylinder #3 Misfire detected

89694637

Diagnostic Trouble Code (DTC) Definitions

DTC	Definitions
P0304	Cylinder #4 Misfire detected
P0305	Cylinder #5 Misfire detected
P0306	Cylinder #6 Misfire detected
P0307	Cylinder #7 Misfire detected
P0308	Cylinder #8 Misfire detected
P0320	Ignition Engine Speed (Profile Ignition Pickup (PIP)) input circuit malfunction
P0325	Knock Sensor (KS) 1 circuit malfunction
P0326	Knock Sensor (KS) 1 circuit performance
P0331	Knock Sensor (KS) 2 circuit malfunction
P0331	Knock Sensor (KS) 2 circuit performance
P0340	Camshaft Position (CMP) sensor circuit malfunction (CID)
P0350	Ignition Coil primary circuit malfunction
P0351	Ignition Coil A primary circuit malfunction
P0352	Ignition Coil B primary circuit malfunction
P0353	Ignition Coil C primary circuit malfunction
P0354	Ignition Coil D primary circuit malfunction
P0385	Crankshaft Position (CKP) sensor malfunction
P0400	Exhaust Gas Recirculation (EGR) flow malfunction
P0401	Exhaust Gas Recirculation (EGR) flow insufficient detected
P0402	Exhaust Gas Recirculation (EGR) flow excess detected
P0411	Secondary Air Injection system incorrect upstream flow detected
P0412	Secondary Air Injection system switching valve A malfunction
P0413	Secondary Air Injection system switching valve A circuit open
P0414	Secondary Air Injection system switching valve A circuit shorted
P0416	Secondary Air Injection system switching valve B circuit open
P0417	Secondary Air Injection system switching valve B circuit shorted
P0420	Catalyst system efficiency below threshold (Bank #1)
P0430	Catalyst system efficiency below threshold (Bank #2)
P0440	Evaporative emission control system malfunction (Probe)
P0442	Evaporative emission control system small leak detected
P0443	Evaporative emission control system purge control solenoid or vapor management valve circuit malfunction
P0446	Evaporative emission control system Canister Vent (CV) solenoid control malfunction
P0452	Evaporative emission control system Fuel Tank Pressure (FTP) sensor low input
P0453	Evaporative emission control system Fuel Tank Pressure (FTP) sensor high input
P0455	Evaporative emission control system control leak detected (gross leak)
P0500	Vehicle Speed Sensor (VSS) malfunction
P0603	Vehicle Speed Sensor (VSS) circuit intermittent
P0505	Idle Air Control (IAC) system malfunction
P0552	Power Steering Pressure (PSP) sensor circuit low input
P0553	Power Steering Pressure (PSP) sensor circuit high input
P0603	Powertrain Control Module (PCM) - Keep Alive Memory (KAM) test error
P0605	Powertrain Control Module (PCM) - Read Only Memory (ROM) test error
P0703	Brake On / Off (BOO) switch input malfunction

89694638

Diagnostic Trouble Code (DTC) Definitions

DTC	Definitions
P0704	Clutch Pedal Position (CPP) switch input circuit malfunction
P0707	Transmission Range (TR) sensor circuit low input
P0708	Transmission Range (TR) sensor circuit high input
P0712	Transmission Fluid Temperature (TFT) sensor circuit low input
P0713	Transmission Fluid Temperature (TFT) sensor circuit high input
P0715	Turbine Shaft Speed (TSS) sensor circuit malfunction
P0720	Output Shaft Speed (OSS) sensor circuit malfunction
P0721	Output Shaft Speed (OSS) sensor performance (noise)
P0731	Incorrect ratio for first gear
P0732	Incorrect ratio for second gear
P0733	Incorrect ratio for third gear
P0734	Incorrect ratio for fourth gear
P0736	Reverse incorrect gear ratio
P0741	Torque Converter Clutch (TCC) mechanical system performance
P0743	Torque Converter Clutch (TCC) electrical system malfunction
P0746	Electronic Pressure Control (EPC) solenoid performance
P0750	Shift Solenoid # 1 (SS1) circuit malfunction
P0751	Shift Solenoid # 1 (SS1) performance
P0755	Shift Solenoid # 2 (SS2) circuit malfunction
P0756	Shift Solenoid # 2 (SS2) performance
P0760	Shift Solenoid # 3 (SS3) circuit malfunction
P0761	Shift Solenoid # 3 (SS3) performance
P0781	1 to 2 shift error
P0782	2 to 3 shift error
P0783	3 to 4 shift error
P0784	4 to 5 shift error
P1000	OBD II Monitor Testing not complete
P1001	Key On Engine Running (KOER) Self-Test not able to complete. KOER aborted
P1100	Mass Air Flow (MAF) sensor intermittent
P1101	Mass Air Flow (MAF) sensor out of Self-Test range
P1112	Intake Air Temperature (IAT) sensor intermittent
P1116	Engine Coolant Temperature (ECT) sensor out of Self-Test range
P1117	Engine Coolant Temperature (ECT) sensor intermittent
P1120	Throttle Position (TP) sensor out of range low
P1121	Throttle Position (TP) sensor inconsistent with MAF Sensor
P1124	Throttle Position (TP) sensor out of Self-Test range
P1125	Throttle Position (TP) sensor circuit intermittent
P1127	Exhaust not warm enough, downstream Heated Oxygen Sensors (HO2Ss) not tested
P1128	Upstream Heated Oxygen Sensors (HO2Ss) swapped from bank to bank
P1129	Downstream Heated Oxygen Sensors (HO2Ss) swapped from bank to bank
P1130	Lack of upstream Heated Oxygen Sensor (HO2S 11) switch, adaptive fuel at limit (Bank # 1)
P1131	Lack of upstream Heated Oxygen Sensor (HO2S 11) switch, sensor indicates lean (Bank # 1)
P1132	Lack of upstream Heated Oxygen Sensor (HO2S 11) switch, sensor indicates rich (Bank # 1)

Diagnostic Trouble Code (DTC) Definitions

DTC	Definitions
P1137	Lack of downstream Heated Oxygen Sensor (HO2S 12) switch, sensor indicates lean (Bank # 1)
P1138	Lack of downstream Heated Oxygen Sensor (HO2S 12) switch, sensor indicates rich (Bank # 1)
P1150	Lack of upstream Heated Oxygen Sensor (HO2S 21) switch, adaptive fuel at limit (Bank # 2)
P1151	Lack of upstream Heated Oxygen Sensor (HO2S 21) switch, sensor indicates lean (Bank # 2)
P1152	Lack of upstream Heated Oxygen Sensor (HO2S 21) switch, sensor indicates rich (Bank # 2)
P1157	Lack of downstream Heated Oxygen Sensor (HO2S 22) switch, sensor indicates lean (Bank # 2)
P1158	Lack of downstream Heated Oxygen Sensor (HO2S 22) switch, sensor indicates rich (Bank # 2)
P1220	Series Throttle Control system malfunction
P1224	Throttle Position Sensor B (TP-B) out of Self-Test range
P1230	Fuel Pump low speed malfunction
P1231	Fuel Pump secondary circuit low with high speed pump on
P1232	Low speed Fuel Pump primary circuit malfunction
P1233	Fuel Pump Driver Module disabled or offline
P1234	Fuel Pump Driver Module disabled or offline
P1235	Fuel Pump control out of Self-Test range
P1236	Fuel Pump control out of Self-Test range
P1237	Fuel Pump secondary circuit malfunction
P1238	Fuel Pump secondary circuit malfunction
P1260	THEFT detected - engine disabled
P1270	Engine RPM or vehicle speed limiter reached
P1285	Cylinder Head over temperature sensed
P1288	Cylinder Head Temperature (CHT) sensor out of Self-Test range
P1289	Cylinder Head Temperature (CHT) sensor circuit high input
P1290	Cylinder Head Temperature (CHT) sensor circuit low input
P1299	Engine over temperature condition
P1351	Ignition Diagnostic Monitor (IDM) circuit input malfunction
P1356	PIPs occurred while IDM pulsewidth indicates engine not turning
P1357	Ignition Diagnostic Monitor (IDM) pulsewidth not defined
P1358	Ignition Diagnostic Monitor (IDM) signal out of Self-Test range
P1359	Spark output circuit malfunction
P1390	Octane Adjust (OCT ADJ) out of Self-Test range
P1400	Differential Pressure Feedback EGR (DPFE) sensor circuit low voltage detected
P1401	Differential Pressure Feedback EGR (DPFE) sensor circuit high voltage detected
P1405	Differential Pressure Feedback EGR (DPFE) sensor upstream hose off or plugged
P1406	Differential Pressure Feedback EGR (DPFE) sensor downstream hose off or plugged
P1408	Exhaust Gas Recirculation (EGR) flow out of Self-Test range
P1409	Electronic Vacuum Regulator (EVR) control circuit malfunction
P1411	Secondary Air Injection system incorrect downstream flow detected
P1413	Secondary Air Injection system monitor circuit low voltage
P1414	Secondary Air Injection system monitor circuit high voltage

Diagnostic Trouble Code (DTC) Definitions

DTC	Definitions
P1442	Evaporative emission control system small leak detected
P1443	Evaporative emission control system - vacuum system, purge control solenoid or vapor management valve malfunction
P1444	Purge Flow (PF) Sensor circuit low input
P1445	Purge Flow (PF) Sensor circuit high input
P1449	Evaporative emission control system unable to hold vacuum (Probe)
P1450	Unable to bleed up fuel tank vacuum
P1452	Unable to bleed up fuel tank vacuum
P1455	Evaporative emission control system control leak detected (gross leak)
P1460	Wide Open Throttle Air Conditioning Cut-off (WAC) circuit malfunction
P1461	Air Conditioning Pressure (ACP) sensor circuit low input
P1462	Air Conditioning Pressure (ACP) sensor circuit high input
P1463	Air Conditioning Pressure (ACP) sensor insufficient pressure change
P1464	Air condition (A/C) demand out of Self-Test range
P1469	Low air conditioning cycling period
P1473	Fan secondary high with fan(s) off
P1474	Low Fan Control primary circuit malfunction
P1479	High Fan Control primary circuit malfunction
P1480	Fan secondary low with low fan on
P1481	Fan secondary low with high fan on
P1483	Power to fan circuit overcurrent
P1484	Open power ground to Variable Load Control Module (VLCM)
P1500	Vehicle Speed Sensor (VSS) circuit intermittent
P1501	Vehicle Speed Sensor (VSS) out of Self-Test range
P1504	Idle Air Control (IAC) circuit malfunction
P1505	Idle Air Control (IAC) system at adaptive clip
P1506	Idle Air Control (IAC) overspeed error
P1507	Idle Air Control (IAC) underspeed error
P1512	Intake Manifold Runner Control (IMRC) malfunction (Bank #1 stuck closed)
P1513	Intake Manifold Runner Control (IMRC) malfunction (Bank #2 stuck closed)
P1516	Intake Manifold Runner Control (IMRC) input error (Bank #1)
P1517	Intake Manifold Runner Control (IMRC) input error (Bank #2)
P1518	Intake Manifold Runner Control (IMRC) malfunction (stuck open)
P1519	Intake Manifold Runner Control (IMRC) malfunction (stuck closed)
P1520	Intake Manifold Runner Control (IMRC) circuit malfunction
P1530	Air Condition (A/C) clutch circuit malfunction
P1537	Intake Manifold Runner Control (IMRC) malfunction (Bank #1 stuck open)
P1538	Intake Manifold Runner Control (IMRC) malfunction (Bank #2 stuck open)
P1539	Power to Air Condition (A/C) clutch circuit overcurrent
P1550	Power Steering Pressure (PSP) sensor out of Self-Test range
P1605	Powertrain Control Module (PCM) - Keep Alive Memory (KAM) test error
P1625	B(+) supply to Variable Load Control Module (VLCM) fan circuit malfunction
P1626	B(+) supply to Variable Load Control Module (VLCM) Air Condition (A/C) circuit malfunction
P1650	Power Steering Pressure (PSP) switch out of Self-Test range

89694G41

Diagnostic Trouble Code (DTC) Definitions

DTC	Definitions
P1651	Power Steering Pressure (PSP) switch input malfunction
P1701	Reverse engagement error
P1703	Brake On/Off (BOO) switch out of Self-Test range
P1705	Transmission Range (TR) Sensor out of Self-Test range
P1709	Park or Neutral Position (PNP) switch is not indicating neutral during KOEO Self-Test
P1711	Transmission Fluid Temperature (TFT) sensor out of Self-Test range
P1728	Transmission slip fault
P1729	4x4 Low switch error
P1741	Torque Converter Clutch (TCC) control error
P1742	Torque Converter Clutch (TCC) solenoid failed on (turns on MIL)
P1743	Torque Converter Clutch (TCC) solenoid failed on (turns on TCIL)
P1744	Torque Converter Clutch (TCC) system mechanically stuck in off position
P1746	Electronic Pressure Control (EPC) solenoid open circuit (low input)
P1747	Electronic Pressure Control (EPC) solenoid short circuit (high input)
P1749	Electronic Pressure Control (EPC) solenoid failed low
P1751	Shift Solenoid #1 (SS1) performance
P1754	Coast Clutch Solenoid (CCS) circuit malfunction
P1756	Shift Solenoid #2 (SS2) performance
P1761	Shift Solenoid #3 (SS3) performance
P1780	Transmission Control switch (TCS) circuit out of Self-Test range
P1781	4x4 Low switch out of Self-Test range
P1783	Transmission overtemperature condition
P1788	3-2 Timing/Coast Clutch Solenoid (3-2/CCS) circuit open
P1789	3-2 Timing/Coast Clutch Solenoid (3-2/CCS) circuit shorted
U1021	SCP indicating the lack of Air Condition (A/C) clutch status response
U1039	SCP indicating the vehicle speed signal missing or incorrect
U1051	SCP indicating the brake switch signal missing or incorrect
U1073	SCP indicating the lack of engine coolant fan status response
U1131	SCP indicating the lack of Fuel Pump status response
U1135	SCP indicating the ignition switch signal missing or incorrect
U1256	SCP indicating a communications error
U1451	Lack of response from Passive Anti-Theft system (PATS) module - engine disabled

89694G42

General Description

The Powertrain Control Module (PCM) is given responsibility for the operation of the emission control devices, cooling fans, ignition and advance and in some cases, automatic transmission functions. Because the EEC-5 oversees both the ignition timing and the fuel injector operation, a precise air/fuel ratio will be maintained under all operating conditions. The PCM is a microprocessor or small computer which receives electrical inputs from several sensors, switches and relays on and around the engine.

Based on combinations of these inputs, the PCM controls outputs to various devices concerned with engine operation and emissions. The control module relies on the signals to form a correct picture of current vehicle operation. If any of the input signals is incorrect, the PCM reacts to what ever picture is painted for it. For example, if the coolant temperature sensor is inaccurate and reads too low, the PCM may see a picture of the engine never warming up. Consequently, the engine settings will be maintained as if the engine were cold. Because so many inputs can affect one output, correct diagnostic procedures are essential on these systems.

One part of the PCM is devoted to monitoring both input and output functions within the system. This ability forms the core of the self-diagnostic system. If a problem is detected within a circuit, the control module will recognize the fault, assign it an Diagnostic Trouble Code (DTC), and store the code in memory. The stored code(s) may be retrieved during diagnosis.

While the EEC-5 system is capable of recognizing many internal faults, certain faults will not be recognized. Because the control module sees only electrical signals, it cannot sense or react to mechanical or vacuum faults affecting engine operation. Some of these faults may affect another component which will set a code. For example, the PCM monitors the output signal to the fuel injectors, but cannot detect a partially clogged injector. As long as the output driver responds correctly, the computer will read the system as functioning correctly. However, the improper flow of fuel may result in a lean mixture. This would, in turn, be detected by the oxygen sensor and noticed as a constantly lean signal by the PCM. Once the signal falls outside the pre-programmed limits, the control module would notice the fault and set an trouble code.

Additionally, the EEC-5 system employs adaptive fuel logic. This process is used to compensate for normal wear and variability within the fuel system. Once the engine enters steady-state operation, the control module watches the oxygen sensor signal for a bias or tendency to run slightly rich or lean. If such a bias is detected, the adaptive logic corrects the fuel delivery to bring the air/fuel mixture towards a centered or 14.7:1 ratio. This compensating shift is stored in a non-volatile memory which is retained by battery power even with the ignition switched **OFF**. The correction factor is then available the next time the vehicle is operated.

➡If the battery cable(s) is disconnected for longer than 5 minutes, the adaptive fuel factor will be lost. After repair it will be necessary to drive the truck at least 10 miles to allow the processor to relearn the correct factors. The driving period should include steady-throttle open road driving if possible. During the drive, the vehicle may exhibit driveability symptoms not noticed before. These symptoms should clear as the control module computes the correction factor.

MALFUNCTION INDICATOR LAMP (MIL)

The Malfunction Indicator Lamp (MIL) is located on the instrument panel. The lamp is connected to the control unit and will alert the driver to certain malfunctions within the EEC-5 system. When the lamp is illuminated, the PCM has detected a fault and stored an DTC in memory.

The light will stay illuminated as long as the fault is present. Should the fault self-correct, the MIL will extinguish but the stored code will remain in memory.

Under normal operating conditions, the MIL should illuminate briefly when the ignition key is turned **ON**. This is commonly known as a bulb check. As soon as the PCM receives a signal that the engine is cranking, the lamp should extinguish. The lamp should remain extinguished during the normal operating cycle.

Diagnostic Link Connector (DLC)

The DLC is located under the left side of the instrument panel. The connector is trapezoidal in shape and can accommodate up to 16 terminals.

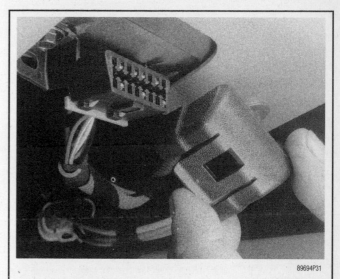

89694P31

The diagnostic link connector is covered by a protective cap

Reading Codes

The EEC-V equipped engines utilize On Board Diagnostic II (OBD-II) DTC's, which are alpha-numeric (they use letters and numbers). The letters in the OBD-II DTC's make it highly difficult to convey the codes through the use of anything but a scan tool. Therefore, to read the codes on these vehicles it is necessary to utilize an OBD-II compatible scan tool.

TCCS4P10

Inexpensive scan tools, such as this Auto Xray®, are available to interface with your Ford vehicle

Among other features, a scan tool combines many standard testers into a single device for quick and accurate diagnosis

When using a scan tool, make sure to follow all of the manufacturer's instructions carefully to ensure proper diagnosis

Since each manufacturers scan tool is different, please follow the manufacturer's instructions for connecting the tool and obtaining code information.

Clearing Codes

CONTINUOUS MEMORY CODES

These codes are retained in memory for 40 warm-up cycles. To clear the codes for the purposes of testing or confirming repair, perform the code reading procedure. When the fault codes begin to be displayed, de-activate the test by either disconnecting the jumper wire (meter, MIL or message center) or releasing the test button on the hand scanner. Stopping the test during code transmission will erase the Continuous Memory. Do not disconnect the negative battery cable to clear these codes; the Keep Alive memory will be cleared and a new code, 19, will be stored for loss of PCM power.

KEEP ALIVE MEMORY

The Keep Alive Memory (KAM) contains the adaptive factors used by the processor to compensate for component tolerances and wear. It should not be routinely cleared during diagnosis. If an emissions related part is replaced during repair, the KAM must be cleared. Failure to clear the KAM may cause severe driveability problems since the correction factor for the old component will be applied to the new component.

To clear the Keep Alive Memory, disconnect the negative battery cable for at least 5 minutes. After the memory is cleared and the battery reconnected, the vehicle must be driven at least 10 miles so that the processor may relearn the needed correction factors. The distance to be driven depends on the engine and vehicle, but all drives should include steady-throttle cruise on open roads. Certain driveability problems may be noted during the drive because the adaptive factors are not yet functioning.

VACUUM DIAGRAMS

Following are vacuum diagrams for most of the engine and emissions package combinations covered by this manual. Because vacuum circuits will vary based on various engine and vehicle options, always refer first to the vehicle emission control information label, if present. Should the label be missing, or should the vehicle be equipped with a different engine from the vehicle's original equipment, refer to the diagrams below for the same or similar configuration.

If you wish to obtain a replacement emissions label, most manufacturers make the labels available for purchase. The labels can usually be ordered from a local dealer.

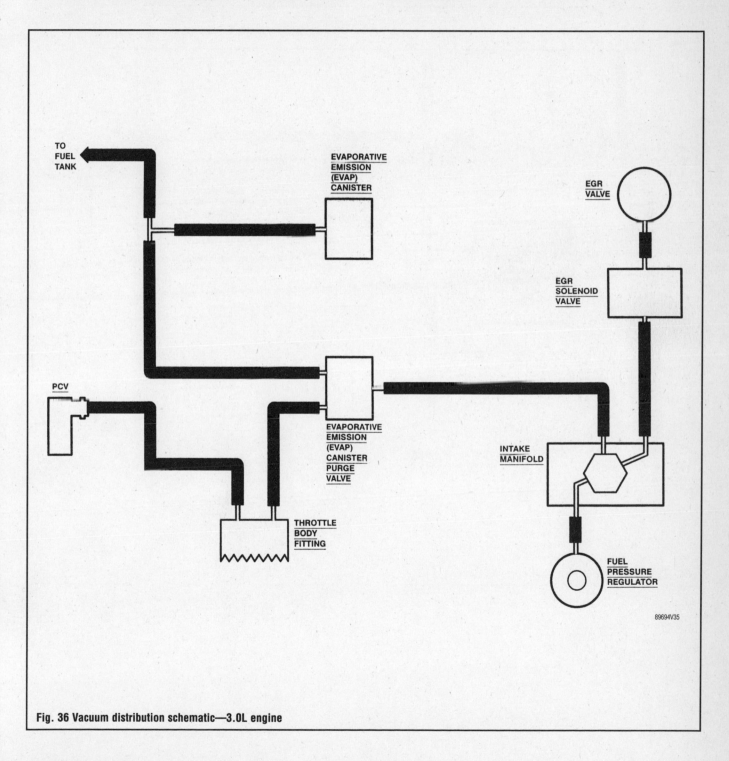

Fig. 36 Vacuum distribution schematic—3.0L engine

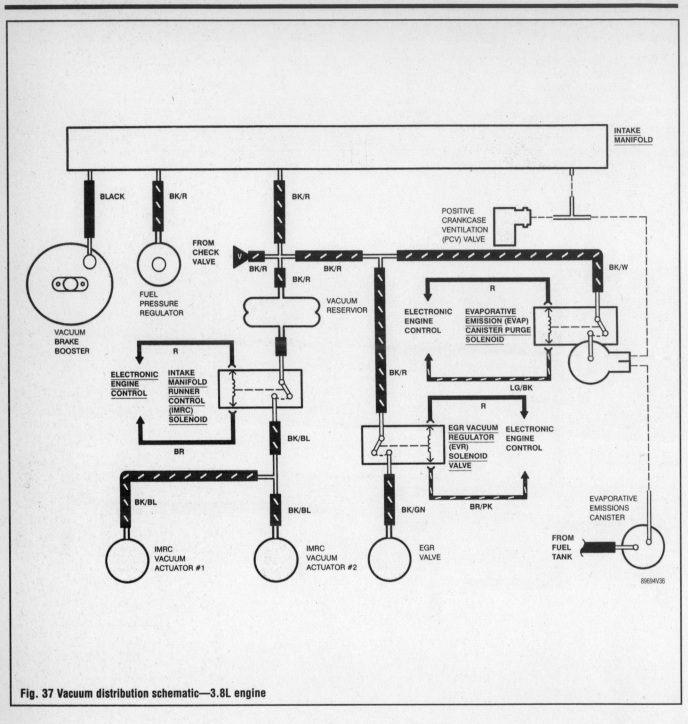

Fig. 37 Vacuum distribution schematic—3.8L engine

5

FUEL SYSTEM

BASIC FUEL SYSTEM DIAGNOSIS

When there is a problem starting or driving a vehicle, two of the most important checks involve the ignition and the fuel systems. The questions most mechanics attempt to answer first, "is there spark?" and "is there fuel?" will often lead to solving most basic problems. For ignition system diagnosis and testing, please refer to the information on engine electrical components and ignition systems found earlier in this manual. If the ignition system checks out (there is spark), then you must determine if the fuel system is operating properly (is there fuel?).

FUEL LINES AND FITTINGS

General Information

➡Quick-connect (push type) fuel line fittings must be disconnected using proper procedure or the fitting may be damaged. There are two types of retainers used on the push connect fittings. Line sizes of ⅜ and ⁵⁄₁₆ in. diameter use a hairpin clip retainer. The ¼ in. diameter line connectors use a duck-bill clip retainer. In addition, some engines use spring-lock connections, secured by a garter spring, which require Ford Tool T81P-19623-G (or equivalent) for removal.

Hairpin Clip Fitting

REMOVAL & INSTALLATION

▶ **See Figures 1 and 2**

1. Clean all dirt and grease from the fitting. Spread the two clip legs about ⅛ in. (3mm) each to disengage from the fitting and pull the clip outward from the fitting. Use finger pressure only; do not use any tools.

2. Grasp the fitting and hose assembly and pull away from the steel line. Twist the fitting and hose assembly slightly while pulling, if the assembly sticks.

3. Inspect the hairpin clip for damage, replacing the clip if necessary. Reinstall the clip in position on the fitting.

4. Inspect the fitting and inside of the connector to ensure freedom from dirt or obstruction. Install the fitting into the connector and push together. A click will be heard when the hairpin snaps into the proper connection. Pull on the line to insure full engagement.

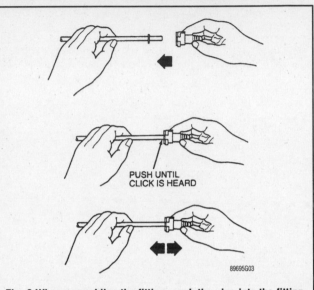

Fig. 2 When assembling the fitting, push the pipe into the fitting until a click is heard

Duckbill Clip Fitting

REMOVAL & INSTALLATION

▶ **See Figure 3**

1. A special tool is available from Ford and other manufacturers for removing the retaining clips. Use Ford Tool T90T-9550-B or C or equivalent. If the

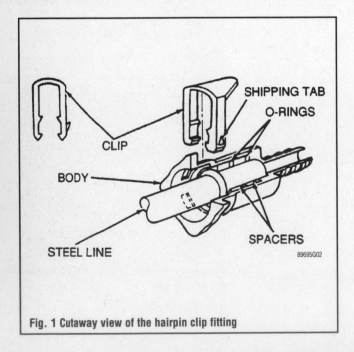

Fig. 1 Cutaway view of the hairpin clip fitting

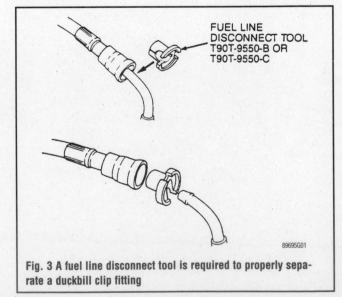

Fig. 3 A fuel line disconnect tool is required to properly separate a duckbill clip fitting

tool is not on hand, go onto step 2. Align the slot on the push connector disconnect tool with either tab on the retaining clip. Pull the line from the connector.

2. If the special clip tool is not available, use a pair of narrow 6-inch slip-jaw pliers with a jaw width of 0.2 in (5mm) or less. Align the jaws of the pliers with the openings of the fitting case and compress the part of the retaining clip that engages the case. Compressing the retaining clip will release the fitting, which may be pulled from the connector. Both sides of the clip must be compressed at the same time to disengage.

3. Inspect the retaining clip, fitting end and connector. Replace the clip if any damage is apparent.

4. Push the line into the steel connector until a click is heard, indicating the clip is in place. Pull on the line to check engagement.

Spring Lock Coupling

REMOVAL & INSTALLATION

▶ See Figures 4, 5 and 6

The spring lock coupling is held together by a garter spring inside a circular cage. When the coupling is connected together, the flared

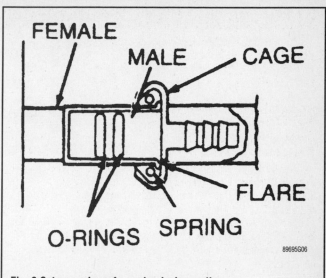

Fig. 6 Cutaway view of a spring lock coupling

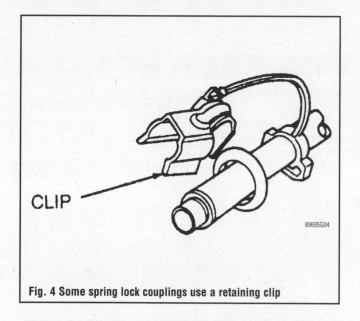

Fig. 4 Some spring lock couplings use a retaining clip

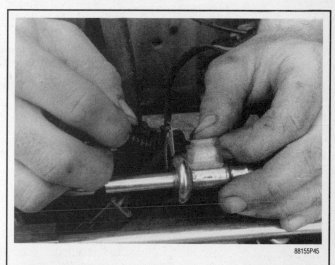

To disengage a spring lock coupling, pull the clip back off the coupling after cleaning the area . . .

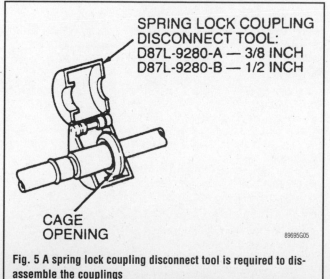

Fig. 5 A spring lock coupling disconnect tool is required to disassemble the couplings

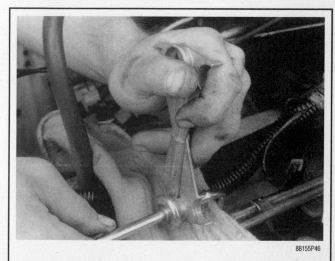

. . . then insert a removal tool into the coupling to release the spring

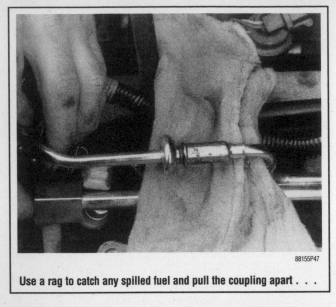

88155P47

Use a rag to catch any spilled fuel and pull the coupling apart . . .

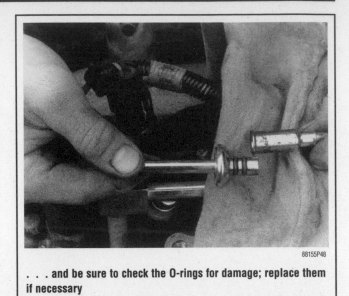

88155P48

. . . and be sure to check the O-rings for damage; replace them if necessary

end of the female fitting slips behind the garter spring inside the cage of the male fitting. The garter spring and cage then prevent the flared end of the female fitting from pulling out of the cage. As an additional locking feature, most vehicles have a horseshoe-shaped retaining clip that improves the retaining reliability of the spring lock coupling.

GASOLINE FUEL INJECTION SYSTEM

General Information

▶ **See Figures 7, 8 and 9**

The Sequential Fuel Injection (SFI) system includes a high pressure, inline electric fuel pump mounted in the fuel tank, a fuel supply manifold, a throttle body (meters the incoming air charge for the correct mixture with the fuel), a pressure regulator, fuel filters and both solid and flexible fuel lines. The fuel supply manifold includes 6 electronically-controlled fuel injectors, each mounted directly above an intake port in the lower intake manifold. Each injector fires once every other crankshaft revolution, in sequence with the engine firing order.

The fuel pressure regulator maintains a constant pressure drop across the injector nozzles. The regulator is referenced to intake manifold vacuum and is connected in parallel to the fuel injectors; it is positioned on the far end of the fuel rail. Any excess fuel supplied by the fuel pump passes through the regulator and is returned to the fuel tank via a return line.

➡ **The pressure regulator reduces fuel pressure to 35–40 psi under normal operating conditions. At idle or high manifold vacuum condition, fuel pressure is further reduced to approximately 30 psi.**

The fuel pressure regulator is a diaphragm-operated relief valve, in which the inside of the diaphragm senses fuel pressure and the other side senses manifold vacuum. Normal fuel pressure is established by a spring preload applied to the diaphragm. Control of the fuel system is maintained through the Powertrain Control Module (PCM), although electrical power is routed through the fuel pump relay and an inertia switch. The fuel pump relay is normally located in the power distribution box, under the hood, and the inertia switch is located on the toe-board, to the right of the transmission hump, in the passenger-side footwell. The inline fuel pump is mounted in the fuel tank.

The inertia switch opens the power circuit to the fuel pump in the event of a collision or roll over. Once tripped, the switch must be reset manually by pushing the reset button on the assembly.

➡ **Check that the inertia switch is reset before diagnosing power supply problems to the fuel pump.**

The fuel injectors used with SFI system are electro-mechanical (solenoid) type, designed to meter and atomize fuel delivered to the intake ports of the engine. The injectors are mounted in the lower intake manifold and positioned so that their spray nozzles direct the fuel charge in front of the intake valves. The injector body consists of a solenoid-actuated pintle and needle-valve assembly. The control unit sends an electrical impulse that activates the solenoid, causing the pintle to move inward off the seat and allow the fuel to flow. The amount of fuel delivered is controlled by the length of time the injector is energized (pulse width), since the fuel flow orifice is fixed and the fuel pressure drop across the injector tip is constant. Correct atomization is achieved by contouring the pintle at the point where the fuel enters the pintle chamber.

➡ **Exercise care when handling fuel injectors during service. Be careful not to lose the pintle cap and always replace O-rings to assure a tight seal. Never apply direct battery voltage to test a fuel injector.**

The injectors receive high-pressure fuel from the fuel supply manifold (fuel rail) assembly. The complete assembly includes a single, pre-formed tube with four, six or eight connectors, the mounting flange for the pressure regulator, mounting attachments to locate the manifold and provide the fuel injector retainers and a Schrader® quick-disconnect fitting used to perform fuel pressure tests.

The fuel manifold is normally removed with the fuel injectors and pressure regulator attached. Fuel injector electrical connectors are plastic and have locking tabs that must be released when disconnecting the wiring harness.

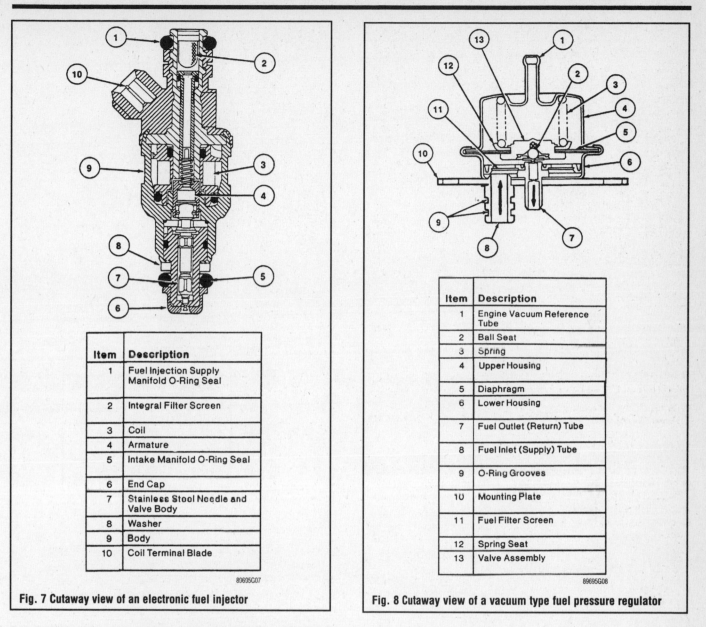

Fig. 7 Cutaway view of an electronic fuel injector

Item	Description
1	Fuel Injection Supply Manifold O-Ring Seal
2	Integral Filter Screen
3	Coil
4	Armature
5	Intake Manifold O-Ring Seal
6	End Cap
7	Stainless Steel Needle and Valve Body
8	Washer
9	Body
10	Coil Terminal Blade

80695G07

Fig. 8 Cutaway view of a vacuum type fuel pressure regulator

Item	Description
1	Engine Vacuum Reference Tube
2	Ball Seat
3	Spring
4	Upper Housing
5	Diaphragm
6	Lower Housing
7	Fuel Outlet (Return) Tube
8	Fuel Inlet (Supply) Tube
9	O-Ring Grooves
10	Mounting Plate
11	Fuel Filter Screen
12	Spring Seat
13	Valve Assembly

89695G08

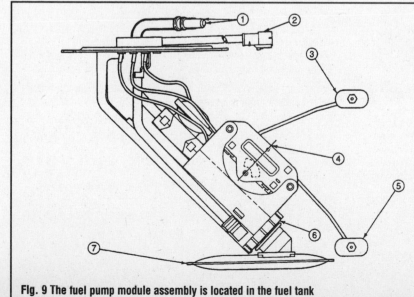

Fig. 9 The fuel pump module assembly is located in the fuel tank

Item	Description
1	Fuel Supply and Return Tubes
2	Electrical Connector
3	Sender Float at Full Position
4	Fuel Gauge Sender
5	Sender Float at Empty Position
6	Fuel Pump, Electric
7	Inlet Filter Sock

89695G09

FUEL SYSTEM SERVICE PRECAUTIONS

Safety is the most important factor when performing not only fuel system maintenance, but any type of maintenance. Failure to conduct maintenance and repairs in a safe manner may result in serious personal injury or death. Work on a vehicle's fuel system components can be accomplished safely and effectively by adhering to the following rules and guidelines.

• To avoid the possibility of fire and personal injury, always disconnect the negative battery cable unless the repair or test procedure requires that battery voltage by applied.

• Always relieve the fuel system pressure prior to disconnecting any fuel system component (injector, fuel rail, pressure regulator, etc.) fitting or fuel line connection. Exercise extreme caution whenever relieving fuel system pressure to avoid exposing skin, face and eyes to fuel spray. Please be advised that fuel under pressure may penetrate the skin or any part of the body that it contacts.

• Always place a shop towel or cloth around the fitting or connection prior to loosening to absorb any excess fuel due to spillage. Ensure that all fuel spillage is quickly remove from engine surfaces. Ensure that all fuel-soaked cloths or towels are deposited into a flame-proof waste container with a lid.

• Always keep a dry chemical (Class B) fire extinguisher near the work area.

• Do not allow fuel spray or fuel vapors to come into contact with a spark or open flame.

• Always use a second wrench when loosening or tightening fuel line connections fittings. This will prevent unnecessary stress and torsion to fuel piping. Always follow the proper torque specifications.

• Always replace worn fuel fitting O-rings with new ones. Do not substitute fuel hose where rigid pipe is installed.

Relieving Fuel System Pressure

All SFI fuel injected engines are equipped with a pressure relief valve located on the fuel supply manifold. Remove the fuel tank cap and attach fuel pressure gauge T80L-9974-B, or equivalent, to the valve to release the fuel pressure. Be sure to drain the fuel into a suitable container and to avoid gasoline spillage.

If a pressure gauge is not available, disconnect the vacuum hose from the fuel pressure regulator and attach a hand-held vacuum pump. Apply about 25 in. Hg (84 kPa) of vacuum to the regulator to vent the fuel system pressure into the fuel tank through the fuel return hose. Note that this procedure will remove the fuel pressure from the lines, but not the fuel. Take precautions to avoid the risk of fire and use clean rags to soak up any spilled fuel when the lines are disconnected.

An alternate method of relieving the fuel system pressure involves disconnecting the inertia switch. Follow the procedures outlined later in this section.

Inertia Switch

GENERAL INFORMATION

◢ **See Figure 10**

This switch shuts off the fuel pump in the event of a collision. Once the switch has been tripped, it must be reset manually in order to start the engine.

The inertia switch is located on the toe-board, to the right of the transaxle hump, in the passenger-side footwell.

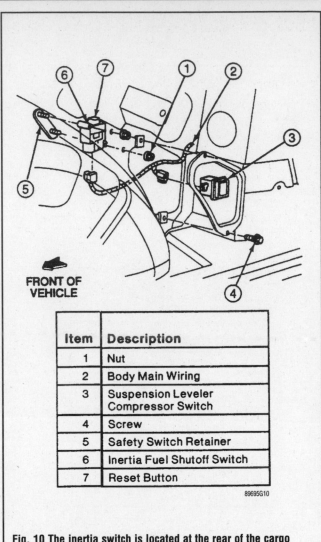

FRONT OF VEHICLE

Item	Description
1	Nut
2	Body Main Wiring
3	Suspension Leveler Compressor Switch
4	Screw
5	Safety Switch Retainer
6	Inertia Fuel Shutoff Switch
7	Reset Button

89695G10

Fig. 10 The inertia switch is located at the rear of the cargo compartment on the passenger's side

RESETTING THE SWITCH

1. Turn the ignition switch **OFF**.

2. Ensure that there is no fuel leaking in the engine compartment, along any of the lines or at the tank. There should be no odor of fuel as well.

3. If no leakage and/or odor is apparent, reset the switch by pushing the reset button on the top of the switch.

➥**You may need to pull the carpet down and away from the instrument panel in order to access the switch.**

4. Cycle the ignition switch from the **ON** to **OFF** positions several times, allowing five seconds at each position, to build fuel pressure within the system.

5. Again, check the fuel system for leaks. There should be no odor of fuel as well.

6. If there is no leakage and/or odor of fuel, it is safe to operate the vehicle. However, it is recommended that the entire system be checked by a professional, especially if the vehicle was in an accident severe enough to trip the inertia switch.

11. Check for fuel leaks at the fittings.
12. Remove the pressure gauge.
13. Start the engine and check for fuel leaks.

Fuel Pump

REMOVAL & INSTALLATION

♦ See Figures 11, 12 and 13

➡To gain access to the fuel pump, it is necessary to remove the fuel tank.

1. Depressurize the fuel system and remove the fuel tank from the vehicle.
2. Remove any dirt that has accumulated around the fuel pump module attaching flange, to prevent it from entering the tank during service.
3. Turn the fuel pump module locking ring counterclockwise using a locking ring removal tool or a brass drift and remove the locking ring.
4. Remove the fuel pump module.
5. Remove the seal gasket and discard it.

To install:

6. Put a light coating of grease on a new seal ring to hold it in place during assembly. Install it in fuel tank ring groove.
7. Insert the fuel pump module into the fuel tank, then secure it in place with the locking ring. Tighten the ring until secure.
8. Install the tank in the vehicle.
9. Install a minimum of 10 gallons of fuel and check for leaks.
10. Install a pressure gauge on the throttle body valve and turn the ignition **ON** for 3 seconds. Turn the key **OFF**, then repeat the key cycle five to ten times until the pressure gauge shows at least 30 psi.

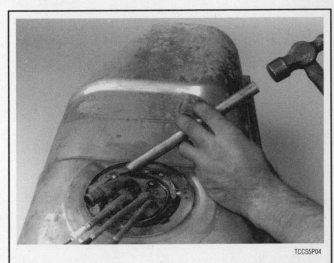

Fig. 12 A brass drift and a hammer can be used to loosen the fuel pump locking cam

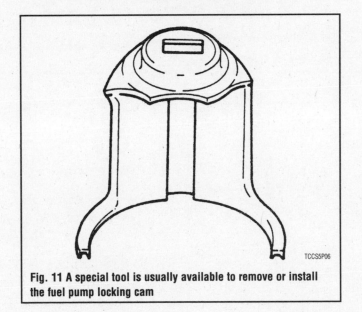

Fig. 11 A special tool is usually available to remove or install the fuel pump locking cam

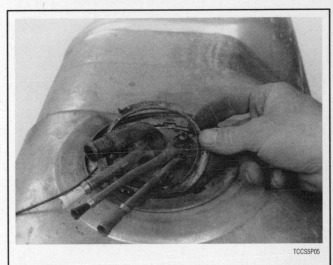

Fig. 13 Once the locking cam is released, it can be removed to free the fuel pump

FUEL DELIVERY SYSTEM DIAGNOSIS CHART (1 of 4)

	TEST STEP	RESULT	ACTION TO TAKE
HC1	**CHECK SYSTEM INTEGRITY** • Key off. • Visually inspect the complete fuel delivery system, including fuel lines, connections, pump, pressure regulator and injector areas for leaks, looseness, cracks, kinks, pinching, or abrasion caused by an accident, collision, mishandling, etc. • Visually inspect electrical harness and connectors for loose pins, corrosion, abrasion, or other damage from accident, mishandling, etc. • Verify Inertia Fuel Shutoff (IFS) switch set. • Verify vehicle battery is fully charged. • Verify electrical / fuse integrity. • Verify sufficient fuel in the tank. • Verify vehicle has followed maintenance schedule. • **Has any problem been found?**	Yes No	▲ SERVICE as necessary. ▲ GO to HC2 .
HC2	**CHECK FUEL PRESSURE** **WARNING: BEFORE SERVICING OR REPLACING ANY COMPONENTS IN THE FUEL SYSTEM, REDUCE THE POSSIBILITY OF INJURY OR FIRE BY FOLLOWING DIRECTIONS IN FUEL SYSTEM "CAUTION, HANDLING AND WARNING" AT THE BEGINNING OF THIS PINPOINT TEST.** • Key off. • Release the fuel pressure. • Install fuel pressure tester. • Scan Tool connected. • Key on, engine off. • Enter Output Test Mode and run the fuel pump to obtain maximum fuel pressure. • **Is fuel pressure between 35 and 40 psi (240-280 kPa)?**	Yes No	▲ GO to HC3 . ▲ GO to HC9 .
HC3	**CHECK FUEL PRESSURE LEAKDOWN** • Fuel pressure tester installed. • Scan Tool connected. • Key on, engine off. • Enter Output Test Mode and run fuel pump to obtain maximum fuel pressure. • Exit Output Test Mode, key off. • Verify fuel pressure remains within 5 psi of the maximum pressure for 1 minute after turning pump off. • **Does fuel pressure remain within 5 psi?**	Yes No	▲ GO to HC5 . ▲ GO to HC4 .

89G65G15

FUEL DELIVERY SYSTEM DIAGNOSIS CHART (2 of 4)

	TEST STEP	RESULT	ACTION TO TAKE
HC4	**CHECK PRESSURE REGULATOR DIAPHRAGM** • Key off. • Fuel pressure tester installed. • Start and run engine for 10 seconds. • Key off, wait 10 seconds. • Start and run engine for 10 seconds. • Key off, remove vacuum hose from fuel pressure regulator. • Inspect for fuel in the vacuum hose or regulator port. • **Is vacuum hose and regulator port free of fuel?**	Yes No	▲ GO to HC11 . ▲ REPLACE fuel pressure regulator.
HC5	**CHECK FUEL PRESSURE, ENGINE RUNNING** • Key off. • Fuel pressure tester installed. • Disconnect vacuum hose at the fuel pressure regulator and plug it. • Drive vehicle with heavy accelerations while observing fuel pressure gauge reading. • **Does fuel pressure reading hold steady within 3 psi during test?**	Yes No	▲ UNPLUG vacuum hose and RECONNECT to the regulator. GO to HC6 . ▲ GO to HC8 .
HC6	**CHECK FUEL PRESSURE REGULATOR RESPONSE TO VACUUM** • Key off. • Fuel pressure tester installed. • Install vacuum gauge to intake manifold. • Start engine and observe both gauges. • Accelerate and decelerate engine speed to vary the vacuum gauge reading. • **Does fuel pressure gauge reading increase as vacuum gauge reading decreases, or does fuel pressure gauge reading decrease as vacuum gauge reading increases?**	Yes No	▲ REMOVE vacuum gauge and fuel pressure tester. Problem is elsewhere. ▲ GO to HC7 .
HC7	**CHECK FUEL VACUUM SUPPLY** • Key off. • Fuel pressure tester installed. • Vacuum hose disconnected and plugged at the regulator. • Install hand held vacuum pump to the fuel pressure regulator. • Start engine, run at idle. • Observe fuel pressure while applying vacuum. • **Does the fuel pressure change as the vacuum changes?**	Yes No	▲ SERVICE vacuum system. UNPLUG vacuum hose and RECONNECT to the pressure regulator. ▲ REPLACE fuel pressure regulator.

89G65G16

FUEL DELIVERY SYSTEM DIAGNOSIS CHART (4 of 4)

TEST STEP	RESULT	ACTION TO TAKE
HC11 CHECK FUEL INJECTOR LEAKAGE AND FLOW • Key off. • Check injectors for leakage and flow rate, using Rotunda Injector Tester 113-00001 and Rotunda Fuel Pump Check Valve-Pressure Regulator and Injector Leakage Tool 113-00010 SBDS Injector Tester or equivalent. • **Is the flow rate for each injector within specification?**	Yes No	▲ VERIFY no other leaks. If none are found, REPLACE fuel pump assembly. ▲ REPLACE the defective injector. RECONNECT all components.
HC12 CHECK FUEL PUMP VOLTAGE • Key off. • Scan tool connected. • Disconnect the electrical fuel pump vehicle harness connector. Inspect for damaged or pushed out pins, corrosion, loose wires, etc. Service as necessary. • Key on, engine off. • Enter Output Test Mode and turn on the fuel pump circuit • Use DVOM to check voltage to the fuel pump, at the fuel pump connector, fuel pump relay, VCRM or CCRM. • **Is the voltage greater than 10.5 volts?**	Yes No	▲ CHECK for fuel pump ground connection. REPAIR as required. If OK, REPLACE fuel pump. RECONNECT all components. GO to HC2 for verification. ▲ LOCATE cause of low voltage in fuel pump circuit. REPAIR as required. GO to HC2 for verification.

8969G18

FUEL DELIVERY SYSTEM DIAGNOSIS CHART (3 of 4)

TEST STEP	RESULT	ACTION TO TAKE
HC8 CHECK FUEL FILTER • Key off. • Scan Tool connected. • Replace in-line fuel filter, if not replaced recently (check maintenance log). • Key on, engine off. • Enter Output Test Mode (OTM) (refer to Section 2) to run the fuel pump. • Check fuel pressure. • **Is fuel pressure within specification?**	Yes No	▲ GO to HC3. ▲ GO to HC12.
HC9 CHECK REGULATOR FOR HIGH PRESSURE CAUSE • Key off. • Scan Tool connected. • Remove fuel return line at the fuel rail and connect a short hose from rail to a measured container of at least one quart capacity. • Key on, engine off. • Enter Output Test Mode (OTM) and run the fuel pump. • Record fuel pressure and note whether fuel is being returned to the measured container. Exit OTM to shut off the fuel pump, key off. • **Is fuel pressure between 35 and 40 psi (240-280 kPa) and is fuel returning to the container?**	Yes No	▲ GO to HC10. ▲ REPLACE fuel pressure regulator.
HC10 CHECK FUEL RETURN SYSTEM • Key off. • Fuel line disconnected at the fuel pressure regulator. • Check the fuel return system for restriction due to blockage, kinking, or pinching. • Disconnect the fuel return line near the fuel tank. • Apply 3-5 psi regulated shop air to the return line at the pressure regulator side. • **Does air flow freely through the line?**	Yes No	▲ REPLACE the fuel pump assembly. ▲ SERVICE the fuel return line.

8969G17

Throttle Body

REMOVAL & INSTALLATION

3.0L Engine

The throttle body for this engine is an integral part of the upper intake manifold and is not serviceable separately.

The throttle body is coated with an anti-sludge film. Never clean the inside of the throttle body with solvent

3.8L Engine

▶ See Figure 14

1. Remove the air cleaner outlet tube.
2. Disconnect the accelerator cable.
3. Label and disconnect the fuel charging wiring harness.
4. Remove the accelerator cable bracket retaining bolts and position the bracket aside.
5. Remove the throttle body retaining buts and two retaining bolts.
6. Remove the throttle body and discard the gasket.

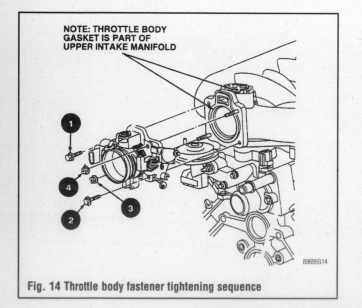

NOTE: THROTTLE BODY GASKET IS PART OF UPPER INTAKE MANIFOLD

Fig. 14 Throttle body fastener tightening sequence

➡Place a rag over the throttle body opening in the intake manifold to prevent the entry of dirt while the throttle body is removed.

To install:

7. Clean the gasket mating surfaces thoroughly.
8. Install the throttle body using a new gasket and tighten nuts and bolts to 90–122 inch lbs. (8–11 Nm) in the illustrated sequence.
9. Install accelerator cable bracket. Tighten bolts to 90–122 inch lbs. (8–11 Nm).
10. Connect the fuel charging wiring harness.
11. Connect the accelerator cable.
12. Install the air cleaner outlet tube.

Fuel Injectors

REMOVAL & INSTALLATION

1. Remove the upper intake manifold.
2. Remove the fuel injection supply manifold.
3. Carefully remove the fuel charging wiring harness connectors from the fuel injectors.

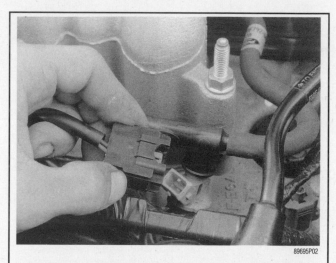

Fuel injectors are attached to the fuel charging wiring harness with two-terminal connectors

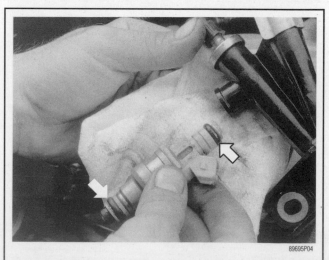

Fuel injectors use two O-rings which should be carefully inspected prior to assembly

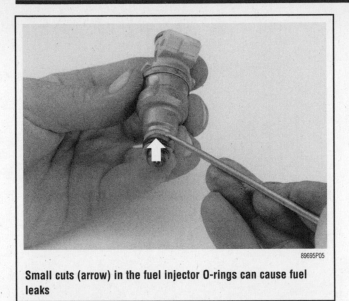

Small cuts (arrow) in the fuel injector O-rings can cause fuel leaks

On some engines, it is necessary to remove the upper intake manifold to gain access to the injectors

4. Pull fuel injector body up while gently rocking fuel injector from side to side.

To install:

5. Inspect fuel injector O-rings for signs of deterioration and replace as required.

➥**Never use silicone grease on fuel injectors.**

6. Lubricate O-rings with clean engine oil and install fuel injectors using a slight twisting motion.
7. Install fuel injection supply manifold.
8. Install the fuel charging wiring connectors.
9. Install the upper intake manifold.

TESTING

▶ **See Figure 15**

1. Disconnect the engine wiring harness from the injector.

➥**This may require removing the upper intake manifold or other engine components.**

2. Measure the resistance of the injector by probing one terminal with the positive lead and the other injector terminal with the negative lead of a multimeter.

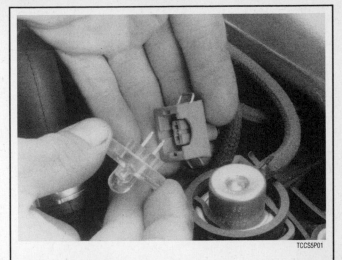

Fig. 15 A noid light can be attached to the fuel injector harness in order to test for injector pulse

3. Resistance should be between 11–18 ohms.
4. If the resistance is not within specification, the fuel injector may be faulty.
5. If resistance is within specification, install a noid light and check for injector pulse from the PCM while cranking the engine.
6. If injector pulse is present check for proper fuel pressure.

Fuel Charging Assembly

REMOVAL & INSTALLATION

▶ **See Figures 16 and 17**

1. Properly relieve the fuel system pressure.
2. Remove the upper intake manifold.
3. Remove the spring lock coupling retaining clips form the fuel inlet and return fittings.
4. Using the proper tool, disconnect and plug the fuel lines from the fuel charging assembly.
5. Remove the four charging assembly retaining bolts.
6. Carefully disconnect the charging assembly manifold from the fuel injectors and remove the assembly from the engine.

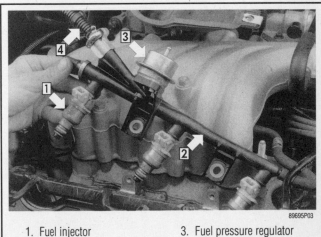

1. Fuel injector
2. Fuel rail
3. Fuel pressure regulator
4. Fuel feed hose

The fuel charging assembly consists of the fuel hose, fuel rail, fuel pressure regulator and fuel injectors

To install:

➡ **When installing the fuel charging assembly, pay special attention to proper O-ring seating to make sure no fuel leaks exist.**

7. Install fuel charging assembly and push down to make sure all fuel injector O-rings are fully seated in the cups and cylinder head pockets.

8. Install retaining bolts and tighten to 71–97 inch lbs. (8–11 Nm).

9. Connect spring lock couplings to fuel inlet and return fittings.

10. Install the upper intake manifold.

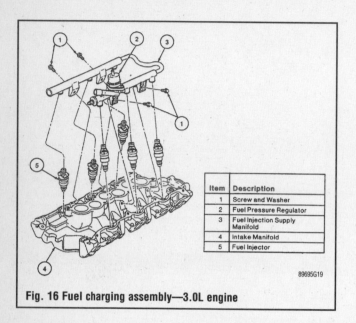

Item	Description
1	Screw and Washer
2	Fuel Pressure Regulator
3	Fuel Injection Supply Manifold
4	Intake Manifold
5	Fuel Injector

89695G19

Fig. 16 Fuel charging assembly—3.0L engine

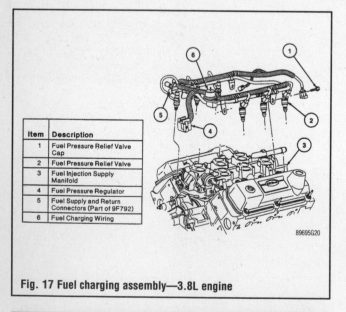

Item	Description
1	Fuel Pressure Relief Valve Cap
2	Fuel Pressure Relief Valve
3	Fuel Injection Supply Manifold
4	Fuel Pressure Regulator
5	Fuel Supply and Return Connectors (Part of 9F792)
6	Fuel Charging Wiring

89695G20

Fig. 17 Fuel charging assembly—3.8L engine

Fuel Pressure Regulator

REMOVAL & INSTALLATION

1. Properly relieve the fuel system pressure.
2. Remove the vacuum line at the fuel pressure regulator.
3. Remove the regulator retaining screws and discard.
4. Remove the fuel pressure regulator, return seal and O-rings. Discard the seal and O-rings.

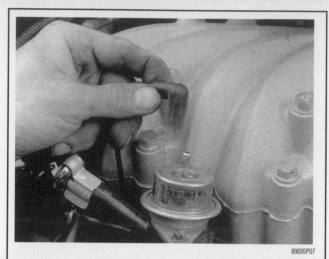

89695P07

Carefully remove the plastic vacuum hose connected to the fuel pressure regulator

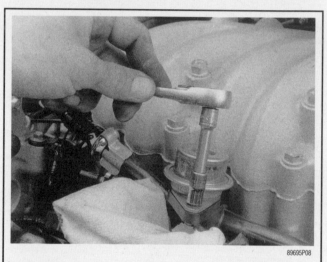

89695P08

Always install the fuel pressure regulator with new retaining screws. Never reuse the old screws

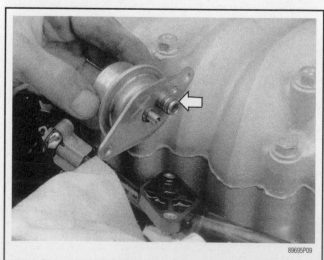

89695P09

The fuel pressure regulator is sealed to the fuel charging assembly with several O-rings

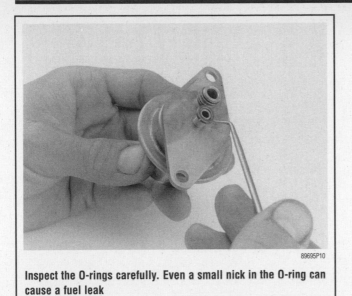

Inspect the O-rings carefully. Even a small nick in the O-ring can cause a fuel leak

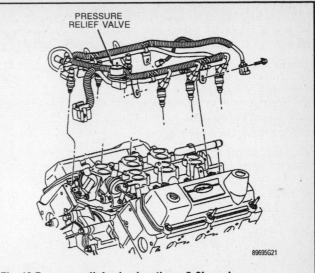

Fig. 18 Pressure relief valve location—3.8L engine

To install:

5. Clean the gasket mating surfaces thoroughly.

➡**Never use silicone grease to lubricate the O-rings.**

6. Lubricate the new fuel pressure regulator O-rings with clean engine oil.
7. Install the fuel pressure regulator using new O-rings, seals and retaining screws.
8. Tighten retaining screws to 34 inch lbs. (4 Nm).
9. Install the vacuum line at the fuel pressure regulator.

Pressure Relief Valve

REMOVAL & INSTALLATION

▶ **See Figures 18 and 19**

1. Remove the fuel cap.
2. Properly relieve the fuel system pressure.
3. Using an open end wrench or suitable deep well socket, remove the fuel pressure relief valve.
4. Installation is the reverse of removal. Please note the following important steps.
5. Install the fuel pressure relief valve and tighten to 69 inch lbs. (8 Nm).
6. Start the engine and check for fuel leaks.

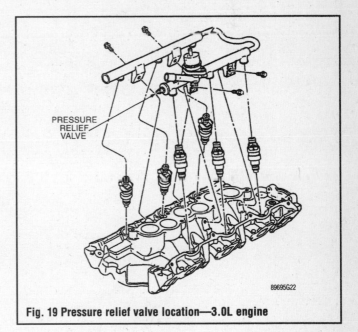

Fig. 19 Pressure relief valve location—3.0L engine

FUEL TANK

Tank Assembly

▶ See Figure 20

REMOVAL & INSTALLATION

1. Properly relieve the fuel system pressure.
2. Drain fuel from fuel tank.

➡The fuel tank has reservoirs inside to maintain fuel near the pickup during vehicle cornering and under low fuel operating conditions. these reservoirs could block siphon tubes or hoses from reaching the bottom of the fuel tank.

3. Raise and support the vehicle safely.
4. Disconnect the fuel tank filler pipe and vent hoses.
5. Place a safety support under the fuel tank and remove the support strap bolts.

6. Lower the fuel tank slightly.
7. Label and disconnect the fuel tubes, electrical harness connectors and vacuum lines from the fuel tank.
8. Remove the fuel tank from the vehicle.

To install:
9. Position the fuel tank in the vehicle.
10. Connect the fuel tubes, electrical harness connectors and vacuum lines.
11. Raise the fuel tank into position and tighten the support strap bolts to 321–39 ft. lbs. (41–54 Nm).
12. Connect the fuel tank filler pipe and vent hoses. Tighten clamps to 27–35 inch lbs. (3–4 Nm).
13. Lower the vehicle.
14. Fill the tank with fuel.
15. Start the engine and check for leaks.

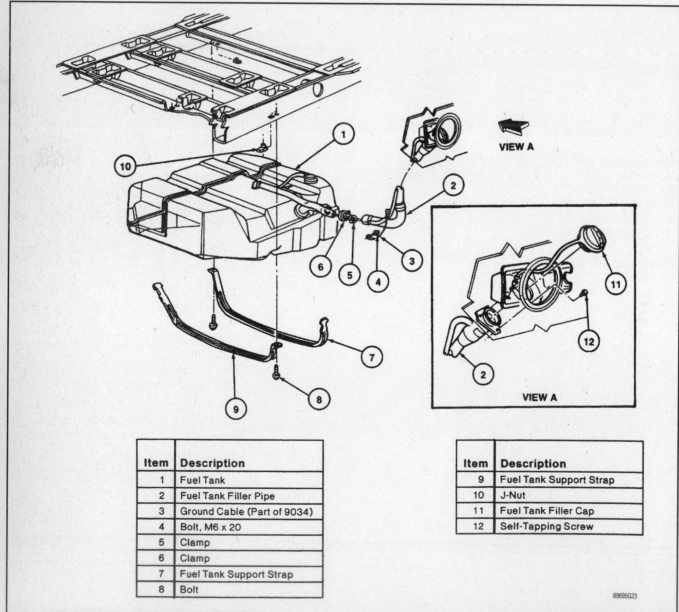

Item	Description
1	Fuel Tank
2	Fuel Tank Filler Pipe
3	Ground Cable (Part of 9034)
4	Bolt, M6 x 20
5	Clamp
6	Clamp
7	Fuel Tank Support Strap
8	Bolt

Item	Description
9	Fuel Tank Support Strap
10	J-Nut
11	Fuel Tank Filler Cap
12	Self-Tapping Screw

89695G23

Fig. 20 Exploded view of the fuel tank and filler pipe

6

CHASSIS ELECTRICAL

UNDERSTANDING AND TROUBLESHOOTING ELECTRICAL SYSTEMS

Basic Electrical Theory

▶ **See Figure 1**

For any 12 volt, negative ground, electrical system to operate, the electricity must travel in a complete circuit. This simply means that current (power) from the positive terminal (+) of the battery must eventually return to the negative terminal (-) of the battery. Along the way, this current will travel through wires, fuses, switches and components. If, for any reason, the flow of current through the circuit is interrupted, the component fed by that circuit will cease to function properly.

Perhaps the easiest way to visualize a circuit is to think of connecting a light bulb (with two wires attached to it) to the battery one wire attached to the negative (-) terminal of the battery and the other wire to the positive (+) terminal. With the two wires touching the battery terminals, the circuit would be complete and the light bulb would illuminate. Electricity would follow a path from the battery to the bulb and back to the battery. It's easy to see that with longer wires on our light bulb, it could be mounted anywhere. Further, one wire could be fitted with a switch so that the light could be turned on and off.

The normal automotive circuit differs from this simple example in two ways. First, instead of having a return wire from the bulb to the battery, the current travels through the chassis of the vehicle. Since the negative (-) battery cable is attached to the chassis and the chassis is made of electrically conductive metal, the chassis of the vehicle can serve as a ground wire to complete the circuit. Secondly, most automotive circuits contain multiple components which receive power from a single circuit. This lessens the amount of wire needed to power components on the vehicle.

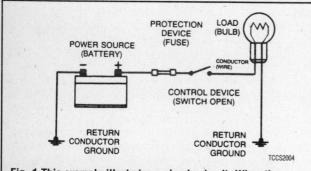

Fig. 1 This example illustrates a simple circuit. When the switch is closed, power from the positive (+) battery terminal flows through the fuse and the switch, and then to the light bulb. The light illuminates and the circuit is completed through the ground wire back to the negative (-) battery terminal. In reality, the two ground points shown in the illustration are attached to the metal chassis of the vehicle, which completes the circuit back to the battery

THE WATER ANALOGY

Electricity is the flow of electrons—hypothetical particles thought to constitute the basic "stuff" of electricity. Many people have been taught electrical theory using an analogy with water. In a comparison with water flowing through a pipe, the electrons would be the water.

The flow of electricity can be measured much like the flow of water through a pipe. The unit of measurement used is amperes, frequently abbreviated as amps (a). When connected to a circuit, an ammeter will measure the actual amount of current flowing through the circuit. When relatively few electrons flow through a circuit, the amperage is low. When many electrons flow, the amperage is high.

Just as water pressure is measured in units such as pounds per square inch (psi), electrical pressure is measured in units called volts (v). When a voltmeter is connected to a circuit, it is measuring the electrical pressure. The higher the voltage, the more current will flow through the circuit. The lower the voltage, the less current will flow.

While increasing the voltage in a circuit will increase the flow of current, the actual flow depends not only on voltage, but also on the resistance of the circuit. Resistance is the amount of force necessary to push the current through the circuit. The standard unit for measuring resistance is an ohm (W or omega). Resistance in a circuit varies depending on the amount and type of components used in the circuit. The main factors which determine resistance are:

• Material—some materials have more resistance than others. Those with high resistance are said to be insulators. Rubber is one of the best insulators available, as it allows little current to pass. Low resistance materials are said to be conductors. Copper wire is among the best conductors. Most vehicle wiring is made of copper.

• Size—the larger the wire size being used, the less resistance the wire will have. This is why components which use large amounts of electricity usually have large wires supplying current to them.

• Length—for a given thickness of wire, the longer the wire, the greater the resistance. The shorter the wire, the less the resistance. When determining the proper wire for a circuit, both size and length must be considered to design a circuit that can handle the current needs of the component.

• Temperature—with many materials, the higher the temperature, the greater the resistance. This principle is used in many of the sensors on the engine.

OHM'S LAW

The preceding definitions may lead the reader into believing that there is no relationship between current, voltage and resistance. Nothing can be further from the truth. The relationship between current, voltage and resistance can be summed up by a statement known as Ohm's law.

Voltage (E) is equal to amperage (I) times resistance (R): $E = I \times R$
Other forms of the formula are $R = E/I$ and $I = E/R$

In each of these formulas, E is the voltage in volts, I is the current in amps and R is the resistance in ohms. The basic point to remember is that as the resistance of a circuit goes up, the amount of current that flows in the circuit will go down, if voltage remains the same.

Electrical Components

POWER SOURCE

The power source for 12 volt automotive electrical systems is the battery. In most modern vehicles, the battery is a lead/acid electrochemical device consisting of six 2 volt subsections (cells) connected in series, so that the unit is capable of producing approximately 12 volts of electrical pressure. Each subsection consists of a series of positive and negative plates held a short distance apart in a solution of sulfuric acid and water.

The two types of plates are of dissimilar metals. This sets up a chemical reaction, and it is this reaction which produces current flow from the battery when its positive and negative terminals are connected to an electrical load. The power removed from the battery is replaced by the alternator, which forces electrons back through the battery, reversing the normal flow, and restoring the battery to its original chemical state.

GROUND

Two types of grounds are used in automotive electric circuits. Direct ground components are grounded through their mounting points. All other components use some sort of ground wire which is attached to the body or chassis of the vehicle. The electrical current runs through the chassis of the vehicle and returns to the battery through the ground (-) cable; if you look, you'll see that the battery ground cable connects between the battery and the body or chassis of the vehicle.

➡It should be noted that a good percentage of electrical problems can be traced to bad grounds.

PROTECTIVE DEVICES

◗ See Figure 2

It is possible for large surges of current to pass through the electrical system of your vehicle. If this surge of current were to reach the load in the circuit, it could burn it out or severely damage it. To prevent this, fuses, circuit breakers and/or fusible links are connected into the supply wires of the electrical system. These items are nothing more than a built-in weak spot in the system. When an abnormal amount of current flows through the system, these protective devices work as follows to protect the circuit:

• Fuse—when an excessive electrical current passes through a fuse, the fuse "blows" (the conductor melts) and opens the circuit, preventing the passage of current.

• Circuit Breaker—a circuit breaker is basically a self-repairing fuse. It will open the circuit in the same fashion as a fuse, but when the surge subsides, the circuit breaker can be reset and does not need replacement.

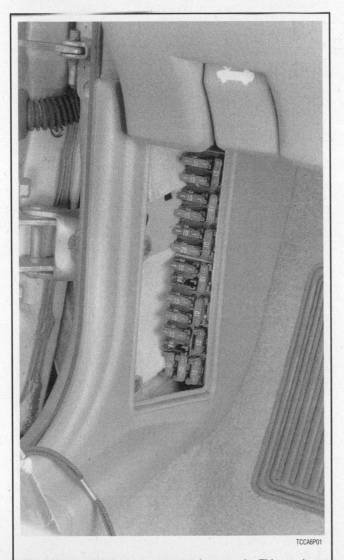

Fig. 2 Most vehicles use one or more fuse panels. This one is located in the driver's side kick panel

• Fusible Link—a fusible link (fuse link or main link) is a short length of special, Hypalon high temperature insulated wire that acts as a fuse. When an excessive electrical current passes through a fusible link, the thin gauge wire inside the link melts, creating an intentional open to protect the circuit. To repair the circuit, the link must be replaced. Some newer type fusible links are housed in plug-in modules, which are simply replaced like a fuse, while older type fusible links must be cut and spliced if they melt. Since this link is very early in the electrical path, it's the first place to look if nothing on the vehicle works, but the battery seems to be charged and is properly connected.

✴✴ CAUTION

Always replace fuses, circuit breakers and fusible links with identically rated components. Under no circumstances should a component of higher or lower amperage rating be substituted.

SWITCHES AND RELAYS

◗ See Figures 3 and 4

Switches are used in electrical circuits to control the passage of current. The most common use is to open and close circuits between the battery and the various electric devices in the system. Switches are rated according to the amount of amperage they can handle. If a sufficient amperage rated switch is not used in a circuit, the switch could overload and cause damage.

Some electrical components which require a large amount of current to operate use a special switch called a relay. Since these circuits carry a large amount of current, the thickness of the wire in the circuit is also greater. If this large wire were connected from the load to the control switch on the dashboard, the switch would have to carry the high amperage load and the dash would be twice as large to accommodate the increased size of the wiring harness. To prevent these problems, a relay is used.

Relays are composed of a coil and a switch. These two components are linked together so that when one operates, the other operates at the same time. The large wires in the circuit are connected from the battery to one side of the relay switch and from the opposite side of the relay switch to the load. Most relays are normally open, preventing current from passing through the circuit. Additional, smaller wires are connected from the relay coil to the control switch for the circuit and from the opposite side of the relay coil to ground. When the control switch is turned on, it grounds the smaller wire to the relay coil, causing the coil to operate. The coil pulls the relay switch closed, sending power to the component without routing it

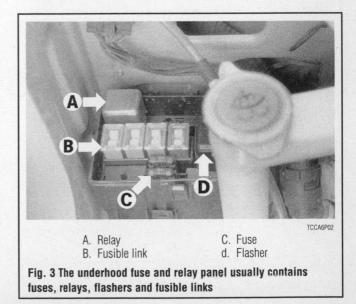

A. Relay   C. Fuse
B. Fusible link   d. Flasher

Fig. 3 The underhood fuse and relay panel usually contains fuses, relays, flashers and fusible links

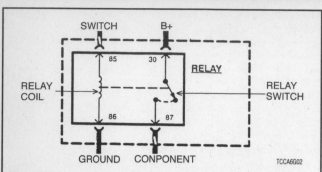

SWITCH   B+

85   30

RELAY

RELAY COIL

RELAY SWITCH

86   87

GROUND   CONPONENT

TCCA6G02

Fig. 4 Relays are composed of a coil and a switch. These two components are linked together so that when one operates, the other operates at the same time. The large wires in the circuit are connected from the battery to one side of the relay switch (B+) and from the opposite side of the relay switch to the load (component). Smaller wires are connected from the relay coil to the control switch for the circuit and from the opposite side of the relay coil to ground

through the inside of the vehicle. Some common circuits which may use relays are the horn, headlights, starter, electric fuel pump and rear window defogger systems.

LOAD

Every complete circuit must include a "load" (something to use the electricity coming from the source). Without this load, the battery would attempt to deliver its entire power supply from one pole to another. The electricity would take a short cut to ground and cause a great amount of damage to other components in the circuit by developing a tremendous amount of heat. This condition could develop sufficient heat to melt the insulation on all the surrounding wires and reduce a multiple wire cable to a lump of plastic and copper.

WIRING AND HARNESSES

The average automobile contains about ½ mile of wiring, with hundreds of individual connections. To protect the many wires from damage and to keep them from becoming a confusing tangle, they are organized into bundles, enclosed in plastic or taped together and called wiring harnesses. Different harnesses serve different parts of the vehicle. Individual wires are color coded to help trace them through a harness where sections are hidden from view.

Automotive wiring or circuit conductors can be either single strand wire, multi-strand wire or printed circuitry. Single strand wire has a solid metal core and is usually used inside such components as alternators, motors, relays and other devices. Multi-strand wire has a core made of many small strands of wire twisted together into a single conductor. Most of the wiring in an automotive electrical system is made up of multi-strand wire, either as a single conductor or grouped together in a harness. All wiring is color coded on the insulator, either as a solid color or as a colored wire with an identification stripe. A printed circuit is a thin film of copper or other conductor that is printed on an insulator backing. Occasionally, a printed circuit is sandwiched between two sheets of plastic for more protection and flexibility. A complete printed circuit, consisting of conductors, insulating material and connectors for lamps or other components is called a printed circuit board. Printed circuitry is used in place of individual wires or harnesses in places where space is limited, such as behind instrument panels.

Since automotive electrical systems are very sensitive to changes in resistance, the selection of properly sized wires is critical when systems are repaired. A loose or corroded connection or a replacement wire that is too small for the circuit will add extra resistance and an additional voltage drop to the circuit.

The wire gauge number is an expression of the cross-section area of the

conductor. The most common system for expressing wire size is the American Wire Gauge (AWG) system. As gauge number increases, area decreases and the wire becomes smaller. An 18 gauge wire is smaller than a 4 gauge wire. A wire with a higher gauge number will carry less current than a wire with a lower gauge number. Gauge wire size refers to the size of the strands of the conductor, not the size of the complete wire. It is possible, therefore, to have two wires of the same gauge with different diameters because one may have thicker insulation than the other.

12 volt automotive electrical systems generally use 10, 12, 14, 16 and 18 gauge wire. Main power distribution circuits and larger accessories usually use 10 and 12 gauge wire. Battery cables are usually 4 or 6 gauge, although 1 and 2 gauge wires are occasionally used.

It is essential to understand how a circuit works before trying to figure out why it doesn't. An electrical schematic shows the electrical current paths when a circuit is operating properly. Schematics break the entire electrical system down into individual circuits. In a schematic, no attempt is made to represent wiring and components as they physically appear on the vehicle; switches and other components are shown as simply as possible. Face views of harness connectors show the cavity or terminal locations in all multi-pin connectors to help locate test points.

CONNECTORS

▶ **See Figures 5 and 6**

Three types of connectors are commonly used in automotive applications—weatherproof, molded and hard shell.

• Weatherproof—these connectors are most commonly used in the engine compartment or where the connector is exposed to the elements. Terminals are protected against moisture and dirt by sealing rings which provide a weathertight seal. All repairs require the use of a special terminal and the tool required to service it. Unlike standard blade type terminals, these weatherproof terminals cannot be straightened once they are bent. Make certain that the connectors are properly seated and all of the sealing rings are in place when connecting leads.

• Molded—these connectors require complete replacement of the connector if found to be defective. This means splicing a new connector assembly into the harness. All splices should be soldered to insure proper contact. Use care when probing the connections or replacing terminals in them, as it is possible to create a short circuit between opposite terminals. If this happens to the wrong terminal pair, it is possible to damage certain components. Always use jumper wires between connectors for circuit checking and NEVER probe through weatherproof seals.

• Hard Shell—unlike molded connectors, the terminal contacts in hard-shell connectors can be replaced. Replacement usually involves the use of

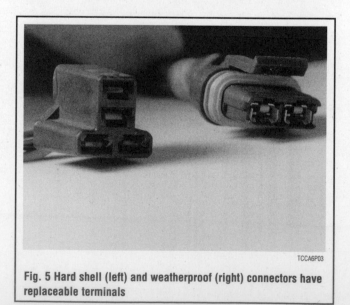

TCCA6P03

Fig. 5 Hard shell (left) and weatherproof (right) connectors have replaceable terminals

Fig. 6 Weatherproof connectors are most commonly used in the engine compartment or where the connector is exposed to the elements

a special terminal removal tool that depresses the locking tangs (barbs) on the connector terminal and allows the connector to be removed from the rear of the connector shell. The connector shell should be replaced if it shows any evidence of burning, melting, cracks, or breaks. Replace individual terminals that are burnt, corroded, distorted or loose.

Test Equipment

Pinpointing the exact cause of trouble in an electrical circuit is most times accomplished by the use of special test equipment. The following describes different types of commonly used test equipment and briefly explains how to use them in diagnosis. In addition to the information covered below, the tool manufacturer's instructions booklet (provided with the tester) should be read and clearly understood before attempting any test procedures.

JUMPER WIRES

✳✳ CAUTION

Never use jumper wires made from a thinner gauge wire than the circuit being tested. If the jumper wire is of too small a gauge, it may overheat and possibly melt. Never use jumpers to bypass high resistance loads in a circuit. Bypassing resistance, in effect, creates a short circuit. This may, in turn, cause damage and fire. Jumper wires should only be used to bypass lengths of wire.

Jumper wires are simple, yet extremely valuable, pieces of test equipment. They are basically test wires which are used to bypass sections of a circuit. Although jumper wires can be purchased, they are usually fabricated from lengths of standard automotive wire and whatever type of connector (alligator clip, spade connector or pin connector) that is required for the particular application being tested. In cramped, hard-to-reach areas, it is advisable to have insulated boots over the jumper wire terminals in order to prevent accidental grounding. It is also advisable to include a standard automotive fuse in any jumper wire. This is commonly referred to as a "fused jumper". By inserting an in-line fuse holder between a set of test leads, a fused jumper wire can be used for bypassing open circuits. Use a 5 amp fuse to provide protection against voltage spikes.

Jumper wires are used primarily to locate open electrical circuits, on either the ground (-) side of the circuit or on the power (+) side. If an electrical component fails to operate, connect the jumper wire between the component and a good ground. If the component operates only with the jumper installed, the ground circuit is open. If the ground circuit is good,

but the component does not operate, the circuit between the power feed and component may be open. By moving the jumper wire successively back from the component toward the power source, you can isolate the area of the circuit where the open is located. When the component stops functioning, or the power is cut off, the open is in the segment of wire between the jumper and the point previously tested.

You can sometimes connect the jumper wire directly from the battery to the "hot" terminal of the component, but first make sure the component uses 12 volts in operation. Some electrical components, such as fuel injectors, are designed to operate on about 4 volts, and running 12 volts directly to these components will cause damage.

TEST LIGHTS

▶ See Figure 7

The test light is used to check circuits and components while electrical current is flowing through them. It is used for voltage and ground tests. To use a 12 volt test light, connect the ground clip to a good ground and probe wherever necessary with the pick. The test light will illuminate when voltage is detected. This does not necessarily mean that 12 volts (or any particular amount of voltage) is present; it only means that some voltage is present. It is advisable before using the test light to touch its ground clip and probe across the battery posts or terminals to make sure the light is operating properly.

✳✳ WARNING

Do not use a test light to probe electronic ignition spark plug or coil wires. Never use a pick-type test light to probe wiring on computer controlled systems unless specifically instructed to do so. Any wire insulation that is pierced by the test light probe should be taped and sealed with silicone after testing.

Like the jumper wire, the 12 volt test light is used to isolate opens in circuits. But, whereas the jumper wire is used to bypass the open to operate the load, the 12 volt test light is used to locate the presence of voltage in a circuit. If the test light illuminates, there is power up to that point in the circuit; if the test light does not illuminate, there is an open circuit (no power). Move the test light in successive steps back toward the power source until the light in the handle illuminates. The open is between the probe and a point which was previously probed.

The self-powered test light is similar in design to the 12 volt test light, but contains a 1.5 volt penlight battery in the handle. It is most often used in place of a multimeter to check for open or short circuits when power is isolated from the circuit (continuity test).

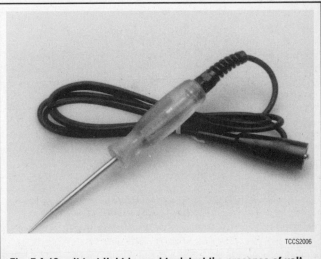

Fig. 7 A 12 volt test light is used to detect the presence of voltage in a circuit

The battery in a self-powered test light does not provide much current. A weak battery may not provide enough power to illuminate the test light even when a complete circuit is made (especially if there is high resistance in the circuit). Always make sure that the test battery is strong. To check the battery, briefly touch the ground clip to the probe; if the light glows brightly, the battery is strong enough for testing.

➡A self-powered test light should not be used on any computer controlled system or component. The small amount of electricity transmitted by the test light is enough to damage many electronic automotive components.

MULTIMETERS

Multimeters are an extremely useful tool for troubleshooting electrical problems. They can be purchased in either analog or digital form and have a price range to suit any budget. A multimeter is a voltmeter, ammeter and ohmmeter (along with other features) combined into one instrument. It is often used when testing solid state circuits because of its high input impedance (usually 10 megaohms or more). A brief description of the multimeter main test functions follows:

• Voltmeter—the voltmeter is used to measure voltage at any point in a circuit, or to measure the voltage drop across any part of a circuit. Voltmeters usually have various scales and a selector switch to allow the reading of different voltage ranges. The voltmeter has a positive and a negative lead. To avoid damage to the meter, always connect the negative lead to the negative (-) side of the circuit (to ground or nearest the ground side of the circuit) and connect the positive lead to the positive (+) side of the circuit (to the power source or the nearest power source). Note that the negative voltmeter lead will always be black and that the positive voltmeter will always be some color other than black (usually red).

• Ohmmeter—the ohmmeter is designed to read resistance (measured in ohms) in a circuit or component. All ohmmeters will have a selector switch which permits the measurement of different ranges of resistance (usually the selector switch allows the multiplication of the meter reading by 10, 100, 1,000 and 10,000). Since the meters are powered by an internal battery, the ohmmeter can be used as a self-powered test light. When the ohmmeter is connected, current from the ohmmeter flows through the circuit or component being tested. Since the ohmmeter's internal resistance and voltage are known values, the amount of current flow through the meter depends on the resistance of the circuit or component being tested. The ohmmeter can also be used to perform a continuity test for suspected open circuits. In using the meter for making continuity checks, do not be concerned with the actual resistance readings. Zero resistance, or any ohm reading, indicates continuity in the circuit. Infinite resistance indicates an opening in the circuit. A high resistance reading where there should be none indicates a problem in the circuit. Checks for short circuits are made in the same manner as checks for open circuits, except that the circuit must be isolated from both power and normal ground. Infinite resistance indicates no continuity to ground, while zero resistance indicates a dead short to ground.

✳✳ WARNING

Never use an ohmmeter to check the resistance of a component or wire while there is voltage applied to the circuit.

• Ammeter—an ammeter measures the amount of current flowing through a circuit in units called amperes or amps. At normal operating voltage, most circuits have a characteristic amount of amperes, called "current draw" which can be measured using an ammeter. By referring to a specified current draw rating, then measuring the amperes and comparing the two values, one can determine what is happening within the circuit to aid in diagnosis. An open circuit, for example, will not allow any current to flow, so the ammeter reading will be zero. A damaged component or circuit will have an increased current draw, so the reading will be high. The ammeter is always connected in series with the circuit being tested. All of the current that normally flows through the circuit must also flow through the ammeter; if there is any other path for the current to follow, the ammeter reading will not be accurate. The ammeter itself has very little resistance to current flow and, there-

fore, will not affect the circuit, but it will measure current draw only when the circuit is closed and electricity is flowing. Excessive current draw can blow fuses and drain the battery, while a reduced current draw can cause motors to run slowly, lights to dim and other components to not operate properly.

Troubleshooting

When diagnosing a specific problem, organized troubleshooting is a must. The complexity of a modern automotive vehicle demands that you approach any problem in a logical, organized manner. There are certain troubleshooting techniques which are standard:

• Establish when the problem occurs. Does the problem appear only under certain conditions? Were there any noises, odors or other unusual symptoms?

• Isolate the problem area. To do this, make some simple tests and observations, then eliminate the systems that are working properly. Check for obvious problems, such as broken wires and loose or dirty connections. Always check the obvious before assuming something complicated is the cause.

• Test for problems systematically to determine the cause once the problem area is isolated. Are all the components functioning properly? Is there power going to electrical switches and motors. Performing careful, systematic checks will often turn up most causes on the first inspection, without wasting time checking components that have little or no relationship to the problem.

• Test all repairs after the work is done to make sure that the problem is fixed. Some causes can be traced to more than one component, so a careful verification of repair work is important in order to pick up additional malfunctions that may cause a problem to reappear or a different problem to arise. A blown fuse, for example, is a simple problem that may require more than another fuse to repair. If you don't look for a problem that caused a fuse to blow, a shorted wire (for example) may go undetected.

Experience has shown that most problems tend to be the result of a fairly simple and obvious cause, such as loose or corroded connectors, bad grounds or damaged wire insulation which causes a short. This makes careful visual inspection of components during testing essential to quick and accurate troubleshooting.

Testing

OPEN CIRCUITS

▶ See Figure 8

1. Isolate the circuit from power and ground.
2. Connect the self-powered test light or ohmmeter ground clip to a good ground and probe sections of the circuit sequentially.

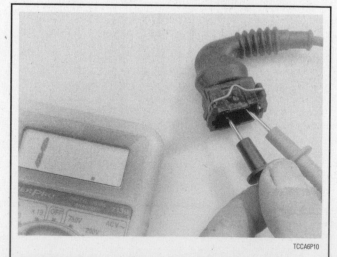

TCCA6P10

Fig. 8 The infinite reading on this multimeter (1 .) indicates that the circuit is open

3. If the light is out or there is infinite resistance, the open is between the probe and the circuit ground.

4. If the light is on or the meter shows continuity, the open is between the probe and end of the circuit toward the power source.

SHORT CIRCUITS

➡**Never use a self-powered test light to perform checks for opens or shorts when power is applied to the electrical system under test. The 12 volt vehicle power will quickly burn out the light bulb in the test light.**

1. Isolate the circuit from power and ground.

2. Connect the self-powered test light or ohmmeter ground clip to a good ground and probe any easy-to-reach test point in the circuit.

3. If the light comes on or there is continuity, there is a short somewhere in the circuit.

4. To isolate the short, probe a test point at either end of the isolated circuit (the light should be on or the meter should indicate continuity).

5. Leave the test light probe engaged and sequentially open connectors or switches, remove parts, etc. until the light goes out or continuity is broken.

6. When the light goes out, the short is between the last two circuit components which were opened.

VOLTAGE

◆ **See Figures 9 and 10**

This test determines voltage available from the battery and should be the first step in any electrical troubleshooting procedure. Many electrical problems, especially on computer controlled systems, can be caused by a low state of charge in the battery. Excessive corrosion at the battery cable terminals can cause poor contact that will prevent proper charging and full battery current flow.

1. Set the voltmeter selector switch to the 20V position.

2. Connect the multimeter negative lead to the battery's negative (-) post or terminal and the positive lead to the battery's positive (+) post or terminal.

3. Turn the ignition switch **ON** to provide a load.

4. A well charged battery should register over 12 volts. If the meter

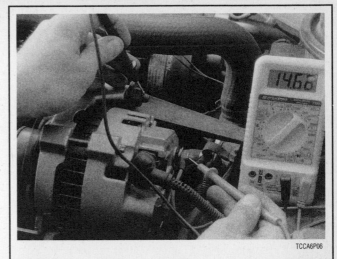

Fig. 10 Testing voltage output between the alternator's BAT terminal and ground. This voltage reading is normal

reads below 11.5 volts, the battery power may be insufficient to operate the electrical system properly.

VOLTAGE DROP

◆ **See Figure 11**

When current flows through a load, the voltage beyond the load drops. This voltage drop is due to the resistance created by the load and also by a small resistance created by corrosion at the connectors and damaged insulation on the wires. The maximum allowable voltage drop under load is critical, especially if there is more than one load in the circuit, since all voltage drops are cumulative.

1. Set the voltmeter selector switch to the 20 volt position.

2. Connect the multimeter negative lead to a good ground.

3. Operate the circuit and check the voltage prior to the first component (load).

4. There should be little or no voltage drop in the circuit prior to the

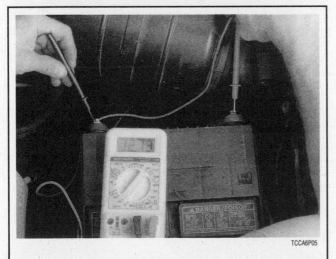

Fig. 9 Using a multimeter to check battery voltage. This battery is fully charged

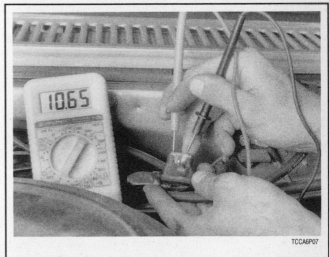

Fig. 11 This voltage drop test revealed high resistance (low voltage) in the circuit

first component. If a voltage drop exists, the wire or connectors in the circuit are suspect.

5. While operating the first component in the circuit, probe the ground side of the component with the positive meter lead and observe the voltage readings. A small voltage drop should be noticed. This voltage drop is caused by the resistance of the component.

6. Repeat the test for each component (load) down the circuit.

7. If a large voltage drop is noticed, the preceding component, wire or connector is suspect.

RESISTANCE

▶ **See Figures 12 and 13**

✳✳ WARNING

Never use an ohmmeter with power applied to the circuit. The ohmmeter is designed to operate on its own power supply. The normal 12 volt automotive electrical system current could damage the meter!

1. Isolate the circuit from the vehicle's power source.

2. Ensure that the ignition key is **OFF** when disconnecting any components or the battery.

3. Where necessary, also isolate at least one side of the circuit to be checked, in order to avoid reading parallel resistance. Parallel circuit resistance will always give a lower reading than the actual resistance of either of the branches.

4. Connect the meter leads to both sides of the circuit (wire or component) and read the actual measured ohms on the meter scale. Make sure the selector switch is set to the proper ohm scale for the circuit being tested, to avoid misreading the ohmmeter test value.

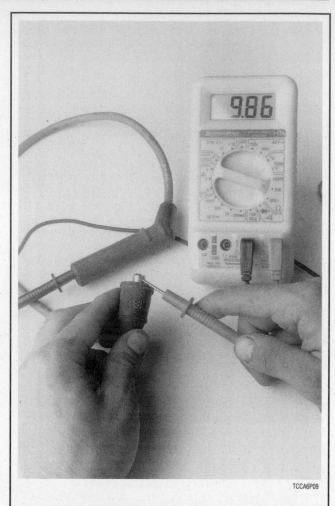

TCCA6P09

Fig. 13 Spark plug wires can be checked for excessive resistance using an ohmmeter

TCCA6P08

Fig. 12 Checking the resistance of a coolant temperature sensor with an ohmmeter. Reading is 1.04 kilohms

Wire and Connector Repair

Almost anyone can replace damaged wires, as long as the proper tools and parts are available. Automotive wire and terminals are available to fit almost any need. Even the specialized weatherproof, molded and hard shell connectors are now available from aftermarket suppliers.

Be sure the ends of all the wires are fitted with the proper terminal hardware and connectors. Wrapping a wire around a stud is never a permanent solution and will only cause trouble later. Replace wires one at a time to avoid confusion. Always route wires exactly the same as the factory.

➡**If connector repair is necessary, only attempt it if you have the proper tools. Weatherproof and hard shell connectors require special tools to release the pins inside the connector. Attempting to repair these connectors with conventional hand tools will damage them.**

BATTERY CABLES

Disconnecting the Cables

When working on any electrical component on the vehicle, it is always a good idea to disconnect the negative (-) battery cable. This will prevent potential damage to many sensitive electrical components such as the Powertrain Control Module (PCM), radio, alternator, etc.

➡**Any time you disengage the battery cables, it is recommended that you disconnect the negative (-) battery cable first. This will prevent your accidentally grounding the positive (+) terminal to the body of the vehicle when disconnecting it, thereby preventing damage to the above mentioned components.**

Before you disconnect the cable(s), first turn the ignition to the **OFF** position. This will prevent a draw on the battery which could cause arcing (electricity trying to ground itself to the body of a vehicle, just like a spark plug jumping the gap) and, of course, damaging some components such as the alternator diodes.

When the battery cable(s) are reconnected (negative cable last), be sure to check that your lights, windshield wipers and other electrically operated safety components are all working correctly. If your vehicle contains an Electronically Tuned Radio (ETR), don't forget to also reset your radio stations. Ditto for the clock.

Also, Ford reports that anytime the battery cables have been disconnected and then reconnected, some abnormal drive symptoms could occur. The is due to the PCM losing the memory voltage and its learned adaptive strategy. The vehicle will need to be driven for 10 miles (16 km) or more until the PCM relearns its adaptive strategy, and acclimates the engine and transmission functions to your driving style.

AIR BAG (SUPPLEMENTAL RESTRAINT) SYSTEM

General Information

▶ **See Figure 14**

The Supplemental Restraint System (SRS) is designed to work in conjunction with the standard three-point safety belts to reduce injury in a head-on collision.

✳✳ WARNING

The SRS can actually cause physical injury or death if the safety belts are not used, or if the manufacturer's warnings are not followed. The manufacturer's warnings can be found in your owner's manual or, in some cases, on your sun visors.

The SRS is comprised of the following components:
* Driver's side air bag module
* Passenger's side air bag module
* Right-hand and left-hand primary crash front air bag sensors
* Air bag diagnostic monitor computer
* Electrical wiring

The SRS primary crash front air bag sensors are hard-wired to the air bag modules and determine when the air bags are deployed. During a frontal collision, the sensors quickly inflate the two air bags to reduce injury by cushioning the driver and front passenger from striking the dashboard, windshield, steering wheel and any other hard surfaces. The air bag inflates so quickly (in a fraction of a second) that, in most cases, it is fully inflated before you actually start to move during an automotive collision.

Since the SRS is a complicated and essentially important system, its components are constantly being tested by a diagnostic monitor computer, which illuminates the air bag indicator light on the instrument cluster for approximately 6 seconds when the ignition switch is turned to the **RUN** position if the SRS is functioning properly. After being illuminated for the 6 seconds, the indicator light should then turn off.

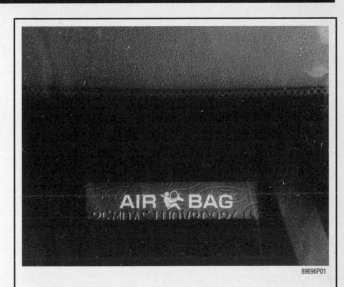

89696P01

Air bag equipped vehicles will be labeled as illustrated

If the air bag light does not illuminate at all, stays on continuously, or flashes at any time, a problem has been detected by the diagnostic monitor computer.

✳✳ WARNING

If at any time the air bag light indicates that the computer has noted a problem, have your vehicle's SRS serviced immediately by a qualified automotive technician. A faulty SRS can cause severe physical injury or death.

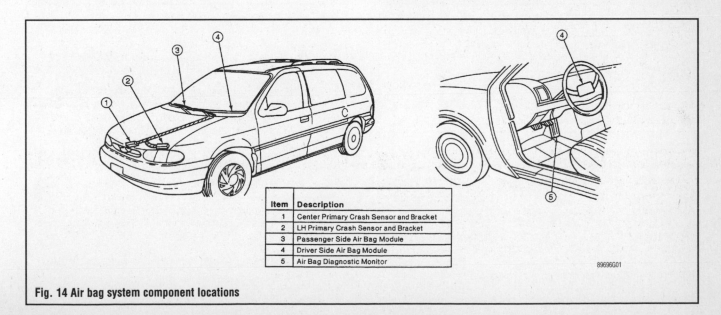

Item	Description
1	Center Primary Crash Sensor and Bracket
2	LH Primary Crash Sensor and Bracket
3	Passenger Side Air Bag Module
4	Driver Side Air Bag Module
5	Air Bag Diagnostic Monitor

89696G01

Fig. 14 Air bag system component locations

SERVICE PRECAUTIONS

Whenever working around, or on, the air bag supplemental restraint system, ALWAYS adhere to the following warnings and cautions.
• Always wear safety glasses when servicing an air bag vehicle and when handling an air bag module.
• Carry a live air bag module with the bag and trim cover facing away from your body, so that an accidental deployment of the air bag will have a small chance of personal injury.
• Place an air bag module on a table or other flat surface with the bag and trim cover pointing up.
• Wear gloves, a dust mask and safety glasses whenever handling a deployed air bag module. The air bag surface may contain traces of sodium hydroxide, a by-product of the gas that inflates the air bag and which can cause skin irritation.
• Be sure to wash your hands with mild soap and water after handling a deployed air bag.
• All air bag modules with discolored or damaged cover trim must be replaced, not repainted.
• All component replacement and wiring service must be made with the negative and positive battery cables disconnected from the battery for a minimum of one minute prior to attempting service or replacement.
• NEVER probe the air bag electrical terminals. Doing so could result in air bag deployment, which can cause serious physical injury.
• If the vehicle is involved in a "fender-bender" which results in a damaged front bumper or grille, have the air bag sensors inspected by a qualified automotive technician to ensure that they were not damaged.
• If at any time, the air bag light indicates that the computer has noted a problem, have your vehicle's SRS serviced immediately by a qualified automotive technician. A faulty SRS can cause severe physical injury or death.

DISARMING THE SYSTEM

✳✳ CAUTION

If you are disarming the system with the intent of testing the system, do not! The SRS is a sensitive, complex system and should only be tested or serviced by a qualified automotive technician. Also, specific tools are needed for SRS testing.

1. Disconnect the negative battery cable from the battery.
2. Disconnect the positive battery cable from the battery.
3. Wait at least one minute. This time is required for the back-up power supply in the air bag diagnostic monitor to completely drain. The system is now disarmed.

ARMING THE SYSTEM

1. Connect the positive battery cable.
2. Connect the negative battery cable.
3. Stand outside the vehicle and carefully turn the ignition to the **RUN** position. Be sure that no part of your body is in front of the air bag module on the steering wheel, to prevent injury in case of an accidental air bag deployment.
4. Ensure that the air bag indicator light turns off after approximately 6 seconds. If the light does not illuminate at all, does not turn off, or starts to flash, have the system tested by a qualified automotive technician. If the light does turn off after 6 seconds and does not flash, the SRS is working properly.

HEATING & AIR CONDITIONING

Blower Motor

REMOVAL & INSTALLATION

Front

▶ **See Figure 15**

1. Disconnect the negative battery cable.
2. Open the glove box door. Gently squeeze the retainers at the rear of the box inward and allow the box to swing downward.

➡**If additional access is required, unfasten the glove box hinge retainers and remove the assembly.**

3. Label and disconnect the electrical harness from the blower motor.
4. Remove the blower motor housing tube and/or blower motor cover.
5. Remove the blower motor retaining screws.
6. Remove the blower motor from the A/C evaporator.

To install:

7. Install the blower motor in the A/C evaporator and tighten the retaining screws securely.
8. Install the blower motor housing tube and/or blower motor cover.
9. Connect the electrical harness to the blower motor.

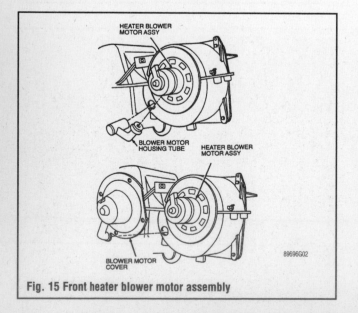

Fig. 15 Front heater blower motor assembly

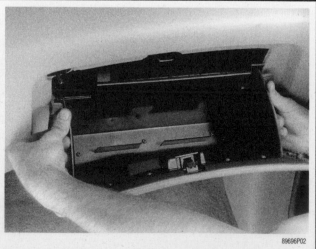

Remove the glove box to access the front blower motor, which is on the firewall

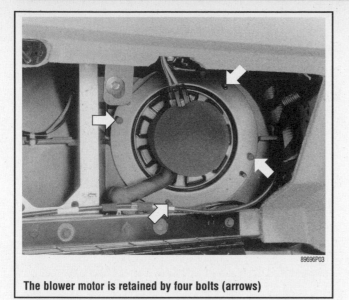

The blower motor is retained by four bolts (arrows)

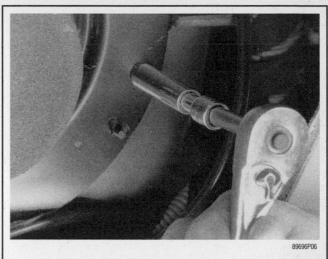

A ratchet with extensions makes removal of the retaining screws easier

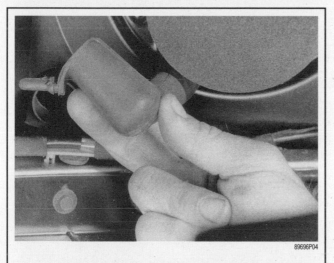

The blower motor vent tube helps to cool the blower motor for efficient operation

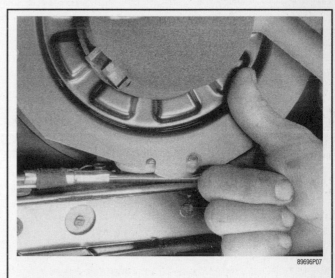

Lift the blower motor over the control cable . . .

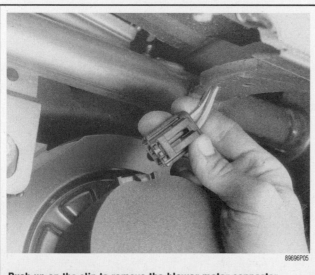

Push up on the clip to remove the blower motor connector

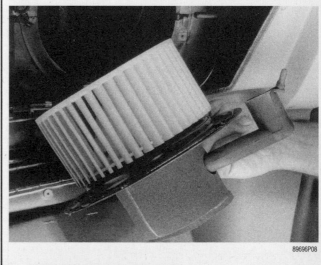

. . . and remove it from the vehicle

10. Reinstall the glove box and close its door.
11. Connect the negative battery cable.

Rear

▶ See Figure 16

1. Disconnect the negative battery cable.
2. Remove both rear passenger seats.
3. Remove the three push pin retainers from the lower edge of the auxiliary heater and air conditioning service cover.
4. Lift the service cover outward and upward to remove.
5. Label and disconnect the electrical harness.
6. Remove the blower motor housing tube.
7. Loosen the three retaining screws and remove the blower motor.

To install:

8. Install the blower motor and tighten retaining screws securely.
9. Install the blower motor housing tube.
10. Connect the electrical harness.
11. Position the service cover and install the three push pin retainers from the lower edge of the cover.
12. Install both rear passenger seats.
13. Connect the negative battery cable.

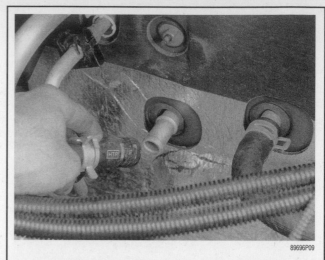

Be careful when removing the hoses from the heater core, as the tubes are easily damaged

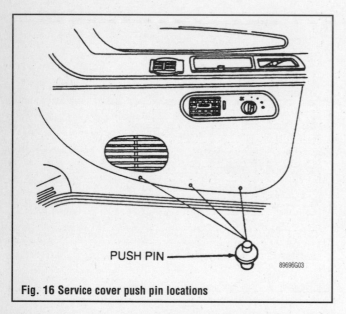

Fig. 16 Service cover push pin locations

PUSH PIN

89696G03

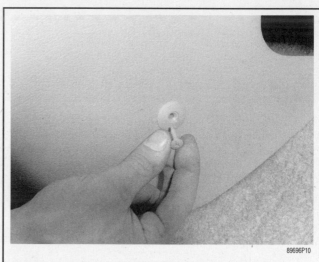

The center instrument panel is attached using special plastic screws

Heater Core

REMOVAL & INSTALLATION

Front

▶ See Figure 17

1. Disconnect the negative battery cable.
2. Drain and recycle the engine coolant.
3. Remove the cowl top vent panel.
4. Disconnect the heater hoses from the heater core inlet and outlet tubes.
5. Remove the ground strap from the heater core tube, as required.
6. Remove the center instrument panel trim.
7. Remove the ashtray.
8. Remove the rear seat airflow duct.
9. Label and disconnect the keyless entry wiring harness, as required.
10. Remove the center instrument panel support brackets.
11. Label and disconnect the climate control vacuum lines.

The rear seat airflow duct carries air to the rear of the passenger compartment

Item	Description
1	Outside Air Seal
2	A/C Air Inlet Duct
3	A/C Air Inlet Door Inner Seal
4	A/C Recirculating Air Duct
5	A/C Damper Door Shaft
6	Vacuum Control Motor
7	Blower Motor Wheel
8	Blower Motor
9	A/C Evaporator Housing
10	Rear Seat Airflow Duct

Item	Description
11	Heater Outlet Floor Duct
12	Heater Housing Core Plate
13	Heater Core
14	A/C Electronic Door Actuator Motor
15	Vacuum Control Motor
16	Shaft — Heater Air Damper Door
17	Windshield Defroster Door Shaft
18	Windshield Defroster Duct Connector

Fig. 17 Front heater housing assembly

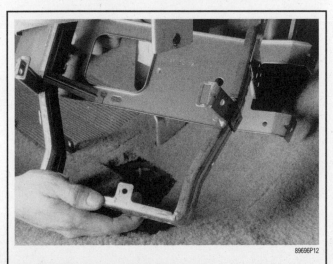

The instrument panel support bracket must be removed to lower the heater core

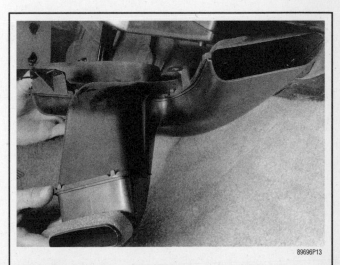

The heater outlet floor duct is attached to the bottom of the housing core

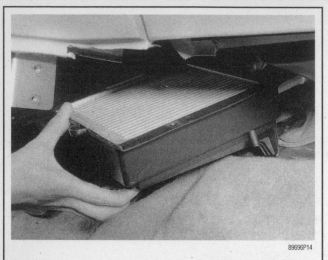

The heater core is located in a box at the bottom of the housing core

A foam liner is used to cushion the heater core

12. Remove the heater outlet floor duct.
13. Remove the housing core plate retaining screws and remove the heater housing core plate.
14. Remove the heater core.
To install:
15. Position the heater core.
16. Install the heater housing core plate and tighten the screws securely.
17. Install the heater outlet floor duct.
18. Connect the climate control vacuum lines.
19. Install the center instrument panel support brackets.
20. Connect the keyless entry wiring harness, as required.
21. Install the rear seat airflow duct.
22. Install the ashtray.
23. Install the center instrument panel trim.
24. Install the ground strap to the heater core tube, as required.
25. Connect the heater hoses on the heater core inlet and outlet tubes.
26. Install the cowl top vent panel.
27. Fill and bleed the cooling system.
28. Connect the negative battery cable.

Rear

▶ **See Figures 18 and 19**

1. Have a qualified technician discharge and recover the refrigerant from the A/C system.

❋❋ WARNING

It is a federal crime to vent refrigerant into the atmosphere. A/C components on your vehicle should be serviced only by a Motor Vehicle Air Conditioning (MVAC) trained, and EPA certified automotive technician.

2. Disconnect the negative battery cable.
3. Drain and recycle the engine coolant.
4. Raise and support the vehicle safely.
5. Place a drain pan under the heater water hose connections for the rear heater assembly.
6. Drain and recycle the engine coolant from the auxiliary heater core and hoses.
7. Disconnect the two A/C spring lock couplings using a Spring Lock Coupling Disconnect Tool (T84L-19623-B) or equivalent.
8. Lower the vehicle.
9. Remove all rear passenger seating.
10. Remove the three push pin retainers from the lower edge of the auxiliary heater and air conditioning service cover.
11. Lift the service cover outward and upward to remove.
12. Label and disconnect the electrical harnesses.
13. Label and disconnect the vacuum lines.
14. Remove the body side trim panels.
15. Disconnect and plug all A/C refrigerant lines.

➡**It is extremely important that the A/C lines be plugged to prevent the entry of dirt or moisture.**

16. Remove the lower A/C recirculation air duct and heater extension air duct.
17. Remove the auxiliary heater and A/C assembly.
To install:
18. Position the auxiliary heater and A/C assembly in the vehicle. Guide the heater water hoses through the floor grommet. Tighten the retaining screws to 16–23 inch lbs. (2–3 Nm).
19. Connect all A/C refrigerant lines.
20. Install the lower A/C recirculation air duct and heater extension air duct. Tighten the retaining screws to 16–23 inch lbs. (2–3 Nm).
21. Install the body side trim panels.

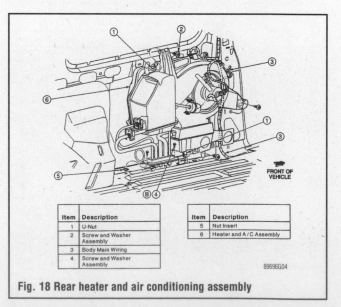

Item	Description
1	U-Nut
2	Screw and Washer Assembly
3	Body Main Wiring
4	Screw and Washer Assembly

Item	Description
5	Nut Insert
6	Heater and A/C Assembly

Fig. 18 Rear heater and air conditioning assembly

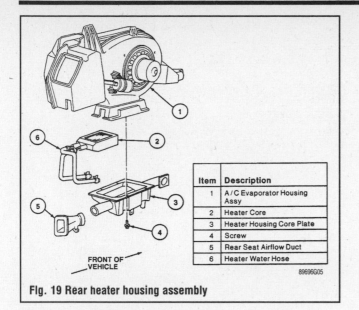

Fig. 19 Rear heater housing assembly

Item	Description
1	A/C Evaporator Housing Assy
2	Heater Core
3	Heater Housing Core Plate
4	Screw
5	Rear Seat Airflow Duct
6	Heater Water Hose

89696G05

22. Connect the vacuum lines.
23. Connect the electrical harnesses.
24. Install the auxiliary heater and air conditioning service cover and secure with three push pin retainers.
25. Install all rear passenger sealing.
26. Raise and support the vehicle safely.
27. Connect the heater water hoses to the heater core tubes.
28. Lower the vehicle.
29. Fill the engine with coolant.
30. Connect the negative battery cable.
31. Have a qualified technician evacuate and charge the A/C system with refrigerant.

Air Conditioning Components

REMOVAL & INSTALLATION

Repair or service of air conditioning components is not covered by this manual, because of the risk of personal injury or death, and because of the legal ramifications of servicing these components without the proper EPA certification and experience. Cost, personal injury or death, environmental damage, and legal considerations (such as the fact that it is a federal crime to vent refrigerant into the atmosphere), dictate that the A/C components on your vehicle should be serviced only by a Motor Vehicle Air Conditioning (MVAC) trained, and EPA certified automotive technician.

➡ If your vehicle's A/C system uses R-12 refrigerant and is in need of recharging, the A/C system can be converted over to R-134a refrigerant (less environmentally harmful and expensive). Refer to Section 1 for additional information on R-12 to R-134a conversions, and for additional considerations dealing with your vehicle's A/C system.

Control Cables

This vehicle uses vacuum control motors, a vacuum harness and an airflow control knob or vacuum selector to control heating and air conditioning airflow through the vehicle. No cables are used.

Control Panel

▶ See Figures 20, 21 and 22

REMOVAL & INSTALLATION

Front

▶ See Figures 23 and 24

1. Disconnect the negative battery cable.
2. Remove the ashtray.
3. Remove the retaining screws over the ashtray cutout in the dashboard.
4. Remove the finish panel by grasping the outer edges and pulling outward until the retaining clips release the panel.
5. Label and disconnect the electrical harness.
6. Remove the control assembly retaining screws.

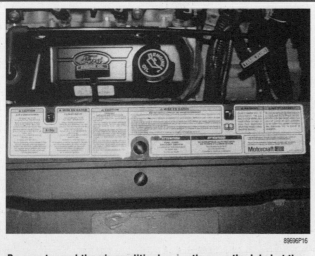

Be sure to read the air conditioning cautions on the label at the front of the engine compartment

89696P16

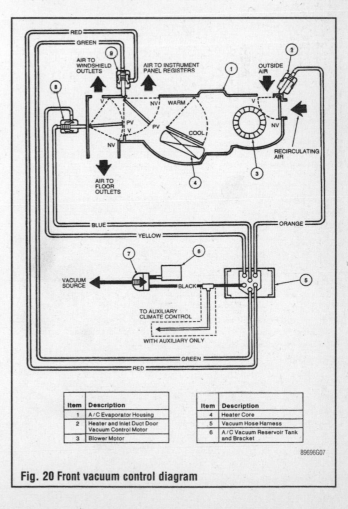

Item	Description
1	A/C Evaporator Housing
2	Heater and Inlet Duct Door Vacuum Control Motor
3	Blower Motor

Item	Description
4	Heater Core
5	Vacuum Hose Harness
6	A/C Vacuum Reservoir Tank and Bracket

89696G07

Fig. 20 Front vacuum control diagram

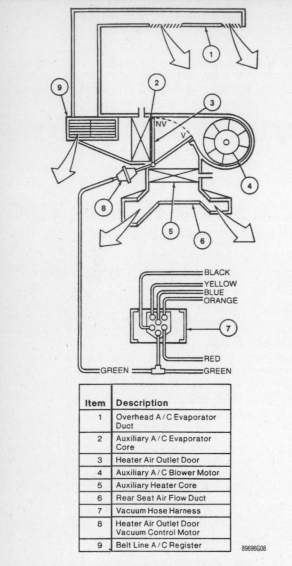

Item	Description
1	Overhead A / C Evaporator Duct
2	Auxiliary A / C Evaporator Core
3	Heater Air Outlet Door
4	Auxiliary A / C Blower Motor
5	Auxiliary Heater Core
6	Rear Seat Air Flow Duct
7	Vacuum Hose Harness
8	Heater Air Outlet Door Vacuum Control Motor
9	Belt Line A / C Register

89696G08

Fig. 21 Rear vacuum control diagram—early production

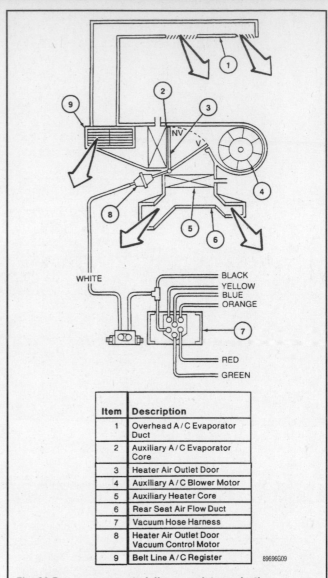

Item	Description
1	Overhead A / C Evaporator Duct
2	Auxiliary A / C Evaporator Core
3	Heater Air Outlet Door
4	Auxiliary A / C Blower Motor
5	Auxiliary Heater Core
6	Rear Seat Air Flow Duct
7	Vacuum Hose Harness
8	Heater Air Outlet Door Vacuum Control Motor
9	Belt Line A / C Register

89696G09

Fig. 22 Rear vacuum control diagram—late production

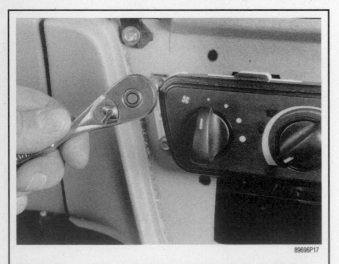

89696P17

The control panel is attached to the instrument panel with four screws

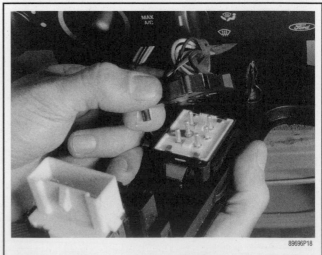

89696P18

Multi-pin connectors are used to control the heating and air conditioning functions

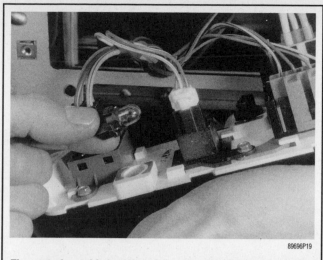

The control panel is backlit with small bulbs. Twist the socket ¼ turn to remove

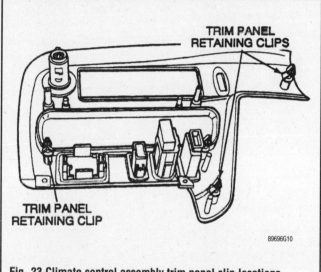

Fig. 23 Climate control assembly trim panel clip locations

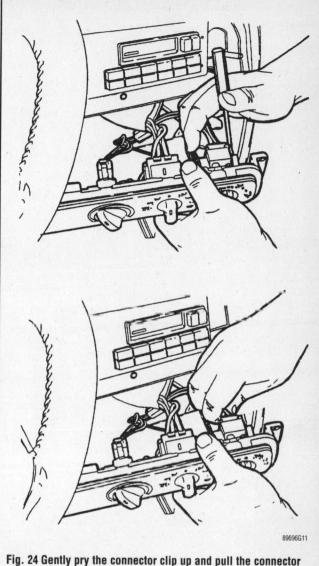

Fig. 24 Gently pry the connector clip up and pull the connector from the control panel assembly

7. Label and disconnect the electrical and vacuum harnesses.
8. Remove the heater control.

To install:

9. Position the heater control.
10. Connect the electrical and vacuum harnesses.
11. Install the control assembly retaining screws and tighten securely.
12. Connect the electrical harness.
13. Install the finish panel by aligning the retaining clips and pushing the panel in place.
14. Install the retaining screws over the ashtray cutout in the dashboard and tighten securely.
15. Install the ashtray.
16. Connect the negative battery cable.

Rear

▶ See Figure 25

1. Disconnect the negative battery cable.
2. Using an appropriate tool, remove the control panel bezel.
3. Label and disconnect the wire harness.
4. Remove the control panel.
5. Installation is the reverse of removal.

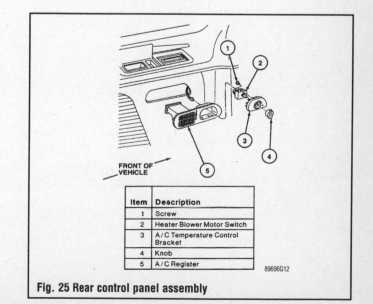

Item	Description
1	Screw
2	Heater Blower Motor Switch
3	A/C Temperature Control Bracket
4	Knob
5	A/C Register

Fig. 25 Rear control panel assembly

CRUISE CONTROL

▶ **See Figure 26**

The electronic cruise control system consists of the following components:
- Control switches
- Servo/control unit (throttle actuator)
- Speed sensor
- Stoplamp switch
- Vehicle Speed Sensor

The throttle actuator/control unit is mounted in the engine compartment and is connected to the throttle linkage with an actuator cable. The control unit regulates the throttle actuator to keep the requested speed. When the brake pedal is depressed, an electrical signal from the stoplamp switch returns the system to stand-by mode. This system operates independently of engine vacuum, therefore no vacuum lines are required.

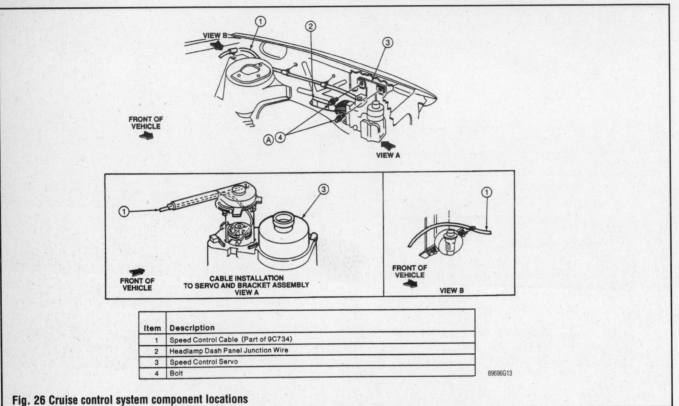

Item	Description
1	Speed Control Cable (Part of 9C734)
2	Headlamp Dash Panel Junction Wire
3	Speed Control Servo
4	Bolt

89696G13

Fig. 26 Cruise control system component locations

CRUISE CONTROL TROUBLESHOOTING

Problem	Possible Cause
Will not hold proper speed	Incorrect cable adjustment
	Binding throttle linkage
	Leaking vacuum servo diaphragm
	Leaking vacuum tank
	Faulty vacuum or vent valve
	Faulty stepper motor
	Faulty transducer
	Faulty speed sensor
	Faulty cruise control module
Cruise intermittently cuts out	Clutch or brake switch adjustment too tight
	Short or open in the cruise control circuit
	Faulty transducer
	Faulty cruise control module
Vehicle surges	Kinked speedometer cable or casing
	Binding throttle linkage
	Faulty speed sensor
	Faulty cruise control module
Cruise control inoperative	Blown fuse
	Short or open in the cruise control circuit
	Faulty brake or clutch switch
	Leaking vacuum circuit
	Faulty cruise control switch
	Faulty stepper motor
	Faulty transducer
	Faulty speed sensor
	Faulty cruise control module

Note: Use this chart as a guide. Not all systems will use the components listed.

TCCA6C01

ENTERTAINMENT SYSTEMS

Radio Receiver

REMOVAL & INSTALLATION

1. Disconnect the negative battery cable.

➡**Do not use excessive force when installing the radio removal tool. This will damage the retaining clips, making radio chassis removal difficult and may cause other internal damage.**

2. Install Radio Removal Tool (T87P-19061-A) or equivalent into the radio face place. Push the tool in approximately 1 in. (25mm) to release the retaining clips.

3. Apply a slight spreading force on both sides and pull the radio chassis out of the instrument panel.

4. Disconnect the radio wiring harness and antenna cable.

5. Remove the radio chassis.

To install:

6. Position the radio chassis in the vehicle.

7. Connect the radio wiring harness and antenna cable.

89696P22

After insertion of the tool, the radio should slide out of the instrument panel easily

89696P20

A Radio Removal Tool (T87P-19061-A) or equivalent is necessary to remove the radio

89696P23

After removing the radio, disconnect the electrical harness and antenna

8. Push the radio chassis inward until the retaining clips are fully engaged.

9. Connect the negative battery cable.

Amplifier

The Premium Sound and JBL® amplifiers are located behind the glove box. The subwoofer amplifier is located behind the left rear quarter panel trim.

REMOVAL & INSTALLATION

1. Remove the glove box or left rear quarter panel trim as required.

2. Disconnect the amplifier electrical harness.

3. Remove the amplifier attaching nuts.

4. Remove the amplifier.

5. Installation is the reverse of removal.

6. Tighten the amplifier attaching nuts to 24–33 inch lbs. (3–4 Nm).

89696P21

The tool fits into special slots on each side of the radio face plate

CD Player

The CD player is an integral part of the radio receiver and is not serviced separately.

Speakers

REMOVAL & INSTALLATION

Front Door

▶ **See Figure 27**

1. Remove the door trim panel.
2. Remove the three screws attaching the speaker to the door panel.
3. Lift the speaker from the door panel and disconnect the electrical harness.
4. Remove the speaker.
5. Installation is the reverse of removal.
6. Tighten the attaching screws to 8 inch lbs. (0.9 Nm).

Quarter Trim Panel

▶ **See Figure 28**

1. Remove the rear quarter trim panel.
2. Remove the three or four screws retaining the speaker.
3. Lift the speaker from the enclosure and disconnect the electrical harness.
4. Remove the speaker.
5. Installation is the reverse of removal.
6. Tighten attaching screws to 8 inch lbs. (0.9 Nm).

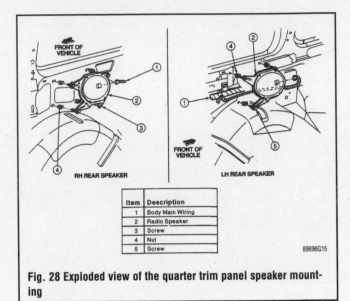

Item	Description
1	Body Main Wiring
2	Radio Speaker
3	Screw
4	Nut
5	Screw

89696G15

Fig. 28 Exploded view of the quarter trim panel speaker mounting

Subwoofer

▶ **See Figure 29**

1. Remove the left rear quarter trim panel.
2. Push back the soft gasket around the radio speaker and remove the four screws attaching the subwoofer to the enclosure.
3. Remove the subwoofer and disconnect the electrical harness.
4. Installation is the reverse of removal.
5. Tighten the attaching screws to 48–60 inch lbs. (5–7 Nm).

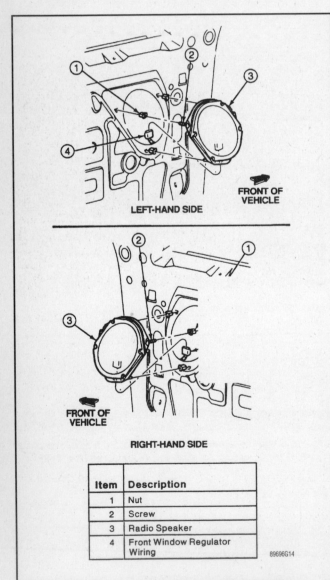

Item	Description
1	Nut
2	Screw
3	Radio Speaker
4	Front Window Regulator Wiring

89696G14

Fig. 27 Exploded view of the front door speaker mounting

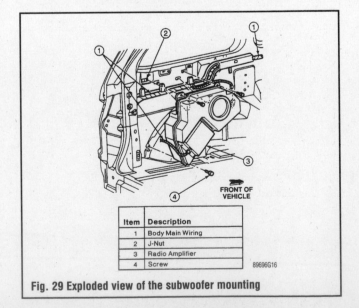

Item	Description
1	Body Main Wiring
2	J-Nut
3	Radio Amplifier
4	Screw

89696G16

Fig. 29 Exploded view of the subwoofer mounting

WINDSHIELD WIPERS AND WASHERS

Wiper Blade and Arm

REMOVAL & INSTALLATION

▶ **See Figures 30 and 31**

Front

➡To prevent glass and paint damage, do not pry the windshield wiper pivot arm from the windshield with a metal or sharp tool.

1. Turn the ignition switch to the **ACC** position. Turn the multi-function switch to **LO**.
2. Allow the windshield wiper motor to move the linkages three or four cycles, then turn the multi-function switch **OFF**.
3. Turn the ignition switch **OFF**.
4. Lift up the cap on the windshield wiper pivot arm to expose the nut that holds the arm to the wiper pivot shaft.
5. Matchmark the wiper arm and the wiper pivot shaft for installation reference.

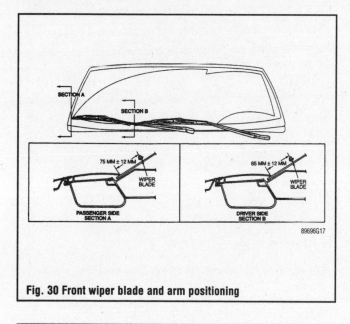

Fig. 30 Front wiper blade and arm positioning

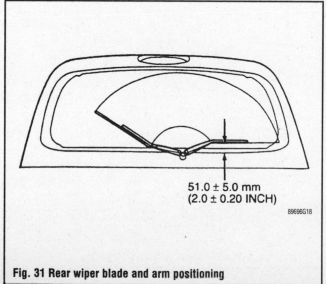

Fig. 31 Rear wiper blade and arm positioning

To maintain proper wiper-to-chassis alignment, always matchmark the wiper to the pivot shaft

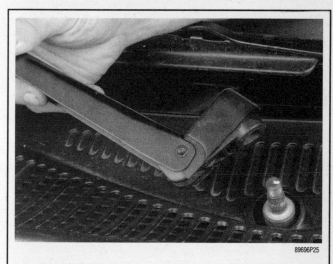

Place the wiper in the service position and rock it back and forth lightly to remove

6. Remove the nuts and lift each wiper arm to the service position, then carefully rock the arm toward the front and rear of the vehicle to loosen the arm from the pivot shaft.
7. Lift the arm off the pivot shaft.

To install:

➡The windshield wiper pivot arms are made of a soft metal and do not have hardened serrations to automatically position the wiper arms.

8. Turn the ignition switch to the **ACC** position. Turn the multi-function switch to **LO**.
9. Allow the windshield wiper motor to move the linkage for 15 seconds, then turn the multi-function switch **OFF**.
10. Turn the ignition switch **OFF**.
11. Align and install the windshield wiper pivot arm. Tighten the nut to 23–29 ft. lbs. (30–40 Nm).

➡Make sure the pivot arms do not contact the cowl top vent panel or A-pillar when they are cycled.

12. Close the cap which covers the attaching nut.

Rear

➡To prevent glass and paint damage, do not pry the wiper pivot arm from the rear window with a metal or sharp tool.

1. Turn the ignition switch to the **ACC** position. Turn the multi-function switch to **LO**.
2. Allow the wiper motor to move the linkage three or four cycles, then turn the multi-function switch **OFF**.
3. Turn the ignition switch **OFF**.
4. Lift up the cap on the wiper pivot arm to expose the nut that holds the arm to the wiper pivot shaft.
5. Matchmark the wiper arm and the wiper pivot shaft for installation reference.
6. Loosen the retaining nut approximately two turns.
7. Using pliers, squeeze the head of the pivot arm and nut until the pivot arm head pops off the shaft.

➡Do not manually rotate the wiper pivot arm. Damage to the wiper motor may result.

8. Remove the nut and wiper pivot arm.

To install:

9. Turn the ignition switch to the **ACC** position. Turn the multi-function switch to **LO**.
10. Allow the wiper motor to move the linkage three or four cycles, then turn the multi-function switch **OFF**.
11. Turn the ignition switch **OFF**.
12. Align and install the wiper pivot arm. Tighten the retaining nut to 106–132 inch lbs. (12–15 Nm).

➡Make sure the pivot arms do not contact any body panels when they are cycled.

13. Install the protective cap.

Wiper Motor

REMOVAL & INSTALLATION

Front

◗ See Figure 32

➡The permanent internal magnets in the windshield wiper motor are made of ceramic. Care must be exercised in handling the windshield wiper motor to avoid damaging these magnets. The windshield wiper motor must not be struck or tapped with a hammer or other object.

The windshield wiper motor uses a 6-pin connector. When disengaging the connector, never pull the wires

The wiper linkage assembly is bolted to the cowl vent in several places

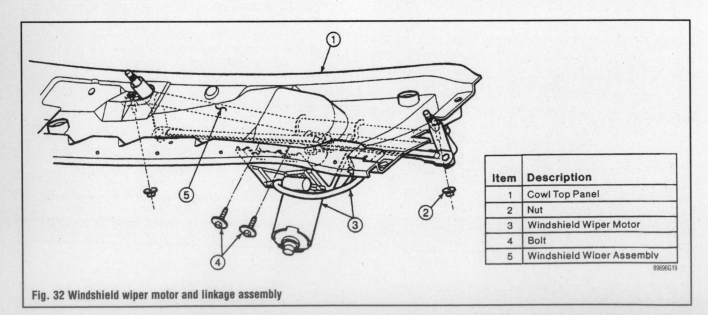

Item	Description
1	Cowl Top Panel
2	Nut
3	Windshield Wiper Motor
4	Bolt
5	Windshield Wiper Assembly

Fig. 32 Windshield wiper motor and linkage assembly

The wiper linkage is connected to the motor using a stud and grommets

The wiper motor is held in position on the cowl vent with three bolts

If removing the wiper motor alone, disconnect the linkage from the motor at the motor's primary shaft

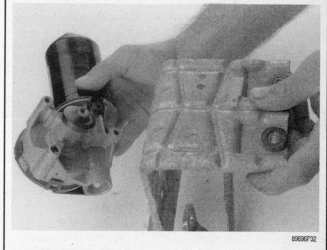

Once the linkage and bolts have been removed, lift the wiper motor from the cowl vent

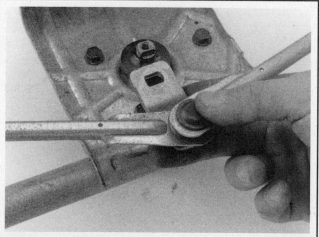

The wiper linkage is keyed with the wiper motor to aid in proper alignment during installation

1. Disconnect the negative battery cable.
2. Remove the windshield wiper pivot arms.
3. Remove the cowl vent top.
4. Remove the five screws retaining the cowl top to the vehicle.
5. Remove the cowl top and windshield wiper assembly from the vehicle.
6. Remove the linkage drive arm from the motor shaft.
7. Remove the three screws retaining the windshield wiper motor to the cowl vent and separate the two parts.
8. Label and disconnect the electrical harness to the wiper motor.
9. Remove the windshield wiper motor.

To install:

10. Position the windshield wiper motor and connect the electrical harness.
11. Install the three screws retaining the windshield wiper motor to the cowl vent and tighten to 115–150 inch lbs. (13–17 Nm).
12. Install the linkage drive arm on the motor shaft.
13. Install the cowl top and windshield wiper assembly on the vehicle.
14. Install the five screws retaining the cowl top to the vehicle and tighten to 115–150 inch lbs. (13–17 Nm).

15. Install the cowl vent top.
16. Install the windshield wiper pivot arms.
17. Connect the negative battery cable.

Rear

▶ **See Figure 33**

1. Remove the rear wiper pivot arm.
2. Remove the liftgate interior trim panel.
3. Label and disconnect the electrical harness.

➡**Pull on the connector only and not on the wires. Pulling on the wires may cause internal damage that may not be apparent to the eye.**

4. Remove the wiper motor retaining screws.
5. Lift off the wiper motor from the liftgate.

To install:

6. Position the wiper motor on the liftgate.
7. Install the wiper motor retaining screws and tighten to 20–29 ft. lbs. (30–40 Nm).
8. Connect the electrical harness.
9. Install the liftgate interior trim panel.
10. Install the rear wiper pivot arm.

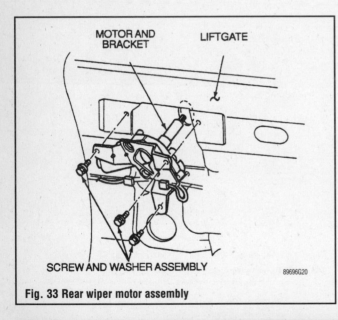

Fig. 33 Rear wiper motor assembly

Windshield Washer Motor

REMOVAL & INSTALLATION

▶ **See Figure 34**

The front and rear washer nozzles are fed by a single washer reservoir and pump located on the driver's side frame rail in the engine compartment.

1. Remove the driver's inner splash shield in the engine compartment.
2. Label and disconnect the electrical harness.

➡**The washer reservoir will drain when the washer hose is disconnected.**

3. Disconnect the washer hose and plug the nipple in the washer reservoir.
4. Remove the washer reservoir from the vehicle.
5. Remove the washer motor from the reservoir.

To install:

6. Install the washer motor on the reservoir.
7. Install the washer reservoir in the vehicle and tighten the attaching bolts securely.
8. Connect the washer hose.
9. Connect the electrical harness.
10. Install the driver's inner splash shield.

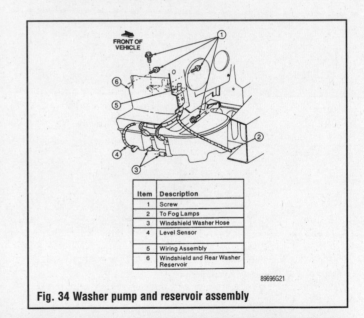

Item	Description
1	Screw
2	To Fog Lamps
3	Windshield Washer Hose
4	Level Sensor
5	Wiring Assembly
6	Windshield and Rear Washer Reservoir

Fig. 34 Washer pump and reservoir assembly

INSTRUMENTS AND SWITCHES

Instrument Cluster

REMOVAL & INSTALLATION

▶ **See Figures 35, 36, 37 and 38**

➡**Federal law requires that the odometer in any replacement speedometer/odometer must register the same mileage as that registered on the removed speedometer/odometer. Service replacement speedometer/odometers and odometer modules with the mileage preset to actual vehicle mileage are available through the dealer. In nearly all cases, the mileage continues to accumulate in the odometer memory even if the odometer does not display mileage. This mileage can usually be verified by the dealer. Contact the dealer for instructions to receive a replacement speedometer/odometer with preset mileage. If the actual vehicle mileage cannot be verified, the dealer will supply a** speedometer/odometer with a display set to zero miles. In addition, an odometer mileage sticker is supplied with the replacement odometer. The sticker must display the estimated vehicle mileage and is to be affixed to the driver's door.

Electronic

1. Disconnect the negative battery cable.
2. Remove the radio.
3. Remove the steering column shroud and upper steering column shroud.
4. Remove the instrument panel steering column cover by removing the attaching two screws and prying the cover off.
5. Remove the lower driver's side instrument panel finish panel.
6. Remove the instrument center panel. Label and disconnect the six electrical harnesses.
7. Remove the panel over the headlamp switch. Label and disconnect the electrical harness.

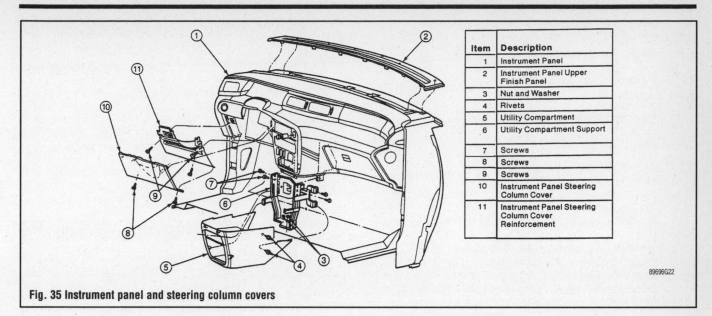

Item	Description
1	Instrument Panel
2	Instrument Panel Upper Finish Panel
3	Nut and Washer
4	Rivets
5	Utility Compartment
6	Utility Compartment Support
7	Screws
8	Screws
9	Screws
10	Instrument Panel Steering Column Cover
11	Instrument Panel Steering Column Cover Reinforcement

89696G22

Fig. 35 Instrument panel and steering column covers

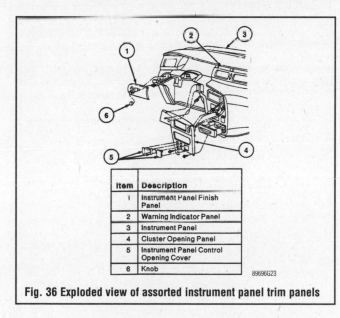

Item	Description
I	Instrument Panel Finish Panel
2	Warning Indicator Panel
3	Instrument Panel
4	Cluster Opening Panel
5	Instrument Panel Control Opening Cover
6	Knob

89696G23

Fig. 36 Exploded view of assorted instrument panel trim panels

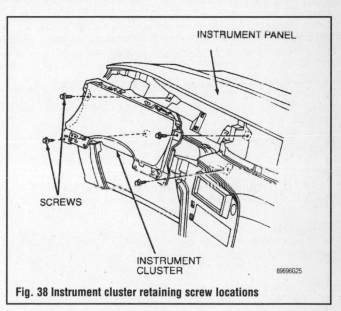

89696G25

Fig. 38 Instrument cluster retaining screw locations

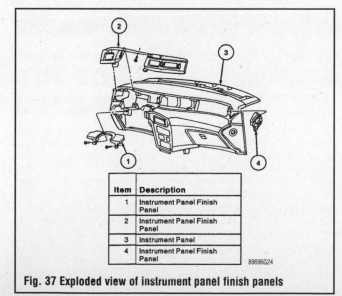

Item	Description
1	Instrument Panel Finish Panel
2	Instrument Panel Finish Panel
3	Instrument Panel
4	Instrument Panel Finish Panel

89696G24

Fig. 37 Exploded view of instrument panel finish panels

8. Remove the two screws above the instrument panel. Unsnap the panel to remove the cluster opening panel.

9. Pull the cluster opening panel forward and remove.

10. Disconnect the transaxle range indicator cable from the column.

11. Remove the screws retaining the instrument cluster to the instrument panel. Allow the cluster to hang loose.

12. Remove the lower dash panel.

13. Remvoe the steering column reinforcement plate.

14. Pull the instrument cluster forward. Label and disconnect the electrical harnesses.

15. Remove the instrument cluster.

To install:

16. Position the instrument cluster, connect the electrical harnesses and tighten attaching screws to 7–12 inch lbs. (0.8–1.5 Nm).

17. Install the steering column reinforcement plate.

18. Install the lower dash panel.

19. Connect the transaxle range indicator cable from the column.

20. Install the cluster opening panel.

21. Snap the opening panel into place and install the two screws above the instrument panel.

22. Connect the electrical harness and install the panel over the headlamp switch.

23. Connect the six electrical harnesses and install the instrument center panel.
24. Install the lower driver's side instrument panel finish panel.
25. Install the instrument panel steering column cover.
26. Install the steering column shroud and upper steering column shroud.
27. Install the radio.
28. Connect the negative battery cable.

Conventional

1. Disconnect the negative battery cable.
2. Remove the steering column cover from below the steering column.
3. Remove the instrument panel steering column cover reinforcement from below the steering column.
4. Loosen the four bolts retaining the steering column and lower the column.
5. Remove the lower steering column shroud from the steering column.
6. Remove the ignition switch lock cylinder.
7. Remove the upper steering column shroud from the steering column.
8. Remove the light switch knob and gently pry the instrument panel finish panel away from the instrument panel.
9. Disconnect the headlamp switch miniature bulb socket from the instrument panel finish panel.
10. Remove the retaining screws and gently pry the cluster opening panel from the instrument panel.
11. Label and disconnect the electrical harnesses and remove the cluster opening panel.
12. Remove the retaining screws and gently pry the instrument panel finish panel from the instrument panel.
13. Disconnect the transaxle range indicator cable from the steering column.
14. Working through the engine compartment, disconnect the upper speedometer cable from the lower speedometer cable.
15. Remove the instrument cluster retaining screws and allow the cluster to hang.
16. Pull the instrument cluster forward to gain access to the electrical harness. Disconnect the electrical harness and upper speedometer cable.
17. Remove the instrument cluster.
To install:
18. Position the instrument cluster and connect the electrical harness and upper speedometer cable.
19. Install the instrument cluster retaining screws and tighten to 18–26 inch lbs. (2–3 Nm).
20. Working through the engine compartment, connect the upper speedometer cable to the lower speedometer cable.

21. Connect the transaxle range indicator cable to the steering column.
22. Install the instrument panel finish panel.
23. Connect the electrical harnesses and install the cluster opening panel.
24. Connect the headlamp switch miniature bulb socket.
25. Position the instrument panel finish panel.
26. Install the light switch knob.
27. Install the upper steering column shroud.
28. Install the ignition switch lock cylinder.
29. Install the lower steering column shroud.
30. Raise and secure the steering column.
31. Install the instrument panel steering column cover reinforcement.
32. Install the steering column cover.
33. Connect the negative battery cable.

Gauges

REMOVAL & INSTALLATION

Gauges on the electronic instrument panel are not serviceable separately. If a gauge is determined to be defective, the instrument panel must be replaced as an assembly.

Gauges on conventional instrument panels are serviceable by removing the instrument panel, removing the instrument panel lens and then removing the gauge.

Headlight Switch

REMOVAL & INSTALLATION

1. Disconnect the negative battery cable.
2. Carefully pull off the headlamp switch knob.
3. Remove the instrument panel finish panel.
4. Remove the two screws retaining the headlamp switch to the instrument panel.
5. Label and disconnect the electrical harness.
6. Remove the switch.
To install:
7. Position the switch in the instrument panel and tighten the retaining screws to 18–27 ft. lbs. (2–3 Nm).
8. Connect the electrical harness.
9. Install the instrument panel finish panel.
10. Install the headlamp switch knob.
11. Connect the negative battery cable.

LIGHTING

Headlights

REMOVAL & INSTALLATION

➡This procedure only applies to replaceable halogen headlight bulbs (such as nos. 9004 and 9005); it does not pertain to sealed beam units.

1. Open the vehicle hood and secure it in an upright position.
2. Unfasten the locking ring which secures the bulb and socket assembly, then withdraw the assembly rearward.
3. If necessary, gently pry the socket's retaining clip over the projection on the bulb (use care not to break the clip.) Separate the bulb from its socket.
To install:
4. Before installing a light bulb into the socket, ensure that all electrical contact surfaces are free of corrosion and dirt.

5. Line up the replacement headlight bulb with the socket. Firmly push the bulb into the socket until the bulb is seated. If so equipped, make sure the spring clip latches over the bulb's projection.

❋ WARNING

Do not touch the glass bulb with your fingers. Oil from your fingers can severely shorten the life of the bulb. If necessary, wipe off any dirt or oil from the bulb with rubbing alcohol before completing installation.

6. To ensure that the replacement bulb functions properly, activate the applicable switch to illuminate the bulb which was just replaced. (If this is a combination low and high beam bulb, be sure to check both intensities.) If the replacement light bulb does not illuminate, either it too is faulty or there is a problem in the bulb circuit or switch. Correct if necessary.

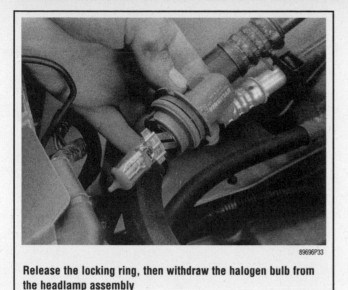

Release the locking ring, then withdraw the halogen bulb from the headlamp assembly

7. Position the headlight bulb assembly and secure it with the locking ring.
8. Close the vehicle hood.

AIMING THE HEADLIGHTS

▶ See Figures 39 thru 44

The headlights must be properly aimed to provide the best, safest road illumination. The lights should be checked for proper aim and adjusted as necessary. Certain state and local authorities have requirements for headlight aiming; these should be checked before adjustment is made.

❊❊❊ CAUTION

About once a year, when the headlights are replaced or any time front end work is performed on your vehicle, the headlights should be accurately aimed by a reputable repair shop using the proper equipment. Headlights not properly aimed can make it virtually impossible to see and may blind other drivers on the road, possibly causing an accident. Note that the following procedure is a temporary fix, until you can take your vehicle to a repair shop for a proper adjustment.

Headlight adjustment may be temporarily made using a wall, as described below, or on the rear of another vehicle. When adjusted, the lights should not glare in oncoming car or truck windshields, nor should they illuminate the passenger compartment of vehicles driving in front of you. These adjustments are rough and should always be fine-tuned by a repair shop which is equipped with headlight aiming tools. Improper adjustments may be both dangerous and illegal.

For most of the vehicles covered by this manual, horizontal and vertical aiming of each sealed beam unit is provided by two adjusting screws which move the retaining ring and adjusting plate against the tension of a coil spring. There is no adjustment for focus; this is done during headlight manufacturing.

➡Because the composite headlight assembly is bolted into position, no adjustment should be necessary or possible. Some applications, however, may be bolted to an adjuster plate or may be retained by adjusting screws. If so, follow this procedure when adjusting the lights, BUT always have the adjustment checked by a reputable shop.

Before removing the headlight bulb or disturbing the headlamp in any way, note the current settings in order to ease headlight adjustment upon

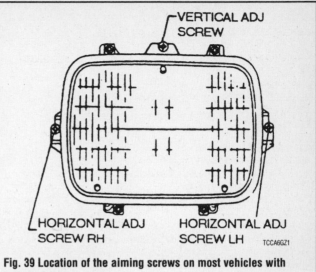

Fig. 39 Location of the aiming screws on most vehicles with sealed beam headlights

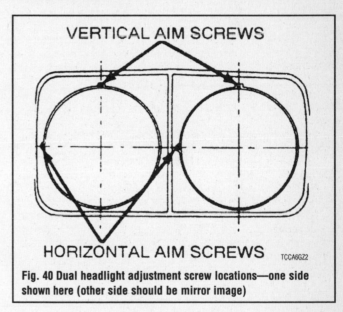

Fig. 40 Dual headlight adjustment screw locations—one side shown here (other side should be mirror image)

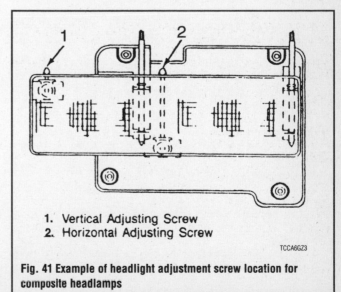

1. Vertical Adjusting Screw
2. Horizontal Adjusting Screw

Fig. 41 Example of headlight adjustment screw location for composite headlamps

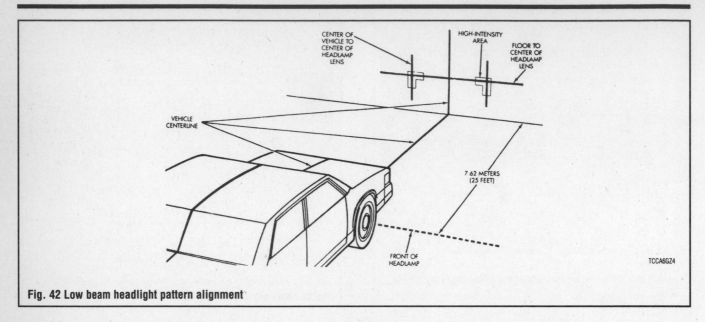

Fig. 42 Low beam headlight pattern alignment

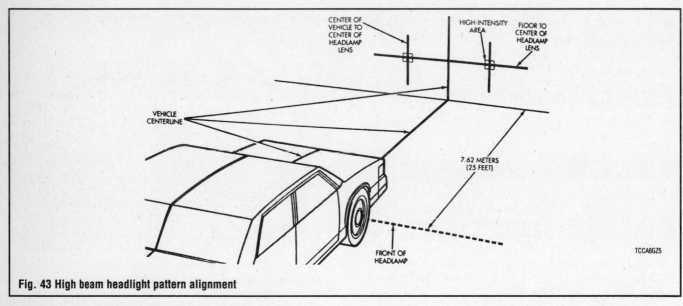

Fig. 43 High beam headlight pattern alignment

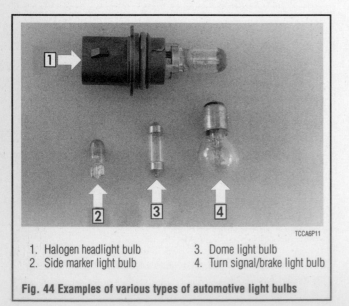

1. Halogen headlight bulb
2. Side marker light bulb
3. Dome light bulb
4. Turn signal/brake light bulb

Fig. 44 Examples of various types of automotive light bulbs

reassembly. If the high or low beam setting of the old lamp still works, this can be done using the wall of a garage or a building:

1. Park the vehicle on a level surface, with the fuel tank about ½ full and with the vehicle empty of all extra cargo (unless normally carried). The vehicle should be facing a wall which is no less than 6 feet (1.8m) high and 12 feet (3.7m) wide. The front of the vehicle should be about 25 feet from the wall.

2. If aiming is to be performed outdoors, it is advisable to wait until dusk in order to properly see the headlight beams on the wall. If done in a garage, darken the area around the wall as much as possible by closing shades or hanging cloth over the windows.

3. Turn the headlights **ON** and mark the wall at the center of each light's low beam, then switch on the high beams and mark the center of each light's high beam. A short length of masking tape which is visible from the front of the vehicle may be used. Although marking all four positions is advisable, marking one position from each light should be sufficient.

4. If neither beam on one side is working, and if another like-sized vehicle is available, park the second one in the exact spot where the vehicle was and mark the beams using the same-side light. Then switch the vehicles so the one to be aimed is back in the original spot. It must

be parked no closer to or farther away from the wall than the second vehicle.

5. Perform any necessary repairs, but make sure the vehicle is not moved, or is returned to the exact spot from which the lights were marked. Turn the headlights **ON** and adjust the beams to match the marks on the wall.

6. Have the headlight adjustment checked as soon as possible by a reputable repair shop.

Signal and Marker Lights

REMOVAL & INSTALLATION

Turn Signal, Side Marker and Brake Lights

1. Disengage the bulb and socket assembly from the lens housing.
2. Gently grasp the light bulb and pull it straight out of the socket.
To install:
3. Before installing the light bulb into the socket, ensure that all electrical contact surfaces are free of corrosion and dirt.

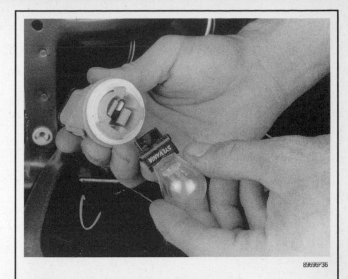

Pull the tail light bulb straight from the socket

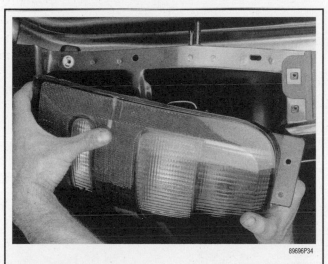

After removing the attaching screws, carefully separate the tail light lens from its mounting

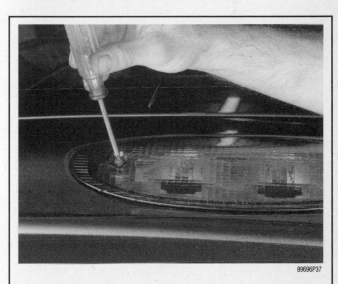

This marker bulb lens is attached with two Torx® head screws

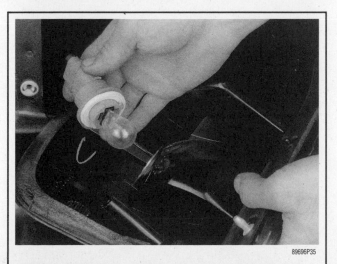

Twist the tail light bulb socket ¼ turn, then withdraw the bulb and socket assembly

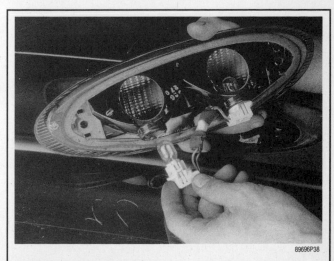

Twist the marker bulb socket ¼ turn, then withdraw the bulb and socket assembly

Pull the marker light bulb straight from its socket

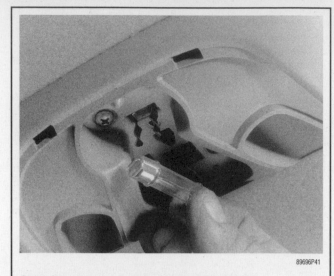

Carefully remove the bulb from the retaining clips

4. Line up the base of the light bulb with the socket, then insert the light bulb into the socket until it is fully seated.

5. To ensure that the replacement bulb functions properly, activate the applicable switch to illuminate the bulb which was just replaced. If the replacement light bulb does not illuminate, either it too is faulty or there is a problem in the bulb circuit or switch. Correct as necessary.

6. Install the socket and bulb assembly into the lens housing.

Dome Light

1. Using a small prytool, carefully remove the cover lens from the lamp assembly.

2. Remove the bulb from its retaining clip contacts. If the bulb has tapered ends, gently depress the spring clip/metal contact and disengage the light bulb, then pull it free of the two metal contacts.

To install:

3. Before installing the light bulb into the metal contacts, ensure that all electrical conducting surfaces are free of corrosion and dirt.

4. Position the bulb between the two metal contacts. If the contacts have small holes, be sure that the tapered ends of the bulb are situated in them.

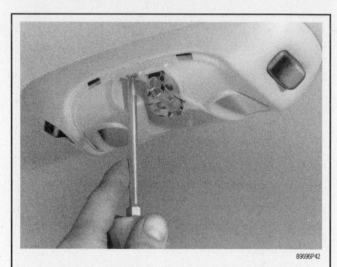

Two map light bulbs can be accessed by removing the dome light assembly

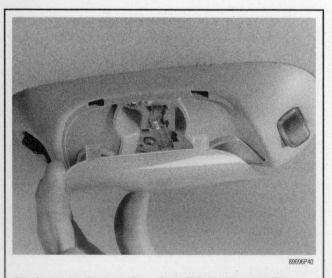

After removing the cover lens, the bulb is easily accessible

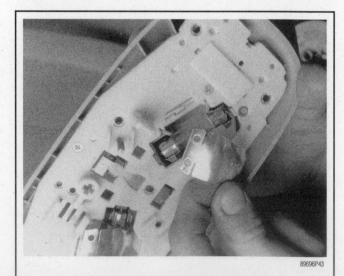

To access the map lights, remove this light shield . . .

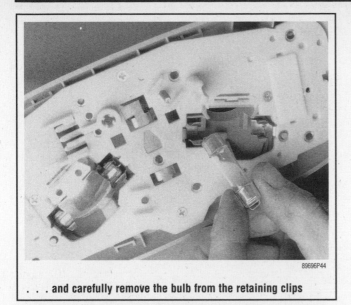

89696P44

. . . and carefully remove the bulb from the retaining clips

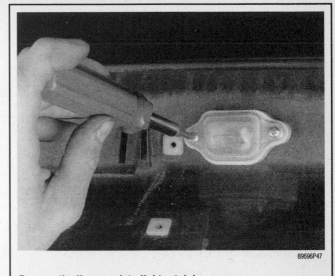

89696P47

Remove the license plate light retaining screws . . .

89696P45

The license plate light is hidden behind a trim panel

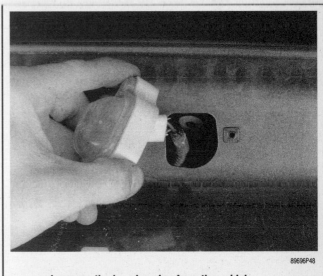

89696P48

. . . and remove the lens housing from the vehicle

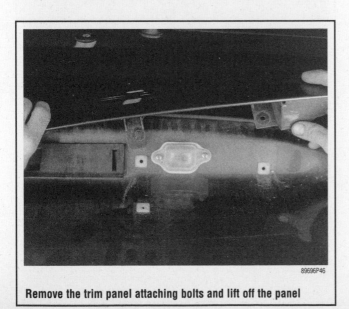

89696P46

Remove the trim panel attaching bolts and lift off the panel

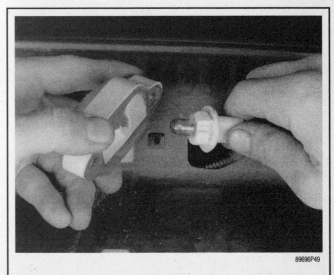

89696P49

Twist ¼ turn, then pull the bulb socket from the lens housing

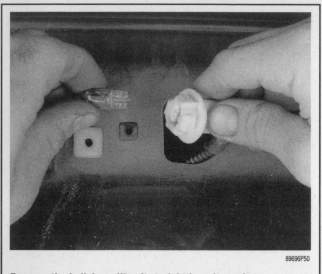

Remove the bulb by pulling it straight from its socket

5. To ensure that the replacement bulb functions properly, activate the applicable switch to illuminate the bulb which was just replaced. If the replacement light bulb does not illuminate, either it is faulty or there is a problem in the bulb circuit or switch. Correct as necessary.

6. Install the cover lens until its retaining tabs are properly engaged.

TRAILER WIRING

Wiring the vehicle for towing is fairly easy. There are a number of good wiring kits available and these should be used, rather than trying to design your own.

All trailers will need brake lights and turn signals, as well as tail lights and side marker lights. Most areas require extra marker lights for wide load trailers. Also, most areas have recently required back-up lights for trailers, and most trailer manufacturers have been building trailers with back-up lights for several years.

Additionally, some Class I, most Class II and just about all Class III trailers will have electric brakes. Add to this number an accessories wire, to operate trailer internal equipment or to charge the trailer's battery, and you can have as many as seven wires in the harness.

Determine the equipment on your trailer and buy the wiring kit necessary. The kit will contain all the wires needed, plus a plug adapter set which includes the female plug, mounted on the bumper or hitch, and the male plug, wired into, or plugged into the trailer harness.

When installing the kit, follow the manufacturer's instructions. The color coding of the wires is usually standard throughout the industry. One point to note: some domestic vehicles, and most imported vehicles, have separate turn signals. On most domestic vehicles, the brake lights and rear turn signals operate with the same bulb. For those vehicles without separate turn signals, you can purchase an isolation unit, so that the brake lights won't blink whenever the turn signals are operated; these units are simple and quick to install.

One, final point, the best kits are those with a spring loaded cover on the vehicle mounted socket. This cover prevents dirt and moisture from corroding the terminals. Never let the vehicle socket hang loosely; always mount it securely to the bumper or hitch.

CIRCUIT PROTECTION

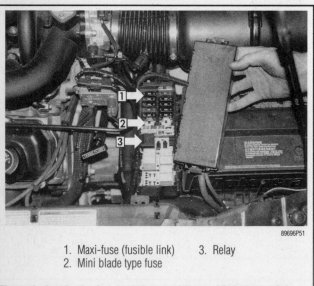

1. Maxi-fuse (fusible link)   3. Relay
2. Mini blade type fuse

The underhood relay box contains maxi-fuses, blade type mini-fuses and relays

To remove the fuse and relay box cover, pull the tabs at each end and lift

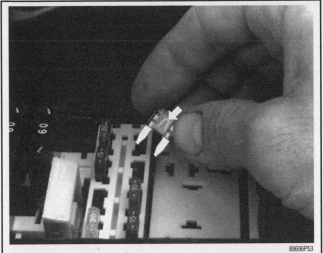

Blade type mini-fuses are blown if the metal portion inside the case (arrow) is broken or burned

The underdash fuse panel (arrow) is a small portion of the underdash relay box

Maxi-fuses are checked in a similar manner to blade type fuses

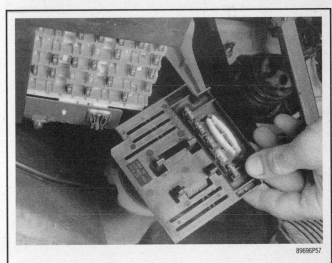

Remove the cover by squeezing the clips together and pulling. A fuse tool and spare fuses are attached

Relays can only be installed in one direction due to the positioning of the terminals

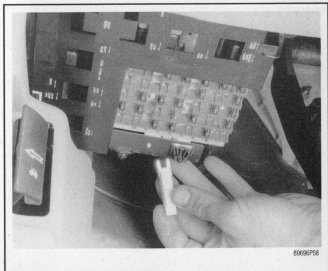

The fuse tool makes removing fuses in tight spots easy

Fuses

REPLACEMENT

Fuses are located either in the engine compartment or passenger compartment fuse and relay panels. If a fuse blows, a single component or single circuit will not function properly.
1. Remove the fuse and relay box cover.
2. Inspect the fuses to determine which is faulty.
3. Unplug and discard the fuse.
4. Inspect the box terminals and clean if corroded. If any terminals are damaged, replace the terminals.
5. Plug in a new fuse of the same amperage rating.

❄❄ WARNING

Never exceed the amperage rating of a blown fuse. If the replacement fuse also blows, check for a problem in the circuit.

6. Check for proper operation of the affected component or circuit.

Maxi-Fuses (Fusible Links)

Maxi-fuses are located in the engine compartment relay box. If a maxi-fuse blows, an entire circuit or several circuits will not function properly.

REPLACEMENT

1. Remove the fuse and relay box cover.
2. Inspect the fusible links to determine which is faulty.

3. Unplug and discard the fusible link.
4. Inspect the box terminals and clean if corroded. If any terminals are damaged, replace the terminals.
5. Plug in a new fusible link of the same amperage rating.

❄❄ WARNING

Never exceed the amperage rating of a blown maxi-fuse. If the replacement fuse also blows, check for a problem in the circuit(s).

6. Check for proper operation of the affected circuit(s).

Flashers

The flashers are located in the passenger compartment fuse and relay box. If the turn signals operate in only one direction, a bulb is probably burned out. If they do not operate in either direction, a bulb on each side may be burned out, or the flasher may be defective.

REPLACEMENT

1. Remove the passenger compartment fuse and relay box cover, noting which position the flasher unit occupies.
2. Unplug and discard the flasher.
3. Inspect the box terminals and clean if corroded. If any terminals are damaged, replace the terminals.
4. Plug in a new flasher of the same type.
5. Operate the turn signals and hazard lights. Check for proper operation.

FUSE AND RELAY APPLICATION CHART (1 of 2)

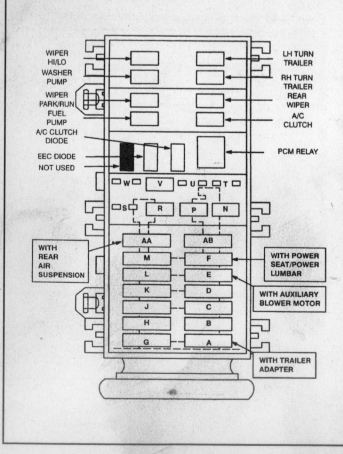

MAXI-FUSE	AMPS	CIRCUITS PROTECTED
A	50	Trailer Adapter
B	60	Engine Cooling Fans High Speed
C	60	Start Motor Solenoid, Ignition Switch, I/P Fuse Panel (Fuses 2, 30, 36)
D	60	Ignition Switch, I/P Fuse Panel (Fuse 8, 12, 14, 18, 20, 21, 24, 27, 33)
E	40	Auxiliary Blower Motor
F	60	Power Seats
G	c.b. 30	Power Windows
H	40	Engine Cooling Fans Low Speed
J	60	Power Accessory, I/P Fuse Panel (Fuses 1, 7, 13, 19, 125, 31, 37)
K	60	Headlamps, I/P Fuse Panel (Fuses 10, 11, 23, 29, 35, 41)
L	60	ABS System
M	60	Rear Window Defrost I/P Fuse Panel (Fuses 16, 22, 28)

MAXI-FUSE	AMPS	CIRCUITS PROTECTED
N	20	Fuel Pump
P	10	Air Bag Diagnostic Monitor
R	30	Powertrain Control Module (PCM)
S	–	NOT USED
T	–	NOT USED
U	–	NOT USED
V	10	Transmission Control Switch, Canister Vent Solenoid
W	–	NOT USED

MAXI-FUSE	AMPS	CIRCUITS PROTECTED
AA	60	Air Ride Suspension
AB	–	NOT USED

89696G27

FUSE AND RELAY APPLICATION CHART (2 of 2)

FOG LAMPS RELAY	TRAILER PARK LAMP RELAY	BRAKE LAMP RELAY
DELAYED ACCESSORY RELAY	START INTERRUPT RELAY	AUXILIARY BLOWER MOTOR RELAY
ONE TOUCH DOWN RELAY	ELECTRONIC FLASHER RELAY	HEATED BACKLIGHT RELAY

		10A	5A	5A	15A	15A	
		1	2	3	4	5	42
		15A	25A	10A	15A	15A	
		6	7	8	9	10	11
		10A	15A	5A		20A	15A
		12	13	14	15	16	17
		25A	15A	25A	10A	20A	15A
		18	19	20	21	22	23	43
		20A	15A	15A	15A	20A	15A
		24	25	26	27	28	29
		15A	10A			15A		10A
		30	31	32	33	34	35	44
		30A	20A	15A				5A
		36	37	38	39	40	41

| DOOR LOCK RELAY | | BATTERY SAVER RELAY | MEMORY LOCK RELAY | INTERIOR LAMP RELAY | DOOR UNLOCK RELAY |
| | DRIVER DOOR UNLOCK RELAY | FRONT BLOWER MOTOR RELAY | HORN RELAY | AUTOLAMPS PARK LIGHTS RELAY | AUTOLAMPS HEADLIGHTS RELAY |

FUSE POSITION	AMPS	CIRCUITS PROTECTED
1	10	Data Link Connector (DLC), Power Mirrors
2	5	Start Interrupt Relay, GEM
3	5	Instrument Illumination
4	15	LH Headlamp (Low Beam)

FUSE POSITION	AMPS	CIRCUITS PROTECTED
5	15	Trailer Park Lamps
6	–	NOT USED
7	15	Brake On/Off (BOO) Switch, Stop Lamps, Trailer RH and LH Relays, Brake Shift Interlock, RAP Module, Speed Control Module, Trailer Electric Brake Module, ABS Module, PCM
8	25	Radio Amplifier, Subwoofer Amplifier
9	10	Park Lamps, Side Marker Lamps, License Lamps, Trailer Park Lamp Relay, Electrick Brake Module
10	15	RH Headlamp (Low Beam)
11	15	I/P Fuses 3 and 9
12	10	GEM, RAP Module, Auxiliary Warning Module, Overhead Console
13	15	Radio, Remote Headphone, CD Disc Changer
14	5	Instrument Cluster, Day/Night Mirror, Auxiliary Warning Module, Air Bag
15	–	NOT USED
16	20	Horns
17	15	Fog Lamps
18	25	Windshield Wiper/Washer System
19	15	GEM, RAP Module
20	25	Ignition Coil, PCM Power Relay
21	10	Shiftlock Actuator, Rear Window Defrost, GEM, Air Bag Module, A/C – Heater Control Switch, Blend Door Actuator
22	20	Power Plug, Rear Cigar Lighter
23	15	Flash to Pass
24	20	Liftgate Wiper/Washer System
25	15	Instrument Cluster, Turn Signal Lamps
26	15	Trailer Turn/Stop/Hazard Lamps
27	15	Electronic Flasher
28	20	Instrument Panel Cigar Lighter
29	15	Interior Lamps, Battery Saver Relay, Delayed Accessory Relay
30	15	ABS Module, Speed Control Module, Brake Pressure Switch
31	10	Rear Air Suspension
32	–	NOT USED
33	15	ABS Lamp Relay, Back-Up Lamps, GEM RAP Module, Day/Night Mirror
34	–	NOT USED
35	15	Instrument Cluster, PCM Power Relay
36	30	Front Blower Motor
37	20	Power Door Locks
38	15	LH and RH High Beams
39	–	NOT USED
40	–	NOT USED
41	5	Autolamp Relay, Day/Night Mirror
42	–	NOT USED
43	–	NOT USED
44	–	NOT USED

89696G28

INDEX OF WIRING DIAGRAMS

89696W01

SAMPLE DIAGRAM: HOW TO READ & INTERPRET WIRING DIAGRAMS

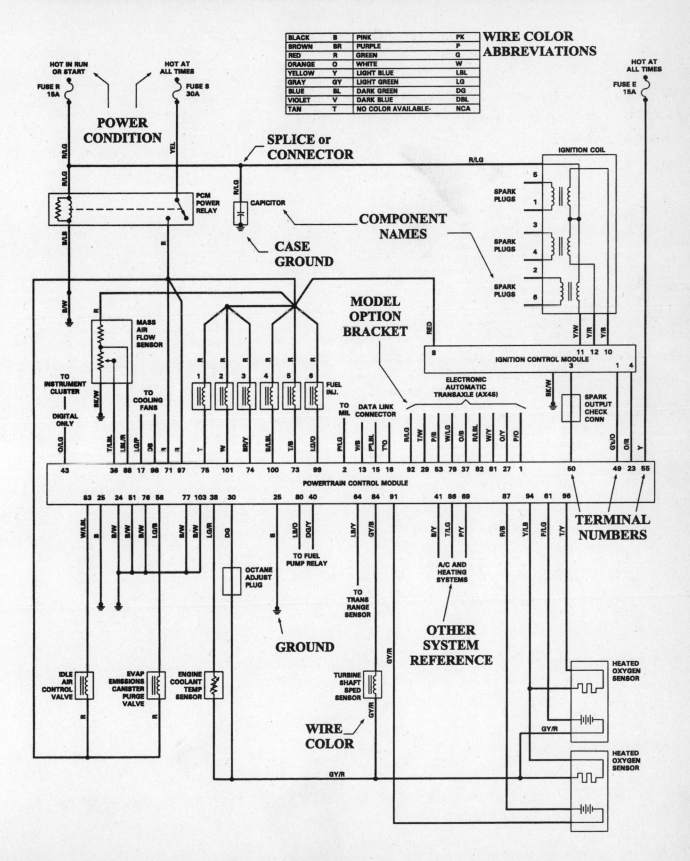

DIAGRAM 1

TCCA6W01

WIRING DIAGRAM SYMBOLS

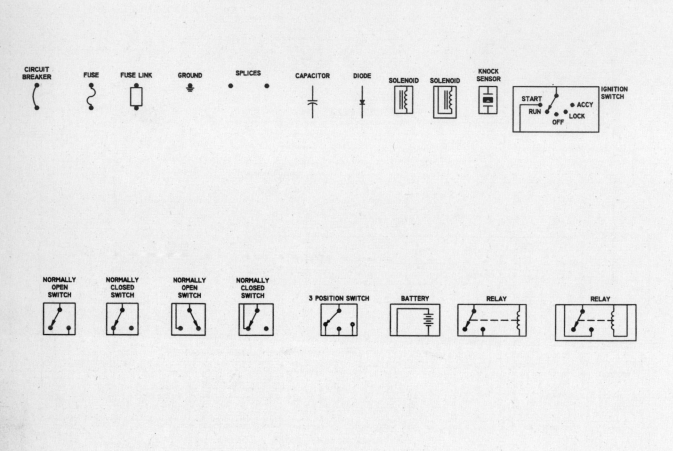

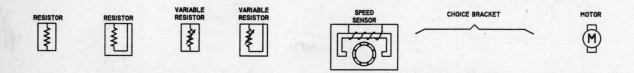

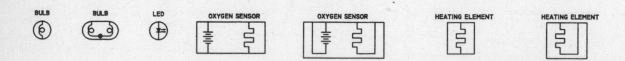

DIAGRAM 2

TCCA6W02

1998 3.0L & 1996-98 3.8L ENGINE SCHEMATIC

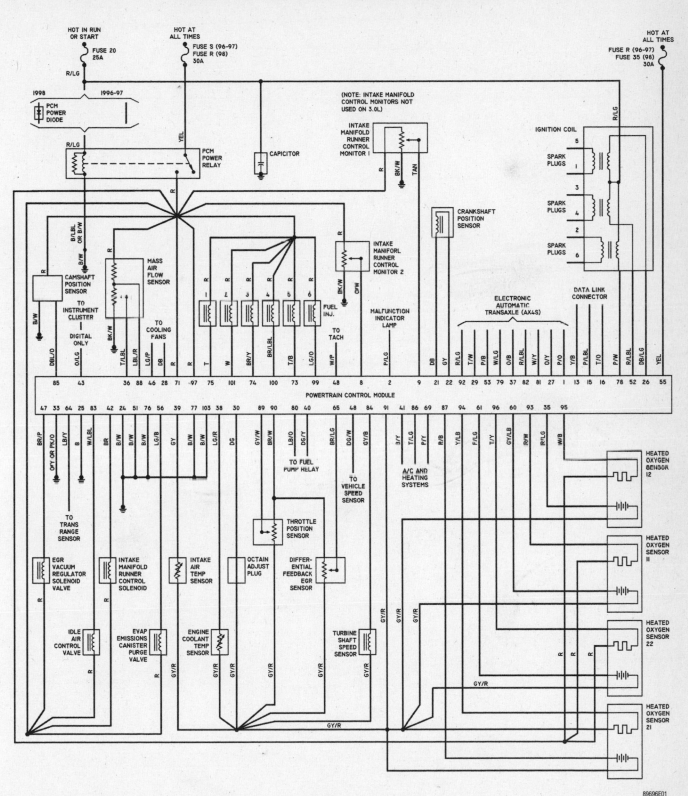

DIAGRAM 3

1996-97 3.0L & 1995 3.8L ENGINE SCHEMATIC

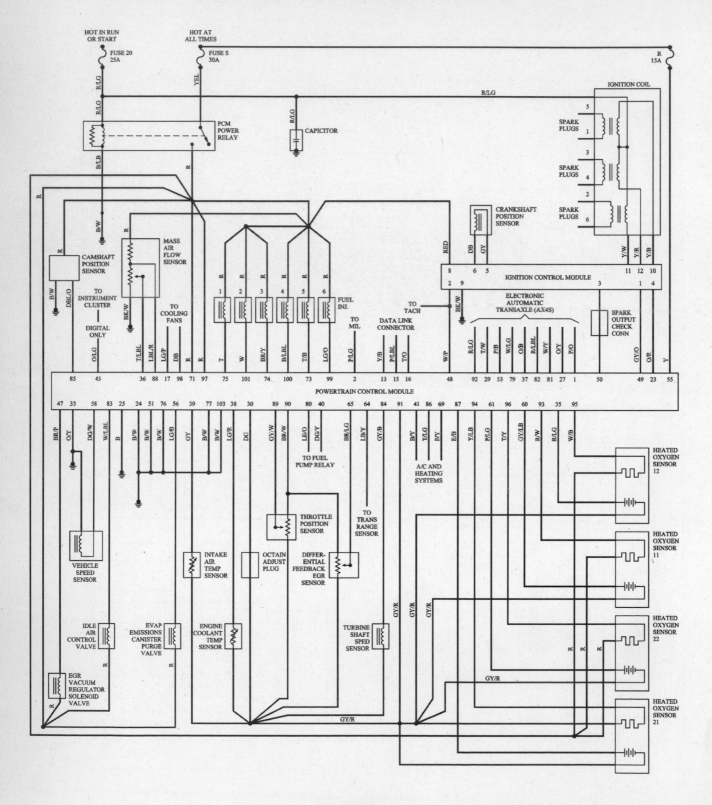

DIAGRAM 4

89696E02

1995-98 CHASSIS SCHEMATICS

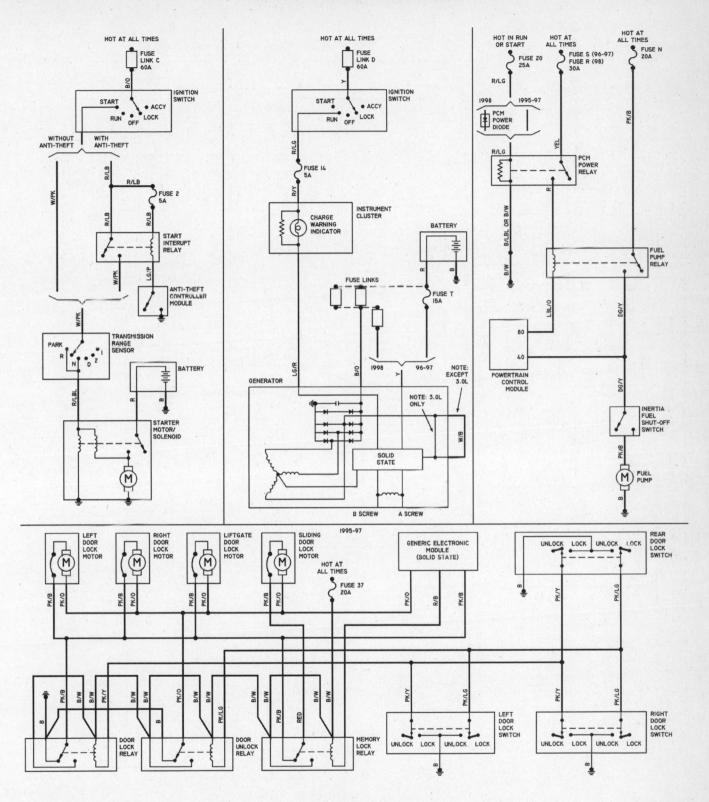

DIAGRAM 5

89696B01

1995-97 CHASSIS SCHEMATICS

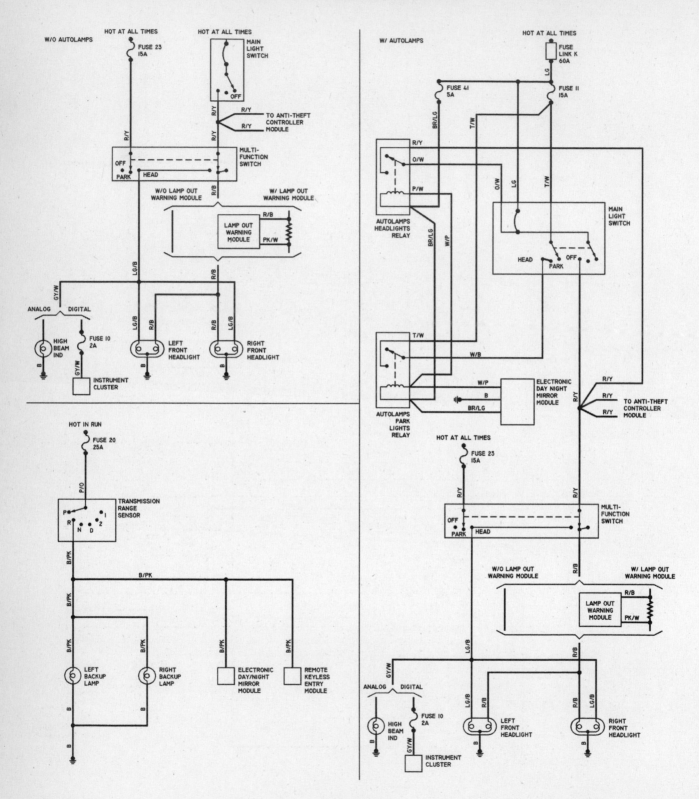

DIAGRAM 6

89696B02

1995-98 CHASSIS SCHEMATIC

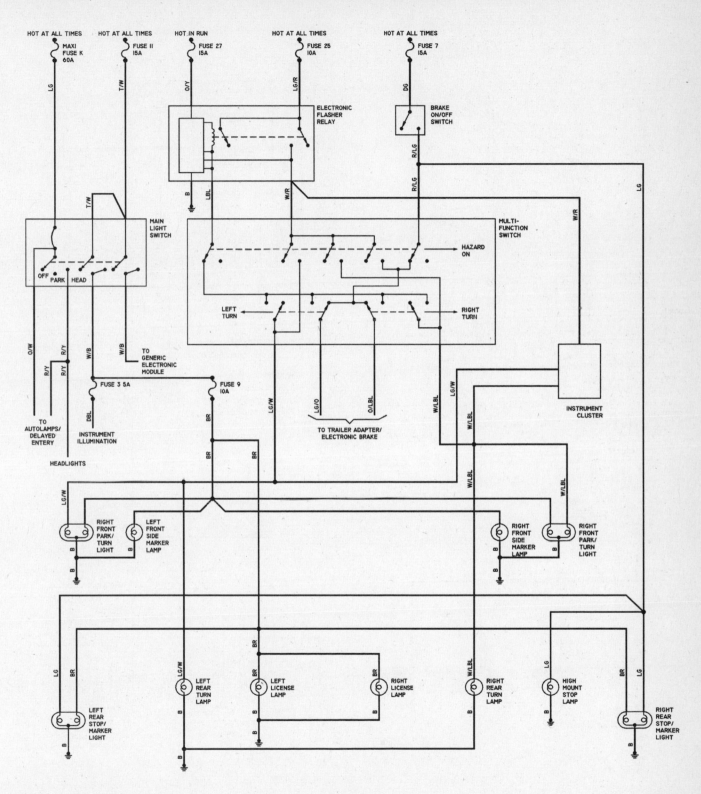

DIAGRAM 7

89696B03

1998 CHASSIS SCHEMATICS

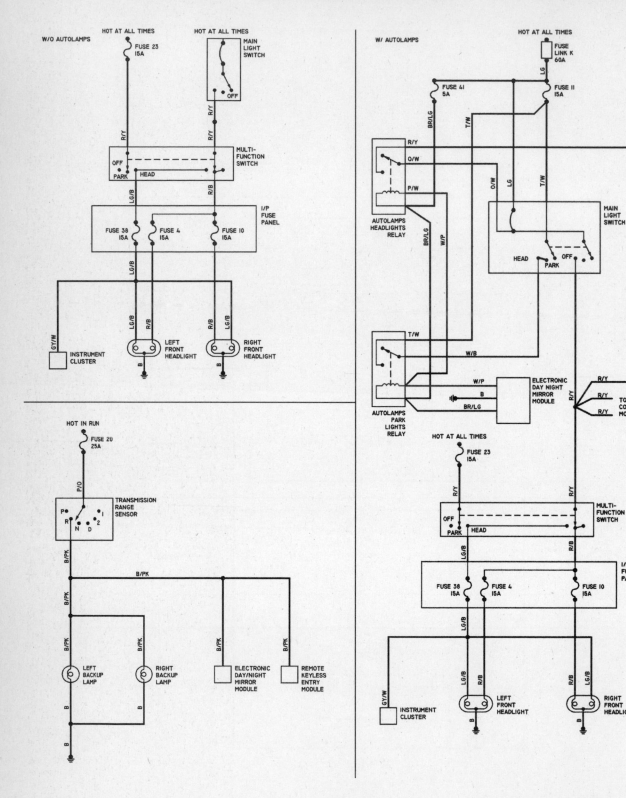

DIAGRAM 8

89696B04

7

DRIVE TRAIN

AUTOMATIC TRANSAXLE

Understanding Automatic Transaxles

The automatic transaxle allows engine torque and power to be transmitted to the front wheels within a narrow range of engine operating speeds. It will allow the engine to turn fast enough to produce plenty of power and torque at very low speeds, while keeping it at a sensible rpm at high vehicle speeds (and it does this job without driver assistance). The transaxle uses a light fluid as the medium for the transmission of power. This fluid also works in the operation of various hydraulic control circuits and as a lubricant. Because the transaxle fluid performs all of these functions, trouble within the unit can easily travel from one part to another. For this reason, and because of the complexity and unusual operating principles of the transaxle, a very sound understanding of the basic principles of operation will simplify troubleshooting.

TORQUE CONVERTER

▶ **See Figure 1**

The torque converter replaces the conventional clutch. It has three functions:

1. It allows the engine to idle with the vehicle at a standstill, even with the transmission in gear.
2. It allows the transmission to shift from range-to-range smoothly, without requiring that the driver close the throttle during the shift.
3. It multiplies engine torque to an increasing extent as vehicle speed drops and throttle opening is increased. This has the effect of making the transmission more responsive and reduces the amount of shifting required.

The torque converter is a metal case which is shaped like a sphere that has been flattened on opposite sides. It is bolted to the rear end of the engine's crankshaft. Generally, the entire metal case rotates at engine speed and serves as the engine's flywheel.

The case contains three sets of blades. One set is attached directly to the case. This set forms the torus or pump. Another set is directly connected to the output shaft, and forms the turbine. The third set is mounted on a hub which, in turn, is mounted on a stationary shaft through a one-way clutch. This third set is known as the stator.

A pump, which is driven by the converter hub at engine speed, keeps the torque converter full of transmission fluid at all times. Fluid flows continuously through the unit to provide cooling.

Under low speed acceleration, the torque converter functions as follows:

The torus is turning faster than the turbine. It picks up fluid at the center of the converter and, through centrifugal force, slings it outward. Since the outer edge of the converter moves faster than the portions at the center, the fluid picks up speed.

The fluid then enters the outer edge of the turbine blades. It then travels back toward the center of the converter case along the turbine blades. In impinging upon the turbine blades, the fluid loses the energy picked up in the torus.

If the fluid was now returned directly into the torus, both halves of the converter would have to turn at approximately the same speed at all times, and torque input and output would both be the same.

In flowing through the torus and turbine, the fluid picks up two types of flow, or flow in two separate directions. It flows through the turbine blades, and it spins with the engine. The stator, whose blades are stationary when the vehicle is being accelerated at low speeds, converts one type of flow into another. Instead of allowing the fluid to flow straight back into the torus, the stator's curved blades turn the fluid almost 90° toward the direction of rotation of the engine. Thus the fluid does not flow as fast toward the torus, but is already spinning when the torus picks it up. This has the effect of allowing the torus to turn much faster than the turbine. This difference in speed may be compared to the difference in speed between the smaller and larger gears in any gear train. The result is that engine power output is higher, and engine torque is multiplied.

As the speed of the turbine increases, the fluid spins faster and faster in the direction of engine rotation. As a result, the ability of the stator to redirect the fluid flow is reduced. Under cruising conditions, the stator is eventually forced to rotate on its one-way clutch in the direction of engine rotation. Under these conditions, the torque converter begins to behave almost like a solid shaft, with the torus and turbine speeds being almost equal.

PLANETARY GEARBOX

▶ **See Figures 2, 3 and 4**

The ability of the torque converter to multiply engine torque is limited. Also, the unit tends to be more efficient when the turbine is rotating at relatively high speeds. Therefore, a planetary gearbox is used to carry the power output of the turbine to the driveshaft.

Planetary gears function very similarly to conventional transmission

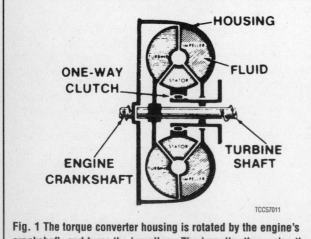

Fig. 1 The torque converter housing is rotated by the engine's crankshaft, and turns the impeller—The impeller then spins the turbine, which gives motion to the turbine shaft, driving the gears

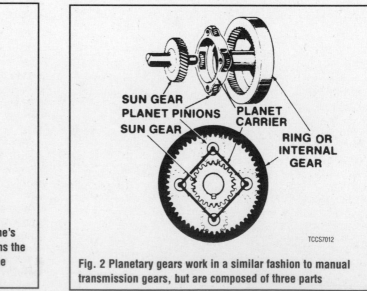

Fig. 2 Planetary gears work in a similar fashion to manual transmission gears, but are composed of three parts

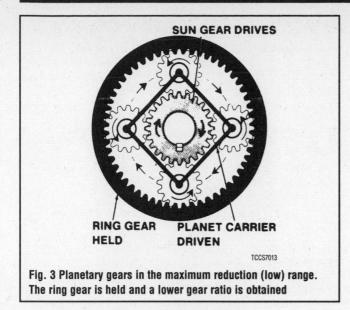

Fig. 3 Planetary gears in the maximum reduction (low) range. The ring gear is held and a lower gear ratio is obtained

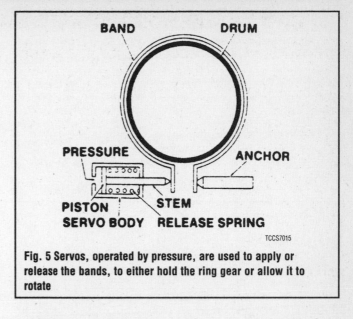

Fig. 5 Servos, operated by pressure, are used to apply or release the bands, to either hold the ring gear or allow it to rotate

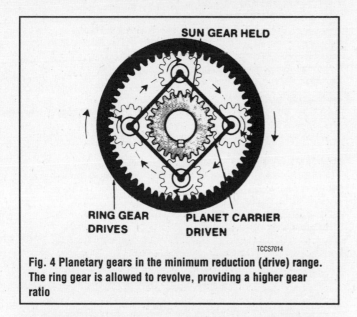

Fig. 4 Planetary gears in the minimum reduction (drive) range. The ring gear is allowed to revolve, providing a higher gear ratio

gears. However, their construction is different in that three elements make up one gear system, and, in that all three elements are different from one another. The three elements are: an outer gear that is shaped like a hoop, with teeth cut into the inner surface; a sun gear, mounted on a shaft and located at the very center of the outer gear; and a set of three planet gears, held by pins in a ring-like planet carrier, meshing with both the sun gear and the outer gear. Either the outer gear or the sun gear may be held stationary, providing more than one possible torque multiplication factor for each set of gears. Also, if all three gears are forced to rotate at the same speed, the gearset forms, in effect, a solid shaft.

Most automatics use the planetary gears to provide various reductions ratios. Bands and clutches are used to hold various portions of the gearsets to the transmission case or to the shaft on which they are mounted. Shifting is accomplished, then, by changing the portion of each planetary gearset which is held to the transmission case or to the shaft.

SERVOS & ACCUMULATORS

♦ See Figure 5

The servos are hydraulic pistons and cylinders. They resemble the hydraulic actuators used on many other machines, such as bulldozers.

Hydraulic fluid enters the cylinder, under pressure, and forces the piston to move to engage the band or clutches.

The accumulators are used to cushion the engagement of the servos. The transmission fluid must pass through the accumulator on the way to the servo. The accumulator housing contains a thin piston which is sprung away from the discharge passage of the accumulator. When fluid passes through the accumulator on the way to the servo, it must move the piston against spring pressure, and this action smoothes out the action of the servo.

HYDRAULIC CONTROL SYSTEM

The hydraulic pressure used to operate the servos comes from the main transmission oil pump. This fluid is channeled to the various servos through the shift valves. There is generally a manual shift valve which is operated by the transmission selector lever and an automatic shift valve for each automatic upshift the transmission provides.

➡**Many new transmissions are electronically controlled. On these models, electrical solenoids are used to better control the hydraulic fluid. Usually, the solenoids are regulated by an electronic control module.**

There are two pressures which affect the operation of these valves. One is the governor pressure which is effected by vehicle speed. The other is the modulator pressure which is effected by intake manifold vacuum or throttle position. Governor pressure rises with an increase in vehicle speed, and modulator pressure rises as the throttle is opened wider. By responding to these two pressures, the shift valves cause the upshift points to be delayed with increased throttle opening to make the best use of the engine's power output.

Most transmissions also make use of an auxiliary circuit for downshifting. This circuit may be actuated by the throttle linkage the vacuum line which actuates the modulator, by a cable or by a solenoid. It applies pressure to a special downshift surface on the shift valve or valves.

The transmission modulator also governs the line pressure, used to actuate the servos. In this way, the clutches and bands will be actuated with a force matching the torque output of the engine.

Transaxle Range Switch

The transaxle range switch permits the engine to start only in the Park and Neutral positions, and activates the back-up lamps in the Reverse position.

REMOVAL & INSTALLATION

▶ **See Figure 6**

1. Disconnect the negative battery cable.
2. Raise and support the vehicle safely.
3. Disconnect the sensor electrical harness.
4. Remove the nut retaining the manual control lever to the shaft. Remove the manual control lever.
5. Remove the two retaining bolts. Remove the transaxle range switch.

To install:

6. Install the transaxle range switch and loosely tighten the retaining bolts.
7. Adjust the sensor slots using a Transaxle Range Sensor Alignment Tool (T92P-70010-AH), or equivalent.
8. Tighten the transaxle range sensor retaining bolts to 80–106 inch lbs. (9–12 Nm).
9. Connect the sensor electrical harness.
10. Install the manual control lever and tighten the retaining nut to 12–16 ft. lbs. (16–22 Nm).
11. Lower the vehicle.
12. Connect the negative battery cable.

ADJUSTMENT

1. Remove the nut securing the manual control lever to the transmission range sensor.
2. Turn the manual control lever to the Neutral position.
3. Loosen the two sensor retaining bolts.
4. Adjust the sensor slots using a Transaxle Range Sensor Alignment Tool (T92P-70010-AH), or equivalent.
5. Tighten the transaxle range sensor retaining bolts to 80–106 inch lbs. (9–12 Nm).
6. Install the manual control lever and tighten the retaining nut to 12–16 ft. lbs. (16–22 Nm).

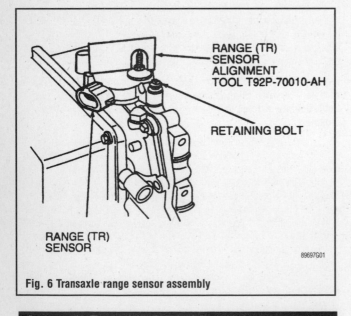

RANGE (TR) SENSOR ALIGNMENT TOOL T92P-70010-AH

RETAINING BOLT

RANGE (TR) SENSOR

89697G01

Fig. 6 Transaxle range sensor assembly

Automatic Transaxle Assembly

REMOVAL & INSTALLATION

▶ **See Figures 7, 8 and 9**

1. Disconnect the negative, then the positive battery cables.
2. Remove the battery and battery tray.

3. Remove the hood and cowl vent.
4. Remove the air cleaner assembly.
5. Label and disconnect all transaxle electrical harnesses.
6. Disconnect the transaxle shift cable from the manual lever by unsnapping the shift cable end from the lever ball stud.
7. Disconnect and plug the transaxle fluid cooler lines.

➡**Leave the two lower engine-to-transaxle bolts in place to hold the transaxle secure against the engine block until a suitable jack can be placed under the transaxle to support it during removal.**

8. Remove the upper transaxle-to-engine bolts.
9. Disconnect the engine electrical harness bracket.
10. Disconnect the battery cable bracket.

➡**Install Engine Lifting Eyes (D94P-6001-A) or equivalent to support the engine during transaxle removal.**

11. Install an Engine Support Kit (014-00792) or equivalent and suitably support the engine.
12. Raise and support the vehicle safely.
13. Loosen the drain pan bolts. Drain and recycle the transaxle fluid.
14. Remove the front wheels.
15. Remove the halfshafts.
16. Remove the bolts retaining the rear engine support to the transaxle.
17. Remove the front subframe.
18. Disconnect the speedometer cable from the vehicle speed sensor.
19. Remove the starter.
20. Remove the transaxle housing cover.
21. Remove the four flywheel-to-converter nuts.
22. Support the transaxle with a suitable jack and remove the remaining transaxle-to-engine bolts.
23. Remove the engine bracket-to-transaxle bolts.
24. Separate the transaxle from the engine block by carefully moving the transaxle rearward until enough clearance exists to remove the transaxle from the engine compartment.
25. Slowly lower the transaxle from the engine compartment.

To install:

26. Place the transaxle on a suitable jack and position it in place.
27. Install the engine bracket-to-transaxle bolts and tighten to 39–53 ft. lbs. (53–72 Nm).
28. Install the lower transaxle-to-engine bolts and tighten to 39–53 ft. lbs. (53–72 Nm).
29. Install the flywheel-to-torque converter bolts and tighten to 20–34 ft. lbs. (27–46 Nm).
30. Install the transaxle housing cover and tighten the bolts to 80–106 inch lbs. (9–12 Nm).
31. Install the starter motor and connect the electrical harness.
32. Connect the speedometer cable.
33. Install and align the front subframe.
34. Install the four bolts retaining the rear engine support and tighten to 39–53 ft. lbs. (53–72 Nm).
35. Install both halfshafts.
36. Install the front wheels and lower the vehicle.
37. Remvoe the engine support kit.
38. Connect the transaxle electrical harnesses.
39. Install the upper transaxle-to-engine bolts and tighten to 39–53 ft. lbs. (53–72 Nm).
40. Connect the fluid cooler to the transaxle lines.
41. Connect the transaxle shift cable to the manual lever ball stud.
42. Install the air cleaner assembly.
43. Install the cowl vent and hood.
44. Install the battery tray and battery.
45. Fill the transaxle with the correct type and quantity of fluid.
46. Connect the positive, then the negative battery cables.

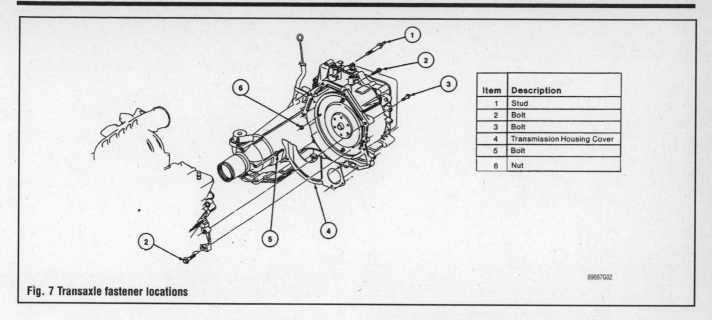

Item	Description
1	Stud
2	Bolt
3	Bolt
4	Transmission Housing Cover
5	Bolt
6	Nut

89697G02

Fig. 7 Transaxle fastener locations

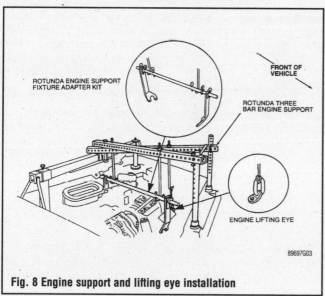

89697G03

Fig. 8 Engine support and lifting eye installation

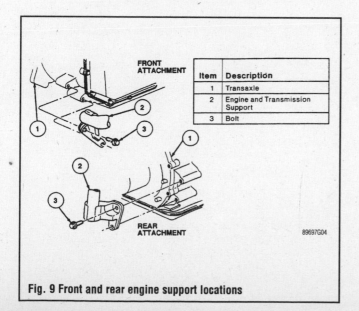

Item	Description
1	Transaxle
2	Engine and Transmission Support
3	Bolt

89697G04

Fig. 9 Front and rear engine support locations

Halfshafts

REMOVAL & INSTALLATION

◗ See Figures 10, 11, 12, 13 and 14

➡Do not begin this removal procedure unless a new wheel hub retainer nut, a new retainer circlip and a new lower ball joint-to-front wheel knuckle retaining bolt and nut are available. Once removed, these parts must not be reused during assembly. Their torque holding ability or retention capability is diminished during removal.

1. Raise and support the vehicle safely.
2. Remove the front wheels.
3. Insert a steel rod into the brake rotor to prevent the rotor from turning and loosen the axle wheel hub nut. Discard the nut.
4. Remove the ball joint-to-front wheel knuckle retaining nut. Drive the bolt out of the front wheel knuckle using a punch and hammer.
5. Remove the front brake anti-lock sensor and position it out of the way.
6. Separate the ball joint from the front wheel knuckle using a prybar. Position the end of the prybar outside of the bushing pocket to avoid damage to the bushing.

➡Use care to prevent damage to the front wheel driveshaft joint boot.

7. Remove the stabilizer bar link at the front stabilizer bar.

➡Make sure the CV-joint puller does not contact the transaxle shaft speed sensor. Damage to the sensor will result.

8. Install a CV-Joint Puller (T86P-3514-A1) or equivalent between the inboard CV-joint and the transaxle case.
9. Install a CV-Joint Extension (T86P-3514-A2) or equivalent into the puller and hand-tighten.
10. Using an impact slide hammer, remove the driveshaft from the transaxle.

➡Do not allow the front wheel driveshaft and joint to hang unsupported. Damage to the front wheel driveshaft joint may result. Do not wrap wire around the front wheel driveshaft joint boot. Damage to the boot may result.

11. Support the end of the driveshaft and joint assembly by suspending it from the chassis using a length of wire.

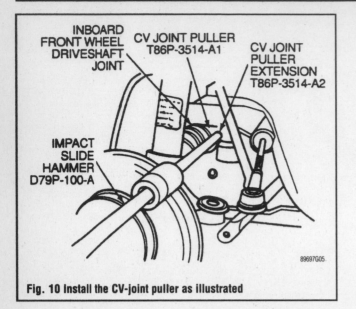

Fig. 10 Install the CV-joint puller as illustrated

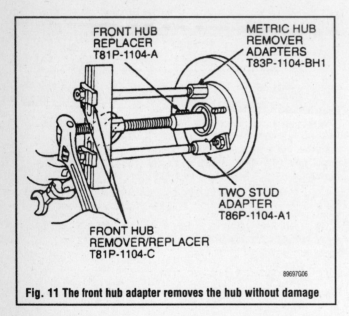

Fig. 11 The front hub adapter removes the hub without damage

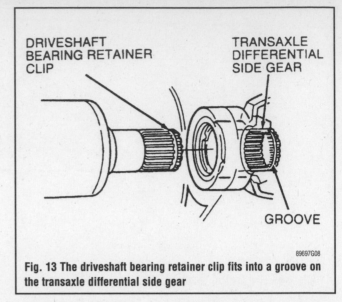

Fig. 13 The driveshaft bearing retainer clip fits into a groove on the transaxle differential side gear

→Never use a hammer to separate the outboard front wheel driveshaft joint from the wheel hub. Damage to the outboard front wheel driveshaft joint threads and internal components may result.

12. Separate the outboard front wheel driveshaft joint from the wheel hub using a Front Hub Remover/Replacer (T81P-1104-C) or equivalent. Make sure the hub remover adapter is fully threaded onto the hub stud.

→Do not move the vehicle without the outboard CV-joint properly installed, as damage to the bearing may occur.

13. Remove the front wheel driveshaft and joint assembly from the vehicle.

To install:

→Do not reuse the retainer circlip. A new circlip must be installed each time the inboard CV-joint stub shaft is installed into the transaxle differential.

14. Install a new retainer circlip on the inboard CV-joint stub shaft by starting one end in the groove and working the retainer circlip over the inboard shaft housing end and into the groove. This will avoid overexpanding the circlip.

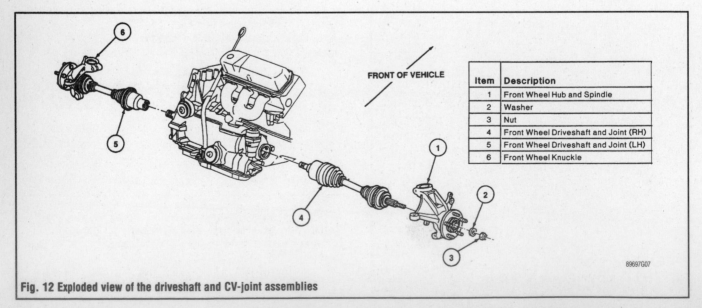

Item	Description
1	Front Wheel Hub and Spindle
2	Washer
3	Nut
4	Front Wheel Driveshaft and Joint (RH)
5	Front Wheel Driveshaft and Joint (LH)
6	Front Wheel Knuckle

Fig. 12 Exploded view of the driveshaft and CV-joint assemblies

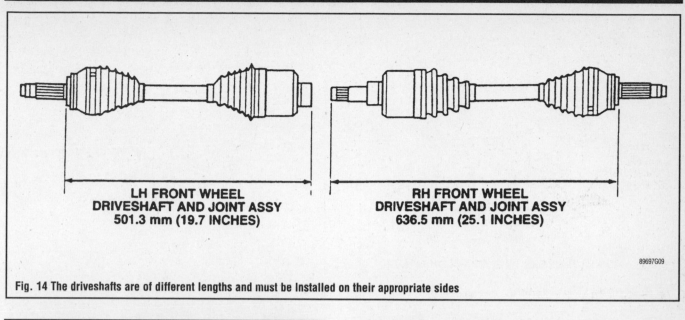

**LH FRONT WHEEL
DRIVESHAFT AND JOINT ASSY
501.3 mm (19.7 INCHES)**

**RH FRONT WHEEL
DRIVESHAFT AND JOINT ASSY
636.5 mm (25.1 INCHES)**

89697G09

Fig. 14 The driveshafts are of different lengths and must be Installed on their appropriate sides

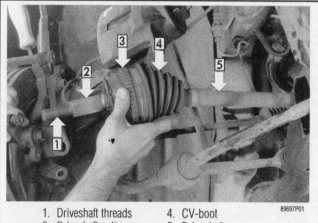

89697P01

1. Driveshaft threads
2. Driveshaft splines
3. Tone ring for anti-
   lock brake system
4. CV-boot
5. Driveshaft

Outboard driveshaft and CV-boot assembly

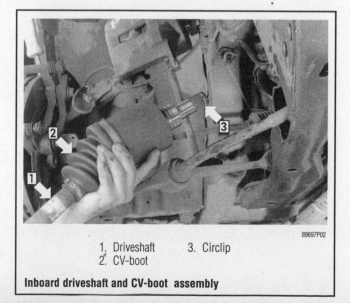

89697P02

1. Driveshaft
2. CV-boot
3. Circlip

Inboard driveshaft and CV-boot assembly

➡A non-metallic mallet may be used to aid in seating the retainer circlip into the differential side gear groove. If a mallet is necessary, tap only on the outboard CV-joint stub shaft.

15. Carefully align the splines of the inboard CV-joint stub shaft housing with the splines in the differential. Exerting some force, push the inboard CV-joint stub shaft housing into the differential until the retainer circlip is felt to seat in the differential side gear. Use care to prevent damage to the inboard CV-joint stub shaft and transaxle seal.

16. Carefully align the splines of the outboard front wheel driveshaft joint with the splines in the wheel hub, and push the shaft into the wheel hub as far as possible.

17. Temporarily fasten the front disc brake rotor to the wheel hub with washers and two lug nuts. Insert a steel rod into the front disc brake rotor and rotate clockwise to contact the front wheel knuckle, to prevent the front disc brake rotor from turning during front wheel driveshaft and joint installation.

➡A new front axle wheel hub retaining nut must be installed.

18. Manually thread the front axle wheel hub retaining nut onto the outboard CV-joint stub shaft housing as far as possible.

➡A new bolt and nut must be used to connect the front suspension arm to the knuckle.

19. Connect the front suspension lower arm to the front wheel knuckle. Tighten the nut and bolt to 40–55 ft. lbs. (54–74 Nm).

20. Install the front brake anti-lock sensor.

21. Connect the front stabilizer bar link and tighten to 35–45 ft. lbs. (47–65 Nm).

➡Do not use power or impact tools to tighten the hub nut.

22. Tighten the front axle wheel hub retaining nut to 157–212 ft. lbs. (213–287 Nm).

23. Install the front wheels and lower the vehicle.

24. Using the recommended type of fluid, fill the transaxle to the proper level.

OVERHAUL

◆ **See Figures 15 thru 28**

Refer to the following photos for an illustration of Halfshaft overhaul.

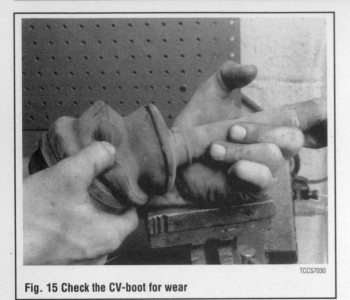

Fig. 15 Check the CV-boot for wear

Fig. 18 Removing the CV-boot from the joint housing

Fig. 16 Removing the outer band from the CV-boot

Fig. 19 Clean the CV-joint housing prior to removing boot

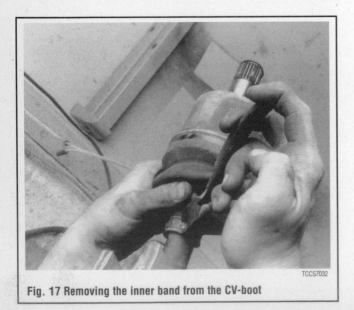

Fig. 17 Removing the inner band from the CV-boot

Fig. 20 Removing the CV-joint housing assembly

Fig. 21 Removing the CV-joint

Fig. 22 Inspecting the CV-joint housing

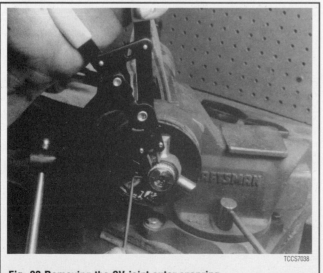

Fig. 23 Removing the CV-joint outer snapring

Fig. 24 Checking the CV-joint snapring for wear

Fig. 25 CV-joint snapring (typical)

Fig. 26 Removing the CV-joint assembly

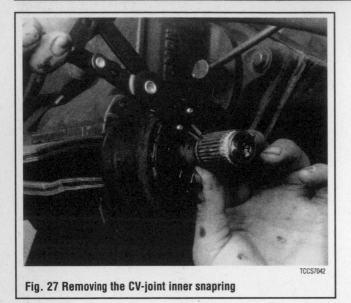

TCCS7042

Fig. 27 Removing the CV-joint inner snapring

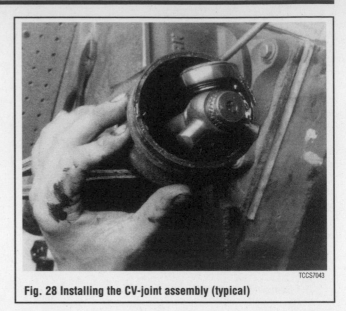

TCCS7043

Fig. 28 Installing the CV-joint assembly (typical)

TORQUE SPECIFICATIONS

Components	Ft. Lbs.	Nm
Transaxle		
Transaxle range sensor	80–106 inch lbs.	9–12 Nm
Manual control lever	12–16 ft. lbs.	16–22 Nm
Automatic Transaxle Assembly		
Engine bracket-to-transaxle bolts	39–53 ft. lbs.	53–72 Nm
Lower transaxle-to-engine bolts	39–53 ft. lbs.	53–72 Nm
Flywheel-to-torque converter bolts	20–34 ft. lbs.	27–46 Nm
Transaxle housing cover bolts	80–106 inch lbs.	9–12 Nm
Rear engine support bolts	39–53 ft. lbs.	53–72 Nm
Upper transaxle-to-engine bolts	39–53 ft. lbs.	53–72 Nm
Halfshafts		
Front suspension lower arm-to-front wheel knuckle	40–55 ft. lbs.	54–74 Nm
Front stabilizer bark link	35–45 ft. lbs.	47–65 Nm
Front axle wheel hub retaining nut	157–212 ft. lbs.	213–287 Nm

89697C01

8

SUSPENSION AND STEERING

WHEELS

Wheels

REMOVAL & INSTALLATION

▶ **See Figure 1**

1. Park the vehicle on a level surface.
2. Remove the jack, tire iron and, if necessary, the spare tire from their storage compartments.
3. Check the owner's manual or refer to Section 1 of this manual for the jacking points on your vehicle. Then, place the jack in the proper position.
4. If equipped with lug nut trim caps, remove them by either unscrewing or pulling them off the lug nuts, as appropriate. Consult the owner's manual, if necessary.
5. If equipped with a wheel cover or hub cap, insert the tapered end of the tire iron in the groove and pry off the cover.
6. Apply the parking brake and block the diagonally opposite wheel with a wheel chock or two.

➡**Wheel chocks may be purchased at your local auto parts store, or a block of wood cut into wedges may be used. If possible, keep one or two of the chocks in your tire storage compartment, in case any of the tires has to be removed on the side of the road.**

7. If equipped with an automatic transaxle, place the selector lever in **P** or Park; with a manual transaxle, place the shifter in Reverse.
8. With the tires still on the ground, use the tire iron/wrench to break the lug nuts loose.

➡**If a nut is stuck, never use heat to loosen it or damage to the wheel and bearings may occur. If the nuts are seized, one or two heavy hammer blows directly on the end of the bolt usually loosens the rust. Be careful, as continued pounding will likely damage the brake drum or rotor.**

9. Using the jack, raise the vehicle until the tire is clear of the ground. Support the vehicle safely using jackstands.
10. Remove the lug nuts, then remove the tire and wheel assembly.

To install:

11. Make sure the wheel and hub mating surfaces, as well as the wheel lug studs, are clean and free of all foreign material. Always remove rust from the wheel mounting surface and the brake rotor or drum. Failure to do so may cause the lug nuts to loosen in service.
12. Install the tire and wheel assembly and hand-tighten the lug nuts.
13. Using the tire wrench, tighten all the lug nuts, in a crisscross pattern, until they are snug.
14. Raise the vehicle and withdraw the jackstand, then lower the vehicle.
15. Using a torque wrench, tighten the lug nuts in a crisscross pattern to 85–105 ft. lbs. (115–142 Nm). Check your owner's manual or refer to Section 1 of this manual for the proper tightening sequence.

❊❊ WARNING

Do not overtighten the lug nuts, as this may cause the wheel studs to stretch or the brake disc (rotor) to warp.

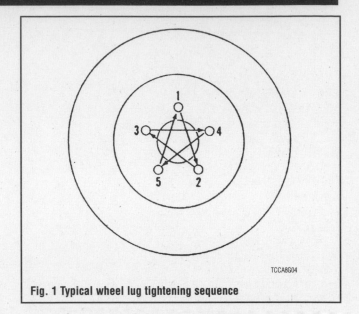

TCCA8G04

Fig. 1 Typical wheel lug tightening sequence

16. If so equipped, install the wheel cover or hub cap. Make sure the valve stem protrudes through the proper opening before tapping the wheel cover into position.
17. If equipped, install the lug nut trim caps by pushing them or screwing them on, as applicable.
18. Remove the jack from under the vehicle, and place the jack and tire iron/wrench in their storage compartments. Remove the wheel chock(s).
19. If you have removed a flat or damaged tire, place it in the storage compartment of the vehicle and take it to your local repair station to have it fixed or replaced as soon as possible.

INSPECTION

Inspect the tires for lacerations, puncture marks, nails and other sharp objects. Repair or replace as necessary. Also check the tires for treadwear and air pressure as outlined in Check the wheel assemblies for dents, cracks, rust and metal fatigue. Repair or replace as necessary.

Wheel Lug Studs

REMOVAL & INSTALLATION

With Disc Brakes

▶ **See Figures 2, 3 and 4**

1. Raise and support the appropriate end of the vehicle safely using jackstands, then remove the wheel.
2. Remove the brake pads and caliper. Support the caliper aside using wire or a coat hanger. For details, please refer to Section 9 of this manual.
3. Remove the outer wheel bearing and lift off the rotor. For details on wheel bearing removal, installation and adjustment, please refer to Section 1 of this manual.
4. Properly support the rotor using press bars, then drive the stud out using an arbor press.

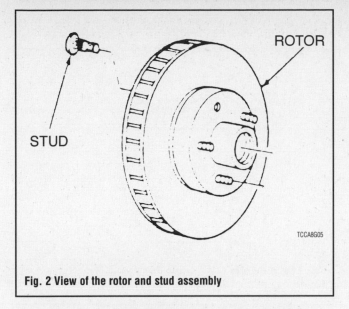

Fig. 2 View of the rotor and stud assembly

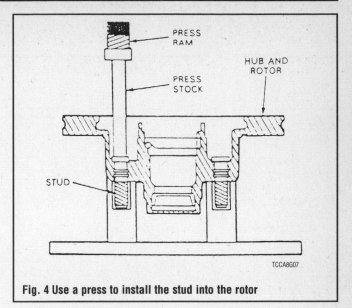

Fig. 4 Use a press to install the stud into the rotor

→If a press is not available, CAREFULLY drive the old stud out using a blunt drift. MAKE SURE the rotor is properly and evenly supported or it may be damaged.

To install:

5. Clean the stud hole with a wire brush and start the new stud with a hammer and drift pin. Do not use any lubricant or thread sealer.

6. Finish installing the stud with the press.

→If a press is not available, start the lug stud through the bore in the hub, then position about 4 flat washers over the stud and thread the lug nut. Hold the hub/rotor while tightening the lug nut, and the stud should be drawn into position. MAKE SURE THE STUD IS FULLY SEATED, then remove the lug nut and washers.

7. Install the rotor and adjust the wheel bearings.

8. Install the brake caliper and pads.

9. Install the wheel, then remove the jackstands and carefully lower the vehicle.

10. Tighten the lug nuts to the proper torque.

With Drum Brakes

♦ See Figures 5, 6 and 7

1. Raise the vehicle and safely support it with jackstands, then remove the wheel.

2. Remove the brake drum.

3. If necessary to provide clearance, remove the brake shoes, as outlined in Section 9 of this manual.

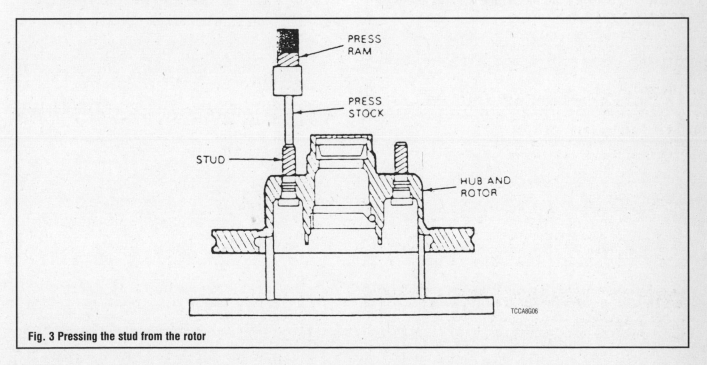

Fig. 3 Pressing the stud from the rotor

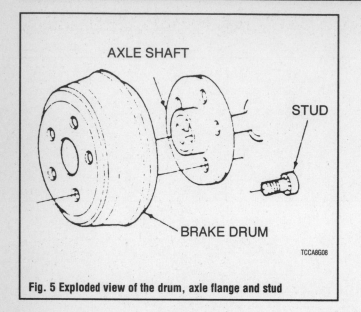

Fig. 5 Exploded view of the drum, axle flange and stud

AXLE SHAFT

STUD

BRAKE DRUM

TCCA8G08

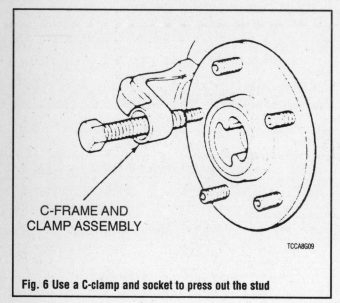

Fig. 6 Use a C-clamp and socket to press out the stud

C-FRAME AND
CLAMP ASSEMBLY

TCCA8G09

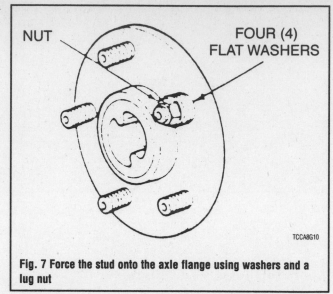

Fig. 7 Force the stud onto the axle flange using washers and a lug nut

NUT

FOUR (4)
FLAT WASHERS

TCCA8G10

4. Using a large C-clamp and socket, press the stud from the axle flange.

5. Coat the serrated part of the stud with liquid soap and place it into the hole.

To install:

6. Position about 4 flat washers over the stud and thread the lug nut. Hold the flange while tightening the lug nut, and the stud should be drawn into position. MAKE SURE THE STUD IS FULLY SEATED, then remove the lug nut and washers.

7. If applicable, install the brake shoes.

8. Install the brake drum.

9. Install the wheel, then remove the jackstands and carefully lower the vehicle.

10. Tighten the lug nuts to the proper torque.

FRONT SUSPENSION

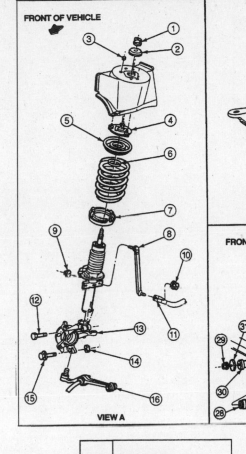

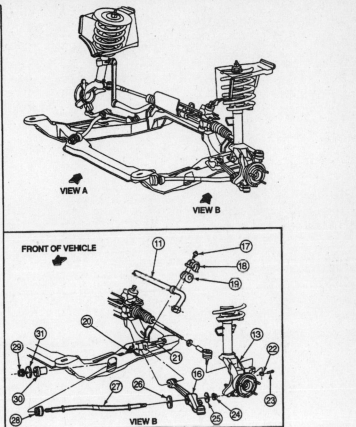

Item	Description
1	Front Shock Absorber Nut
2	Upper Front Shock Absorber Washer
3	Front Shock Absorber Mounting Bracket Nut
4	Front Shock Absorber Mounting Bracket
5	Front Suspension Bearing and Seal
6	Lower Front Shock Absorber Washer
7	Front Spring Insulator
8	Front Stabilizer Bar Link
9	Front Stabilizer Bar Link-to-Front Shock Absorber Nut
10	Front Stabilizer Bar Link-to-Front Stabilizer Bar Nut
11	Front Stabilizer Bar
12	Front Wheel Hub and Spindle-to-Front Shock Absorber Pinch Bolt
13	Front Wheel Hub and Spindle
14	Front Suspension Lower Arm Ball Joint Pinch Bolt Nut

Item	Description
15	Front Suspension Lower Arm Ball Joint Pinch Bolt
16	Front Suspension Lower Arm
17	Stabilizer Bar Bracket Bolt
18	Stabilizer Bar Bracket
19	Stabilizer Bar Bracket Insulator
20	Front Suspension Lower Arm-to-Front Sub-Frame Bolt Nut
21	Front Suspension Lower Arm-to-Front Sub-Frame Bolt
22	Tie Rod End-to-Front Wheel Hub and-Spindle Nut
23	Cotter Pin
24	Front Suspension Lower Arm Strut-to-Front Suspension Lower Arm Nut
25	Washer
26	Washer
27	Front Suspension Lower Arm Strut
28	Front Suspension Strut Insulator
29	Front Suspension Lower Arm Strut-to-Front Sub-Frame Nut
30	Front Suspension Lower Arm Strut Inner Bushing
31	Washer

89698G01

Fig. 8 Exploded view of the front suspension

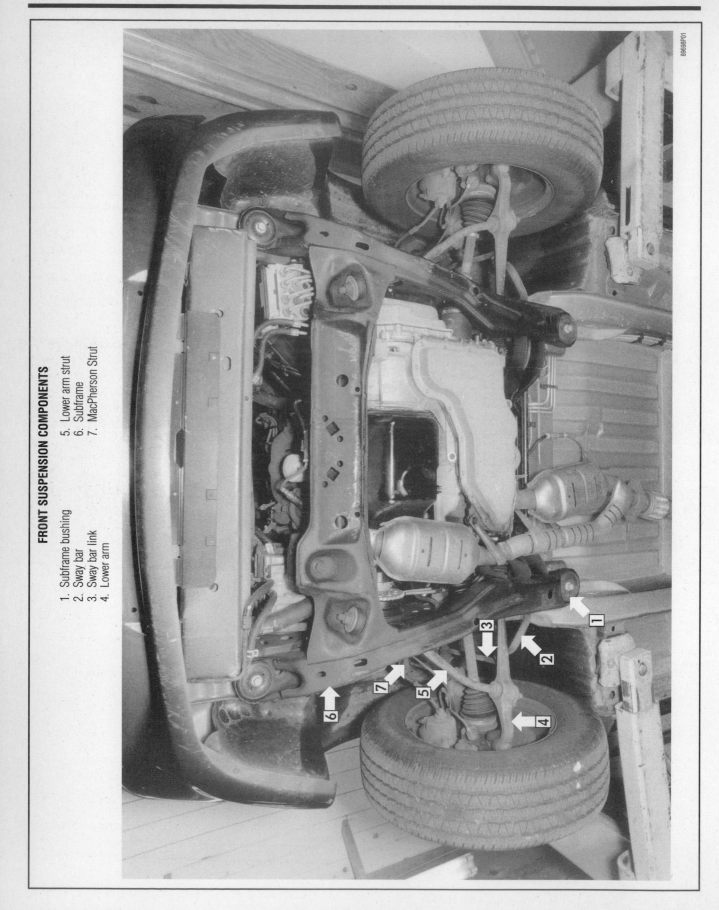

FRONT SUSPENSION COMPONENTS

1. Subframe bushing
2. Sway bar
3. Sway bar link
4. Lower arm
5. Lower arm strut
6. Subframe
7. MacPherson Strut

MacPherson Struts

REMOVAL & INSTALLATION

➡️Do not begin this procedure unless a new front axle wheel hub nut, a new lower arm ball joint pinch bolt and nut, and a new tie rod and knuckle nut and cotter pin are available. Once removed, these parts must not be reused during assembly. Their torque holding ability or retention capability is diminished during removal.

1. Turn the ignition switch **OFF** and place the steering column in the unlocked position.
2. Loosen but do not remove the three front strut-to-tower nuts.

➡️Do not raise the vehicle by the lower arms.

3. Remove the front wheel.
4. Remove the disc brake caliper and suspend it out of the way using a piece of wire.
5. Remove the front disc brake rotor.
6. Remove the front axle wheel hub nut.
7. Using a Front Wheel Hub Remover (T81P-1104-C) or equivalent, remove the front wheel bearing and front wheel knuckle as an assembly.

The stabilizer bar link is attached to the strut assembly using a ball joint

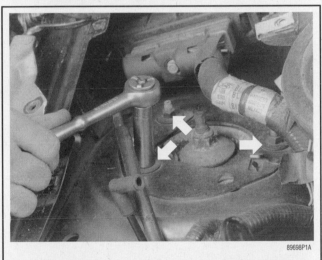

Loosen only the three strut-to-strut tower attaching bolts when removing the strut

Use an Allen wrench to hold the stud steady while removing the stabilizer bar link nut

The strut is attached to the steering knuckle with a pinch joint. Do not reuse the bolt or nut

8. Using a Tie Rod End Remover (TOOL-3290-D) or equivalent, disconnect the tie rod end from the front wheel knuckle.

➡️Use extreme care to not damage the link ball joint boot seal.

9. Remove the stabilizer bar link from the lower arm.
10. Remove and discard the front suspension lower arm-to-front wheel knuckle pinch bolt and nut.
11. Using a prybar, slightly spread the front wheel knuckle-to-lower arm pinch joint and remove the lower arm from the front wheel knuckle.
12. Remove the speed sensor bracket and speed sensor from he front wheel knuckle.
13. Remove the strut-to-front wheel knuckle pinch bolt.
14. Using a prybar, slightly spread the front wheel knuckle-to-front strut pinch joint as required for removal.
15. Remove the front wheel knuckle and wheel hub assembly from the front strut.
16. Remove the three front strut mounting bracket-to-strut tower nuts and remove the front strut assembly from the vehicle.
    To install:
17. Install the front strut assembly and tighten the strut-to-strut tower mounting bolts hand tight.
18. Install the front wheel knuckle and wheel hub assembly.

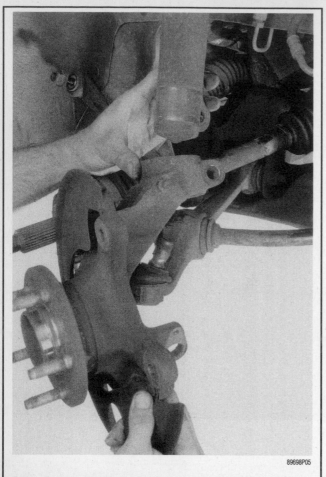

Carefully separate the knuckle from the strut by using a slight twisting motion

19. Install the new strut-to-wheel knuckle pinch bolt and tighten to 85–97 ft. lbs. (115–132 Nm).

20. Install the halfshaft into the wheel hub.

21. Insall the lower arm ensuring that the ball stud groove is properly positioned. use extreme care no to damage the ball joint seal. Install a new pinch bolt and nut. Tighten to 46–52 ft. lbs. (62–71 Nm).

22. Install the front wheel knuckle making sure the front stabilizer bar link is properly positioned. Use care not to damage the ball joint seal.

➡Top left-hand (Top LH) and top right-hand (Top RH) markings are molded into the stabilizer bar link for correct assembly reference.

23. Install a new stabilizer link nut and tighten to 66–74 ft. lbs. (90–100 Nm).

24. Install the tie rod end onto the front wheel knuckle. Tighten the new tie rod slotted nut to 66–74 ft. lbs. (90–100 Nm).

25. Install the front brake anti-lock sensor and bracket on the knuckle.

26. Insatll the front disc brake rotor.

27. Install the front wheel.

28. Tighten the three strut mounting bracket-to-strut tower bolts to 25–30 ft. lbs. (35–40 Nm).

29. Lower the vehicle and tighten the front axle wheel hub nut to 170–202 ft. lbs. (230–275 Nm).

30. Check the wheel alignment.

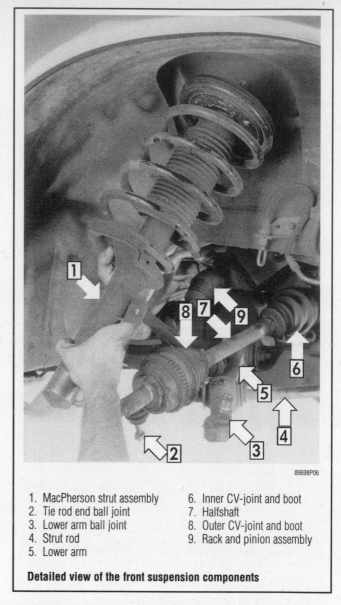

1. MacPherson strut assembly
2. Tie rod end ball joint
3. Lower arm ball joint
4. Strut rod
5. Lower arm
6. Inner CV-joint and boot
7. Halfshaft
8. Outer CV-joint and boot
9. Rack and pinion assembly

Detailed view of the front suspension components

OVERHAUL

❊❊ CAUTION

Never attempt to disassemble the strut without first compressing the coil spring. The spring is under tremendous pressure. Serious injury or death could result.

1. Remove the strut assembly from the vehicle.

2. Compress the front coil spring with a Rotunda Spring Compressor (086-0029B) or equivalent.

➡It is important that the retaining nut be turned and rod held still to prevent fracture of the rod at the base of the hex.

3. Place a 10mm box end wrench on top of the strut shaft and hold while removing the top shaft retaining nut with a 21mm 6-point crow's foot wrench and ratchet.

4. Loosen the spring compressor slowly.

5. Remove the strut mounting bracket, bearing plate and front coil spring.

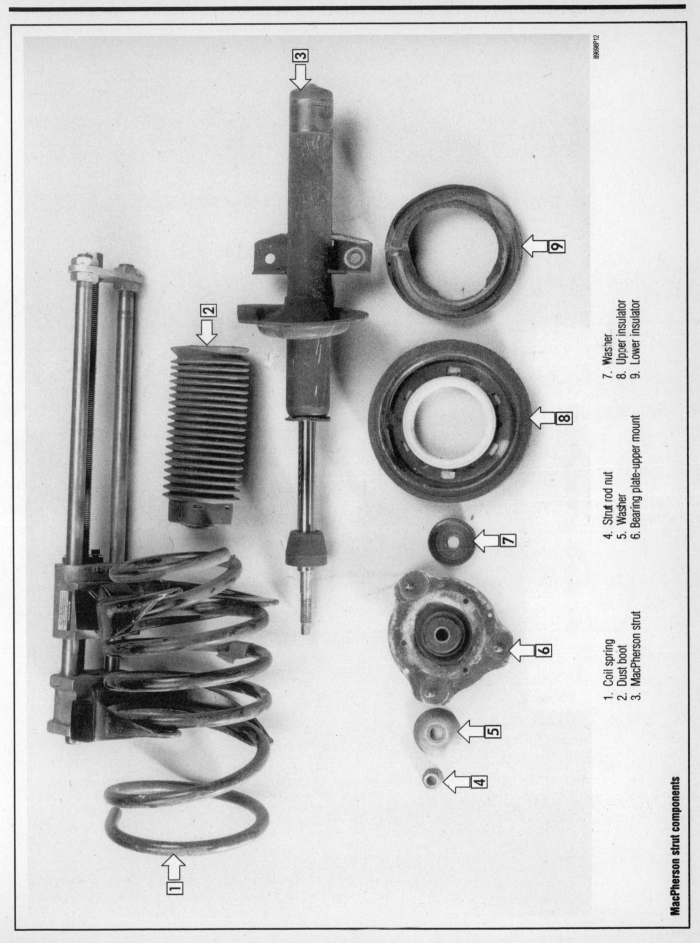

8698P12

1. Coil spring
2. Dust boot
3. MacPherson strut

4. Strut rod nut
5. Washer
6. Bearing plate-upper mount

7. Washer
8. Upper insulator
9. Lower insulator

MacPherson strut components

89698P07

Using a large spring compressor to compress the strut's coil spring

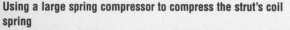

89698P08

Hold the center rod with a wrench while loosening the strut rod nut

89698P09

Remove the strut rod nut and washer

89698P10

The bearing plate provides support for the top of the strut rod and attaches to the strut tower

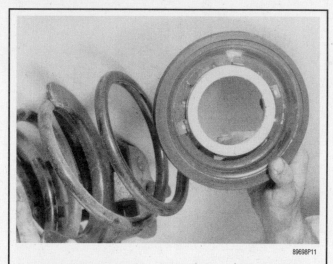

89698P11

Note the insulator position on the spring, as it must be installed in the same position

To install:

→Make sure that the correct assembly sequence and proper positioning of the bearing and seat assembly are followed. The bearing and seat assembly is press fit onto the front strut mounting bracket.

6. Check the front spring insulator for damage. If the outer metal splash shield is bent or damaged, it must be bent back carefully so that it does not touch the locator tabs on the bearing and seal assembly.

7. Install the spring compressor and compress the spring.

8. Install the front spring, lower washer and front strut mounting bracket assembly on the body.

9. Install the upper washer and nut on the strut shaft. Tighten the nut to 40–46 ft. lbs. (55–63 Nm) while holding the shaft to prevent it front turning.

10. Install the strut assembly in the vehicle.

Lower Arm Ball Joint

INSPECTION

◗ See Figure 9

1. Place the vehicle on a level surface.
2. Clean the wear indicator and ball joint cover surfaces.
3. Inspect the wear indicator position relative to the ball joint cover. If the wear indicator protrudes from the checking surface on the cover, the ball joint is functional.

➥**Abnormal tire wear may be caused by faulty ball joints.**

4. If the wear indicator does not protrude from the check surface on the cover, the ball joint is faulty.

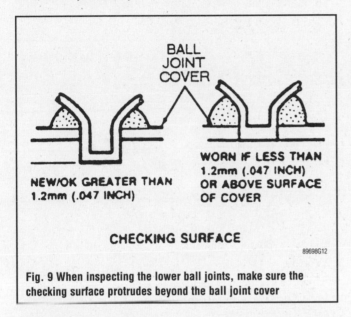

Fig. 9 When inspecting the lower ball joints, make sure the checking surface protrudes beyond the ball joint cover

REMOVAL & INSTALLATION

The lower arm ball joint and seal are an integral part of the lower arm assembly and cannot be replaced separately. If the lower arm ball joint or seal is found to be defective, the lower arm must be replaced as an assembly.

Sway Bar

REMOVAL & INSTALLATION

1. Raise and support the vehicle safely.
2. Support the vehicle with safety stands behind the front subframe.

➥**To avoid damage to the 6mm drive hole in the front stabilizer bar link ball stud, do not use an Allen wrench to break loose, tighten or final tighten the front stabilizer bar link-to-front strut nut.**

3. Using care not to damage the front stabilizer bar link ball stud seal, remove the stabilizer bar link-to-front strut mounting nuts.
4. Using care not to damage the front stabilizer ball link stud seal, remove the stabilizer bar link-to-stabilizer bar nuts.

❊❊ WARNING

Use extreme care not to damage the ball joint boot.

5. With another set of safety stands under the front subframe, remove the two rear subframe retaining bolts. Lower the rear of the front subframe to obtain access to the stabilizer bar brackets.
6. Remove the front stabilizer bar bracket bolts, brackets, insulators and the front stabilizer bar.

To install:

7. Clean the front stabilizer bar to remove dirt and contamination in the area of the insulators.
8. Lubricate the inside diameter of the insulators with Rubber Suspension Insulator Lube (E52Y-19553-A) or equivalent. Do not use any mineral or petroleum based lubricants as they will deteriorate the rubber insulators.
9. Install the stabilizer bar bracket insulators on the bar and position them in their approximate location.
10. Install the stabilizer bar bracket on the insulators and tighten the bolts to 40–46 ft. lbs. (55–63 Nm).
11. Raise the front subframe and install new front subframe-to-body retaining bolts. Tighten the bolts to 85–97 ft. lbs. (115–132 Nm).
12. Install the front stabilizer bar links and tighten the link-to-shock nuts and the link-to-stabilizer bar nuts to 66–74 ft. lbs. (90–100 Nm).
13. Lower the vehicle.

Lower Arm

REMOVAL & INSTALLATION

➥**Do not begin the removal procedure unless a new strut-to-lower arm nut, a new ball joint pinch bolt/nut and a new lower arm-to-front subframe bolt/nut are available.**

1. Raise and support the vehicle safely.
2. Remove the wheels.
3. Remove and discard the lower arm strut nut and dished washer.

➥**Do not use a hammer to separate the ball joint from the front wheel hub and spindle.**

4. Place the steering wheel in the unlocked position.

➥**Do not allow the halfshaft to move outward. Overextension of the halfshaft joint could result in separation of internal parts, causing failure of the halfshaft joint.**

5. Remove and discard the front suspension lower arm ball joint nut and pinch bolt.
6. Using a prybar, slightly spread the pinch joint and separate the lower arm from the front wheel knuckle.

➥**Use extreme care to not damage the ball joint boot seal.**

7. Remove and discard the lower arm-to-front subframe bolt and nut.
8. Remove the lower arm front the vehicle.

To install:

9. Insert the lower arm strut into the lower arm rear strut bushing.
10. Position the lower arm into the front sub-frame bracket.
11. Install a new lower arm-to-front subframe nut and bolt. While holding the lower arm horizontal, tighten to 85–97 ft. lbs. (115–132 Nm).
12. Assemble the ball joint stud-to-wheel hub and spindle, making sure that the ball stud groove is properly positioned.
13. Insert a new lower arm ball joint pinch bolt and nut. Tighten to 46–52 ft. lbs. 62–71 Nm).
14. Clean the lower arm strut threads to remove dirt and contamination.
15. Install the dished washer with the dished side away from the lower arm rear strut bushing.
16. Install the front suspension lower arm strut-to-strut nut and tighten to 85–97 ft. lbs. (115–142 Nm).
17. Install the wheels.
18. Lower the vehicle.

LOWER ARM BUSHING REPLACEMENT

♦ **See Figures 10 and 11**

➡ **Prior to starting this procedure, ensure that new replacement fasteners are available.**

1. Remove the lower arm from the vehicle.
2. Using a Bushing Remover (T86P-5493-A5) or equivalent, remove the bushing from the lower arm using a large C-clamp as a press.

To install:

3. Saturate the lower arm and new bushing in vegetable oil.

➡ **Use only vegetable oil. Any mineral or petroleum based oil or brake fluid will deteriorate the rubber.**

4. Using a Bushing Driver (T86P-5493-A2), or equivalent, press the bushing into the lower arm using a C-clamp as a press.
5. Install the lower arm on the vehicle.

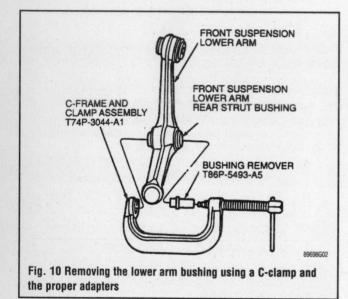

Fig. 10 Removing the lower arm bushing using a C-clamp and the proper adapters

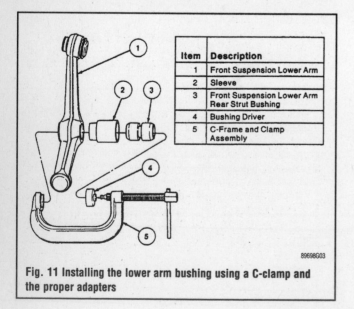

Item	Description
1	Front Suspension Lower Arm
2	Sleeve
3	Front Suspension Lower Arm Rear Strut Bushing
4	Bushing Driver
5	C-Frame and Clamp Assembly

Fig. 11 Installing the lower arm bushing using a C-clamp and the proper adapters

Knuckle and Spindle

REMOVAL & INSTALLATION

♦ **See Figures 12 and 13**

➡ **Do not begin this procedure unless a new front axle wheel hub nut, a new lower arm ball joint pinch bolt and nut, and a new tie rod and knuckle nut and cotter pin are available. Once removed these parts must not be reused during assembly. their torque holding ability or retention capability is diminished during removal.**

1. Turn the ignition switch **OFF** and place the steering column in the unlocked position.
2. Remove the front axle nut.
3. Raise and support the vehicle safely.
4. Remove the wheel.

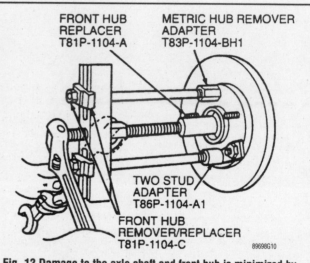

Fig. 12 Damage to the axle shaft and front hub is minimized by using the proper tools

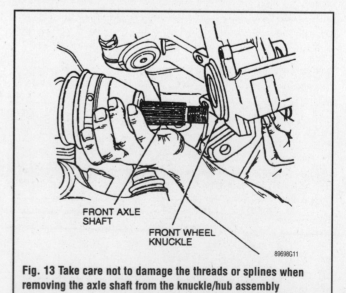

Fig. 13 Take care not to damage the threads or splines when removing the axle shaft from the knuckle/hub assembly

➡**Make sure the steering column tube is in the unlocked position. Do not use a hammer to separate the ball joint from the knuckle. Use extreme care not to damage the ball joint boot seal.**

5. Using a Tie Rod End Remover (TOOL-3290-D) or equivalent, disconnect the tie rod end from the front wheel knuckle.

6. Remove the stabilizer bar link from the lower arm.

7. Remove the disc brake caliper and suspend it out of the way using a piece of wire.

8. Remove the front disc brake rotor.

9. Loosen but do not remove the three top retaining nuts from the strut tower.

10. Remove and discard the front suspension lower arm-to-front wheel knuckle pinch bolt and nut.

11. Using a prybar, slightly spread the front wheel knuckle-to-lower arm pinch joint and remove the lower arm from the front wheel knuckle.

➡**Do not allow the halfshaft to move outboard. Over extension of the CV-joint could result in separation of internal parts causing failure of the halfshaft.**

12. Remove and discard the strut-to-front wheel knuckle pinch bolt and nut.

13. Using a prybar, slightly spread the strut-to-knuckle pinch joint.

14. Using a Front Wheel Hub Remover (T81P-1104-C) or equivalent, remove the front wheel bearing and front wheel knuckle as an assembly.

To install:

15. Install the front disc brake rotor shield, if removed.

16. Replace seal pressed on outboard halfshaft and joint, as required.

17. Install the front wheel bearing, retainer ring and wheel hub.

18. Install the knuckle on the strut assembly and connect the tie rod. Loosely install a new pinch bolt.

19. Install the halfshaft into the front hub.

20. Install the lower arm to the knuckle, making sure the ball stud groove is properly positioned.

21. Tigthen new lower arm nut and bolt to 46–52 ft. lbs. (62–71 Nm).

22. Tighten strut-to-knuckle pinch bolt and nut to 85–97 ft. lbs. (115–132 Nm).

23. Install the front disc brake rotor and caliper. Replace caliper retaining bolts and tighten to 73–97 ft. lbs. (98–132 Nm).

24. Connect tie rod end to knuckle and tighten new castle nut to 66–74 ft. lbs. 90–100 Nm).

25. Install the stabilizer bar link and tighten new nut to 66–74 ft. lbs. 90–100 Nm).

26. Install the front brake anti-lock sensor and bracket.

27. Install the wheel.

28. Lower the vehicle.

29. Tighten the three front strut-to-strut tower retaining nuts to 25–30 ft. lbs. (35–40 Nm).

30. Tighten the front axle wheel nut to 170–202 ft. lbs. (230–275 Nm).

31. Check wheel alignment.

Front Hub and Bearing

REMOVAL & INSTALLATION

▸ **See Figures 14 thru 19**

1. Remove the front wheel knuckle.

➡**Make sure the shaft protector is centered, clears the bearing ID and rests on the end face of the wheel hub journal.**

2. On a workbench, install a 2-jaw puller and Shaft Protector (D80L-625-1) or equivalent, with the jaws of the puller on the knuckle bosses.

3. Separate the front wheel knuckle from the hub.

4. Remove and discard the wheel bearing retainer snapring.

5. Using an hydraulic press, place a Front Bearing Spacer (T86P

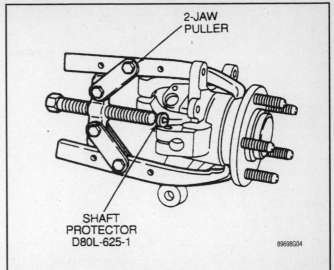

Fig. 14 Separating the knuckle from the hub using a 2-jaw puller

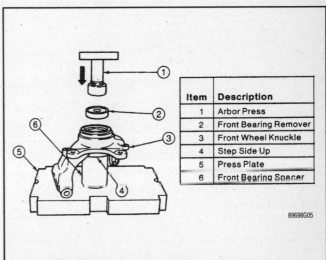

Item	Description
1	Arbor Press
2	Front Bearing Remover
3	Front Wheel Knuckle
4	Step Side Up
5	Press Plate
6	Front Bearing Spacer

Fig. 15 Removing the wheel bearing from the knuckle using an hydraulic press and the proper adapters

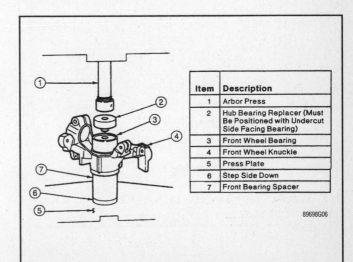

Item	Description
1	Arbor Press
2	Hub Bearing Replacer (Must Be Positioned with Undercut Side Facing Bearing)
3	Front Wheel Bearing
4	Front Wheel Knuckle
5	Press Plate
6	Step Side Down
7	Front Bearing Spacer

Fig. 16 Installing the wheel bearing into the knuckle using an hydraulic press and the proper adapters

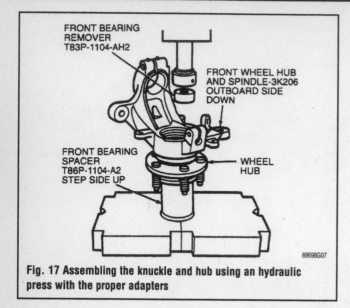

Fig. 17 Assembling the knuckle and hub using an hydraulic press with the proper adapters

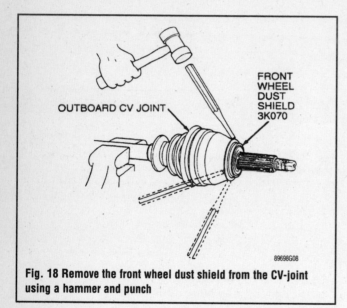

Fig. 18 Remove the front wheel dust shield from the CV-joint using a hammer and punch

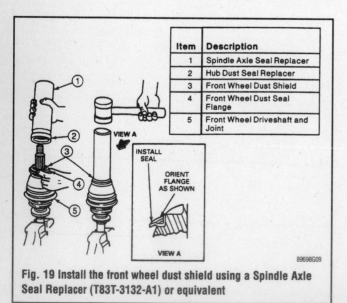

Item	Description
1	Spindle Axle Seal Replacer
2	Hub Dust Seal Replacer
3	Front Wheel Dust Shield
4	Front Wheel Dust Seal Flange
5	Front Wheel Driveshaft and Joint

Fig. 19 Install the front wheel dust shield using a Spindle Axle Seal Replacer (T83T-3132-A1) or equivalent

1104-A2) or equivalent, step side up on a press plate and position the knuckle (outboard side up) on the spacer.

6. Install Front Wheel Bearing Remover (T83P-1104-AH2) or equivalent, centered on the front wheel bearing outer race, and press the front wheel bearing out of the knuckle.

To install:

➡If the wheel bearing journal is scored or damaged, replace the wheel hub. Do not attempt to service. The front wheel bearings are of a cartridge design. Wheel bearings are pregreased, sealed and require no scheduled maintenance. The front wheel bearings are preset and cannot be adjusted. If a front wheel bearing is disassembled for any reason, it must be replaced as an assembly. No individual components are available.

7. Throughly clean the wheel hub and bearing journal to ensure correct seating of the new wheel bearing.

8. Place the Front Bearing Spacer (T86P-1104-A2) or equivalent, step side down on an hydraulic press plate and position the front wheel knuckle (outboard side down) on the spacer.

9. Position a new wheel bearing in the inboard side of the wheel hub and spindle. Install Hub Bearing Replacer (T86P-1104-A3) or equivalent, (with the undercut side facing the bearing) and press wheel bearing into knuckle.

➡Make sure the wheel bearing seats completely against the shoulder of the knuckle bore.

10. Install a new front wheel bearing retainer snapring in the hub and spindle groove.

11. Place Front Bearing Spacer (T86P-1104-A2) or equivalent, on an arbor press plate and position the wheel hub on the front bearing spacer with its lug bolts facing downward.

12. Position the wheel hub and knuckle (outboard side down) on the press. Place Front Bearing Remover (T83P-1104-AH2) or equivalent, flat side down, centered on the inner race of the front wheel bearing and press down until the bearing is fully seated.

13. Ensure that the wheel hub rotates freely in the knuckle after installation.

14. Remove the front halfshaft from the vehicle.

15. Prior to wheel hub, bearing and knuckle installation, replace the front wheel dust shield on the halfshaft.

16. Install the halfshaft and knuckle.

Wheel Alignment

If the tires are worn unevenly, if the vehicle is not stable on the highway or if the handling seems uneven in spirited driving, the wheel alignment should be checked. If an alignment problem is suspected, first check for improper tire inflation and other possible causes. These can be worn suspension or steering components, accident damage or even unmatched tires. If any worn or damaged components are found, they must be replaced before the wheels can be properly aligned. Wheel alignment requires very expensive equipment and involves minute adjustments which must be accurate; it should only be performed by a trained technician. Take your vehicle to a properly equipped shop.

Following is a description of the alignment angles which are adjustable on most vehicles and how they affect vehicle handling. Although these angles can apply to both the front and rear wheels, usually only the front suspension is adjustable.

CASTER

♦ **See Figure 20**

Looking at a vehicle from the side, caster angle describes the steering axis rather than a wheel angle. The steering knuckle is attached to a control arm or strut at the top and a control arm at the bottom. The wheel pivots around the line between these points to steer the vehicle. When the upper point is tilted back, this is described as positive caster. Having a positive caster tends to

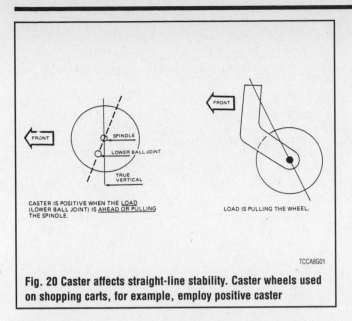

Fig. 20 Caster affects straight-line stability. Caster wheels used on shopping carts, for example, employ positive caster

make the wheels self-centering, increasing directional stability. Excessive positive caster makes the wheels hard to steer, while an uneven caster will cause a pull to one side. Overloading the vehicle or sagging rear springs will affect caster, as will raising the rear of the vehicle. If the rear of the vehicle is lower than normal, the caster becomes more positive.

CAMBER

▶ **See Figure 21**

Looking from the front of the vehicle, camber is the inward or outward tilt of the top of wheels. When the tops of the wheels are tilted in, this is negative camber; if they are tilted out, it is positive. In a turn, a slight

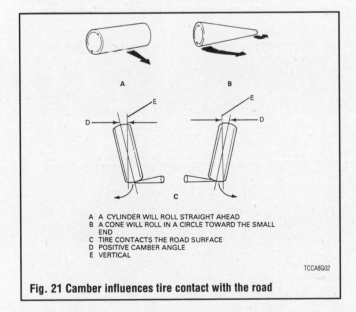

A A CYLINDER WILL ROLL STRAIGHT AHEAD
B A CONE WILL ROLL IN A CIRCLE TOWARD THE SMALL
   END
C TIRE CONTACTS THE ROAD SURFACE
D POSITIVE CAMBER ANGLE
E VERTICAL

Fig. 21 Camber influences tire contact with the road

amount of negative camber helps maximize contact of the tire with the road. However, too much negative camber compromises straight-line stability, increases bump steer and torque steer.

TOE

▶ **See Figure 22**

Looking down at the wheels from above the vehicle, toe angle is the distance between the front of the wheels, relative to the distance between the back of the wheels. If the wheels are closer at the front, they are said to be toed-in or to have negative toe. A small amount of negative toe enhances directional stability and provides a smoother ride on the highway.

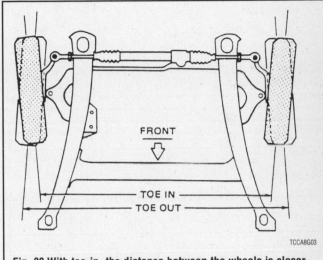

Fig. 22 With toe-in, the distance between the wheels is closer at the front than at the rear

REAR SUSPENSION

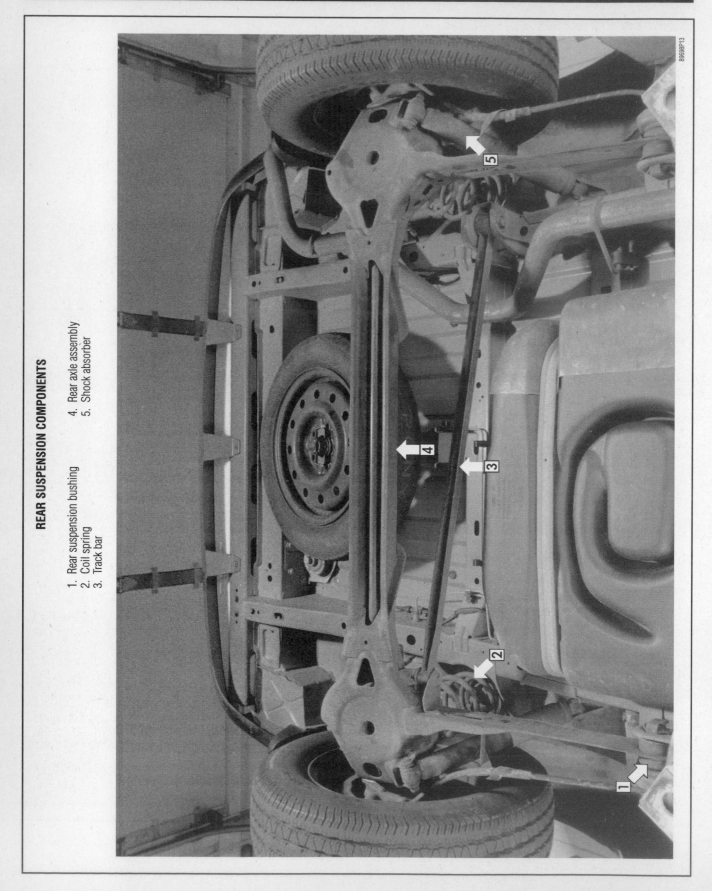

REAR SUSPENSION COMPONENTS

1. Rear suspension bushing
2. Coil spring
3. Track bar
4. Rear axle assembly
5. Shock absorber

89698P13

Coil Springs

REMOVAL & INSTALLATION

▶ **See Figure 23**

➡**If a twin post hoist is used, the vehicle must be supported on jackstands placed under the pads of the underbody, forward of the axle trailing arm bracket.**

    1. Raise and support the vehicle safely.
    2. Remove the wheels.
    3. Remove the shock absorber-to-rear axle nut and disconnect the shock from the rear axle.
    4. Slowly lower the rear axle assembly with a jack until the rear spring can be removed.
    5. Remove the rear spring.

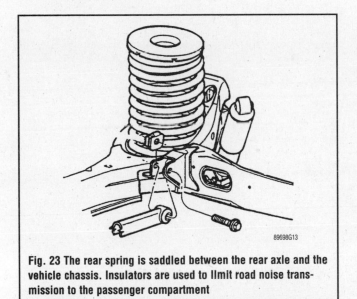

Fig. 23 The rear spring is saddled between the rear axle and the vehicle chassis. Insulators are used to limit road noise transmission to the passenger compartment

To install:

    6. Position the rear spring insulator on the rear axle assembly and press the insulator downward into place. Verify that the rear spring insulator is properly seated in the correct position.
    7. Slowly raise rear axle assembly with a jack and guide the upper rear spring insulator onto the upper spring seat on the underbody.
    8. Position the shock absorber on the lower rear axle assembly and install new nuts and bolts. Tighten to 50–68 ft. lbs. (68–92 Nm).
    9. Install the wheels.
    10. Lower the vehicle.

Shock Absorbers

REMOVAL & INSTALLATION

▶ **See Figure 24**

    1. Raise and support the vehicle safely.
    2. Remove the wheels.
    3. Position a jack under the rear axle assembly and raise it slightly to place the suspension at its normal ride height.
    4. Remove the lower shock absorber bolt/nut and disconnect the shock from the rear axle.
    5. Lower the rear axle slightly to help aid removal of the upper shock absorber bolt/nut.
    6. Remove the shock absorber.

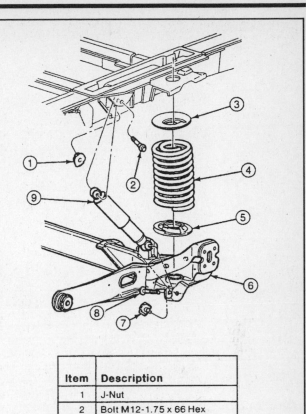

Item	Description
1	J-Nut
2	Bolt M12-1.75 x 66 Hex Flanged Head
3	Rear Spring Insulator (Upper)
4	Rear Spring
5	Rear Spring Insulator (Lower)
6	Axle Assembly
7	Nut
8	Bolt
9	Shock Absorber

Fig. 24 The rear shock absorbers are mounted between the rear axle and the vehicle chassis

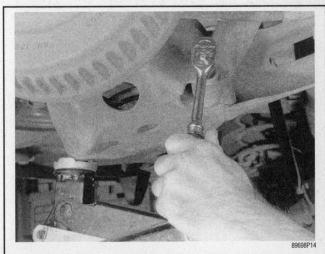

Remove the lower shock absorber-to-rear axle bolt. Note the jack holding the rear axle in position

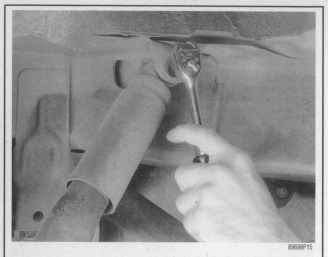

89698P15

Remove the upper shock absorber-to-chassis bolt to release the shock from the vehicle

To install:

7. Attach the shock absorber to the upper mounting bracket and install a new retaining bolt/nut.

8. Slowly raise the rear axle assembly with a jack and guide the lower shock absorber into the bracket on the rear axle assembly. Install a new retaining bolt/nut.

9. Raise the rear suspension to its normal ride height and tighten the shock absorber retaining bolts to 50–68 ft. lbs. (68–92 Nm).

10. Install the wheels.

11. Lower the vehicle.

TESTING

The purpose of the shock absorber is simply to limit the motion of the spring during compression and rebound cycles. If the vehicle is not equipped with these motion dampers, the up and down motion would multiply until the vehicle was alternately trying to leap off the ground and pound itself into the pavement.

Contrary to popular rumor, the shocks do not affect the ride height of the vehicle. This is controlled by other suspension components such as

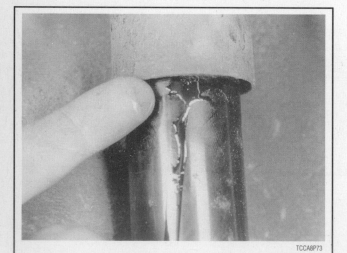

TCCA8P73

When fluid is seeping out of the shock absorber, it's time to replace the shock

springs and tires. Worn shock absorbers can affect handling; if the front of the vehicle is rising or falling excessively, the "footprint" of the tires changes on the pavement and steering is affected.

The simplest test of the shock absorber is to simply push down on one corner of the unladen vehicle and release it. Observe the motion of the body as it is released. In most cases, it will come up beyond it original rest position, dip back below it and settle quickly to rest. This shows that the damper is controlling the spring action. Any tendency toward excessive pitch (up-and-down) motion or failure to return to rest within 2–3 cycles is a sign of poor function within the shock absorber. Oil-filled shocks may have a light film of oil around the seal, resulting from normal breathing and air exchange. This should NOT be taken as a sign of failure, but any sign of thick or running oil definitely indicates failure. Gas filled shocks may also show some film at the shaft; if the gas has leaked out, the shock will have almost no resistance to motion.

While each shock absorber can be replaced individually, it is recommended that they be changed as a pair (both front or both rear) to maintain equal response on both sides of the vehicle. Chances are quite good that if one has failed, its mate is weak also.

Rear Axle Assembly

REMOVAL & INSTALLATION

➡️**If a twin post hoist is used, the vehicle must be supported on jackstands placed under the pads of the underbody, forward of the axle trailing arm bracket.**

1. Raise and support the vehicle safely.
2. Remove the wheels.
3. Disconnect the parking brake cable and anti-lock brake speed sensor cable.
4. Disconnect and cap the brake hydraulic lines
5. Disconnect the shock absorber from the rear axle.
6. Slowly lower the rear axle assembly with a jack until the rear spring can be removed.
7. Remove the rear spring.
8. Support the front of the rear axle assembly with a jack.
9. Remove the trailing arm-to-chassis bolts.
10. Remove the rear axle assembly.

To install:

11. Position the rear axle assembly and install the trailing arm-to-chassis bolts. Tighten the bolts to 50–68 ft. lbs.(68–92 Nm).

12. Install the rear spring.

13. Slowly raise the rear axle assembly.

14. Connect the shock absorber to the rear axle. Tighten the bolts/nuts to 50–68 ft. lbs. (68–92 Nm).

15. Connect the brake hydraulic lines

16. Connect the parking brake cable and anti-lock brake speed sensor cable.

17. Install the wheels.

18. Lower the vehicle.

19. Bleed the brake system.

Track Bar

REMOVAL & INSTALLATION

◆ **See Figure 25**

1. Raise and support the vehicle safely.
2. Remove the bolt retaining the track bar to the rear axle assembly.
3. Remove the bolt retaining the track bar to the track bar mounting bracket at the chassis.
4. Remove the track bar.
5. Installation is the reverse of removal.
6. Tighten the track bar retaining nuts to 50–68 ft. lbs. (68–92 Nm).

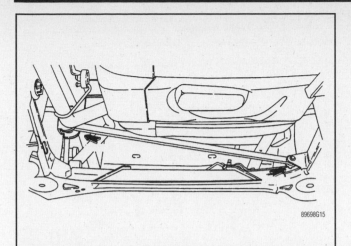

Fig. 25 The track bar ensures that the rear axle assembly is properly located. It is attached between the rear axle assembly and the chassis (arrows)

Rear Hub and Bearing

REMOVAL & INSTALLATION

▶ See Figures 26 and 27

➡Sodium based grease is not compatible with lithium based grease. Do not lubricate the wheel bearings without first thoroughly cleaning all old grease from the bearing. Use of incompatible bearing lubricants could result in premature lubricant breakdown.

1. Raise and support the vehicle safely.
2. Remove the wheels.
3. Remove the brake drum or brake disc.
4. Remove the hub grease cap.
5. Remove the cotter pin retainer, adjusting nut and flatwasher from the rear wheel spindle. Discard the cotter pin.

6. Remove the outer bearing and cone assembly.
7. Remove the rear hub from rear wheel spindle.
8. Using Seal Remover (TOOL-1175-AC) or equivalent, remove and discard the oil seal.
9. Remove the inner bearing cone and roller assembly.
10. Clean the inner and outer bearing cups with solvent. Inspect the bearing cups for scratches, pits, excessive wear and other damage. If the bearing cups are worn or damaged, remove them using a Bearing Cup Puller (T77F-1102A) or equivalent.

To install:

11. Throughly clean old grease from the surrounding surfaces. If a new hub assembly is being installed, remove the protective coating using degreaser.
12. If the inner or outer bearing cups were removed, install replacement cups using Bearing Cup Replacer (T73-1202-A) or equivalent. Seat the cups properly in the hub.

➡If a bearing packer is not available, work as much grease as possible between the rollers and cages. Grease the cone surfaces.

13. Using a bearing packer, pack the bearing cone and roller assemblies with a premium bearing grease.
14. Place inner bearing cone and roller assembly in the inner cup. A light film of grease should be included between the lips of the new grease retainer.
15. Install the retainer with Hub Seal Replacer (T83T-1175-B) or equivalent. Be sure the retainer is properly seated.

➡Keep the hub centered on the spindle to prevent damage to the retainer and spindle threads.

16. Install the hub assembly on the spindle.
17. Install the outer bearing cone and roller assembly on the spindle.
18. Install the flat washer and nut. Tighten the nut to 18–23 ft. lbs. (24–31 Nm) while rotating the hub to set the end-play. Back off the nut and retighten to 18 inch lbs. (2 Nm).
19. Install the new cotter pin.
20. Install hub grease cap.
21. Install brake drum or disc.
22. Install the wheels.
23. Lower the vehicle.

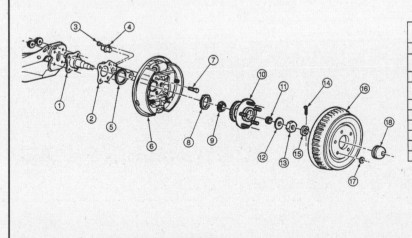

Item	Description
1	Rear Wheel Spindle
2	Anti-Lock Brake Control Module Bracket
3	Bolt
4	Rear Brake Anti-Lock Sensor (RH)
5	Rear Wheel Gasket
6	Drum Brake Assembly (RH)
	Drum Brake Assembly (LH)
7	Bolt
8	Oil Seal
9	Bearing Cone and Roller

Item	Description
10	Rear Hub
11	Rear Wheel Bearing
12	Washer
13	Nut
14	Pin
15	Retainer
16	Brake Drum
17	Nut
18	Hub Grease Cap

Fig. 26 Rear hub assembly with drum brakes

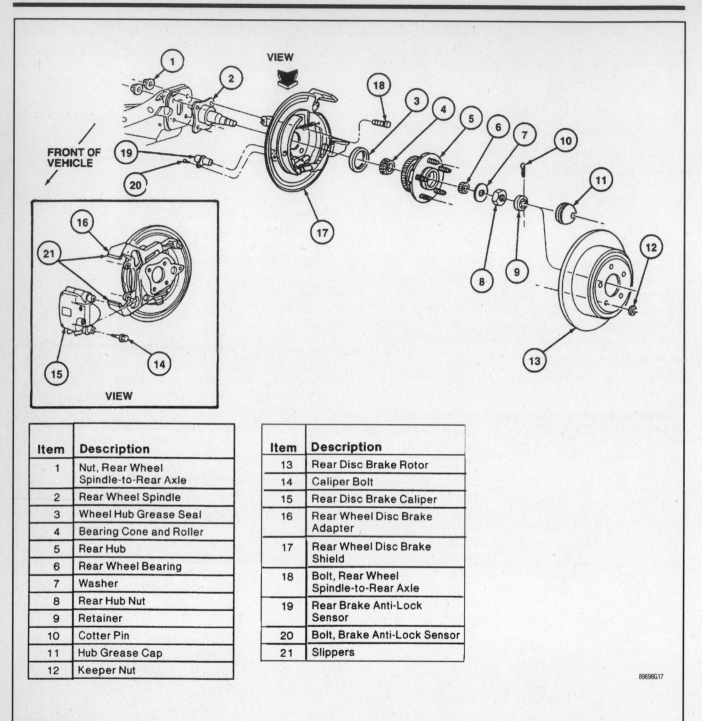

Item	Description
1	Nut, Rear Wheel Spindle-to-Rear Axle
2	Rear Wheel Spindle
3	Wheel Hub Grease Seal
4	Bearing Cone and Roller
5	Rear Hub
6	Rear Wheel Bearing
7	Washer
8	Rear Hub Nut
9	Retainer
10	Cotter Pin
11	Hub Grease Cap
12	Keeper Nut

Item	Description
13	Rear Disc Brake Rotor
14	Caliper Bolt
15	Rear Disc Brake Caliper
16	Rear Wheel Disc Brake Adapter
17	Rear Wheel Disc Brake Shield
18	Bolt, Rear Wheel Spindle-to-Rear Axle
19	Rear Brake Anti-Lock Sensor
20	Bolt, Brake Anti-Lock Sensor
21	Slippers

89698G17

Fig. 27 Rear hub assembly with disc brakes

STEERING

Steering Wheel

REMOVAL & INSTALLATION

❊❊❊ CAUTION

The air bag system must be disarmed prior to service on or around any air bag component. The backup power supply must be disconnected to prevent accidental air bag deployment.

1. Disconnect the positive battery cable from the battery.
2. Wait one minute. This time is required for the back-up power supply in the air bag diagnostic monitor to completely drain. The system is now disarmed.
3. Ensure the steering wheel and the vehicle's front wheels are in the straight ahead position.
4. Disconnect the negative battery cable.
5. Pry out the two steering wheel spoke covers which cover the air bag module screws on the sides of the steering wheel.
6. Remove the air bag module retaining screws on the side of the steering wheel from the driver side air bag module and lift the air bag module away from the steering wheel.
7. Label and disconnect the air bag wire harness, horn control wire and speed control harness.

➡**Ensure the air bag sliding contact assembly wire harnesses do not get caught on the steering wheel when lifting the wheel off of the steering shaft.**

8. Remove the steering wheel retaining bolt and discard.
9. Install Steering Wheel Puller (T67L-3600-A) or equivalent, and remove the steering wheel.
10. Route the contact assembly wire harness through the steering wheel as the steering wheel is lifted off its shaft.

➡**Be sure the air bag sliding contact internal service lock is engaged. The air bag sliding contact should not be turned more than 45 degrees to the right or left to prevent damage.**

11. Rotate air bag sliding contact to the right or left to engage the service lock.

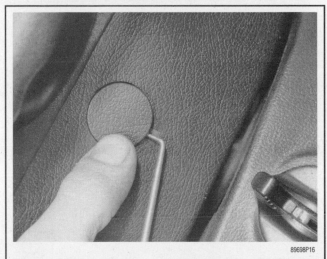

89698P16

Air bag attaching screws are covered by plugs on each side of the steering wheel

89698P18

Carefully slide the air bag from the steering wheel. Take care not to damage the wires

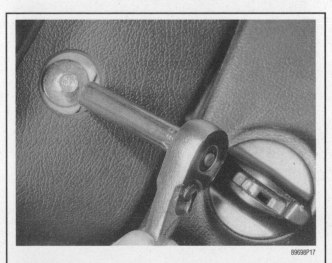

89698P17

Remove the air bag attaching screw using the appropriately sized ratchet

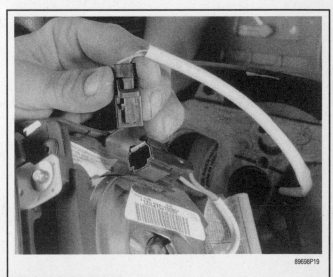

89698P19

Disconnect the air bag . . .

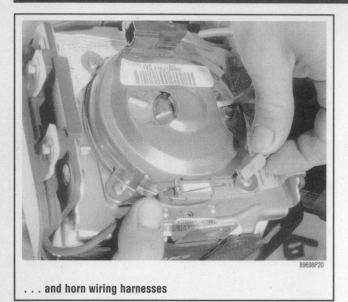

. . . and horn wiring harnesses

Attach a steering wheel puller, then tighten the puller's center bolt to press the wheel from the shaft

The steering wheel nut should not be reused. Discard it after removal

Carefully lift the steering wheel from the steering column. Take care not to snag any wires

It is a good idea to matchmark the steering wheel and steering shaft

If the air bag contact ring becomes uncentered, follow the directions on the ring to recenter it

To install:

12. Ensure that the steering wheel and the vehicle's front wheels are in the straight ahead position.

➡**Be sure wiring does not get caught between steering wheel and air bag sliding contact or air bag monitor will detect a fault.**

13. Route the air bag sliding contact wire harness through the steering wheel opening at the three o'clock position. position steering wheel on steering shaft so the alignment marks are aligned. Be sure air bag contact wire is not pinched.

14. Install a new steering wheel retaining bolt and tight to 25–34 ft. lbs. (34–46 Nm).

15. Connect the air bag wire harness, horn control wire and speed control harness.

16. Ensure all air bag to steering wheel seams are flush and no gaps are visible.

17. Tighten air bag sliding contact retaining screws to 106 inch lbs. (12 Nm). Cover holes in the steering wheel with covers.

18. Connect the negative battery cable and verify the air bag warning indicator is functioning properly.

Multifunction Switch

REMOVAL & INSTALLATION

◆ **See Figure 28**

❋❋ CAUTION

The air bag system must be disarmed prior to service on or around any air bag component. The backup power supply must be disconnected to prevent accidental air bag deployment.

1. Disconnect the negative battery cable.
2. Remove the upper and lower steering column shrouds.
3. Remove the two self-tapping screws retaining the multifunction switch to the steering column tube.
4. Remove the multifunction switch.
5. Label and disconnect the electrical harnesses.

To install:

6. Connect the electrical harnesses.
7. Align the multifunction switch mounting holes with the corresponding holes in the steering column tube casting. Install the two self-tapping screws, making sure to start screws in the previously tapped holes. Tighten the screws to 17–26 ft. lbs. (2–3 Nm).
8. Install the upper and lower steering column shrouds. Tighten the screws to 7–9 inch lbs. (0.7–1.1 Nm).
9. Connect the negative battery cable.

Ignition Switch

REMOVAL & INSTALLATION

◆ **See Figure 29**

1. Disconnect the negative battery cable.
2. Remove the upper steering column shroud.
3. Remove the key release lever, if equipped.
4. Remove the lower steering column shroud.
5. Disconnect the ignition switch electrical harness.
6. Rotate ignition switch lock cylinder to the **RUN** position.
7. Remove the screw retaining the ignition switch.
8. Disconnect the ignition switch from the actuator.

To install:

➡**A new replacement ignition switch assembly will be set in the RUN position when received.**

9. Adjust the ignition switch by sliding the carrier to the ignition switch **RUN** position.

10. Ensure that the ignition switch lock cylinder is in the **RUN** position. The **RUN** position is achieved by rotating the ignition switch lock cylinder approximately 90 degrees from the **LOCK** position.

11. Install the ignition switch into the actuator. It may be necessary to move the ignitions switch slightly back and forth to align the ignition switch mounting holes with the lock cylinder housing threaded holes.

12. Install the retaining screws and tighten to 50–69 inch lbs. (6–8 Nm)

13. Connect the electrical harness.

14. Connect the negative battery cable.

15. Check the ignition switch for proper function including **START** and

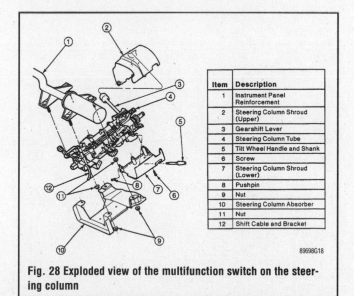

Item	Description
1	Instrument Panel Reinforcement
2	Steering Column Shroud (Upper)
3	Gearshift Lever
4	Steering Column Tube
5	Tilt Wheel Handle and Shank
6	Screw
7	Steering Column Shroud (Lower)
8	Pushpin
9	Nut
10	Steering Column Absorber
11	Nut
12	Shift Cable and Bracket

89698G18

Fig. 28 Exploded view of the multifunction switch on the steering column

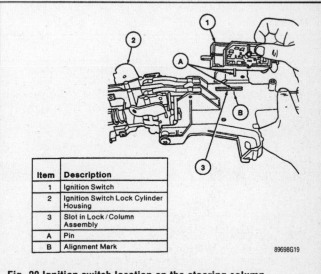

Item	Description
1	Ignition Switch
2	Ignition Switch Lock Cylinder Housing
3	Slot in Lock / Column Assembly
A	Pin
B	Alignment Mark

89698G19

Fig. 29 Ignition switch location on the steering column

ACC positions. Also ensure that the steering column is in the **LOCK** position.

16. Install the key release lever, if equipped.
17. Install the steering column shrouds.

Ignition Lock Cylinder

REMOVAL & INSTALLATION

▶ **See Figure 30**

1. Disconnect the negative battery cable.
2. Turn the ignition switch lock cylinder to the **RUN** position.
3. Place a 0.125 inch (3.17mm) diameter wire pin or small drift punch through the hole in the steering column shroud under the ignition switch lock cylinder.
4. Depress the retaining pin while pulling out on ignitions switch lock cylinder to remove it from the steering column housing.

To install:

5. Install ignition switch lock cylinder by turning it to the **RUN** position and depressing the retaining pin.
6. Insert the ignition switch lock cylinder into the steering column housing.
7. Make sure the ignition switch lock cylinder is fully seated and aligned in the interlocking washer before turning the key to the **OFF** position. This will permit the retaining pin of the ignition switch lock cylinder to extend into the hole of the steering column.
8. Using the key, rotate the ignition switch lock cylinder to make sure of correct mechanical operation in all positions.
9. Connect the negative battery cable.

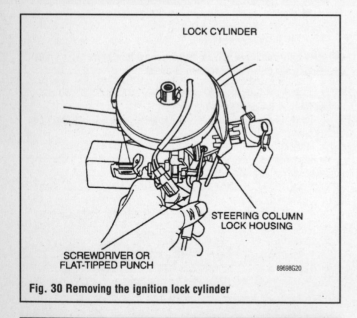

Fig. 30 Removing the ignition lock cylinder

Tie Rod End

REMOVAL & INSTALLATION

1. Raise and support the vehicle safely.
2. Remove the front wheels.
3. Remove the castle nut cotter pin and then remove the castle nut.

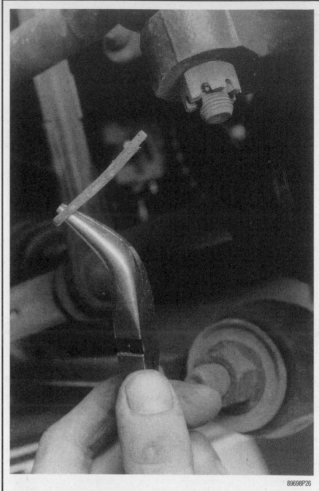

The tie rod end castle nut is retained by a cotter pin

Remove the castle nut from the tie rod end ball joint

Using a tie rod end ball joint separator is highly recommended to ease removal

The ball joint shaft is a taper fit into the steering knuckle bore

4. Disconnect the tie rod ends front the steering knuckle with a Tie Rod End Remover (TOOL-3290-D) or equivalent, as illustrated.
5. Loosen the tie rod locknut.
6. Count the exact number of exposed threads on the tie rod ends and unscrew the tie rod end.

To install:

7. Lubricate the tie rod threads and screw the tie rod ends into place so that the previously noted number of threads are visible with the locknut tightened to 35–46 ft. lbs. (47–63 Nm).
8. Insert the tie rod ball joint stud into the steering knuckle and tighten the castle nut to 35–46 ft. lbs. (48–63 Nm). Install a new cotter pin.
9. Install the front wheels.
10. Lower the vehicle.
11. Check the wheel alignment.

Power Steering Rack

REMOVAL & INSTALLATION

▶ **See Figure 31**

1. Raise and support the vehicle safely.
2. Remove the wheels.
3. Support the vehicle with jackstands under the front jacking pads.
4. Remove the tie rod end cotter pins and castle nuts.
5. Disconnect the tie rod ends from the knuckles.
6. Remove the front stabilizer bar.
7. Position the dash opening weather seal out of the way.
8. Remove the pinch bolt retaining the steering column intermediate shaft coupling.
9. Remove the steering gear retaining nuts/bolts.
10. Remove the rear subframe bolts.

➡**To prevent premature failure, always provide support prior to disconnecting any exhaust system component.**

11. Support the exhaust system flex tube and remove the flex tube-to-dual converter Y-pipe attachment.
12. Lower the vehicle slightly until the rear subframe separates from the body approximately four inches.
13. Remove the heat shield band and fold the heat shield down.
14. Rotate the rack and pinion assembly to clear the bolts from the front subframe and pull toward the driver's side of the vehicle.
15. Place a drain pan under the vehicle and disconnect the power steering lines.
16. Remove the rack and pinion assembly through the driver's side of the vehicle.

To install:

17. Install new Teflon® O-rings on the power steering line fittings.
18. Place the rack and pinion retaining bolts in the gear housing.
19. Install the rack and pinion assembly through the driver's side of the vehicle.
20. Install the power steering lines on the rack and pinion assembly.
21. Position the rack and pinion assembly on the subframe.
22. Install the strap on heat shield.
23. Install the tie rod ends to the front wheel knuckles. Tighten the castle nuts and install the cotter pins.
24. Install the stabilizer bar.
25. Install the rack and pinion assembly retaining bolts and tighten to 85–99 ft. lbs. (115–135 Nm).
26. Raise the vehicle until the subframe contacts the body.

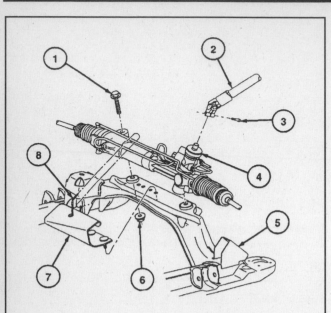

Item	Description
1	Bolt
2	Intermediate Steering Shaft
3	Bolt
4	Power Rack and Pinion Steering Gear
5	Front Sub-Frame
6	Nut
7	Steering Shaft U-Joint Shield
8	Strap

89698G21

Fig. 31 The rack and pinion assembly is mounted to the front subframe of the vehicle

27. Install the rear subframe retaining bolts and tighten to 83–112 ft. lbs. (113–153 Nm).

28. Install the exhaust system flex tube to dual converter Y-pipe.

29. Install the wheels.

30. Using a new pinch bolt, install the steering column intermediate shaft coupling on the rack input shaft. Tighten the pinch bolt to 25–33 ft. lbs. (34–46 Nm).

31. Position the steering column opening weather seal over the steering gear housing.

32. Lower the vehicle.

33. Fill the power steering oil reservoir.

34. Start the vehicle and check for leaks.

35. Check for proper wheel alignment and steering wheel position.

Power Steering Pump

REMOVAL & INSTALLATION

▶ **See Figure 32**

1. Disconnect the negative battery cable.
2. Remove the accessory drive belts.
3. Remove the alternator.
4. Remove the accessory drive belt tensioner.
5. Remove the power steering pump pulley using a Steering Pump Pulley Remover (T69L-10300-B) or equivalent.
6. Position a drain pan under the power steering pump.
7. Disconnect the power steering pump pressure and return hoses.
8. Remove the power steering pump retaining bolts (three in the front, one in the rear) and remove the pump from the support.
9. Remove the pump support from the pump.

To install:

10. Install the pump support on the pump and tighten the fasteners to 30–40 ft. lbs. (40–55 Nm).
11. Install the pump and tighten the retaining bolts to 30–40 ft. lbs. (40–55 Nm).
12. Connect the power steering pump pressure and return hoses.
13. Install the power steering pump pulley using a Steering Pump Pulley Installer (T65P-3A733-C) or equivalent.
14. Install the accessory drive belt tensioner.
15. Install the alternator.
16. Install the accessory drive belts.
17. Connect the negative battery cable.
18. Fill the power steering reservoir with premium power steering fluid to the **COLD FILL** line on the dipstick.

BLEEDING

1. Ensure that the reservoir is full of Premium Power Steering Fluid (E6AZ-19582-AA) or equivalent.
2. Raise and safely support the front wheels of the vehicle.
3. Start the engine.
4. Turn the steering wheel slowly from lock-to-lock to expel air trapped in the system. Continue to turn the steering wheel until no more air bubbles are visible in the reservoir.
5. Confirm that the oil is not milky and that the fluid level is correct.

➡An abrupt rise in the fluid level after stopping the engine is a sign of incomplete bleeding. If this occurs, repeat the bleeding procedure.

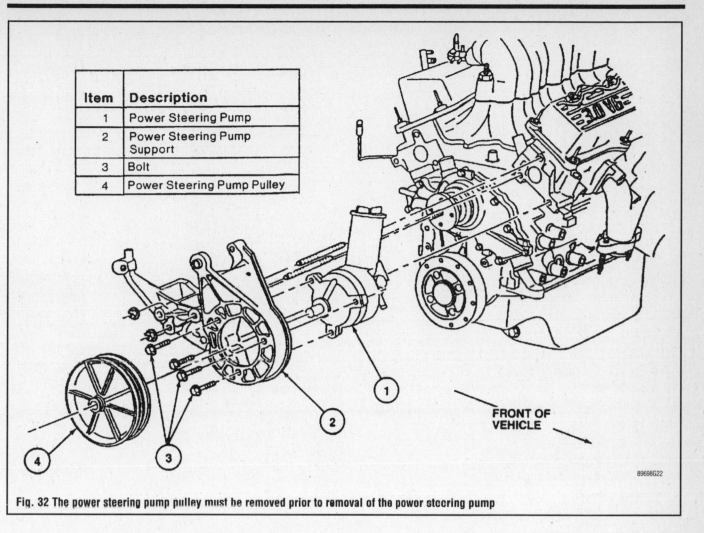

Item	Description
1	Power Steering Pump
2	Power Steering Pump Support
3	Bolt
4	Power Steering Pump Pulley

FRONT OF VEHICLE

89698G22

Fig. 32 The power steering pump pulley must be removed prior to removal of the power steering pump

TORQUE SPECIFICATIONS

Components	Ft. Lbs.	Nm
Front Suspension		
Strut-to-knuckle pinch bolt	85–97 ft. lbs.	115–132 Nm
Lower arm pinch bolt	46–52 ft. lbs.	62–71 Nm
Stabilizer link	66–74 ft. lbs.	90–100 Nm
Tie rod castle nut	66–74 ft. lbs.	90–100 Nm
Strut mounting bracket-to-strut tower	25–30 ft. lbs.	35–40 Nm
Front axle wheel hub	170–202 ft. lbs.	230–275 Nm
Strut shaft locknut	40–46 ft. lbs.	55–63 Nm
Stabilizer bar	40–46 ft. lbs.	55–63 Nm
Front subframe-to-body	85–97 ft. lbs.	115–132 Nm
Front stabilizer bar links	66–74 ft. lbs.	90–100 Nm
Lower arm-to-front subframe	85–97 ft. lbs.	115–132 Nm
Lower arm ball joint	46–52 ft. lbs.	62–71 Nm
Lower arm strut-to-strut	85–97 ft. lbs.	115–142 Nm
Lower arm	46–52 ft. lbs.	62–71 Nm
Strut-to-knuckle pinch bolt	85–97 ft. lbs.	115–132 Nm
Front brake caliper	73–97 ft. lbs.	98–132 Nm
Tie rod end	66–74 ft. lbs.	90–100 Nm
Stabilizer bar link	66–74 ft. lbs.	90–100 Nm
Rear Suspension		
Shock absorber	50–68 ft. lbs.	68–92 Nm
Trailing arm-to-chassis	50–68 ft. lbs.	68–92 Nm
Track bar	50–68 ft. lbs.	68–92 Nm
Rear hub nut		
First step	18–23 ft. lbs.	24–31 Nm
Second step	Back off the nut	
Third step	18 inch lbs.	2 Nm
Steering		
Steering wheel	25–34 ft. lbs.	34–46 Nm
Air bag sliding contact	106 inch lbs.	12 Nm
Multifunction switch	17–26 ft. lbs.	2–3 Nm
Steering column shrouds	7–9 inch lbs.	0.7–1.1 Nm
Ignition Switch	50–69 inch lbs.	6–8 Nm
Tie rod locknut	35–46 ft. lbs.	47–63 Nm
Tie rod ball joint	35–46 ft. lbs.	48–63 Nm
Rack and pinion	85–99 ft. lbs.	115–135 Nm
Steering column shaft coupling	25–33 ft. lbs.	34–46 Nm
Power Steering Pump	30–40 ft. lbs.	40–55 Nm
Wheels		
Lug nuts	85–105 ft. lbs.	115–142 Nm

89698G23

9

BRAKES

BRAKE OPERATING SYSTEM

Basic Operating Principles

Hydraulic systems are used to actuate the brakes of all modern automobiles. The system transports the power required to force the frictional surfaces of the braking system together from the pedal to the individual brake units at each wheel. An hydraulic system is used for two reasons.

First, fluid under pressure can be carried to all parts of an automobile by small pipes and flexible hoses without taking up a significant amount of room or posing routing problems.

Second, a great mechanical advantage can be given to the brake pedal end of the system, and the foot pressure required to actuate the brakes can be reduced by making the surface area of the master cylinder pistons smaller than that of any of the pistons in the wheel cylinders or calipers.

The master cylinder consists of a fluid reservoir along with a double cylinder and piston assembly. Double type master cylinders are designed to separate the front and rear braking systems hydraulically in case of a leak. The master cylinder coverts mechanical motion from the pedal into hydraulic pressure within the lines. This pressure is translated back into mechanical motion at the wheels by either the wheel cylinder (drum brakes) or the caliper (disc brakes).

Steel lines carry the brake fluid to a point on the vehicle's frame near each of the vehicle's wheels. The fluid is then carried to the calipers and wheel cylinders by flexible tubes in order to allow for suspension and steering movements.

In drum brake systems, each wheel cylinder contains two pistons, one at either end, which push outward in opposite directions and force the brake pad into contact with the drum.

In disc brake systems, the cylinders are part of the calipers. At least one cylinder in each caliper is used to force the brake pads against the disc.

All pistons employ some type of seal, usually made of rubber, to minimize fluid leakage. A rubber dust boot seals the outer end of the cylinder against dust and dirt. The boot fits around the outer end of the piston on disc brake calipers, and around the brake actuating rod on wheel cylinders.

The hydraulic system operates as follows: When at rest, the entire system, from the piston(s) in the master cylinder to those in the wheel cylinders or calipers, is full of brake fluid. Upon application of the brake pedal, fluid trapped in front of the master cylinder piston(s) is forced through the lines to the wheel cylinders. Here, it forces the pistons outward, in the case of drum brakes, and inward toward the disc, in the case of disc brakes. The motion of the pistons is opposed by return springs mounted outside the cylinders in drum brakes, and by spring seals, in disc brakes.

Upon release of the brake pedal, a spring located inside the master cylinder immediately returns the master cylinder pistons to the normal position. The pistons contain check valves and the master cylinder has compensating ports drilled in it. These are uncovered as the pistons reach their normal position. The piston check valves allow fluid to flow toward the wheel cylinders or calipers as the pistons withdraw. Then, as the return springs force the brake pads or shoes into the released position, the excess fluid reservoir through the compensating ports. It is during the time the pedal is in the released position that any fluid that has leaked out of the system will be replaced through the compensating ports.

Dual circuit master cylinders employ two pistons, located one behind the other, in the same cylinder. The primary piston is actuated directly by mechanical linkage from the brake pedal through the power booster. The secondary piston is actuated by fluid trapped between the two pistons. If a leak develops in front of the secondary piston, it moves forward until it bottoms against the front of the master cylinder, and the fluid trapped between the pistons will operate the rear brakes. If the rear brakes develop a leak, the primary piston will move forward until direct contact with the secondary piston takes place, and it will force the secondary piston to actuate the front brakes. In either case, the brake pedal moves farther when the brakes are applied, and less braking power is available.

All dual circuit systems use a switch to warn the driver when only half of the brake system is operational. This switch is usually located in a valve body which is mounted on the firewall or the frame below the master cylin-

der. An hydraulic piston receives pressure from both circuits, each circuit's pressure being applied to one end of the piston. When the pressures are in balance, the piston remains stationary. When one circuit has a leak, however, the greater pressure in that circuit during application of the brakes will push the piston to one side, closing the switch and activating the brake warning light.

In disc brake systems, this valve body also contains a metering valve and, in some cases, a proportioning valve. The metering valve keeps pressure from traveling to the disc brakes on the front wheels until the brake pads on the rear wheels have contacted the drums, ensuring that the front brakes will never be used alone. The proportioning valve controls the pressure to the rear brakes to lessen the chance of rear wheel lock-up during very hard braking.

Warning lights may be tested by depressing the brake pedal and holding it while opening one of the wheel cylinder bleeder screws. If this does not cause the light to go on, substitute a new lamp, make continuity checks, and, finally, replace the switch as necessary.

The hydraulic system may be checked for leaks by applying pressure to the pedal gradually and steadily. If the pedal sinks very slowly to the floor, the system has a leak. This is not to be confused with a springy or spongy feel due to the compression of air within the lines. If the system leaks, there will be a gradual change in the position of the pedal with a constant pressure.

Check for leaks along all lines and at wheel cylinders. If no external leaks are apparent, the problem is inside the master cylinder.

DISC BRAKES

Instead of the traditional expanding brakes that press outward against a circular drum, disc brake systems utilize a disc (rotor) with brake pads positioned on either side of it. An easily-seen analogy is the hand brake arrangement on a bicycle. The pads squeeze onto the rim of the bike wheel, slowing its motion. Automobile disc brakes use the identical principle but apply the braking effort to a separate disc instead of the wheel.

The disc (rotor) is a casting, usually equipped with cooling fins between the two braking surfaces. This enables air to circulate between the braking surfaces making them less sensitive to heat buildup and more resistant to fade. Dirt and water do not drastically affect braking action since contaminants are thrown off by the centrifugal action of the rotor or scraped off the by the pads. Also, the equal clamping action of the two brake pads tends to ensure uniform, straight line stops. Disc brakes are inherently self-adjusting. There are three general types of disc brake:

1. A fixed caliper.
2. A floating caliper.
3. A sliding caliper.

The fixed caliper design uses two pistons mounted on either side of the rotor (in each side of the caliper). The caliper is mounted rigidly and does not move.

The sliding and floating designs are quite similar. In fact, these two types are often lumped together. In both designs, the pad on the inside of the rotor is moved into contact with the rotor by hydraulic force. The caliper, which is not held in a fixed position, moves slightly, bringing the outside pad into contact with the rotor. There are various methods of attaching floating calipers. Some pivot at the bottom or top, and some slide on mounting bolts. In any event, the end result is the same.

DRUM BRAKES

Drum brakes employ two brake pads mounted on a stationary backing plate. These shoes are positioned inside a circular drum which rotates with the wheel assembly. The shoes are held in place by springs. This allows them to slide toward the drums (when they are applied) while keeping the linings and drums in alignment. The shoes are actuated by a wheel cylinder which is mounted at the top of the backing plate. When the brakes are applied, hydraulic pressure forces the wheel cylinder's actuating links outward. Since these links bear directly against the top of the brake pads, the tops of the shoes are then forced against the inner side of the drum. This action forces the bottoms of the two shoes to contact the brake drum by rotating the entire assembly slightly (known as servo action). When pressure within the wheel cylinder is relaxed, return springs pull the shoes back away from the drum.

Most modern drum brakes are designed to self-adjust themselves during application when the vehicle is moving in reverse. This motion causes both shoes to rotate very slightly with the drum, rocking an adjusting lever, thereby causing rotation of the adjusting screw. Some drum brake systems are designed to self-adjust during application whenever the brakes are applied. This on-board adjustment system reduces the need for maintenance adjustments and keeps both the brake function and pedal feel satisfactory.

POWER BOOSTERS

Virtually all modern vehicles use a vacuum assisted power brake system to multiply the braking force and reduce pedal effort. Since vacuum is always available when the engine is operating, the system is simple and efficient. A vacuum diaphragm is located on the front of the master cylinder and assists the driver in applying the brakes, reducing both the effort and travel he must put into moving the brake pedal.

The vacuum diaphragm housing is normally connected to the intake manifold by a vacuum hose. A check valve is placed at the point where the hose enters the diaphragm housing, so that during periods of low manifold vacuum brakes assist will not be lost.

Depressing the brake pedal closes off the vacuum source and allows atmospheric pressure to enter on one side of the diaphragm. This causes the master cylinder pistons to move and apply the brakes. When the brake pedal is released, vacuum is applied to both sides of the diaphragm and springs return the diaphragm and master cylinder pistons to the released position.

If the vacuum supply fails, the brake pedal rod will contact the end of the master cylinder actuator rod and the system will apply the brakes without any power assistance. The driver will notice that much higher pedal effort is needed to stop the car and that the pedal feels harder than usual.

Vacuum Leak Test

1. Operate the engine at idle without touching the brake pedal for at least one minute.
2. Turn off the engine and wait one minute.
3. Test for the presence of assist vacuum by depressing the brake pedal and releasing it several times. If vacuum is present in the system, light application will produce less and less pedal travel. If there is no vacuum, air is leaking into the system.

System Operation Test

1. With the engine **OFF**, pump the brake pedal until the supply vacuum is entirely gone.
2. Put light, steady pressure on the brake pedal.
3. Start the engine and let it idle. If the system is operating correctly, the brake pedal should fall toward the floor if the constant pressure is maintained.

Power brake systems may be tested for hydraulic leaks just as ordinary systems are tested.

✳✳ WARNING

Clean, high quality brake fluid is essential to the safe and proper operation of the brake system. You should always buy the highest quality brake fluid that is available. If the brake fluid becomes contaminated, drain and flush the system, then refill the master cylinder with new fluid. Never reuse any brake fluid. Any brake fluid that is removed from the system should be discarded.

Brake Light Switch

REMOVAL & INSTALLATION

▶ **See Figure 1**

➡ **The locking tab of the switch must be lifted before the connector can be removed.**

1. Disconnect the wire harness from the stop light switch.
2. Remove the hairpin clip, then slide the stop light switch, pushrod, nylon washer and brake master cylinder pushrod bushing away from the brake pedal.
3. Since the switch side plate nearest the brake pedal is slotted, it is not necessary to remove the vacuum booster input rod and brake master cylinder pushrod bushing from the brake pedal pin.
4. Remove the brake master cylinder pushrod spacer and then the stop light switch by sliding the switch up or down.

To install:

5. Position the stop light switch so the U-shaped side is nearest the break pedal and directly over/under the pin. Then slide the switch up/down trapping the vacuum booster input rod and brake master cylinder pushrod bushing between the switch side plates.
6. Push the stop light switch and pushrod assembly firmly toward the brake pedal arm.

➡ **Do not substitute other types of pin clips. Use only factory supplied hairpin clips.**

7. Assemble the outside white plastic washer to the pin and install the hairpin clip to hold the entire assembly.

➡ **The stop light switch wire harness must have sufficient length to travel with the stop light switch during full stroke of the brake pedal. If the wire length is too short, reroute or repair the harness as required.**

8. Connect the wire harness to the stop light switch.
9. Check the stop light switch for proper operation. The brake lights should illuminate with less than 6 lbs. (27 N) of force applied to the brake pedal pad.

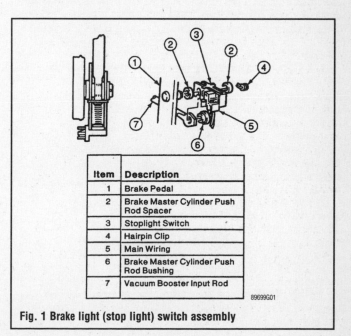

Item	Description
1	Brake Pedal
2	Brake Master Cylinder Push Rod Spacer
3	Stoplight Switch
4	Hairpin Clip
5	Main Wiring
6	Brake Master Cylinder Push Rod Bushing
7	Vacuum Booster Input Rod

89699G01

Fig. 1 Brake light (stop light) switch assembly

Master Cylinder

REMOVAL & INSTALLATION

▶ **See Figure 2**

1. Disconnect the negative battery cable.
2. Disconnect the brake warning lamp indicator wire from the plastic reservoir low fluid level warning switch socket.
3. With the engine **OFF**, push the brake pedal down to expel vacuum from the power brake booster.
4. Disconnect and plug the brake tubes.
5. Remove the wraparound clip and attaching nut from the master cylinder mounting stud.
6. Remove the power brake booster-to-master cylinder nuts.
7. Remove the brake master cylinder.

To install:

8. Before installing the brake master cylinder, check the distance from the outer end of the power brake booster pushrod to the front face of the power brake booster as follows:
    a. With the engine idling, gauge and adjust the pushrod length.
    b. A force of approximately 5 lbs. (22 N) supplied to the pushrod with the gauge will make sure that the pushrod is seated with the power brake booster.
9. Position the brake master cylinder over the power brake booster pushrod and onto the two studs on the brake booster. Tighten attaching nuts to 18–26 ft. lbs. (25–35 Nm).
10. Loosely connect the brake master cylinder tubes.
11. Position the wraparound clip on the mounting stud. Install and tighten the retaining nut.
12. Tighten the master cylinder attaching nuts to 11–15 ft. lbs. (15–20 Nm).
13. Connect the fluid level indicator switch.

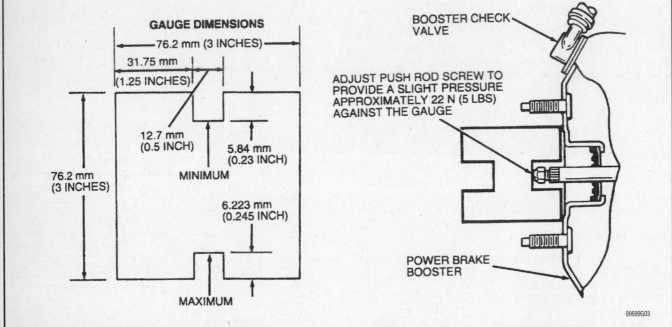

Fig. 2 Checking and adjusting the power brake booster pushrod length is a necessary part of master cylinder replacement

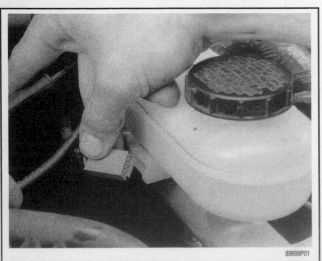

The low fluid level warning switch socket is located on the side of the reservoir

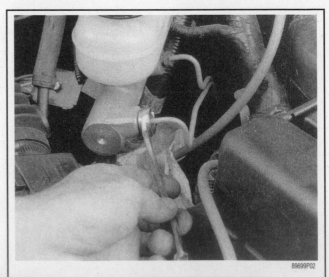

Always use line wrenches when servicing brake tubes

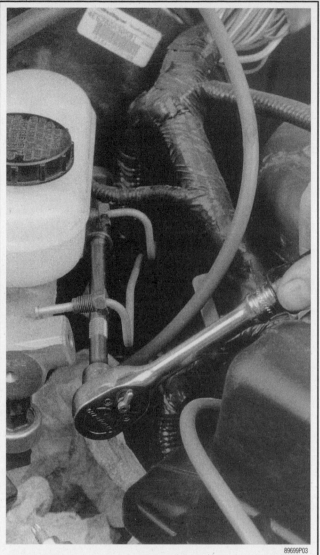

A long socket extension is needed to reach the master cylinder attaching nuts

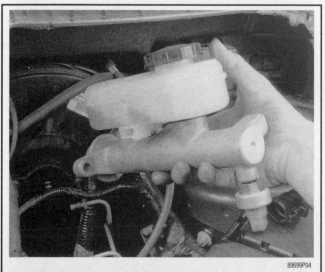

Carefully lift the master cylinder from the brake booster

14. Bleed the brake system.
15. Connect the negative battery cable.

Power Brake Booster

REMOVAL & INSTALLATION

♦ **See Figure 3**

1. Disconnect the negative battery cable.
2. Remove the cowl top vent panel.
3. Label and disconnect the manifold vacuum hose from the brake booster.
4. Remove the master cylinder-to-booster attaching nuts. Slide the master cylinder forward and provide support to prevent damage the brake lines.
5. From inside the vehicle, remove the stop light switch from the brake pedal.
6. Remove the four booster-to-dash nuts.
7. Remove the brake booster from the vehicle.
To install:
8. Position the brake booster in the vehicle.
9. Install the four booster-to-dash nuts and tighten to 15–20 ft. lbs. (21–29 Nm).
10. Install the stop light switch on the brake pedal.
11. Install the master cylinder and tighten the attaching nuts to 18–26 ft. lbs. (25–35 Nm).
12. Connect the manifold vacuum hose to the brake booster.
13. Install the cowl top vent panel.
14. Connect the negative battery cable.

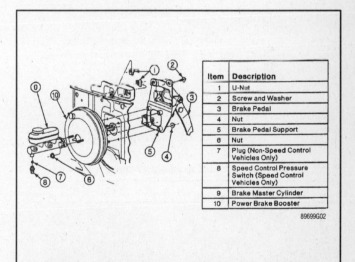

Item	Description
1	U-Nut
2	Screw and Washer
3	Brake Pedal
4	Nut
5	Brake Pedal Support
6	Nut
7	Plug (Non-Speed Control Vehicles Only)
8	Speed Control Pressure Switch (Speed Control Vehicles Only)
9	Brake Master Cylinder
10	Power Brake Booster

Fig. 3 Exploded view of the brake master cylinder and power brake booster attachment

Proportioning Valve

REMOVAL & INSTALLATION

1. Label, disconnect and cap the four brake lines attached to the brake pressure control valve.
2. Remove the brake pressure control valve attaching bolt.
3. Remove the brake pressure control valve from the vehicle.
To install:
4. Install the brake pressure control valve on the vehicle and tighten the attaching bolt to 91–122 inch lbs. (11–13 Nm).

5. Connect the four brake lines to the brake pressure control valve.
6. Tighten brake line fittings to 11–14 ft. lbs. (15–20 Nm).
7. Fill the master cylinder reservoir with fresh brake fluid.
8. Bleed the brake system.

Brake Hoses and Lines

Metal lines and rubber brake hoses should be checked frequently for leaks and external damage. Metal lines are particularly prone to crushing and kinking under the vehicle. Any such deformation can restrict the proper flow of fluid and therefore impair braking at the wheels. Rubber hoses should be checked for cracking or scraping; such damage can create a weak spot in the hose and it could fail under pressure.

Any time the lines are removed or disconnected, extreme cleanliness must be observed. Clean all joints and connections before disassembly (use a stiff bristle brush and clean brake fluid); be sure to plug the lines and ports as soon as they are opened. New lines and hoses should be flushed clean with brake fluid before installation to remove any contamination.

REMOVAL & INSTALLATION

1. Raise and safely support the vehicle on jackstands.
2. Remove any wheel and tire assemblies necessary for access to the particular line you are removing.
3. Thoroughly clean the surrounding area at the joints to be disconnected.
4. Place a suitable catch pan under the joint to be disconnected.
5. Using two wrenches (one to hold the joint and one to turn the fitting), disconnect the hose or line to be replaced.
6. Disconnect the other end of the line or hose, moving the drain pan if necessary. Always use a back-up wrench to avoid damaging the fitting.
7. Disconnect any retaining clips or brackets holding the line and remove the line from the vehicle.

➡If the brake system is to remain open for more time than it takes to swap lines, tape or plug each remaining clip and port to keep contaminants out and fluid in.

To install:
8. Install the new line or hose, starting with the end farthest from the master cylinder. Connect the other end, then confirm that both fittings are correctly threaded and turn smoothly using finger pressure. Make sure the new line will not rub against any other part. Brake lines must be at least 1/2 in. (13mm) from the steering column and other moving parts. Any protective shielding or insulators must be reinstalled in the original location.

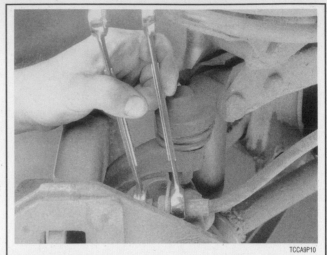

TCCA9P10

Use two wrenches to loosen the fitting. If available, use flare nut type wrenches

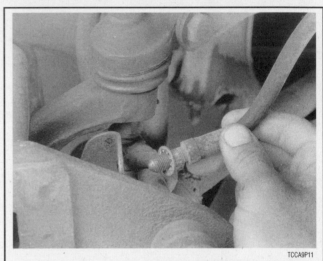

TCCA9P11

Any gaskets/crush washers should be replaced with new ones during installation

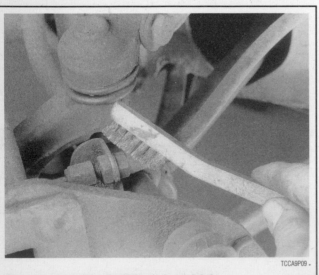

TCCA9P09

Use a brush to clean the fittings of any debris

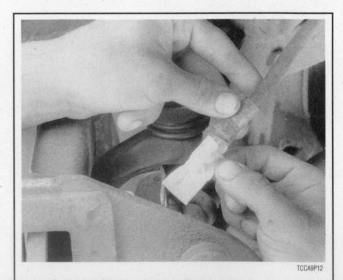

TCCA9P12

Tape or plug the line to prevent contamination

Bleeding the rear drum brakes using the method described in the text

Make sure the hose is NOT kinked or touching any part of the frame or suspension after installation. These conditions may cause the hose to fail prematurely.

9. Using two wrenches as before, tighten each fitting.
10. Install any retaining clips or brackets on the lines.
11. If removed, install the wheel and tire assemblies, then carefully lower the vehicle to the ground.
12. Refill the brake master cylinder reservoir with clean, fresh brake fluid, meeting DOT 3 specifications. Properly bleed the brake system.

Bleeding Brake System

When any part of the hydraulic system has been disconnected for repair or replacement, air may get into the lines and cause spongy pedal action (because air can be compressed and brake fluid cannot). To correct this condition, it is necessary to bleed the hydraulic system to be sure all air is purged.

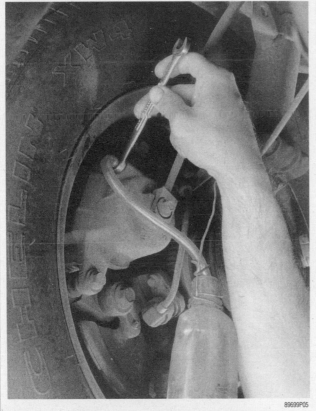

Bleeding the front disc brake caliper using the method described in the text

When bleeding the brake system, bleed one brake cylinder at a time, beginning at the cylinder with the longest hydraulic line (farthest from the master cylinder). ALWAYS Keep the master cylinder reservoir filled with brake fluid during the bleeding operation. Never use brake fluid that has been drained from the hydraulic system, no matter how clean it is.

The primary and secondary hydraulic brake systems are separate and are bled independently. During the bleeding operation, do not allow the reservoir to run dry. Keep the master cylinder reservoir filled with brake fluid.

1. Clean all dirt from around the master cylinder fill cap, remove the cap and fill the master cylinder with brake fluid until the level is within $FR1/4 in. (6mm) of the top edge of the reservoir.
2. Clean the bleeder screws at all 4 wheels. The bleeder screws are located on the back of the brake backing plate (drum brakes) and on the top of the brake calipers (disc brakes).
3. Attach a length of rubber hose over the bleeder screw and place the other end of the hose in a glass jar, submerged in brake fluid.
4. Open the bleeder screw $FR1/2–$FR3/4 turn. Have an assistant slowly depress the brake pedal.
5. Close the bleeder screw and tell your assistant to allow the brake pedal to return slowly. Continue this process to purge all air from the system.
6. When bubbles cease to appear at the end of the bleeder hose, close the bleeder screw and remove the hose. Tighten the bleeder screw to 61–87 inch lbs.(7–9 Nm).
7. Check the master cylinder fluid level and add fluid accordingly. Do this after bleeding each wheel.
8. Repeat the bleeding operation at the remaining 3 wheels, ending with the one closet to the master cylinder.
9. Fill the master cylinder reservoir to the proper level.

DISC BRAKES

Older brake pads or shoes may contain asbestos, which has been determined to be a cancer causing agent. Never clean the brake surfaces with compressed air! Avoid inhaling any dust from any brake surface! When cleaning brake surfaces, use a commercially available brake cleaning fluid.

Brake Pads

REMOVAL & INSTALLATION

Front

1. Remove the brake master cylinder reservoir cap. Siphon and recycle approximately half the fluid from the reservoir.
2. Raise and support the vehicle safely.

3. Remove the wheels.
4. Remove the disc brake caliper guide pins.

➡**It is not necessary to disconnect the hydraulic lines.**

5. Lift the disc brake caliper from the anchor plate.
6. Position the disc brake caliper out of the way by suspending with a wire.
7. Remove the brake pads from the anchor plate.

To install:

8. Inspect the rotor surfaces for scoring or buildup of lining material. Minor imperfections do not require machining. Hand sand the glaze from the rotor using 150 grit aluminum oxide sand paper.
9. Use a C-clamp and wooden block to seat the disc brake caliper hydraulic piston in its bore, as illustrated. This must be done to provide clearance for the disc brake caliper to fit over the front rotor during installation.
10. Remove all built-up rust from the inside of the brake caliper pad contact area.
11. Install the brake pads, with the clip on insulators, into the front brake caliper anchor plate.
12. Install the disc brake caliper onto the anchor plate.
13. Install the disc brake caliper guide pins and tighten to 23–38 ft. lbs. (31–38 Nm).

➡**Failure to tighten the lug nuts to the proper torque in a star pattern may result in damage to the brake rotor.**

14. Install the wheel and tighten lug nuts to 83–112 ft. lbs. (113–153 Nm).
15. Lower the vehicle.
16. Pump the brake pedal to seat the brake pads.

Rear

1. Remove the brake master cylinder reservoir cap. Siphon and recycle approximately half the fluid from the reservoir.
2. Raise and support the vehicle safely.
3. Remove the wheels.

➡**Do not press against the brake pad spring clip.**

4. Position the C-clamp frame on the inboard side of the rear disc brake caliper housing. Position the clamp screw on the outboard brake pad backing plate.
5. Tighten the C-clamp sufficiently to press the rear disc brake caliper piston to the bottom of the caliper bore.
6. Remove the caliper bolts.

➡**Do not allow the caliper to hang by the rear brake hose.**

7. Work the caliper off the rear disc brake rotor and brake adapter.
8. Remove the slippers from the anchor plate abutments by gently prying them of the rails. Discard the old slippers.
9. Remove the brake pads.

To install:

➡**New slippers must be used on the rail abutments for proper operation of the caliper assembly.**

10. Inspect the anchor plate rail abutments for wear or damage. Replace as necessary.
11. Install new anti-wear slippers on the rail abutments by snapping them into place.
12. Position the brake pads on the caliper and rotate it down until the locating lugs and retainer spring are fully seated.
13. Install the rear disc brake caliper on the rotor. Make sure the notches on the upper ends of the brake pad are seated over the upper ledge of the adapter and the brake pad lower tabs are positioned on the lower ledge of the adapter.

14. Lubricate the caliper bolts with Disc Brake Caliper Slide Grease (D7AZ-19590-A) or equivalent. Install and tighten to 11–14 ft. lbs. (15–20 Nm).

➡**Failure to tighten the lug nuts to the proper torque in a star pattern may result in damage to the brake rotor.**

15. Install the wheel and tighten the lug nuts to 83–112 ft. lbs. (113–153 Nm).
16. Lower the vehicle.
17. Pump the brake pedal to seat the brake pads.

INSPECTION

◆ **See Figure 4**

Inspect the brake pads for wear using a ruler or Vernier caliper. Compare measurements to the brake specifications chart. If the lining is thinner than specification or there is evidence of the lining being contaminated by brake fluid or oil, replace all brake pad assemblies (a complete axle set).

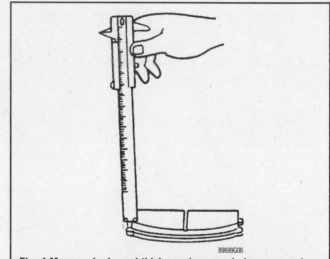

89699G06

Fig. 4 Measure brake pad thickness in several places around the pad

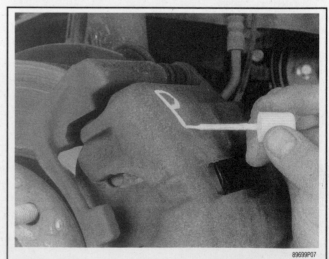

89699P07

Matchmark the caliper prior to removal. "P" is for passenger side

Calipers are secured to the anchor plates by two caliper bolts

89699P08

The brake pads ride in the caliper anchor. Make sure the ledges in the anchor are clean

89699P10

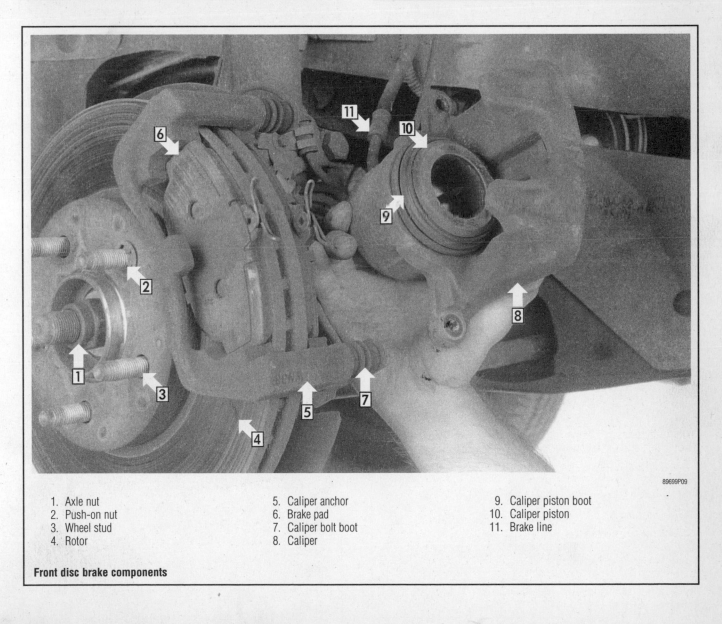

89699P09

1. Axle nut
2. Push-on nut
3. Wheel stud
4. Rotor
5. Caliper anchor
6. Brake pad
7. Caliper bolt boot
8. Caliper
9. Caliper piston boot
10. Caliper piston
11. Brake line

Front disc brake components

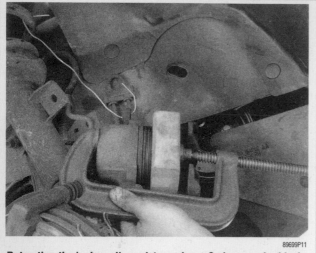

Retracting the brake caliper piston using a C-clamp and a block of wood

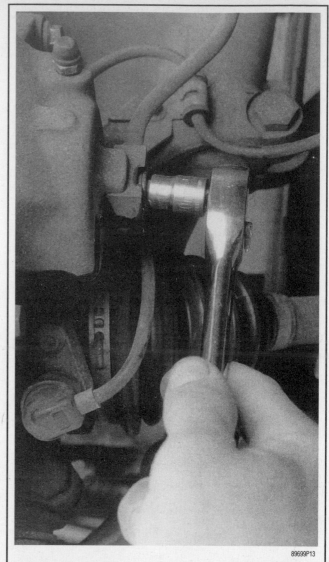

The brake line is attached to the caliper with a hollow "banjo bolt"

When service requires removal of the caliper, always suspend it using a piece of wire

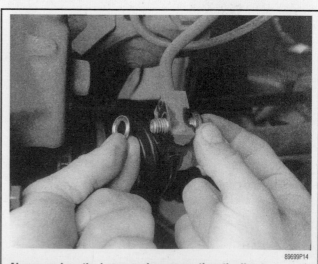

Always replace the brass washers every time the line is removed

Brake Caliper

REMOVAL & INSTALLATION

◆ **See Figures 5 and 6**

Front

1. Remove the brake master cylinder reservoir cap. Siphon and recycle approximately half the fluid from the reservoir.
2. Raise and support the vehicle safely.

3. Remove the wheels.
4. Matchmark the brake caliper to ensure it is installed on the proper side of the vehicle during installation.
5. Place a drain pan under the caliper to catch dripping brake fluid.
6. Remove the hollow retaining bolt that connects the hose to the caliper. Discard the copper washers.
7. Remove the brake hose and cap to prevent the entry of moisture or dirt.
8. Remove the disc brake caliper guide pins.
9. Lift the disc brake caliper from the anchor plate.

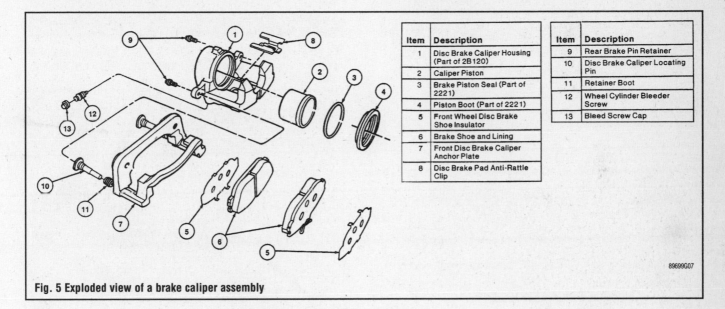

Item	Description
1	Disc Brake Caliper Housing (Part of 2B120)
2	Caliper Piston
3	Brake Piston Seal (Part of 2221)
4	Piston Boot (Part of 2221)
5	Front Wheel Disc Brake Shoe Insulator
6	Brake Shoe and Lining
7	Front Disc Brake Caliper Anchor Plate
8	Disc Brake Pad Anti-Rattle Clip

Item	Description
9	Rear Brake Pin Retainer
10	Disc Brake Caliper Locating Pin
11	Retainer Boot
12	Wheel Cylinder Bleeder Screw
13	Bleed Screw Cap

89699G07

Fig. 5 Exploded view of a brake caliper assembly

Item	Description
1	Nut, Rear Wheel Spindle-to-Rear Axle
2	Rear Wheel Spindle
3	Wheel Hub Grease Seal
4	Bearing Cone and Roller, Rear
5	Rear Hub
6	Rear Wheel Bearing
7	Washer
8	Rear Hub Nut
9	Retainer
10	Cotter Pin
11	Hub Grease Cap
12	Keeper Nut

Item	Description
13	Rear Disc Brake Rotor
14	Caliper Bolt
15	Rear Disc Brake Caliper
16	Rear Wheel Disc Brake Adapter
17	Rear Wheel Disc Brake Shield (Part of 2C220)
18	Bolt, Rear Wheel Spindle-to-Rear Axle
19	Rear Brake Anti-Lock Sensor
20	Bolt, Rear Brake Anti-Lock Sensor
21	Slippers

89699G08

Fig. 6 Exploded view of a rear disc brake assembly

To install:

10. Use a C-clamp and wooden block to seat the disc brake caliper hydraulic piston in its bore, as illustrated.

11. Clean the brake rotor and caliper of all contaminates using commercially available brake cleaning fluid. If brake pads have become contaminated replace them with a new set.

12. Install the disc brake caliper onto the anchor plate.

13. Install the disc brake caliper guide pin and tighten to 23–38 ft. lbs. (31–38 Nm).

14. Connect the brake hose, using two new copper washers and tighten hollow bolt to 35–46 ft. lbs. (47–63 Nm).

15. Fill the master cylinder fluid reservoir with clean, fresh brake fluid meeting or exceeding DOT 3 specifications.

16. Bleed the brake system.

➡Failure to tighten the lug nuts to the proper torque in a star pattern may result in damage to the brake rotor.

17. Install the wheel and tighten lug nuts to 83–112 ft. lbs. (113–153 Nm).

18. Lower the vehicle.

Rear

1. Remove the brake master cylinder reservoir cap. Siphon and recycle approximately half the fluid from the reservoir.

2. Raise and support the vehicle safely.

3. Remove the wheels.

4. Matchmark the brake caliper to ensure that it will be installed on the proper side of the vehicle.

5. Place a drain pan under the caliper to catch dripping brake fluid.

6. Remove the hollow retaining bolt that connects the hose to the caliper. Discard the copper washers.

7. Remove the brake hose and cap to prevent the entry of moisture or dirt.

➡Do not press against the brake pad spring clip.

8. Position the C-clamp frame on the inboard side of the rear disc brake caliper housing. Position the clamp screw on the outboard brake pad backing plate.

9. Tighten the C-clamp sufficiently to press the rear disc brake caliper piston to the bottom of the caliper bore.

10. Remove the caliper bolts.

➡Do not allow the caliper to hang by the rear brake hose.

11. Work the caliper off the rear disc brake rotor and brake adapter.

To install:

➡To prevent interference with rear disc brake caliper operation, verify correct caliper bolt length. The shank portion including the threads of the caliper bolt should not be more than 2.613–2.661 in. (66.4–67.6mm).

12. Install the rear disc brake caliper on the rotor. Make sure the notches on the upper ends of the brake pad are seated over the upper ledge of the adapter and the brake pad lower tabs are positioned on the lower ledge of the adapter.

13. Lubricate the caliper bolts with Disc Brake Caliper Slide Grease (D7AZ-19590-A) or equivalent. Install and tighten to 11–14 ft. lbs. (15–20 Nm).

➡Failure to tighten the lug nuts to the proper torque in a star pattern may result in damage to the brake rotor.

14. Connect the brake hose, using two new copper washers and tighten the hollow bolt to 35–46 ft. lbs. (47–63 Nm).

15. Fill the master cylinder fluid reservoir with clean, fresh brake fluid meeting or exceeding DOT 3 specifications.

16. Bleed the brake system.

17. Install the wheel and tighten lug nuts to 83–112 ft. lbs. (113–153 Nm).

18. Lower the vehicle.

OVERHAUL

◗ **See Figures 7 thru 14**

➡Some vehicles may be equipped dual piston calipers. The procedure to overhaul the caliper is essentially the same with the exception of multiple pistons, O-rings and dust boots.

1. Remove the caliper from the vehicle and place on a clean workbench.

✳✳ CAUTION

NEVER place your fingers in front of the pistons in an attempt to catch or protect the pistons when applying compressed air. This could result in personal injury!

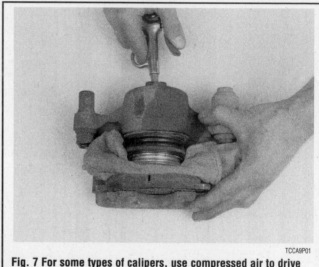

Fig. 7 For some types of calipers, use compressed air to drive out the piston, but be sure to keep your fingers clear

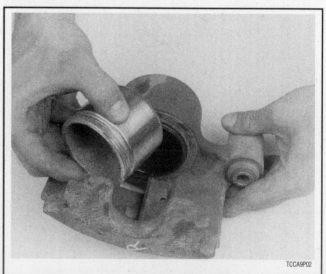

Fig. 8 Withdraw the piston from the caliper bore

TCCA9P03

Fig. 9 On some vehicles, you must remove the anti-rattle clip

TCCSA9P04

Fig. 10 Use a prytool to carefully pry around the edge of the boot . . .

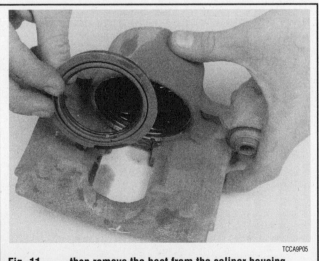

TCCA9P05

Fig. 11 . . . then remove the boot from the caliper housing, taking care not to score or damage the bore

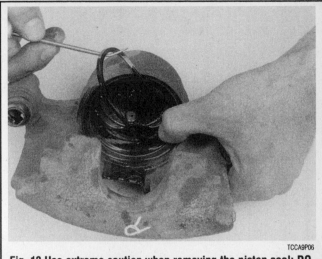

TCCA9P06

Fig. 12 Use extreme caution when removing the piston seal; DO NOT scratch the caliper bore

TCCA9P07

Fig. 13 Use the proper size driving tool and a mallet to properly seal the boots in the caliper housing

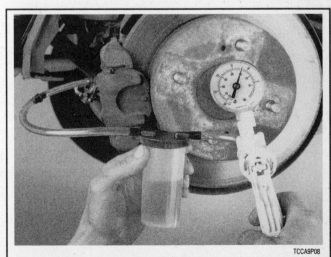

TCCA9P08

Fig. 14 There are tools, such as this Mighty-Vac, available to assist in proper brake system bleeding

➡Depending upon the vehicle, there are two different ways to remove the piston from the caliper. Refer to the brake pad replacement procedure to make sure you have the correct procedure for your vehicle.

2. The first method is as follows:

    a. Stuff a shop towel or a block of wood into the caliper to catch the piston.

    b. Remove the caliper piston using compressed air applied into the caliper inlet hole. Inspect the piston for scoring, nicks, corrosion and/or worn or damaged chrome plating. The piston must be replaced if any of these conditions are found.

3. For the second method, you must rotate the piston to retract it from the caliper.

4. If equipped, remove the anti-rattle clip.

5. Use a prytool to remove the caliper boot, being careful not to scratch the housing bore.

6. Remove the piston seals from the groove in the caliper bore.

7. Carefully loosen the brake bleeder valve cap and valve from the caliper housing.

8. Inspect the caliper bores, pistons and mounting threads for scoring or excessive wear.

9. Use crocus cloth to polish out light corrosion from the piston and bore.

10. Clean all parts with denatured alcohol and dry with compressed air.

To assemble:

11. Lubricate and install the bleeder valve and cap.

12. Install the new seals into the caliper bore grooves, making sure they are not twisted.

13. Lubricate the piston bore.

14. Install the pistons and boots into the bores of the calipers and push to the bottom of the bores.

15. Use a suitable driving tool to seat the boots in the housing.

16. Install the caliper in the vehicle.

17. Install the wheel and tire assembly, then carefully lower the vehicle.

18. Properly bleed the brake system.

Brake Disc (Rotor)

REMOVAL & INSTALLATION

Front

1. Raise and support the vehicle safely.

2. Remove the wheels.

3. Remove the brake caliper and suspend it out of the way using a piece of wire.

➡If excessive force must be used during front disc brake rotor removal, the front disc brake rotor should be checked for lateral run-out prior to installation.

4. Remove the front disc brake rotor by pulling it evenly from the hub.

5. If additional force is required to remove the rotor from the hub, apply a penetrating oil to the front and rear rotor-to-hub mating surfaces. Strike the rotor using a plastic hammer between the studs. If this does not work, remove the rotor using a 2–3 jaw puller.

Rotors are retained using push-on nuts. Use wire cutters to remove the nuts

The rotor is removed by simply sliding it off the studs

To install:

➡Failure to clean rust and foreign material from the rotor and hub mounting faces when installing a rotor will result in high rotor lateral run-out.

6. If a new rotor is being installed, remove the protective coating with brake cleaning fluid. If this coating is not removed, it will contaminate the brake pads.

7. Apply a small amount of silicone grease to the pilot diameter of the front disc brake rotor.

8. Install the brake rotor on the front wheel hub.

9. Install the brake caliper.

➡**Failure to tighten the lug nuts to the proper torque in a star pattern may result in damage to the brake rotor.**

   10. Install the wheel and tighten lug nuts to 83–112 ft. lbs. (113–153 Nm).

   11. Lower the vehicle.

   12. Pump the brake pedal to seat the brake pads.

Rear

   1. Raise and support the vehicle safely.

   2. Remove the wheels

   3. Remove the brake caliper and suspend out of the way using a piece of wire.

   4. Remove the press-on nuts from the rotor, if equipped.

   5. Using a suitable tool, contract the parking brake pad by turning the parking brake adjuster clockwise for the driver's side and counter clockwise for the passenger's side.

   6. Remove the rear disc brake rotor.

To install:

   7. Position the rotor on the hub and install the press on nuts to secure it into place.

   8. Install the brake caliper.

➡**Failure to tighten the lug nuts to the proper torque in a star pattern may result in damage to the brake rotor.**

   9. Install the wheel and tighten lug nuts to 83–112 ft. lbs. (113–153 Nm).

   10. Lower the vehicle.

   11. Pump the brake pedal to seat the brake pads.

INSPECTION

◆ **See Figures 15 and 16**

Using a brake rotor micrometer or Vernier caliper measure the rotor thickness in several places around the rotor

Mount a magnetic base dial indicator to the strut member and zero the indicator stylus on the face of the rotor. Rotate the rotor 360 degrees by hand and record the run-out.

Compare measurements to the brake specifications chart. If the thickness and run-out do not meet specifications, replace the rotor.

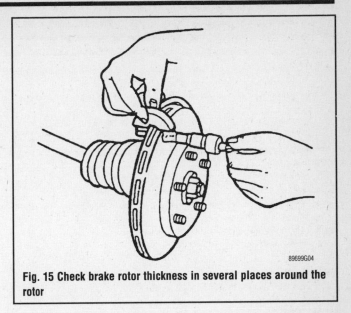

Fig. 15 Check brake rotor thickness in several places around the rotor

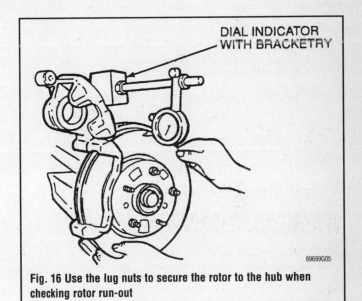

Fig. 16 Use the lug nuts to secure the rotor to the hub when checking rotor run-out

DRUM BRAKES

REAR DRUM BRAKE COMPONENTS

1. Brake shoe hold-down spring
2. Brake shoe (rear)
3. Adjusting lever
4. Adjusting spring

5. Adjuster assembly
6. Retracting spring
7. Brake shoe (front)

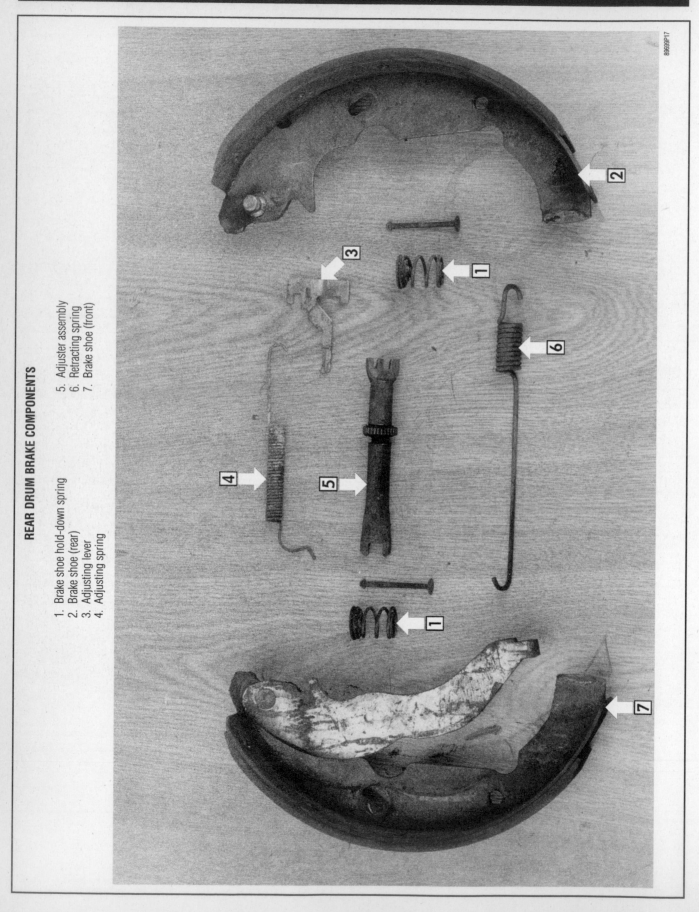

brake surfaces with compressed air! Avoid inhaling any dust from any brake surface! When cleaning brake surfaces, use a commercially available brake cleaning fluid.

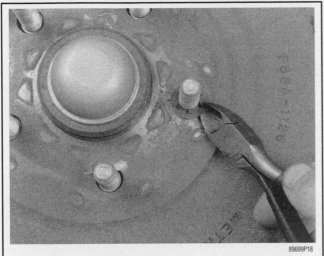

89699P18

Brake drums are held in place with push-on nuts. Cut the nut using wire cutters to remove

89699P19

The brake shoe adjuster may need to be loosened in order to remove the drum

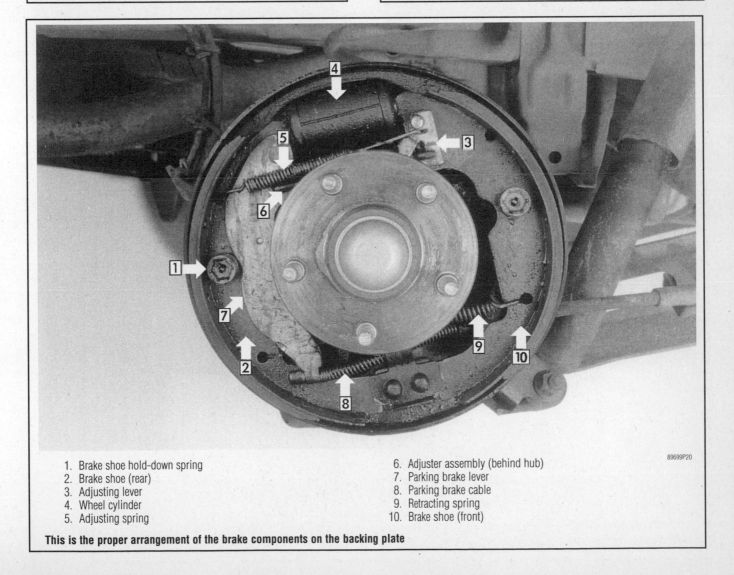

89699P20

1. Brake shoe hold-down spring
2. Brake shoe (rear)
3. Adjusting lever
4. Wheel cylinder
5. Adjusting spring
6. Adjuster assembly (behind hub)
7. Parking brake lever
8. Parking brake cable
9. Retracting spring
10. Brake shoe (front)

This is the proper arrangement of the brake components on the backing plate

Always start your brake service by spraying the components with brake cleaning fluid

This tool eases brake shoe hold-down spring removal. Depress and twist the retainer . . .

Special tools, like these brake spring pliers, are invaluable when performing brake service

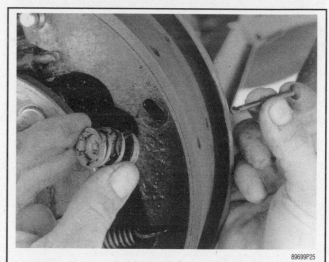

. . . then separate the hold-down spring and retainer from the pin at the rear of the backing plate

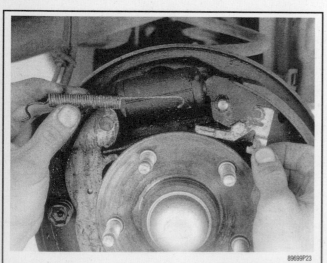

The brake adjusting lever and spring are located at the top of the brake assembly

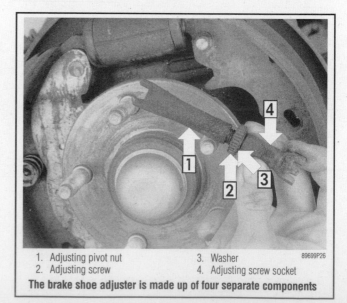

1. Adjusting pivot nut
2. Adjusting screw
3. Washer
4. Adjusting screw socket

The brake shoe adjuster is made up of four separate components

The brake shoe retracting spring attaches between the bottom of the brake shoes

89699P27

The parking brake lever connects the secondary shoe with the parking brake cable

89699P28

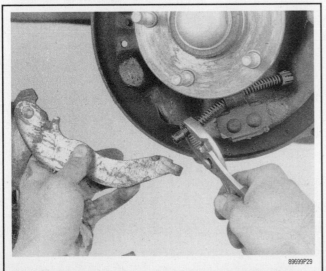

Use pliers to separate the parking brake lever from the cable

89699P29

Brake Drums

REMOVAL & INSTALLATION

1. Raise and support the vehicle safely.
2. Remove the wheel.
3. Remove the push-on nuts, if equipped.

➡It may be necessary to back off the brake shoe adjustment in order to remove the brake drum. This is because the drum might be grooved or worn from being in service for an extended period of time.

4. If the brake drum will not slide off the hub easily, remove the brake adjusting hole cover from the backing plate. Insert a screwdriver and a Brake Adjustment Tool (D81L-1103-C) or equivalent.
5. Disengage the brake shoe adjusting lever and loosen the brake adjuster screw.
6. Remove the brake drum.

To install:

7. If the inside of the drum has a coating of rust or a ridge, clean it with a piece of coarse sandpaper before installation.
8. Before installing a new brake drum, be sure to remove any protective coating with brake cleaner or a suitable fast-drying cleaner.
9. Install the brake drum.
10. Adjust the brakes.
11. Install the wheel.
12. Lower the vehicle.

INSPECTION

Check that there are no cracks or chips in the braking surface. Excessive bluing indicates overheating and a replacement drum is needed. The drum can be machined to remove minor damage and to establish a rounded braking surface on a warped drum. Never exceed the maximum oversize of the drum when machining the braking surface. The maximum inside diameter is stamped on the rim of the drum.

Brake Shoes

REMOVAL & INSTALLATION

▶ **See Figure 17**

1. Raise and support the vehicle safely.
2. Remove the brake drum.

➡It is a good idea to only disassemble and assemble one side at a time, leaving the other side intact as a reference.

3. Raise and support the vehicle safely.
4. Remove the brake drum.
5. Disconnect the parking brake rear cable and conduit.
6. Remove the brake shoe hold-down springs and brake shoe hold-down pins.
7. Remove the brake shoe adjusting screw spring.
8. Remove the brake shoe adjusting lever and adjuster screw.
9. Remove the brake shoe retracting spring.
10. Remove the brake shoes from the backing plate.
11. Remove and discard the parking brake lever clip. Remove the washer.
12. Remove the parking brake lever from the rear brake shoe.

To install:

13. Thoroughly clean the backing plate with brake cleaning solvent and dry completely.
14. Use silicone grease to lubricate the brake backing plate-to-brake shoe contact areas.

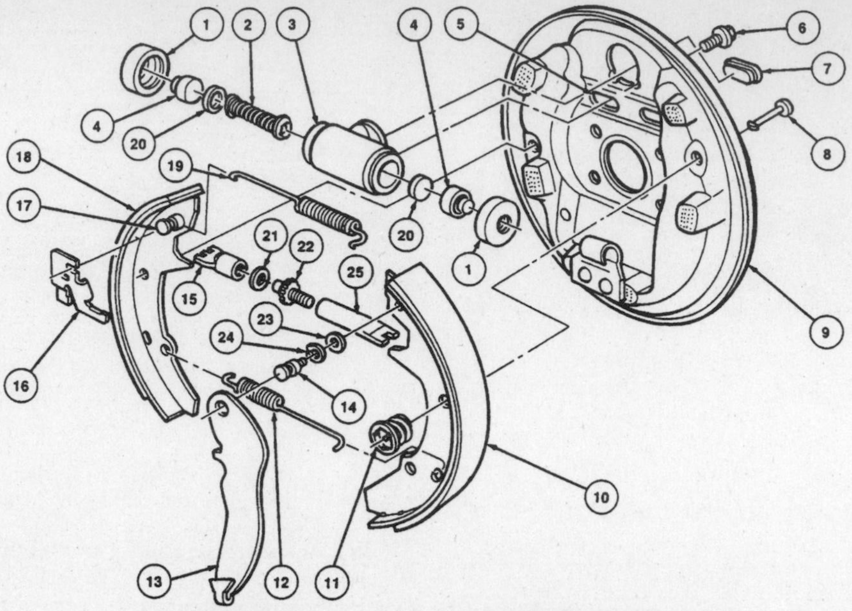

Item	Description	Item	Description
1	Boot (Part of 2261)	14	Parking Brake Lever Pin (Inner)
2	Spring Expander (Part of 2261)	15	Brake Shoe Adjusting Screw Socket
3	Rear Wheel Cylinder	16	Brake Shoe Adjusting Lever
4	Piston and Insert (Part of 2261)	17	Parking Brake Lever Pin (Outer)
5	Shoe and Adjustment Access Hole	18	Leading Shoe and Lining (Part of 2200)
6	Wheel Cylinder Retaining Screw (2 Req'd)	19	Brake Shoe Adjusting Screw Spring
7	Brake Adjusting Hole Cover	20	Cup (Part of 2261)
8	Brake Shoe Hold-Down Spring Pin	21	Washer
9	Brake Backing Plate	22	Adjusting Screw (Part of 2261)
10	Trailing Shoe and Lining (Part of 2200)	23	Washer
11	Brake Shoe Hold-Down Spring	24	Parking Brake Lever Pin Retainer
12	Brake Shoe Retracting Spring	25	Adjusting Pivot Nut (Part of 2048)
13	Parking Brake Lever		

89699G09

Fig. 17 Exploded view of the rear drum brake components

15. Apply a light coating of premium grease to the threaded areas of the adjuster. Turn the adjuster in and out to spread the lubricant. Turn the adjuster all the way down on the screw and loosen one-half turn.

16. Install the parking brake lever to the rear (secondary) brake shoe with a new clip.

17. Position the brake shoes on the backing plate and install the brake shoe hold-down springs.

18. Attach the parking brake rear cable and conduit to the parking brake lever.

19. Attach the brake shoe retracting spring.

➡The socket end of the brake adjuster screw is stamped with "R" or "L" to indicate that it is to be installed either on the right (passenger's side) or left (driver's side) of the vehicle. The adjuster nuts can be distinguished by the number of grooves machined around the body of the nut. Two grooves indicate a right-hand adjuster nut and one groove indicates a left-hand adjuster nut. Another way to identify brake adjuster assemblies is to check thread pitch. The right side adjuster assembly has right-hand threads and the left side has left-hand threads. If installed correctly, the brake adjuster assembly will increase in length when the brake shoe adjusting lever is operated.

20. Install brake adjuster screw in the slots on the brake shoes. The wider slot on the socket end must fit in the slot on the front (primary) brake shoe.

21. Install the brake shoe adjusting lever on the lever pin.

22. Install the brake adjusting screw in the slot on the secondary brake shoe and in the slot on the brake shoe lever. The brake shoe adjusting lever should contact the brake adjuster screw.

23. Adjust the brake shoes.

24. Install the drums.

ADJUSTMENTS

The drum brakes are self-adjusting and require a manual adjustment only after the brake shoes have been replaced, or when the length of the adjusting screw has been changed while performing some other service operation.

Drum Installed

1. Raise and support the vehicle safely.
2. Remove the rubber plug from the adjusting slot on the backing plate.
3. Insert a Brake Adjustment Tool (D81L-1103-C) or equivalent into the

slot and engage the lowest possible tooth on the starwheel. Move the end of the brake spoon downward to move the starwheel upward and expand the adjusting screw. Repeat this operation until the brakes lock the wheels.

4. Insert a small screwdriver or piece of firm wire (coat hanger wire) into the adjusting slot and push the automatic adjusting lever out and free of the starwheel on the adjusting screw and hold it there.

5. Engage the topmost tooth possible on the starwheel with the brake adjusting spoon. Move the end of the adjusting spoon upward to move the adjusting screw starwheel downward and contract the adjusting screw. Back off the adjusting screw starwheel until the wheel spins freely with a minimum of drag. Keep track of the number of turns that the starwheel is backed off, or the number of strokes taken with the brake adjusting spoon.

6. Repeat this operation for the other side. When backing off the brakes on the other side, the starwheel adjuster must be backed off the same number of turns to prevent side-to-side brake pull.

7. When the brakes are adjusted, make several stops while backing the vehicle to equalize the brakes on both of the wheels.

8. Lower the vehicle.

Drum Removed

▶ See Figure 18

1. Remove the brake drum.
2. Make sure that the shoe to contact pad areas are clean and properly lubricated.
3. Using a Brake Adjustment Gauge (D81L-1103-A) or equivalent, check the inside diameter of the drum.
4. Measure across the diameter of the assembled brake shoes, at their widest point.
5. Turn the adjusting screw so that the diameter of the shoes is 0.030 in. (0.76mm) less than the brake drum inner diameter.
6. Install the drum.

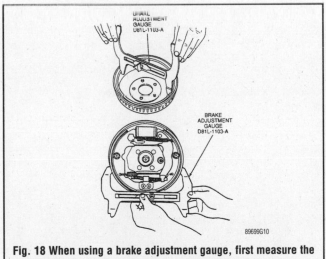

Fig. 18 When using a brake adjustment gauge, first measure the inside diameter of the drum (top) and then adjust the brake shoes to the proper outside diameter (bottom)

INSPECTION

▶ See Figure 19

Inspect the brake shoes for wear using a ruler or Vernier caliper. Compare measurements to the brake specifications chart. If the lining is thinner than specification or there is evidence of the lining being contaminated by

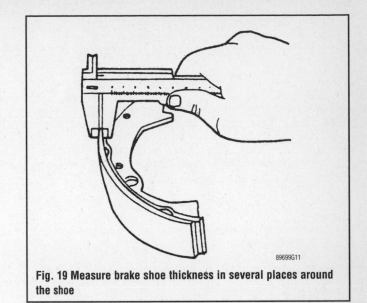

Fig. 19 Measure brake shoe thickness in several places around the shoe

brake fluid or oil, replace all brake pad assemblies (a complete axle set).

Wheel Cylinders

REMOVAL & INSTALLATION

1. Remove the rear brakes.
2. Disconnect and plug the wheel cylinder brake hose.
3. Remove the wheel cylinder attaching bolts.
4. Remove the wheel cylinder.

To install:

5. Position the wheel cylinder and tighten the attaching bolts to 9–13 ft. lbs. (12–18 Nm).
6. Connect the wheel cylinder brake hose and tighten the fitting to 11–14 ft. lbs. (15–20 Nm).
7. Install the rear brakes.
8. Bleed the brake system.

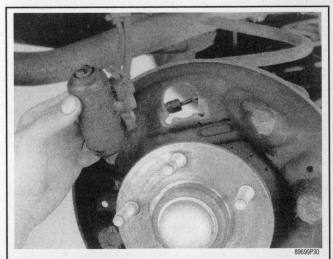

The wheel cylinder is attached to the backing plate with two small bolts

OVERHAUL

▶ **See Figures 20 thru 29**

Wheel cylinder overhaul kits may be available, but often at little or no savings over a reconditioned wheel cylinder. It often makes sense with these components to substitute a new or reconditioned part instead of attempting an overhaul.

If no replacement is available, or you would prefer to overhaul your wheel cylinders, the following procedure may be used. When rebuilding and installing wheel cylinders, avoid getting any contaminants into the system. Always use clean, new, high quality brake fluid. If dirty or improper fluid has been used, it will be necessary to drain the entire system, flush the system with proper brake fluid, replace all rubber components, then refill and bleed the system.

1. Remove the wheel cylinder from the vehicle and place on a clean workbench.

2. Remove and discard the old rubber boots, then withdraw the pistons. Piston cylinders are equipped with seals and a spring assembly, all located behind the pistons in the cylinder bore.

3. Remove the remaining inner components, seals and spring assem-

Fig. 22 Remove the pistons, cup seals and spring from the cylinder

Fig. 20 Remove the outer boots from the wheel cylinder

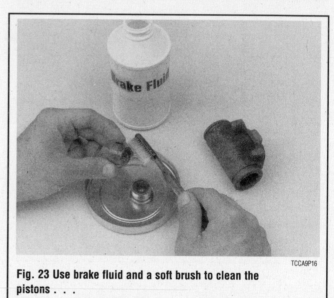
Fig. 23 Use brake fluid and a soft brush to clean the pistons . . .

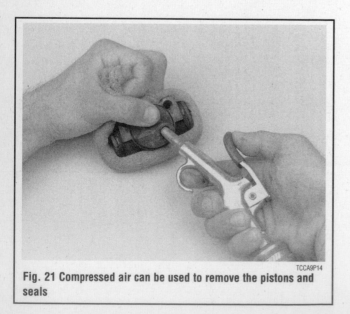
Fig. 21 Compressed air can be used to remove the pistons and seals

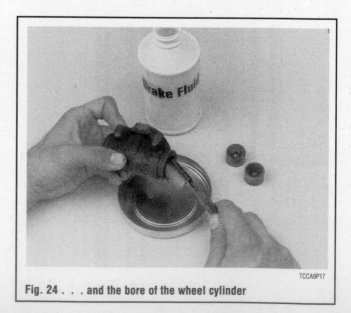
Fig. 24 . . . and the bore of the wheel cylinder

Fig. 25 Once cleaned and inspected, the wheel cylinder is ready for assembly

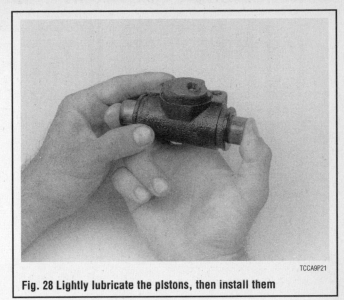

Fig. 28 Lightly lubricate the pistons, then install them

Fig. 26 Lubricate the cup seals with brake fluid

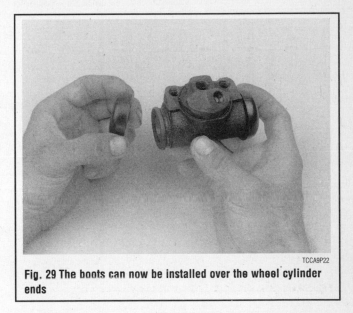

Fig. 29 The boots can now be installed over the wheel cylinder ends

Fig. 27 Install the spring, then the cup seals in the bore

bly. Compressed air may be useful in removing these components. If no compressed air is available, be VERY careful not to score the wheel cylinder bore when removing parts from it. Discard all components for which replacements were supplied in the rebuild kit.

4. Wash the cylinder and metal parts in denatured alcohol or clean brake fluid.

❊❊ WARNING

Never use a mineral-based solvent such as gasoline, kerosene or paint thinner for cleaning purposes. These solvents will swell rubber components and quickly deteriorate them.

5. Allow the parts to air dry or use compressed air. Do not use rags for cleaning, since lint will remain in the cylinder bore.

6. Inspect the piston and replace it if it shows scratches.

7. Lubricate the cylinder bore and seals using clean brake fluid.

8. Position the spring assembly.

9. Install the inner seals, then the pistons.

10. Insert the new boots into the counterbores by hand. Do not lubricate the boots.

11. Install the wheel cylinder.

PARKING BRAKE

Cable

REMOVAL & INSTALLATION

♦ **See Figures 30 and 31**

1. Place the parking brake control in the released position.
2. Remove the parking brake lever boot.
3. Using a screwdriver, push down on the tension arm until it is fully depressed. Lock down the tension arm with the spring lock-out pin or a screwdriver.
4. Raise and support the vehicle safely.
5. Disconnect the parking brake rear cable and conduits from the parking brake equalizer.
6. Lower the vehicle.
7. Working inside the vehicle, lift the base of the parking brake lever boot by pushing the base toward the rear of the vehicle and lifting the back of the parking brake lever boot.

8. Remove the front parking brake cable and conduit from the control lever.
9. Lift the carpet slightly and snap the front cable grommet out of the floor.
10. Remove the front cable by pulling the equalizer through the hole in the floor.

To install:

11. Route the front parking brake cable and conduit around the guide and insert the cable in the hole in the tensioner arm. Insert the front cable and equalizer through the hole in the floor and snap the grommet into place.
12. Raise and support the vehicle safely.
13. Conenct the equalizer to the rear cables.
14. Lower the vehicle.
15. Remove the lock pin from the parking brake control to apply cable tension.
16. Positio the parking brake lever boot over the parking brake control assembly. Snap the base over the spring clip on the control assembly.
17. Apply and release the parking brake control lever several times. Make sure the parking brakes are applied and not dragging when released.

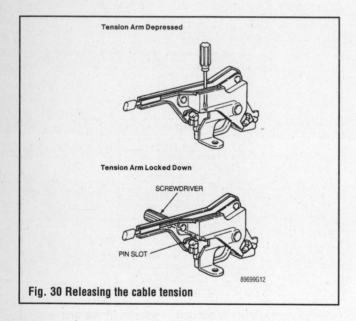

Fig. 30 Releasing the cable tension

Using a wrench to compress the clip, remove the parking brake cable from the backing plate

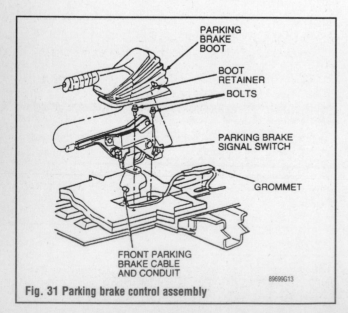

Fig. 31 Parking brake control assembly

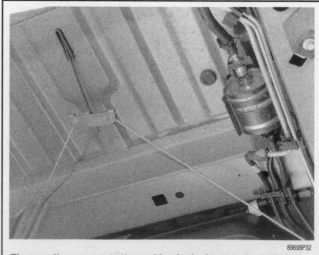

The equalizer connects the parking brake lever to the individual parking brake cables

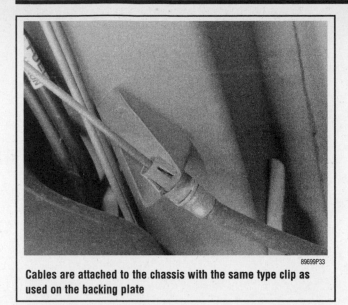

89699P33

Cables are attached to the chassis with the same type clip as used on the backing plate

ADJUSTMENT

The parking brake cable tension is automatically adjusted by a mechanism in the parking brake control assembly.

Brake Shoes

▶ See Figure 32

Separate parking brake shoes are only used on vehicles with rear disc brakes.

REMOVAL & INSTALLATION

1. Place the parking brake control in the released position.
2. Remove the parking brake lever boot.
3. Using a screwdriver, push down on the tension arm until it is fully depressed. Lock down the tension arm with the spring lock-out pin or a screwdriver.
4. Raise and support the vehicle safely.
5. Remove the rear disc brake caliper and rotor.
6. Disconnect the parking brake rear cable and conduit from the parking brake lever.
7. Remove the brake shoe adjusting spring.
8. Remove the upper return spring.
9. Remove the brake shoe hold-down springs and pins.
10. Remove the parking brake adjuster.
11. Pull the parking brake lever out of the rear wheel disc brake adapter.
12. Installation is the reverse of removal.
13. Adjust the parking brake shoes and check for proper operation.

ADJUSTMENT

Adjustment is necessary only on vehicles equipped with rear disc brakes.

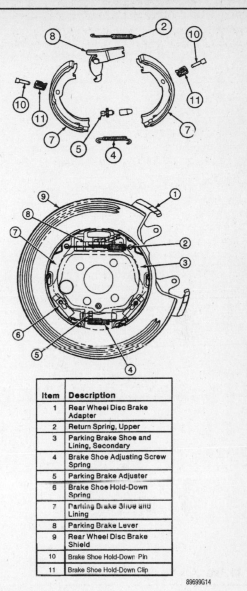

Item	Description
1	Rear Wheel Disc Brake Adapter
2	Return Spring, Upper
3	Parking Brake Shoe and Lining, Secondary
4	Brake Shoe Adjusting Screw Spring
5	Parking Brake Adjuster
6	Brake Shoe Hold-Down Spring
7	Parking Brake Shoe and Lining
8	Parking Brake Lever
9	Rear Wheel Disc Brake Shield
10	Brake Shoe Hold-Down Pin
11	Brake Shoe Hold-Down Clip

89699G14

Fig. 32 Parking brake components—models with rear disc brakes

1. Raise and support the vehicle safely.
2. Remove the rubber plug from the parking brake adjuster access hole.
3. Insert a suitable tool into the adjuster access hole and expand the parking brake adjuster while turning the wheel.
4. Expand the parking brake shoe until resistance is felt while turning the wheel assembly.
5. Back off the parking brake adjuster one turn.
6. Lower the vehicle.
7. Test the parking brake for proper operation.
8. Pull up on the parking brake control and listen to the clicks from the pawl in the control assembly. Resistance should be felt after five clicks from the pawl.

ANTI-LOCK BRAKE SYSTEM

General Information

▶ **See Figure 33**

The 4-Wheel Anti-lock Brake System (ABS) is an electronically operated, all wheel brake control system. Major components include the master cylinder, vacuum power brake booster, ABS Control Module, Hydraulic Control Unit (HCU) and various control sensors and switches.

The brake system is a two channel design. The primary circuit (rear) feeds the RH front and LH rear brakes. The secondary circuit (front) feeds the LH front and RH rear brakes.

The system is designed to retard wheel lockup during periods of high wheel slip when braking. Retarding wheel lockup is accomplished by modulating fluid pressure to the wheel brake units.

TESTING

The ABS module performs system tests and self-tests during startup and normal operation. The valve, sensor and fluid level circuits are monitored for proper operation. If a fault is found, the ABS will be deactivated and the amber ANTI LOCK light will be lit until the ignition is turned OFF. When the light is lit, the Diagnostic Trouble Code (DTC) may be obtained. Under normal operation, the light will stay on for about 2 seconds while the ignition switch is in the ON position and will go out shortly after.

The Diagnostic Trouble Codes (DTC) are an alphanumeric code and a scan tool, such as Rotunda NGS Tester 007-00500 or its equivalent, is required to retrieve the codes. Refer to the manufacturer's instructions for operating the tool and retrieving the codes.

Trouble Codes

A scan tool, such as Rotunda NGS Tester 007-00500 or its equivalent, is required to retrieve the codes. Refer to the manufacturer's instructions for operating the tool and retrieving the codes.

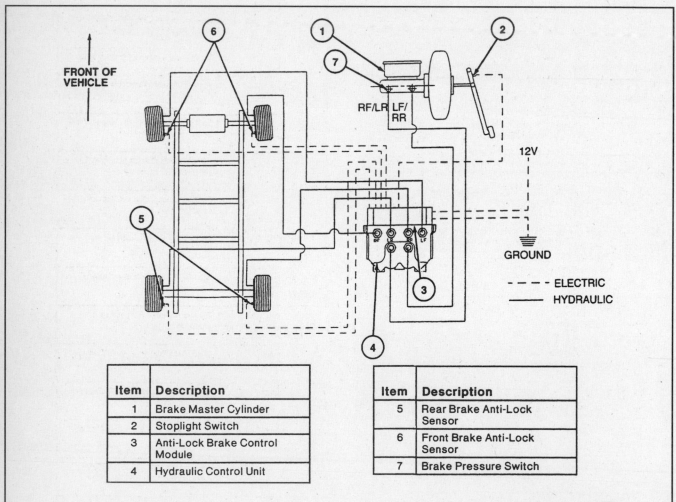

Item	Description
1	Brake Master Cylinder
2	Stoplight Switch
3	Anti-Lock Brake Control Module
4	Hydraulic Control Unit

Item	Description
5	Rear Brake Anti-Lock Sensor
6	Front Brake Anti-Lock Sensor
7	Brake Pressure Switch

Fig. 33 Anti-lock brake system schematic

89699G17

ANTI-LOCK BRAKE SYSTEM (ABS) DIAGNOSTIC
TROUBLE CODE (DTC) INDEX

DTC	Source
B1342	ECU is defective
C1095	ABS Hydraulic Pump Motor Circuit Failure
C1096	ABS Hydraulic Pump Motor Circuit Open
C1103	Hydraulic Brake Pressure Switch Circuit Failure
C1104	TRAC Active Lamp—Circuit Short to Battery
C1105	TRAC OFF Lamp—Circuit Short to Battery
C1113	ABS Power Relay Coil Short Circuit to Battery
C1115	ABS Power Relay Output Short Circuit to Battery
C1140	Lamp Brake Warning Output Circuit Short to Ground
C1141	Wheel Speed Sensor LF front brake anti-lock sensor indicator Tooth Missing Fault
C1142	Wheel Speed Sensor RF front brake anti-lock sensor indicator Tooth Missing Fault
C1143	Wheel Speed Sensor LR front brake anti-lock sensor indicator Tooth Missing Fault
C1144	Wheel Speed Sensor RR front brake anti-lock sensor indicator Tooth Missing Fault
C1145	Speed Wheel Sensor RF Input Circuit Failure
C1148	Speed Wheel Sensor RF Coherency Fault
C1155	Speed Wheel Sensor LF Input Circuit Failure
C1158	Speed Wheel Sensor LF Coherency Fault
C1165	Speed Wheel Sensor RR Input Circuit Failure
C1168	Speed Wheel Sensor RR Coherency Fault
C1175	Speed Wheel Sensor LR Input Circuit Failure
C1178	Speed Wheel Sensor LR Coherency Fault
C1184	ABS System is Not Operational
C1185	ABS Power Relay Output Circuit Failure

ANTI-LOCK BRAKE SYSTEM (ABS) DIAGNOSTIC
TROUBLE CODE (DTC) INDEX (Cont'd)

DTC	Source
C1194	ABS Dump Valve Coil LF Circuit Failure
C1196	ABS Dump Valve Coil LF Circuit Short to Battery
C1198	ABS Isolation Valve Coil LF Circuit Failure
C1200	ABS Isolation Valve Coil LF Circuit Short to Battery
C1210	ABS Dump Valve Coil RF Circuit Failure
C1212	ABS Dump Valve Coil RF Circuit Short to Battery
C1214	ABS Isolation Valve Coil RF Circuit Failure
C1216	ABS Isolation Valve Coil RF Circuit Short to Battery
C1220	Lamp ABS Warning Output Circuit Short to Battery
C1222	Speed Wheel Mismatch
C1225	Lamp Brake Warning Output Circuit Short to Battery
C1226	Lamp Brake Warning Output Circuit Short to Ground
C1233	Speed Wheel LF Input Signal Missing
C1234	Speed Wheel RF Input Signal Missing
C1235	Speed Wheel RR Input Signal Missing
C1236	Speed Wheel LR Input Signal Missing
C1242	ABS Dump Valve Coil LR Circuit Failure
C1244	ABS Dump Valve Coil LR Circuit Short to Battery
C1246	ABS Dump Valve Coil RR Circuit Failure
C1248	ABS Dump Valve Coil RR Circuit Short to Battery
C1250	ABS Isolation Valve Coil LR Circuit Failure
C1252	ABS Isolation Valve Coil LR Circuit Short to Battery

89699G15

ANTI-LOCK BRAKE SYSTEM (ABS) DIAGNOSTIC TROUBLE CODE (DTC) INDEX (Cont'd)

DTC	Source
C 1254	ABS Isolation Valve Coil RR Circuit Failure
C 1256	ABS Isolation Valve Coil RR Circuit Short to Battery
C 1265	Lamp Warning Relay Circuit Short to Ground
C 1446	Brake Switch Circuit Failure

89699G16

ABS Control Module

TESTING

There is no practical way to test the ABS control module in the field. If a preliminary check of all power and ground circuits is negative and all components connected to the control module are functioning properly, the ABS control module may be faulty.

REMOVAL & INSTALLATION

1. Disconnect the negative and positive battery cables.
2. Remove the battery and battery tray.
3. Drain and recycle the engine coolant.
4. Disconnect the upper radiator hose and remove the radiator fan shroud.
5. Label and disconnect the ABS wiring harnesses.
6. Remove the four module retaining screws.
7. Pull the module straight forward to clear the coils away from the valve solenoids.
8. Lift the module out of the engine compartment.
To install:
9. Position the module so the coils line up directly with the solenoid valves and push together.
10. Install the four module retaining screws and tighten to 35—44 inch lbs.(4—5 Nm).
11. Connect the ABS wiring harnesses.
12. Install the radiator fan shroud.
13. Connect the upper radiator hose.
14. Fill the engine with coolant.
15. Install the battery tray and battery.
16. Connect the positive, then the negative battery cable.

Hydraulic Control Unit

TESTING

1. Visually inspect the brake lines to each wheel for damage and replace as necessary.
2. Remove the rubber caps from the hydraulic control unit lower pressure accumulators located on the bottom center of the unit.

3. Insert a clean steel paper clip into each low pressure chamber.
4. Have an assistant press hard on the brake pedal.
5. If the paper clip does not move, the hydraulic control unit is faulty.

REMOVAL & INSTALLATION

1. Disconnect the harness from the anti-lock brake control module.
2. Disconnect the 2-pin power and ground harness from the anti-lock brake control module.
3. Disconnect and cap the tubes from the inlet and outlet ports on the hydraulic control unit.

➡**The hydraulic control unit is removed from below the vehicle.**

4. Remove the hydraulic control unit retaining bolts and lower the assembly down and out of the engine compartment.

➡**Do not pry apart the anti-lock brake control module and hydraulic control unit. Carefully detach the components by pulling them straight apart.**

5. Separate the anti-lock brake control module from the hydraulic control unit by removing the four screws and disconnecting the pump motor harness.

89699P34

The hydraulic control unit is located under the battery in the engine compartment

To install:
6. Assemble the anti-lock brake control module to the hydraulic control unit by carefully lining up the coils with the solenoid valves and push together.
7. Install the four retaining screws and tighten to 35—44 ft. lbs. (4—5 Nm).
8. Reinstall the mounting bracket and install the retaining bolts. Tighten to 71—97 inch lbs. (8—11 Nm).
9. Connect the tubes to the inlet and outlet ports on the hydraulic control unit.
10. Connect the 2-pin power and ground harness to the anti-lock brake control module.
11. Connect the harness to the anti-lock brake control module.
12. Bleed the brake system.

Brake Sensors

TESTING

1. Raise and support the vehicle safely.
2. Disconnect the anti-lock brake sensor harness.
3. Measure the resistance between the terminals on the brake sensor.
4. If resistance is greater than 2200–2500 ohms for the front sensors or 2500–2900 ohms for the rear sensors, the sensor is faulty.
5. If resistance is within specification, check circuit continuity back to the control unit.
6. If continuity exists, the ABS control module may be faulty.

REMOVAL & INSTALLATION

Front

1. Raise and support the vehicle safely.
2. Disconnect the sensor harness.

89699P36

On front disc brakes, the ABS sensor is located near the outer CV-boot

3. Remove the sensor harness retainer from the front wheel knuckle.
4. Remove the sensor retaining bolt and slide the sensor from its bore.
To install:
5. Install the sensor and tighten the retaining bolt to 71–88 inch lbs. (8–10 Nm).
6. Install the sensor harness retainer on the front wheel knuckle.
7. Connect the sensor harness.
8. Lower the vehicle.

Rear

1. Raise and support the vehicle safely.
2. Disconnect the sensor harness.
3. Separate the sensor harness from the brake hose clips and feed it through the frame.
4. Remove the sensor retaining bolt and slide the sensor from its bore.

To install:
5. Install the sensor and tighten the retaining bolt to 71–88 inch lbs. (8–10 Nm).
6. Feed the sensor harness through the frame and attach the harness to the brake hose clips.
7. Connect the sensor harness.
8. Lower the vehicle.

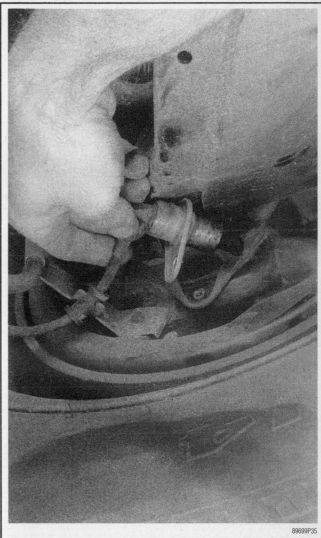

89699P35

On rear drum brake vehicles, the ABS sensor is attached to the backing plate

Bleeding The ABS System

The bleeding procedure for vehicles with conventional braking systems and ABS is the same. Refer to the brake bleeding procedure earlier in this section.

BRAKE SPECIFICATIONS

All measurements in inches unless noted

Year	Model	Master Cylinder Bore	Brake Disc Original Thickness	Brake Disc Minimum Thickness	Brake Disc Maximum Runout	Brake Drum Diameter Original Inside Diameter	Brake Drum Diameter Max. Wear Limit	Brake Drum Diameter Maximum Machine Diameter	Minimum Lining Thickness Front	Minimum Lining Thickness Rear
1995	Windstar	—	—	0.974	0.0003	9.84	9.90	—	0.125	0.059
	Windstar ①			0.409	0.0005	—	—	—	—	0.125
1996	Windstar	—	—	0.974	0.0003	9.84	9.90	—	0.125	0.059
	Windstar ①			0.409	0.0005	—	—	—	—	0.125
1997	Windstar	—	—	0.974	0.0003	9.84	9.90	—	0.125	0.059
	Windstar ①			0.409	0.0005	—	—	—	—	0.125
1998	Windstar	—	—	0.974	0.0003	9.84	9.90	—	0.125	0.059
	Windstar ①			0.409	0.0005	—	—	—	—	0.125

① With rear disc brakes

89699C01

10

BODY & TRIM

EXTERIOR

Doors

REMOVAL & INSTALLATION

Front

▶ See Figure 1

➡To prevent damage to the vehicle, two people should perform this procedure.

1. Open the front door and support it using a Rotunda Flexi-Work Table (156-00070) or equivalent. This is where a helper comes in handy.
2. Matchmark the door hinge for installation reference.
3. Label and disconnect the electrical harnesses.
4. Remove the front door attaching bolts and washers.
5. Remove the door from the vehicle.

To install:
6. Position the door on the vehicle and hand-tighten the attaching bolts.

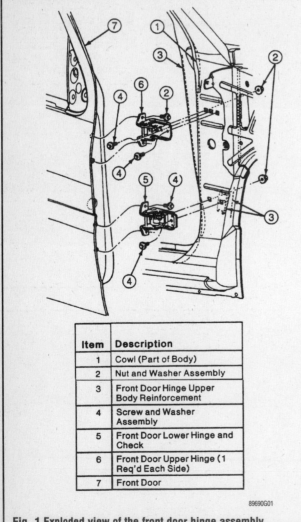

Item	Description
1	Cowl (Part of Body)
2	Nut and Washer Assembly
3	Front Door Hinge Upper Body Reinforcement
4	Screw and Washer Assembly
5	Front Door Lower Hinge and Check
6	Front Door Upper Hinge (1 Req'd Each Side)
7	Front Door

89690G01

Fig. 1 Exploded view of the front door hinge assembly

7. Align the matchmarks and tighten the door attaching bolts to 18–26 ft. lbs. (25–35 Nm).
8. Carefully close the door to check for proper alignment.
9. Readjust door alignment as necessary.

Side

▶ See Figure 2

➡To prevent damage to the vehicle, two people should perform this procedure.

1. Remove the interior trim panel.
2. Remove the bolt attaching the lower guide bracket and roller.
3. Remove the bolt attaching upper guide bracket and roller.
4. Remove the guide bracket and roller from the door.
5. Remove the hinge from the door.
6. Remove the door from the vehicle.

To install:
7. Position the door on the vehicle.
8. Install the hinge from the door.
9. Install the guide bracket and roller on the door.
10. Install the bolt attaching upper guide bracket and roller.
11. Install the bolt attaching the lower guide bracket and roller.
12. Tighten bolts to 89–124 inch lbs. (10–14 Nm).
13. Install the interior trim panel.

ADJUSTMENT

Front

1. Determine which hinge bolts must be loosened to move the door in the desired direction.
2. Matchmark the hinge and the door for reference.
3. Loosen the hinge bolts just enough to permit movement of the door with a padded prybar.
4. Move the front door the distance estimated to obtain the desired fit.
5. Tigten the bolts to 18–26 ft. lbs. (25–35 Nm).
6. Check the door to ensure there is no bind or interference with the adjacent panel.
7. Repeat the operation until the desired fit is obtained.
8. Check the striker alignment for proper door closing and adjust as necessary.

Side

➡For proper sliding door operation, it is critical that the door adjuster wedge and striker on the body pillar fit smoothly into the wedge pocket and latch in the side door. If any adjustments are made, realignment of the wedge and striker may also be necessary.

1. To adjust the front of the side door, loosen the two nuts retaining the side door bracket to the upper guide roller assembly.
2. Move the roller assembly in or out as required to obtain a flush fit of the door to body.
3. To adjust the lower part of the side door in or out, loosen the nut on the lower guide assembly and move the door in or out as required to obtain a flush fit.
4. To adjust the side door up or down, remove the door latch control rod knob. Using a door handle clip tool, spread the ends of the hidden door handle clip and remove the door handle. Remove the door trim panel and moisture barrier.
5. Loosen the four guide to door screws and adjust the door up and down as needed.

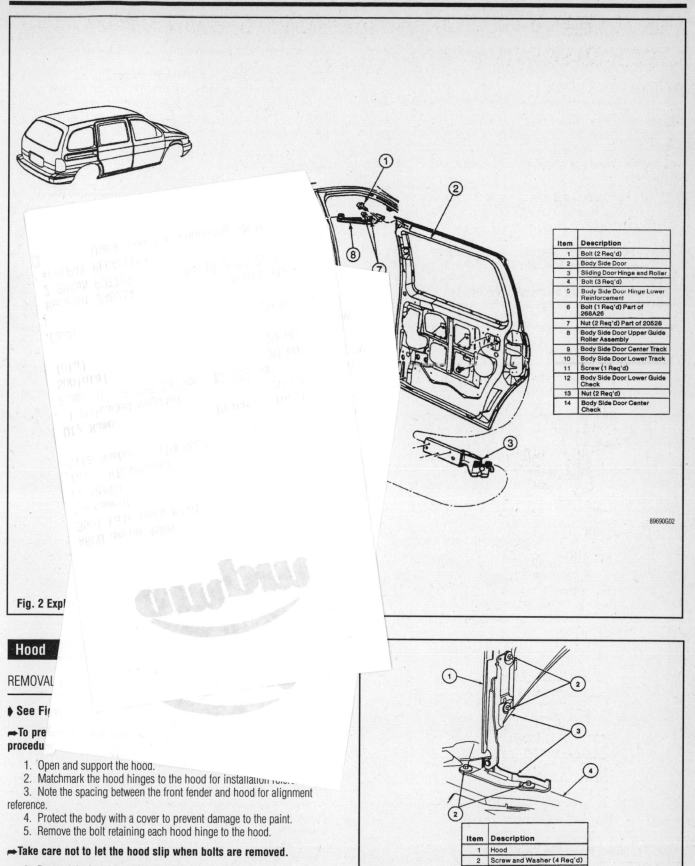

Item	Description
1	Bolt (2 Req'd)
2	Body Side Door
3	Sliding Door Hinge and Roller
4	Bolt (3 Req'd)
5	Body Side Door Hinge Lower Reinforcement
6	Bolt (1 Req'd) Part of 268A26
7	Nut (2 Req'd) Part of 20528
8	Body Side Door Upper Guide Roller Assembly
9	Body Side Door Center Track
10	Body Side Door Lower Track
11	Screw (1 Req'd)
12	Body Side Door Lower Guide Check
13	Nut (2 Req'd)
14	Body Side Door Center Check

89690G02

Fig. 2 Expl

Hood

REMOVAL

▶ **See Fi**

➡ **To pre**

procedu

1. Open and support the hood.
2. Matchmark the hood hinges to the hood for installation ref
3. Note the spacing between the front fender and hood for alignment reference.
4. Protect the body with a cover to prevent damage to the paint.
5. Remove the bolt retaining each hood hinge to the hood.

➡ **Take care not to let the hood slip when bolts are removed.**

6. Remove the hood from the vehicle.
To install:
7. Position the hood on the vehicle and hand tighten the retaining bolts.

Item	Description
1	Hood
2	Screw and Washer (4 Req'd)
3	Hood Hinge
4	Front Fender

89690G03

Fig. 3 Hood hinge retaining bolts

8. Align the matchmarks and tighten the hood retaining bolts to 97–115 inch lbs. (11–13 Nm).

9. Carefully lower the hood to check for proper alignment.

10. Readjust the hood alignment as necessary.

ALIGNMENT

1. The hood can be adjusted fore-and-aft and side-to-side by loosening the hood hinge retaining bolts. Reposition the hood as required and tighten the hood hinge retaining bolts to 97–115 inch lbs. (11–13 Nm).

2. A 3.5–5.5mm clearance should be maintained between the hood and front fenders.

3. To raise or lower the rear of the hood, loosen the hood hinge pivot nut. The pivot can now move up or down. Raise or lower the hood to obtain a flush fit at the rear of the hood with the front fenders. Tighten the pivot bolts to 16–25 ft. lbs. (22–34 Nm).

Liftgate

REMOVAL & INSTALLATION

♦ **See Figure 4**

➥**To prevent damage to the vehicle, two people should perform this procedure.**

1. Open the liftgate.
2. Remove the upper rear header molding.
3. Support the liftgate in the open position.
4. Disconnect the lift assemblies.
5. Move the roof trim panel out of position and remove the nut attaching the hinge to the body.
6. Label and disconnect the wiring harnesses going to the liftgate.
7. Remove the retaining bolts from the liftgate hinge on each side of the liftgate.
8. Remove the liftgate from the vehicle.

To install:

9. Position the liftgate on the vehicle.
10. Install the retaining bolts and hand-tighten.
11. Connect the lift assemblies.
12. Connect the wiring harnesses going to the liftgate.
13. Install the nut attaching the hinge to the body.
14. Move the roof trim panel into position.
15. Install the upper rear header molding.
16. Close the liftgate slowly and ensure alignment is within tolerance.

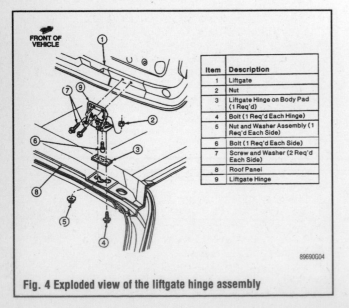

Item	Description
1	Liftgate
2	Nut
3	Liftgate Hinge on Body Pad (1 Req'd)
4	Bolt (1 Req'd Each Hinge)
5	Nut and Washer Assembly (1 Req'd Each Side)
6	Bolt (1 Req'd Each Side)
7	Screw and Washer (2 Req'd Each Side)
8	Roof Panel
9	Liftgate Hinge

89690G04

Fig. 4 Exploded view of the liftgate hinge assembly

17. Tighten the liftgate-to-hinge bolts to 71–89 inch lbs. (8–10 Nm).
18. Tighten the body-to-hinge nuts to 14–19 ft. lbs. (19–26 Nm).
19. Tighten the body-to-hinge bolts 19–25 ft. lbs. (26–35 Nm).

ALIGNMENT

1. The liftgate can be adjusted in or out and side-to-side by loosening the bolt and washer assemblies attaching the liftgate hinge to the roof trim panel.

2. The liftgate can be adjusted up or down by loosening the bolts on the roof trim panel and moving the liftgate up or down.

➥**Adjustment is minimal.**

3. The liftgate should be adjusted for even and parallel fit with the liftgate opening and surrounding sheet metal.

Grille

REMOVAL & INSTALLATION

♦ **See Figure 5**

The radiator grille is an integral part of the front bumper cover. The following procedure describes the front bumper assembly removal and installation.

1. Remove the rivets retaining the front bumper cover to the top of the radiator grille opening panel reinforcement.
2. Remove the screws retaining the cover to the bottom of the radiator support.
3. Remove the screws (5 on each side) retaining the cover to the front fender splash shield.
4. Remove the left and right side marker light assemblies.
5. Remove the screws (one each side) attaching the corner of the front fender to the cover behind the side marker lights.
6. Remove the nuts and washers (two each side) retaining the cover to the front fenders.
7. Depress the two tabs on each side of the cover underneath the headlights.
8. Pull the ends of the cover away from the front fenders to clear the retaining studs.
9. Remove the cover from the vehicle.

To install:

10. Position the cover on the vehicle.
11. Push the ends of the cover over the front fenders.
12. Ensure that the two tabs on each side of the cover underneath the headlights are properly positioned.
13. Install the nuts and washers (two each side) retaining the cover to the front fenders.
14. Install the screws (one each side) attaching the corner of the front fender to the cover behind the side marker lights.
15. Install the left and right side marker light assemblies.
16. Install the screws (5 on each side) retaining the cover to the front fender splash shield.
17. Install the screws retaining the cover to the bottom of the radiator support.
18. Tighten the cover screws to 9–17 inch lbs. (1–2 Nm) and the nuts to 80–123 inch lbs. (9–14 Nm).
19. Install the rivets retaining the front bumper cover to the top of the radiator grille opening panel reinforcement.

Outside Mirrors

REMOVAL & INSTALLATION

♦ **See Figure 6**

Manual

1. Remove the front door trim panel.
2. Remove the mirror mounting hole cover by using a flat bladed tool to carefully pry it off.

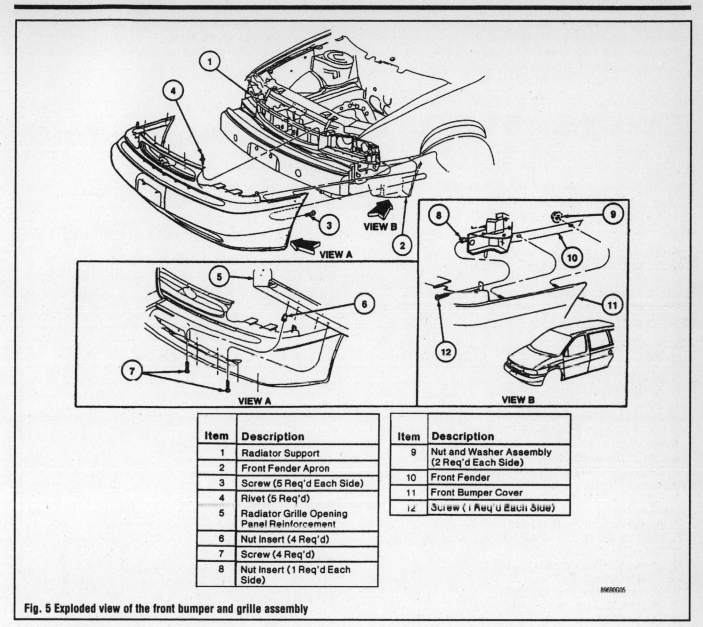

Item	Description		Item	Description
1	Radiator Support		9	Nut and Washer Assembly (2 Req'd Each Side)
2	Front Fender Apron		10	Front Fender
3	Screw (5 Req'd Each Side)		11	Front Bumper Cover
4	Rivet (5 Req'd)		12	Screw (1 Req'd Each Side)
5	Radiator Grille Opening Panel Reinforcement			
6	Nut Insert (4 Req'd)			
7	Screw (4 Req'd)			
8	Nut Insert (1 Req'd Each Side)			

89690G05

Fig. 5 Exploded view of the front bumper and grille assembly

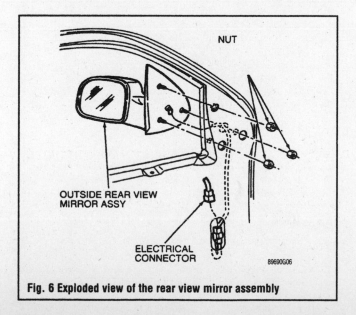

NUT

OUTSIDE REAR VIEW MIRROR ASSY

ELECTRICAL CONNECTOR

89690G06

Fig. 6 Exploded view of the rear view mirror assembly

3. Remove the three nuts retaining the mirror on the door.

4. Remove the mirror and gasket.

To install:

5. Position the mirror and gasket.

6. Install the three nuts retaining the mirror on the door and tighten to 27–44 inch lbs. (3–5 Nm).

7. Install the mirror mounting hole cover.

8. Install the front door trim panel.

Power

1. Remove the front door trim panel.

2. Peel back the water shield, as necessary, to gain access to the mirror electrical harness.

3. Label and disconnect the mirror electrical harness.

4. Remove the mirror mounting hole cover by using a flat bladed tool to carefully pry it off.

5. Remove the three nuts retaining the mirror on the door.

6. Remove the mirror and gasket.

7. Carefully guide the wiring out of the front door.

To install:

8. Carefully guide the wiring into the front door.

9. Position the mirror and gasket.
10. Install the three nuts retaining the mirror on the door and tighten to 27–44 inch lbs. (3–5 Nm).
11. Install the mirror mounting hole cover.
12. Connect the mirror electrical harness.
13. Install the front door trim panel.

Antenna

REPLACEMENT

▶ See Figure 7

1. Remove the cowl top vent panel.
2. Remove the antenna mast from the base.
3. Unsnap the radio antenna base cap and remove from the base.
4. Remove the three antenna base attaching screws.
5. Disconnect the antenna cable from the base.

To install:

6. Connect the antenna cable to the base.
7. Position the base on the vehicle and tighten the base screws to 22 inch lbs. (2.5 Nm).
8. Install the radio antenna base.
9. Install the antenna mast on the base.
10. Install the cowl top vent panel.

Fenders

REMOVAL & INSTALLATION

▶ See Figure 8

1. Remove the front bumper cover.
2. Remove the bolts retaining the radiator grille opening panel to the front fender.
3. Remove the bolt retaining the fender to the upper front fender mounting bracket.

89690P01

The antenna mast is easily removed from its base

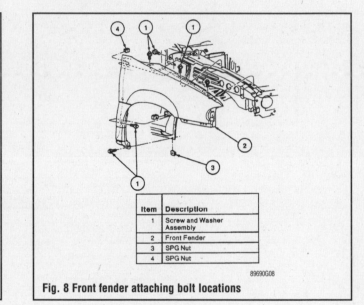

Item	Description
1	Screw and Washer Assembly
2	Front Fender
3	SPG Nut
4	SPG Nut

89690G08

Fig. 8 Front fender attaching bolt locations

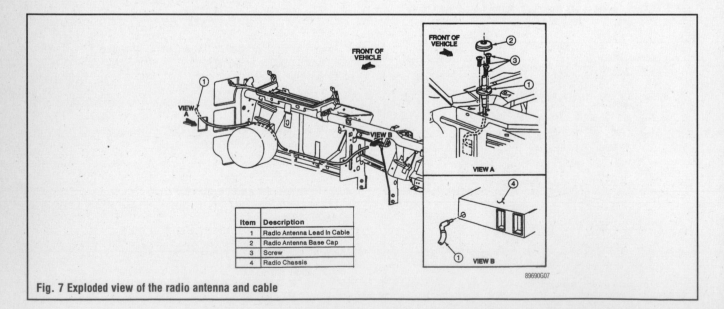

Item	Description
1	Radio Antenna Lead In Cable
2	Radio Antenna Base Cap
3	Screw
4	Radio Chassis

89690G07

Fig. 7 Exploded view of the radio antenna and cable

4. Remove the bolt retaining the fender to the front fender mounting bracket.

5. Remove the bolts retaining the fender to the body side.

6. Remove the bolts retaining the upper and lower front fender.

7. Remove the bolts retaining the upper lid area of the fender to the apron.

8. Remove the fender from the vehicle.

To install:

9. Position the fender on the vehicle.

10. Install the bolts retaining the upper lid area of the fender to the apron.

11. Install the bolts retaining the upper and lower front fender.

12. Install the bolts retaining the fender to the body side.

13. Install the bolt retaining the fender to the front fender mounting bracket.

14. Install the bolt retaining the fender to the upper front fender mounting bracket.

15. Install the bolts retaining the radiator grille opening panel to the front fender.

16. Align the fender and tighten all bolts to 44–62 inch lbs. (5–7 Nm).

17. Install the front bumper cover.

Cowl Top Vent Panel

REMOVAL & INSTALLATION

▶ **See Figure 9**

1. Remove the windshield wiper pivot arms.

2. Remove the seven screws securing the panel.

3. Remove the four plastic rivets securing the bottom of the panel.

4. Lift the panel and disconnect the windshield washer hose from the panel.

5. Remove the panel.

6. Installation is the reverse of removal.

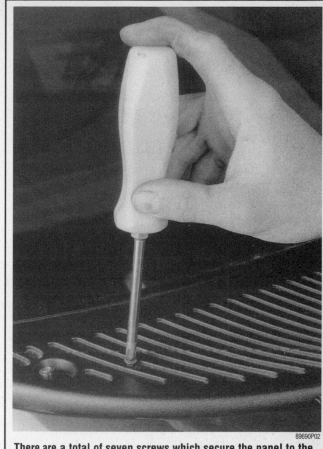

89690P02

There are a total of seven screws which secure the panel to the body

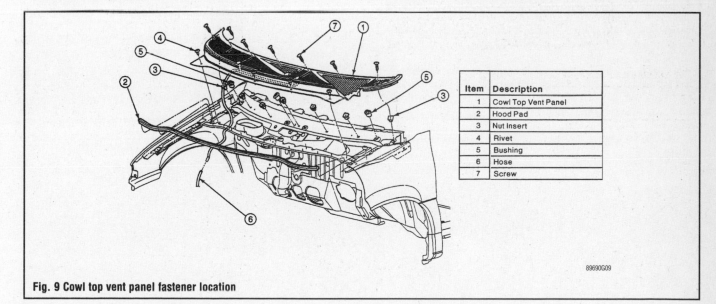

Item	Description
1	Cowl Top Vent Panel
2	Hood Pad
3	Nut Insert
4	Rivet
5	Bushing
6	Hose
7	Screw

89690G09

Fig. 9 Cowl top vent panel fastener location

Carefully lift the panel away from the body, but do not remove it all the way

89690P03

Once the panel is lifted sufficiently, disconnect the washer pump hose

89690P04

INTERIOR

Instrument Panel

REMOVAL & INSTALLATION

▶ **See Figures 10, 11 and 12**

➡ **To prevent damage to the vehicle, two people should perform this procedure.**

1. Disconnect the negative, then the positive battery cable.
2. Loosen the two main wire harness connector bolts in the engine compartment at the left side of the dash panel and separate the main wire harness connectors. Depress the locking tabs on the main wire harness connectors and push the main wire harness connectors into the passenger compartment.
3. Remove the left and right A-pillar moldings.
4. Remove the glove compartment.
5. Disengage the Christmas tree wiring retainers from the left side of the glove compartment support. Label and disconnect the electrical harness.
6. Disconnect the electrical harness from the air bag control module on the left side of the glove compartment support.

7. Remove the right and left cowl side trim panels.
8. At the right cowl, disengage the Christmas tree wiring retainer from the sheet metal. Label and disconnect the electrical harness.
9. At the left cowl, pull back the carpeting and remove the wiring shield. Label and disconnect the electrical and vacuum harnesses.
10. At the left cowl, disengage the Christmas tree wiring retainer from the sheet metal.
11. Remove the lower instrument panel finish panel.
12. Remove one screw to disconnect the transmission indicator cabal from the steering column.
13. Remove the four screws retaining the instrument cluster.
14. Pull the instrument cluster slightly away from the instrument panel. Disconnect the wiring and the speedometer cable.
15. Remove the instrument cluster.
16. Remove the instrument panel steering column cover by removing two screws along the bottom.
17. Pull on the instrument panel steering column cover to unsnap the three slips across the top of the part.
18. Remove the instrument panel steering column cover reinforcement by removing three screws.

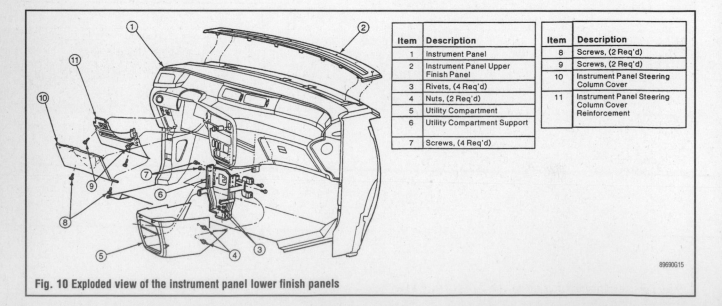

Item	Description		Item	Description
1	Instrument Panel		8	Screws, (2 Req'd)
2	Instrument Panel Upper Finish Panel		9	Screws, (2 Req'd)
3	Rivets, (4 Req'd)		10	Instrument Panel Steering Column Cover
4	Nuts, (2 Req'd)		11	Instrument Panel Steering Column Cover Reinforcement
5	Utility Compartment			
6	Utility Compartment Support			
7	Screws, (4 Req'd)			

Fig. 10 Exploded view of the instrument panel lower finish panels

89690G15

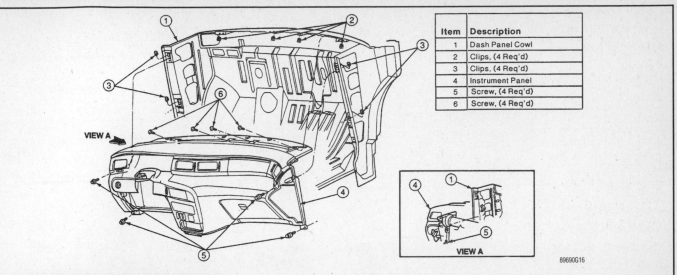

Item	Description
1	Dash Panel Cowl
2	Clips, (4 Req'd)
3	Clips, (4 Req'd)
4	Instrument Panel
5	Screw, (4 Req'd)
6	Screw, (4 Req'd)

VIEW A

89690G16

Fig. 11 Instrument panel fastener locations

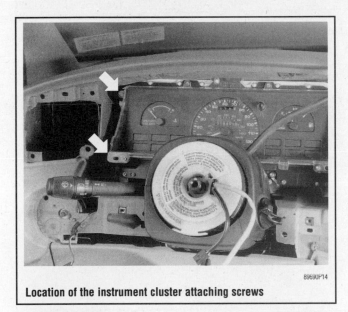

Location of the instrument cluster attaching screws

89690P14

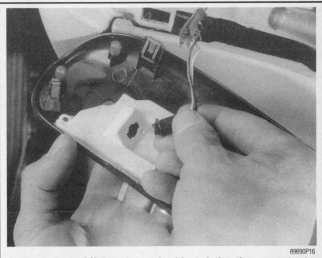

Instrument panel lights are serviced by twisting the connector to remove it . . .

89690P16

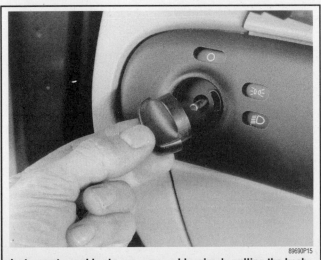

Instrument panel knobs are removed by simply pulling the knob from the switch

89690P15

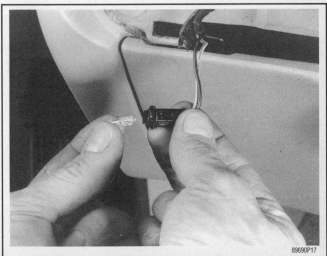

. . . the bulbs are removed by pulling them straight from the socket

89690P17

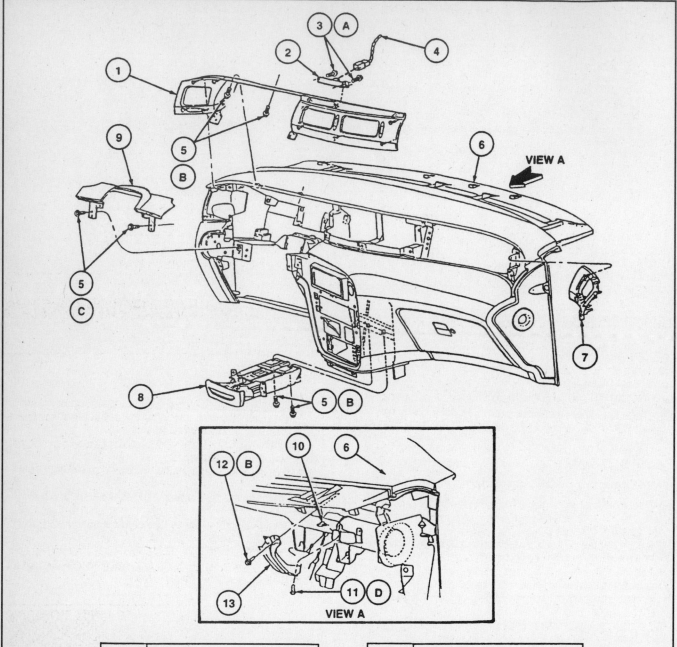

Item	Description
1	Instrument Panel Finish Panel
2	Instrument Panel Control Opening Cover
3	Screw (2 Req'd)
4	Warning Indicator Wiring
5	Screw (6 Req'd)
6	Instrument Panel
7	Instrument Panel Finish Panel
8	Instrument Panel Ash Receptacle

Item	Description
9	Instrument Panel Finish Panel
10	U-Nut
11	Screw
12	Screw
13	Instrument Panel Cowl Bracket

89690G17

Fig. 12 Exploded view of the instrument panel upper finish panels

19. Remove two screws and the wiring connector from the steering column opening brace. Also remove the two bolts that attach the steering column opening brace to the instrument panel.

20. Remove the steering column opening brace.

21. Remove the four screws retaining the steering column shroud.

22. Disconnect the electrical harness from the switches at the top and bottom of the steering column.

23. While supporting the steering column, remove the four steering column assembly retaining nuts.

24. Carefully lower the steering column assembly to the front seat.

25. Disconnect the air conditioning heater vacuum lines from the left side of the evaporator case.

Open the glove box to full open, past the stops, and remove the three screws at the bottom retaining the hinge and glove box assembly to the instrument panel.

26. Remove the glove box from the instrument panel.

27. Separate the radio antenna two-piece lead underneath the instrument panel.

28. Remove one screw to the left of the heater blower motor attaching the instrument panel brace to the evaporator case.

29. Remove the four screws attaching the center of the instrument panel to the storage bin support.

30. Remove the two bolts on each side that attach the instrument panel to the cowl side.

➡**Protect the instrument panel during the following procedure.**

31. Using a putty knife or similar tool, insert under the left or right rear corner of the instrument panel upper finish panel and pry up the panel to release one snap clip.

32. Unsnap the remaining door clips pulling up by hand, working toward the opposite side of the vehicle. Disconnect electrical harnesses as necessary.

33. Remove the nut attaching the right side of the instrument panel cowl side.

34. Remove the four screws retaining the top of the instrument panel to the cowl top.

➡**The following step requires two people.**

35. Carefully pull the instrument panel away from the windshield while checking for and disconnecting any remaining electrical harnesses.

To install:

36. If the instrument panel is being replaced, transfer all components, wiring and retaining hardware the new instrument panel.

37. Installation is the reverse of removal. However, please note the following important steps.

38. Tighten the instrument panel-to-cowl top screws to 62–80 inch lbs. (7–9 Nm).

39. Tighten the instrument panel-to-cowl side bolts to 89–106 inch lbs. (10–12 Nm).

40. Tighten the glove compartment hinge screws to 80–124 inch lbs. (9–14 Nm).

41. Tighten the steering column assembly retaining nuts to 15–20 ft. lbs. (21–28 Nm).

42. Tighten the steering column shroud screws to 7–10 inch lbs. (0.6–1.1 Nm).

Console

REMOVAL & INSTALLATION

▶ **See Figure 13**

1. Remove the cupholder mats from the cupholders.

2. Remove the four screws retaining the console panel. Two screws are located in each cupholder.

3. Lift the console panel and disconnect the electrical harness.

4. Installation is the reverse of removal.

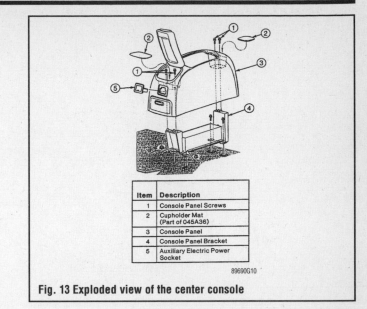

Item	Description
1	Console Panel Screws
2	Cupholder Mat (Part of 045A36)
3	Console Panel
4	Console Panel Bracket
5	Auxiliary Electric Power Socket

89690G10

Fig. 13 Exploded view of the center console

Door Panels

REMOVAL & INSTALLATION

Front

▶ **See Figure 14**

1. Remove the door latch cover by pulling the trim free of the retaining clips and sliding the trim away from the latch.

2. Remove the portion of the armrest containing the door lock switch and window regulator control switch.

3. Remove the screw attaching the front door trim panel to the front door.

4. Remove the screw located at the bottom of the front door trim panel.

5. Disconnect the door lock switch and window regulator control switch electrical harnesses.

6. Remove the door window regulator handle by unsnapping the handle cover from the base in order to expose the retaining screw. Remove the screw from the door window regulator handle.

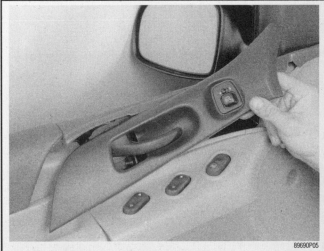

89690P05

The door latch cover is attached by retaining clips. Pull off the cover to remove it

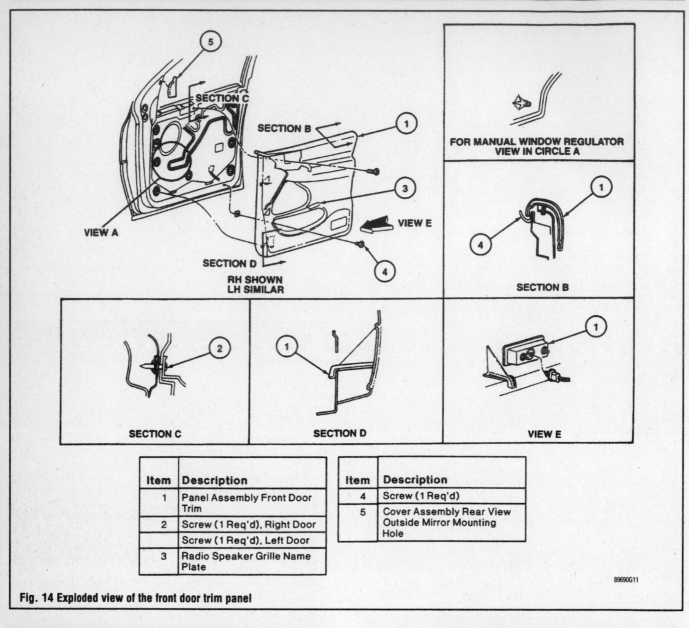

FOR MANUAL WINDOW REGULATOR VIEW IN CIRCLE A

SECTION C

SECTION B

SECTION D

VIEW A

VIEW E

RH SHOWN
LH SIMILAR

SECTION B

SECTION C

SECTION D

VIEW E

Item	Description
1	Panel Assembly Front Door Trim
2	Screw (1 Req'd), Right Door
	Screw (1 Req'd), Left Door
3	Radio Speaker Grille Name Plate

Item	Description
4	Screw (1 Req'd)
5	Cover Assembly Rear View Outside Mirror Mounting Hole

89690G11

Fig. 14 Exploded view of the front door trim panel

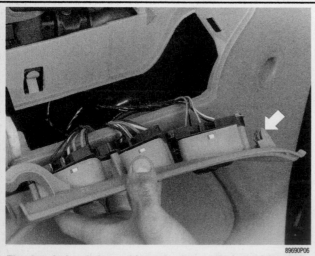

The door lock switch panel is retained by a clip (arrow) located at the front of the panel

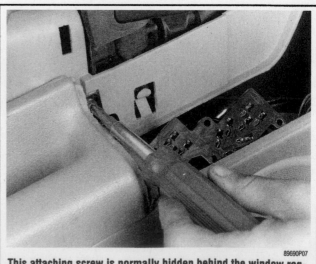

This attaching screw is normally hidden behind the window regulator control panel

Other screws are hidden at the lower end of the door panel

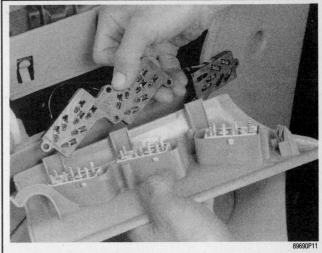

Carefully lift the electrical connector off the pins of the window regulator switches

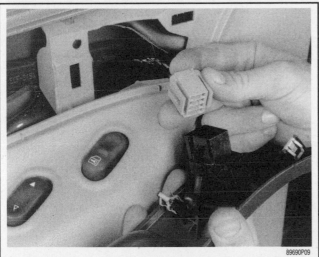

Prior to removing the door panel, disconnect the door lock electrical harness

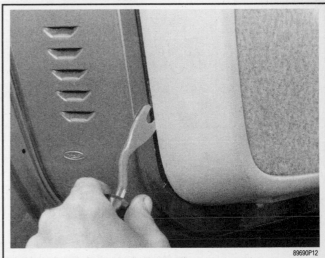

Using a Molding/Trim Removal Kit (Part 107-R0401) or equivalent, remove the door panel

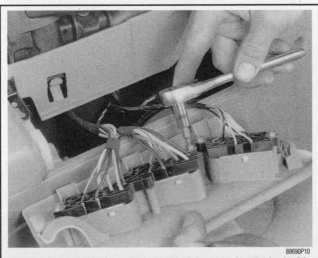

The window regulator control electrical harness is attached with several screws

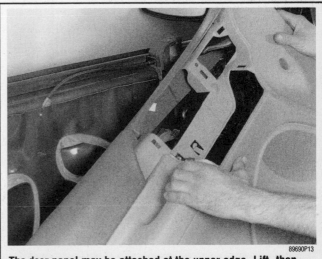

The door panel may be attached at the upper edge. Lift, then remove the panel

7. Remove the door window regulator handle, if equipped.
8. Pull the front door trim panel from the top to release the fasteners from the front door.
9. Remove the front door trim panel.
10. Installation is the reverse of removal.
11. Replace any bent or damaged fasteners.

Side

♦ **See Figure 15**

1. Remove the door handle retaining clip by sliding a shop towel between the handle and door trim. With tension on the cloth, pull one end of the cloth so it slides between the handle and the door trim. If the handle does not come out, reverse direction.
2. Gently pry the door latch bezel from the door trim.
3. Pull the trim panel from the door.
4. Installation is the reverse of removal.
5. Replace any bent or damaged fasteners.
6. Install the clip on the door handle. Install the handle on the shaft and snap it into place.

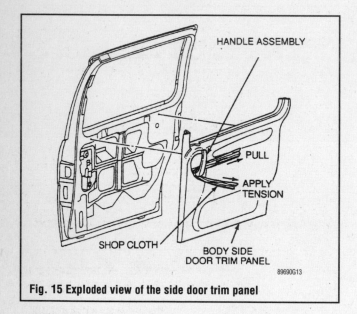

Fig. 15 Exploded view of the side door trim panel

Liftgate

♦ **See Figure 16**

1. Disconnect the rear window defroster electrical harness.
2. Remove the liftgate window garnish molding.
3. Remove the screws attaching the liftgate handle to the trim panel.
4. Using a Molding/Trim Removal Kit (107-R0401) or equivalent, pry the push pins retaining the liftgate trim from the liftgate.
5. Remove the liftgate tram from the liftgate.
6. Installation is the reverse of removal.
7. Replace any bent or damaged fasteners.

Door Locks

REMOVAL & INSTALLATION

♦ **See Figure 17**

➡ **When a lock cylinder is replaced, all door lock cylinder should be replaced in a set or have a qualified locksmith rekey the replacement door lock cylinder. This will eliminate carrying an extra key which will only fit one lock. If a key is to be replaced, the new key code number is stamped on a metal tag attached to the new key.**

1. Close the window.
2. Remove the front door trim panel.
3. Pull the watershield away from the door.
4. Disconnect the front door latch control cylinder rod from the door lock retainer clip.
5. Slide the door lock cylinder retainer away from the lock cylinder.
6. Remove the lock cylinder from the vehicle.
To install:
7. Insert the lock cylinder in the door and connect the lock cylinder retainer.
8. Connect the front door latch control cylinder rod to the lock cylinder retainer.
9. Install the watershield using gasket and trim adhesive. Cement the top and side edges of the watershield to the inner surface of the panel.
10. Install the front door trim panel.

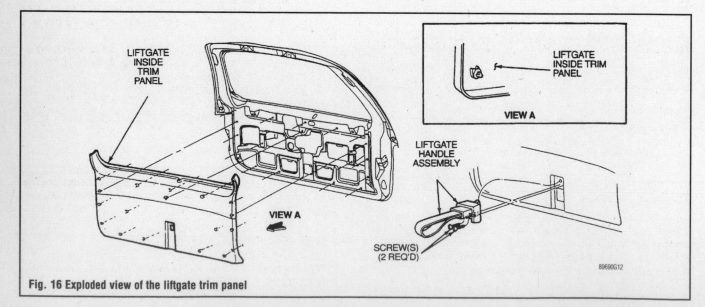

Fig. 16 Exploded view of the liftgate trim panel

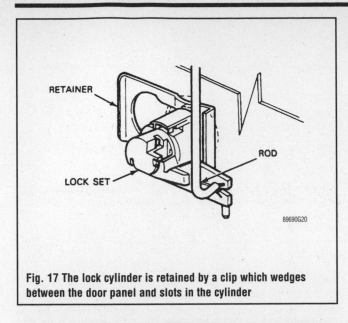

Fig. 17 The lock cylinder is retained by a clip which wedges between the door panel and slots in the cylinder

Liftgate Lock

REMOVAL & INSTALLATION

➡When a lock cylinder is replaced, all door lock cylinder should be replaced in a set or have a qualified locksmith rekey the replacement door lock cylinder. This will eliminate carrying an extra key which will only fit only lock. If a key is to be replaced, the new key code number is stamped on a metal tag attached to the new key.

1. Remove the liftgate door trim panel.
2. Pull the watershield away from the door.
3. Disconnect the liftgate latch control cylinder rod from the retainer clip.
4. Slide the retainer away from the lock cylinder.
5. Remove the lock cylinder from the vehicle.

To install:

6. Insert the lock cylinder in the door and connect the lock cylinder retainer.
7. Connect the liftgate control cylinder rod to the lock cylinder retainer.
8. Install the watershield using gasket and trim adhesive. Cement the top and side edges of the watershield to the inner surface of the panel.
9. Install the liftgate door trim panel.

Door Glass and Regulator

REMOVAL & INSTALLATION

Manual

▶ See Figure 18

1. Remove the front door trim panel.
2. Remove the front door window glass.

➡Use care not to enlarge the sheet metal holes in the door inner panel during drilling.

3. Remove the center pin from the front door window regulator attaching rivets with a drift punch. Then, drill out the remainder of the rivet heads using a 0.125 in. drill bit.
4. Slide the equalizer arm out the end of the equalizer arm bracket.
5. Remove the front door window regulator.

To install:

6. Position the front door window regulator in the door and align the retention holes to the door inner panel.

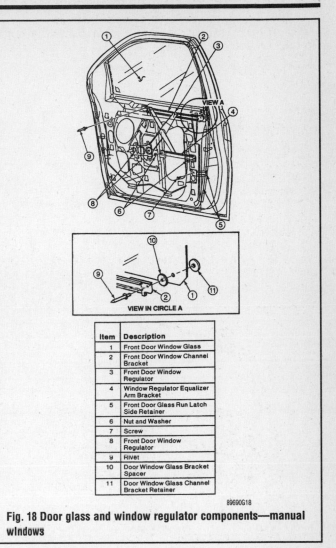

Item	Description
1	Front Door Window Glass
2	Front Door Window Channel Bracket
3	Front Door Window Regulator
4	Window Regulator Equalizer Arm Bracket
5	Front Door Glass Run Latch Side Retainer
6	Nut and Washer
7	Screw
8	Front Door Window Regulator
9	Rivet
10	Door Window Glass Bracket Spacer
11	Door Window Glass Channel Bracket Retainer

Fig. 18 Door glass and window regulator components—manual windows

7. Install the four rivets retaining the front door window regulator to the door inner panel. A screw and washer assembly may be used if rivets are unavailable.
8. Insert window regulator equalizer arm bracket through door access hole. Slide window regulator equalizer arm bracket onto the front door window regulator arm slides and the two retaining studs through the door inner panel.
9. Install two nut and washer assemblies to the window regulator equalizer arm bracket retaining studs and tighten to 62–89 ft. lbs. (7–10 Nm).
10. Install front door window glass.
11. Scheck operation of window regulator.
12. Install front door trim panel.

Power

▶ See Figure 19

➡If the regulator counterbalance spring must be removed or replaced for any reason, make sure that the regulator arms are in a fixed position prior to removal to prevent possible injury during C-spring unwind.

1. Remove the front door trim panel.
2. Remove the inside weatherstrip.
3. Remove the front door window glass.
4. Remove the two nut and washer assemblies attaching the window regulator equalizer arm bracket.
5. Remove the four rivets retaining the front door window regulator base plate to the door inner panel.

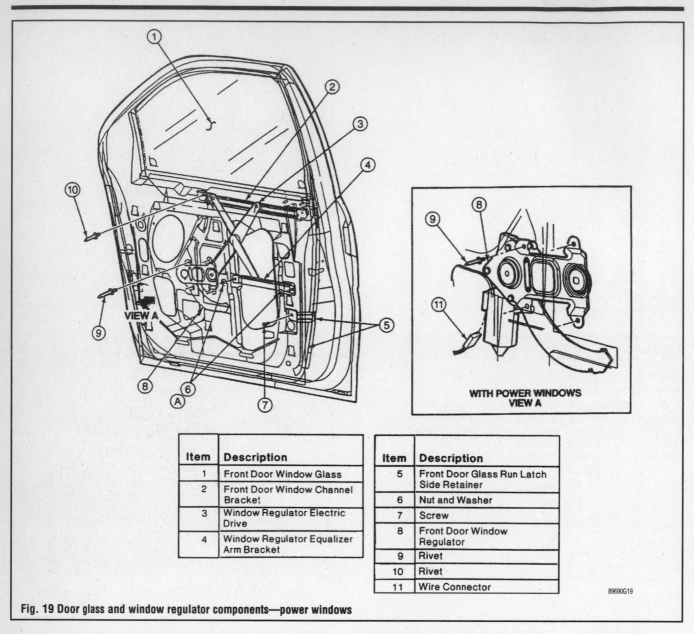

Item	Description
1	Front Door Window Glass
2	Front Door Window Channel Bracket
3	Window Regulator Electric Drive
4	Window Regulator Equalizer Arm Bracket

Item	Description
5	Front Door Glass Run Latch Side Retainer
6	Nut and Washer
7	Screw
8	Front Door Window Regulator
9	Rivet
10	Rivet
11	Wire Connector

89690G19

Fig. 19 Door glass and window regulator components—power windows

6. Remove the front door window regulator and front door window channel bracket from the vehicle.

7. Working on a bench, carefully bend the tabs flat to remove the front door window regulator arm slides from the front door window channel bracket.

➡**Use care not to break the tabs. If the tabs are cracked or broken, replace the front door window channel bracket. Make sure the rubber bumper is installed properly on the new front door window channel bracket, if replacement is made.**

8. Install new front door window regulator arm plastic guides into front door window channel bracket and bend tab back to 90 degrees.

To install:

➡**The front door window channel bracket and window regulator electric drive are installed into the vehicle as one assembly.**

9. Install the window regulator electric drive with the preassembled front door window channel bracket into the vehicle. Set the regulator base plate into the door inner panel using the base plate locator tab as a guide.

10. Install the four rivets retaining the front door window regulator to the door inner panel. A screw and washer assembly may be used if rivets are unavailable.

11. Install window regulator equalizer arm bracket.

12. Lower the front door window regulator arms into the access holes in the door inner panel.

13. Install the front door window glass.

14. Adjust the front door window glass to make sure it is properly aligned with the glass run.

15. Check window for smooth operation.

16. Install the door inner trim panel.

Electric Window Motor

REMOVAL & INSTALLATION

The front door window channel bracket and window regulator electric drive are installed into the vehicle as one assembly. Refer to the Door Glass and Regulator procedure, earlier in this section, for details.

Windshield and Fixed Glass

REMOVAL & INSTALLATION

If your windshield, or other fixed window, is cracked or chipped, you may decide to replace it with a new one yourself. However, there are two main reasons why replacement windshields and other window glass should be installed only by a professional automotive glass technician: safety and cost.

The most important reason a professional should install automotive glass is for safety. The glass in the vehicle, especially the windshield, is designed with safety in mind in case of a collision. The windshield is specially manufactured from two panes of specially-tempered glass with a thin layer of transparent plastic between them. This construction allows the glass to "give" in the event that a part of your body hits the windshield during the collision, and prevents the glass from shattering, which could cause lacerations, blinding and other harm to passengers of the vehicle. The other fixed windows are designed to be tempered so that if they break during a collision, they shatter in such a way that there are no sharp or pointed edges on the glass pieces. The professional automotive glass technician knows how to install the glass in a vehicle so that it will function optimally during a collision. Without the proper experience, knowledge and tools, installing a piece of automotive glass yourself could lead to additional harm if an accident should ever occur.

Cost is also a factor when deciding to install automotive glass yourself. Performing this could cost you much more than a professional may charge for the same job. Since the windshield is designed to break under stress, an often life saving characteristic, windshields tend to break VERY easily when an inexperienced person attempts to install one. Do-it-yourselfers buying two, three or even four windshields from a salvage yard because they have broken them during installation are common stories. Also, since the automotive glass is designed to prevent the outside elements from entering your vehicle, improper installation can lead to water and air leaks. Annoying whining noises at highway speeds from air leaks or inside body panel rusting from water leaks can add to your stress level and subtract from your wallet. After buying two or three windshields, installing them and ending up with a leak that produces a noise while driving and water damage during rainstorms, the cost of having a professional do it correctly the first time may be much more alluring.

We here at Chilton, therefore, advise that you have a professional automotive glass technician service any broken glass on your vehicle.

WINDSHIELD CHIP REPAIR

There is something, however, that you can do to prolong or even prevent the need for replacement of a chipped windshield. There are many companies, such as Loctite®, which offer windshield chip repair products, such as the Bullseye™ Windshield Repair Kit (Part No. 16067). These kits are not meant to correct cracks or holes in your windshield, only chips caused by gravel or stones.

➡**Check with your state and local authorities on the laws for state safety inspection. Some states or municipalities may not allow chip repair as a viable option for correcting stone damage to your windshield.**

To fix a stone chip in your windshield with the Loctite® Bullseye™ Windshield Repair Kit, perform the following:

➡**Loctite Corporation recommends that their repair kits should be applied outside in the sunlight, which, evidently, helps cure the repair solution much faster. In one of our experiments with these kits, performed in a shop using fluorescent lights and without any sunlight, the solution had not cured even after 18 hours. Therefore, it is highly recommended that the solution be allowed to cure in sunlight.**

1. Clean the damaged area of your windshield with glass cleaner, then dry the area completely.

Small chips on your windshield can be fixed with an aftermarket repair kit, such as the one from Loctite®

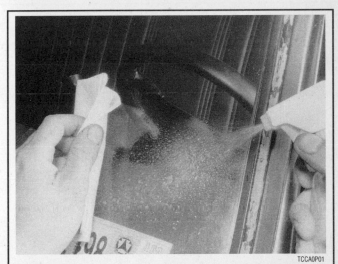
To repair a chip, clean the windshield with glass cleaner and dry it completely

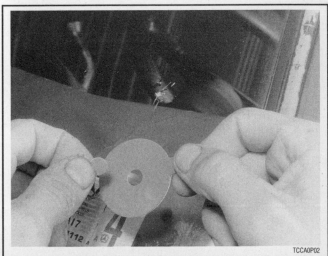
Remove the center from the adhesive disc and peel off the backing from one side of the disc . . .

. . . then press it on the windshield so that the chip is centered in the hole

TCCA0P03

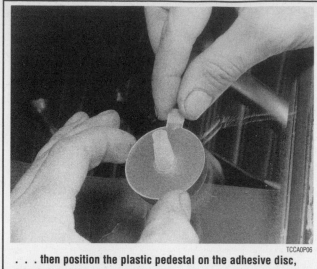

. . . then position the plastic pedestal on the adhesive disc, ensuring that the tabs are aligned

TCCA0P06

Be sure that the tab points upward on the windshield

TCCA0P04

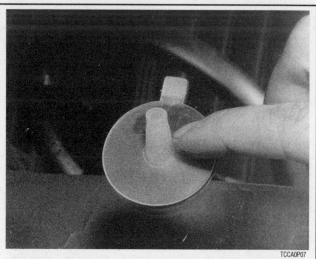

Press the pedestal firmly on the adhesive disc to create an adequate seal . . .

TCCA0P07

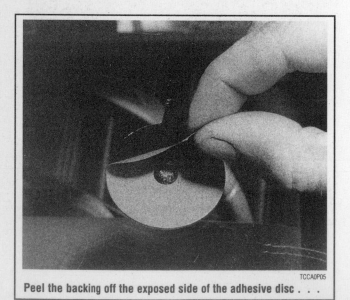

Peel the backing off the exposed side of the adhesive disc . . .

TCCA0P05

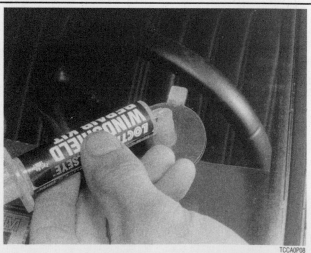

. . . then install the applicator syringe nipple in the pedestal's hole

TCCA0P08

☀ WARNING

The fluid contained in chip repair kits may damage paint; be sure to cover any exposed areas with clean shop rags.

2. Cover any painted surfaces with a clean shop rag, because the chip repair fluid may damage or remove paint.

3. Remove the adhesive disc from the kit, then remove the center hole plug from the disc.

4. Peel the backing off of one side of the disc, then, with the disc tab pointing upward, line up the hole in the disc with the center of the chip on the windshield. Press the disc onto the windshield.

5. Remove the plastic pedestal from the kit. Peel the paper off of the other side of the disc, then align the pedestal with the disc, making sure that the tabs are also aligned. Press the pedestal firmly onto the disc.

6. Remove the fluid applicator (syringe) from the kit and remove the cap from its tip.

7. Thread the syringe into the pedestal tube.

➡**During the next step, pull the plunger back until you feel it hit the stop on the inside of the syringe.**

8. While holding the syringe with one hand, gently pull back the syringe's plunger with the other hand, hold it there for 5–10 seconds, then abruptly release the plunger. Repeat this step 10 times.

9. Allow the entire assembly to sit, undisturbed, for 30 minutes.

10. From inside the vehicle, inspect the damaged area for any residual air bubbles. A flashlight may be necessary. If any air bubbles remain, repeat Steps 8 and 9.

11. Allow the repair kit to sit undisturbed until the solution has fully hardened or set. The light level where you are performing the repair largely dictates the length of time the repair solution needs to completely set. If the

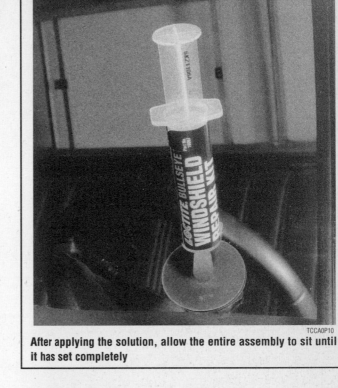
After applying the solution, allow the entire assembly to sit until it has set completely

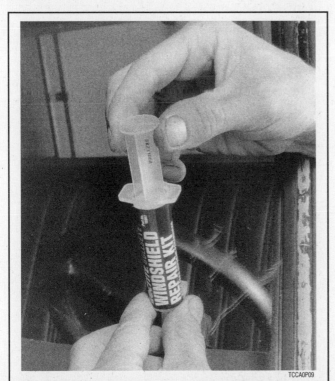
Hold the syringe in one hand while pulling the plunger back with the other hand

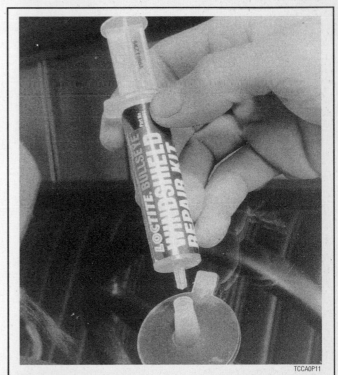
After the solution has set, remove the syringe from the pedestal . . .

repair is performed in a bright, sunny area, it should set up in approximately 1 hour. If the repair is performed inside or on a cloudy day, allow 4–5 hours for it to fully set.

➡️**If the repair must be performed indoors and it does not set in a few hours, an ultraviolet lamp may help expedite the curing process. However, according to the manufacturer, this should not be necessary.**

12. Remove the syringe from the pedestal.

13. Using a pair of pliers or a utility knife, if necessary, remove the pedestal and adhesive disc from the windshield.

14. Clean up any excess compound with glass cleaner.

➡️**For other brands of windshield repair kits, follow the manufacturer's instructions enclosed with the kit.**

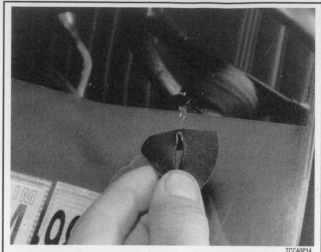

The chip will still be slightly visible, but it should be filled with the hardened solution

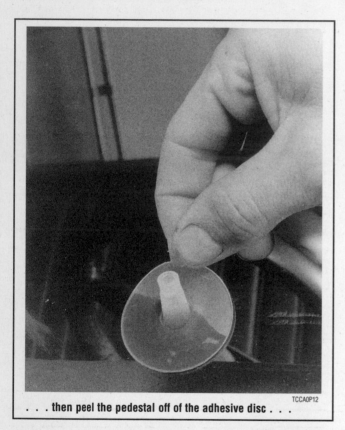

. . . then peel the pedestal off of the adhesive disc . . .

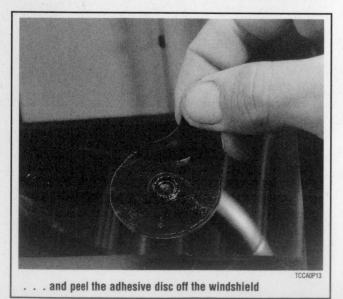

. . . and peel the adhesive disc off the windshield

Inside Rear View Mirror

REPLACEMENT

◗ **See Figure 20**

➡️**Breakaway mounts are used with the inside rear view mirrors. The breakaway mounts are designed to detach from the mirror bracket in the event of an air bag deployment during a collision. Excessive force, up-and-down, or side-to-side movement can cause the mirror to detach from the windshield glass.**

1. Mark the mirror mounting bracket location on the outside surface of the windshield with a wax pencil.

2. Loosen the mirror assembly setscrew.

3. Remove the mirror assembly by sliding it upward and away from the mounting bracket.

4. If the bracket mounting pad remains on the windshield, apply low heat from an electric heat gun until the glue softens. Peel the mounting pad off the windshield and discard.

   To install:

5. Make sure the glass, bracket and adhesive kit are at least at a room temperature of 65–75° F (18–24° C).

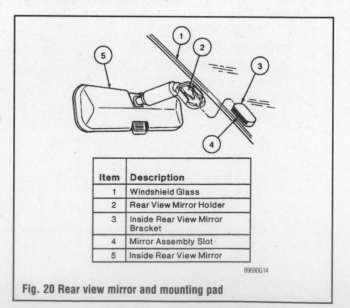

Item	Description
1	Windshield Glass
2	Rear View Mirror Holder
3	Inside Rear View Mirror Bracket
4	Mirror Assembly Slot
5	Inside Rear View Mirror

Fig. 20 Rear view mirror and mounting pad

6. Thoroughly clean the bonding surfaces of the glass and bracket to remove the old adhesive. Use a mild abrasive cleaner on the glass and fine sandpaper on the bracket to lightly roughen the surface. Wipe it clean with the alcohol-moistened cloth.

7. Crush the accelerator vial of the rear view mirror repair kit, and apply the accelerator to the bonding surface of the bracket and windshield. Follow directions on drying time.

8. Apply two drops of adhesive to the mounting surface of the bracket. Quickly spread the adhesive evenly over the mounting surface of the bracket using the applicator.

9. Quickly position the mounting bracket on the windshield. The ⅜ in. (10mm) circular depression in the bracket must be facing you. Press the bracket firmly against the windshield and hold for the appropriate dry time stated in the directions.

10. Allow the bond to set. Remove any excess bonding material from the windshield with an alcohol dampened cloth.

11. Attach the mirror to the mounting bracket and tighten the setscrew to 10–20 inch lbs. (1–2 Nm).

Seats

REMOVAL & INSTALLATION

This procedure is for servicing permanently attached seating. Seating which is designed to be repositioned is removed and installed by operating a lever to release the seat latching mechanism and lifting the seat from the vehicle.

1. Remove the seat track mounting bolts.
2. Fold the seat back forward and tilt the seat assembly back.
3. Disconnect the electrical leads and remove the seat from the vehicle. Remove components from the seat as needed.
4. Install the seat assembly into the vehicle. Connect the electrical leads and install the seat track mounting bolts. Tighten the nuts to 35–46 ft. lbs. (47–63 Nm) and the bolts to 14–19 ft. lbs. (19–26 Nm).
5. Test the operation of the seat on the track.

TORQUE SPECIFICATIONS

Components	Ft. Lbs.	Nm
Front door	18–26 ft. lbs.	25–35 Nm
Side door	89–124 inch lbs.	10–14 Nm
Hood	97–115 inch lbs.	11–13 Nm
Liftgate		
Liftgate-to-hinge bolts	71–89 inch lbs.	8–10 Nm
Body-to-hinge nuts	14–19 ft. lbs.	19–26 Nm
Body-to-hinge bolts	19–25 ft. lbs.	26–35 Nm
Bumper Cover		
Bolts	17 inch lbs.	1–2 Nm
Nuts	80–123 inch lbs.	9–14 Nm
Outside mirror	27–44 inch lbs.	3–5 Nm
Antenna	22 inch lbs.	2.5 Nm
Fender	44–62 inch lbs.	5–7 Nm
Instrument panel		
Instrument panel-to-cowl	62–80 inch lbs.	7–9 Nm
Instrument panel-to-cowl side bolts	89–106 inch lbs.	10–12 Nm
Glove compartment	80–124 inch lbs.	9–14 Nm
Steering column	15–20 ft. lbs.	21–28 Nm
Steering column shroud	7–10 inch lbs.	0.6–1.1 Nm

89690C01

How to Remove Stains from Fabric Interior

For rest results, spots and stains should be removed as soon as possible. Never use gasoline, lacquer thinner, acetone, nail polish remover or bleach. Use a 3' x 3" piece of cheesecloth. Squeeze most of the liquid from the fabric and wipe the stained fabric from the outside of the stain toward the center with a lifting motion. Turn the cheesecloth as soon as one side becomes soiled. When using water to remove a stain, be sure to wash the entire section after the spot has been removed to avoid water stains. Encrusted spots can be broken up with a dull knife and vacuumed before removing the stain.

Type of Stain	How to Remove It
Surface spots	Brush the spots out with a small hand brush or use a commercial preparation such as K2R to lift the stain.
Mildew	Clean around the mildew with warm suds. Rinse in cold water and soak the mildew area in a solution of 1 part table salt and 2 parts water. Wash with upholstery cleaner.
Water stains	Water stains in fabric materials can be removed with a solution made from 1 cup of table salt dissolved in 1 quart of water. Vigorously scrub the solution into the stain and rinse with clear water. Water stains in nylon or other synthetic fabrics should be removed with a commercial type spot remover.
Chewing gum, tar, crayons, shoe polish (greasy stains)	Do not use a cleaner that will soften gum or tar. Harden the deposit with an ice cube and scrape away as much as possible with a dull knife. Moisten the remainder with cleaning fluid and scrub clean.
Ice cream, candy	Most candy has a sugar base and can be removed with a cloth wrung out in warm water. Oily candy, after cleaning with warm water, should be cleaned with upholstery cleaner. Rinse with warm water and clean the remainder with cleaning fluid.
Wine, alcohol, egg, milk, soft drink (non-greasy stains)	Do not use soap. Scrub the stain with a cloth wrung out in warm water. Remove the remainder with cleaning fluid.
Grease, oil, lipstick, butter and related stains	Use a spot remover to avoid leaving a ring. Work from the outisde of the stain to the center and dry with a clean cloth when the spot is gone.
Headliners (cloth)	Mix a solution of warm water and foam upholstery cleaner to give thick suds. Use only foam—liquid may streak or spot. Clean the entire headliner in one operation using a circular motion with a natural sponge.
Headliner (vinyl)	Use a vinyl cleaner with a sponge and wipe clean with a dry cloth.
Seats and door panels	Mix 1 pint upholstery cleaner in 1 gallon of water. Do not soak the fabric around the buttons.
Leather or vinyl fabric	Use a multi-purpose cleaner full strength and a stiff brush. Let stand 2 minutes and scrub thoroughly. Wipe with a clean, soft rag.
Nylon or synthetic fabrics	For normal stains, use the same procedures you would for washing cloth upholstery. If the fabric is extremely dirty, use a multi-purpose cleaner full strength with a stiff scrub brush. Scrub thoroughly in all directions and wipe with a cotton towel or soft rag.

TCCA0G01

GLOSSARY

AIR/FUEL RATIO: The ratio of air-to-gasoline by weight in the fuel mixture drawn into the engine.

AIR INJECTION: One method of reducing harmful exhaust emissions by injecting air into each of the exhaust ports of an engine. The fresh air entering the hot exhaust manifold causes any remaining fuel to be burned before it can exit the tailpipe.

ALTERNATOR: A device used for converting mechanical energy into electrical energy.

AMMETER: An instrument, calibrated in amperes, used to measure the flow of an electrical current in a circuit. Ammeters are always connected in series with the circuit being tested.

AMPERE: The rate of flow of electrical current present when one volt of electrical pressure is applied against one ohm of electrical resistance.

ANALOG COMPUTER: Any microprocessor that uses similar (analogous) electrical signals to make its calculations.

ARMATURE: A laminated, soft iron core wrapped by a wire that converts electrical energy to mechanical energy as in a motor or relay. When rotated in a magnetic field, it changes mechanical energy into electrical energy as in a generator.

ATMOSPHERIC PRESSURE: The pressure on the Earth's surface caused by the weight of the air in the atmosphere. At sea level, this pressure is 14.7 psi at 32°F (101 kPa at 0°C).

ATOMIZATION: The breaking down of a liquid into a fine mist that can be suspended in air.

AXIAL PLAY: Movement parallel to a shaft or bearing bore.

BACKFIRE: The sudden combustion of gases in the intake or exhaust system that results in a loud explosion.

BACKLASH: The clearance or play between two parts, such as meshed gears.

BACKPRESSURE: Restrictions in the exhaust system that slow the exit of exhaust gases from the combustion chamber.

BAKELITE: A heat resistant, plastic insulator material commonly used in printed circuit boards and transistorized components.

BALL BEARING: A bearing made up of hardened inner and outer races between which hardened steel balls roll.

BALLAST RESISTOR: A resistor in the primary ignition circuit that lowers voltage after the engine is started to reduce wear on ignition components.

BEARING: A friction reducing, supportive device usually located between a stationary part and a moving part.

BIMETAL TEMPERATURE SENSOR: Any sensor or switch made of two dissimilar types of metal that bend when heated or cooled due to the different expansion rates of the alloys. These types of sensors usually function as an on/off switch.

BLOWBY: Combustion gases, composed of water vapor and unburned fuel, that leak past the piston rings into the crankcase during normal engine operation. These gases are removed by the PCV system to prevent the buildup of harmful acids in the crankcase.

BRAKE PAD: A brake shoe and lining assembly used with disc brakes.

BRAKE SHOE: The backing for the brake lining. The term is, however, usually applied to the assembly of the brake backing and lining.

BUSHING: A liner, usually removable, for a bearing; an anti-friction liner used in place of a bearing.

CALIPER: A hydraulically activated device in a disc brake system, which is mounted straddling the brake rotor (disc). The caliper contains at least one piston and two brake pads. Hydraulic pressure on the piston(s) forces the pads against the rotor.

CAMSHAFT: A shaft in the engine on which are the lobes (cams) which operate the valves. The camshaft is driven by the crankshaft, via a belt, chain or gears, at one half the crankshaft speed.

CAPACITOR: A device which stores an electrical charge.

CARBON MONOXIDE (CO): A colorless, odorless gas given off as a normal byproduct of combustion. It is poisonous and extremely dangerous in confined areas, building up slowly to toxic levels without warning if adequate ventilation is not available.

CARBURETOR: A device, usually mounted on the intake manifold of an engine, which mixes the air and fuel in the proper proportion to allow even combustion.

CATALYTIC CONVERTER: A device installed in the exhaust system, like a muffler, that converts harmful byproducts of combustion into carbon dioxide and water vapor by means of a heat-producing chemical reaction.

CENTRIFUGAL ADVANCE: A mechanical method of advancing the spark timing by using flyweights in the distributor that react to centrifugal force generated by the distributor shaft rotation.

CHECK VALVE: Any one-way valve installed to permit the flow of air, fuel or vacuum in one direction only.

CHOKE: A device, usually a moveable valve, placed in the intake path of a carburetor to restrict the flow of air.

CIRCUIT: Any unbroken path through which an electrical current can flow. Also used to describe fuel flow in some instances.

CIRCUIT BREAKER: A switch which protects an electrical circuit from overload by opening the circuit when the current flow exceeds a predetermined level. Some circuit breakers must be reset manually, while most reset automatically.

COIL (IGNITION): A transformer in the ignition circuit which steps up the voltage provided to the spark plugs.

COMBINATION MANIFOLD: An assembly which includes both the intake and exhaust manifolds in one casting.

COMBINATION VALVE: A device used in some fuel systems that routes fuel vapors to a charcoal storage canister instead of venting them into the atmosphere. The valve relieves fuel tank pressure and allows fresh air into the tank as the fuel level drops to prevent a vapor lock situation.

COMPRESSION RATIO: The comparison of the total volume of the cylinder and combustion chamber with the piston at BDC and the piston at TDC.

CONDENSER: 1. An electrical device which acts to store an electrical charge, preventing voltage surges. 2. A radiator-like device in the air conditioning system in which refrigerant gas condenses into a liquid, giving off heat.

CONDUCTOR: Any material through which an electrical current can be transmitted easily.

CONTINUITY: Continuous or complete circuit. Can be checked with an ohmmeter.

COUNTERSHAFT: An intermediate shaft which is rotated by a mainshaft and transmits, in turn, that rotation to a working part.

CRANKCASE: The lower part of an engine in which the crankshaft and related parts operate.

CRANKSHAFT: The main driving shaft of an engine which receives reciprocating motion from the pistons and converts it to rotary motion.

CYLINDER: In an engine, the round hole in the engine block in which the piston(s) ride.

CYLINDER BLOCK: The main structural member of an engine in which is found the cylinders, crankshaft and other principal parts.

CYLINDER HEAD: The detachable portion of the engine, usually fastened to the top of the cylinder block and containing all or most of the combustion chambers. On overhead valve engines, it contains the valves and their operating parts. On overhead cam engines, it contains the camshaft as well.

DEAD CENTER: The extreme top or bottom of the piston stroke.

DETONATION: An unwanted explosion of the air/fuel mixture in the combustion chamber caused by excess heat and compression, advanced timing, or an overly lean mixture. Also referred to as "ping".

DIAPHRAGM: A thin, flexible wall separating two cavities, such as in a vacuum advance unit.

DIESELING: A condition in which hot spots in the combustion chamber cause the engine to run on after the key is turned off.

DIFFERENTIAL: A geared assembly which allows the transmission of motion between drive axles, giving one axle the ability to turn faster than the other.

DIODE: An electrical device that will allow current to flow in one direction only.

DISC BRAKE: A hydraulic braking assembly consisting of a brake disc, or rotor, mounted on an axle, and a caliper assembly containing, usually two brake pads which are activated by hydraulic pressure. The pads are forced against the sides of the disc, creating friction which slows the vehicle.

DISTRIBUTOR: A mechanically driven device on an engine which is responsible for electrically firing the spark plug at a predetermined point of the piston stroke.

DOWEL PIN: A pin, inserted in mating holes in two different parts allowing those parts to maintain a fixed relationship.

DRUM BRAKE: A braking system which consists of two brake shoes and one or two wheel cylinders, mounted on a fixed backing plate, and a brake drum, mounted on an axle, which revolves around the assembly.

DWELL: The rate, measured in degrees of shaft rotation, at which an electrical circuit cycles on and off.

ELECTRONIC CONTROL UNIT (ECU): Ignition module, module, amplifier or igniter. See Module for definition.

ELECTRONIC IGNITION: A system in which the timing and firing of the spark plugs is controlled by an electronic control unit, usually called a module. These systems have no points or condenser.

END-PLAY: The measured amount of axial movement in a shaft.

ENGINE: A device that converts heat into mechanical energy.

EXHAUST MANIFOLD: A set of cast passages or pipes which conduct exhaust gases from the engine.

FEELER GAUGE: A blade, usually metal, or precisely predetermined thickness, used to measure the clearance between two parts.

FIRING ORDER: The order in which combustion occurs in the cylinders of an engine. Also the order in which spark is distributed to the plugs by the distributor.

FLOODING: The presence of too much fuel in the intake manifold and combustion chamber which prevents the air/fuel mixture from firing, thereby causing a no-start situation.

FLYWHEEL: A disc shaped part bolted to the rear end of the crankshaft. Around the outer perimeter is affixed the ring gear. The starter drive engages the ring gear, turning the flywheel, which rotates the crankshaft, imparting the initial starting motion to the engine.

FOOT POUND (ft. lbs. or sometimes, ft.lb.): The amount of energy or work needed to raise an item weighing one pound, a distance of one foot.

FUSE: A protective device in a circuit which prevents circuit overload by breaking the circuit when a specific amperage is present. The device is constructed around a strip or wire of a lower amperage rating than the circuit it is designed to protect. When an amperage higher than that stamped on the fuse is present in the circuit, the strip or wire melts, opening the circuit.

GEAR RATIO: The ratio between the number of teeth on meshing gears.

GENERATOR: A device which converts mechanical energy into electrical energy.

HEAT RANGE: The measure of a spark plug's ability to dissipate heat from its firing end. The higher the heat range, the hotter the plug fires.

HUB: The center part of a wheel or gear.

HYDROCARBON (HC): Any chemical compound made up of hydrogen and carbon. A major pollutant formed by the engine as a byproduct of combustion.

HYDROMETER: An instrument used to measure the specific gravity of a solution.

INCH POUND (inch lbs.; sometimes in.lb. or in. lbs.): One twelfth of a foot pound.

INDUCTION: A means of transferring electrical energy in the form of a magnetic field. Principle used in the ignition coil to increase voltage.

INJECTOR: A device which receives metered fuel under relatively low pressure and is activated to inject the fuel into the engine under relatively high pressure at a predetermined time.

INPUT SHAFT: The shaft to which torque is applied, usually carrying the driving gear or gears.

INTAKE MANIFOLD: A casting of passages or pipes used to conduct air or a fuel/air mixture to the cylinders.

JOURNAL: The bearing surface within which a shaft operates.

KEY: A small block usually fitted in a notch between a shaft and a hub to prevent slippage of the two parts.

MANIFOLD: A casting of passages or set of pipes which connect the cylinders to an inlet or outlet source.

MANIFOLD VACUUM: Low pressure in an engine intake manifold formed just below the throttle plates. Manifold vacuum is highest at idle and drops under acceleration.

MASTER CYLINDER: The primary fluid pressurizing device in a hydraulic system. In automotive use, it is found in brake and hydraulic clutch systems and is pedal activated, either directly or, in a power brake system, through the power booster.

MODULE: Electronic control unit, amplifier or igniter of solid state or integrated design which controls the current flow in the ignition primary circuit based on input from the pick-up coil. When the module opens the primary circuit, high secondary voltage is induced in the coil.

NEEDLE BEARING: A bearing which consists of a number (usually a large number) of long, thin rollers.

OHM: (Ω) The unit used to measure the resistance of conductor-to-electrical flow. One ohm is the amount of resistance that limits current flow to one ampere in a circuit with one volt of pressure.

OHMMETER: An instrument used for measuring the resistance, in ohms, in an electrical circuit.

OUTPUT SHAFT: The shaft which transmits torque from a device, such as a transmission.

OVERDRIVE: A gear assembly which produces more shaft revolutions than that transmitted to it.

OVERHEAD CAMSHAFT (OHC): An engine configuration in which the camshaft is mounted on top of the cylinder head and operates the valve either directly or by means of rocker arms.

OVERHEAD VALVE (OHV): An engine configuration in which all of the valves are located in the cylinder head and the camshaft is located in the cylinder block. The camshaft operates the valves via lifters and pushrods.

OXIDES OF NITROGEN (NOx): Chemical compounds of nitrogen produced as a byproduct of combustion. They combine with hydrocarbons to produce smog.

OXYGEN SENSOR: Use with the feedback system to sense the presence of oxygen in the exhaust gas and signal the computer which can reference the voltage signal to an air/fuel ratio.

PINION: The smaller of two meshing gears.

PISTON RING: An open-ended ring with fits into a groove on the outer diameter of the piston. Its chief function is to form a seal between the piston and cylinder wall. Most automotive pistons have three rings: two for compression sealing; one for oil sealing.

PRELOAD: A predetermined load placed on a bearing during assembly or by adjustment.

PRIMARY CIRCUIT: the low voltage side of the ignition system which consists of the ignition switch, ballast resistor or resistance wire, bypass, coil, electronic control unit and pick-up coil as well as the connecting wires and harnesses.

PRESS FIT: The mating of two parts under pressure, due to the inner diameter of one being smaller than the outer diameter of the other, or vice versa; an interference fit.

RACE: The surface on the inner or outer ring of a bearing on which the balls, needles or rollers move.

REGULATOR: A device which maintains the amperage and/or voltage levels of a circuit at predetermined values.

RELAY: A switch which automatically opens and/or closes a circuit.

RESISTANCE: The opposition to the flow of current through a circuit or electrical device, and is measured in ohms. Resistance is equal to the voltage divided by the amperage.

RESISTOR: A device, usually made of wire, which offers a preset amount of resistance in an electrical circuit.

RING GEAR: The name given to a ring-shaped gear attached to a differential case, or affixed to a flywheel or as part of a planetary gear set.

ROLLER BEARING: A bearing made up of hardened inner and outer races between which hardened steel rollers move.

ROTOR: 1. The disc-shaped part of a disc brake assembly, upon which the brake pads bear; also called, brake disc. 2. The device mounted atop the distributor shaft, which passes current to the distributor cap tower contacts.

SECONDARY CIRCUIT: The high voltage side of the ignition system, usually above 20,000 volts. The secondary includes the ignition coil, coil wire, distributor cap and rotor, spark plug wires and spark plugs.

SENDING UNIT: A mechanical, electrical, hydraulic or electro-magnetic device which transmits information to a gauge.

SENSOR: Any device designed to measure engine operating conditions or ambient pressures and temperatures. Usually electronic in nature and designed to send a voltage signal to an on-board computer, some sensors may operate as a simple on/off switch or they may provide a variable voltage signal (like a potentiometer) as conditions or measured parameters change.

SHIM: Spacers of precise, predetermined thickness used between parts to establish a proper working relationship.

SLAVE CYLINDER: In automotive use, a device in the hydraulic clutch system which is activated by hydraulic force, disengaging the clutch.

SOLENOID: A coil used to produce a magnetic field, the effect of which is to produce work.

SPARK PLUG: A device screwed into the combustion chamber of a spark ignition engine. The basic construction is a conductive core inside of a ceramic insulator, mounted in an outer conductive base. An electrical charge from the spark plug wire travels along the conductive core and jumps a preset air gap to a grounding point or points at the end of the conductive base. The resultant spark ignites the fuel/air mixture in the combustion chamber.

SPLINES: Ridges machined or cast onto the outer diameter of a shaft or inner diameter of a bore to enable parts to mate without rotation.

TACHOMETER: A device used to measure the rotary speed of an engine, shaft, gear, etc., usually in rotations per minute.

THERMOSTAT: A valve, located in the cooling system of an engine, which is closed when cold and opens gradually in response to engine heating, controlling the temperature of the coolant and rate of coolant flow.

TOP DEAD CENTER (TDC): The point at which the piston reaches the top of its travel on the compression stroke.

TORQUE: The twisting force applied to an object.

TORQUE CONVERTER: A turbine used to transmit power from a driving member to a driven member via hydraulic action, providing changes in drive ratio and torque. In automotive use, it links the driveplate at the rear of the engine to the automatic transmission.

TRANSDUCER: A device used to change a force into an electrical signal.

TRANSISTOR: A semi-conductor component which can be actuated by a small voltage to perform an electrical switching function.

TUNE-UP: A regular maintenance function, usually associated with the replacement and adjustment of parts and components in the electrical and fuel systems of a vehicle for the purpose of attaining optimum performance.

TURBOCHARGER: An exhaust driven pump which compresses intake air and forces it into the combustion chambers at higher than atmospheric pressures. The increased air pressure allows more fuel to be burned and results in increased horsepower being produced.

VACUUM ADVANCE: A device which advances the ignition timing in response to increased engine vacuum.

VACUUM GAUGE: An instrument used to measure the presence of vacuum in a chamber.

VALVE: A device which control the pressure, direction of flow or rate of flow of a liquid or gas.

VALVE CLEARANCE: The measured gap between the end of the valve stem and the rocker arm, cam lobe or follower that activates the valve.

VISCOSITY: The rating of a liquid's internal resistance to flow.

VOLTMETER: An instrument used for measuring electrical force in units called volts. Voltmeters are always connected parallel with the circuit being tested.

WHEEL CYLINDER: Found in the automotive drum brake assembly, it is a device, actuated by hydraulic pressure, which, through internal pistons, pushes the brake shoes outward against the drums.

MASTER
INDEX